THE GATES OF HORN

THE

A STUDY OF FIVE FRENCH REALISTS

GATES OF HORN

BY HARRY LEVIN

Two gates for ghostly dreams there are: one gateway
of honest horn, and one of ivory.
Issuing by the ivory gate are dreams
of glimmering illusion, fantasies,
but those that come through solid polished horn
may be borne out, if mortals only know them.

—Homer, *The Odyssey*
(translated by Robert Fitzgerald), xix, 560-65

New York   OXFORD UNIVERSITY PRESS   1963

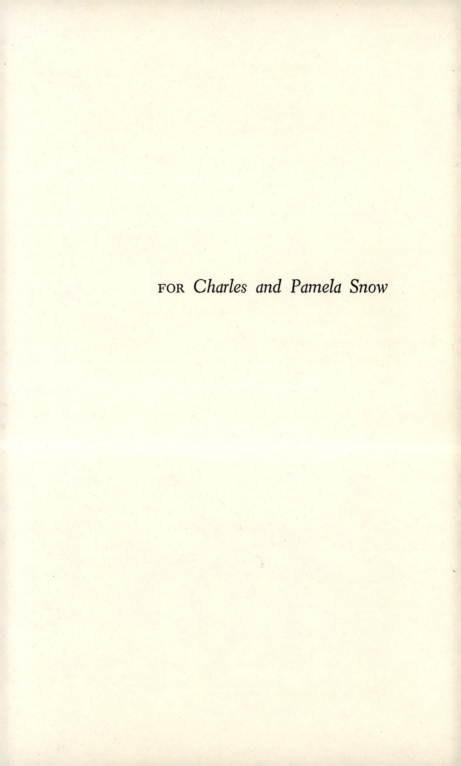

FOR *Charles and Pamela Snow*

Preface

THE PAGES THAT FOLLOW may require some word of apology—
whether because they have been long delayed, or because they are
finally published, it is for the reader to determine. It is now about
twenty-five years since the theme of this book first occurred to me,
and more than fifteen years since my preliminary studies for it
began to appear in print. Those intervals are not to be weighed in
its favor, since it has been an intermittent effort, and rather more
of a personal avocation than a professional assignment. Nor, I
hope, will they be counted against it, since it turns out to be one
of those projects which only youth could conceive and only age
could complete. Today I should hardly be rash enough to undertake it; and, when I did, I was too ignorant to carry it through. In
the process I, at least, have learned something; but it must be confessed that I had nearly everything to learn; I was not even a
specialist, and indeed have yet to become one, in the language and
culture that I was presuming to interpret. The attractions they
harbored, nonetheless, helped to overcome my hesitations, what
with the pleasure of revisiting France, the chance to read more
widely in French literature, the stimulus of new friends and welcoming colleagues.

The French, being such past masters of cultural machinery,
could be relied upon to have organized and provided access to the
available materials. These an outsider cannot claim to have much
augmented, though their domain of scholarship is so rich that he
would be very unobservant if he could not pick up a stray detail
here or adduce a marginal document there. And of course, from his
particular distance, he might be expected to gain a somewhat different perspective, both on the individual authors considered and
upon the sequence as a whole. In any case, my choice of subject-

matter was incidental to a broader concern with the theory of realism and, more precisely, its way of tightening the relation between art and life. Insofar as it comprised a movement, there was no other segment of it which seemed as central—or as classic in the exemplary, rather than the chronological, sense—as the five novelists I proposed to analyze. The unspecialized reader may well prefer those concrete illustrations, which constitute the body of the book, to the three more compendious chapters that frame them with theoretical implications. The scholar, finding much of the ground familiar that has been critically retraversed, might still be interested in the framing arguments, semantic formulations, or historical inferences.

The underlying interest—broadly speaking, as I have elsewhere tried to define it—is fabulation: man's habitual interest in telling stories to summarize his experiences and crystallize his attitudes, while ultimately passing them on to us. My first occasion for discussing this pervasive instinct on any scale was posed by one of its most sophisticated exponents. The work of James Joyce, I argued, in a little book written shortly after his death two decades ago, represented an ultimate point of convergence between the methods of naturalism and symbolism. It consummated a realistic tradition which stretched back through the nineteenth and eighteenth centuries toward the source of all other novels, Don Quixote. It also gave renewed expression to the other, the older tradition, which had persisted into the contemporary period, running largely underground. That symbolic undercurrent had come to the surface in the peculiar genre of American fiction known as the romance, a genre which I studied in The Power of Blackness: Hawthorne, Poe, Melville. This was primarily a study in literary iconology, in the adaptation of archetypal themes to given circumstances close at hand. It emphasized the obverse side of the story-telling faculty, its deep immersion in myth, as opposed to its sharp confrontation with actuality.

But the major tendency of the novel, in the modern West, has been that deliberate resolve on the part of writers to confront, to reflect, and to criticize life which may be prefigured for our purposes by the gate of horn, even as their more fantastic constructs have an emblem in the ivory gate. How far the freely ranging imagination can, or should, be disciplined to the canons of strict observation is one of our most problematic questions. Our recurrent paradox is that fiction, though by definition far removed from empirical reality, can be made to subserve the demand for truth. This demand itself has been responsive to scientific inquiries in the philosophical sphere and to liberal orientations in the social order. Realism is a literary mode which corresponds, more directly than most of the others, to a stage of history and a state of society. Thus it raises a methodological issue, which can be sidestepped by the more oblique modes, as to the exact degree of relationship between literature and society. As a middle term between the two, I have ventured to suggest the institutional concept in my first chapter, from which an early abridgment has been occasionally reprinted— mainly, I think, because it respects the complexity of a problem which has too often been oversimplified, overlooked, or overruled.

In the late 1930's, when I was starting to think about the present undertaking, criticism seemed under pressure to reduce all that came within its ken to sociological factors. That position, in turn, had been a reaction against a prior attitude of esthetic indifference, which regarded the arts as plaster casts, sealed off by time—and, in America, space—from human affairs at large. It had seemed important, if obvious, to recognize the claims of society; and many critics, under political influences, recognized little else; hence literature had its counterclaims to assert. To treat it as an institution, I believed, would render unto Caesar whatever was due, while guaranteeing its autonomous nature, its artistic technique, and its unique conventions. But the pendulum of critical fashion has more recently been swinging in the opposite direction: formal qualities are given careful attention, while once more the social aspect is slighted. This regression seems to be in keeping with an apparent decline in realism, and possibly with a current retreat from the pressures of history itself. History is not less relevant, however, when its impact is less overt; an institutional point of view might now be invoked as its guarantee; for criticism is bound to abhor a vacuum as much as a wind-tunnel.

At all events, I cannot regret the train of procrastination that has kept my book from drifting with topical currents, and has meanwhile been exposing me to a variety of approaches and opinions which I have found instructive or suggestive. My obligations have mounted beyond the point where they could be acknowledged in this place. Those that can be specified by bibliographical reference are included in the notes at the rear, which may be identified by key-phrases from the text. The notes should also make clear how closely the text, through quotation, translation, paraphrase, and commentary, is based upon the writing under scrutiny. All the English renderings are my own, unless otherwise noted. My debts to individuals and institutions, for help and encouragement, are recorded in a special note of acknowledgment. There, too, a record of publication has been briefly set down, since about half of the material in this volume has previously appeared in periodical form. These sections have been fully revised, albeit they were originally designed for the situation they occupy here. Of the many valuable contributions to the field that have lately been appearing, I have taken some cognizance in my revisions, though not so much as I would have liked. A standing invitation to enlargement, and to intellectual diversification, is inherent in the subject before us.

HARRY LEVIN

Bound Brook Island
Wellfleet, Massachusetts
18 September 1962

Table of Contents

V FLAUBERT

VI ZOLA

VII PROUST

VIII REALISM AND REALITY

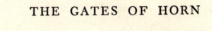

THE GATES OF HORN

I

PREMISES

Stendhal and Flaubert, and to them might be added Balzac, are analysts
of the individual soul as it is found in a particular phase of society; and
in their work is found as much sociology as individual psychology. Indeed, the two are aspects of one thing; and the greater French novelists,
from Stendhal to Proust, chronicle the rise, the regime, and the decay of
the upper bourgeoisie in France.

—T. S. ELIOT

1. Toward a Critical Method

THE SUBJECT OF THIS BOOK, to state it at the outset in the very
broadest and boldest terms, is the relation between literature and
life. Most of the imaginative arts, by Aristotle's primary definition,
strive to imitate nature in their respective ways; but perhaps literature, since it makes use of what can be the most expressive medium, can give the most convincing imitation. And to press the
point toward a conclusion which Aristotle could not be expected
to have foreseen, perhaps the novel, since it has become the most
resourceful of literary forms—"most independent, most elastic,
most prodigious," in the proud vaunt of Henry James—has come
closest to the real thing. Life itself, however, is too protean and
fugitive to be kept in sight for long by the artist without a conscious and a continuous effort. That effort, that willed tendency of
art to approximate reality, which critics call realism, has nowhere
been more clearly recognized or more expertly cultivated than in
modern France. A great tradition, reaching down from the French
Revolution into our own day, has been sustained with conspicuous mastery by at least one novelist in each of five interlinked

generations: notably by Stendhal, Balzac, Flaubert, Zola, and Proust. This book, in the most concrete and pragmatic terms, is a study of their work.

Five of the following essays will approach the same object via another route. If there is any single generalization which they are all designed to support, which is sketched in the next chapter and supplemented in the last, it is that realistic fiction has been a characteristic expression of bourgeois society. The character of our culture is so pervasively middle-class, and our novels are so thoroughly immersed in our social problems, that the correlation seems obvious today. But, if it can no longer be regarded as a discovery, it may now be accepted as an axiom, and the adumbrations and observations that suggest and confirm it may be fully utilized. Art may be said to differ from science by starting from general assumptions and working toward specific applications; hence criticism, which could aspire to be the science of art, is less obliged to expound a thesis than to demonstrate a method. The present demonstration, if it holds, should define the concept of realism in more precise detail than critical usage has heretofore provided. So far as it goes it should also compile, out of the expert testimony at our disposal, a running commentary upon the greatness and decline of the bourgeoisie.

Now it cannot be too explicitly stated that, in attempting to fulfill this double purpose, we shall be operating on two different planes. We shall be dealing immediately with matters of literary craftsmanship, and incidentally with questions of historical perspective. But our subject, realism, would mean very little if it did not signify one of the ways, the most direct way of all, in which literature adapts itself to history, in which literature on occasion makes history. "A vital sense of circumstances and the power to express them"—such, according to Goethe, ought to be the twofold qualification of the imaginative writer. Though critics have contributed much to our comprehension of both these qualities, all too often they have emphasized one at the expense of the other. They have hammered away at the writer's circumstances until we have forgotten what he wrote, or else they have refined upon his power of expression until we have forgotten what it expresses. We are led to forget, in either case, that criticism should be broad enough to extend from the plane of technical scrutiny to the plane of human experience, and that its most useful function may well be to improve the relations between them.

The dilemma set up by such conflicting schools of critical thought does not deserve to be taken as seriously as it has been in academic debate. If they are both one-sided, they can be balanced against one another. Both proceed from the same misleading abstraction, the question-begging dichotomy of form and content. Both agree in tacitly conceiving form as some kind of container, disagreeing as to the relative importance of the substance contained. From one extreme, subject-matter seems an artistic irrelevance; from the other, technique seems an artificial embellishment. Esthetic critics, on the one hand, show little concern for "separable content." Literary historians, on the other, have shown small patience with "belletristic philandering." Neither side has seemed to realize that content and form are not detachable and, by themselves, apart from such discussions, have no existence at all. Metaphysical dualists, having posited a separation between the soul and the body, have never been able to account for consciousness to one another's satisfaction. The analogy that James proposed is much humbler and happier: "The story and the novel, the idea and the form, are the needle and thread, and I never heard of a guild of tailors who recommended the use of the thread without the needle, or the needle without the thread."

But the happiest exemplar for the literary critic may be the critic of the plastic arts, to whom ideas must present themselves in the guise of images. Accordingly, he cannot fail to recognize that themes are basic components of structure, no less intrinsic than lines and colors in forming a part of the composition he studies. The adaptation of a given subject to a particular medium, however complicated, cannot but be one integrated process. The artistry is already manifest in the choice of a theme, and the style itself—as the natural historian, Buffon, announced to the French Academy —is finally a manifestation of personality. James himself could scarcely have engaged his readers in the punctilious amenities of his prose unless it had been animated by a vital flicker of intensely human curiosity. And even Theodore Dreiser, so often singled out as the very paragon of formlessness, the crudest purveyor of life in the raw, had an artist's eye for the shape of events, a power to express the patterns of circumstance. Both novelists, across a world of differences, had to satisfy both of Goethe's requirements in varying degrees.

Again referring these extreme cases back to Aristotle, we might recall that he traced the motivation for poetry to the collaboration between two instincts, *mímesis* and *harmonía:* imitation, by which men learn, and harmony, in which men delight. He may have overemphasized the former instinct because it established a closer connection between the arts and reality than the Platonic arguments had allowed. Nonetheless he authorizes us, if we seek the sanction of classical authority, to require of a work of imagination not only that it be true to life but that it shape life into a pattern, that it stylize its mimicry. If we look more directly at primitive art, we find that it oscillates between two such opposing tendencies: one of them increasingly representational, the other characterized by the psychoanalyst Otto Rank as an urge toward abstraction. Truth and beauty are the hallowed watchwords for this opposition —or is it a fusion? Let us accept them as equally valid criteria. Poets are permitted to confound them, and mystics to identify both with goodness, whereas critics are expected somehow to discover the truth about beauty. Yet the esthetician's question, "What is beauty?," has proved so much more seductive than the scientist's question, "What is truth?," that criticism since Aristotle has seldom stayed for an answer.

When Francis Bacon mapped out the developing provinces of modern knowledge, he left a considerable place for literary studies. Ernest Renan, after the two to three centuries that divide *The Advancement of Learning* from *L'Avenir de la science,* could not report much definitive exploration in that field of research. He compared "the science of literatures" to the old-fashioned botany of an amateur, who cultivates his garden and admires the flowers, gathering pretty bouquets and distinguishing mushrooms from toadstools. Many species, awaiting their Linnaeus, were still unnamed and unclassified; here was a potential discipline without even a taxonomy. There were appreciative essays, gilding the lily no doubt, plus an accretion of scholarly monographs, counting the streaks of the tulip. But, so long as critics feared that dissection would blight admiration, there could be no prospect of further unfoldment—no conception of anything comparable to cell-structure, pollination, or photosynthesis. Serious criticism would not have been so afraid of analyzing the soil, exhorted Renan, "of plucking the flower to study its roots." Such analysis could only end by fostering a more genuine appreciation, for "only reality is admirable."

Renan's exhortation, set down at the beginning of his career in 1848, was not published until 1890, shortly before his death. During his eventful lifetime the French mind had intensified its constant endeavor to sift the subsoils of culture, investigate the propagation of ideas, and trace the organic growth of the various arts. Professing himself a literary disciple of Bacon, Sainte-Beuve accumulated, by a method he casually described as "botanizing," the most varied and voluminous series of case histories that any eminent critic has ever passed in review. To read them is to be reminded that Sainte-Beuve had begun by studying medicine, and that medicine is considered at once an art and a science. He is always the man of the world, the empiric of talent, who shies away from doctrines, and works by his own combination of insight and experience. Whereas Taine, who belonged to a younger generation, and who had taken a doctorate in letters, is the literary scientist for whom Renan longed, the dogged researcher, the man of theories. Esthetics, he literally believed, was "a kind of botany," which treated books like plants and studied their roots. When his history of English literature appeared, it smelled—to a contemporary reader, H. F. Amiel—like the exhalations from a laboratory. To that sensitive Swiss idealist, it conveyed a whiff of "the literature of the future in the American style," of "the death of poetry flayed and anatomized by science."

This "intrusion of technology into literature," as Amiel was shrewd enough to observe, constituted a responsibility which Taine shared with Balzac and Stendhal. As Taine self-consciously remarked, "From the novel to criticism and from criticism to the novel, the distance at present is not very great." Taine's critical theory is grounded upon the practice of the realists, while their novels are nothing if not critical. His recognition of the social forces behind literature coincides with their resolution to convey those forces through their works. Sainte-Beuve, for all the sympathy that he brought to the portrayal of so many writers from so many periods, displays a certain coldness toward his contemporaries. Their critic is, inevitably, Taine. Where Sainte-Beuve be-

trays the disappointment of having lived through romanticism,
Taine shares the aspirations of the pioneering realists. The first to
acknowledge Stendhal as a master, he had welcomed Flaubert as
a colleague, and he lived to find Zola among his disciples. "When
M. Taine studies Balzac," Zola acknowledged, "he does exactly
what Balzac himself does when he studies Père Grandet." There
is no more appropriate way to bridge the distance between criticism and the novel, or to clear the ground for this sequence of
studies, than by a brief reconsideration of Taine's critical method.

2.   Taine and His Influence

"Literature is the expression of society, as speech is the expression
of man." In this aphorism the Vicomte de Bonald summed up
one of the mordant lessons that the French Revolution had taught
the world: the power of rhetoric, the impact of ideology. With the
opening year of the nineteenth century, and with the return of the
Emigration, coincided a two-volume treatise by Madame de Staël,
*De la littérature considérée dans ses rapports avec les institutions
sociales.* This was not the very first time, of course, that some degree of relationship had been glimpsed. Herder, in the eighteenth
century, had laid the foundations for a comparative and a genetic
view of the past. Renaissance humanism long before, fighting out
the invidious quarrel between ancient and modern literatures, had
concluded that each was the unique creation of its period, and had
adumbrated a historical point of view. Romantic nationalism,
seeking to undermine the prestige of the neo-classic school and
to revive the native traditions of the various countries, was now
elaborating a series of geographical comparisons. It was left for
Hippolyte Taine—in the vanguard of a third intellectual movement, scientific positivism—to formulate a sociological approach.
To the historical and geographical factors, the occasional efforts of
earlier critics to discuss literature in terms of *moment* and *race,* he
added a third conception, which completed and finally eclipsed
them. *Milieu,* as he conceived it, is the link between literary criticism and the social sciences. Thus Taine raised a host of new
problems by settling an old one.

A tougher-minded reader than Amiel, Flaubert noted in 1864

that, whatever the *Histoire de la littérature anglaise* left unresolved, it got rid of the old uncritical notion that books dropped
down like meteorites out of the sky. The social basis of art might
thereafter be overlooked, but it could hardly be denied. Any lingering belief in poetic inspiration could hardly withstand the sort
of higher criticism that had disposed of spontaneous generation
and proposed to deal similarly with divine revelation. When
Renan, proclaiming his disbelief in miracles and mysteries, depicted Jesus as the son of man and analyzed the origins of Christianity, then confidently Taine could depict genius as the out-
growth of environment and analyze the origins of literature. On
the whole, though critics have deplored the crudity of his analyses
and scholars have challenged the accuracy of his facts, his working
hypothesis has gained widespread acceptance. For some he has
become the stock example of a rigid determinist, especially for
those who think of determinism as a modern version of fatalism.
Taine's determinism, however, is simply an intensive application
of the intellectual curiosity of his age. It is no philosopher's attempt to encroach upon the freedom of the artist's will; it is simply
a historian's awareness of what the past already has determined.
    As for Taine's rigor, a more thoroughgoing historical materialist,
the Marxist theoretician George Plekhanov, has gone so far as to
accuse him of arrant idealism. Speaking from his Existentialist
viewpoint, Jean-Paul Sartre would prefer to describe Taine's empiricism as an unsuccessful effort to set up a realistic system of
metaphysics. Actually his position is that which most realists have
occupied in their time, outrageous to early readers and tame to
later critics. His method explained too much to satisfy his contemporaries; it has not explained enough to satisfy ours. Confronted
with the provocative statement, "Vice and virtue are products like
vitriol and sugar," we are not shocked by the audacity that reduces
moral issues to chemical formulas; we are amused at the naïveté
that undertakes to solve them both by a single and simple equa-
tion. Taine's introduction to his history of English literature, which
abounds in dogmas of this sort, is rather a manifesto than a meth-
odology. Indeed it first appeared in the form of an article entitled
"History, Its Present and Future." If—after reading it as a prolegomenon to a book about literature—we expect the history itself
to practise what the introduction preaches, we are rather pleas-

antly disappointed. Each successive author is more freely individualized. How does Taine's all-determining scheme meet its severest
test? With Shakespeare, he explains, after canvassing the material
factors, "all comes from within—I mean from his soul and his
genius; circumstances and externals have contributed but slightly
to his development."

The loophole that enables Taine to avoid the strict consequences
of his three determinants is a fourth, an easygoing system of psychology. Psychology takes over where sociology has given up, and
this sociologist has shown surprisingly little interest in social classes
or institutions. He has viewed the course of history as a parade of
influential individuals, themselves the creatures of historic influences. To understand their achievements becomes "a problem in
psychological mechanics." The psychologist must disclose their
ruling passions; he must hit upon that magnificent obsession, that
"master faculty" which conditions have created within the soul of
every great man. Let us not be put off by the circular logic, the
mechanical apparatus, and the pseudo-scientific jargon: Taine, the
conscientious child of his own temperament and time, was himself
an ardent individualist. His theory of character owes quite as much
to Balzac as, we shall be noticing, his theory of environment owes
to Stendhal. Had it been the other way around, had he combined
Stendhal's psychological insight with Balzac's sociological outlook,
he would have been by far a sounder critic. His portrait of Balzac,
for better or worse, is no less monomaniacal than Balzac's depiction of Père Grandet.

Psychology is a knife, Dostoevsky would warn us, which cuts
two ways. We may look for a man in his books, or we may look
to the man for the explanation of his books. Taine's is the more
dangerous way: to deduce the qualities of a work from a presup-
position about the author. The entire *Comédie humaine* is made
to follow from the proposition that Balzac was a business man
working his way out of debt, and Livy's history is just what you
might expect from a man of letters who was at heart an orator.
This mode of critical characterization must perforce be limited to
a few broad strokes, much too exaggerated and impressionistic to
be compared with the detailed nuances of Sainte-Beuve's portraiture. Most of Taine's figures bear a strong family likeness. He is
most adroit at bringing out the generic traits of English literature:

the response to nature, the puritan strain, the tautological fact—
in short—that it was written by Englishmen. He himself, true to
his theories, remains an intransigent Frenchman; and his history,
up to the point where he abandons Tennyson for Musset and re-
crosses the British Channel, remains a traveller's survey of a foreign
culture. Why, in spite of all temptations to interpret other cultures, should Taine have been attracted to England? Wherein
would Taine's Englishman differ from the picturesque barbarian
of Thierry or the stalwart burgher of Guizot?

Taine's critical faculties had been conditioned not by science
but by romanticism, and who was Taine to repudiate his own conditioning? Madame de Staël had been drawn to Germany, and
Melchior de Vogüé would soon be seeking the Russian soul, even
as Matthew Arnold was then evoking the Celtic spirit. Yet English
was, for most Frenchmen, the typically romantic literature. France
had been the Bastille of classicism, while Britain had never been
enslaved to the rules; untamed nature, in Saxon garb, resisted the
shackles of Norman constraint. It took very little perception of the
meters of English poetry for Taine to prefer blank verse to rhym-
ing alexandrines. Form, as he construed it, was a body of artificial
restrictions which inhibited free expression, and which English
men of letters had somehow succeeded in doing without. One
might almost say that they had developed a literature of pure
content. "Not in Greece, nor in Italy, nor in Spain, nor in France,"
said Taine, "has an art been seen which has tried so boldly to express the soul and the most intimate depths of the soul, reality and
the whole of reality." What seemed to him so unprecedented turns
out, upon closer scrutiny, to be a complex tradition. Elizabethan
drama is so much more baroque than the succinct tragedies of
Racine that Taine missed its pattern altogether, and believed he
was facing a chaos of first-hand and unconstrained realities. His
impressions were like those of Fielding's barber at the play, wholly
taken in by theatrical make-believe, naïvely mistaking the actors
for the characters they represent, and quixotically confusing life
with literature.

If we call to mind Lamb's famous essay upon the artificiality of
Restoration comedy, we cannot share Taine's facile assumption
that the English stage received and retained "the exact imprint of
the century and the nation." We cannot accept this free transla-

tion of Hamlet's injunction to give "the very age and body of the time his form and pressure." We can allow that Taine was less of a critic than a historian, but we cannot forgive him for being such an uncritical historian. His professed willingness to trade quantities of charters for the letters of Saint Paul or the memoirs of Cellini does not indicate a literary taste; it merely states a preference for human documents as against constitutional documents. In exploiting literature for purposes of historical documentation, Taine uncovered a new mine of priceless source material. But he never learned the difference between ore and artifice. In his later *Philosophie de l'art*, to be sure, he could no longer sidestep the need for esthetic and technical discussion. There he was forced to concede that art could be idealistic as well as realistic, and to place Greek sculpture at a farther remove from reality than Flemish painting. This concession permitted him to turn his back on the sculpture, and to reconstruct, with a freer hand than ever, the moment, the race, and the milieu of ancient Greece.

The serious objection to environmentalism is that it failed to distinguish, not between one personality and another, but between personality and art. It encouraged scholars to write literary histories which, as Ferdinand Brunetière could point out, were nothing but chronological dictionaries of literary biography. It discouraged the realization, which Brunetière called the evolution of genres, that literary technique had a history of its own. It advanced a brilliant generalization, and established—as first-rate ideas will do in second-rate minds—a rule of thumb. The incidental and qualified extent to which books can epitomize their epoch may vary greatly from one instance to the next. Taine's successors made no allowances for the permutation of forms; rather, they industrialized his process for extracting the contents of books. The prevailing aim of literary historiography, under the quasi-official sponsorship of Gustave Lanson in France and of other professors elsewhere, was a kind of illustrated supplement to extra-literary history. Academic research concentrated so heavily upon the backgrounds of literature that the foreground was all but obliterated; and Flaubert's gloomy prediction, that literature would be absorbed by history, was all but realized. "What shocks me in my friends, Sainte-Beuve and Taine," he had confessed to Turgenev, "is that they do not pay sufficient attention to Art, the work in itself, composition, style, briefly what makes for Beauty."

Meanwhile Taine's influence had been felt in the wider areas of criticism, and here it was subordinated to political ends. Taine himself had been bitterly and indiscriminately anti-political. He did not realize the importance of ideas until he had lost faith in his own: originally he had been a proponent of the materialistic doctrines of the *philosophes*, which he blamed in his later studies, *Les Origines de la France contemporaine*, for instigating the revolution of 1789. Meanwhile socialism, expounded by such theorists as Proudhon, was insisting on "the social destination of art." It was a Danish critic, closely associated with Ibsen, Nietzsche, and the controversies of the 'eighties, who broadened the range and narrowed the tendency of literary history. For politics, and for literature too, Georg Brandes had more feeling than Taine. A cosmopolitan liberal, deeply suspicious of the ascendancy of militant Prussia, he found a touchstone for the romanticists in their struggles or compromises with clerical reaction and the authority of the state. Byron and Heine were his urbane prophets, the Schlegel brothers were apostates, and the revolution of 1848 was the anticlimax toward which his *Main Currents in Nineteenth Century Literature* so intrepidly moved. Whereas a book had been an end-product to Taine, to Brandes it was a continuing force, and the critic's added function was to chart its repercussions.

Both of these aspects, origin and destination, have been duly stressed in the historico-critical discussion of American writers: their reactions to their environment and their contributions to the liberal tradition. Our pioneering literary historian, V. L. Parrington, extended and modified Taine's formula to fit our national problems, dramatizing New England puritanism from the standpoint of western populism, and pitting a heroic Jefferson against a sinister Hamilton. His title, *Main Currents in American Thought*, offered a fraternal salute to Brandes, and denoted an additional qualification. Parrington got around Taine's stumbling-block, the difficulty of using imaginative writers as historical sources, by drawing heavily on the moralists and the publicists. His chapters on Roger Williams and John Marshall are ample and rewarding; his accounts of Edgar Allan Poe and Henry James are so trivial that they might better have been omitted. The latest period is unavoidably the hardest to interpret; and Parrington's last volume was posthumous and fragmentary; but it seemed to register an increasing conflict between artistic and political standards. Granville Hicks, going over the same ground in the 1930's, was able to resolve that conflict by the simple device of discarding artistic standards.

Mr. Hicks, who no longer assumes responsibility for the conception he never quite formulated of *The Great Tradition*, was then a Marxian critic in the sense that Parrington had been a Jeffersonian critic. The choice between those two positions is largely a matter of political standards. Jeffersonianism, naturally the most favorable climate in which to discuss American literature, has been taken in vain so often that it has come to resist definition. Marxism, by redefining milieu in economic terms, presented a more rigorous theory of historical causation than Taine's and a more ruthless canon of political allegiance than Brandes'. It introduced criticism to a sociological system which could be highly illuminating and to a social doctrine which had to be highly controversial. It tightened the relations between literature and life by oversimplifying them beyond recognition. In this respect Karl Marx, as he had occasionally admitted, was no Marxist: he had repeatedly cautioned his followers against expecting the arts to show a neat conformity with his ideological views. Possibly, if he had ever written his projected study of Balzac, he would have bequeathed to them a critical method. For lack of one, they took what was most available. Marxist criticism superimposed its socialistic doctrine upon the deterministic method, and judged according to Marx what it had interpreted according to Taine.

Consequently extension and modification have added their corollary to Taine's method: the relations between literature and society are not unilateral but reciprocal. Literature is not only the effect of social causes; it is also the cause of social effects. The critic may investigate its causes, as Taine tried to do; or he may, like Brandes and others, be more interested in its effects. So long as he is correlating works of art with trends of history, his function is relatively clear. It becomes less clear as he encounters his contemporaries, and as the issues become more immediate. He is then concerned, no longer with a settled past, but with a problematic future. An unsettling present may commit him to some special partisanship, Marxist or otherwise, and incline him to judge each new work by its possible effect—whether or not it will advance or hinder his party's program. Since art can be a weapon, among other things, it will be judged in the heat of the battle by its polemical potentialities. We need not deny the relevance or significance of such judgments; we need only recognize that they carry us beyond the limits of esthetic questions into the field of moral values. There are times when criticism cannot conveniently stop at the border. So long as we know where the argument is leading us, we need not fear to venture afield in pursuit of it.

Indeed we can scarcely proceed very far without running into boundary disputes of one kind or another: patronage and regulation, propaganda and censorship, the issues raised whenever literary activities are promoted or constricted by party lines. More often than not, throughout its history, art has subserved some didactic purpose or other. Ethics has generally held the upper hand over esthetics, which has only secured its occasional periods of independence through the mutual opposition of differing ethical codes. Since goodness is thus no more absolute a criterion than beauty, matters of opinion and taste being equally relative, we fall back upon truth, which—when the particular instance lies open to investigation—can become a matter of fact. What critics consider beautiful may be quite subjective; but that they consider it so is also a fact; and why they consider it so is a question which may lead, via detailed observations, to further truths. Their canons of the good and the bad may be similarly transposed to the objective plane of true or false. Dr. Johnson himself would caution them to proceed "not dogmatically but deliberately." Not evaluation but analysis—"neither to pardon nor proscribe, but to explain and verify"—consummated, for Taine, the critical process. We might sharpen the difference between his contribution and the divagations of his more partisan successors by distinguishing between sociological and social criticism. The former uses society to explain and verify literature; the latter uses literature to pardon or proscribe society.

3. *Literature as an Institution*

It was as if Taine had discovered that the earth was round, without realizing that another continent lay between Europe and Asia. The distance was longer, the route more devious, than sociological criticism could have anticipated. Not that the intervening territory was unexplored; but those who had explored it most thoroughly were isolationists. Those who were most familiar with the techniques and traditions of literature had been least conscious of its social aims or responsibilities. Many of them were writers themselves, lacking in critical method perhaps, yet possessing the very skills and insights that the methodologists lacked. A few were philosophers striving, usually upon some high plane of idealism, toward a historical synthesis of the arts. Their concept of expressive form, inherited by the esthetic of Croce from the metaphysic of Hegel and the literary history of Francesco De Sanctis, resembles that organic principle which Anglo-American criticism inherits from the theory of Coleridge, the preaching of Emerson, and the practice of Thoreau. By whichever name, it is too sensitive an instrument to be used effectively, except by acute critics on acknowledged masterpieces. With cruder material, in unskilled hands, its insistence upon the uniqueness of each work of art and its acceptance of the artist at his own evaluation dissolve into esthetic impressionism and romantic hero-worship. Moreover, while certain German estheticians and cultural historians have been deeply cognizant of forms and styles and parallels among the various arts, they have hedged them about with misleading conceptual schemes.

Conceiving art as the fullest expression of individuality, or else as some emanation of the time-spirit, these schools have incidentally fostered some admirable critiques; but they have disregarded the empirical approaches. Meanwhile, there has been an intensively formalistic reaction, which has gone so far as to turn its back upon history. Under the aegis of New Criticism, it has cogently elucidated the more formal and compact verbal structures; but so far it seems to have been put off by the very informality of the novel, its impenitent intercourse with the outer world. Taine's school, obsolete though its premises may seem, has continued to

prove influential, because it has kept alive the conception of art
as a collective expression of society. The fallacy in this conception
—as we have been seeing—is to equate art with society, to assume
a one-to-one correspondence between a book and its subject-matter,
to accept the literature of an age as a complete and exact replica
of the age itself. Bernard De Voto labelled this "the literary fallacy." One way or another, literature is bound to tell the truth
more or less; but it has told the whole truth very seldom, and nothing but the truth hardly ever; some things are bound to be left
out, and others to be modified, in the telling. Sins of omission can
usually be traced to some restriction in the artist's freedom of
speech, his range of experience, or his control of his medium. Certain sins of commission are inherent in the nature of his materials.
The literary historian must reckon with these changing degrees of
constraint and exaggeration. Literary history, if it is to be accurate,
must be always correcting its aim.

To mention one conspicuous case, the relations between the
sexes have received a vast, if not disproportionate, amount of attention from writers. From their miscellaneous and contradictory
testimony it would be rash to infer very much, without allowing
for the artistic taboos of one period or the poetic licenses of another. An enterprising sociologist, by measuring the exposed portions of the human physique in hundreds of paintings, has arrived
at a quantitative historical index of comparative sensuality. What
inference could not be drawn, by some such future sciolist, from
the preponderance of detective stories on the shelves of our circulating libraries? Those volumes testify, for us, to the colorless
comfort of their readers' lives. We are aware, because we are not
wholly dependent on literary evidence, that ours is no unparalleled
epoch of domestic crime—of utterly ineffectual police, of criminals
who bear all the earmarks of innocence, and of detectives whose
nonchalance is only equalled by their erudition. These, we are
smugly aware, may have no more validity than the counters of a
fascinating game. Nevertheless, it is disturbing to imagine what
uncritical critics might deduce retrospectively, when the players
are dead and the rules of the game have been forgotten. It suggests that we ourselves may be misreading the books of earlier
periods through our ignorance of the lost conventions on which
they may hinge.

Convention may be tentatively described as a necessary difference between art and life. Many of the differences, strictly speaking, may be quite unnecessitated: deliberate sallies of the imagination, unconscious effects of miscalculation or misunderstanding. But art must also differ from life for technical reasons: limitations of form, difficulties of expression. The artist, powerless to overcome these obstacles by himself, must have the assistance of his audience. They must agree to take certain formalities and presuppositions for granted, to take the word for the deed or the shading for the shadow. The result of their unspoken agreement is a compromise between the possibilities of life and the exigencies of art. Goethe might have been speaking of convention when he said, "In der Beschränkung zeigt sich erst der Meister." Mastery emerges through constriction. Limitation has often been a source of new forms, and difficulty—as the defenders of rhyme have argued, from Samuel Daniel to Paul Valéry—has prompted poets to some of their most felicitous expressions. Without some measure of conventionalization, art could hardly exist. It exists by making virtues of necessities; after the necessities disappear, we forget the conventions. After perspective is invented, we misjudge the primitives; after movable scenery is set up, we challenge the unities; and Schiller thereupon pleads for the reintroduction of the tragic chorus as a gesture "against naturalism in art." Yet Taine, forgetting that feminine roles were played by boys, is momentarily overwhelmed by the masculine straightforwardness of certain Elizabethan heroines.

His former classmate, Francisque Sarcey, who became—through forty years of playgoing—the most practical of critics, might have supplied the needed correction for Taine's theories. "It is inadequate to repeat that the theater is a representation of human life," Sarcey had learned. "It would be a more precise definition to say that dramatic art is the sum of those conventions, universal or local, eternal or temporary, which help, when human life is represented on the stage, to give a public the illusion of truth." This illusion may be sustained in the novel more easily than on the stage; but it is still an illusion, as Guy de Maupassant so frankly admitted, when he suggested that the realists ought rather to be known as the illusionists; José Ortega y Gasset would suggest, more warily, that realism be known as apparentism.

Although drama may be the most conventional of literary forms, and fiction the least, even fiction is not entirely free from such encumbrance. Even Proust, one of the most unconventional of novelists, must resort to the convention of eavesdropping in order to sustain the needs of first-person narrative. We shall not condone such melodramatic stratagems; we can observe that the modern novel has tried, both earnestly and ingeniously, to get along without them; upon further consideration we may even conclude that the movement of realism, technically considered, is an endeavor to emancipate literature from the sway of conventions.

That provisional conclusion would explain why literary historians, under the influence of realism, have consistently slighted the attributes of form. In their simplistic impatience to lay bare the so-called content of a work, they have missed a more revealing characteristic: the way the artist handles the appropriate conventions. Whether it is possible, or even desirable, to eliminate artifice from art—that is one of the larger questions before us. But realistic novelists who declare their intentions of transcribing life have an obvious advantage over realistic critics who expect every book that comes their way to be a literal transcript. Stendhal, when he declares that "a novel is a mirror riding along a highway," is in a position to fulfill his picaresque intention. When Taine echoes this precept, defining the novel as "a kind of portable mirror which can be conveyed everywhere, and which is most convenient for reflecting all aspects of nature and life," he puts the mirror before the horse, so to speak. He is then embarrassed to discover so few reflections of the *ancien régime* in French novels of the eighteenth century. His revulsion from neo-classical generalities and his preference for descriptive details carry him back again across the Channel, from Marmontel and Crébillon *fils* to Fielding and Smollett. Some mirrors, Taine finally discovered, are less reliable than others.

The metaphor of the glass held up to nature, the idea that literature reflects life, was mentioned by Plato only to be rejected. By the time of Cicero it was already a commonplace of criticism. It was applied by the ancients to comedy, the original vehicle of realism: the mirror of custom, *speculum consuetudinis*. Later it became a byword for artistic didacticism, for the medieval zeal to see vice exposed and virtue emulated. When Shakespeare invoked it, he had a definite purpose which those who quote him commonly ignore. Hamlet is not merely describing a play, he is exhorting the players. His advice is a critique of bad acting as well as an apology for the theater, a protest against unnatural conventions as well as a plea for realism. Like modern critics who derive their metaphors from photography, he implies a further comparison with more conventionalized modes of art— particularly with painting. To hold up a photograph or a mirror, as it were, is to compare the "abstract and brief chronicles of the time" with the distorted journeywork that "imitated humanity so abominably." Art should be a reflection of life, we are advised, not a distortion—as it has all too frequently been. Criticism, in assuming that art invariably reflects and forgetting that it fre- quently distorts, wafts us into a looking-glass world, more logical than likely. The nineteenth-century resistance to realism, accord- ing to Oscar Wilde, was "the rage of Caliban seeing his own face in a glass." Irish art, according to James Joyce, was "the cracked lookingglass of a servant." The visage continues to vary along with the mirror, and with the gazer as well.

In questioning the attempts of scholars to read Shakespearean drama as the mirror of its time, the late E. E. Stoll reminded them that their business was to separate historical fact from literary illusion, to distinguish the object from its reflected image. Literature, instead of reflecting life, we might better say, refracts it. Part of our task, in any given case, is to determine the angle of refraction. Since that angle depends upon the density of the medium, it is always shifting, and its determination is never easy. We are aided today, however, by a more flexible and accurate kind of critical apparatus than Taine was able to employ. An acquaintance with artistic conventions, which can best be acquired through comparative studies in technique, should com- plement an awareness of social backgrounds. "Literature is com- plementary to life." This formula of Lanson's is broad enough to include the significant proviso that there is room in the sphere of art for ideals and phantasmagoria, shapes and sounds which do not ordinarily find a habitation in the world of reality. But, in recognizing that literature may add something to life or that it may subtract something from life, we must not overlook the most important consideration of all—that literature is at all times an integral part of life. It is, if we can work out the implications of Leslie Stephen's phrase, "a particular function of the whole social organism."

The organic character of this relationship has been most suggestively formulated by a statesman and historian, Prosper de Barante. In writing about the ideas behind the French Revolution while they were still fresh in men's minds, his comprehension of their political dynamics was broader than Taine's. "In the absence of regular institutions," wrote Barante, "literature became one." The fact, though it has long been obscured by a welter of personalities and technicalities, is that literature has always been an institution. Like other institutions, like the church or the law, it cherishes a unique phase of human experience and controls a special body of precedents and devices; it incorporates a self-perpetuating discipline, while responding to the main currents of each succeeding period; it is continually accessible to all the impulsions of life at large, but it must translate them into its own terms and adapt them to its peculiar forms. Once we have grasped this fact, we begin to perceive how art may belong to society and yet be autonomous within its own limits, and we are no longer puzzled by the apparent polarity of sociological and formal criticism. These, in the last analysis, are complementary frames of reference whereby we may discriminate among the complexities of a work of art. In multiplying these discriminations between external pressures and inbred properties —in other words, between the response to environment and the observance of convention—our ultimate justification is a clearer understanding of the vital process to which they are both indispensable. This, in turn, should reinforce the linkage between the given artist and ourselves.

To consider the novel as an institution, then, imposes no dogma, exacts no sacrifice, and excludes none of the critical methods that have proved illuminating in the past or may be proving effective today. If it tends to subordinate the writer's personality to his achievement, that requires no further apology, for criticism has long been unduly subordinated to biography: *Lives of the Poets*. The tendency of the romanticists to live their writings and write their lives, and the consequent success of their critics as biographers, did much to justify this sub-ordination; but even Sainte-Beuve's "natural history of minds," though it unified and clarified an author's works by fitting them into the pattern of his career, was too ready to dismiss their purely artistic qualities as "rhetoric" in the pejorative. More recently the doctrines of Freud, while imposing a top-heavy vocabulary upon the discussion of art, have been used to corroborate and systematize the sporadic intuitions of artists; but the psychoanalysts, like the sociologists, have been more interested in utilizing books for documentary purposes than in analyzing their intrinsic nature. An inquiry into Flaubert's childhood, suggests M. Sartre, would particularize the salient circumstance of his bourgeois origin. A more searching inquiry would take us into the workshop of Flaubert's maturity. Meanwhile the confusion between a novelist and his novels has, on the popular level, been deliberately exploited. A series of novelized biographies, *Le Roman des grandes existences*, has been succeeded by volumes of excerpts in which the author is assumed to be his own biographer: *Zola par lui-même*, *Proust par lui-même*.

If fiction has seldom been discussed on a level commensurate with its achievements, it is because we are too often sidetracked by such displacements. If we recognize the novelist's intention as a Jamesian figure in a carpet, we must also realize that he is guided not by inscrutable caprice but by his material, his training, his commission, by the size and shape of his loom, and by his imagination to the extent that it accepts and masters those elements. Psychology, illuminating though it has been, has treated literature too often as a record of personal idiosyncrasies, too seldom as the basis of a shared consciousness. Yet it is on that basis that the greatest writers have functioned. Their originality has been an ability to "seize on the public mind," in Walter Bagehot's opinion; conventions have changed and styles have developed as lesser writers caught "the traditional rhythm of an age." The irreducible element of individual talent would seem to play the same role in the evolution of genres that natural selection plays in the origin of species. Amid the mutations of modern individualism, we may very conceivably have overstressed the private aspects of writing. One convenience of the institutional method is that it gives due credit to the audience, and to the never-ending collaboration between writer and public. It sees no reason to ignore what is relevant in the psychological prepossessions of the craftsman, and it knows that he is ultimately to be rated by the technical resources of his craftsmanship; but it attains its clearest and fullest scope by centering on his craft, upon his social status and his historical function as participant in a skilled calling and a living tradition.

When Edgar Quinet announced a course at the Collège de France in *La Littérature et les institutions comparées de l'Europe méridionale*, he was requested by Guizot's ministry to omit the word "institutions," and to limit himself to purely literary discussion. When he replied that this would be impossible, his course was suspended, and his further efforts went directly into those reform agitations which culminated in the democratic revolution of the following year, 1848. Thereby proceeding from sociological to social criticism, he demonstrated anew what French critics and novelists have understood particularly well: the dialectical interplay between ideas and events. In a time which has seen that demonstration repeated upon so overwhelming a scale, the institutional forces that impinge upon literature are self-evident. The respect that literature owes to itself, and the special allegiance that it exacts from us readers, should become no less apparent when we view it as an institution in its own right. When we come to appreciate the strategic part that convention is able to play, we shall be better equipped to discern the originality of individual writers. And, after we have made due allowance for the nature of their medium, we can then add their observations to the comprehensive record of humanity's self-knowledge. Between these two aspects of our subject, between life and art, it is fortunate that nothing compels us to choose; for, though the one is inseparably with us so long as we are ourselves, it would be almost meaningless and all too quickly lost without the other.

II

ROMANCE AND REALISM

> The curious thing about art-speech is that it prevaricates so terribly, I mean it tells such lies. I suppose because we always all the time tell ourselves lies. And out of a pattern of lies art weaves the truth . . . Truly art is a sort of subterfuge. But thank God for it, we can see through the subterfuge if we choose.
>
> —D. H. LAWRENCE

1. *Truth and Fiction*

To SHIFT THE EMPHASIS from criticism to the novel should not narrow our focus appreciably; for fiction, as Alfonso Reyes has declared, is the literary process *par excellence*; and the career of the novel itself, though comparatively short, has been versatile and multiform. On occasion it has assimilated the exterior features of many other literary forms: essays and letters, memoirs and chronicles, dialogues and rhapsodies, religious tracts and revolutionary manifestoes, sketches of travel and books of etiquette, every kind of prose and some kinds of verse. It has been so polymorphic that it now seems amorphous, so informal that it seemed "lawless" to André Gide, who deliberately borrowed the English word to underline its unconventionality: "The sole progress that it envisages is to come closer and closer to nature." It can therefore be distinguished not by uniformities of structure but by variations of growth, not by morphology but by physiology. None of the handbooks has managed to establish a structural norm. Many of them identify a story with its plot, the reader with its characters, and the vicarious experience it conveys with its technical means of conveyance. Some of them simply moralize over what happens. The best of them, like Percy Lubbock's

Craft of Fiction, codify the technique of a few examples by emphasizing the novelist's point of view; but laws which may be perfectly adapted to *The Ambassadors* are flagrantly violated by *War and Peace*. James himself would have reaffirmed that the house of fiction had many windows, while the less fastidious Kipling was even more broadly permissive:

> There are nine and sixty ways of constructing tribal lays,
> And-every-single-one-of-them-is-right!

Under such conditions, the exceptions are bound to outweigh whatever rules there may be. "All rules of construction hold good only for novels which are copies of other novels," as D. H. Lawrence perceived. We may set up models for the drama, and even for poetry; but our highest recommendation for a work of fiction is that it be as unlike fiction as possible. Hence realistic fiction, which goes out of its way to avoid the appearance of the fictitious, is bound to involve a contradiction in terms, which comes out tersely in the French *roman réaliste*. The Baconian definition of poetry as "feigned history," in which the imagination redresses the imperfections of literal history, "submitting the shows of things to the desires of the mind," approaches the same paradox from the other side. Poets have long been looked askance at as liars; in their defense it has been urged that their flattering myths could turn this brazen existence of ours into what Sir Philip Sidney called a golden world, such as that of his own romance, *Arcadia*. But therein lay the hazards of escapism, since fictions could be so much more agreeable than facts, as the humanists clearly recognized: "Quanto sunt illa iucundiora ficta quam facta?" Dr. Johnson explained allegorically that Truth, in order to vie with Falsehood in this world, must assume the garb of Fiction. The dangerous prevalence of imagination is for most of us, as it was for him, perennially alluring and suspect. Nor are we completely reassured by the neo-classic touchstone of *vraisemblance*, which has a tricky way of decomposing into the true and the seeming, *vrai* and *semblance*.

Science distinguishes, where magic confounds. *Fictio*, which is roughly the Latin equivalent of the Greek-derived *poíesis*, signifies "making" but also "feigning." The two meanings come together in "make-believe"—or better, because more equivocal, "fabrication." This must be a precarious coalescence, a pseudo-creation in which what is formed is feigned, and therefore subsists in our minds or not at all. "Art is a lie," says Pablo Picasso, "that makes us realize truth." Alfred de Vigny, in prefixing his *Réflexions sur la vérité dans l'art* to the 1829 edition of his historical novel *Cinq-mars*, distinguished two perennial needs of the human heart, seemingly opposed yet intermingled: "one is a love of the true, the other a love of the fabulous." Insofar as the former dominates the latter, we might add, a work of art is realistic. But the sense of wonder is at least as fundamental as the zeal for truth, and when it predominates we have what Vigny terms "the fable." He does not mean that the fabulous is wholly untrue, or that the fictitious is necessarily false; fact, not truth, is the opposite of fiction. He means that, although the fable may deviate from factual truth, it may still be true in its own way. It is never created out of nothing, and the psychologists would agree with Vigny that subconscious fantasy often reveals as much as conscious realism. "Man creates true fiction because he cannot observe anything outside himself and surrounding nature, but he creates true fiction out of a very special truth."

There has been much epistemological speculation, in Bentham's theory of fictions and Vaihinger's philosophy of "as if" and elsewhere, upon the nature of this special truth. It was categorized by Emile Hennequin, in an attempt to apply the canons of science to the novel, as subjective rather than objective. Obviously any work of literature is more dependent on feelings than on facts. From the days of *The Tale of Genji* it has been recognized that the novelist is a witness who is emotionally involved. Incidental details may be discredited without seriously affecting the novel's veracity; it must finally submit to the more searching verification of a total response. It must satisfy our mingled interest in the exotic and the familiar; it must convince us that what seems fabulous is, for the moment, true; it must enlarge, as well as corroborate, our purview by accrediting what may seem incredible. But Pooh Bah's trick of tossing in corroborative detail, "intended to give artistic verisimilitude to a bald and unconvincing narrative," is not enough. The narrative as a whole should carry conviction. Poetry may count upon a willing suspension of disbelief, but prose fiction can afford to take little on faith. The form of the novel, or rather its apparent formlessness, bases an implicit intimacy between the novelist and his reader on certain attitudes and reactions to life which they must both recognize and, in some measure, accept. This mutual recognition should verify the documentary value of the novel. The measure of acceptance, however, is all too frequently the reader's naïveté or the writer's conventionality.

These reservations should confirm our reluctance to entrust ourselves to the mirror fallacy. Two French writers, to whom we are indebted for an object-lesson, once undertook—on the evidence afforded by contemporaneous novels—a sociological survey of the Third Republic. They classified the hero of J. K. Huysmans' *A rebours*, one of the most fantastic creatures in fiction, as a typical aristocrat of his period. Paying small attention to talent, bias, or any of the variables that determine the difference between one book and another, they achieved a meaningless composite. If objectivity is ever to be achieved, it is not by ruling out such distinctions, but by taking them into account; not by uncritically accepting a mass of undifferentiated material, but by calling upon those writers who have been acute observers and would be trustworthy witnesses, by appraising their talent and correcting their bias. Preserving for us the quintessence of history, they present facts as feelings. Instead of the taxes and treaties, they record the values and textures of a period, the dates that frame individual lives, the events that touch immediate sensibilities. The novel is the most tangible of historical documents, Flaubert told Maxime Du Camp: without Balzac's testimony the annals of Louis-Philippe's reign would have been incomplete. To resurrect as much of the past as possible, to reintegrate its dispersed endeavors, to place ideas in their original setting—these objectives of modern historians were first approximated by modern novelists. Michelet and Thierry were the followers of Chateaubriand and Scott.

A great novel, though authenticated by personal observation, never speaks for the novelist alone. To be truer to the normal experience of his readers, Proust deliberately falsified one aspect of his own experience. Any resemblance between a writer's life and his work, unquestionably, can be no coincidence; but the discrepancies between them are possibly even more significant. Though fiction records a history of the sentiments, it is not to be confused with autobiography. In his *Confessions* Rousseau is speaking for himself; in *La Nouvelle Héloïse* he is a spokesman for his contemporaries. The hero of his novel, he confessed to Bernardin de Saint-Pierre, "is not quite what I was, but what I wished to be." In idealizing himself he realized a larger, and hitherto unexpressed, set of ideals. His fable was no private means of escape, no mere revery of a solitary stroller. Rather it expressed the wish-dream of his epoch, the release of bourgeois emotions too long held in check by aristocratic formalities. The literary imagination, as it refracts the real world, is likely to show either a wishful or else an anxious tendency, to emphasize the aspirations or the revulsions of its epoch, to produce an idyll or a satire. It is likely, as Schiller said of Rousseau in his essay *On Naïve and Sentimental Poetry*, "either to seek nature or to avenge itself upon art." Perhaps Rousseau tends toward the idyllic and the utopian because he died eleven years before the Revolution, and had little chance to practise the more direct modes of social criticism. Balzac, who was born a decade after that turning-point, is more obsessed by nightmares than by wish-dreams.

The way in which the imagination idealizes was first suggested by Aristotle, when he maintained that poetic truth is superior to historical truth. He was defending poetry against the strictures of Plato, who, as a metaphysical idealist, held a less idealistic conception of art. When nature is conceived as an imitation of ultimate ideas, then the imitation of nature is only the dream of a shadow. Aristotle, regarding nature itself as the reality, regarded art as the embodiment of a higher reality. The historian might concern himself with particulars, with what has happened; the poet was concerned with universals, with what might happen. To decide what was universal and what was particular, to differentiate the probable from the unlikely, would be the concern of the critic. The canon of verisimilitude, as expounded by Aristotelians, attained its highest level of generality by restricting the subject-matter of literature, fixing the characters and standardizing the themes that were considered worthy of literary treatment. Nature, as an esthetic norm, is subject to no less than eighteen definitions, by Professor Lovejoy's reckoning; but it was fixed in its most idealized manifestation by the classical doctrine of *la belle nature*, the notion that artists should limit themselves

to copying the beautiful. Whenever realists have attempted the
unrestricted reproduction of the ugly or the trivial, traditionalists
have reasserted the principle of artistic selection. In the sense
that art is inherently selective, they have been right. In the sense
that the selective process could represent a wider range of probabilities than they were willing to admit, they have been wrong.
In a world where truth is many-sided and still changing, the
eternal verities need to be reformulated from time to time.

Uniformity is no criterion for universality. "Esthetics would
profit today," writes an esthetician of the novel, Jean Hytier,
"by dealing with conditions instead of rules." The timelessness
of Homer's heroes for us, to a large extent, is contingent upon
the remoteness of the Mycenaean age. Shakespeare's Romans
have often been viewed as thinly disguised Elizabethans, and
Boileau accused contemporary romancers of turning Cato and
Brutus into fops who might have adorned the salon of Mademoiselle de Scudéry. The appeal of neo-classicism has proved less
general than it claimed to be. On the other hand, romanticism,
though it widened the repertory, did not dispense with stock
types. It invoked Ossian more regularly than Homer, ranked
Cromwell above Louis XIV, and preferred the accompaniment
of the *guzla* to that of the lyre. In a word, it had its own conventions, which developed gradually, retarded by the inherent
conservatism of language, the vested interest of the classics, and
the cultural lag. Roger Fry was surprised to observe that the
French Revolution provoked no corresponding upheaval among
the arts. It might be further observed—from the statuesque
painting of David and the oratorical cult of Plutarch, from the
pedantic criticism of La Harpe and the gelid verse of Lebrun-
Pindare, from Talma's tragic revival and Napoleon's Empire
furniture—that post-revolutionary art became more classical than
the classics. It was as if the revolutionists were seeeking to justify
themselves by appealing to tradition. Having broken the heaviest
chains, Benjamin Constant told Vigny, they were preserving the
lightest, "the literary rules." In England, where the political
line was unbroken, Wordsworth was able to precipitate a literary
revolution. In France, where the same impulses were latent, the
appropriate forms of expression had yet to be devised.

The Jeune-France *cénacle*, lagging a generation behind the

Lake Poets, did not emerge until the middle years of the French Restoration. The neo-classicists finally abdicated along with the house of Bourbon; the romantic movement came to power with the July Revolution of 1830; and it is from that year that Arnold Hauser would date the retarded nineteenth century. It was then that Berlioz, having tried three times without success, won the prize of the Conservatory, and completed his *Symphonie fantastique*; Delacroix, who had been scandalizing the Salons, sold his painting of the barricades, *La Liberté guidant le peuple*, to the newly enthroned Citizen-King; Victor Hugo published *Hernani*, whose stormy first night had anticipated the street-fighting by six months, with a preface announcing that romanticism was now a synonym for liberalism; and Auguste Comte brought out the first volume of his tough-minded *Cours de la philosophie positive*. In that same year Balzac published the first *Scènes de la vie privée*, Stendhal began to publish *Le Rouge et le noir*, and fiction began its controlled and detailed analyses of society. Romanticism, Zola would announce from the retrospect of another generation, had been an early stage of that realistic movement which led toward naturalism. Now if art were simply the mirror of reality, then realism would be a constant, and the turbulence of the Revolution would have been immediately reflected in the novel. But realism itself is a historical development: it registers the impact of social changes upon artistic institutions, brings about the breakdown of old conventions and the emergence of new techniques, and accelerates the momentum of the novel toward an increasing scope and flexibility.

Truth, increasingly circumstantial and matter-of-fact, is calculated to prevail over fiction, which gets to look more and more fabulous and conventionalized as it recedes into the past. A more pragmatic outlook implies, of course, a more prosaic worldview, a disappearance of marvels and miracles and consequently tales of the supernatural. But we should be disappointed if we expected realism, after discovering facts and dispelling fables along the way, ever to reach a definite goal. The goals keep moving, too. Some have maintained that, as literature develops, it conforms more strictly to the logic of science: that it progresses from the impossible to the improbable, from the improbable to the probable, and from the probable to the inevitable. To insist very strongly upon this progression is to ignore the inevitabilities of Greek tragedy and the impossibilities of science fiction. The probabilities and improbabilities of art are relative to the minds of its audience. Since the effectiveness of Shakespeare's ghosts depended upon their seeming probable to the superstitious spectator, it would be irrelevant for us to insist that they are not realistic. It is wiser to agree with Johnson: "Shakespeare approximates the remote, and familiarizes the wonderful." The progress of realism can only be charted by its concurrent relationship to the history of ideas. Scientists give us little justification for viewing our present scheme of things, or any given worldview, as the absolute actuality. They have given us relativity, not revelation; they have revealed truths by exposing falsehoods; by trial and error they have learned to improve our observations and revise our hypotheses. All acquisition of knowledge can be described as the continual revision of hypotheses. The possibilities of experience are always vaster than our efforts to account for them, be they literary or scientific; and, to that extent, truth will always be stranger than fiction. Yet fiction serves its turn, as Boileau conceded, by bringing out truth:

> Rien n'est beau que le Vrai. Le Vrai seul est aimable.
> Il doit règner partout, et même dans la fable:
> De toute fiction l'adroite fausseté
> Ne tend qu'à faire aux yeux briller la Vérité.

2. The Third Estate

Granted that fiction is a means of representation, what then— or perhaps we should say whom then—does it represent? Perhaps, in trying to define the ontological status of literature, we have been treating life more as a fixed philosophical abstraction than as a changing social situation. Clearly, it was by responding to social changes that fiction became the most representative—we might even say most democratic—of artistic institutions. The novel, though it already flourished in the eighteenth century, had as yet gained little recognition from critics; neo-classical standards, backed by aristocratic prejudices, had scorned it as a bastard genre. After the Revolution it was gradually legitimatized;

it became, by Hegel's definition, "the modern burgher epic"; it was to become, as Zola boasted, the "forme par excellence" of the nineteenth century. Even Hugo, with all the lyric responsiveness that swept him from the royalism of his youth toward the socialism of his old age, turned from romantic drama to more or less realistic fiction. The ascendancy of fiction over the other arts is illustrated by such popular forms as program music and pictures that tell a story—which critics, curiously enough, call genre-painting. And there is a succinct acknowledgment in the commonest classification of bookshops or public libraries, which reduces all literature to two categories: "Fiction" and "Non-Fiction."

At the beginning such a distinction would have been inconceivable. The art of story-telling, in its primitive attempts to express man's sentiments and transmit his memories, could hardly distinguish truth from fable. Hesiod's Muses, to be sure, could sing: "We know how to speak many fictions as if they were true; but we know how, when we wish, to utter truths." But fiction could not be disengaged until history had appeared, and historians like Thucydides had endeavored to sift the facts. Between the mythical histories of Herodotus and the historic myths of Homer, the line is not too sharply drawn. The epic, preserving an oral type of verse which may have antedated written prose, had been a legend of arms and the man, a celebration of tribal heroes, a tradition incarnate. In comparison with later narratives, especially with the romance, it was less fictitious than historical, less preoccupied with personal adventures than with legendary events. In his illuminating study, *Epic and Romance*, W. P. Ker analyzed these two forms by referring them back to their respective states of society, to the heroic and the chivalric ages. An analysis of the third significant form of fiction, the novel, should be no less dependent on continued cross-reference to the bourgeois age, and to our own state of social organization. Epic, romance, and novel are the representatives of three successive estates and styles of life: military, courtly, and mercantile.

In a seventeenth-century essay on the phylogenesis of the romance, Huet, the scholarly bishop of Avranches, remarked that it had left the theme of war behind with the epic and devoted itself—as its very name would subsequently suggest—to the theme of love. Under the patronage of the Virgin, feminine roles were more prominent in medieval than in classical literature. Dante's Beatrice had intervened to modify Vergil's *Arma virumque cano*, when Ariosto could celebrate "ladies and knights, arms and loves." The lady novelist, no anomaly, made her European debut in the land of Marie de France and Marguérite de Navarre. One of the first English novelists, John Lyly, addressed his books "to the ladies and gentlewomen of England." More often than not, by the time of the French Revolution, novels were written of, by, and for women. But the most articulate woman in post-revolutionary Europe, Madame de Staël, remarked that the novel could now leave romance behind and exploit new themes: ambition, pride, avarice, and vanity. Her *Essai sur les fictions* reads like a preview to Stendhal and Balzac. Love and war could hardly be expected to disappear; but human relations, formerly organized around them, would be decentralized. Feudal allegiances, spiritual sanctions, or flesh-and-blood connections would gradually yield to the cash nexus. Courtship would give place to marriage, exploits to possessions, and happy endings would combine the two. "Fortune" to Jane Austen, or "living" to Trollope, losing all their cosmic connotations, would mean income.

It has since been, in E. M. Forster's words, "The Age of Property." The central motive of the middle class, which novelists may claim—with John Galsworthy—to have "preserved in its own juice," has been the sense of property. By and large, the bonds of interest have been looser, if more intricate, than the institutional ties that held earlier societies together, and have allowed the novelist much more leeway than the epic poet or the romancer. The problems of men without, or with, women have been complicated by their propensities to have or have not, by the tactics and intrigues of acquisition and dispossession. Taking the audit of human affairs, Balzac divided his subjects into three main species: men, women, and things. In *Robinson Crusoe*, the first book that Rousseau recommended to his model pupil, Emile, man had asserted his mastery over things. While fiction moves from Balzac to Proust, things are in the saddle, riding mankind at a swifter and swifter pace. Sterne could include a single prophetic "chapter of things" among the all-too-human vagaries of *Tristram Shandy*; but when the brothers Goncourt, inspired by a reading of Poe, tried to foresee the literature of the twentieth

century, they saw "things having more of a role than men."
Men and women would meanwhile have undergone a process of
reification. Sister Carrie would be stared at as if she were a
package, and Uncle Tom would be advertised as "The Man
That Was a Thing." Social factors, in the system of Emile
Durkheim, are virtually synonymous with *les choses*.

Etymologically, realism is thing-ism. The adjective "real" derives
from the Latin *res*, and finds an appropriate context in "real
estate." The first definition of "real" in Johnson's dictionary, with
a significant citation from Bacon, is bluntly explicit: "relating to
things, not persons." One of the chief ends of language, according
to Locke, is "to convey the knowledge of things." This view
presupposes a nominalistic theory of knowledge. Platonic idealists
and scholastic "realists"—and let us not be confused by the mis-
nomer—had believed in the priority of universals, *universalia ante
rem*. Specific objects were mere accidents, or at best symbolic
correspondences with the actualities of a transcendant otherworld.
That they should be valued for their own sake, that things should
have meaning in themselves, marked the triumph of empiricism,
materialism, and worldliness. Now books are, among other things,
goods and chattels. The novel itself is a negotiable commodity,
unlike the epic in this respect. An epic, as originally recited, was
a kind of public ceremony; a novel, printed and sold and reserved
for private perusal, could be technologically and commercially
exploited upon a wholesale scale. The invention of printing and
the spread of literacy—a diffusion which, culturally considered,
has thinned while it spread—coincided with the accession of
the middle class. William Caxton had early discovered the profits
that lay in the publication of prose romances. Little by little,
in the open market that Sainte-Beuve would designate as "industrial literature," fiction became the favored competitor.

Commerce is a school of realism. The rising cities of the
Middle Ages, as Joseph Bédier pointed out, preferred the chicanery
of Reynard the Fox to the chivalry of the Table Round. Romance
was a prerogative of the barons; the burghers had pre-novels,
their *fabliaux*, their own domesticated anecdotes of double-dealing
or marital mischance. Christianity, with its official contempt for
the world, supported an artistic idealism. The Council of Nicea
had decreed that dogma—not observation—should guide the

painter, and the Iconoclastic Controversy had put down a realistic revolt. But, when the gilds were secularized, the drama came out of the church and into the market-place. When trade thrived in the Low Countries, painting got down to business: the saint stepped aside to make room for the donor, and for a peek into his prosperous household. "The mercantile habits so early introduced into Italy repressed a romantic spirit," explains John Dunlop, the historian of fiction, in discussing the unchivalrous character of the *novella*. The Milesian tale, which was its ancient counterpart, underlay the novels of Petronius and Apuleius. Similar circumstances, in the bazaars of the Middle East, produced the *Arabian Nights*—or, in the geisha quarters of seventeenth-century Japan, the gay tales of "the floating world." Evidently it is no mere freak of association which has linked bawdy stories with travelling salesmen.

To gloss over economic motives is a luxury which students of realism could ill afford. Sociological historians have traced a parallel course for Protestantism and capitalism, and have correlated political revolutions with the Industrial Revolution. If we find that the novel, like other products of our civilization, betrays its commercial background, the intention is not to discredit but to describe. *Bourgeois*, significantly a loan-word from the French, has been overloaded with abusive connotations, by aristocrats and proletarians and intellectuals alike; but it is still, for our use, a descriptive term. It connotes primarily the culture of cities; a novelist, as Thomas Mann told his fellow citizens of Lübeck, is "a burgher story-teller." Its classical synonym, "citizen," was a revolutionary shibboleth; Rousseau proudly inscribed *Citoyen de Genève* on the title-pages of his books; and the objectives of the bourgeoisie were sublimated into the Rights of Man. The progressive watchword of citizenship, liberty, has been contextually defined in liberal politics and laissez-faire economics: free speech and free trade, freedom from certain restrictions and exactions, from arbitrary imprisonment and unjust taxation, the *lettre de cachet* and the *gabelle*. The Revolution virtually imposed individual enterprise on society. When it abolished feudalism, it also prohibited the organization of labor. Abolishing responsibilities along with privileges, it made property an absolute value and competition a way of life. Promoting an ethic of self-interest, it opened up an unprecedented era of social mobility. In older societies, where institutions were more stable, conventions seemed permanent; now, if literature was to keep pace with life, they had to be discarded and replaced. The novel had to be, above all, mobile.

As a vehicle for individualism, it was free to concentrate on character, with wider variety and richer detail than previous fiction. Previously, characterization had been regarded as a specialty of the comic stage. Tragedy, like the epic, had presented myths and idealized its protagonists. Comedy had dealt with private lives and urban types: misers, spendthrifts, parasites, courtesans, domestics. Measured by the exclusive decorum of the neo-classicists, its plane of behavior was low; its attitudes were those of the upper class toward the middle class, so memorably delineated in Molière's *Bourgeois gentilhomme*. When we consider that the early novel dwelt upon the same class distinctions, we should also remember how many novelists had written comedies: Cervantes and Gogol, Lesage and Marivaux, Fielding and Goldsmith. This transition is exemplified in one of the earliest French novels, Scarron's *Roman comique*, which follows a troupe of strolling comedians behind the scenes. Within the privacy of print, the comic spirit can be more sympathetic to the bourgeoisie and more critical of the nobility. The comic factotum, or clever servant, can rise in the world. Starting as a lackey, Lesage's Gil Blas could figure successively as highwayman, steward, doctor, secretary to a bishop, and favorite of the king's favorite. His theatrical descendant, Hugo's Ruy Blas, could even presume to be a tragic hero, a lackey who loves a queen. But a century had passed in the meantime, and that prince of interlopers, Julien Sorel, had arrived. The bourgeois, having crept into fiction through the servants' entrance, had become the master.

Before he could be taken seriously, he had to be taught to behave like a gentleman. Hence eighteenth-century literature was intensively preoccupied with manners, and may be read as a courtesy-book for successful merchants and their families. Addison, like other essayists and character-writers, was a teacher of good taste and even etiquette, frankly serving a didactic purpose. Richardson, a professional printer, teaching female correspondents how to write letters, thereby became a professional observer of manners, a novelist. His epistolary narration was more intimate than conventional narrative in the third person; it was more immediate than autobiography; and it had access to fields of observation that his contemporaries, jauntily posing as Turkish spies or Shandyan eccentrics, had not yet penetrated. Since a novel is essentially an inside story, full of domestic atmosphere and family matters, the point of view has often been associated with the servant in the house. The typical heroine is Richardson's Pamela who, with her irresistible mixture of calculation and sentiment, goes into service and marries the squire. To Fielding, speaking for the country gentry, such a situation could only provide low comedy: Pamela's brother, Joseph Andrews, is put back into his place. To middle-class novelists, on the other hand, the landowner himself is not hearty but sinister: the wicked squire becomes a typical villain, ranging the countryside until the Brontë sisters finally tame him. At length, with the arrival of Thackeray's *Newcomes*, the position of the bourgeois gentleman is so secure that the old Colonel can snub *Tom Jones* by declaring, "I won't sit in the kitchen and boose in the servants' hall."

With the nineteenth century, there is a compromise between the landed and the moneyed interests, as Addison termed them; his Sir Andrew Freeport holds, so to speak, a mortgage on Coverley Hall. Ruined estates—Castle Rackrent, Ravenswood, Wuthering Heights—are the emblematic graveyards of the manorial system. For the picaresque novelists, all roads led to the city; for the romanticists, the novel becomes an excursion to the countryside. It was Scott who reversed the itinerary, and guided trippers through the landmarks of restored Gothic and the outposts of local color. Dickens demonstrated that the cockney cut a ridiculous figure afield, and that his nostalgia for coaching days on the highroad was a protest against a pedestrian circuit of narrow streets and reeking slums. Possibly the centrifugal tendency of English culture, whether the nature-loving example be George Eliot or D. H. Lawrence, has been a reaction against its prevailing industrialism. Conversely France, which remained more agrarian, became more centripetal in its fixation upon the metropolis. Though French and English fiction have developed side by side, they differ much as indoors does from outdoors. England, the pioneer nation of shopkeepers, contributed more heavily to the early development of the novel; Richardson was translated by the Abbé Prévost, imitated by Rousseau, and eulogized by Diderot. But the uncompromising forces behind the French Revolution were to revolutionize the genre. In contrast to the metropolitan and cosmopolitan qualities of the French realists, the great Victorians may seem slightly provincial and insular.

If Taine found little to transcribe in pre-revolutionary French fiction, it was because romance, at the behest of the court, had prolonged itself through the seventeenth century. With heroic flourishes and pastoral refinements, it had mirrored no recognizable landscape but the allegorical map of the "Land of Tenderness." The most striking exception, *La Princesse de Clèves* by Madame de la Fayette, had more in common with the maxims of La Rochefoucauld and the plays of Racine than with the interminably labyrinthine romances of Urfé and La Calprenède. Printed fiction belonged, could only belong, to a leisure class. The eighteenth-century attack upon that class used the literary weapons of philosophy, pamphlets, and encyclopedias. Moral tales, in the manner of Voltaire, darted many a shaft of topical allusion; yet when the philosophers condescended to write novels, realities were subordinated to ideas. When Bernardin de Saint-Pierre sought to bring together a hero and a heroine of different classes, in *Paul et Virginie*, he transported them to an island paradise in the Indian Ocean. Even here, "far from the prejudices of Europe," an egalitarian regime was based upon Negro slavery; and though the heroine, a child of nature, could have saved herself by removing her dress and swimming, she preferred to drown decorously. Ideas can be ahead of their time, but conventions lag behind. Time, however, can revivify certain conventions. Figaro, a servant cleverer than his master, could be welcomed as a harbinger of the bourgeois revolution. Valmont, the profligate villain of *Les Liaisons dangereuses*, could be detested as the representative of a corrupt aristocracy.

Realism asserted the predominance of citizen over courtier. In order to criticize society, Rousseau had glorified nature, and had thereby reawakened the idyllic strain in fiction. The novelist, in the artless phrase of the Marquis de Sade, was "the child of nature, created by her to be her painter." Yet, while Bernardin was painting the natural goodness of man, another disciple of Rousseau was depicting the other side of his doctrine—the corrupting influence of social institutions. This was a more suggestive premise for the novelist: Paris was the new Babylon, and Restif de la Bretonne was stimulated to expose the pitfalls of the capital. *Les Contemporaines*, the forty-two volumes that he filled with case histories of Parisian women are, as the booksellers say, curious; but his life of his peasant father is obviously sincere, *Le Paysan perverti* is the history of his own case, and *Les Nuits de Paris* is his first-hand approach to the people. Thus the old wish-dream of the country yields to nightmares of the city, as it has always done in realistic fiction, ever since Robert Greene interrupted his last Arcadian romance to satirize his competitors. Behind satire there is always pastoral: behind the denunciation of a corrupt Rome, in the histories of Tacitus, there was the vision of a primitive Germany. The major conflict of Italian literature in the Renaissance was between the bucolic and the satiric, according to De Sanctis, "between the idyll and the carnival." When the Great Plague devastated the city of Florence, Boccaccio's ladies and gentlemen could escape to a pleasant country retreat, and beguile the time by telling stories. For later story-tellers there would be no such escape. Defoe, Manzoni, and Albert Camus would discover that the plague itself was a grander theme than all the gallantry and gossip of the *Decameron*. And for those deadlier plagues which devastate man's spirit, the Russian realists would patiently compound their antitoxins.

3. Anti-Romance

The word that denotes the novel in French and several other European languages, *roman*, recalls the vernacular literature of the Middle Ages. Our word, stemming from the Italian *novella* and closely akin to "news," suggests a new kind of anecdotal narrative which purports to be both recent and true. "What is a novel," Goethe asked Eckermann, "but the occurrence of an unprecedented event?" Despite this inclination toward modern journalism, it is still deeply rooted in medieval romance. The difference is a matter of degree, of the varying emphasis placed on truth and on fable. Romance emphasized "marvellous and uncommon incidents," according to Scott; novels emphasize "the ordinary train of human events and the modern state of society." As the old order changed, its sustaining forms outlived their usefulness; as its hierarchies were levelled, its symbols lost their meaning. Particular facts came to the fore and universal myths faded into the distance. "As a country became civilized, their narrations were methodized, and moderated to probability," wrote the historical novelist, Clara Reeve, in her rather complacent dialogue, *The Progress of Romance*. The canon of probability now became a justification for enlarging the domain of fiction. The pre-novel was seeking its own level. "The novel gives a familiar relation of such things as pass every day before our eyes, such as may happen to our friends or to ourselves," wrote Miss Reeve, a generation before Scott, "and the perfection of it is to represent every scene in so easy and natural a manner, and to make them appear so probable, as to deceive us into a persuasion (at least while we are reading) that all is real, until we are affected by the joys or distresses of the persons in the story as if they were our own."

The romance—from verse to prose, from manuscript to print— was a transitional form, standing somewhere between the idealism of the epic and the realism of the novel. With Tasso, Renaissance poetry had aspired, by way of heroic romance, to return to the epic; but it proved to be too short a step from the ridicule of Pulci to the sublimity of Ariosto, and no long journey from *The Faerie Queene* to *The Rape of the Lock*. Neo-classical criticism had set such high standards that it finally collapsed into Pope's art of sinking, with a wild carnival of burlesques, travesties, and mock-heroics. When the grand manner of the *roman d'aventures* became so inflated that—as Boileau declared—Greek mythology seemed bourgeois by comparison, it was time for the *chronique scandaleuse* and for a farewell to heroics. The process of deflation had begun long before in the early centers of trade. Knaves like Tyl Ulenspiegel, created in the unheroic image of the folk, had perpetrated sly jests against the established order. Chaucer's tale of Sir Topas had shown that the flat landscape of the Low Countries was an incongruous setting for romantic adventures. *The Canterbury Tales* had given a realistic twist to a sequence of conventional narratives by drawing the narrators out of their frame. Once the Reeve and the Miller had associated on equal terms with the Knight and the Franklin, the *fabliau* was free to compete with the romance. And the romance seemed more improbable with the passage of years. By the end of the Elizabethan period, English literature was more at home among the gulls and coney-catchers of London than with the nymphs and shepherds of Arcadia.

We may wonder why it was Spain, the most traditionalistic culture of western Europe, that first perfected the novel. Though Spanish enterprise had been first to exploit the new world, the Iberian peninsula was—as indeed it still is—the last citadel of feudalism. The resulting extremes of wealth and poverty, the fanatic effort to preserve medieval institutions in the midst of the Renaissance, and the punctilious formality in keeping up appearances which often masked desperation, could nowhere have been more exaggerated. No background could have provided greater occasion for irony, which plays appearance off against reality and highlights contrasts between the ideal and the real. But, where religious irony had viewed life as a dance of death, humanistic irony praised folly and popular irony glorified roguery. The rogue, who took in everyone he met, and the fool, who was taken in by everyone he met, were complementary figures, deceiver and deceived; their act was a comedy of deception, performed for the benefit of an age which faced unexpected realities and was beginning to question outmoded ideals. Fiction, fallen among thieves and beggars and such-like low company, flouted the knightly code of honor. The hidalgo, with little except pride to support his pretensions, no longer qualified as a hero; he was ill served by the anti-hero of the earliest picaresque novel, *Lazarillo de Tormes*. Thereafter the picaroon, serving many masters, proceeded on his vagabond course through the ranks of society. With Gil Blas and Figaro, the Spanish rogue emigrated to France, where his successes continued and multiplied. With Grimmelshausen's *Simplicissimus*, Head's *English Rogue*, Brackenridge's *Modern Chivalry*, and Gogol's *Dead Souls*, he invaded more distant lands.

Don Quixote travelled in a new direction down the picaresque highway: folly took up the challenge of roguery, and their encounter led to mutual undeception. To mediate between his peculiar imagination and a more pedestrian point of view, the foolish knight was accompanied by a roguish squire; and Sancho Panza had his peculiar foible, the desire to rule a province, which insisted upon being satisfied in a sequel. If Don Quixote's head was in the clouds, Sancho Panza's feet were on the ground. If the master was a feeble champion of the decaying nobility, the servant was a pushing advocate of the lower classes. The pair prefigured—for Stendhal —the conflict between the aristocracy and the third estate, as well as the larger antitheses of past and present or poetry and prose.

> The master tall and pale, the squire plump and ruddy; the former all heroism and courtesy, the latter all egoism and servility; the former always full of romantic and poignant fantasies; the latter a model of the spirit of accommodation, a collection of highly prudent proverbs; the former always feeding his soul on some heroic and daring speculation; the latter ruminating some highly prudent plan, and not failing to take into careful account the influence of all the shameful and egoistic little motives of the human heart. At the very moment when the former should be undeceived by the failure of yesterday's fantasies, he is already preoccupied with today's castles in Spain.

While the former looks back toward the romance, transfiguring commonplace windmills into chimerical foes, the latter looks ahead to the novel, wryly squinting and dryly asking, "What giants?" Their point of departure, then, is the basic disparity between fiction and truth. "The fictitious is all the greater, the more it appears to be true," says the Canon of Toledo, in his diatribe against romances. The ingenious hidalgo of La Mancha, his brain addled by long hours in his library, has forgotten how to distinguish. Thus he is in a position to test the chivalric ideal by acting upon it, and the anticlimax that invariably follows his action renews our sense of reality by sharpening the distinction. "He believed to be truth what is only beauty," Unamuno regretfully commented.

Cervantes was proposing, not without regret, a pragmatic test for a waning chivalry; he was also finding the formula for realism. An unlucky soldier of fortune, "better versed in misfortunes than in verses," writing fiction for money, he himself was not to be taken in by fictitious enchantments. He had ranged the roads, not as a knight errant, but as a tax collector; he had encountered the Moors, not in a puppet show, but in battle and prison. As the author of the sylvan *Galatea*, he too may have yearned for the fabled Golden Age; but his own orbit had been even more adventurous than that to which he assigned his *Persiles and Sigismunda*; and raffish examples jostle cheek by jowl against noble ones in his *Exemplary Novels*. Don Quixote has equal praise for arms and letters, but Cervantes played them off against each other. When he allowed his hidalgo to be dubbed by the innkeeper, a retired picaroon with a head full of balladry, he bound romance over to the picaresque, fully aware that the contrast would prove invidious. He made his readers aware that, after all, inns were more comfortable than castles, kitchen-maids more accommodating than great ladies, barber's basins more useful than enchanted helmets, and workhorses more robust than fabulous steeds. He made *Don Quixote* an ironic commentary on *Amadís of Gaul*, and on the *Orlando* of Ariosto as well. Chapter by chapter, he undercut the precedents of knighthood with Sancho's peasant lore.

A practical man can refute the philosophers, to his own satisfaction, by kicking a stone; the only way in which a writer can refute other writers, however, is to write yet another book. Cervantes, who was both a practical man and a writer, discovered that he could give his book the special effect of vividness and solidity by repudiating all bookish precedent. By disenchanting his readers, he could cast a spell of his own. By attacking literary illusions, he could capture the illusion of reality. He could attain realism by challenging the conventions that gave literature its frequent air of unreality. The barrier that always separates words from deeds, expression from experience, was never more keenly apprehended than in the Renaissance. Travesty, which vulgarized classical subjects, and mock epic, which classicized vulgar subjects, could only reinforce that barrier. Before it could be crossed, the style had to be adjusted to the subject; literature had to be attacked directly in the name of life. Yet literature is a mode of expression, and life is something else; therefore the attack had to be carried out in literary terms. Though Cervantes could not kick the stone, he could appeal to common sense by inviting readers to compare their reading with their experience; he could turn literary criticism, as Américo Castro has shown, into a "critique of reality." He could gauge man's awareness of circumstances, as Ortega defines them: "the mute things that surround us most closely." He could satirize an institution by parodying a convention, by using fiction to break down fictitious barriers, by composing a romance to end all romances.

"Cervantes smiled Spain's chivalry away." Perhaps; but Byron may have overstated the point; elsewhere there remained other windmills to tilt at. In France the vogue of such pastoral romances as Urfé's *Astrée* provoked Charles Sorel's *Anti-roman, ou le berger extravagant*, the story of a shopkeeper's son who sets up as a shepherd, changing his name from Louis to Lysis. Sorel's title, "Anti-romance," generalized Cervantes' formula. Don Quixotes of both sexes, divers professions, and sundry nationalities went adventuring down the bypaths of the eighteenth century. Defoe was proud to acknowledge "the Quixotism of R. Crusoe." Marivaux's first novel, *Pharsamond*, was subtitled *Le Don Quichotte français*. Fielding brought out a comedy, *Don Quixote in England*, before announcing—on the title-page of *Joseph Andrews*—that his first novel had been "written in imitation of the manner of Cervantes." And Julius von Voss was merely one of several Germans who attempted *Der deutscher Donquixott*. Smollett, who had translated Cervantes, was still grinning at chivalry in *The Adventures of Sir Launcelot Greaves*; meanwhile other novelists were advancing the same prescription for other follies. Charlotte Lennox, in *The Female Quixote*, ridiculed the sentimental heroine; Richard Graves, with *The Spiritual Quixote*, hoped to smile away the evangelical movement; and *The Romantic Don Quixote*, better known as *Doctor Syntax*, caricatured the craze for picturesque scenery with drawings by Thomas Rowlandson and hudibrastic verses by William Combe.

Realistic tendencies, we note, had made an early appearance in English literature: Falstaff had abjured honor a few years before Sancho Panza. But even as the middle class was making its presence felt in the Jacobean playhouse, Francis Beaumont, who regularly collaborated with John Fletcher in more elegant drama for the court, exhibited the boorishness of a London apprentice against the charm of a romantic setting in *The Knight of the Burning Pestle*. Cervantes had invented a device for reducing ideas to absurdity, and had applied it to old-fashioned adherences. Samuel Butler applied it to late innovations, and enlisted *Hudibras* in the Cavalier reaction against the Commonwealth. The English compromise, dulling issues which were sharp on the Continent, en-

couraged writers to sympathize with lost causes or indulge in
topsy-turvy humor. The tendency of English fiction is not so much
a clear-cut realism as a shamefaced idealism, varying from the
satire of Swift to the sentimentality of Dickens. *The Pickwick
Papers*, with their bourgeois hidalgo and their cockney picaroon,
make the closest approach to an English *Don Quixote*. Industrialism had provoked a nostalgia for the Middle Ages which Scott,
reversing the role of Cervantes, had cultivated. His was a dual role:
the last minstrel and the first best-seller. If there was something
quixotic about the antiquarian laird of Abbotsford, the author-
publisher of *Waverley* had some of Sancho's shrewdness. His con-
ducted tours of the highlands, starting from the library and returning to the counting-house, compromised discreetly between
Jacobite adventure and Hanoverian comfort. Romance became his
business.

The romantic revival could be interpreted as a mood of collective quixotry, a poetic reaction against the more prosaic attitudes
of the eighteenth century. Diderot, in his *Eloge de Richardson*,
signalized a break in continuity which ambiguous usage might have
glossed over, when he called for a new term to mark a new genre.
But French had no term for differentiating the verse narration of
Chrétien de Troyes from the prose narration of Marivaux—even
though the latter apologized to the readers of *Marianne* for disappointing their courtly expectations by descending to the purlieus
of trade. With the discrediting of the romances, *roman* seems to
have dropped out of sight for a while, and to have been replaced
on French title-pages by such neutral headings as *histoire*. The
word *romanesque*, which had voiced a scorn for the romance-rid-
den mind, was displaced by the English-born *romantique*, which
expressed a sympathy for the same thing. A similar echo from
noun to adjective, in German, prompted Friedrich Schlegel to
sketch his romantic theory of the novel: "Ein Roman ist ein roman-
tisches Buch." A sentimental Swiss novelist—who has described,
in his *Confessions*, how fiction had colored his own attitudes—was
accepted as the international authority, not merely on love, but on
religion and politics, education and ethics. "Jean-Jacques Rousseau
was my Amadís of Gaul," confessed Heinrich Heine, and the nineteenth century confessed with him. Yet Rousseau himself, as he
intimated in the dialogue prefixed to the second edition of *La*

Nouvelle Héloïse, was shrewdly aware that *l'esprit romanesque* can both exalt and delude.

German romanticism was, of course, able to read problematic and subterranean meanings into Cervantes' novel. Knight and squire embodied, for Hegel and Schopenhauer, the everlasting dilemmas of metaphysics; Oswald Spengler would later regard them as rival historiographers; and Franz Kafka would not be the last to meditate a sequel. Not in his wildest delusions had Don Quixote claimed such homage as the romanticists were willing to yield. No longer a figure of fun, he was an object of admiration, nay, of veneration; he stood out, against the triumph of the bourgeoisie, as the tragic hero of the saddest story ever told. Among the Russians, Turgenev considered him a nobler character than Hamlet, and Dostoevsky envisaged him—along with Jesus—as that "positively good man" on whom *The Idiot* was modelled. To Dostoevsky, Cervantes had spoken "the last and greatest expression of human thought . . . the bitterest irony which man was capable of conceiving." To the Soviet playwright Anatol Lunacharsky, *The Emancipated Quixote* was nonetheless a revolutionary hero. Meanwhile, in America, where the frontier had conditioned a unique series of cultural contrasts, the mock-heroic guffaw was heard again. Mark Twain raised the problem of "Castles and Culture" in *Life on the Mississippi*, and mopped up a few late vestiges of romance with the motorized cavalry of *A Connecticut Yankee in King Arthur's Court*. Melville, pursuing his obsession around the world, cited Cervantes and Bunyan as exemplars for the democratic novelist, while William Dean Howells demanded a great American novel built along similar lines, and William Faulkner testified of *Don Quixote*, "I read that every year, as some do the Bible."

But it was in nineteenth-century France that the example of *Don Quixote* proved to be most fruitful, and this is why it so much concerns us here. It was the original stimulus for Stendhal and Flaubert, as they both admitted, and as *Le Rouge et le noir* and *Madame Bovary* should amply reveal. Explicitly or implicitly, again and again, our study should lead us back to the knight of the rueful countenance and his earthy squire. We should feel something of the fascination that led Daumier to paint them, whenever he was not occupied by his lithographic record of the period. We should comprehend through them the split personality that Alphonse Daudet attributed to the French bourgeois: "Don Quixote and Sancho Panza in the same man." When the Don says, "Cover thyself with glory, Tartarin," and Sancho replies, "Tartarin, cover thyself with flannel," their colloquy should account for the romantic idealization of Don Quixote and the hostility of the realists toward Sancho Panza. In an age of flannel, the glory of romance is definitely past, and epic beauty is inconceivably remote. "The conscience of mankind has changed since Homer," sighed Flaubert. "The belly of Sancho Panza has burst the girdle of Venus." The self-contradictory task of the novel had been evident, from the very beginning, in such paradoxes as Furetière's *Roman bourgeois* and such apologetics as Fielding's "comic epic poem in prose" —the very phrase re-echoes from Cervantes. They may have protested too much, but it was the protest of common sense against literary convention.

Defoe prefaced each of his novels with a disclaimer, invidiously differentiating the facts he was about to relate from the fictions of other writers. Diderot boldly called one of his tales *Ceci n'est pas un conte*. Similarly, Thomas Mann warns us, "Dies ist kein Roman," and Henry Miller: "This is not a book." Such, in essence, is what every realist tells his readers in his own way, and what makes *Don Quixote* the prototype of all realistic novels. Though romance can never be conclusively smiled away, every time it reappears in another shape, another writer rises to protest. It cannot be an accident that realism, from Rabelais' burlesque of the Arthurian legend to Jane Austen's glances at Fanny Burney and Anne Radcliffe, has so often originated in parody; that the genre of the "parody-novel," as it remained for the Russian formalists to point out, was so fully developed in *Tristram Shandy*; that so many novelists, like Thackeray, have started as parodists, playing the sedulous ape to their seniors. The writer who has a real contribution to make, even while he is assimilating the craft of fiction, is already disclaiming the conventions of his predecessors. André Malraux would argue that every artist commences with *pastiche*. We need not maintain that all realists have imitated Cervantes, but it is surprising how many have done so. We are all at liberty to observe for ourselves what Bernard Shaw calls "the conflict between real

life and the romantic imagination," but Shaw himself admits that
he picked up the formula at third hand, in a forgotten novel of
Charles Lever's. Whenever and wherever that conflict breaks out,
realism parodies romance, and Don Quixote rides again.

4. The Gates of Ivory

If the posthumous adventures of Don Quixote and Sancho Panza
have led us this far, it is because the duality they present, after one
fashion or another, is always with us. Irving Babbitt's comment
gives us a hint of its inexhaustible meaning: *"Engaño* and *desen-
gaño,* illusion and disillusion, eternal themes of Spanish poetry!"
Eternal themes of Greek tragedy, Nietzsche would have said. The
works and lives of all poets, as Goethe had deduced from his own
work and life, would seem to oscillate between the poles of *Dichtung* and *Wahrheit.* Innocence and experience, sensibility and
sense, appearance and reality—different writers have set forth their
dilemmas in their own ways, and yet their terms overlap and interlink. More recently, criticism and scholarship have put forward a
number of parallel formulations, differing considerably in substance and intent, and yet converging upon that peculiar perspective for which Cervantes provided a working model: the literary
technique of systematic disillusionment. Thus Georg Lukács took
the Hegelian dialectic as a basis for his early theory of the novel,
which he has subsequently reversed in a classic Marxist maneuver.
Christopher Caudwell, in a similar vein, sketched an ideological
approach to poetry under the title *Illusion and Reality.* Pierre
Abraham, from a point of view oriented to anthropology and psychology, has endeavored to distinguish the creations from the
clichés of fiction. Students of the French novel have not overlooked what, in the light of their investigations, appears more and
more to be its most ingrained trait. What should be more surprising is that a recent study of the German novel discerns a
comparable tendency in such dissimilar material. And when the
application can be extended to great writers working in other
forms, notably to Shakespeare, we are encouraged to seek a common denominator.

Assuming then that some more basic process lies behind these individual patterns, our venture is to outline its principles in this present chapter, and to exemplify them in the chapters that follow. It has long been recognized that the ways of the imagination are bifurcated. Homer described twin gates: the one of opaque ivory, through which pass fictitious dreams, and the other of transparent horn, which lets out nothing but truth. Archaeologists have traced the gate of ivory to the symbolism of Olympus and the sun; the gate of horn, which is older, has taken them back to the lore of the East and the cult of the dead. Characteristically, Vergil elaborated the Homeric description into an allegory of the soul, and Rabelais scented a punning connection between the gate of horn and the realm of ribald anecdote. Sainte-Beuve adapted the concept to critical purposes when, in an article on Musset and the beginnings of romantic poetry, he characterized the work of Chénier and Lamartine as "two ivory gates to the new domain." He was somewhat disillusioned with the romanticists four years later, in 1837, when he wrote a poetic epistle to the literary historian Villemain, deploring—among other things—the premature retirement of Vigny into his *tour d'ivoire*. Here too, perhaps, was the faintly blended echo of Vigny's resonant *cor d'ivoire*. Sainte-Beuve's phrase, now a byword for artistic isolation, also echoes the Song of Songs, where the Shulamite's neck is likened to a tower of ivory; but the scriptural hyperbole, which had symbolized erotic dalliance in Sainte-Beuve's novel *Volupté*, here acquires overtones from the Vergilian tradition of the ivory gate. With the decline of romanticism, we are left to infer, that gate is closing. With the advent of realism the gate of horn opens wider than before, and bodies forth its most portentous truths.

The parable is vastly oversimplified. Truth and fiction seldom, if ever, come to us unadulterated and clearly labelled. Even sociological critics, as we have seen in the case of Taine, are prone to mistake the one for the other and to confuse the true with the fabulous. This may well be termed the quixotic confusion, and it did not wane with the romances. Characters less volatile than Don Quixote, such as Dr. Johnson, found novels unsettling. Goethe, conflating *Wahrheit* with *Dichtung*, re-enacted *The Vicar of Wakefield* in an episode of his autobiography. As books and readers have multiplied, as we have become more dependent on the printed word and less conscious of its limitations, our heads have all been slightly muddled. We have all been what Jules Vallès called *les victimes du livre*, and have suffered from what Renan diagnosed as the *morbus litterarius*. The contagion would not have been so widespread, and our resistance would not have been so weak, if we were as receptive to fact as we are to fiction. "A fictive covering," in Wallace Stevens' phrase, "Weaves always glistening from the heart and mind." Romance is an inherent weakness of human nature—if indeed we should consider it a weakness, when it has so often been a source of imaginative power. As revived and redefined by Hawthorne, it held a particular attraction for American writers, anxious to unite the present with the past and the actual with the imaginary. Dickens, who purposely "dwelt on the romantic side of familiar things," has maintained a stronger appeal than sterner realists. Even Cervantes momentarily succumbed to self-hallucination in the bewildering cave of Montesinos. The poetic temperament, preferring romantic madness to suffocating reality, is like Baudelaire's portrait of Tasso:

> l'Ame aux songes obscurs
> Que le Réel étouffe entre ses quatre murs!

One of Joubert's maxims asserts that illusion is an integral part of reality. In that case, the part is easier to define than the whole. The significance of reality, as Carlyle complained, "is too apt to escape us." The stuff of illusion, to the extent that we recognize it as such, has already been pinned down. It is an artificial world, which may be discredited by comparison with the real world, but which exists concretely enough on paper; whereas our printed record of the real world consists, to a surprising degree, of objections and exceptions to this artificial world. On paper, where romance may seem concrete, realism is elusive; for romance works with a definite repertory of symbols and conventions, which realism—in the name of undefined and unexpressed realities—shows to be inadequate. "Canst paint a doleful cry?," the suffering hero asks a painter in Thomas Kyd's *Spanish Tragedy*. Obviously, he cannot; for no one can; his medium is not adequate to the emotion. Yet, by deprecating the medium, the playwright implies the emotion, and cuts through the formalities of theatrical dialogue to a sense of living actuality. He relays that sense to us by illusory means, because these are the only means at the writer's disposal.

Dante conveys the same sort of effect by an analogous device, in implicitly contrasting the literary romance of Sir Launcelot with the felt passion of Paolo and Francesca. That is literature, he seems to say as the lovers put down their book, and this is life . . . In each instance the writer has convinced us, for a moment, that his artificial world coincides with our real world. He has all but accomplished Whitman's intention of expressing the inexpressible.

"True eloquence makes fun of eloquence," said Pascal. True literature, we might continue, deprecates the literary. *Le vrai roman se moque du roman.* Fiction approximates truth, not by concealing art, but by exposing artifice. The novelist finds it harder to introduce fresh observations than to adopt the conventions of other novelists, easier to imitate literature than to imitate life. But a true novel imitates critically, not conventionally; hence it becomes a parody of other novels, an exception to prove the rule that fiction is untrue. By and large, it is the rule that prevails. Fiction congeals, truth is obscured, and the exceptional writer is compelled to cut his way through the rules. Victor Hugo sought critical sanction, in his challenging preface to *Cromwell,* for introducing comedy into tragedy and juxtaposing the sublime and the grotesque: "beauty and the beast." In *Les Misérables* he applied this formula to the novel: "mire, and yet soul." By that time Hugo's innovations had lost some of their vitality, and he was congratulating Baudelaire upon the creation of "a new shudder," a fuller expression of life's complexities as felt by a younger generation. Literature, left to itself, is in danger of going dead; like language, it must be kept alive by assimilating new elements and recharging old ones. Each generation, finding it harder to be original, strives harder for shocks and novelties, contrasts and juxtapositions. With pointed irrelevance or offhand profanity, with a quotation that rings suddenly false or a detail that has not heretofore been recorded, contemporary realists keep striving to break the crust of accumulated literary tradition. Byron's proverbial line gains meaning from its poetic context:

> 'Tis strange,—but true; for truth is always strange;
>   Stranger than fiction; if it could be told,
> How much would novels gain by the exchange!
> How differently the world would men behold!

Hugo, a past master of illusion, knew that absolute reality could never be put into writing. "As a matter of fact, will the novel ever reproduce the strange combinations of life?" asked Gérard de Nerval, comparing the fiction with the stranger journalism of their day. "We invent man because we don't know how to observe him." Earlier critics had preferred invention to observation. Modern novelists pride themselves on being trained observers, but there are many moments when even Balzac is still the visionary. Paul Valéry sustained the paradox, apropos of Stendhal, that it is quite unnatural for a writer to tell the truth. The mind falls naturally into quixotic habits, idealizes and embellishes, creates false perspectives and geometrical misconceptions, against which French philosophers—from Pascal to Bergson—have repeatedly protested. Taine's own theory of knowledge was a belated attempt to correct this propensity. "Two main processes are employed by nature," he wrote in *De l'intelligence*, "to produce in us that operation we call cognition: one consists in creating illusions, the other in rectifying them." This is a simple psychological principle, yet it reconciles the polarities we have encountered, and indicates how fiction can objectify inner conflicts. Literature sees life, not steadily and whole, but fitfully and fragmentarily, through the painful workings of disillusion. Let us assume that reality is an unknown quantity, x, and that romance comprises our whole heritage of literary conventions. These things, when they are known to be illusions, are rectified by the operation of that unknown quantity, and this process of rectification is realism.

Courbet's definition, "the negation of the ideal," is less negative than it sounds, if we construe ideals as *idées fixes*, evanescent Dulcineas who lead men's minds astray. More positively, the novel of disillusionment thus becomes a novel of development, a *Bildungsroman*. Every great novelist since Cervantes has played his own variation on the theme that Balzac epitomized in *Illusions perdues*. Voltaire's is perhaps the neatest and the most schematic: Candide is sent forth, armed with his optimistic philosophy, to lose another illusion in each successive episode. Meredith's is altogether different, yet Richard Feverel is also suspended between the aprioristic and the actual, appealing to feminine influences and woodland retreats in an unsuccessful effort to get away from paternal systems and doctrinaire categories. Tolstoy expands the pattern to the enormous scale of *War and Peace*, turning the proverbs of the Russian peasantry against the French prattle of Saint Petersburg, the comradeship of prison against the ritual of freemasonry, the sensibilities of Prince Andrey against the strategies of the German generals, the pragmatism of Kutuzov against the theatricality of Napoleon. Warfare, with its overt alignment of humane ideals against brutal conditions, provides an exemplary situation. Those who deplored the disillusioned novels about the first World War forgot that it has always been the method of realistic fiction to undermine a series of preconceptions. Romantic presuppositions, like those which Scott attributed to his Waverley, are tested under trying circumstances. The protagonist has been "an imaginist," like Jane Austen's Emma—or, for that matter, Flaubert's. And the test is invariably severe, because, as T. S. Eliot reminds us,

> Human kind
> Cannot bear very much reality.

Realists have always been regarded as pessimists, and accused of seeing through a glass darkly, of underscoring the bestial and ignoring the beautiful. The rejoinder has been that we live in an age when the grotesque is more in evidence than the sublime. We could hardly expect an ebullient reaction from Remarque's schoolboys, marching out of a classroom to death in battle, or from Hemingway's heroes, in retreat from the exploded slogans. "Abstract words such as glory, honor, courage, or hallow were obscene beside the concrete names of villages, the numbers of roads, the names of rivers, the numbers of regiments and the dates."

The novelist must feel a peculiar tension between the words, conventions, and ideas that the masters of his craft have handed on to him and the facts, impressions, and experiences that life continues to offer. We do not wonder that the novel is such a self-conscious form, or that so many novels have been written about novels. No writer has carried literary self-consciousness farther than André Gide, who believed that the novelist's notebooks are more interesting than his novels, and who acted on this belief by publishing *Le Journal des Faux-monnayeurs*. The hero of *Les Faux-monnayeurs* is likewise a novelist, and the core of the novel itself is his notebook. "I begin to glimpse what I shall call the profound subject of my book," he notes. "It is, it will doubtless be, the rivalry between the real world and the representation of it that we construct for ourselves." It would be hard to hit on a better summary of *Don Quixote* in a single sentence. "The way the world of appearances imposes itself upon us, and the way we try to impose our own interpretation on the external world, shape the drama of our lives. The stubbornness of the facts tempts us to transpose our ideal construction into dream, hope, future life, and our belief in these is fed by all our disappointments in this life. The realists begin with facts and accommodate their ideas to the facts." But Gide's hero ends by accommodating the facts to his ideas, and the world of appearances—the counterfeit world—imposes itself upon Edouard's. Meanwhile Gide's novel, by dramatizing the novelist's predicament, by acknowledging the reality that cannot quite be expressed, has given us our subtlest demonstration of realism at work, and has reasserted the genuine world in the end.

The ultimate question, Pilate's question, "What is truth?," we may leave to the epistemologists—though without much confidence, for they too are encumbered by the limitations of language. By applying the label of realist to philosophers as far apart as Thomas Aquinas and Bertrand Russell, they have given us leave to define our subject in strictly relative terms. Nor have the art critics been able to persuade us that their more tangible realism can be supported by any absolute standard. On the contrary, the most persuasive discussion of the problem from a visual angle, E. H. Gombrich's *Art and Illusion*, offers closer parallels to the problem of fiction than might have been suspected. "There is no neutral naturalism," Professor Gombrich assures us, and again: "No art is ever free of convention." Pictorial representation, as he richly illustrates and aptly elucidates it, is shown to have been achieved by the correction and modification of pre-existing schemata. This would corroborate the view of André Malraux, that realism in the plastic arts is less a system than it is a sequence of "stylistic rectifications"—the very word that Taine used to describe the mental process involved. It is not a single style, Malraux makes clear, but an orientation reflected by various styles. "Every realistic ideology, applied to painting, has been a polemic against the latest idealism." Appearances are as deceptive to the eye as to the mind; the phrase *trompe-l'oeil* should be sufficient to warn us against the illusionistic trickery that tempted foolish birds to peck at painted grapes. Even photography, as Baudelaire perceived, is incapable of exact reproduction.

"By what art or mystery, what craft of selection, omission or commission, does a given picture of life appear to us to surround its theme, its figures and images, with an air of romance, while another picture close beside it may affect us as steeping the whole matter in an element of reality?" One pertinent answer to James's question would be to stress the invidious comparison between the two complementary pictures or attitudes. Without attempting to define reality, we have assigned the unrealistic phenomena of literature to the sphere of romance, and have accepted the anti-thesis—which so many others have discussed in their own contexts —between romance and reality. We may consequently begin to think of realism as a synthesis: the imposition of reality upon ro-mance, the transposition of reality into romance. "Thus a novel starts in us all sorts of antagonistic and opposed emotions," Vir-ginia Woolf reassures us. "Life conflicts with something that is not life." To this degree, the analogy of the twin gates seems to be psychologically valid. Man cannot be completely objective without becoming indifferent; what has meaning to him has value for him; his emotions, however confused or crowded, vibrate to the polarity of desire and fear. Freud has rehabilitated the ivory portal by re-lating the motives of wish-fulfillment to the interpretation of dreams. As for the hornéd gate, its darker ghosts are anxiety neu-roses which psychoanalysis cannot exorcise, since they enunciate the reality principle.

Both the wish-dream and the nightmare can be shared by a so-ciety, as well as introjected by an ego; they can take on the guise of public myths as well as private fantasies. So Karl Mannheim has interpreted the collective impulse that shapes utopias and, con-versely, the critical consciousness that exposes ideologies. His inter-pretation of bourgeois liberalism corresponds closely to the realistic temper that we shall be confronting. In both cases, the truth is approximated by means of a satirical technique, by unmasking cant or debunking certain misconceptions. In neither case does truth exist in a vacuum: to unmask the misconception might disturb the vested interests, but it would decidedly advance the claims of certain other groups. To be able to gauge these pressures and ob-stacles is to apprehend, however dimly, what is real behind what is realistic. Moreover, it is to agree with Disraeli's dictum: "Nine-tenths of existing books are nonsense, and the clever books are the refutation of that nonsense." Thus the history of culture becomes a succession of unmasked ideologies and lost illusions, obsolete fables and corrected hypotheses, of which literature comprises the record and commentary. The novel, viewed against its institutional setting, becomes a satire as well as a parody. It penetrates beyond literary convention to social convention, as *Don Quixote* penetrated beyond romance to chivalry itself. In criticizing literature, it criticizes life. It rebounds from fantasy into knowledge.

5. *From Priam to Birotteau*

Life has infinite variety and art has limited resources. The artist, faced with an endless problem of invention and adaptation, coins symbols. His coinages, when they are imitated by other artists, become stereotypes. When new phases of experience emerge, old techniques of expression prove inadequate. A symbol is more or less adequate to a given situation. In a dynamic society, where the situation is always changing, symbols quickly lose their meaning, and artists are thrown back on literal details. In a static society, where artistic convention is stabilized by social convention, art tends to be symbolic rather than realistic. Forces of social change, always clamoring for artistic recognition, are resisted by conservative forces which have already reached a cultural equilibrium. This resistance, vested in such official forms as academies or censors, produces a "petrification of taste." It tries, as William Dean Howells has said, "to preserve an image of a smaller and cruder and emptier world than we now live in." Such a world, for the opponents of realism, is real enough. For the realists, on their side, it is sheer delusion. To dispel the delusion they open abysses and uncover irregularities which, on the other side, their opponents reject as improbable. Each side sets up its own way of life as a canon of probability, and the question is reduced to a conflict of interests.

Realism has the pluralistic advantage of recognizing that there are more things in heaven and earth than any one system can comprehend. To treat literature as a closed system is to cut it off from ever-changing reality. Other changes will take place elsewhere, pressures will gather force, until the inertia of tradition is overcome by deliberate revolt. The literary counterpart of the French Revolution emerged in England when, with the publication of *Lyrical Ballads*, Wordsworth celebrated humbler lives, and Coleridge explored stranger experiences, than classical poetry had been willing to recognize. When romanticism, which began by revolting against classicism, froze into an orthodoxy, it was the turn of the realists to revolt. Realism itself is now an obsolescent slogan, sufficient unto its day but long outdated; later realists have tried to bring their efforts up to date by calling themselves naturalists, naturists, verists, veritists, or super-realists. Yesterday's realism is today's convention; today's revolutionists are notoriously the academicians of tomorrow. Every classic, Stendhal aphorized, has been romantic in its day. Every generation, like the mythical giant, has to renew its strength by touching the earth, tapping new sources of vitality, themes "hitherto ignored by the associations of polite and refined society"—as Harriet Beecher Stowe said of Negro slavery in her preface to *Uncle Tom's Cabin, or Life Among the Lowly*. Even in *The Scarlet Letter*, Hawthorne tried "to give a faint representation of a mode of life not heretofore described." As society extends its privileges, literature gives increasing representation to the newly enfranchised elements. The development of the novel runs parallel to the history of democracy, and results in a gradual extension of the literary franchise.

When the private citizen had achieved wealth and a certain degree of power, literacy and a certain degree of taste, it was no longer seemly to represent him as a comic figure. The more advanced writers of the eighteenth century campaigned for a more serious treatment. Comedy, with Cervantes, had dared to ridicule the nobility. Tragedy, with Lessing, attempted to exalt the middle class. In 1767 Beaumarchais published an essay on *le genre dramatique sérieux*, protesting against the tragic decorum that sympathized exclusively with unfortunate kings, while citizens—overwhelmed by such catastrophes as fell to their lot—were considered merely ridiculous. By 1866, if we may judge from an entry in the Goncourt journal, all that had been changed: "Everything goes to the people and deserts the kings: the interest of novels shifts from royal misfortunes to private misfortunes, from Priam to Birotteau."

From Homer's god-like patriarch to Balzac's wholesale and retail perfumer—the contrast invokes a mock-heroic irony to which Edmond and Jules de Goncourt, with their nostalgia for the *ancien régime*, were poignantly sensitive. The falls of princes and the rises of merchants had blurred the distinction between tragedy and comedy. The word "villain," which originally denoted a person of the lowest rank, could be attached to the nobly born. The hero, originally a person of the highest rank, could be a man of the people.

> I want a hero: an uncommon want,
>   When every year and month sends forth a new one,
> Till, after cloying the gazettes with cant,
>   The age discovers he is not the true one.

Byron opened his mock-epic, *Don Juan*, by voicing the reiterated demand of the age. It was an age of disappointed hero-worship and intermittent iconoclasm, of manufactured myths and exploding hypotheses. A *Hero of Our Time*—the title of the episodic novel by Byron's ill-fated Russian admirer, Lermontov—voices these ambiguities. Thackeray's subtitle for *Vanity Fair*, A *Novel Without a Hero*, would be equally fitting for most other novels. Their protagonist remains a hero in a purely technical sense; his bourgeois environment affords little scope for exploits and passions on the epic or romantic scale. Captain Dobbin and George Osborne are poor substitutes for Achilles or Tristram. Yet even a realistic age has its archetypes, and its art is still dominated by what Taine calls "the ruling personage—that is, the model that contemporaries invest with their admiration and sympathy." Such an idealized role was played in ancient Greece by the athlete, and in the Middle Ages by a saint or a knight; in modern literature, Taine goes on to suggest, it is enacted by a Faust or a Werther. Goethe himself may be, as Thomas Mann affirmed, the principal representative of bourgeois culture; but it is significant that neither of those latter-day heroes was a burgher. If Faust is not the intellect itself, he personifies the intellectual: poet, scholar, scientist, reformer. And what is Werther, ostracized from the polite drawing-rooms of Wetzlar, excluded from the family circle of Lotte and Albert, but the outsider?

The ruling personage of the generation brought up on *The Sor-*

rows of Young Werther, Napoleon Bonaparte, objected to the note
of social protest in Goethe's bread-and-butter romance. Where
could we find a more impressive testimonial to the significance of
that note? The man of destiny hated to be reminded that he too
had been an outsider, before the Revolution had opened careers
to talents and multiplied alternatives to Werther's suicide. Napoleon's career was partly shaped by literary precedent: wagons full
of fiction accompanied all his campaigns, and he once remarked
that France owed some of its heroic deeds to Corneille. His own
lengthening shadow was to overcast French literature and to inspire legends that Béranger or Hugo could hardly magnify. On
the very eve of the nineteenth century, he wrote from Egypt to
his brother Joseph: "I need solitude and isolation; grandeur wearies
me; the fount of feeling is dried up; glory itself is insipid. At
twenty-nine years of age I have exhausted everything. It only remains for me to become a thorough egoist." Self-diagnosis has
never put its finger so firmly on the symptoms of the *maladie du
siècle*. The emulation of Napoleon became, to speak it profanely,
what the imitation of Christ had been to the Middle Ages. We
shall observe its effects upon Fabrice del Dongo and Eugène de
Rastignac. Not until Tolstoy had made Napoleon a kind of imperial Quixote, and exposed him to the mother wit of the Russian
peasantry, did the legend begin to fade.

If Thomas Hardy could look down on him as a cosmic puppet in
The Dynasts, it was because later generations were responding to
another mentor, less spectacular but farther reaching, Darwin. By
the end of the century the novel was more concerned with man's
place in nature than with man's place in history, and no man could
be a hero to the naturalist. It had been apparent, ever since the
Empire, that the eagles and the trumpets were things of the past.
Beethoven's Eroica Symphony was a lament, not for Napoleon,
but for heroism itself. The most effectual survivals of the Napoleonic regime were not military glories but administrative arrangements. The ruling personage, whoever he might become, had to
be militantly civilian. He was not likely to be a captain or a king,
distinguished from his fellow men by prowess or rank; some personal trait, some striking idiosyncrasy, set him apart from the
others. In *complet bourgeois*, without spurs or epaulettes, he was
still distinguished by his ghastly pallor, his piercing eye, and the

restless attributes of his world-weary cosmopolitanism. When not haloed by a supernatural aura, he was stigmatized by some unnatural sin; when not marked by physical deformity, he was alienated by psychological maladjustment. Novelists showed a good deal of morbid ingenuity in marking their men. Sometimes the hero appeared in the guise of a demon, vampire, leper, hunchback, deaf-mute, hermaphrodite, or idiot; at other times as an anchorite, prisoner, conspirator, outlaw, bastard, pariah, or Negro; almost, at times, a villain.

Invariably, he was a man of mystery. The *homme fatal* has had many incarnations, from the earliest rites to the latest films; the Ancient Mariner, as was demonstrated by John Livingston Lowes, reincarnated the Wandering Jew. Legend provides a conventionalized body of recurrent types and irrational motifs, which literature manipulates and rationalizes to the purpose at hand. When Frankenstein's monster sat down to read, his favorite books were *Paradise Lost*, Plutarch's *Lives*, and *Werther*. Not unnaturally, he read Goethe for *Weltschmerz*, Plutarch for republican precedents, and Milton for the romantic diabolism that was brought out by Blake's interpretation and Chateaubriand's translation. The romanticists, rallying to long-lost causes, generously turned villains into heroes. They lost no occasion to repeat the grand gestures of rebellion: to ratify Faust's compact with the devil, to take Cain's curse upon themselves, to revive the ancient struggle of Prometheus. Even the Gothic novel, for the Marquis de Sade, was not without revolutionary implications; its haunted castles symbolized the dilapidations of feudalism. Certainly *The Monk* was a libel on popery, and *Caleb Williams* a brief for William Godwin's brand of political justice. As the *roman noir* was supplanted by the *roman policier*, the sense of mystery was relegated to the underworld of crime. Rationalism, personified by the impersonal detective, brought to book the anti-social energies of the hero-villain.

"Set man apart from society, and you isolate him." This pronouncement of M. Joseph Prudhomme, the very archetype of the bourgeoisie, as Henry Monnier limned him with pen and pencil, has the redundant ring of inevitability. So long as Mr. Prudhomme—or his *confrère*, M. Birotteau—was speaking for society, romantic literature would speak for solitude. M. Prudhomme's janitress would read *Coelina, ou l'enfant du mystère*, a popular novel in the Gothic style that Ducray-Duminil had imported from England to France. If she ever reached the end, where the foundling's secret is revealed by a mute, she might then have followed the adventures of an orphan and a hermit through the equally popular historical novel of the Vicomte d'Arlincourt, *Le Solitaire*. Moral isolation, whether seraphic or satanic, was also the plaintive theme of the tired young poetic school. Its heroes were all powerful and solitary, like Vigny's Moses; they had come too late into a world too old, like Musset's Rolla; they felt lonely in the midst of crowds, like Childe Harold himself. One Byronic attitude persists through all their vagaries, according to the chronicler of Byronism, Edmond Estève: "proud, uncompromising, absolute individualism." From the outside their titanic insubordination looks much like quixotry: it pits the isolated individual against the rest of the world. But Don Quixote was making a comic effort to maintain an old order which society had outgrown. The romantic individualist makes a tragic effort to resist the new order that, in the meantime, has taken possession of society. Cervantes' own values were essentially worldly. The romantic values are essentially private, and can only be approached from the inside.

It is this subjective approach, more than anything else, that distinguishes the literary progeny of Rousseau. Some of them, with Chateaubriand, had been emigrés from the Revolution, and they brought to the Empire and the century their expatriate feelings of dispossession and disinheritance. His *René* contrasted the guilty conscience of the old world with the austere virtues of the new. Sénancour's *Obermann* isolated the romantic sensibility on a mountain top, and draped it in the cult of nature. Constant's *Adolphe*, at the beginning of the Restoration, attempted to draw the egoist out of his shell; but love left him passive, acutely conscious of his weaknesses, yet powerless to act. Where the sons of Priam had been superior men of action, the sons of Rousseau made pageants of their inferiority complexes. The first person, which would have been impossible for epic or romance, was suited to more introspective fiction. Novels resembled confessions more and more, and their heroes were more closely identified with their authors. Although this self-consciousness narrowed their point of view, it improved their facilities for psychological analysis. Goethe, with *Wilhelm Meister*, had refined the tradesman's notion of apprenticeship into a pattern for spiritual autobiography, and established the artist's life as his primary subject-matter. Conversely, the idea of progress, which to Bunyan had meant the Christian's journey from this world to the next, to Flaubert would mean the material well-being of the bourgeois he fulminated against.

The technique of realism is iconoclastic; it breaks down symbols more effectively than it builds them up. It could not regard Louis-Philippe as a ruling personage in any meaningful sense, nor accept his umbrella as a symbol of authority. If anything occupied a central position, comparable to Homeric combat or courtly love, it should have been business; but the mere suggestion is anticlimactic enough to explain why fiction, from *The Satyricon* to *The Rise of Silas Lapham*, has not idealized the business man. If he was not a comic miser, he was nonetheless a figure of fun. Sancho Panza, in the girdle of Venus, is more of a buffoon than ever. Balzac's would-be Napoleons win their triumphs on the stock-market, and his arch-criminals join the forces of law and order; but César Birotteau, though no portrait of a shop-keeper could be more objective or sympathetic, is only half a hero. The rest is anticlimax, like M. Homais' decoration. No definition of a bourgeois could be more antipathetic or subjective than Flaubert's byword, "whoever thinks basely"—which he might have borrowed almost verbatim from an eighteenth-century definition of *le peuple* by the Marquise de Lambert. Flaubert transposed the revolt of the individual against society into a personal quarrel between the artist and the bourgeoisie. If the modern artist—as Mann has appraised him—is "a burgher gone astray," he has strayed so far from middle-class society that he must seek his heroes elsewhere. He still remembers Goethe's prototypes, and often rehearses the strivings and stray-ings of the Faustian consciousness. Most pertinently, he recalls the outsider Werther, whose strongest sympathies were for the lower class, and who was attended to his suicide's grave by workmen.

The worker and the artist, Zola's hero and Proust's, pose the dilemma of twentieth-century literature: its Hamlet-like hesitation between an active and a passive role, between participation and withdrawal—*solidaire* or *solitaire*, in Hugo's equivocation.

In pursuing the quest for a hero from the First Empire to the Third Republic, we shall see that, when the bourgeois regime and the realistic movement came in, the romantic individualist went underground. As early as 1831, the year that saw the publication of *Le Rouge et le noir* completed, Dumas had given the stage his *Antony*, a hero less remarkable for his demonic peculiarities than for his plebeian birth. In 1838 Flora Tristan, a disciple of Fourier, published *Méphis, ou le prolétaire*; her hero, in other respects not unlike Dumas' Count of Monte-Cristo, happened to be a socialist; his name retains the Mephistophelian stigma, but his sobriquet warrants the designation of this book as the first proletarian novel. Eugène Sue, growing more socialistic with the Second Republic, retraced the footsteps of his *Juif errant* with his chronicles of the proletariat. Victor Hugo, exiled from the Second Empire, answered the fading imperial legend with the myth of Jean Valjean—enemy, victim, and savior of society. Hugo's grotesque characterizations were sublimated into the noble convicts and virtuous prostitutes of Dostoevsky. And Dostoevsky wrote, apropos of *Notre-Dame de Paris*, "The basic idea of the art of the nineteenth century is the rehabilitation of the oppressed social pariah."

The art of the twentieth century, whether it flouts the bourgeois or champions the oppressed, whether it continues to practise detachment or engagement, must draw upon materials it has inherited. Consider the portrait of the intellectual in *Point Counter Point*. Maurice Spandrell is as jaded and sinister and wilful and perverse as any of the demons that we have encountered along the way, and his conversation is just as self-consciously modern as Aldous Huxley could make it *circa* 1928. His last act, to the music of an ultimate Beethoven quartet, is to sacrifice himself by assuming responsibility for the murder of a fascist leader. But neither the phonograph record nor the pistol shot can drown out the rumbling of the Dickensian tumbril and the voice of Sidney Carton murmuring at the end of *A Tale of Two Cities*, "It is a far, far better thing that I do ..." None of the sad young men of contemporary fiction, the anti-heroes of our time, is exempted from paying his respects to his predecessors after this fashion. As for the heroines, except for their numerous changes of costume, they have changed surprisingly little since

Madame de Staël introduced the Byronic bluestocking or since George Sand domesticated the *femme fatale*. From that perspective the characters of the novel, for all their mobility and their heterogeneity, may be likened to the members of a stock company playing in a conventional repertory, which the truly percipient novelist modifies in the light of first-hand observation.

Repeated modification is the strategic, the realistic feature of the process; yet it has to be superimposed upon underlying thematic continuities. Thus *Wuthering Heights* might be viewed at long range as a variant of the demon-lover motif, or *Good Soldier Schweik* as one of many folk-tales about shrewd simpletons. Realism has enjoyed its own folklore, and has been indebted to romance for the basic themes and stylized gestures that it has recombined and adapted to the demands of cultural change. Happily, we need not try to decide which is finally the more important: persistence of tradition or emergence of novelty. But we should remember, while concerned with innovations, that even the most individualized and sophisticated art can never proceed very far in advance of pre-existing conventions. Here it has seemed relevant to sketch the vicissitudes of one particular convention—perhaps the central one for the novel, given the centrality of its protagonist and the distance or closeness of the reader's relationship to him—as an excursus on literary typology and a point of return for further discussion. These rough preliminary sketches will serve as groundwork, if they underline a few traits which recur among many novelists. Our deeper concern is with the differentiating factors that make for the special trajectory of the novel, as it moves from the Napoleonic battlefields of Stendhal toward the insulated sick-room of Proust.

6. *The Context of Realism*

We are dealing with a general tendency, and not a specific doctrine. Since no hard and fast definition of realism will cover all the manifestations occurring under its name, we must examine them for its pertinent meaning in each case. "'Realism,'" says Karl Mannheim, "means different things in different contexts." The same word, Benedetto Croce points out, is applied by some

critics in praise and by others in blame. Zola's meat was Brunetière's poison. "Men and women as they are," as they are for
Howells, barely exist for his successors. *Jane Eyre*, which preserves
a schoolgirlish innocence for us, so shocked its reviewers that
they could not believe it had been written by a respectable
woman. Charlotte Brontë, for her part, found Jane Austen's
fiction "more *real* than *true*." Diderot praised Richardson for
achieving "toute la réalité possible." Fielding would not have
agreed. The history of taste, by lending its comparative standards,
may resolve these conflicts of opinion. It suggests a sense in
which Racine, though we do not ordinarily classify him as a
realist, could be more realistic than Corneille. But, as between
two contemporaries, one refining the analysis and the other
broadening the scope of literature, which is the realist? Is it
Trollope, with his accurate notations of provincial or parliamentary
life, or Dickens, with his exaggerated efforts to delve in dust
heaps which Trollope so quietly ignored? Is the penetrating
self-portrait of *Adolphe* less realistic than the panoramic irreality
of *Les Misérables?* Some novelists, evidently, go as far as they
can within a restricted sphere; others, in enlarging those restrictions, overstep the borderline of romance. Every novel is realistic
in some respects and unrealistic in others. Criticism can but
try to estimate the proportions by comparing what the writer
endeavors to show with what the reader is able to see.

When realism appeals neither to ontological argument nor
to scientific experiment but to human experience, philosophers
consider it "naïve." This is the kind of everyday realism that
interests us most, but it would be naïve indeed if we expected
reality to be the same for everyone. And we should be disappointed, like the princess in the fairy tale, if we supposed that
nature could be perfectly reproduced by any artifice. Even the
purely visual reproduction of the painter or the sculptor is
admittedly angled, heightened, foreshortened. The brand of realism that has had the widest application in recent years is the
politician's, which, instead of committing itself to a set of
principles, rather implies the rejection of principle. The political
objective of bourgeois society, freedom, seems to be undefinable
in positive terms. "Freedom from what?" is the question that
liberalism undertakes to answer, and its answers constitute a

negative catalogue of our age's problems. Absolute liberty is as meaningless as realism in a vacuum. Both are relative terms, referring us back to a definite series of restraints from which we have managed to secure some degree of release. When we call a book realistic, we mean that it is relatively free from bookish artificialities; it convinces us, where more conventional books do not. It offers us *realiora*, if not *realia*, as Eugene Zamyatin succinctly put it: not quite the real things, but things that seem more real than those offered by others. By rereading those other books too and reconstructing their conventions, we can relate them to our comparatively realistic book and specify its new departures more precisely. We can define realism by its context.

Our excuse for studying literary history is that the mediocre works help us to place the masterpieces. By establishing the rules we learn to recognize the exceptions. It is the exceptional writer who changes the context of literature, and who—from generation to generation—readjusts it to the vicissitudes of life. Among such writers, Rabelais is doubly exceptional, one of the most original of originals, and he should be saluted in passing as a realist by any criterion, historical or otherwise. Though he preached a naturalistic ethic, he adorned it with an extravagant learning which could scarcely have belonged to a child of nature. Such an attitude is never primordial or spontaneous; it is always a stringent revision of more complicated views. When Schiller ascribed *Realism*—his word was not *Realismus*—to the Greeks, he meant that their outlook was not as idealistic as that of himself and his romantic contemporaries; but this was premised upon his nostalgic contrast between the self-consciousness of the moderns and the simplicity of the ancients. It remained for the twentieth century to perceive, with Léon-Paul Fargue: "There is no genuine simplicity; there are only simplifications. The natural in literature presupposes the utmost effort, or else mannerism." Insofar as realism presupposes an idealism to be corrected, a convention to be superseded, or an orthodoxy to be criticized, George Moore is right: "No more literary school than the realists has ever existed." No writers have been more intensely conscious of what was already written. We can measure their contributions by a sliding scale which moves from literature toward life, but which likewise gravitates in the opposite direction under the counter-influence of romance.

Any work of imagination is likely to exhibit both tendencies, romantic and realistic; they are by no means confined to those historical movements which we respectively associate with the première of *Hernani* in 1830 and the prosecution of *Madame Bovary* in 1857. "Realism had existed long before this great controversy," Baudelaire had written in 1846, under the caption "What is Romanticism?" Nor can we assume, without considerable qualification, that romanticism and realism are historically opposed. "Romanticism is the most recent, the most up-to-date expression of the beautiful ... To say romanticism is to say modern art." In their eagerness to garner local color, to tackle forbidding subjects, and to break down classical genres, the romanticists anticipated the realists; while the realists, we must bear in mind, took over a considerable residue of romance. These intermixtures are strikingly evident in the romantic realism of Dickens, the "fantastic" realism of Dostoevsky, and the "poetic" realism of Otto Ludwig and Adalbert Stifter. In France there was Victor Hugo; but, on the whole, the transition was more homogeneous. Yet, when Georges Pellissier stressed the continuities in a suggestive study, *Le Réalisme du romantisme*, Emile Faguet repeated the usual textbook distinctions by way of review. Mario Praz does not avoid this verbal impasse by applying the term Biedermeier to the bourgeois romanticism of the mid-Victorians or by illustrating from Dutch genre-paintings. More precise definition should clarify both the extent to which the elder generation paved the way for the younger and the extent to which the younger generation reacted against the elder.

Of the successive generations that have been shaken by literary revolution, only one—the middle generation of the nineteenth century—claims the explicit label of realism. Like most critical categories, the term comes after the fact, and comes later to other languages than to French. English seems to have borrowed it, in 1853, through an article on Balzac in the *Westminster Review*. The first independently relevant instance cited by the *New English Dictionary* came in 1857, when Ruskin criticized the "base grotesque" of Bronzino, the attempt to compensate for lack of imagination by "startling realism." The context here, as in so many early instances, refers to painting and expresses hostility. The previous year Emerson had employed the adjective "realistic," as a synonym for "materialistic" and an antonym for "idealistic," in characterizing Swift. Here the word betrays its ultimately philosophical origin, and its long association with the dualistic arguments of the metaphysicians. In France, though Littré still classifies *réalisme* as a neologism in 1872, the word had been utilized by literary criticism as early as 1826. Through the 'thirties it was used occasionally to designate some of the same things that romanticism stood for; it was consistently attacked, in the *Revue des deux mondes* and other conservative periodicals, as an artistic symptom of the growing radicalism of the epoch. It was usually mentioned in a disparaging sense, until some of the younger bohemians, protesting against the outmoded pomp of the academic tradition, began to pride themselves on the designation. Arsène Houssaye's history of Flemish painting, published in 1846, proved that there was also a realistic tradition. Théophile Gautier and other friendly critics defended the new esthetic by invoking the ancient concept of the imitation of nature.

It was "the landscape-painter of humanity," as Gustave Courbet was known to his admirers, who first proclaimed himself a realist —or rather, accepted the epithet thrust upon him. When the Salons objected to his literal treatment of peasants and laborers and the middle classes, he retorted by issuing manifestoes in the name of realism. When the Paris exposition of 1855 refused to hang his pictures, he erected his own *Pavillon du Réalisme,* and began to publicize the movement on an international scale. Later years brought out the socialistic and anticlerical implications of his work, and he was finally exiled for the part he had taken in the Commune. Whenever his critics complained that he had caricatured his models, he would insist, as Balzac did: "Les bourgeois sont ainsi!" Meanwhile realism was being widely popularized by the quasi-photographic genre-painting of the Barbizon school. The technique of photography, which had been invented by Niepce de Saint-Victor in 1824 and subsequently developed by Jacques Daguerre, had been acquired by the state and divulged to the public in 1839. Neither painters nor writers welcomed the new invention, for it drew them into a competition which they were both destined to lose. Nothing short of the *Comédie humaine* could compete with the daguerreotype; Balzac's ingenuity and facility, in reproducing characters and exhibiting scenes, was hardly less inventive; and Daguerre's other novelty, the diorama, echoes across the dinner-table in *Le Père Goriot*. Once perfected, photography served to demonstrate the difference between artistic means and mechanical processes of reproduction. Its ultimate effect was to discourage photographic realism. Painters became impressionists, writers rediscovered the personality of the observer, and even photographers called art to the aid of technology.

Though Balzac won retrospective recognition as the arch-realist, chronologically he belonged to the romantic generation. And though *Madame Bovary* was the most notable and the most notorious book of the realistic generation, Flaubert cultivated an aloofness from his contemporaries. The fanfares were sounded by a pair of journalists whose own novels stirred up less excitement than their articles on contemporary art and literature. Jules Fleury-Husson, under the pseudonym of Champfleury, collected some of his criticism into a volume, *Le Réalisme*, which came out in 1857. Edmond Duranty edited seven numbers of a little magazine, *Réalisme*, at monthly intervals between November 1856 and May 1857. Both men were acute enough to sense that the trend, which they followed rather than led, was far too fundamental to be identified with the special program of a single group. "That terrible word 'realism' is the reverse of the word 'school,'" announced Duranty. "To say 'realistic school' is nonsense. Realism signifies the frank and complete expression of individualities; it is actually an attack upon convention, imitation, every sort of school." More affirmatively, he went on to describe the envisaged result as "the exact, complete, sincere reproduction of the social milieu and the epoch in which one lives." But this was merely to make the description vary with the individual consciousness of one's place and time. As the slogan of a school, announced Champfleury, realism was only "a transitional term which will last no longer than thirty years."

While it lasted, Balzac and Courbet were avenging gods, and Champfleury was their publicist and prophet. He was also the historian of French caricature, which was even then reaching its height and leaving its incisive mark upon fiction. In an embittered tale of bohemian life, *Chien-Caillou*, he schematized the formula of Cervantes by printing side by side in parallel columns the idealistic expectations of his readers and the disappointments that reality would hold for them. His own laconic definition of realism, "sincerity in art," was based upon one of the most elusive words in the critical vocabulary; but it meant something against a context of artistic affectation, and against the constant enthymeme that the lower classes were more rewarding than upper-class subjects because they were more sincere. Here critical logic is overtaken by revolutionary zeal. Champfleury reminds us that realism is the insurrection of a minority, one of those "religions in -ism" like socialism that gained headway with the Revolution of 1848. Even then, while Marx and Engels were framing *The Communist Manifesto*, Champfleury and Baudelaire were conducting a republican paper. Champfleury's distrust of form, and his attempt to judge works of art by their content, foreshadowed the Marxist critics. Disliking poetry, he distinguished the friends and enemies of realism as *sincéristes* and *formistes*—a distinction which left little room for the ironic interplay of Baudelaire or of Flaubert. Political expression, submerged with the failure of the socialist Republic, came to the surface in controversies over realism. Both *Madame Bovary* and *Les Fleurs du mal* were prosecuted by the imperial regime.

Literature was taking stranger and more sensational shapes, artists were making private gestures of opposition to the Empire, while the realists were expressing, in Champfleury's terms, "a latent and unconscious aspiration toward democracy." These impulses converge in the rejected picture, *L'Atelier du peintre: allégorie réelle*, where Courbet has depicted himself, his easel and canvas, a number of cast-off romantic properties, a nude woman, a group of working-class models, and several friends, including Champfleury, Baudelaire, the folk-poet Büchon, and the socialist Proudhon. Here the real allegory is that of the self-portraying artist, whose world is the studio and whose studio is the world, whose symbols are actualities and whose ideology is his art. Even more paradoxically, the distance between Flaubert's material and his style illustrates the ambivalence of realism, as a characteristic product of middle-class society and an unsparing commentary upon it. "As an expression of manners and social conditions, the school seems to correspond in art with the bourgeois element that has become predominant in the new society, reproducing its spirit and image as the novel does in literature," wrote a hostile critic, Louis Peisse, in 1851, the year that witnessed the enthronement of Napoleon III. In 1857, M. Prudhomme himself, succumbing to the vogue, subscribed a letter with assurances of his "distinguished consideration and realism."

With the predominance of the bourgeoisie, with the grandeur and decadence of Birotteau, it was certainly time to explore fresh fields. In 1864, the year of Claude Bernard's *Introduction à l'étude de la médecine expérimentale*, the Goncourts prefaced their *Germinie Lacerteux* with the usual declaration outdating all previous fiction: "The public likes false novels; this is a true novel." They were now proposing a further extension of the literary franchise, *le droit au roman:* "Living in the nineteenth century, in a time of universal suffrage, of democracy, of liberalism, we have asked ourselves whether those we call 'the lower classes' have not their right to the novel." French literature, in all its critical awareness and circumstantial candor, was ready to investigate the servant problem. "Today, when the novel undertakes the investigations and obligations of science, it may also claim the privileges and freedoms." Realism had fully crystallized by 1858, when Taine's essay on Balzac appeared. After the appearance of Darwin's *Origin of Species* in the following year, every mode of interpreting human experience had to be gradually revised. A younger generation, children of the realists and grandchildren of the romanticists, demanded still another readjustment. During the 'seventies Zola sought to consolidate Taine's critical position with Bernard's experimental method, within the widening —or was it the narrowing?—orientation of Darwin's naturalism.

Heretofore "naturalism" had occasionally figured in the critical vocabulary; on occasion it was loosely synonymous with impressionism; but it had never been sharply differentiated from the connotations of realism, the more inclusive term. Zola, the literary executor of Duranty, sought to reinvigorate the realistic novel by substituting a naturalistic slogan. Just as the realists had adopted Balzac, so the naturalists adopted Flaubert, though

Flaubert had never accepted the label, and Zola admitted in cynical moments that it was mere publicity. In serious moments, his naturalism looked beyond Flaubert's hatred of the bourgeoisie to an interest in the proletariat, and beyond the conventions of art to the investigations of science. A novel, though it might be impeded by political barriers, was free to lose itself in the uncharted contexts of nature. But the naturalistic novel also involved certain deterministic premises that realism ignored, that inhibited freedom of action and relieved the characters from responsibility for the degrading condition in which the novelist found them. The novelist himself was now a passive observer, a rigorous compiler of what Edmond de Goncourt first termed "human documents." Observation, it was presumed, would eliminate imagination and convert the art of fiction into a branch of scientific research. For Zola the realism of the Empire had been "too exclusively bourgeois." He in turn, with greater success than his forerunners, founded a school. He virtually established naturalism as an official doctrine of the Third Republic, a hardening orthodoxy from which the divergent movements of the twentieth century still take their departure.

Neither Stendhal nor Balzac nor Flaubert nor Zola nor Proust belonged to the French Academy—a sequence of omissions which throws light on the relationship of the novel to the establishment. Novelists less distinguished have been admitted, since the immortalization of the bland Octave Feuillet in 1863. Through one of the most carefully managed ironies of literary history, plus a bequest from Edmond de Goncourt, naturalism established its own academy in 1903. The issue is internationally reflected in the terms by which the Nobel Prize has been awarded, from 1901, to an author of idealistic tendency. Nonetheless most of its laureates, like the winners of the Prix Goncourt, have written in what became the naturalistic tradition. Now that the naturalists, the realists, and the romanticists are venerated alike by literary historians, we must not forget how often—during the nineteenth century—they were damned by critics, ignored by professors, turned down by publishers, opposed by the academies and the Salons, and censored and suppressed by the state. Whatever creed of realism they professed, their work was regarded as a form of subversion, and all the forces of convention were arrayed against them. While art propagandized against the middle class, the middle class invoked morality as a weapon against art. Literature had come too close to life for comfort. Brunetière, who led the counter-attack against the naturalists, accused them of overstressing the grosser aspects of reality, and pleaded for a revival of idealism. The naturalists hinted, by way of reply, that the traditionalists preferred the timeless to the timely because they were out of touch with their own time.

We have something to learn from their objections to specific details; traditionalism, however, objected in principle to the use of detail, and predisposed its critics to find realism tedious or trivial, ugly or obscene, decadent or improbable. On the other hand, the realists, in their revolt against tradition, felt impelled to exaggerate "the true in the horrible and the horrible in the true." Jules Janin's horrendous parody, *L'Ane mort et la femme guillotinée*, is worth remembering, if only because it proves that the popular novelists of *le bas romantisme* had scarcely been less sensational than Zola. Incidentally, it characterizes the bourgeois idealist who prefers romance to realism as "a Don Quixote in a cotton nightcap," surmounting his shop with battlements and surrounding it with a moat. Thus realism, as Georg Lukács puts it, moves in cycles. Proust, who used the word pejoratively, put his finger on the impetus: "From age to age a certain realism is reborn, by way of reaction against the art that has been theretofore admired." Consequently Erich Auerbach could range across many ages, cultures, and languages, from the *Odyssey* to Virginia Woolf, in order to show us "the representation of reality in western literature." His *Mimesis* is a magistral explication of a rich and eclectic series of texts. It illustrates the stylistic interplay between the grandiose and the plain-spoken, demonstrates the way symbolic conceptions yield to more materialistic approaches, and indicates the realistic component in the formal artistry of Dante and Shakespeare. A *fortiori* the weight of authority must be accorded to Auerbach's considered opinion that historic realism, fully conscious of socio-politico-economic circumstance, is a strictly modern phenomenon beginning with Stendhal.

7. The Dynasty of Realism

Not every age, unfortunately, can be a great age of poetry; and a flourishing drama seems to require a rare conjunction of time and place. If any literary form has flourished in the modern epoch of the western world, it has been prose fiction. And surely, if this form has any nucleus of tradition, it has been the parallel and interconnected development of the novel in England and France. The Occidental novel harks back to brilliant beginnings in Italy and Spain; perhaps it registers its highest degree of imaginative intensity in Russia and America; and it has some interesting later offshoots in the Scandinavian countries and elsewhere. But it was England which led the way in the eighteenth century, and France in the nineteenth century seems to have taken the lead. The fact that Germany has had so few novelists of distinction is clarified by a remark of André Gide's: "The fatherlands of the novel are the lands of individualism." Admitting that German fiction lacks European significance, a sociological study has concluded that it identified itself too uncritically with the interests of the middle class. No land has been more self-critical or more individualistic than France, and no literature has spoken for all of Europe with more authority. Recognizing this authority, Tolstoy advised Maxim Gorky to read the French realists; Henry James wrote Howells that they were the only contemporaries whose work he respected; and George Moore never ceased to tell English novelists how much they could learn from Balzac, Flaubert, and Zola. "Yes, when I read a novel I mostly read a French one," says one of James's heroines, "for I seem with it to get hold of more of the real thing—to get more life for my money."

Circulating in foreign translations or between its original yellow covers, the French novel has acquired an international notoriety, which is based not merely on its pioneer frankness in the matter of sex but on its intransigent refusal to take any human relationship for granted. Its abiding preoccupation might be summed up in the single word *moeurs*, which must be translated by two different English words, "manners" and "morals," but which retains the impersonality of the Latin *mores*. In English literature, ever since the debate between Congreve and Collier, there seems to have been a gradual divorce between manners and morals. Novels of manners, like Meredith's, have been rather eccentric and superficial; novels of morals, like George Eliot's, have been more earnest and didactic. There has been an irresistible temptation, indelibly exemplified in the happy endings of Dickens, to sacrifice the real to the ideal. Too often, when the novelist has not arranged for the triumph of virtue, or modified the conduct of his characters to suit the ethical prepossessions of his readers, they have held him responsible for immoralities which he has simply attempted to describe. Mrs. Grundy equated "realistic" with "pornographic." Guizot, who was an Anglophile as well as an official spokesman for middle-class morality, publicly regretted that French novels were not as respectable as *The Heir of Redclyffe*. Brunetière — that exponent of universality — preferred George Eliot, and even Rhoda Broughton, to Flaubert and Zola. For Flaubert and Zola there could be no compromise with domesticated taste. Morals were the criteria of manners, and manners the test of morals; and, where the practice failed to live up to the theory, nothing less than an uncompromising realism could deal with the situation.

"French novelists are very lucky in having the French to write about," Stephen Spender has remarked. Supremely articulate and gesticulative, their consistent reactions to concrete situations invite such aphoristic remarks; but an almost proverbial example may prove more illuminating, particularly when it is borrowed from Molière. The very title of his comedy, *L'Amour médecin*, characteristically inclines toward a clinical view of an emotional theme. Sganarelle's daughter, having secretly fallen in love, displays symptoms of melancholia, and the father consults his neighbors in the opening scene. M. Josse recommends some gift to cheer her spirits, a diamond necklace or some piece of jewelry, and the others make various other recommendations. Sganarelle listens patiently until they all have spoken, and then tells them off one by one, pointing out that M. Josse happens to be a jeweler—who would profit by the occasion to sell his wares—and that the advice of the others is no more disinterested. "Vous êtes orfèvre, M. Josse!" The line is more than a gag; it is a flash of revelation. Another writer, taken in by the show of

pathos and benevolence, might have taken M. Josse at his neigh-
borly word; or, having detected the ulterior economic motive,
might have cried out in righteous indignation. Molière, in a
mood which is seldom too far from detached amusement, sees
through the characters, grasps the situation, and lays bare the
moeurs. Now there is nothing about a lovesick girl or a worried
parent or a merchant with his eye on the main chance that
could not be encountered anywhere else. What is characteristic
is not the pattern of behavior but the exposure of motivation:
the dissembled emotions and calculations of the personalities,
the conflicting interests and responsibilities of the group.

French literature has been preoccupied, not so much with the
individual in isolation or with society in the mass, as with the
problem of keeping the balance between them. Psychology and
sociology have contributed in equal measure to whet the analysis.
Long before those twin sciences in -ology had been professionally
exploited, their potentialities had been explored by the self-
knowledge of Montaigne and the introspection of Pascal, by
the maxims of La Rochefoucauld and the memoirs of Saint-Simon.
The method of Descartes had located the ego against its context.
La Bruyère had subtitled his character-sketches *Les Moeurs de ce
siècle*. Voltaire had condensed the history of civilization into
an *Essai sur les moeurs*. Even Rousseau, in probing the subjective,
had retained a quantum of objectivity. We often hear that the
French language is better accommodated to prose than to poetry,
that the Gallic genius rises to greater heights in comedy than
in tragedy, or that the most creative achievements of this particular culture are the most critical. Though these generalizations
are far too sweeping to pass unqualified, they are borne out by
the achievements of French fiction. The comparatively short
distance between fiction and criticism is due, in Harold Laski's
phrase, to "the great French tradition of making criticism a commentary on life." In other countries literature and society are
two distinct things, said Renan. "In our country...they inter-
penetrate." Hence the novelist is *ex officio* a social critic. Theory
without practice or practice without theory might subsist elsewhere, fostered by German metaphysics or British empiricism.
French philosophy, under the aspect of Cartesian dualism, has
insisted upon a clear-cut distinction and a running parallel between

material reality and the realm of ideas. Realism, as we define it, is therefore implicit in the traditional structure of French thought.

An incomparable control of the instruments of culture has made France's experience available to the rest of the world, but it is the experience itself that has made France, and has made it the second fatherland of educated foreigners. Its explicative talents have reinforced its diagrammatic position. Geographically and historically France has played the typical role of *l'homme sensuel moyen*, as Matthew Arnold was so acutely aware, for Arnold faced the thankless task of upholding a critical tradition in a more decentralized culture. The centrality of France among nations strengthened the centripetal position of Paris among cities, making it the geographical and historical capital of bourgeois democracy. "France is at the heart, and is the heart, of Europe; if it beats too hard or too fast, fever and disorder may spread through the whole body," warned Bonald, fearful lest cultural continuities had been destroyed by the Revolution of 1789. The Revolution of 1830 brought to Michelet, at the other extreme of political opinion, a sense of France's mission: to reveal the social Word, as Judea and Greece had revealed the moral Word. "All social and intellectual solutions are fruitless for Europe until France has interpreted, translated, and popularized them." Bonald's organic metaphor differs significantly from Michelet's conception of the French people, piloting the ship of humanity. "But today this ship is navigating in a hurricane; it goes so fast, so fast that dizziness overcomes the sturdiest, and every breast is troubled. What can I do in this beautiful and terrible movement? One thing—understand it. I shall try, at least."

Why should French writers, with such unflinching effort, have dedicated themselves to that comprehensive task? The reason is the salient circumstance of modern history. It was revolution that inspired both the reactionary Bonald and the radical Michelet. Not less than ten times during the hundred and fifty years that divide the *ancien régime* from the Vichy government, Frenchmen were called upon to overthrow their leaders and to establish a new order. Alas, these overturns have since continued, and Michelet's trepidations would be even stronger today. The record, repeating itself with cumulative emphasis, testifies to a high degree of social consciousness, and to an equally high degree of individualism. Revolutionary movements end in Napoleonic careers, and the cult of Napoleon ends in the Commune.

> Napoleon introduces the need for success, unbridled emulation, unscrupulous ambition—crass egoism, in short, primarily his own egoism—as the central motive and the universal spring. This spring breaks, stretched too far, and ruins his machine. After him, under his successors, the same mechanism will operate in the same way, and will break down in the same way after a more or less protracted period. Up to the present day, the longest of these periods has lasted less than twenty years.

When Taine was writing this passage in 1889, just a century after the first revolution, he was expecting another man on horseback, General Boulanger, to trample down the Third Republic. But the democratic regime, having already lasted nineteen years, and having proved more durable than its predecessors, was to live fifty years longer. The statue of Liberty Enlightening the World, its gift to a sister republic, retains an undimmed image in a poem by Marianne Moore, written upon the dark days of collapse and capitulation under Marshal Pétain:

> . . . we with re-
> enforced Bartholdi's
> Liberty holding up her
> torch beside the port, hear France
> demand, "Tell me the truth,
> especially when it is
>   unpleasant." And we
> cannot but reply,
> "The word France means
> enfranchisement. . ."

Enfranchisement prompted mingled reverberations of despair and hope in 1941. "French writers, the freest in the universe"—so began a pamphlet published that year by Kléber Haedens, *Paradoxe sur le roman*, which terminated with the imprimatur of the Vichy censorship. The calculated irony was a bid for independence in the very teeth of disheartening odds.

Fanny Burney, who as Madame d'Arblay had lived under the Napoleonic Empire, declared upon her return to England that it would henceforth be impossible to delineate "any picture of actual human life without reference to the French Revolution." Yet it never occurred to Jane Austen that the young officers, who figure as dancing partners for the heroines of her novels, were on furlough from Trafalgar and Waterloo. One had then to breathe the air of France to be fully conscious of the difference between the eighteenth and nineteenth centuries. The new issues were quite as urgent in England, but not so desperately clear; the French were tearing down and building up institutions, while the English were preserving and adapting them. The English novel was free to go its own way, if it chose, and to be content with domestic life; the French novel, for lack of answerable government, assumed certain quasi-public obligations. In the absence of regular institutions, literature became one, whose leadership was conceded in Europe, if not in France. Since the breakdown of the old Latin republic of letters, French books had kept up a kind of International among the intellectuals. Elsewhere, when modern ideas penetrated, they were recognized and ticketed as overtly French. It was the French Revolution of July 1830, according to the historian of materialism, Friedrich Lange, that subverted German idealism. "It was toward France—'realistic' France—that men loved to look even from a political point of view. But what so specially endeared the July Monarchy and French constitutionalism to the men who now gave the tone in Germany was their relation to the material interests of the moneyed classes."

Revolution secured, not the realization of its own slogans, but the enthronement of the middle class. Writers thereafter could only express their doubts and disappointments, and hope for another revolution. The hopes of the first revolutionists had been dashed by the Terror; the grand illusion of Napoleon's Empire had been lost at Waterloo. The monumental past, with its legend of conquest and its rhetoric of freedom, could only reduce the present to mock-heroic dimensions. Alfred de Musset, in his *Confession d'un enfant du siècle*, gave a first-hand diagnosis of the disillusioned state of mind that was inciting his contemporaries to realism. "All the sickness of the present century comes from two causes: the people who have gone through '93 and 1814 bear two wounds in their hearts. Everything that was is no more; everything that will be is not yet. Look no farther for the secret of our troubles." Though the nobleman had been deprived of his prerogatives, it was not the common man who profited. M. Prudhomme, rushing into the breach, was the man of the hour. Eulogizing himself, he parodied Musset. "No matter what you do or say, everything today is bourgeois. Aristocracy exists no more, democracy does not yet exist, there is nothing but bourgeoisie. Your ideas, your opinions, your manners [*moeurs*], your literature, your arts, your instincts are transitional; then hail to Joseph Prudhomme, the man of transition—that is to say, of the bourgeoisie!" Perhaps Musset, as he himself had confessed, had been born too late. Stendhal, who was old enough to be a child of the previous century, liked to think that he had been born too early. But Prudhomme, emerging between revolutions, was the personification of self-conscious modernity, immune to the disenchantments and undeceptions of the *maladie du siècle*.

When the Goncourts portrayed the generic man of letters in *Charles Demailly*, they confronted him with the generic theme. His novel, *La Bourgeoisie*, would apparently have been a French equivalent of *The Way of All Flesh* or *Buddenbrooks*. But, since it was French, it would also have been a "social synthesis"; it would have traced, through three generations of a single family, the evolution of society and behavior (*moeurs*); it would have depicted "the plutocracy of the nineteenth century in its full expansion." The grandfather would have been "the incarnation of the sense of property," the son an ardent believer in "the religions of human and national solidarity," and the grandson a degenerate embodiment of "all the practical skepticisms of modern youth." And, since Charles Demailly depended on observation rather than imagination, like a dutiful disciple of the Goncourts, his characterizations would have been historically sound. At any rate, other observers confirm the story. They show how, through political agitation and dynastic change, the bourgeois dynasties continued to enrich themselves; how the French nation as a whole enacted, in the ambivalent phrase of the intellectual historian, Bernhard Groethuysen, "a virtual epos of the bourgeoisie." The development of capitalism has been divided by the economic historian, Werner Sombart, into two phases. During the first phase, from the Renaissance to the latter part of the eighteenth century, manners and morals were restricted by the sanctions of orthodox Christianity. The second phase, the period of individual competition in a dynamic society, has been unrestricted and expansive. If we accept Sombart's criteria, the presence or the absence of restrictions, it requires no prophet to point out that, since the second World War, this phase has been moving toward a cyclical ending.

This period of bourgeois capitalism, roughly from 1789 to 1939, happens by no accident to be the heyday of the realistic novel. With due allowance for lag and experiment, we are concerned with exactly a hundred years—from Stendhal's first novel, *Armance*, published in 1827, to Proust's last volume, *Le Temps retrouvé*, published in 1927. Our five novelists, posted at intervals, chronicle the intervening century and bear witness for their interconnected generations. Thus in 1842, when Stendhal died and Flaubert came of age, the foreword to the *Comédie humaine* marked Balzac's prime, and Zola's birth had just occurred. If we consider the symbolist overtones of Proust as an epilogue and the classical origins of Stendhal as a prologue, there is a consistent and continuous tendency from romanticism through realism proper to naturalism, which we can follow through the work of Balzac, Flaubert, and Zola. All five, realists according to their respective lights, explicitly render an account of their day, and address themselves directly to posterity—a title which seems for the moment to have devolved upon ourselves. Looking back upon the total configuration of their work, we can hardly fail to notice its chronological links with politics, and with comparable revolutions in the advancing sciences and the plastic arts. We notice that their respective accounts are soon corroborated: Mérimée refines upon Stendhal, Charles de Bernard emulates Balzac, Maupassant sits at the feet of Flaubert, Zola's disciples form the school of Médan, and the influence of Proust is still with us. The imitators lead us back to the innovators. They are the dynasts of realism, and their authority has outlasted the Bourbons and the Bonapartes. Their books, not less than Vigny's, may be read as successive cantos in an epic poem of disillusionment.

By a series of approximations, we arrive at our subject. Novels are such bulky, opaque, and many-faceted items, so easy to conjure with and so much harder to analyze. We have not analyzed a novel until we have discovered its place in the mind of the novelist, in the movement of the age, and in the tradition of literature. Every great novelist has his own solutions to the technical and historical problems that I have been too summarily reviewing. In touching upon some ancestors of the French realists, some of their rivals in English and other literatures, and some of the efforts to formulate their genre, I have tried to test the generality of certain definitions before applying them to these specific examples. The question remains, for the following chapters to answer as well as they can, whether I have chosen the best examples. It can only be hoped that the choice of this sequence of novelists is not arbitrary, but would agree with the consensus of readers and critics and other novelists over the years. The reasons for literary survival, depending as they do upon a peculiar combination of powers and circumstances, are never single or simple. If popular appeal were our criterion, we should have to discuss Eugène Sue and Georges Ohnet. If every author lived up to his literary pretensions, none would be greater than Edmond de Goncourt or Anatole France. If we wanted skillful story-tellers, and did not want them to tell us very much more, we should find them in Alexandre Dumas and Guy de Maupassant. If we rated authors by their humanitarian sympathies, rather than by their comprehension of human beings, we should rate George Sand and Victor Hugo above the authors on our list.

If all books belonged to their period like furniture and bric-a-brac, Octave Feuillet would be the novelist of the Second Empire. His novels fit as neatly into Louis Bonaparte's world as the boulevards of Haussmann, the opera-house of Garnier, the music of Offenbach, the drama of Meilhac and Halévy, or the painting of Meissonier and Winterhalter. But that world, though self-satisfied, was not self-sustaining. The Salon des Refusés opened more spacious vistas with the art of Manet and Pissarro; the suppressed poems of Baudelaire uncovered gulfs beneath the very pavements of Paris; and the exile of Hugo held out to later writers the alternatives of intransigence and conformity. Convention dried up Mérimée's inspiration and weakened Daudet's talents, but realism stiffened Flaubert's opposition. Where Feuillet belonged, Flaubert detached himself; and *Madame Bovary* is still alive, where *Le Roman d'un jeune homme pauvre* is as dead as the Empress

Eugénie. But Flaubert's detachment, which has kept his work from fading into the debris of his period, is not to be confused with indifference, nor is it an empty gesture; rather it indicates broken attachments, and asserts stronger allegiances to higher standards of integrity. No lack of conviction but too many convictions troubled him, he told George Sand. To conclude that Flaubert and our other realists were misanthropic and negativistic would be to accept the short-sighted view of their contemporaries. Taking advantage of an enlarged perspective, we shall see them—without exception—as men of generous enthusiasms, positive values, and fruitful ideas. They belong, as I would interpret them, to that world which is inhabited by the greatest writers of all time; for all great writers, in so far as they are committed to a searching and scrupulous critique of life as they know it, may be reckoned among the realists.

III

STENDHAL

The writer is primarily a man of his time, an eye-witness, an active personage in his tragedies and dramas. He can remain impartial if he puts up enough resistance to the prejudices and superstitions of the social class to which he belongs, if his observation is honest, if he himself is a portion of the concentrated energy of the epoch. . . Stendhal was the first writer who, almost on the morning after the triumph of the bourgeoisie, was able to depict, with perspicacity and clarity, the symptoms of its decomposition, as well as its absurd myopia.

—MAXIM GORKY

1. *The Pursuit of Happiness*

NOTHING COULD BE more characteristically modern than the preference for some other age than one's own. Thus, in preferring the eighteenth century, Henry Adams proved himself a child of the nineteenth, and *The Education of Henry Adams* proved to be his testament to the twentieth. A first glance at Stendhal is always a temptation to explain him, either by historical anachronism or by psychological paradox, as a belated classicist or a *philosophe manqué*. But a paradox is only the other half of a half-truth, and books like his exist to rectify the half-truths of history and psychology. Admittedly, when writing his first book, *Vies de Haydn, de Mozart et de Métastase*, he was attached to the receding past: "In music, as in many other things, alas, I am a man of another century!" With maturing detachment, however, he grew more conscious of the future. Vigny was conceiving his poems as bottles to be cast into the sea; Stendhal conceived his novels, in an equally characteristic image, as tickets for a posthumous lottery. Unhonored during his lifetime, they would be accepted by the realists and rewarded by the naturalists—recommended by Taine and Sarcey, imitated by Bourget and Barrès, canonized by the antiquarians of the Stendhal Club, and enshrined by Henri Martineau's bookshop and publishing firm, Le Divan. Stendhal's break would come, as he had predicted, around 1880. Sometimes, momentarily doubting himself or posterity, he had postponed the date until 1900, or even a generation after that. Today, four generations after his death, the last scraps of his manuscripts are being edited, the slightest of his minor works translated, and the number of his readers is still increasing. Though he is the oldest novelist before us, he is still the nearest, for we may consider ourselves the audience to whom his appeal is finally addressed.

His confidence in the future and his nostalgia for the past join forces to intensify the present. Extremes meet in his work because he has covered the distance between them, and his wayward course has become a highroad for later writers. Their point of departure is his vivid and unremitting sense of modernity. Literally, Henri Beyle was a child of the eighteenth century. Logically, he expected the nineteenth century to realize those ideals which the philosophers had promised and the revolutionists had guaranteed. Logically, but—as it turned out—naïvely. Those ideals, which Jefferson summed up for Americans in the democratic trinity of life, liberty, and the pursuit of happiness, have meanwhile been losing some of their luster. It is now our turn to be nostalgic, to recapture—in so far as we can—the bright expectancy that lit the minds of the Napoleonic generation. What with thrones tottering everywhere, with humanity on the march, prejudices dying out, and enlightenment spreading, unlimited possibilities seemed to open before the individual. Life and liberty, it seemed, at last could be taken for granted as the means to a single end: *la recherche du bonheur*. Beyle devoted his life to this inviting pursuit and, when it turned out to be a wild-goose chase, Stendhal devoted his work to the resulting disillusionment. Now no man is ever born disillusioned; whenever he becomes so, it is the result of a long-drawn-out process; that process, as exemplified in fiction, is what we have agreed to call realism. Hence every realist is a reformed idealist, whose commentary is to be deduced from the ideals that he has lived down. Stendhal would never have become the past master of disillusion, if Beyle had been less susceptible to the illusions of his time.

Our study begins where modern history begins, with the grand illusion that was dispelled by the Battle of Waterloo. We shall never understand the Empire, or its place in the hopes and fears of European liberalism, if we endorse the ephemeral journalistic analogies between Napoleon Bonaparte and such latter-day tyrants as Adolf Hitler. Napoleon may well have been the last of the enlightened despots, rather than the first of the fascist dictators. At the moment, it must have seemed as if progress—and never have men had better reason to believe in progress—were fighting on the side of his Grand Army. For Beyle, who followed its eagles through twelve campaigns, "he was our sole religion." For contemporary readers, as for Lucien Leuwen, the story of young General Bonaparte at Arcola was more thrilling than Homer or Tasso. Napoleon's career, flashing a swift trajectory from the French Revolution to the Holy Alliance, definitively marked the triumph of individualism. When a Corsican lieutenant could crown himself Emperor of the French, then his new subjects could freely indulge their own ambitions. His staunchest following, historians remind us, was recruited from the bourgeoisie. His declaration, "la révolution c'est moi," was a sentiment which every man could profitably repeat to himself. The slogan, "la carrière ouverte aux talents," was at once the fulfillment and the abandonment of revolutionary principles. In ethics as well as in politics, Ernest Seillière has shown in a series of studies, imperialism was the order of the day. A whole generation had been polarized—to use the sociological term by which Gabriel Tarde denoted the effect of a leader on his followers. "France was propelled by the extreme emulation that Napoleon inspired in all ranks of society . . . ," Stendhal himself commented. "The merest lad, working in the back room of his master's pharmacy, was agitated by the notion of making a great discovery; he would belong to the Legion of Honor and be made a count."

The news of Napoleon's *coup d'état*, 18 Brumaire, 1799, met Beyle on the road to Paris seeking his fortune. His military servitude and grandeur, such as they may have been, were consummated by superintending the ravaged French commissariat through the retreat from Moscow. He took no active part in the campaign of France, though he aided in organizing the defenses of his native Dauphiny. Shortly afterward he left for Italy, whence he did not return for the hundred days of the Grand Army's last campaign.

Instead he compiled his *Histoire de la peinture en Italie,* which he planned to dedicate to his exiled master. "Lacking more serious occupations since 1814," he subsequently remarked, "I write, as one smokes a cigar, to pass the time." He wrote about music and painting, literature and travel, laughter and love, "always about frivolous subjects." His journalistic articles and reviews, most of them contributed to English magazines, and his essayistic books, largely published at his own expense, were read as casually as they had been written. Yet his manual of style, which he formed the habit of consulting every day, he would say, was Napoleon's *Code civil.* Among the pastimes of his own exile was the repeated attempt to write a biography of his fallen idol. And, among his own autobiographical attempts, is one which ends on an article of faith: "He respected a single man, Napoleon." Respect was tempered by harsher afterthoughts: the Jacobin hero had turned into a parvenu dynast, the savior of society had turned out to be a social climber, the defender of the Revolution had become its betrayer. But the promise and the disappointment cannot be divorced, and no connection between history and literature is clearer than that which links the Man of Destiny to the destiny of Stendhal.

No historical novelist, arranging for one of his characters to be present at important events, could have made more opportune arrangements for Beyle's career. He was born half a dozen years before the Revolution of 1789 and died half a dozen years before the Revolution of 1848. Political crises, punctuating a life-span of almost sixty years, divide it roughly into quarters. His first sixteen years, which were the closing years of the eighteenth century, he spent in Grenoble, glimpsing the earliest revolutionary experiments through the wide eyes of a provincial schoolboy. For the next fifteen years, the Napoleonic period, he ranged from Paris through various occupied territories, serving the Empire in various administrative functions. The next quarter, corresponding to the restoration of the Bourbons, by cutting him off from more serious occupations, gave him leisure to cut the jaunty figure that we begin to recognize —the traveler and critic, the frequenter of theaters and salons, the "unsuccessful lover, in love with music and painting." Having witnessed the Revolution of 1830 from the portico of the Comédie Française, he was awarded a consolation prize by the liberalized administration of the new July Monarchy, and he spent his last twelve years attempting to escape from—his reward—the French consulate at Civitavecchia. The leading motives of his first three periods, by his own reckoning, were Childhood, Ambition, and Dilettantism; toward the end of his third period, as an alternative to suicide, he began *Le Rouge et le noir*. In his last period, in a final attempt to escape from what he labelled Boredom, after having dissipated all the other possibilities, he began to regard himself a novelist.

If Stendhal's position seems to face both ways, looking backward and forward, perhaps it is because the descrescendo of the times, dividing the Revolution and the Empire from the Bourbon reaction and the Orleans monarchy, divided the prospects of a would-be from the pretensions of a has-been. His is a part of a larger ambivalence, which is still our perplexing heritage, the dilemma of individualism: self-seeking versus self-searching, ambition versus dilettantism, the career open to talents versus the pursuit of happiness. He was not exempt from the vaulting careerism that bestrides his epoch, yet he slept through the examination that was expected to qualify him for the Ecole Polytechnique. Toward his relative and patron, Pierre Daru—a capable functionary who, by the grace of Napoleon, was promoted to be a general and a count, a minister of state and a member of the Academy—he must have felt something of the envy and scorn that had possessed the youthful Jonathan Swift in the household of Sir William Temple. He watched fellow-townsmen, like Casimir Périer and Félix Faure, astutely weathering Napoleon's downfall and founding opportunistic political dynasties of their own. He too might have enjoyed what he named, in one of his fragments, *Une Position sociale*. He was not above pulling an occasional wire; his was not the sort of temperament that must commit itself to some great refusal; quite frankly, he would rather have been on the inside than on the outside. Yet he could not have whole-heartedly regretted the turn of events that released him from the obligation to be a success. He was free at last to pursue his happiness. And, though he did not find it, he found—by *la voie oblique*, by a long and circuitous irony —a career which lay open to no talent short of genius. To be a ruined man, as T. S. Eliot has observed of Coleridge, is sometimes a vocation.

The old aristocracy had cultivated the art of living, it was commonly believed, had really known *la douceur de vivre*. The Revolution, it was hoped, would extend this privilege. But the newly privileged class, the bourgeoisie, was less concerned with enriching its experience than with a more literal kind of enrichment. Vainly Stendhal, repudiating his solidly bourgeois connections, sought a mode of existence which was either dead or powerless to be born. The object of his search seemed near at hand each morning and far away each night. Pleasures of the moment left him, exhausted by gout and syphilis, no happier than before. Yet he went on assuming, with all the inquisitiveness of a Rasselas and all the elasticity of a Candide, that happiness awaited him in the next episode. "This curious epicurean," Nietzsche would call him, "this human question-mark." His contemporaries had been too busy to take him seriously—that flippant conversationalist, that ungainly dandy, that inveterate poseur. Not until a year or two before his death, when Balzac reviewed *La Chartreuse de Parme*, came the shock of recognition. What amateur ever had a more professional reviewer or a more enthusiastic review? Stendhal's acknowledgment, touching in its eagerness to profit from the advice of the younger novelist, was worthy of Balzac's homage. The ant was generous, the grasshopper conscientious; their brief interchange was all that literary relations should be, and seldom are. Léon Blum would aptly compare Stendhal to a perennial student whose classmates have got on in the world, who has never acquired the responsibilities of maturity but always retains the vivacity of youth. Stendhal had clarified this situation by the diagram of a crossroad in *La Vie de Henry Brulard*. One road leads to the public office of a Daru, another to the riches of a Rothschild; in a third direction lies the artistic glory of a Rousseau or a Mozart; the fourth way madness lies.

But diagrams are misleading if they imply that Stendhal made a deliberate choice, or that he habitually moved in a straight line. The calendar of his life is perforce an itinerary, a restless and far-flung round of coaches and inns and hotel rooms, which the indefatigable Dr. Martineau has been at some pains to retrace. From the day Beyle quit Grenoble to take up headquarters in Paris, he very rarely stayed for an uninterrupted year in any single place. Place, nonetheless, as well as time, he reckoned from a fixed point. He was a man of another country, as well as another century, and his other country could only be Italy. Italy was for him, he liked to think, what Greece had been for Byron. So spontaneous, so responsive, so individualized are Stendhal's impressions that they seemed, to the informed perception of Benedetto Croce, "his dream in Italian costume." For this second lieutenant of dragoons who had crossed the Alps to participate in the Marengo expedition, Milan was an esthetic revelation: sherbets in the cathedral square, pictures at the Brera, a box at the Scala, fascinating women and scintillating conversation. Here, if anywhere, was the *dolce far niente* that the middle class had banished from France. He never outlived the melodious impact of Cimarosa's *Matrimonio segreto*; opera continued to be his favorite art, sociable, decorative, and none too serious; he admired Dante and Leonardo, but he adored Metastasio and Cimarosa. He developed a taste for the dry sparkle of Asti Spumante. But how to explain these discoveries to his compatriots? He would feel like an English sea-captain, trying to tell the natives of Guinea about ice and snow.

Milan, in those strategic years, was one of the true capitals of European culture. Like Weimar and Edinburgh, it was an enclave of eighteenth-century enlightenment in the midst of nineteenth-century turmoil. As the historic seat of French occupation, the capital of Napoleon's quondam Cisalpine Republic, it held a special attraction for Stendhal. Was not Napoleon himself more of an Italian than a Frenchman? Was he not essentially a *condottiere* of the Renaissance? And had he not attained the iron crown of Lombardy in Milan's cathedral? Clearly Stendhal did not put France behind him when he crossed the Alps. His cult of Italy was a critique of France, just as his cult of the eighteenth century covered his own retreat from the nineteenth. These assumptions were made explicit in his *Mémoires d'un touriste*, a shrewd and tired book, lacking the effervescent gusto of his earlier books on Italy. Having posed in Italy as a cavalry officer, he went on to pose in France as a commercial traveler; while his traveling companion, Prosper Mérimée, was making archaeological investigations—while, for that matter, on another plane Jules Michelet was making his majestic survey of the map of France—Stendhal was noting the local gossip and petty politics. The word *touriste*, appro-

priately enough, was among the things he had brought back
to his native country from his foreign travels. As a cicerone for
other tourists, he pointed the way to Murray and Baedeker;
long before Burckhardt and Symonds, he rediscovered the Renaissance. He was on leave from his Italian post when a stroke
of apoplexy overtook him in a Paris street; and, when he was
buried in the cemetery at Montmartre, his epitaph, inscribed
by his directions in Italian, described him as a citizen of Milan.
Unhappily, the grave now lies under a causeway, where the
sunlight never touches it.

"How can you love Correggio at Paris when a north-east wind
is blowing?" he had asked in *Promenades dans Rome*, and had
dryly answered himself by switching from esthetics to economics:
"These days you must read Bentham and Ricardo." It was in
Paris, however, that *La Chartreuse de Parme* was written—or
rather, dictated, in one week less than two months. It was in
France that Stendhal wrote of Italy and in Italy that he wrote
of France. His secret motive, as Albert Thibaudet divined it,
may be "tender revery over something he misses." This might
account for the vicarious enjoyment with which his writing is so
strongly charged, but it overlooks the even stronger motive of
comprehending—and thereby, in his own fashion, mastering—the
circumstances that confront him. His dream of Italy may have
passed through the ivory gate, but his dream of France comes
straight through the gate of horn. If he had been searching
for the usual expatriate escape, he would have written romantic
poetry instead of realistic prose; his haven would have been
some storied medieval town, instead of the lively, cosmopolitan
Lombard city. It is Milan which dominates *Rome, Naples et
Florence*, though his title avoids the name for political reasons.
The Swiss historian Sismondi, from whom he may have learned
more than he cared to acknowledge, had been tracing the origins
of modern liberty to the Italian cities. Stendhal's Milanese
friends—the Abbé di Breme, Silvio Pellico, Alessandro Manzoni,
and other writers and *carbonari*—were preparing for the Risorgi-
mento. His allegiance to a lost revolutionary cause was congenial
to their resistance against the dominance of Austria. Once the
Austrian police expelled him from Milan as a dangerous liberal;

later it was Metternich himself who rejected Stendhal's diplomatic credentials to Trieste. These were somewhat higher distinctions than any to which he had actually aspired.

The incessant clash of reveries and realities, idealistic aspirations hidden beneath ironies, raillery shielding a wounded heart —in such phrases he is characterized by his acquaintances. Their antitheses suggest neither a dual nor a multiple personality, but a single elusive person masking under many disguises. He himself could not have been more conscious of playing a role, more irrepressibly addicted to cults and poses, shrugs and quick changes, masquerades and mystifications. By uncompleted count, he seems to have employed at least two hundred different pseudonyms, including peradventure the modified name of Winckelmann's Prussian birthplace, Stendhal—a name which, because of its supererogatory *h*, has been a shibboleth halting many a printer. The fact that he drew up no less than thirty-two wills, without having very much property to bequeath, scarcely suggests a man who knew his own mind or who was indeed very greatly enamored of life; nevertheless, few men have penetrated more deeply into their own minds or have given more ebullient expression to the joys of living. A more valuable testament—and here again statistics betray emotions—consists of seventy-two folios of manuscript in the library at Grenoble, some of them still unpublished. His drafts and projects, transcriptions and notations, memoranda and marginalia reveal precisely what the pen-names conceal: the intimate, the almost secret interconnection between his life and work, between the realities and the reveries, the unsuccessful pursuit of happiness and the unexpectedly successful pursuit of literature. No writer, unless it be that curiously similar personage, James Boswell, has written more voluminously and unreservedly on the subject of himself, and on that subject Stendhal remains the final authority.

The ironic consequence has been that, in so much of the posthumous discussion centered upon him, his life has claimed more attention than his work. His keenness as an observer and his originality as a novelist have been assumed more often than examined. Professional Stendhalians, reshuffling his papers, have zealously catalogued his mistresses and keyed them to the heroines of his novels. Biographers and psychologists, attracted by the rich legacy of autobiographical documents, have mainly exhibited the details and insights that he more incisively provides. Paul Hazard's *vie romancée*, contrasted with the firm lines and fine shadings of Stendhal's self-portrait, is a mere impertinence—the more so because he took such trouble to distinguish between autobiography and fiction, and expressly to surpass the rigorous candor of Rousseau's confessions. Through the very bulk and multiformity of this body of self-revelation, Stendhal has virtually delivered himself into the hands of his interpreters, many of whom have made him an object of their casuistry. Recently Georges Blin has devoted a massive Sorbonne dissertation to *Stendhal et les problèmes de la personnalité*, heavily documented to reinforce a somewhat extraneous dichotomy between an Existentialist *être* and a Phenomenologist *paraître*. M. Blin is more convincing in his complimentary thesis, where he reaches *Stendhal et les problèmes du roman*, and addresses himself specifically to the problem of narrative point of view. Here a substantial case can be made for Stendhal as the technical innovator who abdicated the narrator's omniscience and attached himself to the protagonist's consciousness.

What is truly remarkable, as has been attested by his twentieth-century Italian disciple, Giuseppe di Lampedusa, is "the total fusion of author, character, and reader." The completeness of this interrelationship fosters that vibrant intimacy of tone which Jean Prévost has so perceptively analyzed, focusing *La Création chez Stendhal* upon the point of conjunction between the writer and his writing, as is indicated by his subtitle: *Essai sur le métier d'écrire et la psychologie de l'écrivain*. For Prévost there are two wholly disparate techniques of literary creation: the more usual technique of elaboration, whether it be practised by Balzac or by Flaubert, and the technique of improvisation as practised by Stendhal, most notably in dictating *La Chartreuse de Parme* at the rate of thirty pages a day. Following the suggestions of Balzac, he labored to revise and correct the style of his published masterpiece; but Prévost demonstrates, by stylistic collation, that Stendhal's second thoughts were seldom as effective as his phrasings off the cuff. He must have astonished his amanuensis as he spoke his breathless tale from day to day, never quite certain as to what would happen in the next chapter. The ability to improvise so effectively presupposes, like the seemingly casual paintings of Whistler, long and arduous years of preparation and practice. The author, while taking the reader into his confidence, limits their mutual field of vision to that of the character; the story gains in rapidity of movement what it loses in density of description; and the net effect is that sprightly prestissimo which so distinctively marks the Stendhalian tempo.

The obverse side of this identification is the never-ending search for identity. In a suggestive essay, *Stendhal pseudonyme*, Jean Starobinski has retraced the shy other self through its succession of protective cloaks and histrionic masks. Stendhal, at fifty-seven, could privately yearn for a wishing-ring which would endow him with money, elegance, good looks, prowess of all sorts, invisibility at will, and—one wish soon granted—a painless death. Despite the evasions of fantasy, sooner or later, he was not afraid to take a hard look at himself. *La Vie de Henry Brulard*, without even a change of initial, is the early life of Henri Beyle, the prelude to his adventures among the masterpieces. It is distinguished from such examples of the *Bildungsroman*, the formative novel, as Goethe's *Wilhelm Meister* or Tolstoy's *Childhood* or Gottfried Keller's *Green Heinrich* by a literal accuracy which embraces dates and genealogies and floorplans. It is shaped, like Butler's *Way of All Flesh*, by a gifted son's recoil from his philistine family, and particularly by his animus against his father. Like Joyce's *Portrait of the Artist as a Young Man*, it records the conflict between esthetic impulses and moral inhibitions within an awakening mind. Unlike Stephen Dedalus, who must struggle profoundly to emancipate himself, Henry Brulard can relegate the Catholic religion, with an airy skepticism, to the bugbears of adolescence. Although a hundred years separate the stately old-fashioned existence of the high provincial bourgeoisie, as Stendhal depicts it, from Joyce's depiction of shabby metropolitan gentility, *La Vie de Henry Brulard* has preserved, with a surprising freshness, amenities which are ruefully absent from the *Portrait of the Artist*.

But Joyce's book is the manifesto of a young man, going forth to encounter "the reality of experience." Stendhal's book is the retrospect of a man of fifty, contemplating his distant youth from the cypress-covered heights of the Janiculum. It may be, as at least one biographer suspects, that he has retroactively darkened the picture in order to throw his discovery of Italy into sunny relief. Grenoble meant his father, its deputy mayor, a prosperous lawyer, to whom he habitually referred as "the bastard"; their tense relationship, terminating in disinheritance, was bound to be reflected in his social attitudes. "As a matter of fact, when I come to think of it, I have not cured myself of an irrational horror for Grenoble; in the true sense of the word, I have *forgotten* it," he confessed. "The magnificent memories of Italy, of Milan, have effaced everything." As a matter of fact, like the returning emigrés, he had forgotten and forgiven nothing. Etched in acid on his memory was the occasion when, having undertaken to serve as Count Daru's secretary, he commenced by misspelling an obvious word: *cella* for *cela*. He confessed his blunder in *La Vie de Henry Brulard*; in *Le Rouge et le noir* the same blunder is attributed to Julien Sorel, when he is entering the service of the Marquis de la Mole. But, though Julien derives his rankling intensity from Henri's early humiliations, further comparison will show that he has been objectified; he belongs to—in fact, he typifies—a lower class and a later generation.

As for Beyle-Brulard, psychoanalysts can do little more than translate his memoirs into Freudian terminology and hail him as a precursor of the Vienna school. They could probe no deeper than Henri-Henry into his rivalry with his father, nor hint at a more sensual motivation for his love of his mother, who had died when he was barely seven years old. His dilemmas were already dramatized in the persons of his grandfather and his great-aunt: the periwigged physician, Henri Gagnon, who had made a classic pilgrimage to Ferney and cherished the bust of Voltaire, and the romantic spinster, Elisabeth Gagnon, who introduced young Henri to Italian literature and whose touchstone was *Le Cid*. His Jesuit tutor, the Abbé Raillane, who insisted on teaching him the Ptolemaic system of astronomy, had inculcated so bitter a distaste for clericalism that the Restoration itself seemed a large-scale repetition of "La Tyrannie Raillane." Conversely, he had identified the distant rumors of revolution with his own revolt against his family, callowly proclaiming himself a Jacobin and rejoicing to hear of the execution

of Louis XVI. "La chasse du bonheur" was associated with his
first remembrance of his mother, and later with a succession of
unhappy love affairs. Still later, in his treatise on love, he defined
beauty as "la promesse du bonheur." Ultimately—hoping that
art, at all events, would fulfill that promise—he remarked that
he had abandoned his mistresses for his works. His works, then,
form a series of program notes to his pursuit of happiness. His
biography need not detain us beyond establishing the themes
and indicating the orchestration.

All writing is related, more or less deviously, to the writer's
experience. Rarely, springing from so personal a need, has it
attained so wide an application. It is a delicate task, even with
Stendhal's help, to disentangle facts from fantasies. To classify
his heterogeneous volumes, more than half of them posthumously
published, we might imagine a number of concentric circles,
revolving around his personality in an ever-widening orbit. At
the core, closest to his central consciousness, would be his journal,
most conscientiously kept before he began to express himself
in other forms, registering ideas and sensations as they occurred
to him, and growing consistently and impressively in self-knowledge. At a second remove we have his extensive correspondence,
varying in tone from one correspondent to the next: close to
the immediacy of a diary in some letters, in others more eccentric,
swayed by certain affectations or weighted by ulterior considerations. In the middle distance, halfway between spontaneity and
self-consciousness, stands the fragmentary record of his middle
years, *Souvenirs d'égotisme*, along with *La Vie de Henry Brulard*,
some necrologies composed for his own amusement, and other
autobiographical manuscripts. As we approach the fourth circle,
Beyle disappears altogether, and Stendhal emerges: the retired
officer who strolls along the boulevard at our elbow, the raconteur
who gossips about the other strollers as we sit with him in a
café, the unacclaimed author of potboiling journeywork, critical
essays, and impressionistic books—some of the latter so impressionistic that they might be transcriptions from his journal. In
the fifth and outer sphere, the spacious circuit of his novels, he
succeeds in playing the brilliant and gallant roles for which all his
other pursuits have scarcely been more than awkward rehearsals:
Julien Sorel, Lucien Leuwen, Fabrice del Dongo.

To view Stendhal's books as a projection of his own desires and anxieties is by no means to limit their scope, for his imagination was pervaded by the obsessions of his age, its wish-dreams of empire and nightmares of reaction. In his history of Italian painting, while considering the material preconditions of the Renaissance, he had elaborated a theory of *le beau idéal:* that idealized conception of the beautiful, shared between artist and audience, which underlay the masterpieces of the Renaissance. Though he could not count upon an audience, he professed an esthetic ideal, both for the individual and for society. Every page he ever wrote must be read in the light of his vista of Milan and in the shadow of his image of Napoleon. Writing in the nineteenth century, he found it hard to sustain those ideals; measuring contemporary scenes and characters by that utopian vista and that titanic image, he found himself willy-nilly a realist. In *Le Rouge et le noir* the path of glory leads to crime and humiliation. In *La Chartreuse de Parme,* in the best of possible worlds, everything is for the worst. Happily, it is not the conclusion which matters so much as the pursuit, the buoyant idealism that charms us into accompanying him toward a devastating sequence of implications. Not the fruit of experience, but experience itself is the end—as in the hedonist's credo of Walter Pater. If Stendhal did not quite reach the fruit, at least he never tasted the ashes; and there were unforgettable moments, which he has evoked for us, when it almost dangled within his tantalized grasp. The psychologist Dugas has interpreted his frame of mind as *l'esprit de l'escalier*—the delayed response, the happy second thought, the witty retort that comes too late. But, if one is a writer, it is never too late; with due patience and ingenuity, one can always have the last word.

Psychologists, making the most of the richly documented case history that Stendhal has placed at their disposal, would doubtless speak of maladjustment. But is it not rather a unique adjustment, when a writer faces his frustrations and misadventures with an insight and a gaiety which illuminate his books and exhilarate his readers? Should one not rather speak of a society which was maladjusted, a time which was out of joint? If we talk of failure, let us talk of the failure of the Revolution to live up to its promise. Henri Beyle was able, with great success, to convey this crucial disappointment. When he first arrived at Paris, it had been most disappointing to see no mountains there. "Paris," he had exclaimed, "n'est-ce que ça?" A year later, joining his regiment, he saw the Saint Bernard Pass. "Le Saint-Bernard," he asked his companion then, "n'est-ce que ça?" The next day, before the fortress of Bard, he had his baptism of fire. He compared it to the loss of virginity. "Quoi! n'est-ce que ça?" he added with a swagger. "That exclamation and that rather silly astonishment have pursued me all my life. I believe it comes from imagination." One must indeed be perpetually hopeful in order to be perennially disappointed. When the heroine of his last novel, *Lamiel*, hires a young rustic to relieve her of her virginity, again there is a similar undeception. "Comment, ce fameux amour, ce n'est que ça!" Obviously, there is a great deal more to be said on the themes of sex and war, of beauty and politics, and Stendhal goes on to discuss them at great length and with mature wisdom. Perhaps enough has been said here to indicate the conditions under which his hard-won maturation was achieved. We may go on to discuss the intellectual vicissitudes that transform Henri Beyle, the naïve sentimentalist, into Count Frédéric de Stendhal, the cynical sophisticate. How—we shall then inquire —did this dallier and dilettante, specializing in ambition and intrigue, manage to produce the two novels that leave us with our most acute realization of the ways of the world?

2. *The Comedy of the Nineteenth Century*

Worldly wisdom is the most demanding and the least rewarding of the arts or sciences. *La Chartreuse de Parme*, according to Balzac, could only have been produced by a man in his fifties, and would only be appreciated by politicians, diplomats, great artists, and men and women of the world. "In short, he has written *The Modern Prince*, the novel Machiavelli would write if he were living exiled from Italy in the nineteenth century." Balzac identifies Count Mosca, master of ceremonies in the novel, with his vaunted acquaintance, Prince Metternich. Stendhal, who was apparently glancing at the Austrian minister to the court of Tuscany, did not accept that identification; and he looked upon Metternich as the spokesman for the Machiavellian policies that had frustrated Napoleon's career, and incidentally his own. He looked back on Napoleon, who was already enveloped in a retrospective nimbus of liberal propaganda, as the quixotic champion of a defeated order. Metternich was the villain, as Napoleon had been the hero, of the drama he watched from his box at Milan; while Europe moved from revolution to *Realpolitik*, Stendhal was moving from *Don Quixote* to *The Prince*. This transition is not so abrupt as it may seem to us, for both books—uniquely and unforgettably—had embodied the Renaissance's perception of the incongruities between romance and reality. Cervantes had presented, in the negativistic form of anti-romance, what Machiavelli had analyzed in the positivistic terms of political realism. If the one voices a certain regret for the Middle Ages, the other betrays the disgruntled idealism of an exiled patriot. One satirizes the code of chivalry, the other codifies the tactics of the unchivalrous; one expresses the mood of undeception, the other expounds the technique of deception. Both protagonists, the noblest of fools and the ablest of rogues, belong to the same world; *The Prince* tells how, and *Don Quixote* tells how not, to get on in it.

Le Moyen de parvenir, that facetious old miscellany of Béroalde de Verville, might well have furnished a comprehensive title for Stendhal's work. His outlook might be described as an unexpected combination of Machiavellism and Quixotry, an opportunism which makes a point of missing its opportunities, always arriving and never really getting anywhere. Having wanted to make his name as a poet, he lapsed into a politician in spite of himself. The impulse awakened by his love for his dead mother, inadequately requited by other women, was intermittently diverted to esthetic pursuits. The revulsion aroused by his hatred of his bourgeois father, impelling him toward liberalism, brought him to the stalemate of his Napoleonic career. But, fifteen years after the serious-minded young bureaucrat had become a dilettante, the frivolous middle-aged dilettante became a diplomat: consul of Louis-Philippe, "the most knavish of kings," at Civitavecchia, the miasmal seaport of Rome. He relieved the monotony of his consular duties, which consisted largely of checking imports and exports, by digging at nearby ruins. With a diligence which no one expected from such an anticlerical in such a sinecure, he turned in reports on the intrigues and crises of papal politics—reports which might, in Shakespearean phrase, "set the murderous Machiavel to school." He was annoyed, when he finally received the cross of the Legion of Honor, to be classified as a man of letters rather than as a man of affairs. Experience had augmented his respect for *The Prince*. As a manual of statecraft, a handbook for despots, a "treatise on the art of doing citizens out of their liberties," it exercised an ambivalent fascination; but it failed to account for those irrational motives, those passionate outbursts, "those gusts of sensibility," which could upset the best-laid calculations. Stendhal knew, as well as he knew himself, that man is an imperfectly rational animal. "The heart has its reasons," as Pascal had said, "which the reason does not know." Stendhal, in the vanguard of modern thought, was seeking a rationale of the emotions.

Henry Brulard recalls the very lime tree on his father's estate under which, a truant from the lessons of the Abbé Raillane, he first read *Don Quixote*. "The discovery of this book," he writes, "is perhaps the greatest epoch of my life." It made him laugh for the first time since his mother's death, and sent him to his grandfather's shelves for Molière and other comic writers. When comedy bogged down in an ignoble welter of bourgeois detail, he again took flight into the sphere of romance. What Amadís of Gaul had been to Don Quixote, the Don was to him. He cultivated a kind of "Spanish noble-mindedness" under the influence of his great-aunt Elisabeth, on whom he retrospectively blamed the "abominable illusions" of his first thirty years. That *espagnolisme*, that romantic susceptibility, dampened the comic spirit, as he later realized. "All my life I have been seeing my ideas and not reality." After *Don Quixote* his head had been filled, like the Don's, with the landscapes and heroics of the *Orlando Furioso*. "Ariosto shaped my character." The third book that shaped his character, that marked perhaps an even greater epoch, was *La Nouvelle Héloïse*. He attuned his tears and transports to the sensibilities of Rousseau's hero, who taught him the dangerous habit of self-pity. Sometimes he saw himself in the role of a more effectual lover, the mordant rake of *Les Liaisons dangereuses*, a novel which was traditionally associated with local scandals in Grenoble. "I, who regarded myself as a combination of Saint-Preux and Valmont," he thought, as he went forth to encounter the reality of Paris, "I, who believed that I had an infinite capacity to love and be loved, and that only the occasion was lacking, found myself inferior and awkward in a society which I considered gloomy and sullen."

When Stendhal first went to Italy, he admitted, he knew nothing of the world except what he had learned from novels. He lay in his barracks rereading the thirty volumes he had carried along with him to the Battle of Marengo. When he gathered up his courage and courted a mistress, he felt as if he were the Chevalier des Grieux and she were Manon Lescaut. Fundamentally, all his books had taught him, there were only two types of lovers, the unsuccessful and the successful; the respective counterparts of Saint-Preux and Valmont were Werther and Don Juan, the Quixote and the Machiavel in love. There could be no question as to which came closer to the object of his pursuit. "The trouble," sighed Stendhal, "is that I am always being Saint-Preux." On the cover of a notebook he set down his resolve to "de-Rousseauize" his judgment. "To know men thoroughly, to judge events soundly, is a great step toward happiness." From his *philosophe* grandfather, whose watchword had been "the knowledge of the human heart," he had inherited the classical tastes and encyclopedic appetites of the eighteenth century. Where then, if not from *Don Quixote*, was such knowledge to be obtained? If not from novels, no doubt there were other books. His letters to his sister Pauline, during his early days in Paris, were breathless with references and recommendations. He was especially drawn to subversive authorities like Tacitus and Hobbes, to the most sarcastic historians and the most hard-headed philosophers—in a word, to the Machiavellians. "The imagination," he conceded, "must learn the iron rights of reality." Under the polyglot heading of *Filosofia nova* he recorded his assent to the negations of the great destructive thinkers, along with his Anglicized intention "to do a book of all definitions." He exchanged a tender-minded doctrine for a tough-minded one; but it remained a doctrine, and he remained a doctrinaire.

Though his outside reading had tended to make him a sentimentalist, Stendhal's schooling had been devised to make him a rationalist. His favorite teacher had been a mathematician, the earnest young republican Gros. His favorite subject had been mathematics because, he believed, "it left no room for hypocrisy and vagueness." Hypocrisy meant the priest-ridden atmosphere of his family, vagueness meant his tendency to escape into romantic fiction, and mathematics meant an escape from both. "True or false, mathematics could get me out of Grenoble." This is not the most disinterested expression of intellectual zeal, and yet it is noteworthy that his confused feelings should have sought so rational a channel. It was a notable age of science into which he grew up, and he was not unaware of the revolutions that Lavoisier and Laplace and Monge were fomenting. The years of Stendhal's secondary education happened to coincide with a remarkable educational experiment. The Central Schools, inaugurated by the Directory, with the reformer Lakanal as their national administrator, were locally administered by a committee whose chairman was Dr. Gagnon. At no other period could a French student, preparing for the baccalaureate, have been grounded so thoroughly in the sciences or so superficially in the classics. Retaining the imprint of this curriculum, Stendhal became a lifelong disciple of the philosopher who had framed it, Destutt de Tracy. Now Tracy was, in Jefferson's opinion, "the ablest writer living on intellectual subjects, or the operations of the understanding"; his commentary on Montesquieu and his *Eléments d'idéologie* constituted "The Statesman's Manual." While Jefferson was sponsoring American translations of these works, Napoleon was denouncing them, in language which could hardly have made them less crucial for Stendhal: "Your Ideologues destroy every illusion, and the time of illusions is for peoples and individuals alike the time of happiness."

The new school of Ideology was regarded, by the adherents of the established order, as a source of free-thinking and radicalism. Its own adherents preferred to regard it as that branch of zoology which is devoted to the science of ideas. It falls into place among the materialistic schools of philosophy, somewhere between the eighteenth-century Encyclopedists and the nineteenth-century Positivists. Locke had discovered it, Condillac had developed it, and Tracy was now perfecting it, Stendhal told his sister. The master was bringing together, within his Ideological system, the physiology of Cabanis and the psychology of Maine de Biran. These three Ideologues were united in their endeavor to correlate man's physical and moral natures. Scientists at last had caught up with philosophers, and were striving to advance beyond them by an empirical approach to the mind-body problem. If knowledge was derived from sensation, and not from innate ideas, human nature was no longer reducible to fixed principles; it was the variable product of particular conditions. Faculty psychology was thenceforth discredited, and the way lay open that ultimately led to psychoanalysis. Locke had characterized the mind as a blank tablet on which experience inscribed its lessons; Tracy emphasized the impact of the stylus, the substance of the lesson, the process of conditioning. Education was emphasized, almost to the exclusion of biological factors. It gave a new significance to external facts, and to seemingly insignificant details, if they alone determined psychological traits and motives. The implications of this determinism are so far-reaching that novelists are still engaged in working them out. Sterne, basing *Tristram Shandy* on tricks of circumstance and association of ideas, had thereby parodied Locke. Scott, who had professed no further purpose than to describe "scenery and manners," almost bored Stendhal enough to dissuade him from writing novels. He was, however, to discover and demonstrate the relevance of such dense circumstantial description: manners, so to speak, were conditioned by scenery.

"A human being never seems to me to be anything but the result of what the laws have put into his head and what the climate has put into his heart," Stendhal remarked in a letter, and accepted the consequences of his remark by blaming crime on human institutions, church and state. Ideology had convinced him, and the fall of Napoleon strengthened his conviction, that man was nothing if not the creature of circumstances. To form character we must control environment; to reform character we must improve environment; to understand a character we must investigate his environment. It was left for Taine's environmentalism to push the logic of the Ideologues to its inevitable conclusion. And it had been Stendhal, as Taine enthusiastically acknowledged, who "first noted the fundamental causes, I mean the nationalities, the climates, and the temperaments; in short, he treated the sentiments as they should be treated—that is to say, as a naturalist or a physicist, making classifications and weighing forces." Stendhal was indeed what Amiel considered him, "the novelist after Taine's heart." But what delighted the materialist Taine, in *La Chartreuse de Parme*, repelled the idealist Amiel. "Literature is here subordinated to natural history, to science; it no longer belongs to the humanities; it no longer honors man with a rank apart; it ranks him with the ants, beavers, and monkeys." Hence nature becomes more active, and man more passive; background comes into prominence and characterization becomes fluid. From the inside the senses are approached more directly; from the outside characters come to resemble such conceptions as Condillac's animated statue or La Mettrie's mechanical man. As the older conventions of fiction break down, novelists must stress one or the other, the objective or the subjective approach, the material influences that surround their theme or the consciousness that perceives it. Both potentialities are latent in Stendhal, as he alternates between a Machiavellian and a Quixotic point of view. The obvious alternative, the one Amiel feared, leads to the naturalism of Zola. The other, less obvious but quite as close to Stendhal, leads toward the impressionism of Proust.

On the margin of his own copy of *Le Rouge et le noir* Stendhal has written, "M. de Tracy told me that truth could only be attained by means of the novel." Tracy's philosophy encouraged no one to be a philosopher. Its effect was rather to discourage metaphysical abstraction, to stimulate detailed consideration of specific cases. Its effect on Stendhal was to convert the pursuit of happiness into a search for knowledge, to send him—intellectually disciplined—back to the novel, equipped to use it not as a substitute for reality but as an instrument for observation and analysis. Meanwhile his first-hand acquaintance with reality was improving, and he regarded himself not as a dilettante taking notes but as an Ideologue collecting sense-impressions. As a conscientious hedonist, he tried to regulate his disordered existence by the felicific calculus, hopefully planning each day for a preponderance of pleasure over pain. Bentham and Ricardo were not so far removed from Correggio, after all. The age that reduced ethics to Utilitarianism and economics to laissez-faire would do what it could for esthetics, and Stendhal's books were pioneer contributions to that most individualistic of fields. They were guide-books, not to galleries and concerts, but to the fine art of life. The parvenu classes, more adept at calculating profits and losses than at refining pleasures and discriminating pains, needed to know how to live. Taste, which had previously been the standard of an elite, was now a matter of individual response. Every man could now be an epicurean; the arts of living could become sciences; even cook-books could take the tone of quasi-scientific treatises, like Brillat-Savarin's *Physiologie du goût.*

The passions could not be the subject of an exact science, Stendhal observed in reviewing an exhibition, because they must be felt in order to be painted. Knowledge of the human heart, it would seem, was not book-knowledge; reality must differ from romance. Yet, having felt, one might paint; one might even, with due rigor, depict the most intimate of the passions. Having contemplated a novel upon the subject of love, he decided to write "a book of ideology." *De l'amour* is a gallant effort to take an objective attitude toward the most subjective of phenomena. To keep one's head while losing one's heart is the very essence of what Henri Beyle liked to call Beylism. It was not an easy trick, he confessed: "I am constantly afraid that I have written nothing but a sigh when I wanted to put down a fact." Yet sighs, to the hard-boiled experimentalist, can be data. A hopeless passion for a Matilda Dembowska, if it led nowhere else, was preliminary research for this lover's manual. Passion had been too often confused with vanity, Werther too often mistaken for Don Juan, and Stendhal—who had studied both parts—undertook to distinguish between them. Once at Salzburg he had seen a branch thrown into a salt-pit; crystals had formed and ramified around it until, completely and brilliantly encrusted, it reflected everything else in its peculiar glitter. He was struck by the analogy between this process and the way a beloved object, to the eye of a lover, is obscured with "the accumulation of charming illusions." By transposing the concept of crystallization from chemistry to love, Stendhal penetrated—with more finesse than previous writers—the psychology of delusion, the mechanism of self-deception, the eternal quixotry of the human mind.

The next step was to undertake an equally systematic study

of the process of disillusionment. Was there any means of seeing through the crystals, of resolving the realities, of liberating the mind? If love enslaved the sentiments, it was laughter which released them. The two had fused in Stendhal's precocious aspirations when, at the age of seven, he had desired "to write comedies, like Molière, and live with an actress." In Marseilles, at the age of twenty-two, he attained the second of these desires with a Mademoiselle Louason, who was neither very talented nor very faithful, but was indubitably a professional actress. As for the first, he was so far from attaining it, that he was there employed as a clerk in a wholesale grocery establishment. Nevertheless, he has left many manuscripts and fragments which attest his ambition to be another Molière; and his scattered analyses and comments, collected under the caption of *Du rire*, would make an appropriate sequel to *De l'amour*. His friends complain that, except in rare moments of outspoken sincerity, he was always playing the comedian. The comic mask of Stendhal was the anti-mask of Beyle—if we may draw upon Yeats's conception of how the writer fulfills himself through assuming a complementary personality. It was no caprice which attracted Stendhal to the wings of the Comédie Française and prompted him to study the classical repertory with a retired actor. Perhaps the illusory devices of the theater, perhaps the lines of Alceste in *Le Misanthrope*, showed him the absurdity of trying to play a tragic part in an essentially comic world.

"This world is a comedy to those that think, a tragedy to those that feel." Horace Walpole's epigram neatly poses the dilemma: to be a suffering protagonist or a detached observer, to be overwhelmed by disappointments or to rise above them, to magnify the opposing forces or to belittle them. Accepting Hobbes's definition of humor, which is based upon a sense of superiority, Stendhal added—and went on to prove—that scorn is not incompatible with gaiety. The man who pillaged a volume of Voltaire from the flames of the Kremlin had gone far toward de-Rousseauizing himself. To cure himself of "the habit of viewing society as an impassioned man, in the mode of Rousseau," he consulted Molière and Goldoni. On the flyleaf of his Molière, he jotted the notion that the comic writer should be something of a Machiavelli. Machiavelli, he did not forget, had been very much of a comic writer. The comic stage, like the political scene, was ruled by self-interest and sharp practice. He who would master the rules must be prepared to analyze and generalize and deduce; he must therefore be something of a scientist. A Jussieu, classifying plants, was not altogether dissimilar to a Leporello, cataloguing Don Giovanni's mistresses; whereas the comic method, with its classification of social types, was diametrically opposed to the tragic view, with its concern for the unique individual. Sympathy, as Stendhal recognized, was easier than mockery. "Sensibility happily does not require much intellectual effort. The shallowest novelist succeeds in squeezing out our tears or in keeping us from extinguishing our candles until three o'clock in the morning. It takes a Cervantes or a Lesage or a Mérimée to kindle that delicious smile which is a sign of intellectual pleasure." A French smile, *un sourire*, we must not forget, is a sub-laugh.

These examples were well chosen in their differing ways, for each was a comic writer who had turned from drama to fiction. Stendhal's own advance in that direction is manifested in an article categorically entitled *La Comédie est impossible en 1836*. Comedy relies, more directly than other forms, upon the observation of manners, and upon a vantage-point which the observer shares with his audience. In the eighteenth century, standards of conduct had been particularly clear; in the nineteenth century, manners were changing too fast; it was no time for comedy, Stendhal argued, and a republic was no place for it. "There was gaiety in 1739. The nobility was not afraid; the third estate had not yet become impatient of its bonds, or rather its handicaps; the current of life flowed gently in France. The ambition, the envy, and the atrocious poverty that affect us were then impossible." In 1836, at a performance of *Le Bourgeois gentilhomme*, half the audience would be laughing at young Dorante, and the other half at old Jourdain, "who is too vividly reminiscent of their own family life." Had Stendhal lived until 1851, he would have seen Molière's values completely reversed by *Le Gendre de M. Poirier*, where Augier and Sandeau ridiculed the young aristocrat and sympathized with the bourgeois father-in-law. Comedy, as the middle class prevailed, had been softened and sentimentalized. Though Stendhal was no believer in aristocracy, he continued to find the bourgeoisie ridiculous, and capitalism unworthy of the heroic treatment that its apologists were claiming for it. But to go on laughing was to scoff against the new regime. "You might say that the century of ridicule is past," Stendhal wrote, in a letter to his cousin, Romain Colomb. "Not that there are no more ridiculous people, but that there will soon be no one left to laugh at them."

Yet the very forces that had disintegrated their audience had provided comic writers with the medium for addressing a happy few who might appreciate the joke, a posterity who might be worth the speculation. "Since democracy has filled the theaters with vulgar crowds, incapable of comprehending niceties, I regard the novel as the comedy of the nineteenth century," Stendhal commented on the margin of a novel of his own. "Transform your comedies into novels, and print them!" he therefore advised his contemporaries. Thus his experiments in comedy completed the intellectual discipline that his course in Ideology had begun, and Molière confirmed the suggestion of M. de Tracy. Consequently, we should not be surprised when, even within the ampler framework of prose narrative, Stendhal occasionally resorts to stage effects. With farcical timing, when Lucien Leuwen sits down to meditate on war and civilization, his chair collapses. When he makes a quick calculation as to the relative cost of marrying a Montmorency or a Tremoïlle, we are on a more Proustian plane of high comedy. When Julien Sorel, to engage the jealous affections of Mathilde de La Mole, systematically copies a series of love letters and addresses them to another woman, he is behaving in the convention of a Molièresque suitor, a Léandre or a Valère. When he is first invited out to dinner, another guest quotes Horace, as his bishop had done in a previous conversation; Julien, putting two and two together, concludes that Horace is the single classical author with whom these aristocrats are acquainted. "From that moment," Stendhal concludes, with a Machiavellian succinctness, "he was master of himself." Rereading the chapter in which Madame de Rênal hoodwinks her husband, Stendhal cannot refrain from applauding himself: "Here is a scene of comedy."

Such occasions have that mechanical aspect which Bergson discerns in every humorous situation. But Stendhal cannot fairly be accused of oversimplification; if anything, he over-complicates matters. "Life is simpler," Zola was to shrug. For Stendhal life was a conspiracy. It was the liberal's duty and the comedian's pleasure to expose plots, to impugn motives, to satisfy curiosities, to justify suspicions, to believe the worst. Often his Benthamite calculations and Machiavellian intrigues seem too rational to be reasonable, too bad to be true. We credit them, as we would credit a hypothesis, not because it explains everything, but because it brings to light a pattern of behavior which would otherwise be submerged in irrelevances and trivialities. Albert Sorel, the diplomatic historian, was not much impressed by Stendhal's consular reports: "His processes of observation and description are particularly dangerous and illusory. Stendhal ascribes too much importance to anecdotes and generalizes too easily." A similar scrutiny of his novels, by the economic historian Henri Sée, contrasts Stendhal unfavorably with Balzac. Actually, Stendhal did not have much patience with "the little true facts" on which he so frequently insisted. He could not have scanned the Penal Code as he did the Civil Code, for he permits Julien Sorel to be accused of violating a non-existent article. "More details, more details," Lucien is admonished by the elder Leuwen. "There is no truth or originality except in detail." It is estimated, notwithstanding, that almost half of the names and dates in Stendhal's life of Napoleon are inaccurate. His biographies of painters and musicians are still worth reading, in spite of their numerous inaccuracies, for their critical generalizations. A factual realism, which seemed too vividly reminiscent of his own family life, was the obstacle to his enjoyment of Molière. More analytic than observant, Stendhal is at his best when he is generalizing from experience; he is at his worst when, in his immature work, generalization outruns experience. Consider the memorandum he once drew up, carefully appraising the attractions and inclinations of a certain lady, his patron's wife, and elaborately canvassing all the strategic possibilities. Several years afterward he subjoined this sadder and wiser postscript:

> The only advice to give was:
> Attack!
> Attack!
> Attack!

Balzac grouped French writing into two main categories, the literature of images and the literature of ideas. An eclectic himself, he placed Hugo at the head of the first group and Stendhal at the head of the second. This opinion is fully supported by the hypothetical and schematic qualities of Stendhal's writing, his emphasis on line at the expense of color, his reluctance to catch the eye or charm the ear. It also places him with the minority where he belongs in literary history, as heir of the neo-classicists and forerunner of the realists at a time when the romanticists were in the majority. Sainte-Beuve once defined romanticism as royalism in politics, Catholicism in religion, and Platonism in love. Stendhal, who hated kings and priests, and was Platonic only when all the other approaches had failed, would have been excluded on every count. But each of his books is a surprise, and his two pamphlets on *Racine et Shakespeare*—the first of them published seven years before the première of *Hernani*—constitute the most trenchant manifesto of the romantic movement. It seems to have been inspired by the prospect of a controversy with the pundits of the Academy, and by a genuine enthusiasm for the English actors who were making their first appearance in Paris. Its attack on the dramatic unities seems less audacious, however, when we are reminded that Stendhal borrowed much of his ammunition from Dr. Johnson. His own opinions proceed from a historical relativism toward a theory of literary progress, in which *le romantisme* figures as simply the most recent phase. Its recentness is what appeals to Stendhal. Throughout he sustains the unromantic assumption that the novel has eclipsed all the other genres. Speaking as a classicist, he advises himself, in the guise of a romantic correspondent, to transform his comedies into novels. Hugo's preface to *Cromwell*, a few years later, outlined a more influential program for the romanticists which agreed in almost no particular with Stendhal's. Nothing could more cogently illustrate the basic ambiguity of the term. Had *le réalisme* been more current, it would better have suited his argument.

As if to increase the distance between himself and the rhapsodic poets of the *Cénacle*, Stendhal reiterated his preference for the Napoleonic songs and satirical ballads of Béranger. He submitted the manuscript of *Racine et Shakespeare* to Paul-Louis Courier, the radical pamphleteer and classical translator. Such writers belonged, as he did, to the old sardonic tradition, which had been driven into sharp opposition by the reigning sentimentalism, and which was to contribute its note of social satire to the realistic movement. Most French writers were being influenced by the reactionary German romanticism that Madame de Staël had publicized; in so far as Stendhal was a romanticist at all, it was in the liberal Italian vein, whose outstanding exponent was Manzoni. But Stendhal was twenty years older than the young extremists of Hugo's generation; his sojourn in Milan and his subscription to the *Edinburgh Review* had set for him a tone of enlightened moderation, somewhat advanced in politics and somewhat old-fashioned in taste. He was, if we may preserve a distinction by coining a term, a counter-romanticist. In this respect, Stendhal had his most striking prototype in Byron, with whom he had conversed and corresponded, and other affinities in other countries—notably Pushkin and Heine. All four, in contradistinction to the romanticists, preferred cosmopolitanism to nationalism, rationalism to mysticism, irony to sentiment. They professed the culture of the Enlightenment, the cult of Napoleon, and the pose of a dandy. Now dandyism, as Baudelaire would later define it, elaborating some of Stendhal's notions on the role of heroism in modern life, is "a kind of cult of one's self which can live through the pursuit of happiness by finding it in some one else,— in woman, for example—which can live through all that we call illusions. It is the pleasure of astonishing and the proud satisfaction of never being astonished." The dandy is an unemployed hero, a dismounted knight, who cuts a last dash and registers a last protest against the bourgeois uniformity of modern life. "Dandyism appears particularly in transitional epochs, when democracy is not yet all-powerful and aristocracy is only partially tottering and debased."

In the figure of Euphorion, the brilliant and short-lived offspring of a marriage between classicism and romanticism, "neither classical nor romantic but like the present day itself," Goethe symbolized the art of Byron. Stendhal stated his own intentions by declaring himself, in one of those queer English phrases which besprinkle his journal, a "comic bard." The epithet is paradoxically apt in conveying his final synthesis of observation and imagination.

The perennial student might discard romances for mathematics, the lover might laugh, the philosopher might garner experience; but the writer had still to reckon with the available conventions, which had been cast in a romantic mold. The dramatist of ideas had to use the ideas of his time. *La Vie de Henry Brulard* carries on, from one page to the next, this dialectic between "le romanesque des idées" and "la réalité des faits." The peculiar fervor with which Stendhal liked to repeat the word *logique* did not elude the ironic attention of Mérimée. In this devotion to logic Stendhal disclaimed any pretension to style; he protested, almost too volubly, against literary artifice. Poetry was his antipathy because it seemed "less exact than prose," and he especially abominated the poetic prose of Chateaubriand. Apropos of Madame de Staël, he noted in his marginal English: "I am a warm friend to the Romantick and a warmer enemy to the so caled Romantick stile." His own style has the offhand verve and deliberate indiscretion, the anecdotal flow and epigrammatic turn, the sudden transitions and involved parentheses, the frequent repetitions and occasional inconsistencies of the professional conversationalist. Only in conversation could a characteristic adjective like *affreux*, so colorless in print, be charged with meaning. He never paused to choose a word or to arrange a sentence; his considered revisions were not improvements, as Prévost has conclusively shown. "My talent, if I have any talent, is that of an improviser," he was well aware. The improvisation owes its effectiveness to the comic mask. Yet it is most effective when Stendhal allows us to catch sight of the face behind the mask, the sensibility beyond the logic, the temperament of Rousseau's *Confessions* beneath the discipline of the Civil Code.

"Characters depicted by poets and historians," he notes, "(1) are odious only through their hearts and never through their heads; (2) are ridiculous only through their heads and never through their hearts." This may be the reason why Stendhal's characters are rarely hateful and always amusing, or why there are no villains in his books—or rather, why everyone is a villain, differing from the others in degree of charm and cleverness. Here we are again in the familiar world of the picaresque, where the issue is whether to be a rogue or a fool. Evil, which is rather political than moral, is intellectually grasped rather than emotionally apprehended;

hence villainy can be a source of entertainment and instruction. It is Rousseau's world, seen through the satiric rather than the idyllic imagination. It is Poe's universe, seen through the rationalism of the detective story rather than the mysticism of the supernatural tale. Stendhal is an illusionist who creates mysteries in order to investigate them—in other words, a disillusionist. His five novels, from the vague *Armance* to the clear-cut *Lamiel*, detach themselves from romanticism with increasing sharpness and advance toward a purer refinement of the comic spirit. Both of his two major novels dramatize the predominant idea of his lifetime, the idea of reaction. *Le Rouge et le noir*, written out of his emotions at the climax of the Restoration, is a tragedy of reaction. *La Chartreuse de Parme* is a comedy of reaction, recollected in the full maturity of his intellect. The White Terror has twisted Napoleon into Julien Sorel and Milan into Parma. The tragedy centers upon the individualistic hero; the comedy ranges over the social setting. We, as Stendhal's audience, may accordingly shift our point of view. Following his development, we may foresee the progression of modern fiction from the old Quixotry of the romanticists toward the new Machiavellism of the realists.

3. *The Happy Few*

"It is hard to escape from the malady of one's century," Stendhal observes in his first novel. *Armance, ou quelques scènes d'un salon de Paris en 1827*, as if to illustrate this observation, languishes under the spell of romanticism. Both the elusive Armance de Zohiloff and the melancholy Octave de Malivert suffer from fainting fits; their trysting-place is the tomb of Abelard; and their love is confirmed by a letter written in blood. Stendhal asserts himself here and there by attempting to rationalize the conventions. Octave's noble pallor and cold disdain are marks of caste, supported by two million francs and a viscount's title. His intellectual superiority is accentuated by a diploma from the school that Stendhal had hoped to attend, the Ecole Polytechnique. An engineer by training, Octave is ill at ease in the languid salons of the aristocracy; his own class is "the least energetic because it is the farthest from real needs." An aristocrat by birth, he feels out of place among the teeming enterprises of the century: "Ah, how I'd like to operate a cannon or a steam engine! how I'd love to be a chemist connected with some factory!" Instead he vacillates, even more nervously than Constant's Adolphe; he marries Armance and runs away; he goes to Greece, where he dreams of joining the revolution but ends by committing suicide. His fatal secret, which is barely hinted in the novel, carries the anti-social attitudes of René and Manfred to their most lame and impotent conclusion. For Stendhal's Ideology, rationalizing the *maladie du siècle*, has correlated moral lassitude with physical impotence. No romantic hero ever labored under a severer handicap.

The ruling personage, straying from romantic poetry into sentimental fiction, had to be isolated from society in one fashion if not another, as we have taken note. The Duchesse de Duras, with scandalous success, had introduced a Negro heroine in *Ourika* and a lower-class hero in *Edouard*. In *Olivier*, inspired by a German tale, she had pursued the subject of unhappy love to its ultimate frustration, and presented a eunuch as hero. When she had not dared to publish this novel, Henri de la Touche had published an *Olivier* of his own, and had thereby provided Stendhal with his unspoken premise. In *De l'amour* he had anxiously touched upon the possibility of fiasco, and the apprehension of failure in sexual intercourse. In *Armance* he implied a correlation between the sexual and the political, between Octave's plight and the futility of the Restoration years. Though he scarcely expected his contemporaries to follow the analogy, it should be plainer to us, after a time of indecision whose androgynous prophet was Eliot's Tiresias and whose emasculated playboy was Hemingway's Jake Barnes. In virility and the other Stendhalian virtues, Octave is the very antithesis of Stendhal's subsequent heroes. His immediate successor, Julien Sorel, belongs to that class which is nearest to real needs and therefore most energetic. Lucien Leuwen, under the July Monarchy, is a lapsed Polytechnician who belongs to the new ascendancy of wealth—a circumstance which allows him to vacillate somewhat more purposefully than the scions of the old nobility. Fabrice del Dongo, though he inherits the titled name and special privilege of a Lombard nobleman, is really the illegitimate son of a French soldier. A comparable mystery surrounds the lowly birth of Lamiel, a heroine who is more cold-blooded than any of Sten-

dhal's heroes, who is known to her neighbors as "the devil's daughter" and to her lover as a Machiavellian, but whose portrait rests
incomplete. Novices all, eager to profit from their worldly novitiate, they are pupils of "the professor of energy," as Barrès would
call Napoleon; but, among them, it is Julien Sorel who devotes
himself most energetically to the master's teaching.

Stendhal, like Julien, never really mastered the Horatian lesson
of *nil admirari*. Like Lucien Leuwen, he regarded everyone as either
a hero or a villain. Posing as a misanthrope, he secretly continued
to practise hero-worship. The difficulty was to encounter objects
worthy of his large capacity for admiration. He had set Napoleon
upon the pedestal his own father had never occupied; and when
that colossus came crashing down, he paid homage to other heroes
by writing his books about the arts. He admired Cimarosa, Mozart,
and Shakespeare so much that he wanted their names engraved
upon his tombstone. He worshipped Michelangelo as the personification of *énergie*. This criterion combined the old rhetorical term
for emphasis with the new concept of power, *puissance motrice*,
which Nicolas Carnot and other physicists were then developing.
It might be glossed as the thermodynamics of genius. Certain
countries were congenial, and certain periods had been prolific, in
converting potential ability into kinetic expression—notably the
Italian Renaissance. Accepting Madame de Staël's invidious distinction between the *Midi* and the *Nord*, Stendhal, for his old-
fashioned part, preferred the culture of the Latin south, her
Corinne, ou l'Italie to her *De l'Allemagne*. Like most European
intellectuals, from Chateaubriand to D. H. Lawrence, he played
upon the contrast between the primitive and the hypercivilized.
But, unlike his fellow tourist, Mérimée, he would not appear in
the condescending role of a traveler amused by the natives. Rather,
he hoped that native energies would contribute to the renewal of
an all too effete civilization. Revolution had released the latent
forces of mankind, and Napoleon had given them dynamic leadership; but the Restoration suppressed them again, and the July
Monarchy merely pushed them into the avenues of middle-class
conformity. "In France," Stendhal wrote from Italy, "it is the
galleys that bring together the most remarkable men."

In Italy, where the medieval republics had given way to despotic
governments, Stendhal recognized brigands and bandits as a kind

of underground opposition. The *condottieri* had retreated to the hills, where they led a picturesque existence in the mode of Salvatore Rosa. Charles Nodier, in the tale of *Jean Sbogar*, pictured brigandage as "a state of permanent revolution." The romantic outlaw, as dramatized by Goethe and Schiller, had expressed a revolutionary impulse; and Nietzsche was to define the criminal type as "a strong man amid unfavorable circumstances." The nineteenth century offered comparatively small scope to the superman, unless he chose to exert his talents in the underworld. Stendhal, an assiduous reader of the atrocities reported in the recently established *Gazette des Tribunaux*, paused in the midst of his *Promenades dans Rome* to discuss the latest French crime. One Laffargue, a young carpenter of literary inclinations, had displayed both energy and delicacy in murdering his unfaithful mistress. Stendhal was impressed by his "good education, ardent imagination, and extreme poverty"—qualities which, under more favorable circumstances, had produced Napoleon. "Probably all great men will henceforth emerge from the class to which M. Laffargue belongs." The upper class—for example, Octave de Malivert—was no longer capable of passion or will. The lower class, no longer able to express itself in revolution, would convert its energy into crime. "Crime belongs exclusively to the lower orders," Oscar Wilde would remark. "I don't blame them in the smallest degree. I should fancy that crime was to them what art is to us, simply a way of procuring extraordinary sensations." Wilde's extreme estheticism, the motiveless mischief of Gide's Lafcadio, and the nihilistic perversion of Jean Genet's anti-heroes, are the later refinements of Stendhal's intellectual curiosity. The dramatic gestures of Edmond Dantès and the messianic feats of Jean Valjean were among the more immediate consequences of Julien Sorel's crime, which encountered its living parallel six years later at the trial of the poet-assassin Lacenaire.

Here Dostoevsky, who was even more concerned with guilt than with crime, raises a pertinent question. "How do you distinguish those extraordinary people from the ordinary ones?" the magistrate Porfiry asks the student Raskolnikov in *Crime and Punishment*. And how, we are sometimes minded to ask Stendhal, can you tell an unemployed hero from a common criminal? Sometimes the difference is ominously slight. Granted Stendhal's belief in a natural elite and his contempt for repressive mediocrity, however, it is not surprising that he should have expected more from prisons and galleys than from churches and salons. As a freemason, he believed in signs and passwords; he believed that the extraordinary people could be distinguished by their political loyalties and their artistic tastes. The cult of Napoleon, above all, is the touchstone whereby we can tell his heroes and heroines from the ordinary people. Thus the heroine of *Le Rose et le vert*, Mina Wanghen, is "too ardent a soul to be content with the reality of life"; her father is a German general who refused to fight against the Emperor, while her lover is a French count who was the Emperor's page on the Russian expedition. Romain Rolland has reminded us that the music of Cimarosa, so intimately associated with Stendhal's discovery of Italy, figures as a leitmotif in his amorous passages. The higher freemasonry was not confined to statesmen and artists; it included such notables—oddly assorted by any other criteria—as the revolutionary Madame Roland, the ballet-master Vigano, the mathematics teacher Gros, and the unhappily convicted Laffargue. Such are the "noble and tender souls" to whom Stendhal dedicates his works, and who in turn communicate energy and passion to his creations. *Le Rouge et le noir*, *La Chartreuse de Parme*, and several other volumes are inscribed in English with his vaguely Shakespearean motto, "To the Happy Few."

The central theme of *Lucien Leuwen* is the bittersweet attachment—"à la Don Quichotte," Stendhal adds—between Lucien, who is at heart a liberal Orleanist, and Bathilde de Chasteller, who is jealously guarded by her ultra-royalist connections. In an atmosphere of intrigues and suspicions, not unlike that of Turgenev's *Smoke*, love is similarly the only reality. But how can the lovers distinguish their genuine emotions from the hypocrisies that surround them? How can the happy few, across the barriers of misunderstanding, learn to recognize one another? Through their sensibilities, Stendhal answers, through their sincere responses to art and nature, through *le naturel*. They meet in the forest of Burelviller, named after the captain that Henry Brulard accompanied on his first visit to Italy; they stop at the Chasseur Vert, the coffeehouse that Beyle frequented with his German beloved, Mina de Griesheim; to these associations, and the romantic music—so it sounded in Stendhal's day—of Mozart, their recognition is orchestrated. "Such is the danger of sincerity, of music, and of great forests." After rambling far beyond the length of Stendhal's completed books, the novel breaks off at an appropriate point, when Lucien is revisiting the haunts of Rousseau. Whatever the Ideologues may have put into Stendhal's head, he remained a Rousseauist at heart. He was less certain of human goodness than of institutional evils; but his values, put to the touch, were those of nature and sincerity. Underneath the disguises they are forced by the world to assume, his sympathetic characters—in the parlance of the romanticists—have beautiful souls. "Vous avez une belle âme," says one heroine of *La Chartreuse de Parme* to the other. It is well for us to remember, when launched with Stendhal upon the high seas of doubt, that he now and then returns to these few happy islands of belief.

"Naturalness or lack of hypocrisy" was the basis of the sympathy he continually sought. The struggle in his novels, Auguste Bussière suggested, is between those who are led by passion and those who are led by vanity. Either passion is everything or all is vanity, novelists are tempted to proclaim, depending on how much or how little they sympathize with their characters. Occasionally, like Thackeray, they manage to balance pseudo-morality against callow cynicism. But Thackeray is a domesticated dandy who looks especially mild alongside of Stendhal: Major Pendennis is no counterweight for Count Mosca. For the French novelist, life is more complex: good intentions are misled by worldly values. There are degrees of passion, caprices of vanity, and the real conflict between them is waged within the individual soul. It therefore calls for psychological treatment, which can only be applied at full length to a single personage. Stendhal acknowledged that he could not, like Fielding, treat several personages at once. But Fielding used the external method of comedy, as indeed Stendhal did in his unsympathetic characterizations; it was through his protagonists, characterized so close to himself and his readers, that he brought the introspective tradition into the novel and approximated the internal monologue. To fiction, as well as criticism, his approach was biographical—not to say autobiographical. *Egotisme*, the grammarians' word for recurrence of the first person—not to be confused with *égoisme*, the moralists' word for selfishness—was one of the words he brought into literary usage. Self-knowledge and self-interest are at the opposite poles of his thought, as far apart as the *esprit de finesse* and the *esprit de géométrie*, and as close together as the sublime and the ridiculous. They are united through the person of the Stendhalian hero who, as his consciousness enlarges and his superiority reveals itself, is both a tragic actor and a comic spectator, a sublime individual in a ridiculous society, a Don Quixote in a Machiavellian world. Hence, while the behavior of others can always be calculated, his actions are unpredictable; as Julien's protector says of him, "Il a de l'imprévu."

Most modern novelists would be willing, with Somerset Maugham, to give Stendhal the credit for having shown them "what contrary qualities could exist side by side." Not that the contradictions of human nature had gone unnoticed before: the habit of seeing the better course and pursuing the worse had been lamented by Ovid and taken for granted by Aristotle. Montaigne had dramatized the conflict of the many selves within his own microcosm. It was pre-eminently the eighteenth century, with its sharp dichotomy between reason and emotion, which fostered a literature of self-analysis. Rousseau, though more acutely aware of other men's duplicity than of his own, confessed through his Savoyard vicar: "I am active when I listen to reason, passive when my passions carry me away." Diderot, conscious of "things thought and done but never said," saw to it that some of them were said by Rameau's nephew. The Abbé Prévost was able to deal with a gambler and a courtesan, far more sympathetically than the picaresque novelists had previously done, by professing that *Manon Lescaut* was "a treatise on morality pleasantly reduced to an exercise." Fiction gradually found out how to keep and eat its cake, how to deplore and indulge the same emotions, how the morality of the author could atone for the immorality of his subject. This ambivalence, as author drew closer to subject, tended to split personality, and culminated in the romantic protagonist known as the *Doppelgänger*. Such an ambiguous type as Adolphe, without becoming quite so overtly schizoid, is "a mixture of egoism and sensibility." Such is the Stendhalian hero, who might likewise be described as "the most loyal and cruel of men." But where Constant describes Adolphe as "having always finished by cruelty after having begun by loyalty," Stendhal reverses the description. His heroes, though they have a passive and subjective side which reminds us of their ineffectual predecessors, are ultimately men of action functioning in an objectified sphere.

As a psychological novelist, Stendhal had many models; as a social novelist, he had few. There had been a few fumbling attempts to deal realistically with provincial life, and he had manifested an interest in them. For Mortonval's *Tartuffe moderne*, with its glimpse into the petty politics of a theological seminary, he had his obvious uses. Lemontey's *Famille de Jura*, with its regional setting and its peasant's impression of Paris, was more of a Bonapartist pamphlet than a novel, and all the more stimulating on that account. More and more suspicious of novels, Stendhal had grown particularly fond of memoirs. It is no coincidence that a remarkable triad of human documents—from the courtier Saint-Simon, the philanderer Casanova, and the detective Vidocq—first saw print within a year or two before *Le Rouge et le noir*. In Italian libraries, where he spent long hours copying anecdotes and *novelle* out of Renaissance manuscripts, Stendhal discovered immense reserves of energy. Splendid sinners, like Francesco Cenci or Vittoria Accoramboni, set examples for his characters; and forgotten chroniclers plied a lively, unvarnished, economical style which he has preserved in such Italianate tales as *L'Abbesse de Castro*. His distrust of imagination made him peculiarly dependent upon documentation; this dependence, in his early writing, did not quite stop short of plagiary. He took his property, like Molière, where he found it, and where the Elizabethan dramatists found their subjects. He might have avowed, with André Gide, "I have never been able to invent anything." It was Stendhal who introduced novelists to the habit of clipping their material out of newspapers, particularly out of the crime news. There he came across the case of Antoine Berthet, a student of theology employed as a tutor, who had made advances to one employer's wife and another's daughter; who, having been dismissed, had attempted murder and suicide; and who had then been tried and condemned to death by a court at Grenoble in 1827.

There, unsuspectedly close to home, were the facts, the little true facts, the "odious truths" that would shock Mérimée. The problem was whether the techniques of fiction were adequate to handle them. The most available genre was that which the Waverley novels had so successfully exploited. "The French nation is

mad about Walter Scott," Stendhal had declared, counting two
hundred translations and adaptations and imitations. Young writers
were trying their hands at historical novels: Vigny with *Cinq-mars*
in 1826, Balzac with *Les Chouans* in 1829, Hugo with *Notre-Dame
de Paris* in 1831. Mérimée, who stood closest to Stendhal, made
the Saint Bartholomew massacre a theme for anti-clerical satire
with his 1572, *Chronique du règne de Charles IX*, which appeared
in 1829. In 1830 several chapters from *Le Rouge et le noir* appeared
in periodicals, subtitled *Chronique de 1830*. The year, and the completion of the book, were interrupted by the July Revolution; the
subtitle, to retain its element of timeliness, became *Chronique du
dix-neuvième siècle*. So timely was the book that, although it covers
its hero's life from his nineteenth through his twenty-third year,
an early chapter is headed "Modes of Behavior in 1830." In an
anonymous puff Stendhal praised himself for daring "to recount
an adventure which took place in 1830." The most original feature
of *Armance* had likewise been the note struck by its subtitle,
Quelques scènes d'un salon en 1827; not only was 1827 the date
of publication, but *scènes* was a hint which Balzac would act upon.
Stendhal's journalistic timing, his emphatic contemporaneity, contrasts strikingly with the work of Scott's imitators. In an essay on
Scott and *La Princesse de Clèves* he demurred:

> *Imitate nature* is a piece of advice which is devoid of mean-
> ing. To what extent must one imitate nature in order to
> please the reader? That is the big question... If art is noth-
> ing but a beautiful lie, Sir Walter Scott has been too much
> of a liar.

But this dismissal is cavalierly unfair to the most influential of
novelists. As an antiquarian and a tourist, Scott had broadened the
picaresque novel by taking history and geography in his stride; by
taking a comprehensive survey of a given region of the past, from
court to cottage, he had paved the way for the sociological novel.
Stendhal's contribution—to take the present for his period, to
write a historical novel of his own time was, in the judgment of a
recent Italian critic, "the most important literary innovation of
the century." From the introductory epigraph—Danton's phrase,
"bitter truth"—Stendhal gives an unprecedented twist to Scott's
conventions. We start from the usual topographical presentation:

the little village of Verrières, its red-tiled roofs and its Spanish ruins, the Jura mountains in the background and the river Doubs in the foreground. Then, as the river turns, the tempo changes: water-power, industry, textiles, machines, the fall of Napoleon, and the rise of the bourgeoisie as typified by the figure of the mayor, M. de Rênal. Two further chapters of small-town gossip and business prepare us for a close-up of Julien Sorel, sitting astride a beam in his father's sawmill and reading *Le Mémorial de Saint-Hélène*.

The novel develops, under Ideological auspices, into a case study of Antoine Berthet's motivation, an analysis of the interaction between temperament and environment. For literary purposes the hero is drawn somewhat larger than life, and draped in the attributes of a vestigial romanticism. Like Byron's Manfred, he is attended by an ominous bird; like Lamartine's Jocelyn, he repairs at intervals to a mysterious grotto; but under his seminarist's garb, he is not an angel; he is another *homme fatal*. His fatality, rationally considered, is that of Dumas' Antony or Hugo's Ruy Blas: to be qualified for a dominant role and cast in a subordinate position. But narrative, unlike drama, can present itself through the hero's point of view; and when the hero happens to occupy a domestic position, we can expect an inside story which will upset the more conventional views. Julien is constantly citing the precedent of Saint-Preux, a tutor, and of Rousseau himself, an erstwhile lackey. Julien's knowledge of the world has been precariously gleaned from the *Confessions*. Stendhal's, by this time, is wider. His task is to present his romantic hero in a realistic situation, to inject a confession into his chronicle. Las Cases' *Mémorial de Sainte-Hélène*, being Napoleon's confession and chronicle, is Julien's inevitable favorite among many books. It does not matter that his father knocks it into the mill-race, for Julien has memorized it more assiduously than the New Testament. The old army surgeon, who bequeathed it to him, was the only person toward whom he has been able to behave sincerely; and he uses a surreptitious portrait of Napoleon as a test of Madame de Rênal's sincerity. He cannot take a step without wondering what "the other one" would have done in his shoes; he prepares himself for his amatory conquests by rereading the bulletins of the Grand Army. What will happen, without the Emperor, to those poor devils who have just enough money for an education and not enough for a career?

"Whatever happens," Julien muses, "that fatal memory will prevent us from being happy."

Stendhal recollected, in the preface to *Armance*, an operatic snatch hummed by Napoleon during the Russian campaign: "Whether to be a miller or a notary . . ." It must have seemed, to the young men he led to glory, that the choice was infinite. In those days, some fifteen years before, one was either dead or a general at thirty-six. A glance at the Sixth Dragoons returning from Italy—Stendhal's own regiment—awakens Julien's military ambitions. But his pale and perfervid generation, which Musset interpreted six years after Stendhal in *La Confession d'un enfant du siècle*, a generation whose infant slumbers were broken by the tramp of the returning armies, whose boyish dreams were pervaded by the sands of Egypt and the snows of Russia, was to be bitterly disillusioned: "When children talked of glory, they were told, 'Enter the priesthood.'" The cassock was their "terrible symbol." Hence Julien's boast: "I know how to choose the uniform of my century." The eagles have disappeared; the only career still open to talent is the church. Julien is constrained to hide his worship of Jean-Jacques and Bonaparte; a set of Tacitus, the present of the worldly old bishop of Besançon, is his *moyen de parvenir*; Maistre's *Du pape*, the manual of ultramontane Catholicism, is his careerist's handbook. In the lottery of fortune he plays the alternatives of red and black—the colors of revolution and reaction, the uniforms of the army and the clergy, the genuine ardor that burns in his breast and the cold careerism that governs his conduct. Never is he more himself than in the scene at the restored abbey of Bray-le-Haut. He has ridden in the king's guard of honor, and he feels his spurs beneath his subdiaconal garments. The young bishop of Agde, another clerical career-man, performs the benediction that Julien has watched him rehearse before a mirror. The cannoneers, veterans of the Battle of Leipzig, fire a salute. The whole ceremony costs 3800 francs, and undoes the work of a hundred Jacobin papers.

Le Rouge et le noir is a funeral eulogy over the lost generation that was born during the Empire and came of age under the Restoration. Clericalism has thrown a pall over their hopes. "Under Napoleon, I should have been a sergeant; among these future *curés* I shall be a vicar-general," so the neophyte resolves, when he finds the seminary filled with crass peasants whose sole concern is a comfortable living. Though he is not insensitive to the attractions of religion, though he delights in decorating the cathedral, his brain is too clear to be fuddled by the incense of Chateaubriand's religiosity. He finds, to his surprise, that some priests are sincerely religious; but they are Jansenists like his austere mentor, the Abbé Pirard, suspected of heresy and persecuted by their black-robed brethren. The kindly Chélan, who doubts if Julien's vocation is sincere, loses his parish because he has allowed a reformer to inspect the prison. No local graft is too small and no national policy is too big for the machinations of the Jesuits: from appointing a bigoted imbecile to the lottery office—and ignoring the worthier candidate, Stendhal's old friend Gros—to conspiring with the enemies of France for the return of ecclesiastical property—and making Julien, somewhat anachronistically, the bearer of the notorious secret note that urged the Duke of Wellington to prolong the foreign occupation. The plot is controlled, behind the scenes, by the political strategy of the Jesuit-dominated Congregation; the wires are pulled, from first to last, by its director, the vicar-general Frilair. *Lamiel* continues the exposure with a grotesque account of a Jesuit mission, where a sermon is heightened by fireworks. Stendhal's account of the pageantry at Bray-le-Haut echoes the coronation of Charles X, last of the Bourbons and most extreme of the ultras, at Rheims in 1825—an occasion on which Church and State had managed to travesty one another.

The reign of counter-revolutionary terror thus heralded, which did its utmost to revoke the charter of 1815, to repress the liberties that the Revolution had extended and to restore the privileges it had abolished, is the occasion of Stendhal's novel. Needless to say, the novel could hardly have been printed until that reign was over, and its harsh restrictions on the press had been lifted. Hence Stendhal's climax is appropriately staged in a newly built church during the celebration of the mass. Julien's pistol seems to be specifically aimed at the Jesuitical legislation against sacrilege; the blasphemous reverberations seem to celebrate the downfall of Bourbons and ultras. The Three Glorious Days of the July Revolution were generally likened to the Glorious Revolution that drove the Stuarts from the English throne. The opening chapter of the second volume, wherein the mail-coach brings Julien from country to city, is a debate between a Bonapartist and a Liberal, who speak for the previous and the succeeding regimes. The two volumes proceed, in ascending order, from the provincial bourgeoisie to the Parisian aristocracy, while Julien proceeds from tutor to seminarist and from secretary to officer. In each of the two households that employ him, the servant asserts his mastery through sex; first Louise de Rênal, and then Mathilde de La Mole, becomes his mistress. The ladder, which he formerly climbed to decorate an altar, becomes an accessory to his love-affairs and a symbol of his ascent in the social hierarchy. His successive masters, M. de Rênal and the Marquis de La Mole, find him an apt pupil; for his part, he finds that the difference between chicanery and diplomacy is a matter of scale. In the first excitement of arrival, and the constant fear of ridicule, he expects too much; over-eager to do the correct thing, he makes the mistake of challenging a coachman. Experience is disappointment: when he has fought a real duel, and when he has accomplished his first seduction, his comment is "N'est-ce que ça?"

Passion is intermingled with politics in Stendhal; his lovers are usually members of different parties or antagonistic classes; his projected comedy, Les Deux Hommes, pitted the republican character against the monarchic. Julien, as a lover, is the man of energy converting his force into heat, the Jacobin turned social climber. The author of De l'amour understood that love, in its incipient stages, is almost indistinguishable from self-love. Julien's devoir is primarily a sense of what he owes to himself. When he deliberately grasps Louise's hand, and she impulsively responds, he begins to realize that love has its unselfish aspects. He is not lying when he tells the jury, "Madame de Rênal has been like a mother to me." Because he is motherless, like Stendhal himself, his profoundest desires seek some kind of maternal object. When she accedes to him, he sobs like a child. She writes her fatal letter out of what she thinks is conscience but is actually jealousy; he fires his answering shot out of what he thinks is revenge but is actually longing. Between Julien and Mathilde, the peasant's son and the peer's daughter, the tension is even stronger. Here the devoir is on her side; it is she, in the manner of Bernard Shaw's heroines, who finally takes the initiative. Their conversations are "animated by sentiments of the liveliest hatred." In mutual ambivalence, they fascinate and repel each other; with suspicion on both sides, they arrive at an assignation. And when they arrive at an understanding, it is based on the humiliation of her pride and the assertion of his, the masochism of the aristocrat and the sadism of the revolutionist. "Beware of that young man who has so much energy," her brother has warned her. "If the revolution starts again, he will have us all guillotined." At the ball or the opera, among the gilded youth, he cuts a sinister figure. He will be another Danton, she imagines in her proud humility, perhaps another Robespierre. When he determines to climb her balcony, we see him in his true colors: "the unhappy man at war with the whole of society."

Goethe, though he praised the psychological insight of *Le Rouge et le noir*, considered the feminine characters too romantic. They undoubtedly are, for their function is to understand Julien's true nature. It is because Julien is a romantic at heart that he, figuratively and literally, loses his head. Mathilde's cult of her beheaded ancestor, the lover of Marguérite de Valois, strengthens her for the part of a Dumas heroine, and for the macabre series of last rites that she arranges for her lover. In contrast to the naturalness of the Rênal estate at Vergy, her necrophilic love has ripened in a library, nourished on the chronicles of Brantôme and Aubigné and the novels of Rousseau and Prévost. It should not be too surprising, for those familiar with Stendhal's touchstones, that she ends by boring and irritating Julien, or that the prodigal—torn between his two mistresses, like Dimitri Karamazov between Katya and Grushenka—reverts to Madame de Rênal. It is truly surprising that Emile Faguet should accuse Stendhal of evading the issue, and propose an ending in which Julien either reaches the top of the ladder or else drags Mathilde down to his original level. If Julien had a future, it clearly would not be shared with Mathilde. She has all too clearly become, as Stendhal must have learned to say in Italy, the *terza incomoda*. So far as Stendhal's intentions are concerned, the crime is the issue, and the condemnation is the pay-off. Nothing less than complete failure will prove Julien's sincerity, vindicate his good faith, and demonstrate that he is no mere *arriviste*. Eugène de Rastignac would be too hard, Frédéric Moreau too soft, for such an act. Afterward, after Frilair has been conciliated and the jury has been fixed, Julien's fate again falls into his hands. But the trial, the sight of the assembled bourgeoisie, arouses his peculiar notion of duty. Improvising for the first time,

he loads his speech with the dynamite of class-consciousness. He
pleads guilty to the crime of having risen in the world and pronounces his own verdict. "Gentlemen, I have not the honor of
belonging to your class. You see in me a peasant who has revolted
against the baseness of his fortune..."

Prince Korasoff's advice to him, "Always do the opposite of
what is expected of you," should have prepared us for the denouement. Julien's pent-up heroism betrays itself by one of those gusts
of sensibility which cannot be foreseen by the Machiavellian calculus. Isolated in his impenitent cell, he comes to Hobbesian conclusions about the predatory human animal; he envisions society
as a relentless conspiracy of power and wealth. "No, man cannot
put his trust in man." Often he has naïvely wondered if he too
were not merely another egoist, and often he has acted suspiciously
like one; his last actions, at any rate, are disinterested. "The powerful idea of duty," he trusts, has saved him from living in isolation.
The distinction between duty and interest, in the last analysis, is
the gulf that separates the happy few from the world at large. Yet
it must be admitted that the happy few fare none too happily in
their pursuits; the free spirits are enchained while charlatans prosper; for those that feel, the world is a tragedy. Even Croisenois,
the noble suitor of Mathilde, is killed in a duel by a millionaire
named Thaler. In a world where everything else is for sale, there
is one decoration that distinguishes, one honor that cannot be
bought: it is the death sentence. The revolutionary Count Alta-
mira, who has had a price set on his head, is the one character who
commands Julien's wholehearted respect. Other omens foreshadow
the guillotine: the news of an execution, the sound of a prisoner's
song. The singer Geronimo, named for Lablache's role in *Il Matrimonio segreto*, represents those graces which are rather Italian
than French. Stendhal has a way of fastening on specific details
—a pair of scissors, an ancient sword, a Japanese vase—to evoke a
mood or connote a situation. His most arresting metaphor is that
of a tiger kept as a pet by an Englishman, who took care to keep
a loaded pistol within his reach.

Though later generations of supermen and nihilists and *dera-
cinés* and *immoralistes* pay their respects to Julien, and claim
Stendhal as the founder of their *culte du moi*, no writer has more
cogently insisted that egoism is self-destroying, and that the few

cannot be happy when the many are unhappy. *Le Rouge et le noir,* accepted at its face value, could be made to serve as reactionary propaganda. Paul Bourget has sententiously retold the story in *Le Disciple:* his young upstart, influenced by the experimental doctrines of a philosopher modelled on Taine, seduces a young patrician and incites her to suicide. The labored moral is that new ideas are dangerous, and that the lower classes should be kept in their place. But face values are precisely what Stendhal wished to discount. "What the pride of the rich calls society" is for him a comic phenomenon; and while, in ironic footnotes, he disclaims the radical opinions of his characters, his own sympathies are with the interloper. The tragic resistance of the individual, vainly trying to uphold the integrity of his personality against the conformities and corruptions of the time, is what lends stature to Julien Sorel. At a time when it is difficult not to write satire, it is equally hard to be a hero; and Stendhal's irony fluctuates against the double standard of realistic worldliness and romantic sensibility. Julien surrenders too early and resists too late. The desperate intelligence that guides his steps, nevertheless, is a refutation of Amiel's criticism and an assertion of freedom of the will. In Dreiser's *American Tragedy* a century later, as it happens, we see the same factors at work: bigotry and venality, the climb toward success, the compromising affair, the murderous impulse, the trial and condemnation and execution. Circumstances meanwhile have been closing in, and Clyde Griffiths is their victim. Unlike Julien, he has no elbowroom for heroics, and little responsibility for his actions. Not Ideology but behaviorism offers the key to his character. The novel is no longer the confession of a mind, but has wholly become the chronicle of a milieu.

"Tender and honest" are Stendhal's adjectives for Julien, reconsidered at a distance of ten years, "ambitious, yet full of imagination and illusion." To be a lone champion of modernity, under a regimen which encouraged the shrewd and the stolid to adopt the costumes and revive the customs of the Middle Ages— surely Don Quixote was never confronted with a more preposterous situation. As for Gil Blas, that clever rogue who showed such agility in mounting to high places, what would he have made of a social hierarchy which was itself in motion, of bishops and kings who were merely invested and annointed picaroons?

"O nineteenth century!" In 1823 when the radical orator, Jacques Manuel, invoked the "new energy" that had emerged with the Revolution, he was expelled from the ultra-royalist Chamber of Deputies. This was the energy, submerged again during the Restoration, that Stendhal sought to register; the heat that soon, he warned his contemporaries, would be converted into force. Temporarily it lurked behind the comic mask, the clerical uniform, the antic disposition; Julien's hypocrisy, like Hamlet's madness, was a dramatic device. French logic had frequently speculated on the paradox of the comedian: Diderot maintained that the best acting had the least feeling, while Rousseau drew tragic implications out of Molière's ridicule. From the comedy of the nineteenth century to the tragedy is a step which Julien finally takes; his superiority, which must stoop to conquer, debases itself and foregoes its conquest. The irony of ironies is that Stendhal should pattern his hero upon the classic model of the hypocrite, that sincerity should be driven to *Tartufferie.* Yet Molière's comedy, which Julien committed to memory, had a special meaning for the Restoration; it voiced a protest against the clerical regime, which could not otherwise have been heard. Even Tartuffe had his great scene, when it befell the servant to order the master out of the house. To royalty and nobility, to the clergy and the Third Estate, to the thrones and powers and dominions and vested interests, *Le Rouge et le noir* brought back that scene with all the accelerating impact of a nightmare:

> C'est à vous d'en sortir, vous qui parlez en maître:
> La maison m'appartient, je le ferai connaître . . .

4. *A Pistol-Shot at a Concert*

If you think *Le Rouge et le noir* an immoral book, you are admonished by the author to think again. "A novel is a mirror riding along a highway." This definition, which Stendhal apocryphally attributes to the historian Saint-Réal, is his own apology for realism. Whether the novelist reflects the sky or the ground depends upon his angle of observation, and yours as well. You must not blame the man with the mirror when the road is

muddy; and when it leads through the mire of political controversy, you should pay some heed to his sense of direction. No
one would guess whether the author of *Armance* was an ultra
or a liberal, Stendhal overconfidently assured his publishers; but
the Austrian police were not baffled by the tendency of his
books on Italy. His precautions and disclaimers merely called
attention to his innuendoes. "Politics in a work of literature is
like a pistol-shot at a concert, something crude from which,
however, it is impossible to withhold our attention," he repeats
in *La Chartreuse de Parme*, having voiced the same thought by
the same arresting metaphor in his two other published novels.
In *Le Rouge et le noir* he imagines the publisher replying: "If
your characters don't talk politics ... they are not Frenchmen of
1830, and your book is no mirror..." Even the love scenes
have their political discussions, and the religious tone is desecrated
by a literal pistol-shot. Each of Stendhal's novels, despite its
professed frivolity, is interrupted by some shattering detonation.
Sooner or later the unexpected interruption becomes the inevitable cadenza. The shooting is on the program; the pistol is
in the score; the Stendhalian performance would be incomplete
without it. For *La Chartreuse de Parme*, which was literally an
improvisation, politics provide the theme. Esthetics provide the
orchestration. The dissonant motives of *Le Rouge et le noir*,
esthetic and political, are here at last resolved with subtle and
complex virtuosity.

The individualistic gesture, the social accompaniment; the
Napolionic hero, the Italianate setting; the romantic energy, the
Ideological analysis; the revolt against bourgeois careerism, the
unending pursuit of love; the tragedy of the happy few, the
comedy of the nineteenth century—the emphasis shifts as we
turn to *La Chartreuse de Parme*. Reaction still predominates,
but the nightmare is now a wish-dream. If *Le Rouge et le noir*
was a journalistic recension of *Don Quixote*, *La Chartreuse de
Parme* is an operatic version of *The Prince*. It is not surprising
that the less mature work has been the more popular, especially
with the young, for its romanticism and its realism are both
more obvious; its dissonances are unresolved. The mellower work,
like the works of Montaigne or Jane Austen, improves with
rereading and with improved experience. One must see something

of life, as Balzac perceived, in order to appreciate how much of it Stendhal has seen. Novels, though they are peculiarly urban products, are seldom truly urbane. In this respect, as in many others, _La Chartreuse de Parme_ is exceptional: it is perhaps the most civilized novel ever written. It was written by a diplomat escaping from his post, whereas _Le Rouge et le noir_ was written by a dilettante excluded from office. Neither an esthete nor a politician at heart, Stendhal reproved his contemporaries for neglecting the arts; yet he never forgot that society was the precondition of art. For him the suicide of Chatterton, so bemoaned by the romanticists, had been the result of bad government. Yet good government, which he supported in principle, failed to capture his imagination. In practice he was bored by democracy and fascinated by despotism. He delighted Charles X, of all people, by his memorandum on the papal conclave of 1829. "He would rather pay court to the Minister of the Interior," he professed, "than to the corner grocer."

Thomas Jefferson was one of his heroes, and the government of the United States was a "perfect model." _De l'amour_, however, has a bleakly disparaging chapter on America. Americans, we are told, have no imagination; their springs of sensibility have dried up. "They are just, they are reasonable, and they are not happy." The objection that they think of nothing but dollars and cows is frequently raised. Stendhal had come, without crossing the ocean, to some of Alexis de Tocqueville's conclusions. If the austere virtues of the new republic proved disappointing, one might as well fall back on the comfortable vices of an older civilization. "Washington would have bored me to death," confesses that ardent young republican, Lucien Leuwen, "and I prefer to find myself in the same salon with M. de Talleyrand." In the salon of M. de Tracy, Stendhal found himself in the company of La Fayette, now the elder statesman whose prestige swung the Revolution of 1830 toward the constitutional monarchy of Louis-Philippe. The Orléans regime, though it restored Stendhal to office, was the least satisfactory of compromises. His character had hardened, under the Restoration, as a member of the opposition. He could hate the reactionary Congrégation and admire the revolutionary Charbonnerie, but the muddling policies of the _Juste-milieu_ left him cold. A free press and a democratic legislature had seemed worthier institutions when they were menaced by the symbols of clericalism and royalism, the altar and the throne. Industrial enterprise, as opposed to the privileges of the landed aristocracy, seemed a progressive force. But Stendhal was never a utopian. He could not agree with the Saint-Simonians, who ignored the distinction between capital and labor, that production would solve all social problems. In 1825 he published an acute pamphlet, *D'un nouveau complot contre les industriels*, pointing out that the capitalists, who still claimed to be public benefactors, were serving their own vested interests, and would be proper subjects for some future Molière. But that was to be Balzac's comedy.

Stendhal saw the July Monarchy only upon his occasional furloughs from Civitavecchia; back at his post, in *Lucien Leuwen*, he kept the record of his inverted nostalgia. An alternative title, *Le Rouge et le blanc*, again suggests a love which spans opposing camps. Lucien's dilemma is to spend his life "between raving legitimists, selfish and polite, who adore the past, and raving republicans, generous and tiresome, who adore the future." Between these extremes, dominating the novel and the period, stretches the bourgeois compromise, symbolized by the nightcap, the umbrella, and the pear-shaped head of the Citizen King. In contrast to the solemn mummery of Charles X at Bray-le-Haut, Louis-Philippe is presented as a royal businessman, a "crowned price-list," a "pettifogger from lower Normandy." Lucien, having been expelled from the Ecole Polytechnique for his radicalism, and then garrisoned as a lieutenant among the royalists of Nancy, is sent upon an appropriate series of missions. After trying to fix an election for the Jesuits, after shooting down a crowd of striking workers, after supervising the death of an *agent provocateur*, he looks upon life "with no other sentiment than that of astonishment without pleasure: 'N'est-ce que ça?'" He tries to "combine the profits of an office-holder with the fine sensibility of a man of honor." Like his decade, like his class, he falls betwixt and between; he is neither a criminal like Julien nor a courtier like Fabrice. As the scene changes from the provinces to Paris, and from love to politics, it is Lucien's father and mentor who emerges as the central figure. The bankers and politicians have supplanted the aristocrats and priests at the top of the hierarchy. François Leuwen is Stendhal's portrait of the worldly-wise banker-politician, the friend of Bentham, the rival of Rothschild, "the Talleyrand of the Bourse," whose integrity is famous—"almost as famous as his malice." Everything around him is new: bric-a-brac from the current exhibition, fashionable pictures, modern conveniences. His first act is to request Lucien to press the button of a new-fangled heating device; his next is to express solicitude for his son's career.

> "Think it over: have you enough will-power to be a rogue? That is, to take part in some petty roguery; for during the last four years there has been no occasion to spill blood."
>
> "To steal money, at worst," Lucien interrupted.
>
> "From the poor people," M. Leuwen interrupted in his turn, with a maudlin air. "Or to employ it somewhat differently from the way they would," he added in the same tone. "But they are rather stupid, and their deputies are rather silly, and not particularly disinterested—"
>
> "What do you want me to be?" Lucien asked, with a simple air.
>
> "A rogue," answered his father. "I mean a politician, a Martignac; I won't go so far as to say a Talleyrand. At your age, and in your papers, that is called being a rogue. In ten years you will realize that Colbert, Sully, Cardinal Richelieu, in a word, all politicians—that is to say, rulers of men—have risen by means of that first step in roguery which I am anxious for you to take."

It is significant that Stendhal, more at home with diplomacy than with finance, singularly ill at ease on the Balzacian terrain of contemporary France, should have dropped *Lucien Leuwen* and turned to *La Chartreuse de Parme*. After he completed his masterpiece, he returned to "the French under King Philippe" with *Lamiel*, which he did not live to complete. Meanwhile the businesslike 'thirties had given way to the radical 'forties, and the mood of Balzac to that of George Sand. Lamiel, a female Julien Sorel, is the most energetic of Stendhal's heroines, who have gradually taken the lead over his heroes. Her province is hard-headed Normandy; her sole passion is profound curiosity; her lovers, in descending order, range from a duke to a thief.

The latter, Valbayre, would have involved Stendhal in his furthest excursion into criminology. After Valbayre has escaped from the galleys, and been caught and condemned—we gather from the synopsis—Lamiel is scheduled to burn down the Palace of Justice, immolating herself, by way of revenge. "I make war on society, which makes war on me," he has informed her. "I read Corneille and Molière. I have too much education to work with my hands and earn three francs for ten hours of labor." Lamiel avoids the sentimental education of Stendhal's other characters: she reads chapbooks about highwaymen, subscribes to the *Gazette des Tribunaux*, and is presented with a biography of Talleyrand. Under the tutelage of the hunchbacked dandy, Dr. Sansfin, she learns "the rule of the ivy," a practical exercise in the theory of crystallization. Therewith the mind is compared to a sturdy oak, obscured by a tangle of illusions. Lamiel must learn to distinguish the vine from the tree, the pretext from the motive. "The world," says Sansfin, "is not divided, as nincompoops believe, into rich and poor, good and bad men; but quite simply into dupes and knaves. Here is the key that explains the nineteenth century since the fall of Napoleon."

Why, then, protest? Undisguised calculation, taking for granted that every man or woman has his or her price, and that every conflict ends in a bargain, is the uncontestable order of the day. In the last analysis—and *Lamiel* is Stendhal's last analysis— logic prevails, comedy triumphs, and romanticism is exorcised. The problem of the few and the many is really quite simple, once we admit that the many want to be duped. For the few, who do not, a single course is open: the main chance. The old-fashioned dualism of good and evil, sensibility and selfishness, is suspended in favor of a single-minded opportunism. Whether to be a fool or a rogue, a *dupe* or a *coquin*—that is the question confronting Stendhal's heroes and heroines. Nowadays, as the elder Leuwen exhorts the younger, charlatanism is a highly competitive profession; the antichambers and back-rooms are crowded with would-be rogues, busily endeavoring to make fools of one another. Because *La Chartreuse de Parme* poses the alternatives so sharply and engagingly, it is "the most exquisite treatise on comparative roguery ever written on this planet," according to Charles Maurras, who came to know a good deal about "coquinologie comparée." It is a picaresque novel written between the lines of a court calendar, substituting princes and statesmen for innkeepers and vagabonds. "Everyone is grossly immoral," Henry James demurs, "and the heroine is a kind of monster." But James, with his American innocence and suspicion of foreign intrigue, nonetheless happens to be a country cousin of Stendhal. Sturdily, like the hero of his *Ambassadors*, he weathers the shock, and discerns "that through the magnificently sustained pauses of the narrative we feel at last the influence of the writer's cynicism, regard it as amiable, and enjoy serenely his clear vision of the mechanism of character, unclouded by the mists of prejudice." *La Chartreuse de Parme*, he reassures us, "will always be numbered among the dozen finest novels we possess."

This does not mean that the action takes place in a moral vacuum; Stendhal's opportunists, though they put themselves beyond good, are certainly not beyond evil. To be shocked at their behavior, and the circumstances that inspire it, is just the response that Stendhal intended to stimulate. By polishing the surfaces, he makes us uncomfortably aware of the recesses; by extolling the specious, he enhances our regard for the genuine. Savage indignation is a less effective weapon than the dry irony that shrugs its shoulders at manifest outrages. Realism, we have seen, is implicitly ironic, since it implies an odious comparison between the real and the ideal. Explicit irony is a mocking endeavor to palm off the real as the ideal. Stendhal's method is two-edged: Machiavellian when it pretends that an unsatisfactory state of affairs is the best of all possible situations, Quixotic when it invokes reality to undercut the pretensions of romance. The first five chapters of *La Chartreuse de Parme*, which form a mock-heroic overture, apply the formula of Cervantes to history itself. The novel begins, where *La Vie de Henry Brulard* breaks off, in the heyday of the Cisalpine Republic. With the triumphal entry of Bonaparte's army into Milan, Stendhal's two preoccupations converge—as they do at the climax of his *Mémoires sur Napoléon*. The ragged revolutionaries are contrasted with the elegant Milanese: Lieutenant Robert, whose shoes have no soles, loves the Marchioness del Dongo, whose retainers wear silver buckles. Fabrice del Dongo, their natural son, is a Napoleonic changeling, the scion of French energies and Italian passions.

He is brought up in grim retirement by his nominal father, a stuffily aristocratic tool of the Austrians. After the years of imperial glory, the Congress of Vienna settles down over Europe, and the reactionaries crawl out of their hiding-places. But they are interrupted, for a hundred portentous days, by the return of Napoleon from Elba. The sixteen-year-old Fabrice, setting out to join his hero, manages to arrive on the eve of Waterloo.

"A just posterity will lament the battle of Waterloo for having pushed liberal ideas back a century," Stendhal wrote to Napoleon, in the cancelled dedication of his *Histoire de la peinture en Italie*. It was the anticlimax of history, the dividing line between progress and retrogression, the horn that sounded the death of heroism. "Our hero," as Fabrice is ironically designated, is the standard-bearer of Stendhal's retreating illusions. He is robbed; he loses three successive horses; he is shunted from one side to the other; he simply gets in everybody's way. Having shot his man, he runs like a hunter to the quarry; befuddled with brandy by a motherly *vivandière*, he misses his glimpse of the Emperor; he does not, of course, recognize his father, now a famous general; he is wounded while ineffectually striving, with Stendhal's Sixth Dragoons, to stem the rout of demoralized cavalry across a bridge. Not until the next day, when he reaches Amiens and buys a newspaper, does he learn the answer to the two questions that have been troubling him: "Was what he had seen a battle?" and "Was that battle Waterloo?" Here, in Stendhal's definitive outcry of *Ce n'est que ça*, is anti-romance with a vengeance. Fabrice's naïve expectations, aroused by the chivalry of Tasso and Ariosto, are dashed by the knavery of his comrades in arms. "The amount of blood that he had shed had delivered him from all the romantic aspect of his character." Although his character has been romantic, he has not been characterized romantically. The author's objectivity has detached itself from the character's boyish undeception. If Stendhal viewed Julien subjectively, with mixed emotions, he views Fabrice under the aspect of comedy, feeling with him but also laughing at him. Literally, five feet five inches tall, he is not a hero of commanding stature. He is more impressionable than Julien, if less impressive; more natural, albeit less energetic. If Julien is Michelangelesque, Fabrice reminds Stendhal of Correggio. Julien is the politician in love, Fabrice the lover in politics. Where Julien is active, Fabrice—doubtless because of his higher status—is passive. Fabrice's fortunes devolve less upon himself, and more —as his aunt predicts and proves—upon women. We might say of him, what Stendhal said of Byron's Don Juan, that the larks fall already roasted into his mouth.

War is the test-case for realistic fiction. No other subject can be so obscured by the ivy of tradition, the crystallization of legend, the conventions of epic and romance. No situation can so enslave the individual to reifying forces beyond his control. Civilian conscription and long-range artillery, revolutionizing the technique of modern warfare, seemed to eliminate heroics utterly, to metamorphose people into things, and to minimize the soldier's awareness of what was happening. All he knew was what he could read in the papers afterward. Faced with this predicament, Stendhal deliberately adopted the combatant's point of view, disregarding the history-book outlines of grand strategy and concentrating on the bewildering immediacies in Fabrice's baptism of fire. Other novelists have offered other accounts of the Waterloo episode. In *Vanity Fair* it is an off-stage noise and a stock-exchange report; in *Les Misérables* it is an apocalyptic vision and a tour of the battlefield. In *La Chartreuse de Parme* it is a personal experience. Stendhal was not a combatant, nor even an eye-witness, as it had happened. From other engagements, notably Moscow and Bautzen, he had gained his first-hand impressions of battle: "that is to say, nothing." He was the first to dramatize the Shavian paradox of the unheroic soldier. "Who ever so described war?" asks Tolstoy, acknowledging his own debt to Stendhal. "Described it, that is, as it is in reality?" The open-eyed heroes of *War and Peace*, at Austerlitz and Borodino, retrace the uncertain footsteps of Fabrice. Tactics are further reduced, in Stephen Crane's *Red Badge of Courage*, to a sheer barrage of impressionism. As the pace has accelerated, the bewilderment has increased, and the disillusionment has been still further intensified. "Where are the eagles and the trumpets?" we may well ask with T. S. Eliot. Between the fanfares and posters, on the one hand, and the actualities on the other, lies an inherent difference which honest writers can but observe and chronicle. One of Napoleon's generals at Waterloo, Cambronne, was reported to have grandiloquently declared: "The guard dies but never surrenders." His actual expression, as he later admitted, was much terser and notoriously unprintable. When publicists are apprehensive lest "the validity of the Word" be weakened by the cynicism of war-novels, they should remember the word of Cambronne.

It is not the realists but the idealists who weaken the power of language, not the gross expletive but the grandiose rhetoric which instigates disillusion; for words are verified by their correspondence with deeds; and a realistic novel is, in terms of its period, an attempt at verification. *La Chartreuse de Parme* is to the Napoleonic aftermath what *Don Quixote* was to Europe after the Battle of Lepanto. "The vile Sancho Panzas will always win out in the long run over the sublime Don Quixotes," Count Mosca remarks to Fabrice, explaining the triumph of John Bull over Bonaparte. This time the Don confronts worse foes than windmills, and Sancho governs stranger islands than Barataria. The pistol-shot—this time a cannonade—occurs at the beginning, and the rest is anticlimactic by design. The mock-epic of Waterloo lapses into the travesty of Parma. Fact and fiction disjoin, as they do in Tolstoy, as Manzoni said they must in historical novels. Stendhal's plot, though he clothes it in comparatively modern dress, derives its energy from the Renaissance. Where Manzoni's *Betrothed* evoked the past to satirize current tyrannies, Stendhal carries on the attack by bringing an old *novella* up to date. In a Neapolitan manuscript, while garnering some of the tales retold in his *Chroniques italiennes,* he had discovered a more or less authentic anecdote whose edifying moral was that most noble families could trace their fortunes to a harlot. The intrigues of Vandozza Farnese, mistress of Cardinal Borgia, had launched her favorite nephew, Alessandro, upon a career which culminated in that pinnacle of "worldly happiness," the papacy. It seasons Fabrice's adventures with the spice of anticlericalism to realize that they are modelled on the early escapades of Paul III, the pope who commissioned Michelangelo's Last Judgment and enabled Loyola to found the Society of Jesus. The Farnese dynasty, stemming from Paul's illegitimate son, ruled the duchy of Parma until the eighteenth century, when it was succeeded by the Bourbons. The reigning duchess, even while Stendhal wrote, was Napoleon's former empress, Marie-Louise. The court of Parma, which could boast of Correggio as its painter and of Condillac as its tutor, was thus a focal point for Stendhal's interests, and pseudo-history was corroborated by pseudo-geography.

In spite of his title, it is the citadel of Parma which dominates the book. Now, since this edifice is conspicuous by its absence from the Lombard plain, Stendhal has constructed for himself an exact Parmesan replica of the Castle of Sant'Angelo at Rome. Alessandro Farnese had been imprisoned there for a peccadillo resembling Fabrice's affair with Marietta; later, as Paul III, he had cast Benvenuto Cellini into the same prison. Cellini's memoirs, an energetic testament which Stendhal highly valued, supplied him with many details of the imprisonment—particularly the escape and return. His own recollections of the castle, and its magnificent view, have been woven into the novel; one of the inmates whom Stendhal tried vainly to visit, the *carbonaro* Barbone, has been metamorphosed into a sullen turnkey. Both the cross-hatched images of Piranesi's tenebrous prisons and the enlightened ideas of Beccaria's penal reforms are discernible in Stendhal's pictured citadel. In it the Bastille seems to rise again, a monument to counter-revolution. No contemporary could read of Fabrice's incarceration without also being reminded of the Spielberg, the dread Moravian fortress to which the Holy Alliance consigned its prisoners. Some of them had survived to tell their tale: Stendhal cites Alexandre Andryane's *Mémoires d'un prisonnier d'état*, and he had known the liberal Milanese poet, Silvio Pellico, who agitated Europe with *My Prisons*. The Prisoner of Chillon or the Man in the Iron Mask was then no exotic figment of the past. Liberalism was struggling into its heroic age, and the prisoner was its literary protagonist. The romantic solitary found a haven in prison, and a justification for his grievances against the social system. Stendhal had poignantly touched upon this theme in *Le Rouge et le noir*, and it was widely popularized by Saintine's cloying novel, *Picciola*. Hugo had fully developed it in *Les Derniers Jours d'un condamné*, and Beethoven set it to music in *Fidelio*. It continues to be timely whenever men suffer in the cause of freedom, and wherever the shadow of the concentration camp falls.

André Malraux has noted that Bunyan, Defoe, and Dostoevsky

—jailed, pilloried, and exiled—all returned to write "the book of solitude." *La Chartreuse de Parme*, turning those values upside down, is a book of society, except for its title-page and its last paragraph. The revolutionary quest for the good society, the discussion of Phalanstaries and Icarias, the socialist utopias and brave new worlds were stalemated in 1830, to be renewed in the socialistic 'forties. The lame excuse proposed by La Fayette on behalf of the July Monarchy was to call it "la meilleure des républiques." This is the slogan to which Mosca, whose remark is paraphrased by the epigraph to the second volume, ironically alludes: "With this talk of republic, the fools would keep us from enjoying the best of monarchies." Excess of zeal suggests its own reduction to absurdity. The formula is not too far removed from the self-exposing complacencies of Bernard Shaw's ironic capitalists or David Low's apoplectic colonels, glorying in a *status quo* which is obviously intolerable, and blaming the radicals and reformers when something is rotten. In *Rome, Naples et Florence*, the book that got him into trouble with the Austrian authorities, Stendhal's comment on the despotic policy of the Prince of Modena is a discreet hiatus, capped by a paradox against tolerance and in defense of the auto-da-fé. Machiavellian guidebook and Quixotic civil code, *La Chartreuse de Parme* fills in the hiatus and acts out the paradox. Parma is a principality where the ultras are always in office, and everyone who is neither aristocratic nor pious is in jail; where the Prince turns back the clock and the courtiers powder their hair; where the nineteenth century goes through the motions of the eighteenth; where the only safe direction is right and the only reason is *raison d'état*. By reducing power politics to a Lilliputian scale, by observing the strict protocol of comic opera, Stendhal secures for Parma the hegemony among imaginary kingdoms — Nephelococcygia, Illyria, Gerolstein, Erewhon, Ruritania, Zembla, Poictesme, and the various islands and territories of Cockaigne. If the liberal imagination is flagging today, as Lionel Trilling has convincingly argued, we do well to recall Stendhal's Parma as one of its most brilliant creations. In short, it is the ultra-reactionary utopia.

The difficulties of being a petty despot have augmented since Machiavelli's day. Stendhal, in formulating his *Modern Prince*, has revived the extinct house of Farnese, and set it to rule over subjects who are so misguided as to have read the history of the French Revolution. The anachronistic sovereign, Ranuce-Ernest IV, an absolute prince in an age of Jacobins, patterns himself upon Louis XIV of France or Joseph II of Austria; but he has made the mistake, in a nervous moment, of hanging two liberals; and now he cannot go to sleep until Count Mosca della Rovere has looked under his bed for conspirators. The tactful punctilio with which Mosca performs this courtly office has made him prime minister; his powdered hair is the badge of his political doctrines; he is our guide through the corridors of palace intrigue. Plot and counterplot could scarcely be fitted together without him. European war has surrendered to diplomacy, and the Napoleonic marshals have yielded to the Metternichian statesmen, of whom he is the consummate representative. Though one of Stendhal's revisions admits the resemblance to Metternich, Mosca's original seems to have been Metternich's envoy at Florence, Count Saurau, who exerted a strong counter-revolutionary influence over the states of northern Italy, while the name seems to be a souvenir of Rossini, who was born in the Palazzo Mosca at Pesaro. Every Talleyrand has his Fouché, and Mosca's subtlety is enforced by the dirty work of the minister of justice, Rassi, a comic illustration of Joseph de Maistre's authoritarian thesis that the ultimate pillar of society is the executioner. The court, emulating His Serene Highness, is forever play-acting and never quite up to its parts: the childish heir-apparent collects minerals, the bashful Princess collects botanical specimens, the Prince's mistress collects bribes. *Commedia dell' arte* is the favored pastime, Clélia Conti communicates with Fabrice in recitative, the Duchess of Sanseverina burns her incriminating papers after a trio with the dowager Princess and the young Prince. From her first meeting with Mosca, in a box at the Scala, the novel sustains an operatic atmosphere.

When she tells him that his proposals are immoral, his reply underscores Stendhal's satire: "No more immoral than what happens at our court and at twenty others." At courts, Stendhal warns his readers, happiness is subject to the wiles of chambermaids; in republics, well, alas! the Americans have no opera. Fabrice has a notion of going to America and becoming a republican soldier, but his aunt, who has meanwhile accepted the Count's proposition for a *ménage* at Parma, is able to instruct her nephew in the higher immorality:

> "Imagine that you are learning the rules for the game of whist. Have you any objection to the rules of whist? I have told the Count that you are a believer, and he is delighted; that is useful in this world and the next... Believe blindly in everything they tell you at the Academy. Remember that there are people who will keep strict account of your slightest objections. You will be forgiven a gallant little intrigue if it is well conducted, but not a doubt; our age suppresses intrigue and increases doubt."

This advice accords well with Mosca's favorite conception of eighteenth-century monarchy: "the confessor and the mistress." Indeed it coincides with Bernard Mandeville's perverse argument for a stable order precariously founded on collective selfishness, where luxury is a virtue and private vices are public benefits. Mandeville's couplet could have been a succinct description of Stendhal's Parma:

> Thus every part was full of vice,
> Yet the whole mass a paradise.

Living down his Napoleonic escapade, Fabrice learns to be a rogue, to play the game with adroitness and amusement. Outwardly he conforms to Canon Borda's rules for dashing young clerics, though he does not give up his secret subscription to an advanced French journal. He becomes so Machiavellian that he cannot caress a dog without an ulterior motive. When catechized, he denounces the heresies of liberty, justice, and the greatest good for the greatest number so jesuitically that he incurs the Prince's suspicions. But he wins the good graces of the Archbishop of Parma—first, because that saintly old snob is pleased to have an aristocratic coadjutor; second, because his Grace dislikes Fabrice's ecclesiastical rival; and third, because the prelate genuinely likes Fabrice. Stendhal's account of the Archbishop's motivation is exhaustive, and it does not touch the irrelevant matter of Fabrice's qualifications for his calling. Donning, like Julien Sorel, the uniform of the century, he commences his novitiate as a vicar-general, in the violet stockings of the monsignor. Neither adultery nor assassination will be serious obstacles to his archbishopric. In church he prays sincerely, conscious of many sins, but blandly unaware of the sin of simony. Where Julien's career was shaped by his own intensive efforts, Fabrice's is the effortless and unblushing consequence of nepotism.

Fabrice is likewise exposed to the dilemma that puzzles so many heroes of nineteenth-century fiction—what has been termed the Rebecca-Rowena problem. The heroes of Scott and Cooper, or of Thackeray and Melville, waver between alternating heroines, blonde and brunette embodiments of sacred and profane love. For Stendhal the choice is complicated by his own maternal fixation: Julien prefers Madame de Rênal to Mathilde de la Mole, and the relationship between Fabrice and the Duchess of Sanseverina is a delicate blend of the nepotic and the erotic. The taint of incest, emphasized by a legend connected with the Farnese tower, is neutralized by the consideration that he is not really her brother's son. This lends especial poignance to the fate that constrains her to love him "like a son." Their closest kinship is based on clandestine Bonapartism: Gina's first husband was a general in the imperial armies, and even her second, the parvenu Duke, is indiscreet enough to pay ten thousand francs for a bust of Napoleon by Canova. The Prince suspects, more justly than he realizes, that she is capable of fomenting revolution at Parma, like the notorious Sanfelice at Naples. In moments of repose, while being rowed across Lake Como by Fabrice, she reincarnates Stendhal's idealized passion for his all but unattainable mistress, Angela Pietragrua. Those reveries on the lake, reminiscent of Lamartine and Rousseau, are touchstones for the happy few. Stendhal is still the romanticist whenever he writes about love. Clélia's vow never to see Fabrice again, and her ruse for circumventing it by means of assignations in the dark, are the stuff of folklore, more appropriate to the Tristram romance or *The Duchess of Malfi* than to a historical chronicle. Romance, ever up to its old tricks, superimposes its pattern on reality. An eagle is the omen of Fabrice's military adventure, and his imprisonment fulfills the prophecy of an old astrologer straight out of Dumas' *Henri III et sa cour*.

The citadel has esthetic aspects, as well as political: its chiaroscuro of spacious heights and claustrophobic depths, Alpine landscapes and gloomy *oubliettes,* lovers on the terrace and prisoners in the dungeon. That "aerial solitude," that cloistered overview, with its beauty and loneliness, its signals and makeshifts, stands as a kind of euphoric symbol for Stendhal's Italian exile. Such are the pleasant places, *i luoghi ameni,* which he delights in mapping out, and which are foretold by the initial epigraph quoted from Ariosto. It is characteristic of Fabrice to look down from incarcerating heights, from the Prior's belfry at Grianta or the cell in the tower known as "Passive Obedience." His escape, with its Cellini-like ingenuity and its dizzying sense of release, is characteristically a descent, as contrasted with the habitual climb of Julien Sorel—or with the fall from horseback of the more awkward Lucien Leuwen. It cannot be said, however, that Fabrice regains his freedom without a sigh. The hovering presence of the governor's daughter, Clélia Conti, has made his durance the happiest period of his life. When coincidence had brought them together once before, he had reflected that she would make a charming prison companion. Hence, with a long succession of duchesses, actresses, and chambermaids, he has felt himself incapable of love. Love, which surmounts stone walls and transcends party lines, offers private happiness; but Fabrice's fate has become a public issue over which ministries rise and fall. For a nobleman, he has served an unprecedented sentence. After all, he has only killed a man. Why treat him as if he were a liberal? It must be politics. It is, in fact, a liberal conspiracy, and the liberals are even more reactionary than the ultras. General Fabio Conti, the pompous leader of the liberal party, occupies an embarrassing position as warden of political prisoners. He is Stendhal's devastating sketch of the demagogic time-server, whose reforming zeal disguises an unsatisfied appetite for power, who dissembles the cunning of a Louis-Philippe behind the pose of a La Fayette —a more recognizable type than his opposite, the Stendhalian figure who sheathes his tender soul in an assumed worldliness.

Mosca's position is Conti's turned inside out. Having been released from his Bonapartist convictions by the Peninsular War, he has cynically accepted the court uniform of uncompromising ultracism. The unemployed hero, in compromising his heroism, has found employment. He must now endure the special administrative frustration of being close to the throne and obviously much cleverer than its occupant. He retains one hope: to make a million. His search for happiness has gradually narrowed until it hardly extends beyond himself. The triumph of reason has been the defeat of emotion. Each of Stendhal's novels has its *raisonneur*—a Marquis de La Mole, a François Leuwen, a Dr. Sansfin—who initiates the *ingénu* into the ways of the world. With increasing detachment from the juvenile lead, the author's viewpoint is more closely identified with the middle-aged counsellor. Mosca's avuncular task, as master strategist of the political chessboard on which Fabrice is a pawn, is doubly difficult: he must please the woman he loves by protecting and advancing the protegé she loves. Fleeing from the Sanseverina, like Hippolyte from Phèdre, Fabrice had run headlong into his affair with the actress, Marietta, and his duel with her protector, Giletti, which have finally led him to Clélia and the perilous custody of her father. The mistress, in her grandest manner, has blackmailed an equivocal pardon out of the Prince, who is not above increasing the complications by anonymous letters. When Mosca hesitated for a moment, like Polonius in the role of Hamlet, the scapegrace was caught in the stalemate of passion and interest. No sooner is Mosca's jealousy of Fabrice allayed by seeing him so happily immured, than the Duchess' jealousy of Clélia is stirred to precipitate the crisis. To engineer Fabrice's escape the Duchess must appeal to the one man who understands her, Ferrante Palla, who is neither a fake liberal like Conti nor a cynical conservative like Mosca, but a sincere revolutionist. A great poet and a skilled physician, he has become a highwayman in order "to fulfill his duties as a citizen." Scrupulously issuing promissory notes to his victims, he levies no more than will support his illegitimate family and defray the expense of his seditious pamphlet, *Will (Parma) ever have a Legislature and a Budget?* With this self-constituted "tribune of the people," whom Balzac considered a "sublime republican Don Quixote," Stendhal's cult of the criminal attains its apotheosis. It should go without saying that Palla is distinguished by the death sentence and beloved by the peasantry, that he admires Napoleon and adores the Sanseverina.

The most dazzling heroines are best described by their impact. Stendhal's glamorous Duchess is another Helen of Troy who,

from the walls, directs the strategies of Trojans and Greeks alike;
she is a Cleopatra who beguiles Pompey and Caesar and Antony,
not successively but simultaneously. The pensive Clélia fades
into virtual insignificance beside the charming Gina, yet Fabrice
is the one man who is insensible to her charm. Judged by her
effect on the others—her devoted accomplices in murder, treason,
arson, and whatever else is on her calendar—she is irresistible.
And she can be judged by no other standards: for if any feminine
character was drawn *con amore*, it is she; if any charms or wiles
can sweep the reader off his feet, they are hers. Like her eighteenth-
century prototype, the Princesse des Ursins, she can amuse herself
with the little games of Parmesan etiquette; but her real nature
must betray itself in imperious gestures, unpredictable rebounds,
and passionate vendettas. Fireworks, set off at her country estate,
are a signal for opening the reservoir and flooding the town. The
Parmesans storm the citadel and kill a jailer, then march on the
palace and deface a statue. The people fraternize with the troops,
the courtiers flatter the mob, and Parma has its three glorious
days of revolution. It all occurs too quickly for anyone to notice
that it was the Duchess' jewels which financed the uprising, or
Palla's poison which assassinated the Prince. Not Palla but Mosca
is the man of the hour, riding the counter-revolutionary wave.
He calls out the guard and puts down the rebellion, shooting
sixty people who are quickly buried, and whose families are
ordered—on pain of imprisonment—to announce that their defunct relations are traveling abroad for their health. "Without
me, Parma would have been a republic for two months, with
the poet Ferrante Palla as dictator," he writes to his mistress,
and for once he misses the irony of the situation. Palla, tired
of attempting "to make a republic without republicans," slips
away to America. Shades of the prison-house again close in around
Fabrice; there is no escape from politics. On this occasion it is
the newly enthroned prince, Ranuce-Ernest V, who blackmails
the Sanseverina. In his bed she purchases Fabrice's freedom,
grandly stipulating that the churchly benefice be thrown into the
bargain. The reprieve goes into operation an instant before
Conti's poison. The majesty of the law is upheld by a trial, in
which it is hard to keep the judges from acquitting Fabrice
before they have heard the testimony.

A subdued and belated note of fulfillment is struck when Mosca, temporarily displaced by a liberal cabinet, marries the Duchess, who has retired beyond the Po. Together, they are the powerful and jealous gods whose machinations frame the story, like Valmont and Madame de Merteuil in *Les Liaisons dangereuses*. As she is the prodigal madonna, so he is the paternal mentor, whom Stendhal sought throughout his art and life. Detached from his heroes and hero-worship, he identifies himself with the battle-scarred veteran, the seasoned man of the world, regretting his fifties yet cherishing his ideal. Mosca's debonaire maturity is the quintessence of Beylism. Fabrice, too, maturing, has learned to play the game. Ultimately he has the privilege and pleasure of playing whist at the Prince's table, to the strains of Mozart and Cimarosa, while Clélia furtively watches. Constrained by her vow and by her marriage, she has learned a demure trick or two. Fabrice, to be sure, is bound by vows of his own, and by the duties of his archdiocese. His fashionable sermons, filled with "the perfume of profound melancholy," pack the cathedral and empty the opera-house. The quaint institutions that stand in their way inevitably serve to reunite the lovers. But nature, consummating their reunion with a child, revenges their compromises and casuistries. The catastrophic ending was probably telescoped at the behest of the publisher. The last page of the book, recording the death of the kidnapped infant, Sandrino, followed at short intervals by the deaths of Clélia, Fabrice, and Gina, was actually Stendhal's point of departure. At the point where his model, Alessandro Farnese, founded a dynasty, Fabrice's line dies out; and Fabrice, instead of becoming Pope, takes the unworldly vows of the Carthusian order. He enters the Charterhouse, so much more definitively a solitary confinement than the citadel, where—cultivating his monastic garden—he finishes his brief career. Possibly Stendhal's childhood memories of the Grande Chartreuse near Grenoble made this renunciation a homecoming. "It is better to kill the devil than to have him kill you" is the French maxim that Mosca has taught Fabrice; and perhaps, as Alembert wrote to Voltaire, it should be the motto of monarchs; but the devil is a tough customer. His disciples, Stendhal is happy to announce, still flourish at Parma. His Serene Highness, Ranuce-Ernest V, is as popular as the Grand Dukes of Tuscany—those notorious despots. Mosca is rich—having instituted a new system of bribery. The prisons are empty—all the liberals, if not executed or exiled, having presumably trimmed their sails to the winds of orthodoxy.

John Adams, writing to thank Thomas Jefferson for a book of Destutt de Tracy's, expresses precisely the stimulus and the response that *La Chartreuse de Parme* communicates: "His book was written when the French Experiment was glowing in the furnace not yet blown out. He all along supposes that men are rational and conscientious creatures. I say so too; but I say, at the same time, that their passions and interests generally prevail over their reason and their consciences; and if Society does not contrive some means of contracting and restraining the former, the world will go on as it has done . . ." We begin by thinking that we are poised upon the brink of a better world, and we end by feeling that Machiavelli's description is still the last word. *Plus ça change,* in Alphonse Karr's weathered and weary phrase, *plus c'est la même chose.* The Prince is dead, long live the Prince. Right forever on the scaffold, wrong forever on the throne. Yet this book leaves us with a taste which is rather sweet than bitter, a feeling which is rather hopeful than hopeless. It may be that, because the quality of Stendhal's disillusionment is intellectual rather than emotional, the ultimate promise outshines the immediate disappointment. No great writer, who was alive in 1789, failed to respond to the emotions of the Revolution:

> Bliss was it in that dawn to be alive,
> But to be young was very Heaven! O times
> In which the meager, stale, forbidding ways
> Of custom, law, and statute took at once
> The attraction of a country in romance!

But most of the responses that have come down to us, like Wordsworth's, have been dulled and distorted by backslidings and palinodes. Stendhal's is unique in its clear-eyed immediacy, its penetrating candor, its strong sense of historical direction. Today, as the idea of progress is degraded to the verge of meaninglessness, and the contending dogmas of obscurantism come again into vogue, Stendhal's confidence in ideas is notably refreshing. Along with his maturity, he preserves an eternal youthfulness. He defined the modern ideal, in his history of painting, as "above all, the agile air of youth"—the enthusiasm, the ebullience, the *brio*. His books recapture the lost youth, the lost innocence of our modern world. Though the world itself is already in its old age, the century is brand-new; though conservatism is in authority, liberalism is full of energy. Though the happy few die young, they enjoy their world in their time. Put not your faith in princes or politicians, Henri Beyle advises his posthumous readers, there are better objects of adoration. There is love; there is laughter; there are the arts. There are people, who are invariably fascinating. There are the people, who are usually sound. There is, above all, the human intelligence. And, of course, there are heroes, ready to risk their necks for heroines in high places, and to fire a reckless pistol-shot for the eagles of enlightenment. "What happiness to be young in 1801!" exclaims the envious twentieth-century reader, with Jean Dutourd. With Stendhal we undergo, at first hand, the rites of initiation into the nineteenth century.

IV

BALZAC

The accumulation of so enormous a mass of substantial truth is not possible without organization. The faculty for order is just as much a creative one as the faculty for presentation. Or rather they are simply different aspects of one and the same faculty. Out of the truth of countless isolated phenomena there arises the truth of the relationships existing among them: in this way a world is produced. As with Goethe, I feel myself in a sure relationship to the whole. There is here an imperceptible system of co-ordinates by which I can orient myself. Whatever I read, one of the great novels, one of the short stories, one of the fantastic-philosophic rhapsodies, whether I dip into the secrets of a soul, into a digression on politics, into the description of an office or a shop, I never fail to find this relationship. I feel: around me there is an organized world... Here, behind these books, which in their sum total form the greatest epic conception besides *Don Quixote* of the modern world, the idea of the epic art-form seems to be awakening.

—HUGO VON HOFMANNSTHAL

1. *The Law of Disorganization*

CRITICISM, perhaps because there is so much to be said on both sides of any human situation, tends to pair off the masters of the novel: Dickens and Thackeray, Tolstoy and Dostoevsky, Hawthorne and Melville, Balzac and Stendhal. Against the checks and balances of literary history, Stendhal cuts a highly eccentric figure. He addresses himself, not to a contemporaneous public, but to a future elite; he surrounds the books he published with manuscripts of self-annotation. His approach is leisurely and experimental; his originality resists facile characterization; his long-suspended achievement comes to a head in two compact novels. These, one may hope, are the very considerations that

have made him an accommodating subject for the initial exercise
of a critical method. But it is Balzac who occupies the central
position in any considered account of realism, who claims and
earns and duly receives the title of novelist before all others.
The overwhelming quantity and the substantial quality of his
writing form a monument around which there are no detours.
Its impressive structure and its uneven texture are better appreciated from a distance, where Stendhal's writing invites a closer
scrutiny. Two such disparate temperaments cannot be viewed
through the same focus; two such contrasting talents cannot be
measured by the same scale. Each establishes its distinctive
atmosphere and prescribes the conditions, typical or special, under
which it may best be approached. With Stendhal we must piece
together fragments and draw out implications; Balzac is so thorough and so explicit that he simplifies—threatens to oversimplify
—the problems of his critics. Comprehensive rather than intensive,
deductive rather than inductive, synthetic rather than analytic,
his work carries its own commentary. And few lives can be more
fully accounted for in works. Few writers have repeated, with
such tenacious conviction, *Exegi monumentum* . . .

Stendhal was so nonchalant an amateur, Balzac so inveterate
a professional, that there could be no rivalry between them.
Instead there was a clear and consistent meeting of minds, warmly
attested by Balzac's review of *La Chartreuse de Parme*. The
younger writer, the first to win recognition, was the first to
recognize the importance of the elder, to enroll himself among
the happy few. If the admiration was one-sided, it was a belated
acknowledgment that Stendhal had been the pioneer; for *Le
Rouge et le noir* had made its striking contribution to realism
while Balzac was still enmeshed in the fantasy of *La Peau de
chagrin*; and *Armance, ou quelques scènes d'un salon en* 1827
appeared three years before the first installment of *Scènes de la
vie privée*. But Stendhal's values were unswervingly individualistic,
and his particular domain lay within the individual consciousness;
only in reverse could he create a society, the utopia *au rebours*
of Parma. Balzac, whose values were pre-eminently social, could
put the individuals in their respective places, and—what is more—
could set the entire panorama in motion. Ramifying plot to the
point from which Stendhal had refined character, demonstrating

the external consequences of the motives that Stendhal had treated introspectively, Balzac became the sociologist of the novel as Stendhal had become its psychologist. The two related modes of interpretation, converging upon the same tract of material from opposite points of view, supplement and corroborate each other. The extremes of liberalism and conservatism join forces to interpellate the *Juste-Milieu*, to challenge the mercenary compromises of middle-class rule, and to complete an indelible record of French life between the Battle of Waterloo and the Revolution of 1848. The obverse of Stendhal's medallion, it will be seen, is Balzac's franc. The other side of Julien Sorel's valediction will be Eugène de Rastignac's salute. To Balzac, then, we turn for *L'Envers de l'histoire contemporaine.*

Balzac may not have invented the nineteenth century, but he did more than any other novelist—as Wilde's epigram implies—to exploit it, to cast its fictional matrices, to coin its literary currency. Altogether unlike Henri Beyle, with his classical inheritance and his eighteenth-century childhood, Honoré Balzac was unreservedly a man of his time. He was born at Tours in 1799, the year that witnessed Beyle's arrival at Paris, as well as Napoleon's *coup d'état.* Grandson of peasants in Touraine and small Parisian tradesmen, son of a self-educated government official, Balzac himself rounded out the cycle by marrying into a foreign aristocracy. The half-generation that divides Stendhal from Balzac is a denser barrier than this difference between the higher and the lower bourgeoisie. Stendhal had grown up during the Revolution and served his apprenticeship under the Empire; Balzac grew up during the Empire and served his apprenticeship under the Restoration. Stendhal's work is a critique of the Restoration from the viewpoint of a revolutionary Bonapartist; Balzac's work is a critique of the July Monarchy from the viewpoint of a Catholic royalist. The Restoration, for better or for worse, had flown a flag over the ship of state, and had concealed the cargo by certain moral ideas and patriotic gestures, as Sainte-Beuve pointed out in a far-sighted essay, *De la littérature industrielle.* With the final collapse of the old order, the flag was hauled down, the cargo revealed, and the merchandise offered for sale. Guizot's invitation to his countrymen, "Enrichissez-vous," was the slogan of the new regime, the text on which the *Comédie humaine* provides a running comment: "It is a mistake . . . to believe that it is King Louis-Philippe who reigns, and he is not deceived on that point. He knows, as we all do, that above the Constitution is the holy, venerable, solid, amiable, gracious, beautiful, noble, young, all-powerful five-franc piece!"

Writers have always held money in mingled esteem and contempt, but never have its attractions and repulsions been more powerfully grasped, for Balzac was at once the notorious victim of industrial literature and its most enterprising entrepreneur. From his earliest transactions on Grub Street to his presidency of the Société des Gens de Lettres, he frankly looked upon authorship as a business. "We have no more works," he informs the reader of *Béatrix*, "we have products." Georg Lukács, describing *Illusions perdues* as the *Don Quixote* of bourgeois illusions, has aptly stated its theme: the transformation of literature into goods. Hence this novel, a pivotal installment of *La Comédie humaine*, swings from one to another of its heroes, *Les Deux Poètes*. The professing poet, Lucien de Rubempré, sets out for Paris with a romance in the manner of Scott under his arm, and is gradually corrupted by the seductions of metropolitan journalism. His less poetic friend David Séchard becomes a printer, who perseveres at Angoulême and invents a paper-making process which is exploited by others. Now Balzac, who can be closely identified with both *Un Grand Homme de province à Paris* and *Les Souffrances de l'inventeur*, had tried to be both a poet and a printer, and had hoped to make his fortune by just such an invention. Many times he retells this parable of idle and industrious apprentices, and he usually allows the credits to accrue on the philistine side of the ledger. In *La Maison du Chat-qui-pelote*, one of the preliminary sketches for his great design, the draper's older daughter marries the industrious apprentice, who inherits the shop and lives happily ever after; while the younger sister marries a feckless artist and comes to grief.

Thus the romance of art is duly tempered by the realism of business. In another generation, Flaubert's generation, the artist and the bourgeois will agree to disagree and go their separate ways. Balzac's realism avoids that separation by making a business of art and by dramatizing the romance of business. It pays the stiff surtax that no artist can avoid when he commercializes his talent; but it succeeds in taking an inventory of the bourgeoisie while their stock is at its height, and in painting as rich and massive a Dutch interior as Théodore de Sommervieux's exhibition picture of the shop at the sign of the Cat and Racket. Balzac condenses his tribute to Sir Walter Scott into a punning epithet: "ce trouveur (trouvère) moderne." The modern troubadour, the poet of today, must likewise be a discoverer, an inventor. The Laird of Abbotsford, though he dissembled his joint enterprises as long as he could, had been a novelist and a publisher too. The shadow of bankruptcy, which had darkened the end of Scott's career, hung over Balzac's from the very beginning. Happily for Balzac, financial failure was the beginning of literary success. The middle decade of his fifty-year span was his period of apprenticeship and discovery. In his twenty-first year he left a law-office in order to devote his life to writing. Discouraged in his more ambitious efforts, a tragedy in verse about Cromwell and fragments of more or less philosophical fiction, he thereupon devoted himself to hack-writing. He turned out, under various pseudonyms, more than a dozen slap-dash novels of the neo-Gothic school. When these fell short of the popularity that would have been their sole justification, he sought more direct ways and means of boiling the pot. He set up shop as a printer and publisher.

Printing everything, from patent-medicine advertisements to one-volume editions of the classics, he soon branched out into type-founding and paper-making. He soon got into debt. In 1828, through the aid of his family and friends, a petition in bankruptcy was narrowly averted. After that, though he operated in other fields on an increasingly bullish plane, though his extravagances became proverbial, though he ran a continual risk of landing in the debtor's prison at Clichy, he was never quite solvent. He spent the rest of his life renewing his notes, postponing his bills, and writing his *Comédie humaine*. "Life is a perpetual loan," explains Mercadet, whose perpetual endeavor to shake off a chorus of creditors is the comic evocation of Balzac's own plight; and, though *Mercadet* was the only one of Balzac's plays to be successfully performed, Balzac did not live to see the performance, or to hear the triumphant tag-line that his adapter, Adolphe Dennery, had added: "At last I am a creditor!" Balzac was a debtor to the end; the crown of his exhausting labors was not to die a bankrupt. Bankruptcy and solvency, as no one more keenly felt, were to middle-class morality what dishonor and honor had been in the code of chivalry. "To go bankrupt," declares the miser Grandet, "is to commit the most disgraceful of all actions that can disgrace a man." It meant—in the strict letter of the Civil Code—to be legally humiliated, to be socially ostracized, to be deprived of the rights of citizenship. To regain them against such odds, to rehabilitate one's pecuniary honor, to make good the heraldic device of "paid in full" was re-markable enough to be considered a heroic deed in an age when traditional heroism was largely confined to the theater.

It is in *Histoire de la grandeur et de la décadence de César Birot-teau*, which purports to be "the poem of bourgeois vicissitudes," that the tradesman makes his debut as a serious hero, a Don Quix-ote rather than a Sancho Panza. The first half of this Caesarian poem, as its anticlimactic title suggests with its echo from Montes-quieu, does not rise above the serio-comic conventions of the mock-epic. César, a wholesale and retail perfumer, lays out his advertising like Napoleon planning a campaign; drawing himself up like one of Plutarch's Romans, he delivers a ringing challenge to the manufacturers of Macassar Oil. At his apogee, at the ball that celebrates the opening of his enlarged premises, he is no more than the bumbling parvenu, inflated with mercantile hubris, whose pedigree extends from Trimalchio to M. Jourdain and from M. Prudhomme to George F. Babbitt. But when his real-estate ven-tures fail and his notary absconds, when the invoices come in and the notices go out, in the maze of courts, the abyss of poverty, and the slow, steep climb to rehabilitation, he attains a certain degree of moral superiority. The comedy of the exploiter becomes the tragedy of the exploited. When he dies, "a martyr of commercial probity," and—to the accompaniment of Beethoven's Fifth Sym-phony—is welcomed by Jesus into heaven, the novel sinks into bathos; but it discloses, at all events, the depths of Balzac's sym-pathy. He has deliberately glided over the counter-revolutionary activities of his historic original in order to stake everything upon the wavering balance of debts and credits. César's accounts are meticulously audited, and the legal technicalities are expounded with all the pettifogging circumstantiality of a case-book. A dealer in luxuries, and therefore a staunch royalist, César represents the restricted capitalism of the *ancien régime*. The rise of a new class of speculators and promoters is predicated upon his fall; the sharp practice of these Tillets and Nucingens is based on the good faith of such heretofore unsung and now disappearing heroes.

The bankruptcy and rehabilitation of César Birotteau, like the poet-inventor partnership of *Illusions perdues*, is one of those pivots around which Balzac's intentions appear to revolve. It illustrates that social phenomenon which his philosopher, Louis Lambert, calls the law of disorganization. "When the effect produced is not in direct relation nor in equal proportion to its cause, disorganization sets in." Every inflation is due to have its deflation. Ambitions outrun abilities, debits overbalance credits, supply exceeds demand, growth succumbs to decay, and institutions lose their equilibrium. We are disturbed by the same sense of toppling hierarchies and unrestrained appetites that Shakespeare envisages in his harrowing descriptions of nature run wild and society out of frame. The portentous symptom of these disorders, if not the disorder itself, was—for Balzac and many of his contemporaries—the French Revolution. Eighteenth-century thought had culminated in the disorganization of society, according to the Count de Saint-Simon; the aim of the nineteenth century would be reorganization, and the periodical of the Saint-Simonians was accordingly known as *L'Organisateur*. Another pioneering socialist, Louis Blanc, was formulating plans for a labor movement in his famous article, *L'Organisation du travail*; and Renan was to advance the spacious proposal that science, after it had finished the job of organizing humanity, should organize God. "Organiser," remarks the Russian Prince in Balzac's *Autre Etude d'une femme*, " 'Organize' is a word of the Empire which sums up Napoleon completely." It is a word which Balzac's German biographer, Anton Bettelheim, has invoked to sum up the prodigious task of shaping the *Comédie humaine*.

Balzac's collected works, taken in their most grandiose terms, are a titanic attempt to impose a cosmos on the chaos of contemporary life. Every volume may be ticked off, in more intimate terms, as a debt acquitted. In paying off his obligations to society, which itself had been plunged into a state of moral bankruptcy, he was likewise contributing toward its redemption. The threads of vindication, expiation, and rehabilitation are deeply woven into the specific patterns and the collective fabric of the *Comédie hu-*

maine. Most of its characters have something to live down. The revolutionary executioner, Henri Sanson, for whom Balzac had ghost-written in the suggestively titled *Mémoires d'un paria*, attends a mass for the soul of Louis XVI in *Un Episode sous la Terreur*. In *L'Envers de l'histoire contemporaine* an anti-royalist judge, notorious for his sweeping iteration of the death sentence, is pardoned by his enemies and enabled to vindicate himself by publishing a monumental work on law and order. More familiar with the corruptions of towns than with the countryside, Balzac exhibits his idyllic and utopian strain in two companion studies, *Le Médecin de campagne* and *Le Curé de village*. A protagonist in each case, Doctor Benassis or Madame Graslin, expiates a private sin by setting up a model community, a kind of human reclamation project. Doctor Benassis, the mayor of his village, the father of his people, the Napoleon of his valley, whose biography somewhat parallels Balzac's, dies in the crucial year of 1829. Madame Graslin, like the protagonist of *Crime and Punishment*, ends by submitting to a public confession; but works transcend faith in Balzac's ethical system: "the gospel in action." The Marquis d'Espard, in *L'Interdiction*, acquits a long-standing debt of honor by writing and printing an illustrated history of China; such a book had been among the ill-fated publications of Balzac's actual press.

The liquidation of this establishment did not dampen his commercial zest. Whenever he went on a journey, he came back talking of railway shares and canal concessions, timber rights and mining prospects. He could scarcely pass by a manure pile without undertaking to convert it into a gold mine. His friends vie with one another in their anecdotes of get-rich-quick schemes and glibly munificent speculations, improvised and elaborated with the same admixture of the fantastic and the matter-of-fact that animates his books. Evidently, he drew no distinctions between his literary and his financial interests. He engaged habitually in lawsuits against editors and publishers, and he founded several short-lived periodicals of his own. In his novels he advertised the products of the tradesmen he patronized; he speculated on tickets for his plays; he thought of incorporating his readers into a sort of lottery, a tontine, by combining premiums with subscriptions. Like Defoe, the English novelist whom he most surprisingly resembles, he was a man of innumerable projects. None of them, with the all-important exception of the *Comédie humaine*, ever quite materialized. Taine, as usual, saw the point and overstated it, when he characterized Balzac as "a man of affairs in debt." Balzac was nothing if not a man of letters: literature was his unique stratagem for settling his affairs. His talents and ambitions as organizer, projector, promoter, were finally expressed in his writing. As a writer, he was a consummate business man. Theoretically, he could calculate better than James de Rothschild; we have Balzac's word that his publisher, Souverain, said so. We have also the word of Werdet, one of his previous publishers, that Balzac was not a practical businessman. And, to apply the only canon by which such matters can be tested, we have a significant fact: after Balzac's "Dilecta," his motherly first love, Madame de Berny, had helped to extricate him from the failure of his type-foundry, her son took it over and made a success of it.

Balzac's unsuccessful experiments as a man of affairs confirmed his vocation as a man of letters. Yet it is hard to think of a great writer whose juvenilia are less promising than Balzac's *Oeuvres de jeunesse*. Although their callow sensationalism persists throughout the work of his maturity, they do little to foreshadow his solid accomplishments. "His first operations in mercantile literature," as he candidly termed them, show all of his faults and virtually none of his merits. They bring no new resources to the impoverished conventions of Mrs. Radcliffe and Monk Lewis, or the *bas romantisme* of Pigault-Lebrun and Ducray-Duminil. Indeed it is only the occasional note of parody that detaches them from the gruesome monotony of their models. Only when *Argow le Pirate* supplies the sequel to *Le Vicaire des Ardennes*, and the sinister pirate reappears in the even more sinister guise of a banker, do we catch a first faint glimmering of the Balzacian vision. But Balzac did not discover his subject, nor adjust himself to his métier, until he had been caught in the toils of finance. While Balzac & Cie was being liquidated, he was rusticated to the wilds of Brittany, where he lived "the life of a Mohican." There, a generation before, during the royalist insurrection of the Vendée, the loyal peasants of the Chouannerie had waged partisan warfare against the Revolution. "They were savages who served God and the King by fighting like Mohicans." *The Last of the Mohicans* had lately been translated, and Balzac had begun to regard James Fenimore Cooper as the only novelist worthy of comparison with Scott. One was the historian of nature, the other of humanity, Balzac would write in a later appreciation. Meanwhile, returning to fiction, he felt that he brought to the imitation of both "a passion and spirit which are present in neither." The lost cause he celebrated was that of neither the vanishing redskin nor the Jacobite pretender. It was nothing less than the altar and the throne. It was the old order, to which—brooding over his troubles, and ascribing them to the new disorder—he gradually came to profess allegiance.

In 1829, at the age of thirty, on the eve of the July Revolution, Balzac hit his stride with *Le Dernier Chouan, ou La Bretagne en 1799*. The first of his books to be signed with his own name, its Cooperesque title would subsequently be changed to *Les Chouans*. Simultaneously, and with louder success, *succès de scandale*, he produced another volume which was to be fitted into the embryonic scheme of the *Comédie humaine*. Since Balzac was to be both a romantic *trouvère* and a realistic *trouveur*, his models were to include both the historical novel and the scientific compendium. He had long wanted to do for French history what Scott had done for British. On the other hand, his casual journalism reflects the taste of the time for facetious monographs and burlesque codes, pseudo-scientifically trifling with such topics as landlords and neckties "considered in themselves and in their relation to society and institutions." Everything has its physiology, as gastronomes had been taught by Brillat-Savarin, whose life and work Balzac recounted for a biographical dictionary. For his own *Physiologie du mariage* he chose—wisely in view of his inexperience—to emphasize the social institution at the expense of the psychological relationship. Compared with the penetrating insight of Stendhal's *De l'amour*, or the more thoroughgoing esthetic naturalism of Remy de Gourmont's *Physique de l'amour*, it can hardly be taken seriously. To advise other men not to marry until they have dissected at least one woman is all very well for an irresponsible bachelor who is not even a medical student, but it holds up a standard of rigorous empiricism which could not be fulfilled by any of his novels except by the three classed as *Les Célibataires*. A sequence of married mistresses, over whom his biographers archly linger, seems to have mitigated his bachelorhood. If he could not write of love, as Lytton Strachey asserted, it was not for lack of first-hand acquaintance. It was rather from a strongly masculine tendency to reduce love to sex, to be less interested in the psychological variables than in the physiological constants, to be less at home in the boudoir than in the smoking-room. The complicated liaisons of the *Comédie humaine* are often less convincing than the single-minded *fablieaux* of the *Contes drolatiques*.

In 1830 the hero of *La Peau de chagrin*, Raphaël de Valentin, having gambled away his last sou, wanders along the Quai Voltaire in suicidal mood, when he chances upon a magic talisman which renews his lease on life. Similarly Lucien de Rubempré, dangling on the brink of suicide at the end of *Illusions perdues*, is rescued by a mysterious Spanish priest and launched upon the incredible adventures of *Splendeurs et misères des courtisanes*, which waft him from the *haut monde* to the *demi-monde* and back to suicide in 1830. The reprieve from folly, the vicarious existence, the posthumous and anonymous career figure again in the story of Balzac's feminine namesake, *Honorine*—much as they do in "Wakefield," Hawthorne's curiously similar story of an "Outcast of the Universe." Such were the last twenty years of Balzac's own career, desperately preoccupied with the creation of the *Comédie humaine*, or more specifically the hundred-odd novels and tales that constitute about two-thirds of the projected series. Like the Spanish priest, who turns out to be the master criminal Vautrin, he led many lives beside his own; he "realized the German superstition of the Double by a phenomenon of moral paternity." Like Ferragus, the proscribed father of *Les Treize*, he exercised an invisible supervision over his progeny. Since he had no legitimate children, and since his main hope for flesh-and-blood immortality seems to have been still-born, he satisfied his paternal instincts by peopling his books with more than two thousand different characters. By creating, as critics say less pertinently of other novelists, a world of his own, with the most lavish demiurgy that any artist has ever practised, he gratified his worldly ambitions. In the preface to the *Histoire des Treize*, he speaks of the satisfactions of playing God. In one of his penny-dreadfuls, *Le Centenaire*, he attributes the longevity of its Faustian protagonist to a certain vital fluid. That essence, as he enumerates its effects, seems to contain the innermost secret of the artist's powers:

Today clothed in the rags of misery, tomorrow travelling in a magnificent carriage under the title of an extinct family, saving the lives of the good and allowing the wicked to die—such a man takes the place of *destiny*; he is almost God! . . . He holds in his hands all the secrets of the art of government and the secrets of every state; he learns at last what to believe about religions, man, and institutions. He looks upon the vain debates of this earth as from the height of a cloud; he wanders in the midst of the living like a sun; finally, he traverses the centuries without dying.

This, we may be informed, is the hollow reverberation of Arlincourt's once-popular *Solitaire*, the fustian journeywork of a self-subscribed "public writer and French poet at two francs a page." Yet it does not exaggerate the ultimate range of Balzac's ambition. Napoleon, through conquest, had dominated Europe; Cuvier, through science, espoused the globe; O'Connell, through politics, embodied a people. The admiring Balzac aspired, through literature, to equal the immensity of those three careers, and to leave a comparable mark upon their common century: "As for me, I shall have borne a whole society in my head." Paul Bourget, in hailing Balzac as "our literary Napoleon," corroborated this boast; and Pedro Salinas, in defining the novel as the "imperialistic genre," indicated the grounds for Balzac's leadership. Certainly a Napoleonic complex has never been harnessed to a more constructive purpose. The motto that Balzac inscribed upon his bust of Napoleon, "I shall accomplish with the pen what he could not complete with the sword," suggests a very different task of organization. *Scènes de la vie militaire*, for self-evident reasons, is the weakest and most fragmentary section of the *Comédie humaine*. Balzac's project for presenting a battle at first hand, characteristically, modulated into a humanitarian tract, *Le Médecin de campagne*. To be sure, this includes "The Napoleon of the People," a folk-tale recited by an old soldier to a group of peasants, which is one of the finest chapters in the imperial legend; it is also one of the most elegiac. "No more eagles" is now the watchword. The short story *Adieu*, pathetically re-enacting on French soil the Grand Army's crossing of the Beresina, is another good-bye to all that. There is no homecoming for Colonel Chabert, who has legally been slain at Eylau, and whose remarried wife hounds him back into an asylum. As for Philippe Bridau, the half-pay officer of *La Rabouilleuse*, he returns from a veterans' colony in Texas, the Champ d'Asile, to outswagger the *chevaliers d'industrie* of the Restoration and the July Monarchy. Nucingen and Keller, the bankers—in other words, Rothschild and Laffitte—are now the marshals of France, "massing their securities as Napoleon massed his troops." Nowadays *action* means stock in a corporation.

As for the younger generation, the children of the century, the Napoleonides, "of the same race but somewhat degenerate," who has canvassed their situation more authoritatively than Balzac? Where Stendhal had chronicled the exceptional case, it was Balzac who codified the rules. Stendhal had been a soldier and a diplomat where Balzac had been an unsuccessful business man; but Balzac became, what Stendhal never was, a successful author. Balzac was compelled to use his imagination where Stendhal could rely on his observation. And where the gregarious Stendhal was an intellectualist, the solitary Balzac—to cap the antithesis—was absorbed in physical things. Instead of living his books, he lived in his books —a sedentary mode of existence for a man of Napoleonic indefatigability. Small wonder that he so frequently reverts to the theme of a double life, or that even his crudest fantasies possess an inherent vitality. Since he had begun his battles, he mock-heroically boasted, more than one chair had been shot out from under him. The fields of overt action continued to beckon; he was tempted, on several occasions, to be a candidate for the Chamber of Deputies; but he was no luckier in politics than in commerce. His fellow authors repeatedly refused to grant him official status in the Académie Française, and it was a disappointment not to be awarded the Montyon prize for the conspicuous promotion of virtue. There was never any time for regret, however; there was always another novel waiting to be written. Writing day and night, from twelve to eighteen hours out of every twenty-four, he might well have sighed, with Eliot's Prufrock, "I have measured out my life with coffee spoons." He shut himself in his room for as long as twenty-six days at a stretch; he brought out as many as fourteen volumes within a single year. By the rule of opposites that seems to dictate most writers' conceptions of themselves, there he affected the white robe of a Carthusian. Doubtless he would have been more at home in the Abbey of Thélème than in a charterhouse; but it takes more than affectation to goad a man into blackening so much paper. His debts were his vows, his study was a cell, and composition a monastic regimen.

"Creating, always creating!" he exclaims, in an outburst of complacent blasphemy. "God only created for six days." His own life seemed to hang, like Scheherazade's, on resuming the story each night. Between novels there was little rest; there were restless trips to the provinces of France and the corners of Europe. "Constant work is the law of art as it is of life," he moralized over the young sculptor of *La Cousine Bette*. He gave younger writers the terse advice of a self-made industrialist: "Work!" Toward dilettantes and bohemians and—most effete of all—critics, he adopted the self-righteous tone of a hard-working craftsman, "a galley-slave to pen and ink, a merchant of ideas." The companionship of women, he warned Gautier, was a distraction to the creative artist. There was no objection to a correspondence, he conceded. "It develops one's style." His love letters, as we might have expected, are both voluminous and businesslike. Unlike the unexpectedly intimate revelation of Mérimée's *Lettres à une inconnue*, Balzac's *Lettres à l'Etrangère* merely take us into the wings of the *Comédie humaine*, and share with us the long-drawn-out travails and last-minute anxieties of life's dress rehearsals for art. The role of Eve was played for him, passively and enigmatically, by Eveline Hanska, the cultivated Polish wife of an elderly Ukrainian nobleman. The grand passion that she provoked by a fan letter subsisted for seventeen years on a few brief meetings. In 1850, several years after Count Hanski's death, she consented to become Madame Balzac. Balzac, whose health had been broken and whose output had been tapering off for two or three years, died in his new home at Paris a few months after their marriage. His labors had killed him at the very moment when his twin objectives, power and pleasure, "to be celebrated and to be loved," might securely have been enjoyed. "Mais il paraît que l'histoire de tous les hommes ne sera jamais qu'un roman pour moi," he had prophesied in a letter to Countess Hanska. Fiction was fated to be his reality.

His epistolary romance with the Countess was fictionally consummated in the comic misunderstandings of *Modeste Mignon* and the tragic frustrations of *Albert Savarus*. The latter, having met his mistress in Neuchâtel precisely as Balzac had done, writes a novel about her; but the caprice of fortune—or, rather, of another woman—keeps them apart, and he ends in the lonely obscurity of the Grande Chartreuse. The precedent of Stendhal's Fabrice, atoning for his escapades in a like reclusion, may have been one of the features that attracted Balzac to *La Chartreuse de Parme*. For his country doctor, Benassis, the turning-point between a profligate youth and a benevolent prime had been a retreat to the Grande Chartreuse, where he found himself admonished by a monkish Latin inscription: "Fuge, late, tace . . ." This is not far removed from Stephen Dedalus, and the Joycean admonition of silence, exile, and cunning. Many a sensitive mind has experienced that need to fly from mundane confusions, to hide and be silent. "The best are silent now," so Matthew Arnold paused to meditate in his "Stanzas from the Grande Chartreuse." Arnold's stanzas voice the classic statement of the intellectual pilgrim midway through the nineteenth century, wandering between the divergent worlds of tradition and modernity, between a lost faith and a wavering skepticism. Balzac's generation had its doubts and momentary pauses of indecision, but its energies were still strong enough to resolve contradictions by overriding them, and its silences were distinctly audible. The extreme vicissitudes that frame the destinies of his protagonists testify to an underlying resilience: *Gloire et malheur*, *Grandeur et décadence . . .* , *Splendeurs et misères . . .* The articulate Benassis recoils from the "sublime egoism" of the mute cloister. Resolving to use his repentance for the benefit of the "social world," he becomes a physician instead of a monk, and his rural hiding-place becomes a thriving canton under his professional ministrations.

It was as if Balzac, like one of his characters, had struck some infernal bargain which empowered him to conjure up a society, on condition that he lived and worked in solitude. His biography is an agenda, a calendar of works and days, a tabulation of profits and losses. His interior life has gone into "the perpetual creation that emerges from my inkwell." There is poignance in the fact that the voluptuous setting for the lurid climax of *La Fille aux yeux d'or* was modelled on the boudoir adjoining his own Carthusian study, or that the interrupted love story of *La Grenadière* was located in a home he had wished to buy. "I have written my desires, my dreams," he confessed to his Countess. We are not surprised that so many of his characters are monomaniacs when we trace their peculiar obsessions back to their creator's all-embracing megalomania. It is surprising that there has been so little investigation of Balzac's imaginative processes, for few writers have written so unguardedly. His misunderstood geniuses, his unappreciated artists, his persecuted scientists act out the compulsion that bound him to his desk through the nights. His letters refer to his *grand oeuvre* in the awe-inspiring manner that the Queen's astrologers, of *Le Secret des Ruggieri*, assume when they discuss the philosophers' stone. *La Recherche de l'absolu* intensifies this note by contrasting the comfortable bourgeois solidity of its Flemish background with the sublimated alchemical quintessence for which Balthazar Claës experiments in vain. The indifferent reception of Balzac's preposterous drama *Les Ressources de Quinola* must have seemed a confirmation of its thesis—the obsessive Balzacian thesis of the inventor's sufferings. A contemporary of Galileo's, who has had the temerity and ingenuity to invent the steamship, is forced to scuttle it by the Inquisition. "Hell," he concludes, "is paved with good inventions."

Balzac must have touched, in moments of self-questioning, the thin line that separates inspiration from paranoia. To his composer in *Gambara*, and to his tenor in *Massimilla Doni*, their own music sounds divine; to the others it is insane cacophony. The isolated idealists of his *Etudes philosophiques* stand apart from the social realities of his *Etudes de moeurs*. Reality is the never quite attainable absolute toward which his laborious researches tend. It is his own fixed idea that he exposes in *Le Chef-d'oeuvre inconnu*, permitting life itself, in the youthful person of Poussin's mistress, to elude the endeavors of art, personified by the half-mad Frenhofer. Is that painter an incomparable genius or a self-hypnotized charlatan? His encrusted canvas seems to be dismissed by Balzac as a meaningless daub, and yet the reader is left wondering—until he too seems touched by a gleam of madness—whether a more percipient taste would not discern some brilliant innovation. Cézanne identified himself with Frenhofer, while Picasso has published a dazzling series of illustrations. And Balzac's ambiguities have survived to perplex other writers. For Hawthorne, in "The Artist of the Beautiful," the masterpiece of a lifetime takes the shape of a delicate mechanical toy, which a careless gesture of the merest child can crush. For Henry James, in "The Madonna of the

Future," there are further refinements to "that terrible little tale of Balzac's." The hesitant perfectionist, who contemplates his blank easel, while his model waxes buxom and middle-aged, bears a closer resemblance to James than to Balzac. Balzac, after all, has more in common with the ingenious interloper, who takes possession of the impatient madonna and thrives upon prolific caricature. His is the last word: "Cats and monkeys, monkeys and cats —all human life is there."

The allegory should explain why James, probably the least Balzacian of novelists, bore wistful homage again and again to "the first and foremost member of his craft." For Balzac specialized in those bustling combinations of material circumstance, so characteristic of the American scene, which had eluded both Hawthorne and James, and to which they both preferred the quest for ivy-covered romance. Moreover, Balzac's works were translated and circulated in America on a scale which befitted the mass-production of his brothers Cointet and the supersalesmanship of his Gaudissart. Five-foot sets of dusty editions in any second-hand bookshop will bear witness to this national vogue, as well as to a subsequent ebbing of interest. The ephemeral nature of the Balzacian wave that swept our shores may be blamed, at least in large part, upon bungled and garbled translations. In larger part, it was bound to call forth a school of native Balzacians, who would set their sights closer to home. Borrowing *The Wild Ass's Skin* from the Carnegie Library, Dreiser learned to visualize himself through Valentin and Pittsburgh through Paris. Others in other countries, similarly, readjusted the novelistic focus as they extended its panoramic range. To have represented the bourgeoisie so thoroughly was to retain certain defects of their qualities; and Balzac remains, far more obviously than Goethe or such other household gods, an inspired philistine. By way of compensation, he could claim with his Mercadet: "They will never put a stop to speculation. I have understood my epoch." It is often ambiguous, as we try to follow the curve of Balzac's speculations, whether he belongs with the Mercadets or the Galileos, with the jobbers or the discoverers. But to run up a perennial deficit into one of the most amazing success stories in the history of literature is to be paid in kind.

2. Doctor of Social Medicine

Balzac's professionalism, like the efficient theatricalism of Scribe, owes a certain amount to legal training. The future novelist and the future dramatist, while learning to brief human nature, clerked side by side in the office of Guyonnet de Merville. That well-established attorney, under the name of Derville, handles the affairs of many characters in the *Comédie humaine*. "There are three men in our society, the priest, the physician, and the man of justice, who cannot esteem the world," he tells his client in *Le Colonel Chabert*. "They have black garments, perhaps because they wear mourning for all the virtues, all the illusions." So the country doctor, Benassis, talking to the Abbé Janvier and the local justice of the peace, defines their respective functions: "One cures the wounds of the soul, another those of the purse, a third those of the body. They represent society in its principal terms of existence—conscience, property, health." Not that they always live up to Balzac's ideals. Consider the shyster Fraisier and the quack Poulain, picking at the bones of Cousin Pons, or the clerical intrigue of *Le Curé de Tours*, which is differentiated from the milder ironies of Trollope's *Warden* by all the rigor and ardor that differentiate Roman Catholicism from the Church of England. The clergy of Mauriac and Bernanos will be more dedicated to their vocation. But Balzac, in his recoil from big business, put his faith in the old-fashioned notary, the exemplary curate, and the family doctor; their acute sense of social responsibility was good for what ailed him and his contemporaries; he envied their professional competence for playing the detached and ubiquitous witness, for judging life by a set of clear and distinct principles, for reconstructing what others had destroyed. Viewed in this light, his books are law-cases, cases of conscience, case histories. His *opus magnum* is a codification, a confession, a diagnosis.

Having begun his career as a lawyer's clerk, he subsequently draped himself in monkish garments, and was eventually greeted by the diagnostic Sainte-Beuve as "a somewhat medical confessor," whose profession gave him access to the alcoves and the alleys, and enabled him to shock his readers by invading privacies and unveiling secrets. Law and religion, he soon discovered, were being more honored in the breach than in the observance. That, of course, is the sort of discovery that realists cannot but make. "You look for a man as he ought to be," Balzac told George Sand, "I take him as he is." This seemed to her an inverted idealism, but to him it was a clinical method. He associated the writer's function with the surgeon's in *Madame Firmiani*, and prefaced *Les Parents pauvres* by proclaiming himself "a doctor of social medicine." His most eminent practitioner, Doctor Horace Bianchon, appears in twenty-nine stories, almost with the regularity of a trademark, as confidential adviser to the other characters and plenipotentiary of the author. The *Comédie humaine* has been taken for, among its other achievements, a nosography, a systematic description and classification of the many diseases to which flesh is heir. Frequently the novel has profited from an association with medicine, since both combine science with art in varying proportions, and each submits an opportunity for observation to a technique of analysis. Rabelais, Goldsmith, and Chekhov are not the only physicians who have enriched the domain of fiction, and Balzac is not the only novelist whose books contribute to what he terms "The Pathology of Social Life," although he is indeed the main contributor. He is rather a social pathologist than a pillar of state or the church; but we shall not appreciate his scientific and artistic views, or his conception of the *Comédie humaine*, until we have considered his political and religious assumptions. These cannot be separated from one another, inasmuch as Balzac's premise was the conclusion of Bonald's *Théorie du pouvoir*: the joint necessity for the throne and the altar.

The Vicomte de Bonald and Joseph de Maistre—"those two eagles of thought," so un-Napoleonic in their gyrations—had undertaken to answer the *philosophes*, to point the moral to the Revolution, and to formulate a counter-revolutionary philosophy. Balzac was more sympathetic to the somber logic of Bonald, who recommended a Bourbon restoration along imperial lines, than to the ultramontane fervor of Maistre, who looked beyond the monarchy to the papacy. If Bonald had been the first critic to call literature an expression of society, Balzac was the first writer to set up this axiom, consciously and conscientiously, as the touchstone of his own intentions. The revolutionary argument habitually appealed to the state of nature; the reactionary answer was an appeal to the concept of society. It was society, Doctor Bianchon noted in the album of *La Muse du département*, which brought out the two-edged distinction between a water-carrier and a Napoleon. Rousseau had extolled the goodness of natural man because he himself had lived under repressive institutions. Bonald, living through the experiments that swept them away, was more painfully conscious of the unrestrained egoism that reigned in their place. Citing these ethical alternatives in the *Avant-propos* to the *Comédie humaine*, Balzac declares that man is neither good nor bad; that society, far from depraving him, improves and perfects him; that royalism and Catholicism form a complete system for the repression of his depraved tendencies. Thereupon he takes his downright stand: "I write in the light of two eternal verities, religion and monarchy." The question then arises, which he does his best to anticipate, why evil prevails in his work. It cannot be met by instancing virtuous characters, since the Birotteaus and Eugénie Grandets are usually the victims. It can only be understood as a sweeping moral condemnation of a system, or default of system, which tends to loosen restraints and to encourage depravity. Not until the age of William Saroyan would a *Human Comedy* be possible in which pure goodness prevailed.

When the disorder is so serious that nothing good can be expected, it is just as well to know the worst, and not to blame the doctor for the disease. Balzac's treatment aims at a kind of literary homeopathy. Thus the social unit, he repeatedly insists, is not the individual but the family. "The family is society." The trouble, as he more than once diagnoses it, is that "there is no family today ... there are only individuals." Accepting Bonald's fundamental triad of father, wife, and child, he exalts the *père de famille* to the apex; but revolution, undermining the bulwarks of authority, has guillotined him, has cut off the head of the family. *La Rabouilleuse* illustrates this thesis by depicting both a widow's household and an unmarried ménage, and showing the unfilial degeneration that results from the absence of a father. But where are the benefits of his presence, then? What are the paternal virtues? The avarice of Père Grandet or the weakness

of Père Goriot, the lechery of Baron Hulot or the madness of
Balthazar Claës? Again the prescription is homeopathic, confronting evil with evil. Now and then, as in *Mémoires de deux
jeunes mariées*, a good example is brought in to moralize over
a bad one. Renée de Maucombe consents to a marriage of convenience, raises several children, and quietly reads Bonald; while
Louise de Chaulieu is married for love, successively to a foreigner
and a poet, and leads an adventurous, unhappy, and unfecund
existence. Her letters make up the larger and more interesting
part of the tale; her memory is held up to a younger sister, in
Béatrix, as an example not to follow. Balzac's usual mode of
presentation is that of an object-lesson, with the lesson lagging
far behind the object. The lesson is presented didactically, the
object represented dramatically. The medicine is applied externally.
There is too much protest, too often in Balzac's own person,
on behalf of his eternal verities; while the foreground is occupied,
to greater advantage, by all sorts and conditions of sinners against
them. The *Comédie humaine* is predominantly a collection of
bad examples, like Dante's *Inferno* or Madame Tussaud's Chamber of Horrors.

Not the most incorrigible hater of fathers and families, not
Samuel Butler himself, could have treated them more grimly.
Yet bankers and courtesans, spawn of the very corruption that
Balzac laments, he glorifies. And when he attempts to glorify
virtue, to dramatize his doctrines, to modernize the *Imitatio
Christi*, he fails—how completely we may gauge by comparing
his *Médecin de campagne* with Lamennais' *Paroles d'un croyant*,
which appeared the following year in 1834. Both writers would
have agreed with the Abbé Janvier's definition of Catholic communion as "the image of universal social communion"; but the
Christian socialist was backing away from the altar, because he
had not found it there, even as Balzac was approaching, because
he had not found it elsewhere. Tracing his tergiversation, Bernard
Guyon characterizes Balzac's starting position as "liberal in
politics, positivistic in philosophy, anarchistic in sociology." Two
of his earliest fictional efforts, neither of them printed until the
twentieth century, must be ranked among the orphan progeny
of the Enlightenment, harking back to Voltairean rationalism
and groping toward something like Stendhal's Ideology. *Sténie,*

ou les erreurs philosophiques is an epistolary novel in the mode
of *La Nouvelle Héloïse*. *Falthurne: manuscrit de l'Abbé Savonati*
is a cross between a *conte philosophique* and a *roman noir*. Having
tried his hand at a play about regicide, Balzac published an
"impartial" history of the Jesuits, fearing in neither case to deal
with a subject which was then particularly explosive. While the
legitimate dynasty and the Catholic church were in power, he
does not seem to have taken much satisfaction in either, to judge
from his journalism and correspondence. Like a good bourgeois,
he detested Charles X and welcomed the Glorious Days.

Having been somewhat to the left of center during the Restoration, he moved rightward under Louis-Philippe. He adopted
the aristocratic particle *de*, to which his family had no claim
whatsoever: his father's surname, before it was assimilated to
that of the seventeenth-century letter-writer, had been plain
Balssa. As elder son of a widowed mother who showed an obvious
partiality for a scapegrace younger brother, he sharply sympathized
with the royalists on the mooted issue of primogeniture. His
failures, as their candidate for deputy, must have confirmed his
distrust of democratic elections. But it would be unfair to attribute
his legitimism to snobbery, to dub him a venal turncoat like
Lucien de Rubempré, or to derive his conservative principles from
his titled mistresses, as does his current biographer, André Billy.
Balzac's conservatism is primarily an undeception, a reaction
against the July Monarchy, a gesture of opposition, a frame of
ethical reference. The stages of his conversion can be traced
through the parable of *Jésus-Christ en Flandre*. As it appeared
originally in 1831, this was a brief *exemplum* representing the
estates of modern society as passengers on a sinking boat, some
of them drowned in the shipwreck, some of them saved by a
miracle. During the previous year he had published two mordant
sketches, criticizing the church and dismissing it as a figment of
the past. In 1832 these were incorporated into *L'Eglise*, where
a dream vision is set against the ecclesiastical background that
shadowed his youth and reappears in his writing, the Cathedral
of Tours. There the hostile arguments are eloquently refuted,
and the voice of the personified church is heard crying for help:
"Defend me! Defend me!" That cry went unanswered until 1845,
when Balzac attached *L'Eglise* to *Jésus-Christ en Flandre* as a

hortatory epilogue, terminating with this profession of faith: "Believing is living. I have just watched the funeral procession of a monarchy. The church must be defended!"

To the defense Balzac, increasingly vocal, had meanwhile been devoting his skills in polemic and propaganda. As a lay apologist for Christian culture, or as a prescient spokesman for social Catholicism, his stand was explicit enough. But a credo is not a catechism. "The religion of Balzac was truly his own; he had composed it for his use," the Abbé Bertault has concluded after a thorough survey. "The church to which he belonged exacted no obedience; he was the founder, he was the sole adept." In a letter to Countess Hanska he professes himself a Catholic "politically." His Catholicism, he writes again, is poetry; and again, it is "wholly terrestrial." Its sanctions are merely formalistic observances, like the empty carriages at Goriot's funeral—a device repeated in Gogol's *Dead Souls* and Dickens' *Bleak House,* where outworn institutions are satirized. Now and then Balzac seems to be satirizing himself, as when he allows the Duchesse de Langeais to assert: "Religion is intimately allied to property— Priest and King are you and I and the Princess, my neighbor— in a word, all the personified interests of the best people." Religion, for Balzac, is a code of morality; for his Duchess, going a step farther, it is a code of immorality. She might be enunciating the clerical opportunism of Julien Sorel, or the Catholic atheism of the Action Française. The difference between these varieties of religious experience and Balzac's emerges from *La Messe de l'athée,* where the atheistic surgeon Despleins, one of Balzac's saints, orders masses to the memory of a pious water-carrier—and this, too, by way of discharging a debt. What matters, then, are not the articles of belief, but principled patterns of behavior: not the controversies of theology nor enhancements in the manner of Chateaubriand, but a unique means of counter-acting the forces of self-interest.

Hence Balzac displays, not the intolerance and fanaticism that have agitated some later exponents of his creed, but a true catholicity. A favorite pattern, the reunion of opposites, is exemplified by the warm friendship of Daniel d'Arthez and Michel Chrestien, which runs unbroken through the *Comédie humaine.* Arthez, a great author and royalist deputy, who looks like Napoleon and sounds like Balzac, is seduced by the Princesse de Cadignan, and gradually retires from literary and political life. Meanwhile Chrestien, an intransigent republican, has escaped from her toils, and dies gloriously at the Cloître Saint-Merry in the insurrection of 1832. His similarity to Ferrante Palla helps to explain why Balzac acclaimed *La Chartreuse de Parme* and admired the anticlerical Stendhal. From their opposite poles they both attack the regime, for Balzac's politics are rather a frontal attack on the house of Orléans than a rear-guard defense of the Bourbons. If he defends counter-revolution in *Les Chouans*, he also follows Scott's conventions of the generous foe and the enemy lovers. If his position is inconsistent, it is impartial; it has room for extremes, but not for compromises. If the *Juste-Milieu* is an *aurea mediocritas*, it is less a golden mean than a gilded mediocrity, a government— as Balzac is fond of saying—by "mediocracy." Seeking a vantage-point from which to condemn it, he entertained the numerous proposals then in the air, a plurality of possible worlds, including Fourier's socialism. And, despite his final adherence to traditionalism, Hugo and Zola and Friedrich Engels united to hail the radical strain in his books. On the other side, the reactionary historian Thureau-Dangin branded them a pernicious influence, and the church they supported still places some of them on its *Index Librorum Prohibitorum*. Extremes meet here to agree about the effect, and to disagree with Balzac's purpose.

It would be idle to deny the authoritarian tendency of his expressed opinions. The striking fact is that, holding them sincerely, he should depict the issues of the day in terms which win the approbation of democrats and radicals. Yet Balzac held one commitment that went deeper than any partisanship. "The opinion of an artist," he says in *Les Comédiens sans le savoir*, "should be faith in his work." Against such conviction as his, mere opinion seems arbitrary and superimposed. The up-to-date apologist for orthodoxy is driven, sooner or later, to paradox. *Sur Catherine de Médicis* brings together the extremists of the right and the left, starting from a diatribe against the France of the 'forties, and concluding with a eulogy of that Machiavellian queen by none other than Robespierre. The destruction of the Saint Bartholomew Massacre and the Terror of 1793 are justified as necessary preliminaries to construction. The inevitable parallel in Balzac's own fortunes is the liquidation that prepared the way for his constructive labors. But art, single-handed, cannot reorganize a disorganized society; the best it can do is to expose the sources of disintegration. The chief of these, according to Félix Davin, who wrote the authorized introduction to the *Etudes philosophiques*, is thought. It is thought which undoes the precocious Louis Lambert. As for the antiquated but admirable Baron du Guénic, in *Béatrix*: "Religion and institutions thought for him." Vilfredo Pareto, whose ancestor, the Marquis Damaso Pareto, has a dedicatory niche in the *Comédie humaine*, would categorize these opposing influences as "combinations" and "residues." People and periods tend toward one or the other, a flair for speculation and innovation or an adherence to custom and stability. Paretan sociology, completing the paradoxical retreat from reason that began with Bonald, vacillates between those "magnificent combinations," intellectual or financial, toward which Balzac's characters strive, and that backward swing of the historical pendulum toward the intuitive and the secure.

Such were the cross-purposes at work in Balzac's eclectic mind —the gambler's yearning for security, the intellectual's revulsion from the intellect, and the genius of novelty pledged to the service of tradition. He had few occasions to practise what he preached, and formalism means little when the forms are neglected. "I am by no means orthodox, and I don't believe in the Roman church," he confessed to Countess Hanska, "...Swedenborgianism is my religion." Balzac's Catholicism was too formal, too political, too terrestrial to satisfy his need for a personal theology. Seeking to disencumber his ideas of the materialism that was their native element, he veered toward the remote extreme of spirituality. The mystic Emanuel Swedenborg, who had once been a scientist, had described the streets of heaven and the garments of the angels with a matter-of-fact conviction which could not but impress Balzac. This was the quintessence of Christianity, for Louis Lambert, the sociology of the supernatural. Balzac, however, was better initiated in the diabolic than in the seraphic arcanum; his androgynous angel, Séraphitus-Séraphita, belongs to that tawdry school of church decoration which the French call *sulpicerie*; yet he, or she, still manages to bedazzle such uncloistered spirits as Henry Miller. Otherworldliness was not Balzac's forte. He was "less of a natural mystic than any other great writer," as Aldous Huxley remarked, in the days when he could afford to deal uncharitably with pretensions of that sort. The stories that constituted *Le Livre mystique* seem improbable rather than miraculous. The theosophy of Sweden-borg and the illuminism of Saint-Martin intervene to solve the domestic and financial complications of *Ursule Mirouët*; but there the ghost walks in a Balzacian direction, and reveals the whereabouts of missing bonds.

Mysticism is Balzac's middle term between religion and science. Science, which had fostered Stendhal's skepticism, reinforced Balzac's will to believe: to believe in virtually everything, alchemy as well as electricity, elixirs as well as medicines, angelic hierarchies as well as stock-market tips. His was an age of reawakening cre-dulities, in which scientific experiment was a miracle and religious ceremony a convenience. The distance between a Perrault fairy tale and a Jules Verne thriller was not excessive, as Balzac proved by an early effort, *La Dernière Fée*. Realism, ever since Chaucer cast the horoscopes of his characters, has consulted the scientific auspices of its time. Too often it has been unduly influenced by the pseudo-scientists, who have made the most sensational claims or advanced the simplest explanations. Balzac's characters respond too readily, we must admit, to the animal magnetism of Mesmer, the physiognomy of Lavater, the phrenology of Gall, and other outmoded theories. But in the great zoological debate, the controversy between Cuvier and Geoffroy Saint-Hilaire, which Goethe considered vastly more important than the July Revolution of the same year, 1830, Balzac saw the issue and accepted the consequences of evolution. Cuvier, though Balzac regarded him as "the greatest poet of our century," had lacked the imagination to conceive how one species could develop out of another. Geoffroy, to whom *Le Père Goriot* is dedicated, antic-ipated Darwin by introducing "the principle of the unity of organic composition." The universal process of composition, of putting fragments together, imparting life—here was a biological corollary to Balzac's law of disorganization. If the varied mani-festations of nature could be unified by a single hypothesis, what of society? Traditionalists, from Montesquieu to Bonald, had emphasized the natural growth of social institutions. Balzac, as

Jean Cassou observes, identified the social order with the natural order. If society was an organic whole, the family was a molecular cell, and the transgressing individual was unnatural as well as anti-social.

Balzac's point of departure, and the basis for his most vivid images, is the analogy between the human race and the animal kingdom. A dense underbrush of metaphor, where naked appetites and brute antagonisms snap and snarl, luxuriates beneath the literal surface of his narrative. "Financially speaking," Monsieur Grandet, the avaricious mayor of Saumur, is as predatory as a tiger and as cold-blooded as a boa-constrictor. *La Vieille Fille* investigates the human molluscs that cling to provincial villages, while *César Birotteau* exhibits the curious lichens that make Parisian roofs their habitat. Marche-à-terre, in *Les Chouans*, may owe the rhythm of his name to the French Leatherstocking, Bas-de-cuir; but his attributes, lithely foreshadowing Mowgli or Tarzan, are compared no less than fifty times to those of different animals. Balzac pushes such comparison to the point where it becomes a blood relationship, and man himself is firmly linked to the fauna and flora of the naturalists' chain of being. In that strange story, *Une Passion dans le désert*, a female panther is susceptible to human emotions; more frequently human beings elsewhere yield to bestial instincts. After marriage has been reduced to physiology, "the chemistry of the will" invites research. "Look," exclaims the alchemist Claës as his wife weeps, "I have decomposed tears. Tears contain a little phosphate of lime, some sodium chloride, mucus, and water." Though the decomposition, in this case, had been verified by two members of the Académie des Sciences, Balzac did not pursue the analytic approach very far. His need, his aim, his method was synthesis. Bankruptcy had taught him the meaning of organization; revolution had taught him the value of dogma; zoology taught him the unity of created things. The doctor, putting into practice what the lawyer and the priest formulated, treated his material as an evolving and expanding organism. In 1834, with *Etudes de moeurs dans le dix-neuvième siècle*, he served notice on the public that each of his novels was merely a fragment of a more systematic undertaking. By 1842, when the *Avant-propos de la Comédie humaine* was written, it was already supported by the bulk of his achievement.

The scope of that achievement is vast but not unique, if we bear in mind the productivity of Balzac's period and the gigantism of his literary generation—a generation which, tearing a leaf from Heine's book, liked to think of Vesuvius as its inkwell. Hugo, Dumas, Scribe, Sue, and George Sand in their turn left five-foot shelves of their respective works. What distinguishes Balzac's from these is an integrating force, inherent in everything he wrote, which ultimately attains the resonance of a manifesto. The *Avant-propos*, which is not so much a foreword as a postscript, leaves few loose ends. Though the developing structure was subject to many changes, to amplifications and curtailments and transpositions and revisions over the years, the *Comédie humaine* adhered staunchly to its basic program. Science and philosophy alone could not integrate a work of art; Bonald, Swedenborg, and Geoffroy would have meant little to Balzac if he had lacked a concrete and capacious medium. It was Walter Scott, *trouveur* and *trouvère*, who merited his profoundest acknowledgment, for having "elevated the novel to the philosophic value of history." But the Waverley Novels, which he had long admired for their explorations into "the social movement" of the past, had lacked continuity. Balzac saw life as a continued story, of which each chapter was a novel and each novel an epoch. By co-ordinating fiction, as Geoffroy had co-ordinated natural history, the novelist could write social history; nay more, he could synthesize humanity, even as Humboldt was synthesizing the cosmos. Stendhal had recognized the psychological importance of environment, but Balzac—following Scott—implemented his descriptions with detailed inventories and atmospheric backgrounds. Following Buffon's natural history, he even subdivided his dramatis personae into men, women, and things, "persons and the material representation that they give to their thoughts." It was Balzac who introduced into literature the physical term *milieu*, which he had borrowed from Geoffroy, and who handed it on to Comte and the sociologists, to Taine and the critics, and to Zola and the other novelists.

Balzac's *Avant-propos*, which put the term into currency, was to realism what Hugo's *Préface de Cromwell* had been to the romantic movement. A shift in emphasis, from the drama to the novel and from imagination to observation, had made the writer more directly responsible to his enlarging subject. "French society was going to be the historian," Balzac roundly declared. "I had only to become its secretary." Conceiving his task as a problem of documentation, he compiled—in Taine's phrase— "the greatest storehouse of documents that we have on human nature." In his own phrase, he endeavored to write the history that so many historians had forgotten, that of *les moeurs*. He penetrated beyond manners to morals, beyond public events to private lives, by assuming an omniscient curiosity, an omnipresent detachment, and an omnipotent judgment. The doctor attending his patients became a caliph of the *Arabian Nights*, a Haroun-al-Raschid strolling incognito through the bazaars of his modern Bagdad, or—coming closer to home—a Louis XI, "deliberately mingling his royal majesty with scenes of bourgeois life." Did Balzac's jewel-headed walking-stick confer invisibility upon him, and thereby equip him to gather his stories by eavesdropping? So Delphine Gay alleged in her amusing fantasy, *La Canne de M. de Balzac*. Previous fictions, notably *The Turkish Spy* in the seventeenth century and Lesage's *Diable boiteux* in the eighteenth, had used keyholes and chimneys and similar narrative ruses for detaching the observer and conveying him from one domestic establishment to another. Sébastien Mercier, in *Le Tableau de Paris*, had surveyed the city in the last days of the *ancien régime*; and Etienne de Jouy, in *L'Ermite de la Chaussée d'Antin*, had sketched Parisian habits under the Empire. Restif de la Bretonne, more exhaustively than any of Balzac's predecessors, had adumbrated the range and liveliness of the *Comédie humaine*. And the great work did not lack such contemporary rivals as Frédéric Soulié's *Mémoires du diable* or Eugène Sue's *Mystères de Paris*. Mysteries, no longer confined to Udolpho or other haunted castles, were popularized by addresses on city streets.

Hugo took a bird's-eye view of the medieval roof-tops in *Notre-Dame de Paris*; in *Les Misérables*, under the modernizing influence of Balzac, he carried his municipal inspection into the sewers. A typical Hugolian vista, a building in the shape of an elephant, betrays his penchant for monstrosities. Balzac is more concerned with the monsters that nestle behind inconspicuous façades, with the hidden treasure in the house next door, the erotic adventure waiting around the corner, the inevitable coincidence. He opens

Ferragus with an apostrophe to the lights and shadows, the grand boulevards and blind alleys of Paris, "that monstrous marvel, astonishing assemblage of movements, machines, and thoughts, city of a hundred thousand novels, head of the world." Other capitals have their literary reconstructions; the London of Dickens and the Dublin of Joyce attract their passionate pilgrims; but its centripetal attraction makes Paris—for even so late a comer as Henry James—an iridescent jewel, a loadstone of cultural values. Where could a novelist find a more perfect setting for *"The Thousand and One Nights* of the Occident?" Esthetically, it was at an ideal midpoint between the Bourbon monuments and the Haussmann demolitions. Apartments were beginning to supersede the *hôtel particulier*, cafés and shops were exfoliating, modes and *articles de Paris* exhibiting themselves, *lorettes* and dandies sauntering, tilburies attended by *tigers* passing by, all diffusing an air of urbanity which could be encountered nowhere else—an atmosphere which, spiced and sentimentalized in the *romans gais* of Paul de Kock, seemed especially seductive to foreign readers. All of France was divided into two zones: "the province jealous of Paris, Paris only thinking of the province when it needed money." Balzac, acutely aware of this "social antithesis," endowed his work with a geography as well as a genealogy. Surveying Tours or Besançon, Saumur or Angoulême, he showed how post-revolutionary centralization had levelled the old provincial capitals, and he registered the flow of brains and resources toward the metropolis. Paris might be, as he observes in *Melmoth réconcilié*, "a branch office of hell"; but then, as Leslie Stephen is said to have remarked, hell is the only place worth living in.

It is his own apprenticeship that Balzac recalls in *Facino Cane*, when he speaks of writing in a mansard, taking long walks, and observing forgotten dramas, "admirable scenes, tragic or comic, masterpieces begotten by chance." Among his journalistic pieces are a dictionary of Parisian sign-boards, a treatise on the theory of walking, and other contributions to the pedestrian field mapped out by John Gay's *Trivia, or the Art of Walking the Streets*. A group of early sketches is entitled *La Comédie du diable* and the *Physiologie* posits a "divine comedy of marriage." *La Fille aux yeux d'or*, with its blindfold ride over cobblestones which feel and sound familiar, elaborates the parallel between the infernal circles and the Parisian faubourgs, and promises that the damned souls of the business world will have their Dante. A glimpse of the exiled Florentine poet himself, brooding nostalgically over the Ile de la Cité, is the surprise ending of *Les Proscrits*. Just as his *Divine Comedy* subsumed the culture of the Middle Ages, so Balzac envisages an encyclopedic poem of the "stupid"—the all too human—nineteenth century. The topographical opening of *Le Père Goriot* issues a Dantesque warning to abandon hope on entering the lower regions. "The peculiarities of this scene, full of observation and local color, could only be appreciated between the slopes of Montmartre and the heights of Montrouge . . ." To us, in our armchairs, the author will present the realistic dramaturgy of metropolitan circumstance. "This drama is neither fiction nor a novel." Lest we remain unconvinced, after this anti-romantic disclaimer, he adds in English: "All is true." Thereupon the Rue Neuve Sainte-Geneviève is projected upon our minds like an approaching camera-shot, and the house of Madame Vauquer, *née* de Conflans, is disclosed. We catalogue its appurtenances, outside and inside, and even sniff its *odeur de pension*; we proceed, from room to room and floor to floor, into the lives of its inmates. The several plots and counterplots of the drama involve the four estates of Balzacian society: the aristocratic connection with the Restauds through one of Goriot's daughters, the banking affiliation with the Nucingens through the other, the student life of the young intellectual, Rastignac, and the outlaw existence of Vautrin.

Care is taken that the different classes, fluctuating with the fortunes of Parisian real estate, are housed in appropriate quarters: the upper circles in the Faubourg Saint-Germain, the middle class in the Chaussée d'Antin, the bohemians in the Latin Quarter, and the underworld in that elusive Thirteenth Arondissement which then subsisted everywhere and nowhere. The *Comédie humaine* has been likened, for sheer heterogeneous inclusiveness, to a department store and to the Tower of Babel, but most aptly to Paris itself. The development of the *roman-feuilleton* and the precedent of the frame-story may have suggested certain techniques of literary articulation; for Balzac published much of his writing serially, and had started a small-scale

collection in *Les Contes drolatiques*. But the impulse to comprehend a series of individual items within some large-scale collective
enterprise was most concretely exemplified by the city itself, and
Balzac's realism was firmly based upon its burgher foundations.
Had not Cervantes extinguished chivalry with "a written comedy?" he asked. Though he looked with complacency upon Cervantes and Sterne as writers of a single novel apiece, and boasted
of having multiplied Richardson's accomplishment a hundredfold,
Balzac could still be *homo unius libri*. The acts and scenes of
his collected works were bound to be incomplete because he
had attempted nothing less than to transcribe the spectacle of
life in its gargantuan totality—an attempt which one of his most
prolific successors, Jules Romains, has named "unanimism." Balzac's actual title was in the air. It may be that *The Undivine
Comedy* of the Polish poet Krasiński had something to do with
his choice. It may have been crystallized by Vigny's *Maison du
berger*, where the poet, eternal spectator, addresses himself to
Eva, his personification of nature, impassive playhouse for the
enactment of the human comedy. The pile of unsuccessful scripts
left by Balzac testifies that he shared the aspiration of all poets
and novelists toward the stage. Having once contemplated a
dramatization of *The Prince*, and again a Napoleonic redaction
of *Don Quixote*, he was in a receptive mood for *La Chartreuse
de Parme*. It may well have occurred to him, writing his *Avant-
propos* a few months after the death of Stendhal, that the comedy
of the nineteenth century was scheduled to be his own big
production.

Balzac's opinion, expounded in *A combien l'amour revient aux
vieillards*, seems to coincide with Stendhal's: "Henceforth our
comedies will be narrated..." Books will take the place of the
theater because the bourgeoisie cannot afford to watch themselves
being lampooned; Tartuffe has now gone into politics and Turcaret
sits on the throne. Louis-Philippe's government, as if to prove
this point, had stopped the performance of Balzac's *Vautrin*
because the dashing actor, Frédérick Lemaître, in the villainous
title-role, had made himself up to resemble the Citizen-King.
Yet no edict could prevent his subjects from going through their
routines, the humor of which could be pointed out to the passer-
by; this is literally done, in *Les Comédiens sans le savoir*, by two

of Balzac's irrepressible painters. His sense of the dramatic was keen enough to justify the running title used for subdivisions: "Scenes from . . . Life." The scenic, the pictorial, the photographic is a prime element of his craft; his less dramatic episodes often give the effect of *tableaux vivants;* and he claimed to have foreshadowed Daguerre's epoch-marking invention. In an epoch which had also welcomed the invention of lithography, the comic spirit, inhibited on the stage, won militant expression in the press. There we must seek for the closest analogues to Balzac's talent, for a pictorial supplement—as Baudelaire saw—to the *Comédie humaine.* Two caricaturists stand out, in this respect, from an incomparably brilliant generation: Honoré Daumier, artistically the most gifted of all, for his lawyers and laundresses, for *Les Bons Bourgeois, Moeurs conjugales,* and *Croquis parisiens,* for endless variations on the theme of *Don Quixote,* and for that prince of sharpers, Robert Macaire; Henry Monnier, whose lesser gifts were rather more journalistic than artistic, for having illustrated *Le Rouge et le noir,* having struck the note of realism as early as 1830 in *Scènes populaires,* having posed for Balzac's portrayal of the bohemian mimic, Bixiou, having given an epigrammatic twist to the fatuities of the bourgeoisie, and above all having created Joseph Prudhomme. Prudhomme and his creator were to enjoy a theatrical career, and Macaire himself had been adapted from one of Lemaître's most popular roles. They stand together as *bon bourgeois* and *chevalier d'industrie,* guardian of residues and projector of combinations, as the Sancho Panza and Don Quixote of the period, the prototypes of César Birotteau and Maxime de Trailles and the other heroes and villains of the *Comédie humaine.*

It was difficult for the novelist not to be a caricaturist, as Dickens and Thackeray were finding under similar circumstances. Balzac contributed verbal cartoons to Daumier's periodical, *La Caricature,* and Daumier delineated his own interpretation of *La Comédie humaine.* And, if Balzac had borrowed some traits of Birotteau from Monnier, Monnier was to return the compliment in *Grandeur et décadence de Joseph Prudhomme.* The truth, we may suspect, is that their shrewd eyes were fixed on the same models, and that the picture society offered—in the words of Balzac's Duchesse de Beauséant—was an assembly of rogues and fools. To effect a comic demonstration of this truism, a reversion to type of characters who had other pretensions, a denouement in which everybody got fleeced, was a timeless trick of the trade. The moneybags of Harpagon, the stratagems of Sganarelle, the jealousies of Géronte, the impertinences of Toinette, the lovers, whatever their names were—could it be the same old troupe, forced to improvise, over and over again, from the well-worn scenarios with an occasional change of costume? Balzac enjoys bringing out the resemblance of a detective to Figaro, a salesman to Scapin, and other figures to their counterparts in the classical repertory. Molière is mentioned and cited more frequently than any other author; and the epithet *Molière médecin*, when we remember Molière's notorious distrust of doctors, is paradoxically apt for Balzac; but Balzac's medicine is stronger stuff than the horrendous purgatives of Dr. Diafoirus. The social comedy consists of many individual tragedies: Goriot's agony is a cynical lesson for Rastignac. The relationship between age and youth is one of the subtlest lines that Balzac traces, since it leads us into the middle age of the century. For the youthful romanticist, life is large, albeit fragmentary; for the adult realist, the astronomical perspectives have scaled down to convenient landmarks. Balzac's world is ultimately a small one. How else could he have managed to set it all down? Familiarity with it breeds contempt for it. The astringent experience it holds for us, which Baudelaire has so poignantly caught, is the shrivelling of a generation's values from the Titanic to the Lilliputian.

> Pour l'enfant, amoureux de cartes et d'estampes,
> L'univers est égal à son vaste appétit.
> Ah! que le monde est grand à la clarté des lampes!
> Aux yeux du souvenir que le monde est petit!

3. Subtracting the Discount

If disorganization was the cause of Balzac's troubles, his peculiar sort of unified composition was the cure. We have seen his project assigned to him by circumstances, and have tried to conceive it—and them—in his own terms; we have annotated his preface by glancing at his table of contents. The plot and characters of the human comedy, the methods and results of his component "studies," their contribution to the technique of realism and their transcription of social history are matters that invite our further attention. The very bulk of the work is a warrant for emphasizing its total configuration, even though such an emphasis may slight the particularities of its novels and tales. Magniloquently heralded and hastily composed, there was bound to be an immeasurable gap between the conception and the execution of the *Comédie humaine*. Organization, for Balzac, meant all-embracing inclusion rather than discriminating selection. As secretary of society by his own appointment, it was his duty to describe exhaustively and his privilege to digress sententiously. His inevitable failure to complete the survey, to exploit every claim he had staked, is more excusable than the effort to incorporate a number of stories and episodes which were hardly worthy of his maturing plans. Few great structures have been filled out with so dangerous a proportion of rubble. If only Balzac's style had lived up to his conception, sighed Lamartine, then France would really have had another Molière. That Stendhal should have asked Balzac for stylistic advice is one of the ironies of their relationship; for Balzac, whose gamut does not stop short at either banality or hyperbole, carries the traditions of French prose to a demotic and somewhat overripe stage, while Stendhal initiates the modern revulsion from rhetoric. In a revealing letter to Countess Hanska, Balzac defines style as "a garment"—in other words, as something which can be put on or taken off at will, like his Carthusian dressing-gown.

Style, in his case, is not the man himself so much as the exigencies that pressed him. His debts could only be floated by accelerating his rate of production. The *mot juste* is necessarily the fruit of leisure, and Balzac did not write—complains Thackeray—"like a gentleman." He once planned to turn out a novel a month; and, though no one could have maintained that deadline steadily for very long, he met and surpassed it on numerous occasions. *César Birotteau* was written, rewritten, and on the press in twenty days. The pen that claimed to have dashed off *Le Secret des Ruggieri* in a single night could never have hesitated an instant nor blotted a line. Yet there were at least six states to the text of *Illusions perdues*. It was as if the organic process of writing had been caught up in the mechanical process of printing. The roughest of drafts went, chapter by chapter, to the compositor, and came back over and over again for revision in proof. An endless and almost illegible sequence of printer's corrections broke into the galleys as often as twenty times, and all but consumed the profits the author had counted upon. What was worse, he acquired the habit of interpolating and elaborating, of separating the substance from the form of his work, of applying the style to the surface by a process of overlay. Sometimes it seems to be laid on pretty thick, with a display of allusions and a bandying of epithets which leave the reader feeling like Macaulay's schoolboy. Balzac's imagery, which Taine has critically scrutinized, is "a gigantic chaos"; and yet that chaos, like the encyclopedia, is somehow organized. "Chemistry expounds love, cookery borders on politics, music or groceries are related to philosophy." Nothing human is irrelevant to Balzac's purview; everything is related, deviously if not directly; in tracing those relationships, through whatever channels they may lead, he is at his best.

He is at his worst when he conjures with names or airily mentions far-fetched works of art, in the naïve hope of enhancing his artistic tone. He reaches the nadir of taste in the hypertrophied last sentence of *Massimilla Doni*, where muses, angels, sylphs, and a varied assortment of famous madonnas are invited to lament—at the foot of his heroine's bed—her departing virtue. In effectual contrast, because it runs so much closer to Balzac's vein, is the metaphor that runs through *Le Cousin Pons:* "Let us borrow an image from the railways, if only to compensate for their borrowings from us . . ." Society is there envisaged, as it is by Tennyson, "Launched on its metallic path with the swiftness of a locomotive." Despite his metaphorical intimations of wildness hiding behind tame exteriors, Balzac remains the inveterate city-dweller, embarrassed at being confronted directly with nature. Confronted with the scenery of his native Touraine, he crowds fifteen figures of speech into the first page of *Le Lys dans la vallée*, and suffuses a hothouse atmosphere throughout. He is more at home with landmarks than with landscapes, utterly fascinated by street scenes and domestic arrangements, anxious to bring household interiors and family groups within the range of his flash photography. If Barbey d'Aurevilly complained that Balzac made description "a skin disease of the realists," if Flaubert campaigned for a more rigorous selectivity, it was because Balzac had managed to reproduce so many familiar objects, to put so many recognizable sights into words for the first time. To include everything, to be all-embracing, is—as Whitman found—both a continual incentive and an unattainable goal. Exuberance clutters Balzac's narrative with Homeric catalogues and Rabelaisian lists; two steps forward and one step backward is his regular pace. But there are frequent variations, largely colloquial, when he stops speaking and lets us listen to his characters: their smart table-talk and shrill curtain-lectures, their genial *blague* and surreptitious *argot*.

Dramatic dialogue and photographic description, relieving and highlighting what James calls foreshortened narration, often lend the effect of solidity to flimsy materials. Balzac faced the handicap of having learned his profession in an undistinguished literary school. His apprentice novels, as a historian of the *roman noir* reminds us, are among the very blackest of the lot. Yet life itself holds mysteries which outshadow Mrs. Radcliffe's, we are reminded by the preface to the *Histoire des Treize*. Chance is the greatest novelist, we read in the *Avant-propos*; but Balzac was overanxious to collaborate with chance. When he cast off such youthful pseudonyms as Lord R'hoone and Horace de Saint-Aubin, he did not abandon the disguises, the coincidences, and the conventionalized sensations of popular fiction. *Une Femme de trente ans* reverts to the themes of *Argow le Pirate*, and *Splendeurs et misères des courtisanes* is no more credible than *Clothilde de Lusignan* or *Jane la pâle*. Balzac's firm had meanwhile printed the third edition of Vigny's *Cinq-mars*, and the *Comédie humaine* had found reputable models in the Waverley and Leatherstocking volumes. A novel entitled *L'Archer de Charles IX* wins Lucien de Rubempré his brief success as "the ape of Walter Scott," and poor old Cousin Pons misses his opportunity by dying before he can compose the operatic score for a libretto from Cooper's *Dernier Mohican*. Balzac's hall of fame embraces the works of previous novelists, on which he is constantly drawing for mythological comparisons. Laurence de Cinq-Cygne, the dashing horsewoman of *Une Ténébreuse Affaire*, is another Diana Vernon; Maxence Gilet, the small-town bravo of *La Rabouilleuse*, has the hawklike vision of Natty Bumppo. Scott's influence is gradually neutralized by Balzac's maturity, but Cooper's hold—as we shall see—is annually strengthened.

Challenging Scott on his own terrain—and Balzac's sister tells us that *Maître Cornélius* is a matter-of-fact rejoinder to the intolerable picturesqueness of *Quentin Durward*—he deliberately based his own fifteenth-century story upon a folk-tale, and solidly built it around the establishment of a medieval usurer. The characterization that stands out from the wraiths of *Le Martyr calviniste* is a Balzacian portrait of the sixteenth-century surgeon, Ambroise Paré. *Le Succube,* the most ambitious of the *Contes drolatiques,* amasses a portfolio of legal documents. By reviving the elemental bourgeois conventions of the *fabliau,* Balzac's realism invades the most hallowed regions of romance; though his droll tales show the crudities of stylistic *pastiche* at too long a range, they seem to penetrate the blood and bones and marrow of the Middle Ages more comfortably than any historical novel. His search for better masters had guided Balzac to Rabelais, and to their compatriot Béroalde de Verville, whose *Moyen de parvenir* was more emulated than imitated. Balzac, however, had not forgotten the lurid vistas contrived by the Gothic novel. No book haunted him more than *Melmoth the Wanderer,* that bizarre and episodic medley of thriller and sermon, by the Reverend Charles Maturin. Its Byronic hero-villain, an Anglo-Irish squire, found many reasons to repent of his pact with the devil, but could not die in peace until some one else was willing to exchange his hope of salvation for Melmoth's supernatural powers. Balzac's cynical epilogue, *Melmoth réconcilié,* conveys the aged wanderer to Paris, where his dubious bargain is snapped up at once by the cashier of the Nucingen bank. There the combination to the vault is like the "Open Sesame!" of the *Arabian Nights;* souls circulate, like bills, at increasing discounts, on the stock-exchange; "the principle of honor is replaced by the principle of money."

Melmoth réconcilié, slight and neglected though it be, is strategic in Balzac's development, since it reconciles fantasy with fact. Up to a certain phase, he can still be regarded as a rival of Charles Nodier, a professed imitator of E. T. A. Hoffmann, a specialist in the grotesque and the arabesque. Some of his short stories bear a striking resemblance to Poe's: compare *La Grande Bréteche* with

"The Cask of Amontillado." But motiveless suspense is never sufficient for Balzac; here he motivates the denouement with both
sexual intrigue and religious irony. The underlying duality of his
genius, his alternating dependence on observation and imagination,
was pointed out by Philarète Chasles and amplified by Sainte-
Beuve. To take Balzac at his face value was to regard him as an
observer and analyst; his romantic contemporaries, like Gautier
and Baudelaire, chose to emphasize his visionary side. They considered him to be, like Louis Lambert, a *voyant*. The brothers
Goncourt, carrying this view to the extreme, describe him as a
somnambulist. Yet if he was dreaming, he kept his eyes open; his
hallucinations are distinguished by circumstantial exactitude and
pictorial concreteness. "My sole ambition has been to see," says
his emissary in *La Peau de chagrin*, "Voir n'est-ce pas savoir?" Seeing is knowing; and believing is seeing, when the mind can project
its beliefs into such vivid imaginings, when the inward eye becomes
a camera eye, focussed on outer phenomena. Scores of anecdotes
vouch for his absorption in the imaginary lives of his characters:
"Let us get back to reality; let us talk about Eugénie Grandet." Or
again, the dying request: "Consult Doctor Bianchon." He did not
seem to be escaping from the concerns of his fellow men, but
rather to be pursuing them with a special concentration. With no
responsibilities but debts and no means of expression but writing,
he had just enough worldly intercourse to substantiate his dreams
and not enough to satisfy his appetites. That he created a vicarious
world is not surprising. The surprise is that it should correspond
so elaborately with the actual world.

To what extent the foremost of the realists was in touch with
reality is obviously the decisive question: what is historicity, what
is phantasma? Psychologically it is also a delicate question, the
investigation of which has revealed too little beyond the preconceptions of Balzac's critics. Sociologically we are on somewhat
firmer ground, since it is the ground that Balzac himself has chosen.
Since he so proudly boasted of competing with the civil registry,
since historians speak of his "demographic authenticity," Pierre
Abraham is justified in tabulating a statistical analysis of the population of the *Comédie humaine*. In stature, pigmentation, and
other physical traits, they differ exceedingly from what anthro-
pometrists might expect of a few thousand French men and women.

In fact, as ordinary readers might expect, the exceptions tend to overbalance the norms. Balzac tends, like any journalist, to take the average for granted and to play up the angles. His account of daily life is exaggerated, like that of any newspaper. Furthermore, in his busier moments, he is likely to substitute bookish clichés for independent observations. This, of course, is what all romancers are licensed to do; but it impairs his pretensions as an archivist. As a pathologist, a physician reports, Balzac's expertise is "une pathologie romancée." Extensive as his command of the law may seem to laymen, to lawyers he is a "juriste romantique." Countless dissertations and monographs have retraversed his topography, and assiduously verified his backgrounds. While the academic sense of reality is not to be identified with the absolute, it guarantees the substantial accuracy and completeness of Balzac's realism on the guidebook level. On the more complex levels of human behavior, we are forced to admit that some of his personages are more readily encountered in books than in the streets. Of them Howells has remarked: "Balzac, when he imagined these monsters, was not Balzac, he was Dumas; he was not realistic, he was romantic."

But the author of *The Rise of Silas Lapham* begs the question. His own kind of realism, the notation of the normal, "the truthful treatment of material," was inconceivable to Balzac. There was then no ready-made alternative to Dumas; there was only the method that Balzac finally achieved. Both writers had started with conventional equipment, an equipment designed for pleasantly adventurous sorties into a romanticized past, and Balzac's problem was to utilize this for the treatment of contemporary society. How he solved it is suggested by Croce's remark that Balzac set the Three Musketeers up in business, endowing his inventors and investors with the spirit of d'Artagnan and his dashing companions. By presenting these creatures of romance against a realistic setting, he approximated "le romanesque réel que présente notre société." Life itself was inextricably mingling "those elements of the epic, the marvellous and the true." Chimeras were changing into realities, as the *Avant-propos* announces; the scientists were outstripping the romanticists. There are times when a grasp of the facts requires an exercise of the imagination, when inventive energies must be measured by wildcat schemes and coffee-drugged fantasies. Though Balzac's projected novel *L'Histoire et le roman* was never written, we may safely assume that it would have been another illustration of his major premise, that truth is stranger than fiction. The local colorists were calling attention to the dramatic aspects of everyday existence; they went so far as to seek among the common people for heroes and heroines of Shakespearean stature. Russia, for example, would reveal itself in A *Hamlet of the Shchigri District* or A *Lady Macbeth of Mtsensk*. Turgenev was to rediscover King Lear on the Russian steppes, as Balzac had already rediscovered him at a French *pension* in the person of a retired noodle manufacturer, Jean-Joachim Goriot.

Balzac, we have noted, is fond of providing his characters with literary precedents. His is not the traditional formula of anti-romance, though he pauses to parody the Radcliffian novel in *La Muse du département*. Habitually, instead of appealing to realism against romanticism, his technique is to romanticize reality: to make the vulgar illustrious rather than to mock the heroic. Like Tartarin, he combines Don Quixote with Sancho Panza. Unlike the deflationary Stendhal, Balzac is in style and temperament an inflationist; he puffs up everything he touches, heightens the commonplace, distorts for effect. The resulting perspective, in its grotesquerie, is akin to such tragicomic street scenes as Gogol's Nevsky Prospekt or Dickens' Chancery Lane. Its feeble imitation is the attempt to convert sordidness into quaintness, as in Murger's *Scènes de la vie de Bohème*—the very title an echo of Balzac's scenes from life. Its end-product is the prefabricated fiction of that Broadway Balzac, O. Henry. The secret of the real Balzac's clairvoyance is a genuine and unflagging curiosity about the lives of others. When he was shown a certain painting, Baudelaire tells us, he exclaimed: "How lovely it is! But what are they doing in that hut? What do they think about, what are their troubles? Have the crops been good? No doubt they have bills to pay." Here, where the shoe pinches, is the Balzacian touch. Bills become as universal as crops, as fateful as death and taxes. A writer whose researches are ways of dramatizing his doctrines cannot be very much of an empiricist; but there is a point in Balzac when life and work, observation and imagination coalesce—the point where the bills come in. "He has learned everything, both good and evil, from the observation of facts or the contemplation of ideas, not at all from experience." So George Sand testifies, forgetting the crucial experience that Balzac could never forget. And since, in a capitalist economy, the dread of insolvency is almost as powerful as the love of money, he may be said to have undergone the cycle of his age.

If—as the dollar-conscious James, among others, has said—the protagonist of the *Comédie humaine* is the twenty-franc piece, it is rather the villain than the hero; its ubiquitous and diabolical fascination, rather than any set of proclaimed principles, is Balzac's *moteur social*. The Golden Calf has indeed usurped the altar and the throne. Behind the dynasts and statesmen stand the bankers and business men, and behind them—in the very back-room of society—sits the money-lender Gobseck, flashing the mesmeric glance of the Wandering Jew and convulsed with the soundless laughter of Leatherstocking. Given Balzac's careful habits of nomenclature, the very name could mean "gulp-dry," *gobe-sec*. Passions, "aggrandized by the play of social interests," parade before Gobseck; financial experience has qualified him for "the penetration of all the springs that move humanity." Believing in nothing, he is still a poet; for he comprehends the significance of millions, contemplates the cities and peoples of the earth, and commands— like Marlowe's Barabas—"infinite riches in a little room." After his profit has been duly deducted, he retains a harsh integrity, which he vindicates by saving the fortune of the Restauds from the depredations of Goriot's daughter, now the dowager Countess. He is the Balzacian devil's advocate, the spokesman of the franc, the Vergilian guide through the fiscal inferno. "Keep your illusions if you can," he advises Derville, then a hopeful novice of the law. "I will subtract the discount from life for you." Thereupon he translates the *moeurs* into a handful of trenchant maxims. Moral convictions are valueless phrases; the only valid instinct is self-interest. "Man is the same everywhere. Everywhere the battle between the rich and the poor is entrenched; everywhere it is inevitable. Hence it is better to be the exploiter than the exploited . . ." Everywhere the ego, all is vanity. "Power and pleasure sum up your whole social order." It is money that operates the machinery of life. "Gold contains everything in essence, and gives everything in reality."

The sharp theories of Gobseck, put into sharp practice, supply the plots for dozens of Balzac's other stories. We have recognized that *Le Père Goriot* seeks to be a bourgeois redaction of *King Lear*.

But how can so lofty a tragedy be transposed to the middle plane? The answer is indicated by a jotting from Balzac's notes: "A fine man—middle-class boarding-house—600 francs income—despoiled by his daughters who both have 50,000 francs income, dying like a dog." From this meager basis, mostly economic, the plot ramifies into a series of transactions, as carefully audited as Birotteau's. What is lacking is not only grandeur but compassion, which revisited Shakespeare's Lear in the person of a third daughter, painfully absent here. The dying Goriot concludes that "money is life"; the miser Grandet assumes that "life is a business." In the business of exploitation, where Père Goriot is one of the plotted against, Père Grandet is one of the plotters. His name could be an anagram of *d'argent*; his philosophy is Bentham's theory of interest; his Midas-touch turns everything into francs and centimes. "Poor young man," cries Madame Grandet, when their nephew's ruined father commits suicide. "Yes, poor," agrees Grandet. "He hasn't a sou." If *Eugénie Grandet* were a comedy like *L'Avare*, the poor young man would end by marrying his rich young cousin. Nor is it a tragedy for Eugénie, since she remains untouched by the means of corruption: the portagues, genovines, Dutch ducats, double Napoleons, and rupees of the Grand Mogul. Her quiet firmness, through the long ordeal of the provincial years, makes her the moral antithesis of Emma Bovary, and explains why Flaubert— who was no great admirer of Balzac—held a high opinion of this novel. The really tragic figure is the poor young man, grown rich and corrupt in the Indian slave trade, jilting his cousin and the values she preserves. "He perceived that the best means of attaining fortune, in the tropical regions as well as in Europe, was to buy and sell men."

Going beyond the classical or biblical premise that money is the root of evil, Balzac chronicles—in terms of its impact on hundreds of private lives—the growth and ramification and flowering and blight of capitalism. Swaying with the satirist's ambivalence, he seems to enjoy the cake he renounces, to revel in what he condemns—in Nucingen's deals and Gaudissart's bargains, in Grandet's hoard and Gobseck's usury. When John Ruskin asserted that "a miser cannot sing of his lost money," he was overlooking the lyric rapture that coin of the realm could awaken in Balzac. This lyricism, like the romantic prose of our advertising agencies, parodies itself; it inflates itself, like Ben Jonson's verse, in order to become satire. The art-dealer boasts, in *La Peau de chagrin,* pointing at Raphael's Christ, "I have covered this canvas with gold-pieces." And, under that blasphemous implication, the whole antique-shop depreciates; the jumbled inheritance of the ages is worth no more than a Russian kopek or a Scotch farthing or a Levantine piastre. A sequel, *L'Auberge rouge,* reaching back into the career of the millionaire Taillefer, uncovers a murder at the base of his fortunes, and implies that such wealth is tainted with original sin. As for poverty, it is always with us, and the odds that favor the exploiter disappoint the exploited. Madame Descoings, in *La Rabouilleuse,* plays the same lottery number for twenty years, and is robbed on the day it turns up. The religion of Louis-Philippe's charter, which takes nothing into consideration except property, enshrines the money-changers in their temple, the Bourse, and sanctifies a thriving traffic in bodies and souls. So long as values are pegged to the gold standard, taste is ruled by pecuniary canons. Balzac's shrewd insight affixes to everything its plainly marked price-tag. The cost of passion can be computed in cab fares and tailor bills.

"Gradually the ideas of exchange, of devaluation, of inflation invaded his book . . . where they usurped the place of the characters." These words are André Gide's, referring to *Les Faux-monnayeurs,* and to the final discounting of the debased coinage against which Balzac had warned his contemporaries. He had regretted that property, "the most vividly materialized of human ideas," should be the sole remaining bond between man and man. The running inventory, the interior decoration, the insistent materialism, the visual and audible and tangible and olfactory and gustatory detail of the *Comédie humaine* are his means of subtracting the realistic discount from the gross exaggerations of romance. Attaching as much importance to things as to men and women is his most devastating innovation. "He narrates the ornaments of the chimney-piece, the clock and the candelabra, and they live with strange intensity. . . ," George Moore observes. "There is life in Balzac's hats and neckties." The Goncourts had accused him of paying more heed to furniture than to people. If the story seems strained in *La Fille aux yeux d'or,* it may be looked upon as an abstract painting in golds and whites and reds. Things are virtually human; humans, on the other hand, are enslaved to their goods and chattels—a lesson from Balzac which Henry James studiously applies in *The Spoils of Poynton*. Balzac himself was an impassioned collector of bric-a-brac, and some of his prized possessions are catalogued with the collection of Cousin Pons. Like the predatory animals of Jonson's *Volpone*, or—in Balzac's reductive simile —like crows around a corpse, the presumptive heirs flock to the old musician's deathbed. After his third-class funeral, a salesman palms off a tombstone on Pons's faithful colleague Schmucke. Its three allegorical figures, designed to mark the grave of a politician, were supposed to represent the Glorious Days; proposed again, and again rejected as a monument to a banker, they served as the Army, Finance, and the Family; now, for the poor relation, they are Music, Painting, and Sculpture. And *Le Cousin Pons*, the last novel Balzac completed, is his mordant allegory of the destiny of the arts in a commercial civilization.

Flaubert foresaw that Balzac's methods of literal representation —"a novel on chemistry, another on banking, another on the printing press"—would sooner or later reduce novels to monographs. "We shall have them on every trade and on all the provinces, then on all the towns and on the floors of each house and on each individual—which will no longer be literature but statistics and ethnography." Conversely, no writer would be able to stray beyond his first-hand sphere of reportage without running the risks of journalistic superficiality. Balzac, having taken all society for his province, proves to be less versatile than his pretensions; his documentation falls necessarily short of his program. His visits to battlefields did not result in any full-scale depiction of war. Even his scenes from political life, contrasted with Stendhal's, redound to the advantage of the *livre vécu*. Out of Balzac's disappointments as a candidate, he painted an unfinished picture of carpet-baggers and rotten boroughs in *Le Député d'Arcis*; but his statesmen are not nearly so convincing as his business men. We take it on faith that Henri de Marsay has been, or will become, prime minister, but whenever we meet him, in the pages of the *Comédie humaine*, he is merely engaged in gossiping or philandering. Faults have been found in Balzac's presentation of the upper classes: his fashionable milieux are unexpectedly vague or incredibly flamboyant. It is with the middle class that he is thoroughly at home, and that realism lavishes its gifts on its favorite subject. Though he proposed to set

forth the multifarious aspects of "social man," he is more concerned with the tactics of enrichment than with the conditions of
poverty. The lower class is even more remote from him than the
upper: not the proletarian slums, but the lowest depths of the
underworld solicit the romanticist in Balzac. He shares Stendhal's
preoccupation with the criminal, and Baudelaire's with the prostitute as well. There is still room, in the interstices between his pavements, for flowers to spring up or abysses to open. He is enticed
by "the poetry of evil."

The devil in the machine is Jacques Collin, alias Vautrin, alias
Trompe-la-Mort, alias the Abbé Carlos Herrera, who emerges from
these incarnations as the most dynamic and yet elusive character
in the *Comédie humaine*. When everyone is a villain, more or less,
the arch-villain becomes the hero. Vautrin, as François Mauriac
notices, has shouldered Goriot out of the leading part, thereby
shifting the drama from age to youth, and from Goriot's agony
to Rastignac's temptation. In paying his respects to the romantic
outlaw, Balzac out-Herods his contemporaries and himself. He exhausts the repertory of demonic analogies, from Satan and Cain
to Robespierre and Napoleon. Vautrin is quite literally a marked
man; for when the police strip the shirt from his shoulders, the
brand of the galleys is revealed. He is also a poet who acts out his
poems, an artist in crime as Molière is in literature and Cuvier in
science. As a philosopher, he is a disciple of Rousseau, protesting
against the infractions of the social contract. Balzac is less concerned with a credible characterization than with a sinister influence, with the devil's bargains that waylay ambitious young men;
yet there is more than a hint of homosexuality in Vautrin's pater-
nalistic surveillance of Rastignac, Rubempré, and other protegés.
It is in the cards that the reformed convict will go over to the
police, and emerge as head of the Sûreté Générale, since Balzac
has been following the adventures of the famous detective, Vidocq.
Both Stendhal's Valbayre and Hugo's Valjean were similarly influenced by Vidocq's memoirs. Balzac, too, may have been impressed by the Count de Saint-Hélène, the original of Dumas'
Monte-Cristo. A significant conversation is on record, in which
Vidocq taxed Balzac with evading reality. "It is we who create
reality," retorted the novelist. Certainly he preferred his own creations to the commonly accepted versions of it, as he showed by

rushing into the notorious Affaire Peytel. There we behold the realist setting aside the sordid and obvious motives for the crime, advancing a farfetched and highly colored explanation of his own, and convincing nobody that the accused was not guilty of murdering his wife.

As we pass from the upper and middle worlds into Balzac's underworld, the tragic emotions and the comic machinations are interlocked in melodrama. Good and evil, no longer present as ethical alternatives, are hypostasized into secret societies of not very human beings: either benefactors, like the Confrérie de la Consolation in L'Envers de l'historie contemporaine, or—more typically—malefactors, like the Dévorants in the Histoire des Treize. Balzac's suspicious mind, forever deducing causes from effects, traces upheavals to subterranean agencies. Agents and spies are endlessly machinating behind the scenes of the Comédie humaine. Its plots are plots in more than one sense. As the mere task of probing their complications, by deductive methods, becomes an end in itself, Balzac is pushed, like Dickens, in the direction of the detective story; his logical successors are Gaboriau, Ponson du Terrail, and the perpetrators of the roman policier. The mystery of Une Ténébreuse Affaire is overshadowed by the shady genius of Fouché; royalists and Bonapartists alike are double-crossed by the police. The all-seeing and all-knowing policeman is eulogized, in language reminiscent of Maistre's panegyric on the hangman, at the conclusion of Les Petits Bourgeois; although this passage was probably added by Balzac's collaborator, Charles Rabou, Balzac had shown himself an old admirer of the guillotine. Finally, above the fallen dynasties and the corrupted bourgeoisie, looms the survival of sheer amoral power. When Balzac's arch-criminal turns out to be the final incarnation of law and order, when Vautrin's theatrical disguise is the full uniform of Louis-Philippe, values are completely overturned; the peace is kept and the throne is occupied, it is implied, by thieves. Lawyers and bankers are classified with pickpockets and highwaymen, in Balzac's youthful lampoon, Code des gens honnêtes. He supports, with unexpected authority, the sweeping declaration of the socialist Proudhon that property is theft.

Elements of the factual and the fictitious are so mixed in Balzac's writing that it is never quite certain which will prevail. Some of his later fiction is even more sensational than his *Oeuvres de jeunesse*. The progress of his realism was retarded by the competition of such popular romanticists as Dumas and Sue; public apathy persuaded him to abandon the hard actualities of *Les Paysans* for the easy excitations of *Splendeurs et misères des courtisanes*; his interest in the underworld waxed as his hope for the good society waned. But pornography is by no means excluded from the range of his serious thought. "Prostitution and theft are two living protests, male and female, of the natural state against the social state." Through the darker and dimmer regions of the picaresque and the rocambolesque, we struggle back into the glaring light of comedy; we particularize the generalization that everything has its price, that at heart every man is a thief and every woman a whore, that the *haut monde* is no better than the *demi-monde*. Balzac is better at portraying the fundamental sluttishness of the *grande dame* than at exhibiting the virtuous harlot; his Esthers and Coralies are pallid sisters to Marion Delorme and Sonia Marmeladova. *Les Marana* argues the superiority of a courtesan to her bourgeois husband. *La Cousine Bette* is dominated by the adventuress Valérie Marneffe, whose seductive role is the feminine counterpart of Vautrin's and whose path is strewn with broken families, wasted talents, and spent fortunes. On the other hand we have Adeline Hulot, a paragon of virtue, indignantly rejecting the advances of the boorish Crevel, who resembles a provincial comedian in the role of Tartuffe. But when her husband is ruined by Madame Marneffe, Madame Hulot is compelled to play the seductress—an inept and pitiful performance which offers Crevel his revenge. Rejecting her plea and offer, he returns to his old mistress, Valérie, and the climactic scene is Valérie's. She plays it with her most cloying wiles, then suddenly interrupts herself to subtract the discount, and—here our cheap cynicism echoes Balzac's dearly bought shrewdness—this is the pay-off:

> Madame Marneffe left Crevel and knelt again before her chair, clasping her hands in a ravishing posture and repeating with unbelievable unction this prayer: "Ah, Saint Valérie, my kind patron, why don't you visit the bedside of your entrusted child more often? Oh, come this evening, as you came this morning, to inspire me with virtuous thoughts, and I shall leave these evil paths; like Mary

Magdalene I shall renounce the misleading delights, the false attractions of the world—even the one I love so much!"

"Sweetheart," said Crevel.

"Sweetheart no longer, sir!" She turned proudly, like a virtuous woman, and, her eyes wet with tears, she seemed dignified, cold, indifferent. "Leave me," she said, pushing Crevel away. "What is my duty? To belong to my husband. That man is dying, and what am I doing? I am deceiving him on the brink of the grave. He believes your son is his. I am going to tell him the truth, first asking his pardon and then God's. Let us part. Goodbye, M. Crevel," she repeated, rising and holding out an icy hand. "Goodbye, my friend, we shall not see each other until we meet in a better world. You have given me some inexcusable pleasures; now I want—yes, I shall have—your respect."

Crevel was weeping warm tears.

"You big oaf," she shrieked, breaking out in infernal laughter. "That's the way these pious women go about it, to wheedle you out of two hundred thousand francs!"

4. The Thirty-third Mandarin

The weakness of the demiurge or megalomaniac, when he takes the trouble to superimpose a cosmos upon his private share of the public chaos, is that he wants to create a better world, an unrecognizable utopia, a fool's paradise. It is here that Balzac exhibits his strength, by creating a microcosm which—if anything—is rather worse than this world. Exact reproduction, except in such simple matters as stage properties and scenic effects, is impractical; what the realist must do is to stir his readers out of their preconceived and conventional worlds, if necessary by darkening his pictures and exaggerating his strokes, with the murk of Doré and the sweep of Delacroix. Romanticism thus contributes to realism in the sense that commonplace reality does not, in the Aristotelian sense that poetry is more philosophic than history. Which, philosophically speaking, is the true Balzac: the porcine face that stares myopically

out of Nadar's daguerreotype, or the leonine head that tosses restlessly back from Rodin's colossus? The artist in Balzac, taking his
cue from the moralist, goes beyond the scientist and the business
man. When he transubstantiates values into prices, he is not selling out; he is harshly reminding us that there are other standards
than gold. For a man who could never make both ends meet, who
was capable of making a dowerless marriage, whose intellectual
appetites were as vast and undiscriminating as his literary energies,
there were more important things than money—or, at any rate,
there should have been. What should be, of course, is the province
of moralists, such as Thomas Carlyle. But when Carlyle points the
moral of the French Revolution or the Middle Ages, when he
preaches hero-worship or the gospel of work, he is adorning a tale
which Balzac has already told. And Balzac has graphically illustrated Carlyle's strongest contention: that the laissez-faire society
of industrial capitalism discounts all obligations except the cash
nexus.

It is Balzac's zeal for tracing financial relationships that links
cause to effect, plot to character, and volume to volume in the
Comédie humaine. Although "the great social force is character,"
it can only be activated by material forces. Hence sociology comes
first and last for Balzac, with psychology crowded in between. "Tell
me what you have and I will tell you what you think." Property
conditions thought and thought produces action. Balzac begins by
telling us what his characters have; their incomes and addresses,
their houses and furnishings, their clothes and accessories, their
bodies and faces are chosen to fit with unique propriety. He then
tells us what they think, with special reference to the pseudo-sci-
ences of mesmerism and phrenology, which provide him with the
easiest and most external means of characterization. The influence
of one personality upon another—for example, of Vautrin upon
Rubempré—is explained away by a kind of hypnosis; and psychological characteristics are manifested through their corresponding
physical traits, such as Goriot's hypertrophied bump of paternity.
Emotions are so externalized that ladies not infrequently die of
love, and fortunes are predetermined by physiognomies. The comic
decorum of every man in his humor is preserved by type-casting,
and by salting the dialogue with *mots de caractère*. "You are too
much of a Marneffe, M. Marneffe," says Baron Hulot. A few pages

afterward, when the blackmailing husband has gained the upper hand, he retorts, "You are too much of an Hulot, M. Hulot." So it might be said, of all Balzac's characters, that they are rather too insistently themselves. This egoistic insistence, by selecting in each case the prime specimen of a class, animates a series of stock types with Balzac's driving megalomania. All of them, says Maurice Bardèche, are *avares* and *absents:* avid for something and absent-minded about everything else. Everyone, it would seem, is a nonpareil. "Even the concierges," Baudelaire averred, "have genius."

Balzac describes his method as "individualizing the type and typifying the individual," as lending concreteness to abstractions in the *Etudes philosophiques* and lending generality to particulars in the *Etudes de moeurs.* More often than not he proceeds deductively, starting from first principles and picking up incidental details. In *Une Fille d'Eve,* having mentioned the "secret saturnalia of literature and art mingled with politics and finance," where "Desire reigned as a sovereign" and "Spleen and Fantasy were sacred," he proceeds to list the guests, filling in each category with its appropriate representatives. He recruits his cast from the virtues and vices, the talents and interests, by a process of personification. When he characterizes a stalwart peasant as "the Milo of Crotona of the valley," or Vautrin as "the Cromwell of the prison," or Goriot as "the Christ of paternity," he may be establishing what Arnold Bennett termed a "frame of conventionalization." He may, as Ernst Robert Curtius suggested, be attributing the most diversified forms of human experience to the same primordial energy. He is also asserting the timelessness of certain historic patterns and moral problems. Concurrently, he is adapting them to his own time. As his work accumulates and his scope enlarges, he discovers objects of comparison in his previous books, and introduces his own creations side by side with the real people in the walk-on parts. Not Talleyrand but Gondreville becomes his byword for political intrigue; not Don Juan but Maxime de Trailles is the paragon of erotic dalliance. Balzac, in sum, has created his own mythology, fixing the archetypes of literature and affecting the conventions of society for many years to come. Jules Vallès has left a vivid account of the impression Balzac made upon a younger generation whose Amadís de Gaul was Vautrin, whose ambition was to succeed in everything and believe in nothing, who wanted decorations in their buttonholes, duchesses in their arms, and millions in their bank-accounts.

Whether we choose to regard Balzac as a creator of myths, as-signing a tutelary genius to every sphere, or as a compiler of statis-tics, competing with the civil registry, it is not the individuality but the typicality of his characters that stays with us. They do not seem to step out of his books and into our lives, like some of the memorable characters in fiction. Rather it is we who remain de-tached, while they become increasingly involved in the trammels of circumstance; but circumstance is so many-sided and far-reach-ing that it transcends the limits of any single volume; and it is here that Balzac introduces what Michel Butor would call his principle of artistic economy. The brilliant device that integrates Balzac's volumes, the *retour des personnages*, cannot be called his invention; it is as old as the first writer who hit upon a success and wrote a sequel; it may even have been suggested to Balzac by the reappearances of Leatherstocking through five of Cooper's novels. But heretofore no novelist had made it an instrument for catching the facets of personality, for recording the passage of years, for registering the shifts and compromises and realignments that inter-relate a series of careers. If psychology added a third dimension to the flat, old-fashioned technique of characterization, Balzac's sys-tem of cross-reference added a fourth—the dimension of time and change and growth in which Proust was to move. This discovery was first utilized in *Le Père Goriot*, which gathers up the loose ends of preceding stories and plants the presuppositions for further ones. It proved so suggestive that it seems to have been largely responsible for the extraordinary fruitfulness of Balzac's next few years. It provided him with a backlog for his dramatis personae; each minor character demanded a larger part in a new story. *César Birotteau* makes use of 104 reappearing characters and *Illusions perdues* of 116, by Miss Ethel Preston's computation. With *Splen-deurs et misères* no fewer than 155 old friends put in an appear-ance, crowding the novel into shapelessness.

Here the law of diminishing returns sets in, and Balzac, drawing less upon his stock-company for his later productions, replenishes his personnel. *Les Parents pauvres*, comprising his two maturest novels, came along almost as an afterthought: neither *La Cousine Bette* nor *Le Cousin Pons* had a place in his original plan. They are more self-contained than the earlier installments of the *Comédie humaine*, which are designedly fragmentary and interdependent. Though Balzac recapitulates and moralizes, he seldom commences or concludes; he is always, like life itself, in the midst of things. Thus *Le Père Goriot* presupposes *Gobseck* and *L'Auberge rouge*, and is consummated by *La Maison Nucingen* and *Splendeurs et misères des courtisanes*. And thus, because its continuing interrelationships are more significant than its characters in any given situation, the whole of Balzac's work is greater than the sum of its parts. It is no more than a coincidence that both the alchemist Claës and the perfumer Birotteau should purchase their supplies from the same chemical firm. To recognize Birotteau's brother in the title role of *Le Curé de Tours* does little more, perhaps, than underline the generalization that the world is small indeed. But to observe that Eugénie Grandet's lover was swindled by the very notary who precipitated Birotteau's bankruptcy is to score a Balzacian point. To follow the rise of Birotteau's successor, Célestin Crevel, is to realize the decay of bourgeois standards between the Napoleonic generation and the 1840's. And it is statistically impressive that the largest number of *retours*—thirty-one—is made by the arch-financier, the Baron de Nucingen. "Do you know whom Félix de Vandenesse is marrying?" Balzac once asked his sister. "One of the Granville girls. He is making a fine match. The Granvilles are wealthy, in spite of what that Mlle de Bellefeuille has cost the family." The reader can watch the outcome of this marriage in *Une Fille d'Eve*; he may trace the gossip to *Une Double Famille*; he will remember Félix's first love from *Le Lys dans la vallée*, and piece together Granville's legal career from half a dozen other novels.

There are many possible sequences for reading Balzac. To plunge in somewhere, to try again elsewhere, putting two and two together, accumulating impressions and implications, is to approach the conditions of actual experience, more immediately than in the usual narrative sequence where the middle is limited by the beginning and end. *Les Misérables*, by contrast, is a thin piece of work, thickened by rhetorical and theatrical devices: every other person turns out to be the detective Thénardier in disguise. Balzac's advantage is grounded on the multiplicity and consistency of his characters. His cross-references, biographically rearranged and alphabetically catalogued by Cerfbeer and Christophe, and more recently by M. Lotte, form a *répertoire* which is scarcely less fascinating or convincing than Who's Who? Character is stamped, in each instance, by acts and affiliations, by words rather than by thoughts. Except on a behavioristic plane, it cannot be maintained that Balzac's extroverts offer much opportunity for psychological exploration. Taine's metaphor is crude but not inappropriate when he sums them up as pedestals, on which the respective passions are poised like statues. In statuesque repose, in static arrangement, they would be heavy and lifeless; they are brought to life by the interplay of dynamic energies. Balzac's method, to use his own metaphor, is physiological rather than anatomical; he is more concerned with movement than with form. His books are intricately geared together in order to convey a sense of movement, which in turn conveys the social mobility of the epoch. An apprentice attains the Bourse, a streetwalker the Opera. An inventor goes bankrupt, a *grande dame* is seduced. The poet is in debt to the tradesman, who is in debt to the banker, we read in one book; the banker is in love with the courtesan, who is in love with the poet, we read in the next volume. Everything moves in vicious circles, but it keeps moving.

The philosopher of motion, Louis Lambert, investigates the chemistry of the will. The *Avant-propos* sweepingly asseverates that "passion is all humanity." Passion and will, which are as closely identified with bodily mechanisms as they are in the James-Lange theory of the emotions, function as response and stimulus in the Balzacian psychology. Will is a kind of avarice or concupiscence, depending upon the nature of its object. Passion is motivated by the object's magnetic attraction. When this motivation is unworldly, artistic or scientific, it usually leads to monomania; when it has a material basis, it is usually connected with money or sex. Business connections are the usual link between Balzac's personages because business, as the younger Dumas was to note, is "other people's money." Balzac's mode of analysis, equating self-interest with financial interest, simply ascribes the profit motive—*Vous êtes orfèvre, Monsieur Josse*—to the butcher, the baker, the candlestick-maker and every other calling. As for the alternate connection, the sexual liaison, it is even more universal, and therefore less characteristic of Balzac. It is the major premise in the *Contes drolatiques,* where the joke reduces everything to a common denominator of carnality, and the minor premise in the *Comédie humaine,* where finance is the major. Yet the affairs of the Princesse de Cadignan are no less a cross section of society than the affairs of the Baron de Nucingen. Where marriage itself is a transaction, as in *Le Contrat de mariage,* adultery becomes the natural relationship between the sexes, and a scandalously high proportion of Balzac's characters are born out of wedlock. Marriage is treated sociologically, sex physiologically, and a psychological treatment of love completes the triangle in *Le Lys dans la vallée.* This is Balzac's exacerbated commentary on the bloodless Platonism of Sainte-Beuve's *Volupté.* The romance of Félix de Vandenesse with the Countess de Mortsauf is as idyllic as Petrarch's with Laura. But the repressed passion reveals itself at her deathbed, and this model of virtuous womanhood dies with ghastly coquetries and obscene imprecations on her lips.

All women, to the lover of Eveline Hanska, were daughters of Eve, from the romantic schoolgirl Modeste Mignon to the *sandiste* writer Camille Maupin. The habit of elopement, in *La Femme de trente ans,* is handed down from mother to daughter. Frequently Balzac protests against Scott's virginal heroines: the chill of the Protestant North, he feels, is upon them. Thackeray might archly overlook the open secret of Becky Sharp's charm, referring to her as "that wretched woman," and apologizing for the scales of the mermaid beneath the surface of the water; but Balzac, and along with him Taine, was frankly swept off his feet by Valérie Marneffe. She is the real protagonist of *La Cousine Bette.* Her accomplice, Lisbeth Fischer, is much deadlier than the masculine "poor relation," Silvain Pons; she is the grasping peasant, the smouldering artisan, "Hatred and Vengeance" personified, "the Mohican whose snares are inevitable." But these snares are set through the gold-digging maneuvers of Valérie. The comic scene in which Valérie's two middle-aged suitors, Crevel and Hulot, are locked out in the street together is as grimly passionate as that tragic scene in *The Idiot* where Myshkin and Rogozhin are found with the body of Nastasya Filippovna. After Valérie has married Crevel, a terrible retribution overtakes them; yet even at the last stages of a leprous disease, she runs true to type, in her confidence that she will be able to "get around God." Her principal victim, the Baron Hulot d'Ervy, survives his dyed whiskers and cast-off corsets, his costly philanderings and fraudulent army contracts, the very ruin of his family, to descend with each successive mistress into a lower circle of sensual degradation. To bring home the object-lesson, by way of Plutarchan parallel, we recognize in his brother, old Marshal Hulot, the stern young revolutionary soldier of *Les Chouans*.

As the prodigal father, Baron Hulot stands at the apex of that inverted pyramid which represents, for Balzac and Bonald, an overturned social hierarchy. "Society—the world—revolves around fatherhood," exclaims Père Goriot, who is plainly obsessed with his role as a latter-day Lear, and whose abject paternalism does not stop short at playing the pander for his daughters. "Everything collapses if children do not love their parents." His daughters are too busy to attend his deathbed, and his landlady is too stingy to waste clean sheets upon a dying man. Nothing could indicate more sharply than these grim death-watches, in which Balzac seems to delight, the displacement of family ties by the bonds of interest—particularly when, as in *Ursule Mirouët* or *Le Cousin Pons*, the heirs fall out over the will. *Martin Chuzzlewit* is comparatively benign in this respect. Concentrating each set of his *études* upon a different age group, Balzac was already aware of the tension that would be felt between the generations in the second half of the century. If the fathers had eaten sour grapes, what could be expected of the sons? The unprincipled opportunism of Henri II's maxim: "There is no such thing as absolute virtue; there are only circumstances." *L'Elixir de longue vie* is concocted out of patricide; the unfilial hero-villain, Don Juan, like Faust or Melmoth or Mirabeau or Bonaparte, is an image of evil, more specifically of the individualism that disintegrates families. As he canvasses the ranks and niches of society, discovering no sanction except the economic, Balzac's heart goes out to the unattached and the celibate, the old maid or the elderly bachelor, victims of worldly intrigue like the good-natured Abbé Birotteau or the pathetic slavey Pierrette. His Niobe-like mothers, the Countess de Dey in *Le Réquisitionnaire* or the widow Bridau in *La Rabouilleuse*, mourn for the children of the century.

His real protagonists are the *enfants du siècle*, the young lions. The main direction of the *Comédie humaine* is pointed by their careers, contemporary and concurrent with his own. The mediocrities, like Oscar Husson in *Un Début dans la vie*, live down their legal and military escapades to become solid citizens. "C'est enfin le bourgeois moderne," Balzac breaks off with a shrug. A high-principled and highly competent public servant, like Xavier Rabourdin in *Les Employés*, is quite exceptional; his reward is to see incompetents and intriguers promoted over his head. The self-effacing Z. Marcas, his brains picked by unscrupulous politicians, dies prematurely and obscurely. His legacy is a Stendhalian warning: "Pent-up youth will burst out like the boiler of a steam engine." As long as the regime can buy off the rising talents, however, that explosion will be postponed; the mounting pressures will be controlled by what Dr. Benassis calls for, "a perpetual pact among those who possess against those who do not possess." Two voices beset Lucien de Rubempré on the road to Paris. "Intelligence is the lever that moves the world," cries one. But the other flatly declares that the prop of intelligence is money. And the young poet from the provinces, finding Paris a "lupanar of thought," is faced with the option of starving in a garret or coming to terms with the literary market. A candidate for posthumous honors, an Arthez or another of his *cénacle*, might choose the hard way; but Lucien's feet are soon on the primrose path. Having abandoned poetry for journalism, he soon abandons liberal principles for royalist bribes. The moral of *Splendeurs et misères des courtisanes* is that the talented writer who sells his mind prostitutes himself more abysmally than the pathetic women who sell their bodies on his behalf. As a devastating study in the ways and means of intellectual prostitution, *Illusions perdues* is still authoritative and still pertinent.

John Dos Passos has vividly restated the attractions and repulsions of *The Big Money* for the last generation of Americans. Balzac had the advantage of gauging these effects while they were freshly observable, and of appealing to an ethical code which had not been altogether upset by materialism. Stendhal, himself a materialist and a hedonist, could sympathize with his careerist heroes. Balzac's careerists engage our sympathies only through their failures; as they succeed, they become unsympathetic. When we first encounter Eugène de Rastignac, he is the hope of his mother and sisters, who have pawned their jewels that he may

study law. Two of his fellow boarders at the Pension Vauquer exert
their counter-influence upon his eager southern temperament, good
and bad angels wrestling over his soul. Vautrin tempts his ambition
by framing a duel which leaves Mademoiselle Taillefer an heiress,
but Rastignac is honest enough to reject this temptation. Goriot
offers love, but his daughters' rejection of his own love is an example which fosters egoism rather than altruism. A lone mourner
at Goriot's grave, Rastignac looks down from the cemetery of
Père-Lachaise as the lights begin to glitter along the banks of the
Seine. The column of the Place Vendôme and the cupola of the
Invalides define the ground he has chosen for his post-Napoleonic
duel with society. As he goes off to dine with the Baroness de
Nucingen, née Goriot, he utters his grandiose challenge: "A nous
deux maintenant." This open ending so unnerved the first American translator of *Father Goriot* that he demurely added: "The
reader may believe that Eugene returned to the Maison Vauquer
thoroughly cured of his fancy for Parisian high-life and female
patronage, and that in due time he married Victorine and took up
his abode in the provinces." Nothing could be less Balzacian.
Through Balzac's later volumes we catch glimpses of Rastignac's
social ascent and rake's progress; finally, in *La Maison Nucingen*,
he makes his killing in the shadiest of stock-market deals and marries the daughter of his old mistress, the Baroness. The political
side of his career seems to parallel that of Thiers, who began as a
radical leader in the Revolution of 1830, and would end—after putting down the Commune—as first president of the Third Republic.

One of Balzac's favorite walks, during his early explorations of
Paris, lay among the tombstones of Père-Lachaise. From the epi-
taphs he wryly inferred, in the preface to *Le Vicaire des Ardennes*,
that the city of the dead reverses the customs of the living metropolis; here, at any rate, husbands are honest and wives faithful. The
cemetery is therefore an appropriate setting for the reversal of
values, when Rastignac buries his lost illusions with Goriot and
dedicates himself to the main chance. In a case of conscience,
attributed to the master of modern casuistry, Rousseau, he has
already put the problem to his friend Bianchon. Supposing one
could get rich by a simple act of will, merely by willing the death
of an aged mandarin in China? "Bah!" is the retort. "I am going
on my thirty-third mandarin." When Rastignac insists that the

question is serious, Bianchon hesitates, asks the presumable age
of the mandarin, and finally renounces the bargain. Dostoevsky,
recounting the episode, self-revealingly exaggerates this final renunciation, and forgets the magnificent cynicism of Bianchon's
immediate response. For the uncompromising Dostoevsky, no one
can be happy while others are suffering. For Balzac compromise is
the precondition of happiness, which is invariably paid for by
others. Instead of renouncing the bargain, he computes the cost;
instead of sparing the mandarins, he reckons the casualties. The
raisonneur Bianchon, in spurning Rousseau's hypothetical offer, is
more scrupulous than his fellow denizens of the *Comédie humaine*. Rastignac learns, under the tutelage of Vautrin, to dispense
with principles and take advantage of circumstances. "Fortune is
virtue." Vautrin's maxim, which placed providence in the hands
of the unscrupulous individual, stems from Machiavelli's *Dis-
courses* on the opportunistic policies of Rome. And Rome, as Ben
Jonson describes it in *Sejanus*, is not unlike Balzac's Paris:

> Men's fortune there is virtue, reason their will,
> Their licence law, and their observance skill.
> Occasion is their foil, conscience their stain,
> Profit their lustre, and what else is, vain.

These profaner studies in opportunism are counterweighted by
Louis Lambert, which was classified by Yeats as a sacred book.
It purports to be the biography of a schoolmate, sent through
the patronage of Madame de Staël to Balzac's old college at
Vendôme, where Louis' fledgling treatise on the will has been
confiscated by their Oratorian masters. After he has graduated,
and enlarged his observation of social dynamics, practice continues to frustrate theory. The most serious of Balzac's thinkers,
he finds no room for thought in Paris: "Here the point of departure for everything is money." For the *voyant* who refuses
to compromise his intellectual integrity, the single alternative
is madness. His gradual retreat from the Parisian inferno carries
him into the visionary sphere of Swedenborg's angels. One of
his last unsuccessful acts, the ultimate gesture for a hero who
renounces power, is an attempt to castrate himself. Impotence
and corruption, the respective destinies of Louis Lambert and
Eugène de Rastignac, pose the alternatives of *La Peau de chagrin*.

That philosophical tale, for Goethe, testified to the degeneration of contemporary France. Therein Raphaël de Valentin, another youthful author of a *Théorie de la volonté*, having gambled away his fortune, is rescued from suicide by an antique dealer, another avatar of the Wandering Jew. The terms of their Mephistophelian contract are embodied in a piece of shagreen, which magically fulfills the wishes of its owner, shrinking slightly—and thereby further curtailing his existence—with every wish. Oscar Wilde has presented the same dilemma in *The Picture of Dorian Gray*, where art is made to suffer from nature's transgressions, and has underscored the same conclusion: that there is no experience which does not exact a heavy price.

Between the desire and the fulfillment, between the appetite and the satiety, between the appearance and reality, Valentin is caught in a Schopenhauerian dilemma of the will. Two words contain the secret of human activity, as revealed to him by the dealer: "Vouloir et Pouvoir...Vouloir nous brûle et Pouvoir nous détruit." If frustrated ambition consumes his contemporaries, satisfied ambition destroys them. Power corrupts, and the will to power degenerates. Napoleon was undoubtedly "a prodigious phenomenon of the will"; and Julien Sorel may have been, in Nietzschean phrase, a strong man amid unfavorable circumstances; but Eugène de Rastignac and Lucien de Rubempré are weak-kneed supermen, who arrive by swimming with the current and flounder whenever they resist it. Rastignac expounds "the morality of the comedy that society plays every day" to Valentin at an orgy, and Valentin concedes that society will henceforth be divided into two parties: resistance and movement. Those who moved with their century would reap, during its middle years, the middle-class satisfactions that M. Homais was so complacently to express. Those who resisted the march of progress would temporarily be swept aside. But Balzac, a lifelong student of Bonald's *Théorie du pouvoir*, understood the weakness of power politics. And Nietzsche, whose voluntarism so often reiterates Balzac's, confirmed those paradoxes which reduce the will of the people to anarchy and bestow leadership upon the most adept follower. No reader of Balzac should be altogether unprepared for the venalities and disillusionments of more recent history: such tired lions as Marshal Pétain or such stupid foxes as Pierre Laval are fabled in the *Comédie humaine*. Anatole France was not alone, nor without provocation, when he saluted Balzac as "the greatest historian of modern France." For Antonio Labriola he was a more penetrating sociologist than Comte; he is "the actual inventor of class psychology." Edmond and Jules de Goncourt went even farther:

> No one has called Balzac a statesman, yet he is perhaps the greatest statesman of our time, a great social statesman, the only one who has plumbed the depths of our ills, who has taken a long-range view of the disintegration of France since 1789, of the manners beneath the laws, the fact beneath the word, the anarchy of unbridled interests beneath the apparent order in the competition of talents, abuses replaced by influences, privileges by more privileges, equality before the law annihilated by inequality before the bench—the falsity of that program of 1789, money instead of good name, bankers in place of noblemen, and communism as the last straw, the guillotine of fortunes! What a strange thing that only a novelist could see all this!

The novel that prompted this testimonial, *Les Paysans*, has never been popular. Though Balzac considered it his most substantial work, the public response did not even encourage him to complete it. It was written to clarify "that terrible social question ... that increasingly ardent debate between man and man, between the rich and the poor"—those combatants whose mutual opposition Disraeli had lately proclaimed in *Sybil, or The Two Nations*. Balzac starts out by meeting halfway the arguments of such literary socialists as Sand and Sue. "We have written poetry about criminals, taken pity on hangmen, and almost deified the proletarian. Factions have been stirred up, and all their writers cry: 'Workers, arise!,' just as the Third Estate was told to arise." Thence the doctor of social medicine proceeds to diagnose the "democratic vertigo" as a permanent conspiracy against property-holders on the part of property-seekers. "This unsocial element, created by the Revolution, will some day absorb the bourgeoisie, as the bourgeoisie has devoured the nobility." On a later page this new force is given the more explicit name of "communism, that living and acting logic of democracy." Communists have acknowledged the justice of Balzac's analysis, stern as it is: the Soviet critic, V. R. Grib, characterizes *Les Paysans* as "the *Cherry Orchard* of French literature." Balzac, however, is less concerned with the nostalgic disintegration of the old regime than with the predatory lawlessness of the new. The beleaguered estate of Aigues, after harboring the old age of an eighteenth-century opera-singer, passes to a retired Napoleonic general, who is no match for the depredations of tenants and poachers, conniving stewards and village politicians. When the chateau is razed and the territory divided, the revolution has completed itself and the last outpost of feudalism has surrendered. New owners, former peasants, petty proprietors, rentiers can now move in. *Chacun chez soi!*

Admittedly, *Les Paysans* has nothing in common with the bucolics of Vergil or the pastoralism of George Sand, and little with the rustic utopianism of the earlier *Scènes de la vie de campagne*. The restless burden of Balzac's realism, unrelentingly pushed to its farthest point, is *Qui terre a, guerre a*. Writing shortly before the socialist revolution of 1848, Balzac refers the question of property back to the land itself and to man's primitive warfare over possession. One need not travel to America, remarks the journalist Etienne Blondet, in order to behold Cooper's redskins. "After all, it's an Indian's life surrounded by enemies, and I am defending my scalp," announces Vautrin, when he makes his appearance on the stage. "Paris, you see, is like a forest in the new world, agitated by twenty sorts of savage tribes —Illinois and Hurons living on the products of the different social classes," so he warns Rastignac in *Le Père Goriot*. "You are hunting after millions." His own role is not so much the diabolical tempter as the frontier guide, who teaches younger men to bait their traps and track their prey, and who blazes a trail through the pathless faubourgs. It is ironic that Cooper should have been living in Paris during these very years, trying to recapture the earlier spirit of Natty Bumppo in *The Deerslayer* and *The Pathfinder*. Meanwhile Balzac had been pursuing his own particular tribe of savages—*mohicans en spencer et hurons en redingote*, as they were designated by André Le Breton; *Les Mohicans de Paris*, to borrow an epithet from the elder Dumas; or, to employ a more modern designation, *apaches*. Balzac had come a long way since he modelled *Le Dernier Chouan* on *The Last*

of the Mohicans or prompted Marche-à-Terre to emulate Magua;
but Cooper had come along to provide epic comparisons for
the bourgeoisie and to point, where civilization breaks down,
to the harsher backgrounds of nature.

It is the stark antagonism, the brute ferocity, the endless hos-
tilities, so near to the innocuous surfaces of the Leatherstocking
novels, that account for their continued influence over the
Comédie humaine. The poor relation, Lisbeth Fischer, is the
Mohican in ambush, the eternal revolutionary. Where Tolstoy
idealizes the wisdom of the folk in the peasant figure of Platon
Karataev—who coincidentally recounts a warm-hearted, self-accusing Russian version of *L'Auberge rouge*—Balzac's peasantry is
the soul of invidious guile. Not that he is prejudiced against
them; for he respects the aristocracy, and yet presents them as
debauchees and weaklings. Both the upper and the lower classes
debase themselves, in his opinion, by competing with the middle
class. Only the dispossessed retain their dignity. After the July
Revolution, *Le Curé de village* maintains, "There is no more
patriotism except beneath dirty shirts." Balzac, in the end, is
to be found on neither side, though he has never been far from
the thick of the battle. Rastignac, he tells us, has seen the three
great expressions of society: "Obedience, Struggle, and Revolt:
the Family, the World, and Vautrin." Goriot exemplifies the
domestic virtues; the outlaw speaks for rebellion; between these
extremes lies Balzac's worldly path. The middle way, the way
of most men, is an uncertain struggle. The uncertainties of
Balzac's struggles and their impact on his work can hardly be
exaggerated beyond his own description; *lutte, lutte financière,
lutte acharnée* are the catchwords of his correspondence. To
Countess Hanska he outlined his life as "combat for money,
battle against jealousy, perpetual struggle with my subjects,
physical struggles, moral struggles." It was, as Victor Hugo con-
curred, "a life of storms, struggles, quarrels, combats." Even school,
for Louis Lambert, is "a continual struggle between teachers and
pupils." *Le Curé de Tours* pushes the struggle into the sanctuary
of the church. Marital union, in *Le Contrat de mariage*, is the
battleground for litigation. Rival clans, the Cruchotins and the
Grassinistes, feud for priority in Grandet's Saumur. "I must
struggle," resolves Lucien de Rubempré, approaching Paris. Not

two of Balzac's books, but all of them, might be headed *Les Rivalités*.

As much as life varies, it always remains, in terms of Balzac's early *Code*, "a perpetual combat between the rich and the poor." Balzac was able, while Darwin and Wallace were still experimenting, to depict it as a struggle for existence. And, before Marx and Engels had formulated their slogans, Balzac had completed a powerful depiction of the class struggle. Marx was generous in acknowledging the debt, and Gobseck raises his ugly head in a footnote to *Das Kapital*. Engels, writing to an English novelist, confesses to have learned more from Balzac than "from all the professional historians, economists, and statisticians of the period together." This is high praise for a realist—"a greater master of realism than all the Zolas, past, present, and future"— but it is not the highest. The highest must come from a fellow novelist, an imaginative writer of comparable stature and divergent sensibility, who was less involved in the battles of Balzac's time than in the timeless battle waged between God and the devil that turns every heart into its battlefield. Dostoevsky, whose first published work was a Russian translation of *Eugénie Grandet*, had a profound admiration for Balzac and a special insight into his significance: "His characters are the product of the intelligence of the universe! It is not the spirit of the epoch, but of millions of years of struggle, which have ended by producing this result in a human heart." If the fundamental law of drama is conflict— a conflict, as Brunetière stipulates, of the will—what writer has lodged a stronger bid than the *Comédie humaine* to establish himself as dramatist of humanity? And what higher tribute can we pay Balzac than to accept that comprehensive title which he has so boldly draped over his grand designs and desperate efforts?

V

FLAUBERT

> The writer, however, who shows the conflict between the romantic
> imagination and the real better than either Balzac or Zola, better than
> any other writer perhaps of the modern French movement, is Flaubert...
> He portrays satirically the real and at the same time mocks at the ideal
> that he craves emotionally and imaginatively (this is only one of the
> innumerable forms assumed by the Rousseauistic warfare between the
> head and the heart). He oscillates rapidly between the pole of realism
> as he conceives it, and the pole of romance, and so far as any serious
> philosophy is concerned, is left suspended in the void... It has been
> said that *Madame Bovary* bears the same relationship to esthetic ro-
> manticism that *Don Quixote* does to the romanticism of actual adven-
> ture of the Middle Ages. Yet *Don Quixote* is the most genial, *Madame
> Bovary* the least genial of masterpieces.
>
> —IRVING BABBITT

1. A Sentimental Education

To THE CENTURY that began by proclaiming the Napoleonic
"career open to talents," and continued by accepting Guizot's
invitation, "Enrich yourselves!," the poet-politician Lamartine
gave a watchword for the middle years: "France is bored..." The
umbrageous personification of this state of mind, *L'Ennui*, stalks
even more heavily through Flaubert's prose than through Baudelaire's verse, or through the wilting pages of their already world-
weary forerunners. Every line, writers sighed with Gautier, is
"the coffin of a dead illusion." It is especially Gustave Flaubert
whom moralists have accused of reviving the medieval sin of
sloth, in whom sociologists have discovered the missing link
between genius and madness, whose darker moods have provided
psychologists with a textbook case of *taedium vitae*. Balzac, of

course, had been much too busy to indulge in momentary yawns. Stendhal had feared and fought off the onset of boredom; his tedious moments had been more like hangovers, interludes between the last excess and the next expectation. But Flaubert's was a congenital ennui, a "permanent lassitude" which shadowed him at home and abroad, which figures both early and late in his letters and works. His was, he wrote at the age of twenty-three, "not that common, banal ennui which derives from idleness or illness, but that modern ennui which gnaws at a man's entrails, and turns an intelligent man into a walking shadow, a thinking phantom."

Thus Flaubert, Hamlet-like, blamed his melancholy upon his time. Approaching that time, as we do here, by way of the preceding period, we are conscious of its accumulating reasons for dissatisfaction with itself. The private chagrins that Balzac had rehearsed were framed by a series of public grievances which Louis Blanc chronicled in his *Histoire de dix ans*. The literary history of those ten years—the first decade of the July Monarchy—registers the ebbing of romanticism, superseded in the 'forties by a literature of social consciousness, a barrage of propaganda and exposure, which encompassed the competing socialistic utopias, the anarchistic pamphlets of Proudhon, the pro-revolutionary histories of Michelet, and the increasingly popular serial fiction of George Sand and Eugène Sue. The conflicting ideologies of this movement led to the divided counsels of the provisional government, when revolution came in 1848. The proletariat, having occasioned the downfall of Louis-Philippe in February, was itself put down with the National Workshops in June. The bourgeoisie, which had guaranteed the compromise of 1830, hereafter gravitated toward the right. On the left, whence the "right to work" had vainly been affirmed, the *Communist Manifesto* drastically redefined the aims of the working class and sought to co-ordinate their agitations on an international scale. But Engels conceded that, in contrast to the idealism and energy of previous French revolutions, the Second Republic had lapsed in an "absence of all illusion, of all enthusiasm."

Even the conservative economist Louis Reybaud underlined the trend of those two decades with a pair of satirical novels. In the first, *Jérôme Paturot à la recherche d'une position sociale,* the hero, a simple-minded shopkeeper's assistant, pursues an individualistic course through Balzacian hierarchies. In the second, *Jérôme Paturot à la recherche de la meilleure des républiques*, he is bewildered by social doctrines and doctrinaires. Finally he takes up his abode in Africa, leaving his compatriots to elect a president who is "less a man than a name," namely Louis Bonaparte. After the *coup d'état* of the Prince-President in 1851, and the plebiscite crowning him in 1852, it is easy to understand why—in the metaphor of Edmond and Jules de Goncourt— "unemployed public thought went out on strike." So long as Bonapartism remained a lost cause, refractory writers could afford to draw unflattering comparisons between the umbrella of the Citizen-King and the eagle of the first Napoleon. They could appeal to such high-sounding abstractions as the altar and the throne, while clericalism and militarism lay dormant. But it was both silly and dangerous to play with these authoritarian weapons at the point where they were being pressed into the service of dictatorship. Thus, where Stendhal and Balzac could criticize a regime in the name of an opposition, Flaubert was denied the consolations of any losing cause or political allegiance whatsoever. He could only lament that 'eighty-nine had destroyed the nobility, 'forty-eight the middle class, and 'fifty-one the people.

Such considerations assuredly lay behind his much quoted statement to the same correspondent, Louise Colet, in 1853: that the artist—who is called "a triple thinker," presumably because his thoughts extend in three accustomed directions— "should have no religion nor fatherland nor even any social conviction." Ten years later the brothers Goncourt, after reviewing the broken promises and the booby-traps of recent politics, arrived at a parallel conclusion: "...All this, in the long run, brings disillusionment, an aversion to all belief, a tolerance of any power, an indifference to political passion which I find in my literary colleagues, in Flaubert as well as myself. Hence no cause is worth dying for, any government can be lived with, nothing but art may be believed in, and literature is the only confession." Yet the Second Empire, which could ill afford to tolerate those who refused to take it seriously, proved that it was not indifferent to purely artistic activities by hauling the Goncourts and Flaubert and Baudelaire into police courts—the four purest men of letters in France, as the brothers took pains to protest within the privacy of their journal. The imperial censorship, by a mounting sequence of taxes and fines, regulations and suppressions, peremptorily constrained the press. "What would Beyle and Balzac say if they were here today?" was the rhetorical question that Edmond About asked when *Madame Bovary* was brought to trial. What would they have been permitted to say?

What Victor Hugo said about Napoleon the Little is a more pertinent question, since his freedom of speech was purchased at the price of exile. Flaubert, who vastly admired Hugo's intransigence, helped him to keep in clandestine touch with his fatherland. At the other extreme, Flaubert did not consider himself compromised by the friendship of the Princess Mathilde or the hospitality of her cousin, the quondam Emperor. Disciplined in incongruities, Flaubert could somehow bring himself to accept the red ribbon of the Legion of Honor on the very occasion when that commonplace decoration was also awarded to Ponson du Terrail, the most facile and slipshod writer of the day. It was equally impossible for Flaubert to be an exile or a time-server, since his skepticism undercut all commitments except work and friendship. Deeply as he resented the German invasion, he saw in it a just retribution, a reparation for "the long lie we have lived." As for the faltering new world that opened on the other side of the Commune, he execrated it and breathed more freely. He saw more clearly in retrospect that the nineteenth century, at its midpoint, must have taken the wrong turning. Its socialism was becoming another theology, even while its science was being reinforced by Darwinism. The eloquent, optimistic, ineffectual Europe of 1789–1848 must have gone down, like Turgenev's Rudin, on the Paris barricades. It was hard to explain this discontinuity to a generation which had not lived through the actual experience. "The reaction of 'forty-eight," he wrote to George Sand, "has hollowed out an abyss between two Frances." That abyss haunted Flaubert like the gulf that beset Pascal.

The retreat from liberal humanitarianism, the stalemate of parties and programs, the regimentation of morals, the inflation of values, the entrenchment of interests, the reaction against labor, the commercialization of the arts, the treason of the intellectuals, the failure of nerve—we need scarcely be reminded, in this century of ours, that such tendencies can create a cultural void. What is worth remembering is that personal integrity and technical skill could persist, cut off from normal responsibilities and immediate functions. Better, in an era of stuffed-shirts, to be a hollow man: the reverberations, at all events, might some day reach sentient ears. Not that the sensation of emptiness, which Flaubert so often professed, was the Dead Sea fruit of middle age. "Blasé at eighteen!" he had confessed himself, and at the age of fourteen—writing to his schoolmate, Ernest Chevalier —he had somewhat prematurely dethroned the house of Orléans: "Yes, our century is fertile in bloody upheavals. Goodbye, farewell, and let us concern ourselves always with Art, which is greater than peoples, crowns, and kings . . ." We are not confronted here, then, with the usual conflict between temperament and circumstance. Character seems resolved, from the very outset, to yield as little as possible to environment. It is the epoch which hesitates, is lost, and finds itself again: an embalmed masterpiece of the *genre ennuyeux*. The fundamental conflict takes place in the mind of the master.

He himself has stated it in such terms as can only be echoed by his observers. "In literary terms, there are two different fellows within me: one that is fond of ravings, lyricism, great eagle-flights, all the sonorities of the phrase and exaltations of the idea; another that searches for and digs out the truth as much as he can, that likes to point out the little facts as vigorously as the big ones, that wants to make the things he reproduces felt almost tangibly; the latter likes to laugh and takes pleasure in man's animalities." And Flaubert goes on to tell Madame Colet that the manuscript she has been admiring, his first *Education sentimentale,* is an unsuccessful attempt to fuse those two sides of his nature. That he ultimately effected a fusion would be implied by Zola when he characterized Flaubert as "a poet cold-blooded enough to be clear-sighted." But the poetry and the *sang-froid* are rarely simultaneous; he zigzags mercurially from the former to the latter, with the sunny and rainy days of his *Notes de voyage.* If all of his works were produced by the collaboration between those *deux bonshommes,* we must add that now the one, and again the other, gains the upper hand. Clairvoyance alternates with chiaroscuro. And since these alternations coincide with the chronological transition from the romantic to the realistic school, Flaubert assumes a diagrammatic significance, which looks before and after, and brings the novel into the sharp perspective of modernity.

More personally, this dualism embodies the hybrid strain that would engender Tonio Kröger, the intermixture of Latin and Nordic blood. The atmosphere of Flaubert's books may have been successively influenced by northern mist and Mediterranean sunlight; and his Norman prudence was relieved by impulsive outbursts; but his large and fair appearance, to the admiration of such racial connoisseurs as Gobineau, bore the impress of his Viking ancestry. His mother was a native of Normandy, the daughter and ward of local physicians, and a relative of the Cambremer family—petty provincial nobility who appear in both Balzac and Proust. Flaubert's father—whom he celebrates as Dr. Larivière in *Madame Bovary*—was the son of a veterinary in Champagne, the able pupil of Bichat and Dupuytren, and subsequently director of the municipal hospital at Rouen. There Flaubert was born in 1821. Whether or not he was allowed to play in a dissecting-room during childhood, as he liked to boast, he caught glimpses of surgical procedure which would lend precision and concreteness to his novelistic observations. Compared with his clinical treatment of the croup in *Education sentimentale*, the famine in *Salammbô*, or the operation and poisoning in *Madame Bovary*, Balzac's amateur science is old-fashioned quackery. The positivistic generation of Taine, "radically cured of the malady of René," had introduced a new professionalism which that unfulfilled medico Sainte-Beuve was quick to recognize. In his famous review of *Madame Bovary* he welcomed these would-be anatomists and physiologists into the domain of literature, hailing Flaubert as the son and younger brother of distinguished surgeons, who handled his pen as if it were a scalpel.

Now Flaubert had spoken interchangeably of his novel as "anatomy" and as "criticism." In one of his boyish letters he had envisaged the criticism of poetry as the dissection of a beautiful woman, "with her guts in her face, her leg skinned, and half a burnt-out cigar lying on her foot." Already, it would seem, the two different fellows had become involved in their lifelong argument. But though the critical Gustave had been fortified by his medical background, it cannot be said that the lyrical Gustave received no nourishment. On the contrary, like his friend Chevalier, he was a "child of literature." He could have claimed, like the poet in his play, that he had learned to read in *Hernani* and longed to be Lara. All over France, as an academic re-examination of their exercise-books has latterly revealed, mute inglorious schoolboys were struggling to express Hugolian audacity and Byronic cynicism. This romantic bookishness, suffusing the first attempts of Flaubert and his literary mentor, Alfred Le Poittevin, accounts for a good deal of what Baudelaire might have termed their "précoces ennuis." The subtitle of one such exercise, "an unhealthy tale for sensitive nerves and devoted souls," would seem to account for many. Most of them dwell, with adolescent unction, on the macabre and the erotic, the grotesque and the autumnal. But once we dismiss the mere conventions, we are left with certain themes which preoccupy Flaubert throughout his maturity: ours is a late and benighted phase of history; nothing is worthy of belief except possibly art; love is a snare, life is a cheat, and death is highly alluring.

When Flaubert included an amorous orang-outang among the characters of *Quicquid volueris*, or when he planned to dramatize a duel between a king and an ape, he was not merely trying to outshudder the fantasies of Petrus Borel, the self-styled Lycanthrope. He was motivated by some intimate spring of association which was touched again, on his *Voyage de famille* of 1845, by the sight of a monkey in a poet's garden on the Riviera:

> I never know whether I am looking at the monkey or the monkey is looking at me. Apes are our ancestors. About three weeks ago I dreamed that I was in a large forest full of apes; my mother was walking with me. The farther we advanced, the more of them came up; they were laughing and jumping among the branches; many of them came into the path, larger and larger ones, more and more numerous. They all looked at me until finally I was afraid. They surrounded us in a circle; one wanted to caress me and took my hand; I fired a pistol and made his shoulder bleed; he gave frightful groans. Then my mother said to me: "Why do you wound him? He is your friend. What harm has he

done to you? Don't you see that he loves you? How much
he looks like you!" And the monkey looked at me. This
rent my heart and I woke up . . . realizing that I was of the
same nature as the animals and fraternizing with them in a
very tender and pantheistic communion.

Apart from its Darwinian externals or Freudian recesses of implication, this dream may be read as a perversely narcissistic beast-
fable of the relationship between Flaubert's two selves. The
outgoing self, the fellow that takes pleasure in man's animalities,
obviously takes over when the dreamer awakes into a naturalistic
world. The subconscious self, who projects the dreamwork, is
apparently the fellow that loves ideas and phrases. Notice that,
while his mother endeavors to guide him toward reality, his recoil
is an act of manifest aggression which is also a symbol of sexual
completion. That the idealist should turn away in misanthropic
withdrawal, while the realist inclines toward fraternal embrace
with his kind, is only superficially paradoxical. It is thoroughly
consistent with Flaubert's *oeuvres de jeunesse,* wherein escape
leads not to vicarious realms of self-indulgence but to nightmarish horrors and frustrations. On the other hand, young Flaubert and Le Poittevin put enormous gusto into the invention of
an imaginary character, Le Garçon, who burlesqued for them all
the logical consequences of the stock bourgeois response: *C'est
la vie de garçon.* Later, notably in *La Légende de saint Julien
l'hospitalier,* Flaubert would resume the doubly ambivalent theme
of killing the things one loves and embracing what seems repellent.
Yet even at this stage it is evident that, where Swift had scorned
his fellow men as yahoos, and where Kafka would identify himself with a talking ape, Flaubert's ambivalence mingles the satiric
indignation of the one with the introspective pathos of the other.

For Flaubert's frenetic emphasis on bestiality, mortality, and
the humiliations of the flesh, there was a physical—not to say
a psychosomatic—basis. Like his exact contemporary, Dostoevsky,
he was not only the son of a doctor; he was himself a sick man;
indeed the two patients, in Freud's opinion, may have suffered
from the same complaint. Diagnosis, without agreeing on anything, has ranged from epilepsy to eye-strain; René Dumesnil,
a biographer who is also a physician, decides in favor of "hystero-

neurasthenia," which is still rather vague. Flaubert's own term for his malady was simply "neurosis," an occupational deformation which we almost take for granted in writers today. Our fullest account of the symptoms, which seem to have been mainly psychological, unfortunately depends upon the least dependable of his friends, Maxime Du Camp. More illuminating than the golden flashes that seem to have shot before Flaubert's eyes, however, were the circumstances under which he first beheld them. The family had designated their younger son for the law, which he found much less sympathetic than literature; and after three years of perfunctory study in Paris, he had failed in his examinations. Home for the holidays toward the end of 1843, he was driving with his brother down a country road at night when the seizure came. A semi-invalid regimen was henceforth prescribed, and he gladly shelved the Civil Code for occupations dearer to his taste. Between his laborious projects, in intervals of health, he would emerge to renew his Parisian acquaintances or to embark upon travels southward and eastward. But the crisis had changed and divided his career, as he warned the poetess, Louise Colet: theretofore he had led an active existence, thereafter he was vowed to the contemplative life.

Madame Colet, whose person must have been more seductive than her poetry, did not heed his warning. She had been the mistress of Victor Cousin, and she looked upon herself as the muse of Musset and Vigny. In both of these roles and possibly a third, that of wife, she aspired to play opposite Flaubert. They had an intense affair in the late 1840's and a fascinating correspondence in the early 'fifties. She took her revenge in one of those novels cheaply concocted of literary gossip, where she denounced his "monstrous personality" for "feeling nothing but the throes of art." Flaubert maintained his distance from others through his closeness to his widowed mother and his orphaned niece. With them he lived in comfortable seclusion at the family estate of Croisset on the Seine near the outskirts of Rouen. In 1856, with the publication of his first novel, *Madame Bovary*, he suddenly achieved both fame and notoriety. He took his place now and then at the Magny dinners and other intellectual gatherings, but the only milestones that measured his path were his books: *Salammbô* and *L'Education sentimentale* in the 'sixties,

La Tentation de saint Antoine and *Trois Contes* in the 'seventies. His mother died soon after the upheavals of 1871, and the motherly friendship of George Sand was not there to console him for long afterward. Belatedly, reluctantly, and ineffectually, when the family underwent financial reverses, he tried to gain a living through a government sinecure or pension and a few unlikely flings at theatrical success. He died of an apoplectic stroke in 1880, leaving the uncompleted manuscript of *Bouvard et Pécuchet* and a large number of early and incidental writings, most of which have been published posthumously.

This bald outline, though biographers have enriched it with personal detail, is still quite uneventful. Essentially, it supports Flaubert's assertion that he had no biography. In all modesty, he lived out Hugo's stoical recommendation: "Ami, cache ta vie, et répands ton esprit!" Most of his works, in one way or another, exploit the imaginative resources of that inner life to which his nervous breakdown committed him. A few of them deal more directly with material he has experienced and observed, and these may be considered somewhat autobiographical. A thread of confession runs through the juvenilia, particularly in *Mémoires d'un fou* and *Novembre*, where it may be readily disentangled from the lurid fustian that pieces it out. In a class by itself is the *Education sentimentale* of 1845, quite distinct from the novel published under the same title in 1869, yet readable for its own sake. In pairing off two young provincials, and following them through the classical stages of disillusionment, it resembles its successor. Furthermore, it dramatizes in them the rivalry between the two Gustaves. While the cynic Henry gets along in the world, succeeds in love, elopes to America, and returns to make a rich marriage, the poet Jules fails in the theater, renounces the world for art, concludes that life is a desert, and departs to make a Flaubertian tour of Africa. But his pangs have brought him closest to the author when, having missed a carriage bound for elopement, he falls by the roadside, bruised and gasping in the winter night: "Tout m'a manqué . . ."

Not until twenty years later, when Flaubert had reached his own forties, did he set down his definitive account of the 1840's. Though the full and final *Education sentimentale*, from its flashback of boyhood to its epilogue in middle age, covers thirty-five years, the story itself falls within the crucial decade, 1840–1851, and the central section is closely synchronized with the happenings of 1848. Those dates perforce had broadened Flaubert's subject, assigning to politics a share of the attention that had hitherto been concentrated on love. But the novel parallels his youthful confessions by starting from the grand Platonic passion of Flaubert's lifetime. Though the cherished heroine, Madame Arnoux, "looked like the women in romantic books," she was tenderly drawn from life—or rather, from memory. Her husband, Jacques Arnoux, the proprietor of *L'Art industriel*, seems to have been modelled upon the music publisher Maurice Schlésinger, of whom Wagner has left us a much less amiable portrait. Madame Schlésinger's biography, it would seem, was actually more eventful than Flaubert's delicate version of it would suggest. Indeed, because of an imprudent first marriage, about which he cannot have known, she was not yet married to the father of her child when the three made such a binding impression upon young Flaubert. Life, in this instance more romantic than literature, was tamed and muted by it. His devotion, like his hero's, was kept alive by the necessity of worshipping from afar, where fulfillment would undoubtedly have broken the spell. Frédéric Moreau's revulsion from Marie Arnoux, many years later, is "like the dread of incest." Their reunion, based again on actuality, is a last farewell. Leaving him a lock of her white hair, she kisses him on the forehead "like a mother."

Except for this encircling situation, *L'Education sentimentale* is not an autobiography. Frédéric ceases to be identifiable with Flaubert from the day he passes his law examinations. When he courts the worldly Madame Dambreuse, he seems to be retracing the slippery footsteps of Maxime Du Camp, with whom Flaubert had witnessed the Paris insurrection. Du Camp himself had written *Mémoires d'un suicidé* and *Les Forces perdues*, two weak novels about weak young men, contemporaries of his and Flaubert's and Frédéric's. Flaubert's book was characteristically strong, but it was concerned with the same groping protagonist, the composite post-romantic, the generic veteran of 'forty-eight. "I want to write the moral history—sentimental would be truer—of the men of my generation," he had explained, hesitating significantly over the adjective. The title might apply to all of his novels,

Proust would point out, and not least to *Madame Bovary*. For, in substituting *sentiments* for *moeurs*, the novel shifts from an objective to a subjective approach; and if sentiments may be defined as untested emotions and illusory ideas, then Flaubert proposed to apply the test of reality. "What does that mean, reality?" asks his painter, Pellerin. "Some see black, others see blue, most people see stupidly." Few of them are cold-blooded enough to be clear-sighted; their vision is colored by lovers' reveries or politicians' slogans. The sentimentalist, the man who lives by illusions, has been let down more gently in English fiction than in French. In sounding the hollowness of sentimentality, Flaubert was performing the habitual task of the realist. But instead of pointing his attack at a single illusion, as Brandes acutely remarked, he simultaneously tackled all the contradictions and disappointments of an illusion-ridden age.

Was there anything left that was not illusion, any manifestation of Schopenhauer's countervailing force, the will? Not in that tired liberal, "that man with every weakness," that hero foredoomed to failure, Frédéric Moreau. Henry James's description of him as an abject and inferior human specimen, "positively too poor for his part," bounces back when Edmund Wilson describes him as "a perfect Henry James character." Yet the part calls for indecision and ineffectuality because Frédéric's position is a false one. Because of his emotional involvement with Marie Arnoux, he responds half-heartedly to every other stimulus. Pampered by a private income—and, when he has run through that, a second inheritance—he dabbles as a dilettante among the serious pursuits of other men. Having grown up under the tutelage of Werther and René, having dreamed—like Lucien de Rubempré—of becoming "the Walter Scott of France," Frédéric has been speeded to Paris by the advice of his brash friend Deslauriers, to emulate the heroes of the *Comédie humaine*. Alas, he shows neither the ambition of Rastignac nor, for that matter, the sensibility of Julien Sorel. The young man of the 'thirties, the Amaury of Sainte-Beuve's *Volupté*, had erred with conviction and sinned with enthusiasm. No source of comparison is more revealing than the scene in which Balzac's hero, standing upon the heights of Père-Lachaise between a funeral and a dinner engagement, flings his dramatic challenge to the city. Bearing this in mind, consider the passage where Frédéric walks home from his first dinner with Madame Arnoux, and Flaubert rounds off his sensitive impressions with an irony which is almost a repudiation:

> The gas-lamps gleamed in two straight lines indefinitely, and long red flames wavered in the profundity of the water. It was the color of slate, while the sky, which was clearer, seemed to be upheld by large masses of shadow which arose on both sides of the river. Some buildings, which were hardly noticeable, augmented the darkness. A luminous haze floated over the roofs beyond; all the noises mingled in one monotonous hum; a light breeze stirred.
>
> He had stopped in the middle of the Pont-Neuf. Bareheaded, chest expanded, he breathed in the air. All the while he felt as if something unquenchable were welling up from the depths of his being, a flow of tenderness which left him weak, like the movement of the waves before his eyes. Slowly the clock of a church struck one, like a voice calling to him.
>
> Then he was seized by one of those shudders of the soul in which you seem to be transported to a higher world. An extraordinary power, whose purpose he did not know, had come to him. He seriously asked himself whether to be a great painter or a great poet; and he decided in favor of painting, for the requirements of that profession would bring him close to Madame Arnoux. So he had found his vocation! The aim of his existence was now clear, and the future infallible.

Painting is an anticlimax, as law and literature have been, and as business and politics will turn out to be. Yet if Frédéric does not climb so high as Rastignac, at least he does not sink so low as Rubempré, and his dearly bought failures retain a muddling idealism which would be absent from the cheap successes of *Bel-Ami*. Maupassant's ladies' man will complete the demoralization of the hero, after the Second Empire has dissipated the Napoleonic ideal. For Frédéric the boudoir proves more hazardous than the barricade. While the Reform Banquets are kindling a revolution, he is arranging a rendezvous with Madame Arnoux. She fails to come at the last moment, and he "reforms" on the rebound by spending the night with Arnoux's mistress, Rosanette. Next day that pathetic little tart declares

herself for the Republic "as Monsieur the Archbishop of Paris
had already done," continues Flaubert, "and as would do, with
a marvellous quickness of zeal, the magistracy, the council of
state, the Institute, the marshals of France . . . all the Bonapartists,
all the legitimists, and a considerable number of Orleanists." But,
having preferred the matronly Madame Arnoux to his girlish
fiancée Louise Roque, Frédéric now neglects Rosanette for the
wife of the aristocratic capitalist Dambreuse. It is a far cry from
the bohemianism of the studios to the business transacted in
her salon. "The majority of the men there had served at least
four governments; and they would have sold France or the human
race to guarantee their fortunes, to save themselves trouble or
embarrassment, or even out of simple meanness or instinctive
adoration of power."

As for the people, when Frédéric has the leisure to watch
them fighting in the streets, looting the Tuileries, or sprawling
on the throne itself, he agrees that "heroes smell bad." The
uprising of February gives way to the suppressions of June as
the middle class, dressed in the uniform of the National Guard,
steps in. The crusty Père Roque, after shooting a youth who
has begged for bread, rushes home to lunch, and goes to bed
crying: "Oh, these revolutions! . . . I am too sensitive!" Yet if
power corrupts, for Flaubert, enslavement ennobles, conferring
tragic dignity upon one character in his gallery of radicals. This
is Dussardier, the man of good will who became a revolutionist
because he happened to be walking down the Rue Transnonain
when the bloody reprisals occurred which made that street a
synonym for counter-revolution. His love of simple justice and
hatred of the police are juxtaposed to the rigid theories and
utopian authorities of Sénécal, who combines "the reason of a
geometrician with the faith of an inquisitor." These gifts equip
the latter to rationalize the dialectic of those events which convert
him into a factory-manager and then a police-agent. The climax
arrives with the *coup d'état* of 1851, when Dussardier's last outcry
of "Vive la République!" is cut off by Sénécal's pistol-shot—a
denouement which subsequent events have converted into a
parable. Frédéric, a witness to this episode, has just witnessed
another revelation: the marriage of the opportunistic Deslauriers,
a prefect under the incoming regime, to the heiress Louise. Again,

as when Frédéric missed both Madame Arnoux and the insurrection, private and public frustrations have converged.

Repeatedly and decisively he has missed the boat. Everything has conspired, as it were, to fail him. A feeble duel has been stopped at the first scratch. Rash speculations and friendly loans have cost him his second fortune. His political candidacy has gone by default. After a fraudulent bankruptcy and a disastrous trial, the Arnoux ménage has fled to the provinces. The auction of their effects, so hallowed by his sentiments, is the final disintegration. Every blow of the auctioneer's hammer knocks down an illusion. What, after all, has Frédéric Moreau learned in the school of experience? Not the esthete's "secret of success in life," nor the mellow wisdom that ultimately rewarded the conscientious endeavors of Wilhelm Meister. Though Goethe laid down the pedagogical formula, Flaubert's conclusions have more in common with the self-deprecating ironies of that pedagogue *manqué*, that assistant professor of failure, Henry Adams. For both, the educational process is less a matter of learning than of unlearning, the result of which is negative—even, for Frédéric, nihilistic. Yet for the reader, Flaubert told Du Camp, his book taught history-lessons which, had there been time to meditate upon them, might have prevented France from returning to the barricades in 1870. Was it to be taken as Flaubert's critique of revolution, even as Stendhal's writing had been a critique of reaction? Why then should it evoke such admiration from the syndicalist author of *Réflexions sur la violence*, Georges Sorel? Its pros and contras, its manifestoes and credos, operate to neutralize each other. Rulers and reformers, proletarians and police appear and vanish in turn, like the visions that bedevil Saint Antoine. Instead of Sancho Panza's two eternal parties, the Haves and the Have-Nots, Deslauriers adds the historic dimension by distinguishing three, all of them impelled by the very same motive: "those who have, those who no longer have, and those who try to have."

Flaubert stands aside from all of them. He indicates his own role when he testifies in a letter, "I have been present as a spectator at nearly all the riots of my time." Bored and passive as Frédéric himself, he had marched with the National Guard. Living through the official lies of the Second Empire, he became retrospectively interested in the missed opportunities of the Second Republic. The abyss across which he viewed them interposed a coldness in the most heated debates, a dryness in the most exciting conspiracies. Though *L'Education sentimentale* is subtitled *Histoire d'un jeune homme*, its outlook is replete with weariness and apathy. "Ouf! I have finished my mournful work," he wrote to Du Camp. "Our entire youth has just passed before me. I am broken up over it." In the book, after Frédéric's anticlimactic reunion with Madame Arnoux, he has another with his unfaithful friend Deslauriers, who—always too clever for his own good—is also pretty much the worse for wear. Reverting together nostalgically to anecdotes of their shared adolescence, they recall an occasion when Frédéric's trepidations kept them from entering a local brothel. Now Deslauriers echoes his agreement with Frédéric: "We were better off then!" Thus the last word expresses our perennial yearning for innocence, our universal revulsion from guilty knowledge. It rounds out the book by protesting against wasted years, frustrated loves, corrupted hopes. It throws light on Flaubert's arrested emotional development, his lifelong desire to be sheltered from the contingencies of adult existence, his single-minded concentration on what ordinary men regard as a casual pastime. It suggests explanations for the reduplicating patterns of friendship that run through his work, for the maternal images in which his most impressive heroines are shaped.

Immediately after her husband dies, Madame Dambreuse proposes to Frédéric, who entertains her proposal for mercenary reasons. The sterility of this connection is symbolized when, discovering that the money is bequeathed elsewhere, she sits beside the emptied strong-boxes like "a mother in mourning before an empty cradle." It was a sick child, claiming a mother's attention and incidentally recovering, who thwarted Frédéric's assignation with Madame Arnoux. It is more than coincidental that the token of his relations with Rosanette should be an illegitimate child who dies in infancy. A pitiful and hideous pastel of the dead infant, "a veritable *nature morte*," is sketched by Pellerin—and by Flaubert as well. His notes show that he had prepared himself with particular thoroughness on the pathology of children's diseases. Nothing could more strongly emphasize this Flaubertian trait than the manner in which Octave Feuillet, whose *jeune homme pauvre* is so debonair a contemporary of Frédéric, glides over the scientific details of a similar case: "We shall not dwell upon this scene of poignant cruelty..." The Flaubert that loved animalities was not less strongly attached to such situations by their latent tenderness. In his own childhood he had cultivated a precociously morbid streak; in later life he preserved an ever-youthful sense of wonder. Hence the underlying contradiction of Flaubert's personality reasserts itself in *L'Education sentimentale*, where the dispirited banalities that his theme presents are redeemed by a poet's freshness of perception. When Remy de Gourmont was moved to call it "our *Odyssey*, and the most beautiful poem in French," he was not simply indulging in mock-heroic overstatement. For Flaubert's Dublin disciple, James Joyce, would demonstrate anew how the wanderings of a latter-day Odysseus could be charted against the divagations and distractions of the city.

After the pallid human figures, spectators rather than actors, have been relegated to the sidelines, it is Paris that occupies the foreground of *L'Education sentimentale*—not the flamboyantly romantic metropolis of Balzac, but a more subdued, more subtle, more poetic vista. The narration detaches itself sharply from the characters, while lingering suggestively over the setting. The description is all but untranslatable: words move, lights "balance," shades "descend." Intermittent rain, the rain that beats through the cadences of Verlaine and Rimbaud, dampens the greying soul of Flaubert's protagonist. Through Frédéric we apprehend the sight and smell of gaslight, the rumbling of the omnibuses, the sensation of wet pavements, and—whenever he goes to the country—"a nostalgia for the boulevards." The pace and direction of the novel are set by his dilatory walks through the streets, and accelerated by the march of history to the abortive climax of street-fighting. To render "the great city with all its noises," rustling around his heroine "like an orchestra," Flaubert has utilized every artistic medium. Step back and squint: the ugliest negations of his subject assume a positive beauty of composition; the most embittered controversies dissolve into a mood of esthetic contemplation. The term "impressionism" would not be current until 1874, when Monet exhibited his *Impression: soleil levant*; but members of that school were gathering at Batignolles when Flaubert published his book, and of them it constantly reminds

us: of Pissarro, when Frédéric strolls down the boulevard; of
Manet, when he joins his friends at a café; of Monet, when he
glimpses reflections in the river; of Degas, when he takes Rosanette
to the races; of Renoir, when he kneels at the feet of Madame
Arnoux.

2. *The Martyrdom of Saint Polycarp*

"I have always put myself in what I have written. In place of
Saint-Antoine, for example, it is I who am there; the *Temptation*
has been for me and not for the reader." It is only fair to add
that, in this letter to Louise Colet, Flaubert alludes to the earliest
version of *La Tentation de saint Antoine*; and that later letters,
addressed to less intimate correspondents, stress the impersonality
of his writing. Inevitably he is present, to a greater or lesser
degree, in every single one of his creations; but the quoted
example confirms our suspicion that there is more of him in
Antoine than in any of his other characters—including Frédéric
Moreau. While *L'Education sentimentale* was harder to write
than any of his other works, even harder than *Madame Bovary*,
La Tentation de saint Antoine seems to have come more easily,
even more easily than *Salammbô*—thereby confirming Flaubert's
own opinion that he was "born lyrical" and had resolutely disciplined himself to prose. Frédéric's vocation, so lightly undertaken, so frequently shifted, so aimlessly sidetracked, has little
in common with the great refusal and lifelong resistance of
Flaubert's career, except for certain dates and material details.
Flaubert's spiritual autobiography, from first to last, identifies
itself with the ancient hermit. The *Education* parallels the *Tentation*, and differs from the other books, in completing a sequence
of literary effort which extends from youth into middle age.
But the *Tentation* was, conclusively and comprehensively, its
author's favorite: "the book of my whole lifetime." It is a *livre
vécu* on the mythical, rather than the literal, plane. Though it
may not be history, it is legend in the authentic meaning of the
word, the life of a saint.

It is therefore the work that gives freest scope to Flaubert's
imagination; and, though he stringently revised it, the mere

fact that he kept returning to it attests the power of its recurrent fantasy. "Enthusiasm for works of art which correspond to everyone's dream," he had jotted in his original notes for a rejected passage on the Muses. One of his most interesting pieces of apprentice-work, *La Spirale*, is a study of reality transfigured by hashish and of happiness sustained by illusion. Flaubert himself could see golden fulgurations, could conjure up artificial paradises, without the aid of stimulants. Perhaps it was his neurotic condition that impelled him to lose himself so completely in the lives he wrote about. For the vividness of these projections, Freud coupled *Saint-Antoine* with *Don Quixote* among his literary admirations. Taine's *De l'intelligence*, in expounding a theory of knowledge through disillusionment which is well exemplified in *Madame Bovary*, illustrates the faculty of voluntary hallucination by citing a testimonial from Flaubert. Even uncontrolled hallucination was becoming, with Lautréamont, a literary device; and Rimbaud would shut his eyes to envision mosques in the place of factories. Such reveries condense a lyric impulse and a satiric reservation, equally characteristic of Flaubert, into what Albert Thibaudet has aptly termed a "binocular vision." Flaubert's divided personality, expressing itself in a predisposition for contrasts, dictated not only his choice of subject-matter but his use of verbal antithesis. Nor was this a conventionally romantic union of opposites, since the rhetorical mode of linking them together, which is hyperbole with Hugo, is irony with Flaubert. We need seek no farther for comparison than the street scenes of *Les Misérables* and those of *L'Education sentimentale*.

The latter novel, in a typical metaphor, likens Madame Dambreuse's overloaded sideboard to the altar of a church or an exhibit of silverware. Here the secular application of the religious image, ironic in itself, is underlined by its commercial alternative. Again, the palm trees in the Jardin des Plantes, opening tropical vistas to Frédéric, bring home the colorlessness of local surroundings. Again and again, in Flaubert's letters, the mood recurs. "Ah, some day I shall get intoxicated on Sicily and Greece!" he wrote to Du Camp in 1846. "Meanwhile I stay in bed with boils on my legs." Within a year the two went on a walking trip across the fields and strands of northwestern France, where Flaubert was fascinated by cromlechs and cathedrals but shocked by the newly strung telegraph wires. Two years later, with the same companion, he made an extensive tour of the eastern Mediterranean countries. Like Frédéric, "he came to know the sadness of steamboats, the chill of waking up in a tent, the bedazzlement of landscapes and ruins, the bitterness of interrupted sympathies." Even here the cadence is anticlimactic: "la mélancolie des paquebots." An itinerary which is rather Levantine than Greco-Roman, a sensibility which is rather Alexandrian than Attic, are reflected in his journals. After travelling in the wake of Byron's heroes, he yearned—more earnestly than Childe Harold ever did —to have the desert for his dwelling-place. Since the desert blended the pathos of distance with the attraction of solitude, it provided an exotic setting for that endless soliloquy to which, after all, the terms of his existence predisposed him. There he might say, with Tertullian, "Successi de populo..."

But the Father of the Church whose feast-day Flaubert celebrated, with all the convivial ardor of his contrary nature, was Saint Polycarp. For it had been Polycarp who daily lamented: "My God, my God, in what a country hast Thou made me live!" Or had he said "... in what a century...?" Flaubert varied the litany, depending on whether he happened to feel that his place or his time was out of joint. He eased the geographical displacement by travel; he sought to transcend the historical plight by study. Through the most advanced and erudite scholarship of his tradition-conscious age, he gained acquaintance with other periods. In 1834 Désiré Nisard, through his *Etudes sur la littérature latine de la Décadence*, had made an oblique attack on modern literature. The epithet flung in academic scorn would be picked up and brazenly flaunted by the post-romantic generation. That prince of decadents, the hero of Huysmans' *A rebours*, would rank the *Tentation de saint Antoine* high above the *Education sentimentale*. Flaubert had often expressed his taste and outlook in sentences which Verlaine's sonnet on languor would virtually echo: "Je suis l'empire à la fin de la décadence." Le Poittevin had styled himself "a Greek of the Lower Empire." The obvious disparity between the empires of the first and third Napoleons may well have prompted such reactions, along with their implicit comparison to the Roman republic. Flaubert's researches, like his voyages, led him toward the point of convergence between Christian and classical, Oriental and Occidental cultures. Their points of conflict led him on toward such conclusions as Renan would formulate in his famous prayer from the Acropolis: "Everything here below is but a dream and a symbol. The gods pass, as men do . . ."

This attitude, whether it glorifies myth or sophisticates truth, whether it undermines religion or reinforces art, helps us to understand why *La Tentation de saint Antoine* pursues a symbolic method and an ecclesiastical theme. Where Balzac had taken up theology, and Stendhal had cast it aside, Flaubert was never anything but a freethinker. With the detached curiosity of an archaeologist, he compared his niece's baptism to "some ceremony of a remote religion exhumed from the dust." What belonged to reason he rendered unto the scientific rationalism of his background; his emotions responded nonetheless to ritual and stained glass. "I am mystical at heart," he confessed, "and I believe in nothing." He revered Spinoza as a prophet and Voltaire as a saint, but their kingdoms were too definitely of this world. When he thought of his consecration to his calling, he was bound to fall back on the imagery and terminology of the monastic, the sacerdotal, the anchoritic. Live like a monk; an artist should be priest; the history of the arts is a martyrology—his correspondence reiterates these articles of faith, which thereupon resound antiphonally down the choir of his commentators. The most fanatical of these, Antoine Albalat, hailed Flaubert as "the Christ of literature." Here François Mauriac, intervening to remind all novelists that they are no more than the apes of God, would rather accuse Flaubert's art of attempting to usurp the role of religion. More recent Catholic criticism has been more tolerant, discerning signs of grace in the very aura of religiosity with which he surrounded his priestly task.

M. Mauriac has the awesome habit of judging other writers *devant Dieu*. Logically, as well as theologically, it is not before God, but merely before his own pharisaic opinion, that he has any right to arraign them. Flaubert reserved his faith for Spinoza's deity, immanent, ubiquitous, yet uninvolved in human affairs. As between the creator of the universe and the poet creating a second nature, criticism had been fond of drawing a neo-Platonic analogy. "Like God," exulted Hugo, "the poet is present everywhere in his work." But with Flaubert's better-known corollary, that the artist should be "everywhere present and nowhere visible," the emphasis shifts from omnipresence to invisibility, from the Platonic to the Spinozistic, and from the personality of the demiurge to the fabrication of his little cosmos. The last refinement upon this attitude is Joyce's gesture of depersonalization: "The artist, like the God of the creation, remains within or behind or beyond or above his handiwork, invisible, refined out of existence, indifferent, paring his fingernails." Whether self-portraiture furthers self-effacement is a question we may leave him to ponder, torn between these extremes of egocentricity and aloofness. Plainly Joyce's indifference, in turning from his masterpiece to his manicure, is a part of his artistic pose. Others might challenge the gods or play the oracle; it was to the rigors of sainthood, rather than to the perquisites of divinity, that Flaubert metaphorically aspired. He was more concerned with vocation and sacrifice than with either titanic rivalries or messianic pretensions.

On an earthier level, of course, it is possible to trace his creative activity to a sublimation of the libido; and Theodor Reik's monograph contributes some insights to the fund of self-knowledge; but Flaubert himself started the psychoanalysis when he chose a theme which overtly centered upon the repression of fleshly impulses; and his patristic authorities had known something about the *libido sentiendi* as well as the *libidines sciendi et dominandi*. If *La Tentation de saint Antoine* is to be interpreted as a substitute for both religion and sex, we should not be dizzied by its sudden transitions from austerity to sensuality. When Barbey d'Aurevilly also describes it as a kind of suicide, he superimposes an intolerable load upon its heavy burden of vicarious experience. Though Flaubert's persistent death-wish was counterbalanced by a fitful *joie de vivre*, he told George Sand that he lacked the qualifications for living. He could not have relegated the responsibility to servants, like Villiers de l'Isle-Adam's impossible Axël. But Flaubert's malady, whatever it was—and the Goncourts suspected mere hypochondria—restricted and specialized his relations with the outer world. He was prosperous enough to ignore the problem of money, and to be outraged by the very notion of literary property. He found Croisset, with its gloomy comforts and its bruited traditions of Pascal and the Abbé Prévost, a tolerably livable Thebaid. His niece grew up there in the belief that *La Bovary* meant work, that work meant writing, and that her uncle was—by his own confession—"the last of the Fathers of the Church." A book, while he was working on it, was quite literally a way of life.

He wrote neither for a living, like Balzac, nor for pleasure, like Stendhal; he was too hard-working to be an amateur and too high-minded to be a professional; he was, in short, a perfectionist. Now the will to achieve perfection, though not so rare as it sounds, is all too rarely abetted by leisure and crowned with results. Limbo is paved with the good intentions of the forgotten Frenhofers. Flaubert was lucky to find his peculiar oasis, where projects could ripen in supreme disregard of the pressures and uncertainties that were jeopardizing the status of other writers. Their hand-to-mouth existence, which Balzac had lightly sketched in *Un Prince de la Bohême*, was sentimentalized and popularized in 1851 by Murger's *Scènes de la vie de Bohême*. Apart from the timeless charms of gypsy vagabondage, bohemianism presented a timely protest against the middle-class conformities. Using university slang—the gowns-man's name for the anti-intellectual townsman—which had been imported with Heinrich Heine from Germany, the bohemians termed their enemies philistines. To Bohemia, "the fatherland of my breed," Flaubert professed a theoretical allegiance; but, as Edmond de Goncourt observed, "he practised all the bourgeois virtues"; and *L'Education sentimentale* offers a far from sentimental account of his days in the Latin Quarter. With Murger, however, he shared one dynamic conception: that the man of letters, no less than the practitioner of the plastic arts, should be an artist. If this is today a redundant commonplace of critical discussion, it is due to the fruitful cohabitation of painting and writing during the last hundred years. Thus a master of both media, Eugène Fromentin, impressed by pictorial effects and formal values, praised Flaubert as a painter. And that man for whom the visible world so color-fully existed, Théophile Gautier, edited *L'Artiste*, the review in which fragments of *La Tentation de saint Antoine* were appropriately published.

The rift, the abyss that the Goncourts noted between the artist and the public, had already been felt by the romantic generation when Sainte-Beuve coined the expression that Flaubert lived by, "ivory tower." Musset had bemoaned the poet's solitude in his midnight conversations with the Muse. Vigny, in *Stello*, had adduced a number of eighteenth-century examples to show that the lot of the poet had always been a curse in life, a blessing in death, and a perpetual ostracism. But it had not been until the mid-nineteenth century that genius was invariably linked with misunderstanding; that long-haired intellectuals were recognized, if not accepted, as a social class; that artistic and public standards, diverging more widely than before, reached a point of diametrical opposition. The Impressionists, rejected from official exhibitions, exhibited their paintings in the Salon des Refusés. Flaubert and various friends, all disappointed playwrights, formed a circle of *auteurs sifflés*. The younger generation sought its patron saints in the calendar of *poètes maudits*. Rejections, hisses, and curses were mutual. Perhaps because Gautier had to earn his bread by journalism, he particularly delighted in berating the bourgeoisie, and in championing the arts against those who would subordinate them to didactic or utilitarian ends. He sang that the bust survives the city, and shouted that he would renounce his French citizenship for an authentic Raphael. Yet to Flaubert, who deferred to him as "my master," Arsène Houssaye recalls that he spoke more cynically: "You believe in the mission of the writer, the priesthood of the poet, the divinity of art. The writer sells copy as the dry-goods merchant sells handkerchiefs—only calico pays better than syllables, and it's wrong!"

If art was a commodity, the artist subjected himself to the demands of the bourgeois consumer, as well as to the strictures of the clerical moralist and the political censor. If he refused to purvey their ideologies, he could use his medium to set forth some alternative; but the failure of the 'forties to accomplish the aspirations of the socialists discouraged reliance on art as propaganda. This is the context in which the slogan of "art for art's sake" becomes meaningful. Though its manifesto is Gautier's preface to *Mademoiselle de Maupin* and its gospel is Flaubert's *Correspondance*, though it was based on Kant's delineation of categories and adumbrated by Schiller's insistence upon the disinterestedness of esthetic endeavor, *l'art pour l'art* was actually formulated by the eclectic philosopher, Victor Cousin, in a course of lectures on *Le Vrai, le beau, et le bien*, delivered in 1818 and not published until 1836. Cousin's assertion that art was an end in itself, like religion and morality, helped to free it from extraneous influences; and its proclaimed autonomy gave artists a chance to preoccupy themselves more intensively with form; but Flaubert must have known, when he sat through the trial of *Madame Bovary*, that esthetics can never be completely divorced from ethics. Believing that form and content could not exist apart from each other, he aimed at "truth by means of beauty." His scientific inclinations accorded with the dispassionate objectivity so passionately upheld by the rising Parnassian school of poetry. Since idealism was discredited by its association with lost utopias, if not with the imperial regime, the independent artist inclined toward realism, which—we have seen—was not without its own moral implications.

The triple thinker could not restrict himself to a single category: his work would not be beautiful unless it was well and truly done. In detaching himself from social responsibilities, Flaubert was obliged to set up artistic criteria for the true and the good, which he situated in the precise relationship between things and words. His awareness that words are also things in themselves, like the pigment on an impressionistic canvas, enriched the sensuous texture of his prose; the form came before the idea, he insisted, and sometimes the rhythm came before the phrase; but, much as he admired Chateaubriand, writing for writing's sake was never his aim. If it had been, Flaubert, the man of phrases, would have had to struggle less with Flaubert, the man of facts. That struggle, though fought out on a verbal level, was fundamentally an attempt to clarify particulars and specify nuances that more casual novelists indicate by opaque generalizations and vague clichés. The doctrine of the so-called *mot juste*, which he enunciated in this connection, is most explicitly reported by Guy de Maupassant in his preface to *Pierre et Jean*. "Whatever you want to say, there is only one word to express it, one verb to animate it, and one adjective to qualify it," Flaubert evidently told his disciple, and it is heuristic to begin by making sure of what one wants to say. Yet such advice would seem to imply an almost Cartesian dualism of spirit and matter, or else a transcendental system of correspondences between the two worlds. In one case, the writer would be a rationalist adjusting a mechanism; in the other, he would be a mystic awaiting a revelation. Both take for granted a fixed correlation between the syntax of language and the structure of the universe which is, to say the least, semantically naïve.

But Maupassant, whose own technique derived from a simplification of Flaubert's, may have oversimplified here. Flaubert, by continually redrafting and revising, by correcting and changing his texts even after they appeared in print, seemed to admit that the pursuit of the exact word was a process of gradual approximation; that absolute reality was a never quite attainable ideal; that the control of speech over life, like the efficacy of primitive magic, would be incomplete. In the Balzacian sense, he was not a creator but a visionary. His imperfect tenses renew "our vision of things," re-creating the external world through "the impression of time," in a way which Proust compares to the Kantian categories. When, in rewriting, Flaubert substitutes a different descriptive verb for each reappearance of the verb-of-all-work, *faire*, he assumes with warrant that no two situations are exactly alike. When, in proceeding on this assumption, he waits at least thirty pages before permitting himself to repeat a word, he shackles the potentialities of thought to the limitations of diction. His habits of composition, we may suspect, were regulated by his neurotic compulsions. Those pangs and groans, that panting and sweating, were they the agonies that canonized him—for Pater and so many others—as "the martyr of style"? Was his distrust of imagination and talent a suppression of his own more spontaneous qualities? Or was his cult of labor and patience a compensation for the spontaneity of the born writer, the effortlessness of Stendhal? He was well satisfied when, working seven hours a day, he completed two pages a week. Anthony Trollope, at the other extreme, dashed off ten pages every day. Was it not the precondition of Trollope's fluency that he blandly accepted so many conventions, both social and literary, which Flaubert resisted? Was it not significant that, while Trollope's ecclesiastical theme was sinecure, Flaubert's was martyrdom?

It had possessed him from childhood: from the puppet-show, the pinches and grimaces of the demons and the squeaks of the puppet-saint, begging his torturers to leave him alone. The horrific elaboration of Antoine's visions, in the painting of Brueghel and the engraving of Callot, expanded Flaubert's imagination as the impact of the visual arts always did, and became a sort of icon as he hinted to Louise Colet: "For me the sadly grotesque has an unimaginable charm; it corresponds to the intimate needs of my waggishly bitter nature. It doesn't make me laugh, it makes me dream endlessly." He commenced his lucubrations on the subject in May 1848, a month after the death of Alfred Le Poittevin, to whom they would be finally dedicated. Le Poittevin, to whom Flaubert had also dedicated several of his adolescent experiments, had manifested his affinity in a poem entitled *Le Stylite*, where the youthful poet declaims from a lofty and sequestered column:

> Si je descends, soudain m'assiège,
> Confus et bruyant, le cortège
> Qui troublait Antoine aux déserts . . .

In September 1849, Flaubert read aloud his original draft of *La Tentation de saint Antoine* to Louis Bouilhet and Maxime Du Camp. We must allow for retrospective spite in the latter's account of how cavalierly, after four days of reading, the two advised their friend to throw his manuscript into the fire and never to mention it again. After travelling with Du Camp through the Near East for the greater part of the next two years, Flaubert returned to act upon Bouilhet's advice and write *Madame Bovary*. After completing the novel in 1856, he gravitated to his unburned manuscript, and revised it thoroughly, cutting it nearly in half, pruning down its lyricism, and solidifying its allegory. This is the redaction from which excerpts were published in *L'Artiste*. Thence Flaubert turned to *Salammbô* and then, alternating characteristically, to *L'Education sentimentale*, the more pedestrian recapitulation of his moods and changes. It was not until 1871 that the visitation came again: the third and definitive version of *La Tentation de saint Antoine*, which severely stripped the medieval trappings and chastened the personal overtones of the first and the second versions. Bouilhet, the friend who had succeeded Le Poittevin in Flaubert's affections, the poet who so congenially chanted "le dégoût d'être homme et l'ennui de vivre," had just died. Thus the commencement and the completion of Flaubert's work were shadowed by the deaths of his two closest friends. The cycle of loneliness was rounded out by the deaths of his father and sister in 1846 and of his mother in 1872. Coincident with the Empire, it spanned the years between the Republic and the Commune.

The pedestal on which he placed his saint was of monumental design. To some extent it was modelled on *Faust*, which Flaubert had cultivated since his schoolboy discovery of Gérard de Nerval's prose translation. But no distinction could be more strongly

marked than that which separates Goethe's archetype of modernity, with his ripening zest for many-sided fulfillment, from the
self-mortifying renunciation of Flaubert's emaciated protagonist. A
more immediate model may have been Edgar Quinet's anticlerical
mystery-play *Ahasvérus*, in which the ennuis of the Wandering Jew
are mitigated by rhapsodies in favor of scientific progress and visions
conceived by a bored poet—"pour me désennuyer." The effect of
these expansive influences is felt in a youthful fantasy, *Smarh*,
where the demon Yuk looks upon life as "a shroud stained with
wine," and Flaubert's embittered waggery mixes the grotesque with
the sublime according to Hugo's well-known formula. The impulse
to revive the epic, which counted Hugo's *Légende des siècles* as
its grandest monument, was not wasted on Flaubert. He longed
especially to emulate Chateaubriand's *Martyrs*, not only its poetic
prose but its balance of cultural contrasts: paganism against Christianity, France against Rome. As it happened, Flaubert's instincts
were less epical than lyrical, and meanwhile drama itself was deli-
quescing into indeterminate forms. The poet, moving out of the
theater and toward the novel, was freed from theatrical confine-
ments, at any rate; his scenes could range, as broadly as the minds
of his characters, from the subjective spectacle of Goethe's *Wal-
purgisnacht* toward the psychological cinema of Joyce's *Ulysses*.

Midway in this development stands *La Tentation de saint Antoine*. Though it does not adapt itself readily to formal classification, it is a philosophic closet-drama, an encyclopedic prose-poem.
Substantially, it is a dream: the best example of dream literature
that George Saintsbury could name, in a pioneering English article
which Flaubert lived long enough to appreciate. So far as dreams
recapitulate myths, it comprises a veritable parade of mythologies;
that master mythographer, Renan, congratulated Flaubert for having so comprehensively evoked the dreams of humanity. The
dreamer had not escaped from his private nightmares; he had
objectified them by transposing artistic agony into the sphere of
religious controversy. Historically the first of the monks, Saint
Anthony had dominated the ascetic movement of the fourth century which, not irrelevantly to Flaubert's intentions, had protested
against merging the Christian church with the Roman state. The
tendency of the romanticists to isolate their heroes could proceed
no farther than a play about an anchorite, an expressionistic mono-

drama in which temptation and flagellation were performed by the same actor upon himself: Gustave-Antoine in his habitual dual role. "Quelle solitude! quel ennui!" the opening cry of the Egyptian solitary might well be an echo of self-pity from Croisset. The mirage of a city, a city of light, glittering against the bleakness of the Libyan mountains, might be imperial Paris; but no, it is Alexandria, Byzantium, Babylon, each capital vanishing before another more decadently barbaric. Along with more outlandish deities, the gods of Olympus pass, their cups now emptied of ambrosia; and Jupiter steps down from his throne lamenting that "the folly of crowds, the mediocrity of individuals, the hideousness of races triumph everywhere."

A masochistic, self-bound Prometheus, an introverted, impractical Robinson Crusoe, Flaubert's hero would have nothing to do and little to say if it were not for the distractions, the enticements, the disputations that so spectacularly interrupt his monologue. When his erstwhile disciple argues that "this life apart from others is bad," he replies that "all action is degrading." His tempter retorts that "this scorn for the world is merely the impotence of thy hatred against it," and continues in the same ambivalent vein that moved Flaubert, visiting a Breton church, to ask himself: "Isn't asceticism a superior epicureanism, isn't fasting a refined gluttony?" Isn't the world too much with Antoine in his wilderness? Is his withdrawal, then, an act of possession? The indulgence and the mortification of the body are inseparable for Flaubert, even as they are for Baudelaire: chastity is liable to corruption, even as prostitution is compatible with holiness. It remained for Anatole France's *Thaïs*, wherein the monk is debauched and the courtesan sanctified, to work both sides of that particular paradox. For Flaubert the pleasures of the flesh were pervaded by the smell of mortality. His fondest antitheses are those that wed the carnal to the charnel: the wine-stain on the shroud, the skeleton beneath the nude, the legendary carnival of austere doctrines and erotic images. His love for man's animalities, double-edged from the first, culminates before the hermit's cell in the sisterly embrace of Lechery and Death: the gulf of generation and the irony of dissolution. This, too, was an apparition which Baudelaire beheld: "La Débauche et la Mort sont deux aimables filles . . ."

Lust for knowledge is as dangerous as sexual lust to Antoine's besieged innocence. In earlier versions an eighth deadly sin, Logic, had accompanied the orthodox seven—all of which Flaubert later discarded as anachronisms. He retained the horrendous scene where, succumbing to man's original temptation, Christian rites degenerate into orgies of serpent-worship. When at length the voice of the biblical God thunders forth, it is to lament that "the Holy of Holies is open, the veil is torn." The same ambiguous symbols for profanation and violation, desecrated sanctity and forbidden scrutiny, reappear in *Salammbô* along with the python. The vows that banish Antoine from the presence of women do not exclude them from his imaginings, where the part they play is perforce elusive. Among them he vainly seeks a glimpse of Ammonaria, the pious waif remembered from his youth. He repulses the magniloquent advances of the Queen of Sheba, who is "not a woman but a world." As for Ennoïa, who has also been Helen, Lucrece, and Delilah, by any other name she is still the *femme fatale*. Old yet forever young, pale as memory, vague as a dream— we recognize the face, for we have glimpsed it in Walter Pater's prose-portrait of the Mona Lisa. An even more evanescent and sinister heroine, who glides into the story anonymously and by hearsay, is familiar to readers of Keats's "Lamia." That cross-reference may be specially illuminating, since it poses so clear a choice between beauty and truth. Whereas Keats naïvely delights in enchantment and regrets the disenchantment, Flaubert takes cynical satisfaction in the cold philosophy that dispels the charm and turns the woman back into a serpent.

But the illusionistic art of the enchanter holds no appeal for Antoine. "He believes, like a brute, in the reality of things," says the mage Apollonius, and departs for "the world of Ideas, which" —he claims—"is replete with the Word." The Logos, the key to creation, has been differently construed by the martyrs and the magicians, bitterly debated by the Heresiarchs and the Fathers. Strange gods and heathen idols succeed one another, like priests who slay their predecessors. What is truth, what falsehood, in this pageant of comparative religion? The thunder of the scriptural Jehovah and the flatulence of the apocryphal Crépitus are treated with equal reverence. Out of the *Götterdämmerung* steps the disciple Hilarion, whose stature has enlarged with each episode. Now he is ready to announce his identity: he calls himself Science

and Antoine calls him the Devil. As he unfolds his ultimate panorama—the stars, the sky, space, infinity, nothingness—Antoine falls
back, with the cosmic shudder of Pascal. And after Lechery and
Death have laid bare the weakness of the body, another pair of
phantoms, the Chimera and the Sphinx, expose the inadequacy of
the mind. Fantasy expostulates with the Unknown: fleeting illusion is neutralized by unfathomable mystery. "The continuity of
life" is solemnized by a last procession of monsters, fabulous, pre-
historic, increasingly naturalistic. "But if substance is unique, why
should Forms be varied?" Antoine wonders. The answer, "the bond
between matter and thought, the nature of Being," is unveiled
when he flings himself upon the earth and beholds the multiplying
protozoa. The rocks, the plants, the beasts are all confounded together in primal matter, and Antoine unites his existence with
theirs, as the countenance of Jesus Christ radiates from the sun
rising over the Nile.

"Where is the line between dream and reality?" Antoine wondered in the corresponding passage of Flaubert's first version. In
the second, he was no less bewildered: "How can I tell what an
illusion is, or what constitutes reality?" Science was routed by
Faith, Hope, and Charity; Antoine's closing prayer was mocked by
the Devil's laughter; and both versions ended in a metaphysical
stalemate. Before the third version, however, Darwin's *Origin of
Species* which was to be further elucidated for him by Haeckel's
Natural History of Creation, offered Flaubert a materialistic synthesis. By concretely reaffirming the pantheism that he had learned
from Spinoza, the theory of evolution supplied him with a happy
ending under the aspect of eternity. Fond as he was of animals,
it must have been a sacrifice to suppress Antoine's uncanonical pig;
but he compensated by a wealth of zoological allusion so precise
and up-to-date that Taine himself was overwhelmed. Flaubert kept
up with his century, despite the intercession of his other patron,
poor old Polycarp; and *La Tentation de saint Antoine* is at once
a higher criticism of ancient myth and a modern myth of evolu-
tionary progress. To step down from hagiography to autobiography
is to note how Flaubert's interest in religion and science unified
the contrarieties of his art. Three unshakable beliefs, which he
carried over from one realm into another, served to fortify his disbelief in everything else: first, a pursuit of reality, which was neces-

sarily a campaign against illusions, perfecting the tactics of the realist; second, the most real of all facts, material creation, so vulgarly imitated by procreation, so painstakingly refined upon by the literary creator; and third, a devotion to the word, not as dogma but as the medium in which the writer creates, and by which he approximates reality. "Car le mot, c'est le Verbe," Flaubert believed with Hugo, "et le Verbe, c'est Dieu."

For the skeptical, misogynistic recluse, at whose entrails gnawed the *libido sciendi, sentiendi, et dominandi,* this was the true, the beautiful, and the good life. In setting it down—in becoming, so to speak, his own Bollandist—Flaubert not only immersed himself in rich traditions and rigorous disciplines; he threw out hints of surrealism and flashes of montage which, in their very strangeness, are calculated to touch the more obscure places in the reader's consciousness. The demons that plague most of us are smaller and more numerous, more anxious to compromise and content with petty triumphs. The issues are seldom so clear-cut as they were in the cardinal instance of *Paradise Regained,* or the conclusions so foregone. Flaubert's hero is momentarily in danger of succumbing; Milton's, for all the tension between humanism and puritanism, never was; while T. S. Eliot's, in *Murder in the Cathedral,* proudly succumbs to the temptation to resist temptation. The strength of Antoine's resistance can be gauged, at the other extreme, by the futility of Frédéric Moreau. Tempted by every illusion, the ideologies of 'forty-eight pass before him, like the hallucinations and heresies that distract Antoine. Like Antoine, who suffers more than he acts, Frédéric is less an actor in his drama than a spectator at it. But unlike the Gymnosophist, who "moves no farther than a tombstone," Antoine has not permanently "fled from all contact, all action." As a matter of historical fact, which does not contradict the personal legend, Saint Anthony emerged from his trials in the desert to strengthen the faithful and confound the heretics of Alexandria. In the monastery he had organized, among those who were attracted to the stringencies of his rule, he died a serene and natural death at the age of a hundred and five. Properly speaking, he was not a martyr after all.

3. The Female Quixote

As if to put the finishing touches on Flaubert's self-portrait of the artist as a saint, Anatole France likened him to the gigantic and unswerving figure of Saint Christopher, painfully leaning upon an uprooted oak, and stoutly bearing French literature from the romantic to the naturalistic bank of the stream. The quarrel between his two selves—or, perhaps more precisely, the adaptation of temperament to discipline—fitted him uniquely for that mission. His youth, as he recalled it, seemed like some flamboyant cathedral, interposing its stained-glass windows between him and the world. The fact that his native habitat had been a hospital, in all actuality, sanctioned his later efforts to attain a clinical view. This did not entail a rejection of poetry, since he maintained that disillusion was a hundred times more poetic than illusion. The best way of detaching the one from the other was that which he had learned from our classic source; and to it, to *Don Quixote*, he attributed his artistic origins. To it he returned again and again, smitten with its Spanish malady, savoring its gay melancholy, praising its "perpetual fusion of illusion and reality." The generous streak of quixotry in his own nature did not go unremarked by such friends as Alphonse Daudet. Critics have not been remiss in underlining the close analogy between his masterwork and that of Cervantes. Surveying the state of the novel in 1876, an article by Emile Montégut made Flaubert blush by commenting: "Just as Cervantes dealt the death-blow to the chivalric mania with the very weapons of chivalry, so with the very devices of the romantic school Gustave Flaubert has demolished the false ideal that it brought into the world." The doughty deed would not have been committed, in either of these cases, if the time had not conjoined with the talent. Shortly before 1843, in reviewing a play by Scribe, the prophetic Søren Kierkegaard had paused for a footnote to wonder: "It is remarkable that the whole of European literature lacks a feminine counterpart to *Don Quixote*. May not the time for this be coming, may not the continent of sentimentality yet be discovered?"

Heroines were certainly not lacking, and their scope had somewhat widened since the eighteenth century. Marriage was not so much their happy ending as it was the precondition of their unhappiness and an incentive to their emancipation. Delphine or Corinne, the *femme fatale* of Madame de Staël, was presented as the feminine counterpart—and, consequently, the moral superior —to the *homme fatal* of Byron and Chateaubriand. The trousers, the cigars, and the masculine pseudonym of George Sand were the badges of an upsurging feminism, which met with its travesty in the transvestism of Théophile Gautier's *Mademoiselle de Maupin*. Emerging from the domestic incompatibilities of her *Indiana*, George Sand lived through the adventurous passions of her subsequent protagonists, stopping just short of *Lélia*'s unhappy denouement. Her whole-hearted involvement in her heroine fostered a special empathy with her feminine readers. Transported from their everyday lives to her romanticized sphere, they could view themselves in the role of *la femme incomprise*, the unappreciated wife, the misunderstood woman. That vogue had its *cause célèbre* in 1840, when the pampered and well-connected Madame Lafarge was tried and found guilty of poisoning her vulgar provincial husband. Her defense and her memoirs, clearly nourished by sentimental fiction, gained devout support among the public, and were read by Flaubert on the advice of Louise Colet. They moved such moralists as Alfred Nettement to suggest that the veritable poison must have been an immoral novel. A prize-winning discourse by Menche de Loisne extended this logic by accusing Eugène Sue of fomenting the revolution of 1848. The February uprising was also described by Saint-Marc Girardin as "a scene from *Les Mystères de Paris*." The Second Empire, with its tighter controls and its philistine party-lines, made such reactions official; while Flaubert was completing *Madame Bovary*, the Academy of Moral and Political Sciences was calling for an inquiry into the demoralizing influence of the *roman-feuilleton*. The incidence of adultery is not subject to computation; but crimes of passion seemed to be breaking out more and more shockingly; while the suicide rate more than tripled during the years between 1830 and 1880 in France. How much had literature done to spread the moral contagion?

Flaubert's novel, though it won no prizes, could have been construed as another inquest into this critical problem. His persistent theme, according to Paul Bourget, was the hazard of thought; the reading habit itself was his principle of social disequilibrium; and Bourget retrospectively endeavored to summon Flaubert as a witness for his own anti-intellectualism. On his side Bourget could indeed count the elder Madame Bovary, who seeks to cancel her daughter-in-law's subscription to a circulating library, denouncing the librarian as a poisoner. She is volubly seconded by the opinionated M. Homais in Flaubert's original manuscript, wherein the book trade is similarly denounced by a reactionary aristocrat. But these denunciations were retrenched, and the denouncers were never Flaubert's spokesmen. Bad novels merely reflected that narcissistic indulgence which occupied him more seriously as a target. To set forth what Kierkegaard had spied out, to invade the continent of sentimentality, to create a female Quixote—mock-romantic where Cervantes had been mock-heroic—was a man's job. Jane Austen might have done it, but not George Sand, whose *Elle et lui* was reversed when Alfred de Musset retold their romance in *Lui et elle*. The act of detachment had to be incisive and virile, the gesture of a crusty bachelor interrupting the banns to point out the impediments. The first word of the title proclaims a change of status: instead of *La Princesse* or *La Religieuse*, plain *Madame* without the ennobling *de*. Housewives had rarely played title-roles before, except in the raffish tales of Paul de Kock; Balzac's *Madame Firmiani* stresses its heroine's misalliance; and *Madame Angot*, the revolutionary operetta, is about a parvenu fishwife. *Madame Bovary!* the appellative warns us that our heroine is married, and to a bourgeois—a premise not for romance, but for complications, if she happens to be romance-minded. The latent romanticist within Flaubert had been suppressed when Maxime Du Camp and Louis Bouilhet had advised him to burn the original draft of his *Tentation de saint Antoine*. These friends had advised him to discipline himself by taking up a modern subject, something down to earth, such middle-class stuff as Balzac had just been handling in *Les Parents pauvres*.

Bouilhet, who had studied medicine under Flaubert's father, proposed the local and recent case of another former student. In 1848 at the town of Ry, the second wife of a Dr. Delamare, after a series of adulteries and extravagances, was rumored to have poisoned herself and precipitated her husband's suicide, leaving an orphan daughter. Flaubert acknowledged this suggestion, and the years of critical midwifery that supported it, when he dedicated *Madame Bovary* to Bouilhet. To Du Camp, we are informed by the latter, Flaubert's acknowledgments were appropriately medical: "I was ridden by the cancer of lyricism, and you operated; it was just in time, but I cried out in pain." Part of the cure was their Mediterranean voyage, which left Flaubert bored with the exotic and homesick for the commonplace. From a French hotel-keeper in Cairo, a M. Bouvaret, he picked up a name for his bovine country doctor: *forum bovarium* is a cattle-market. Among his *Notes de voyage* he jotted down an occasional reflection upon his future theme: "The poetry of the adulterous wife is only true to the extent that she is at liberty in the midst of fatality." To the heroine of George Sand, resisting the prose of her environment, such poetry may be subjectively true. But to the extent that she is caught in the network of objective circumstance, that free will is subjected to determining necessity, the truth about her is bound to be unpoetic; what seems beautiful must prove false. To the extent that her intimate fantasies are exposed by the light of external realities, that sense undercuts sensibility, Flaubert's treatment is like that of other realists. But where the fantasy of *Don Quixote* took on the guise of a vanishing heroism, which the heroine did not jeopardize with her presence, the feminine outlook of *Madame Bovary* is consistently belied by its masculine characters. Where romance, to Cervantes, signified knightly adventure, to Flaubert—more narrowly and intensively—it signifies passionate love. The means of exposure, which put Cervantes' realism on a solid and genial basis, was an appeal to the common sense of the bourgeoisie. That would have been, for Flaubert, almost as delusive and fantastic as romanticism itself. Hence he often seems to have taken the realistic method and turned it inside out. "Realism seems to us with *Madame Bovary* to have said its last word," commented Henry James, with a sigh of somewhat premature relief.

In sharpest contradistinction to Don Quixote, whose vagaries were intellectual, Emma Bovary's are emotional. Hence they are counterweighted by no earthbound Sancho Panza, but by the intellectually pretentious M. Homais. The comic relief that he injects into Emma's tragedy is later to be elaborated into the unrelieved comedy of *Bouvard et Pécuchet*. Because it is herself that she misconceives, where Don Quixote's misconception of actuality could be corrected by reference to his fellow men, she remains incorrigibly tragic. This paranoiac attitude of Emma's, this self-hallucination induced by overreading, this "habit of conceiving ourselves otherwise than as we are," is so epidemic that Jules de Gaultier could diagnose the weakness of the modern mind as *Bovarysme*. The vicarious lives that film stars lead for shop-girls, the fictive euphoria that slogans promise and advertisements promote, the imaginary flourishes that supplement and garnish daily existence for all of us, are equally Bovaristic. If to Bovarize is simply to daydream, as everyone does to a greater or lesser extent, the criterion is not how much we do so, but whether our daydreams are egoistic like Emma's or altruistic like Don Quixote's. Every epoch depends upon some verbal medium for its conception of itself: on printed words and private fictions, if not on public rituals and collective myths. The trouble came when, instead of the imitation of Christ or the veneration of Mary, readers practised the emulation of Rastignac or the cult of Lélia. Yet, whatever their models, they were romanticizing a reality which would otherwise have been formless and colorless; for when nature has established norms of conduct, art is called upon to publicize them. "There are people who would not fall in love if they had never heard of love," said La Rochefoucauld. Denis de Rougemont has tried to substantiate that epigram by arguing that the erotic motive was superimposed upon the West through medieval romance. Paolo might never have loved Francesca, in Dante's memorable episode, had not the book of Galeotto acted as a go-between.

But the writer, if not the reader, cannot afford to be swept off his feet by emotions involved in a given story. Thus Flaubert, in his first *Education sentimentale*, describes the youthful reading of his poet, Jules:

> He reread *René* and *Werther*, those books of disgust with life; he reread Byron and dreamed of the solitude of his great-souled heroes; but too much of his admiration was based on personal sympathy, which has nothing in common with the disinterested admiration of the true artist. The last word in this kind of criticism, its most inane expression, is supplied to us every day by a number of worthy gentlemen and charming ladies interested in literature, who disapprove of this character because he is cruel, of that situation because it is equivocal and rather smutty—discovering, in the last analysis, that in the place of such a person they would

not have done the same thing, without understanding the
necessary laws that preside over a work of art, or the logical
deductions that follow from an idea.

It follows that Emma Bovary and her censors, though their ethics
differed, shared the same esthetic approach. Jules on the other
hand would learn, as did Flaubert, to differentiate a work of art
from its subject-matter and the artist from his protagonist. The
anecdote of Cervantes on his deathbed, identifying himself with
his hero, has its much quoted Flaubertian parallel: *Madame Bovary c'est moi*. But this equivocal statement was not so much a
confession as a cautious disclaimer of certain resemblances which
Madame Delamare's neighbors, without indulging in unwarranted
gossip, might have suspected. In so far as Flaubert lived the part,
as any novelist enters into his fully realized characterizations, it was
a *tour de force* of female impersonation. The identification was not
nearly so close as it had been with Saint-Antoine or would become
with Frédéric Moreau. It is true that, on summer days, he worked
in the arbor where he stages trysts between Emma and Rodolphe;
that the cigar-case, the seal inscribed *Amor nel cor*, and other relics
actually commemorate his own affair with Louise Colet; that
Louise may well have suggested aspects of Emma, and Emma's
lovers and husband may have embodied aspects of Gustave. But
the very first premise of the book was the suppression of his own
personality, and his later pronouncements adhere with stiffening
conviction to the principle of *ne s'écrire*. Empathy is seasoned with
antipathy whenever he writes about Emma to Louise; he repeatedly complains that the bourgeois vulgarity of his material disgusts
and nauseates him. He would much prefer to write a book without
a subject; or rather, he would like to abolish the transitions and
obstacles between thought and expression; and he prophesies that
literary convention, like the Marxian concept of the state, will
some day wither away.

Flaubert had chosen the legend of *La Tentation de saint Antoine* in accordance with his personal predilections. Baudelaire,
who preferred the more imaginative work, explained *Madame
Bovary* as a sort of wager. "The budding novelist found himself
facing an absolutely worn-out society—worse than worn-out, brutal
and greedy, fearing nothing but fiction and loving nothing but

property." Deliberately choosing the drabbest setting, the pettiest characters, the most familiar plot, he undertook to create a masterpiece out of them, to turn their shapeless ugliness into formal beauty. He did not quite succeed in assimilating the psychology of his heroine, in the opinion of Baudelaire: "Madame Bovary has remained a man." Now it may be—in fact, it would be Dorothy Richardson's hypothesis—that no masculine novelist can ever quite penetrate the feminine mentality. Nevertheless, as Matthew Arnold perceived, Tolstoy's portrayal of Anna Karenina could be more warmly sympathetic than the "petrified feeling" that went into Flaubert's portraiture. Insofar as he attached his narration to his heroine, Flaubert was detaching himself from those whom she repudiated and from those who repudiated her. Thereby he ostensibly gave up, to the indignation of his critics, the moralistic prerogatives of the narrator. He replaced sentiment, so Brunetière charged, with sensation. He developed the technical device that handbooks term point of view by adapting the rhythms of his style to the movement of his character's thoughts. By limiting what has more precisely been termed the center of consciousness to the orbit of a single character—and, with Henry James, a peculiarly limited character—purists could intensify the focus of the novel still further. Nonetheless *Madame Bovary* begins, as if with a prologue, in the first person; then it switches from an anonymous classmate, of whom we learn no more than that, to Charles Bovary; through Charles's eyes we first glimpse Emma's fingernails, and gradually experience his delayed reaction; thereafter the action is mainly, though by no means exclusively, circumscribed within her range of perception. But toward the end the perspective opens up and detaches itself from Emma more and more; her pantomime interview with the tax-collector is reported as witnessed by a chorus of townswomen; and Flaubert's account of her funeral terminates with the various night-thoughts of the men who have loved her.

And there are such moments as when, having escorted his lovers into a curtained cab, Flaubert draws back a tactful distance and projects a rapid sequence of long-range shots, so that—instead of witnessing their embrace—we participate in a tour of the city of Rouen, prolonged and accelerated to a metaphorical climax. The invisible omnipresence that stage-manages these arrangements is normally expressed by *on*, initially by *nous*, but never by *je*. The

author's commentary is to be inferred from his almost cinematographic manipulation of detail: the close-up of a religious statuette,
for example, which falls from the moving-wagon into fragments on
the road between Tostes and Yonville. Such comment is transposed to a scientific key when, after the unsuccessful operation,
Emma slams the door on Charles and breaks his barometer. Henceforth the incongruous memento of his failure is the patent-leather
shoe affixed to the artificial limb of his patient, the no longer club-
footed stableboy. A silly cap which characterizes Charles on his
first appearance, a pocket-knife which betokens his coarseness in
Emma's eyes—nothing is mentioned that does not help to carry
the total burden of significance. Hence every object becomes, in its
way, a symbol; the novelist seeks the right thing, as well as the
right word; and things are attributes which define their owners,
properties which expedite the stage-business. Charles's first marriage is tellingly summed up by a bouquet of withered orange blos-
soms in a glass jar, while a handsome cigar-case retains the aroma
of fashionable masculinity that Emma has inhaled at the ball.
Such effects are governed by a rigorous process of selection, far
removed from the all-inclusive collection by which Balzac accumulated background. The atmosphere, for Flaubert, is the story; the
province is both his setting and his subject—the colorlessness of
local color. The midland that he depicts is a bastard territory,
somewhere along the borders of Normandy, Picardy, and Ile-de-
France, where the speech has no accent, the landscape no character, the soil no richness. Even the cheese thereabouts is lacking in
savor. Everything seems, like Charles's conversation, "as flat as a
sidewalk."

To render flatness flatly, however, is to risk the stalemate
that confronted Pope when he tried to excoriate dullness without
becoming dull. Flaubert, deploying his full stylistic resources,
relieves the ennui by colorful allusion and invidious comparison.
What is literally boring he renders metaphorically interesting.
The river quarter of Rouen, at first sight, is "a small, ignoble
Venice." The names of famous surgeons are mock-heroically
sounded in connection with Charles's professional activities. Similes, ironically beautiful, frequently serve to underline ugly realities:
thus the pimples on the face of his first wife had "budded like
a springtime." Occasionally Flaubert seems to set thousands of

miles between himself and the situation at hand, as when—with the anthropological objectivity he had shown at his niece's baptism—he notes the similarity between a statue of the Virgin in the village church and an idol from the Sandwich Islands. The gap between the heroine and her chronicler opens wide with a Shakespearean simile, linking her amorous intoxication to the butt of Malmsey in which the Duke of Clarence was drowned. Despite Flaubert's more usual closeness to his dramatis personae, he austerely dissociates himself from their subjective opinions, and italicizes certain expressions which their lack of fastidiousness has forced him to cite. He manages to approximate their points of view, while retaining the detachment of the third person and avoiding the formality of indirect discourse, through his mastery of *le style indirect libre*. Though this term seems to have no English equivalent, it denotes the kind of grammatical figuration, the modulation of tenses, the dropping of pronominal antecedents, and the resulting internalization of narrative which, thanks primarily to Flaubert, are now employed in most of our novels and short stories.

> She gave up music. Why play? Who would listen?

> What sunny days they had had! What fine afternoons, alone in the shade at the depth of the garden!

> Never before had he come across such grace of speech, such good taste in attire, such supple, dovelike poses. He admired the exaltation of her spirit and the lace of her petticoat.

Through the first two quotations we catch the lilt of Emma's internal monologue. In the third, for a sentence, the voice of Léon echoes the naïveté of her previous responses to Rodolphe, and then yields to the voice of Flaubert, with a clear-cut dissociation which makes manifest Léon's confusion. Meaningful juxtaposition is Flaubert's signature, where Balzac's was miscellaneous accretion. Where Balzac's descriptions were like introductory stage-directions, Flaubert introduces objects as they swim into the ken of his personages. His personages, since they are the fluid receptacles of sense-impressions, are much less numerous than the sharply moulded types from the Balzacian mint. In the English novelist's sense, says Elizabeth Bowen, Emma is not a character at all: "She consists in sentiments and sensations, in moments for their own sake." Flaubert's technique of characterization, as he formulated it to Taine, was "not to individualize a generality, like Hugo or Schiller, but to generalize a particularity, like Goethe or Shakespeare."

He forwarded this large intention by deciding to portray a particular individual who also happened to be a universal type— who, as he put it, suffered and wept in twenty French villages. She had actually existed in the ill-fated Madame Delamare; and, as Zola remarked, her sisters went on existing throughout France. Even while Flaubert was writing his novel, her misadventures were being enacted by the wife of his friend, the sculptor Pradier; and some of Louise Pradier's confidences became Emma Bovary's indiscretions. Strangely enough, the latter's fate was to be paralleled by that of the novel's first English translator, Karl Marx's daughter, Eleanor Marx-Aveling. American readers recognize Emma's kinship with Carol Kennicott, the capricious wife of Sinclair Lewis' country doctor in *Main Street*, and are struck by recurring features of small-town subsistence which abridge the spatial and temporal intervals between Gopher Prairie and Yonville-l'Abbaye. Flaubert's preoccupation with his heroine's environment is emphasized by his subtitle, *Moeurs de province*—how far a cry from the sympathetic overview that subtitles *Middlemarch, A Study of Provincial Life!* His social observation, which of course is more precise and analytic than Balzac's, concentrates upon a much smaller terrain and thoroughly exhausts it. His fiction starts from, and returns to, fact; when in a newspaper he came across the very phrase that he had put into his imaginary orator's mouth, he congratulated himself that literature was being reduced to an exact science at last. When *Madame Bovary* appeared, it was saluted by the magazine *Réalisme* as "a literary application of the calculus of probabilities." Though that is a far cry from any classical doctrine of probability, it looks beyond mere particularizing toward some meaningful pattern into which all the particulars must fit, a result which is predictable from the data, the logical deductions that follow from an idea. The concrete details that Flaubert selects, we have noticed, are always typical and often symbolic. We notice too his tendency to multiply the specific instance into a generalization. In his treatment of crowds, at the wedding or the exhibition, traits which were individually observed are collectively stated. Similarly, the plural is applied to immediate experiences which have become habitual, as in this summary of the doctor's routine:

> He ate omelets on farmhouse tables, poked his arm into damp beds, felt the warm spurts of blood-letting in his face, listened for death-rattles, examined basins, turned over a good deal of dirty linen; but every evening he found a blazing fire, a laid-out table, comfortable chairs, and a well-dressed wife, so charming and sweet-smelling that it was hard to say whence the odor came, or whether her skin were not perfuming her chemise.

The second half of this highly Flaubertian sentence brings us home to Emma, balances the attractions of her day against the revulsions of Charles's, and registers the incompatibility of their respective ways of life. A sequence of vividly physical manifestations, ranging through the clinical toward the sensual, unfolds itself for us just as it did for Charles. Strain is compensated by relaxation; pain and suffering give place to comfort and well-being; but, contrasted with the grim concreteness of his own sensations and the tangible solidity of his cases, there is something elusive and possibly deceptive in the person of Emma, which is vaguely hinted by her ambiguous perfume. More commonly we see the uxorious husband, from her vantage-point, as the thick-skinned personification of plodding mediocrity: the medical man well suited to the village of Tostes, whose competence is strained by the town of Yonville. From his earliest entrance into the schoolroom, he falters between the comic and the pathetic; his solitary youth and loveless first marriage prepare him for the ungrateful role of the cuckold; on his visit to the chateau he seems indeed to be playing the bourgeois gentleman. His very schoolmates have found him too unromantic, yet his love is the most devoted that Emma finds—as Flaubert expressly states in his work-sheets, adding: "This must be made very clear." His own devotion to his motherless niece is doubtless reflected in Charles's tenderness toward his daughter, Berthe. In the final retrospect—the analogue of that weary reunion which rounds out

L'Education sentimentale—Charles, over a bottle of beer with his wife's lover, Rodolphe, forgives him and blames the whole affair on "fatality." Rodolphe, though he has blamed fatality in his farewell letter to Emma, was scarcely a fatalist when he took the initiative; while Emma has enjoyed, as long as it lasted, the poetic illusion of liberty. Now that it has yielded to necessity, and the probable has become the inevitable, Charles is left to bear—and it kills him—the unpoetic truth.

The issue is poised between his materialistic plane, which is vulgar but real, and her ideal of refinement, which is illusory. "Charles conjugal night: plans for his career. his child. Emma: dreams of travel. the lover. villa on the shore. until dawn..." This bare notation was expanded by Flaubert into two of his most luminous pages—pages which reveal not only the nocturnal reveries of the doctor and his wife, her Italianate fancies and his Norman calculations, but the conflict within Flaubert's dual personality between lyricism and criticism—or, to use his synonym for the latter, "anatomy." To anatomize Emma's imagination is succinctly to recapitulate the romantic movement itself, moving from the primitive idyll of *Paul et Virginie* through the polychromatic mysticism of Chateaubriand's *Génie du Christianisme* toward the vicarious passions of George Sand and Balzac. Emma's sentimental education, accompanied by the excitations of music and perfumed by the incense of religiosity, is traced back to the convent where she has been schooled. From the drab milieu she has known as a farmer's daughter, her extracurricular reading conjures up the allurements of escape: steeds and guitars, balconies and fountains, medieval and Oriental vistas. Dreaming between the lines, she loses her identity in the heroines of the novels she peruses, the mistresses to whom verses are inscribed, the models in the fashion magazines. The ball at the Château de Vaubyessard lends a touch of reality to her fictitious world, which Flaubert likened—in a discarded metaphor—to "a drop of wine in a glass of water." When she discovers a kindred soul in the young law-clerk Léon, the only person in the community who seems comparably sensitive to boredom and yearning and the arts, their friendship is "a continual traffic in books and romances." And when a neighboring landowner, the sportsman-philanderer Rodolphe, assists her to fulfill her sexual desires, fantasy and actuality seem to merge in the realization: "I have a lover!"

But adultery ends by reasserting "the platitudes of marriage," and neither condition teaches Emma the meaning of "the words that looked so fine in books: 'felicity,' 'passion,' and 'intoxication.'" Here, more explicitly than in *Don Quixote* itself, language is of the essence; the basic misunderstanding, since it is verbal, is regulated by the flow and ebb of Flaubert's prose; and his rhetoric is constantly expanding into purple passages which are trenchantly deflated by his irony. The ensuing style, he feared, might read like "Balzac chateaubrianisé." Yet if that compound means eloquent banality rather than banal eloquence, it is not too inept a summation of what Flaubert attempted and achieved; and those literary auspices are not inappropriate for the incongruity between Emma's high-flown sentiments and Charles's pedestrian bumblings. If we ever forgot that the book was about an ill-matched pair, we should be reminded by the way that sentences double back upon themselves and episodes are paired off against one another. The two turning-points of the first part, the fourth and eighth chapters, frame a significant contrast between the peasantry and the aristocracy. The garish colors of the rustic wedding, the raw haircuts of the farmers, the lengthened communion-dresses of the girls, the boisterous jokes and substantial viands in the manner of Brueghel, are pointedly offset by the grand entertainment at the chateau, where the stately dancers display "the complexion of wealth, that fair complexion which is enhanced by the pallor of porcelain, the shimmer of satin, the veneer of fine furniture." In the second part a similar pairing occurs, which even more fatally brings out the variance between Charles and Emma: the operation versus the opera. On the one hand his surgical incompetence, the gangrenescent cripple, and the amputated foot are portents of Emma's relapse. On the other the romantic libretto from Scott, *Lucia di Lammermoor*, the swaggering tenor Lagardy as Edgar, and the coruscating spectacle would corrupt purer souls than hers; we may recall Natasha in *War and Peace*. Overwhelmed by "Edgar Lagardy," Emma becomes, in effect, Lucia Bovary.

The two antithetical strains are juxtaposed in the central chapters of the book, where the agricultural exhibition takes place in the public square while Rodolphe flirts with Emma in the privacy of the deserted neo-Greek town hall. His amorous pleas are counterpointed by the bureaucratic platitudes of the political orators outside; a prize for the highest quality of manure is awarded at the delicate moment when he grasps her hand; the bifurcation is so thoroughgoing that the National Guard and the fire brigade refuse to march together; and the series of anticlimaxes culminates when nightfall brings a fizzle of dampened fireworks. Now Flaubert built up this scene by writing out continuous speeches for both sets of characters, which he thereupon broke down and rearranged within the larger framework of the situation. By such means he caught that interplay of cross-purposes which is increasingly stressed through the third and last part, above all in the cathedral and at the deathbed. He told Louise Colet that the method of *Madame Bovary* would be biographical rather than dramatic, yet biography seems to branch out into drama at all the crucial stages of Emma's career; and these, in turn, furnish the novel with its six or eight major scenes—several of which are overtly theatrical or, at any rate, ceremonial. Their relation to the rest of the book, and to his ambivalent purpose, may be gathered from his further remark that "dialogue should be written in the style of comedy, narrative in the style of epic." Mock-epic would probably be a more accurate classification of Flaubert's tone, as differentiated from the various inflections he reproduces, and softened by lyrical interludes when he is Emma. The many contrasting strands of discourse are so closely interwoven that the texture is uniformly rich, although it varies from one chapter to the next. Each of them advances the narrative a single step, scores a new point and captures another mood, much as a well-turned short story does in the hands of Flaubert's innumerable emulators.

The chapter, as Flaubert utilizes it, is in itself a distinctive literary genre. Its opening is ordinarily a straightforward designation of time or place. Its conclusion habitually imposes some striking effect: a pertinent image, an epigrammatic twist, a rhetorical question, a poignant afterthought. "She had loved him after all." The succession of episodes, like the articulation of a rosary, shapes the continuity of the work. The three-part structure allows the novelist, with a classicism seldom encountered in novels, to give his conception a beginning, a middle, and an end: to study first the conditions of Emma's marriage, then her Platonic romance and her carnal affair, and finally the train of consequences that leads to her death. Different leading men play opposite her, so to speak, in these three successive parts: Charles in the first, Rodolphe in the second, Léon in the third. The setting broadens with her aspirations, starting from the narrowest horizon, Tostes, proceeding to the main locale, Yonville, and ultimately reaching the provincial capital, Rouen. Not that she wished to stop there. "She wanted simultaneously to die and to live in Paris," Flaubert apprises us in a characteristic zeugma, and he seems to have toyed with the notion of granting her that double-barreled wish. But he wisely decided to confine her to the province, reserving his study of the metropolis for the fortunes of Frédéric Moreau. The chronology of *Madame Bovary*, which spans the decade from 1837 to 1847, roughly corresponds with the period of *L'Education sentimentale*, stopping just short of the mid-century crisis. Each of its subdivisions, conforming to a rough but Dantesque symmetry, covers slightly more than three years. The crucial season would seem to be the autumn of 1843, when Rodolphe fails to elope with Emma and she is plunged into brain fever. Up to that stage, with manic fervor, her illusions mount; after that, with steady disillusionment, she sinks toward her last depression. The dating coincides, more or less, with Flaubert's failure to pass his examinations, and with the neurotic crisis of his personal career.

Between the autumn of 1851 and the spring of 1856 his concentrated labor was the writing of *Madame Bovary*. For those who hold—with André Gide—that the gestation of art is more interesting than the finished product, no record could be more fascinating than Flaubert's correspondence during those four years and a half. The parallel lives of the author and the heroine, daily, weekly, monthly, yearly, charge the novel with their emotional tension. Imaginative effort was reinforced by documentation when Flaubert sought the proper shading for Emma's hallucinations by immersing himself in *Keepsakes* and other feminine periodicals. By plying his brother with queries about surgery and toxicology, he filled in the peculiar symptoms his outline required: "Agony precise medical details 'on the morning of the twenty-third she had vomiting spells again. . .' " He familiarized himself with the children of his brain by drawing a map of Yonville and keeping files on its citizens. He controlled his plot—or should we say he calculated his probabilities?—by carefully drafting and firmly reworking scenarios. The embryonic material for his novel comprised some 3600 pages of manuscript. The demiurgic function of reducing that mass to its present form might be compared to the cutting of a film; and, rather than speak of Flaubert's "composition" in the pictorial sense, we might refer, in kinetic terms, to montage. To watch him arranging his artful juxtapositions, or highlighting one detail and discarding another, is a lesson in artistic economy. To trace his revision of a single passage, sometimes through as many as twelve versions, is the hopeful stylist's *gradus ad Parnassum*. It is therefore a boon to students of literature that Flaubert's drafts and variants have been gathered and printed. But to reincorporate them into a composite text of *Madame Bovary*, interpolating what he excised, reamplifying what he condensed, and thereby undoing much of what he so purposefully did—as has been done in the so-called *Nouvelle version*—is a doubtful service to his intentions. Flaubert might have preferred Bowdlerization.

He did protest against expurgations when the novel was serially published in the *Revue de Paris*; but Du Camp and his editors had not expurgated enough to appease the prudery of the imperial police; and Flaubert, together with the publisher and the printer, was prosecuted for outraging civic and religious morality. The outrage, so the prosecution alleged, was worse than pornography; it was blasphemy. Flaubert's offense was less a concern with sex than an attempt to link sex with religion. It mattered little that the linkage had been effected on the naïve level of Emma's confused motivation, or that his analysis could be corroborated, by such sympathetic clerics as Bishop Dupanloup, from their first-hand remembrance of country confessionals. The ruse of citing passages out of context figured heavily in the trial, and the government staked much of its case on the passage where Emma receives extreme unction. It was a precarious example, since by definition that sacrament hovers ambiguously between the worlds of sense and spirit: shift the emphasis, as Joyce does in *Finnegans Wake*, and it becomes an apology for the flesh. Flaubert's defense, by warily refusing to admit the ambiguity, was able to claim the support of orthodox sanctions, along with the precedent of such diverse French writers as Bossuet and Sainte-Beuve. It argued that *Madame Bovary* as a whole, far from tempting its readers to sensualism, offered them an edifying object-lesson. Considerable stress was laid *ad hominem* on the bourgeois respectability of the Flaubert family. Won by such arguments, the judge acquitted Flaubert and his accomplices, with a parting disquisition on taste and a fatherly warning against "a realism which would be the negation of the beautiful and the good." Six months later, when *Les Fleurs du mal* was condemned, Flaubert must have wondered whether he or Baudelaire was the victim of judicial error. Meanwhile, in April 1857, when *Madame Bovary* came out as a book, its intrinsic ironies were enhanced by a preliminary dedication to Flaubert's lawyer and an appended transcript of the court proceedings.

Great books have their proverbial fates, among which banning and burning may not be the hardest, since these involve downright conflicts of principle. It may be harder for the serious artist, be he Flaubert or Joyce, to emerge from the cloud of censorship into the glare of scandalous success. The public reception of Flaubert's first book, at all events, hardened those equivocal attitudes which had been poured into it. To avoid the accusation of immorality, he was pushed into the embarrassing position of a moralist. If the novel was not pornographic, it must be didactic —or had he stopped beating his wife? Taine spins an amusing anecdote of an English project to translate and circulate *Madame Bovary* as a Methodist tract, subtitled *The Consequences of Misbehavior*. The respectable Lamartine, cited on Flaubert's behalf, declared that Emma's sins were too severely expiated. Why need Flaubert have been so much less merciful than Jesus was toward the woman taken in adultery? Partly because he was not exemplifying justice, partly because he may have been punishing himself, but mainly because her infractions of the seventh commandment were the incidental and ineffectual expression of an all-pervasive state of mind: Bovarism. Her nemesis, as Albert Thibaudet shrewdly perceived, is not a love affair but a business matter: her debt to the usurious merchant, Lheureux. When the bailiffs move in to attach the property, their inventory becomes a kind of autopsy. The household disintegrates before our eyes, as its component items are ticked off, and we think of the auction in *L'Education sentimentale*. This empty outcome, by the Flaubertian rule of opposites, is a sequel to the agricultural exhibition, where rural prosperity smugly dispenses its awards. And the lonely figure of Charles, left to brood among unpaid bills and faded love-letters, has been foreshadowed by Père Rouault after Emma's wedding, "as sad as an unfurnished house."

The vacuum her absence creates for her father and husband echoes the hollowness of her own misapplied affections. Rodolphe's gallantry, after meeting her desires halfway, proves to be no more than a cynical technique of seduction. Léon's sentimentalism is quite sincere, until she seduces him, and then it vanishes like growing pains. "Every notary bears within him the ruins of a poet." Consequently, amid the most prosaic circumstances, there will still be some spark of poetry, and in Yonville-l'Abbaye it is Emma Bovary. It is not, alas, the Princesse de Clèves; nor could that model of all the compunctions have flourished there; for her delicacy presupposes reciprocal comportment on the part of others. Emma's dreams are destined, at the touch of reality, to wither into lies. Is that a critique of her or of reality? If she suffers for her mistakes, shall we infer that those who prosper are being rewarded for their merits? If we cannot, we can hardly assume—with the novel's courtroom apologists—that it preaches a self-evident moral. If it were a play, our reactions would be clearer; we are more accustomed to facing her plight in the theater; we disapprove of Hedda Gabler's intrigues and pity the wistful Katerina in Ostrovsky's *Storm*. Though she possesses the qualities of both those heroines, Emma is essentially a novelistic creation, set forth in all her internal complexities. Entrammelled by them, we cannot pretend to judge her, any more than we can judge ourselves. But, guided by Flaubert, perhaps we can understand her: *Madame Bovary c'est nous*. With her we look down from the town hall upon the exposition, a sordid rustic backdrop for Rodolphe's welcome advances. Again, at her rendezvous with Léon, the lovers occupy the foreground; but this time it is the massive cathedral of Rouen that looks down upon them; and its sculptured warriors and stained-glass saints, too hastily passed by, are the mute upholders of higher standards than those which

Emma and Léon are engaged in flouting. "Leave by the north portico, at any rate," the verger shouts after them, baffled by their indifference to Gothic antiquities, "and see the Resurrection, the Last Judgment, Paradise, King David, and the Condemned in Hellfire!"

The heavy judgment that Flaubert suspends, and which we too withhold, is implicit in this hurried exclamation. It affects the lovers as little as the extinct abbey affects Yonville, in whose name alone it survives. Yet oblique reference accomplishes what overt preaching would not, and those neglected works of art bear an ethical purport. The category of *moraliste*, which is so much more comprehensive with the French than with us, given its condensation of morals and manners, still applied to Flaubert *malgré lui*. Whereas he seemed immoral to those who confused him with his characters, and seems amoral to those who take at face value an aloofness which is his mask for strong emotions, he protested too much when he claimed to be impersonal. If he deserves Maupassant's adjective "impassive," it is because all passion has crystallized beneath the lucent surfaces of his prose. He is not above making sententious and aphoristic pronouncements upon the behavior of his characters: "A request for money is the most chilling and blighting of all the winds that blow against love." Nor does he shrink from stigmatizing Emma's acts as phases of "corruption" and even "prostitution." More positively he betrays his sympathy, when it seems most needed, by the adjective *pauvre*. The crippled groom is a "poor devil," and so is the blind man; the luckless Charles is "poor boy," and the gestures of Emma's agony are made by "her poor hands." The word regains its economic overtones, and Flaubert's tone is uniquely humanitarian, when he pauses before the "poor garments" of Catherine Leroux. The hands of this aged peasant woman, in definitive contrast to Emma, are deformed with toil. On the platform "before those expansive bourgeois," personifying "half a century of servitude," her mute and ascetic presence strikes the single note of genuine dignity amid the pomposities and hypocrisies of the agricultural exhibition. Flaubert deliberately classifies her with the attendant livestock, for whose impassivity he reserves his compassion. His irony intervenes to measure her reward, twenty-five francs for a lifetime of service, against two pigs which have just gained prizes of sixty francs apiece. An earlier and crueller twist, which Flaubert finally left out, pictures her deaf apprehension lest the judges accuse her of stealing the twenty-five francs.

Here is Flaubert's response to those who criticize *Madame Bovary* for its apparent lack of positive values. The human qualities he really admired, the stoic virtues of patience, devotion, work, are not less admirable when they go unrewarded. His careful portrait of Catherine Leroux—together with many landscapes, small and subdued, of his fog-tinted Normandy—belongs with the canvases then being painted by Courbet at Ornans and Millet at Barbizon. Peasant faces, though never conspicuous, are always in the background; they watch Emma through the broken window-panes of the chateau. Animals, too, are sentient characters: her mysterious greyhound, Djali, is almost a demonic familiar, which has its opposite number in the goat Djala, the mascot of *Notre-Dame de Paris*. The people that Flaubert treats sympathetically are life's victims like the clubfooted Hippolyte, those whom Hugo would name *Les Misérables* and Dostoevsky *The Insulted and the Injured*. Surely the kindest person in the story is the druggist's errand-boy, Justin, whose dumb affection is the unwitting instrument of Emma's death, and whose illicit reading-matter is her ironic epitaph: a book entitled *Conjugal Love*. The meek do not inherit Flaubert's earth; the good, by definition, are the ones that suffer; and the unhappy ending, for poor little innocent Berthe, is grim child-labor in a textile factory. The most downtrodden creature of all, the dog-like Blind Man, is linked by a grotesque affinity with Emma herself. Envisaging him as a "monster," a *memento mori*, an incarnation of fleshly frailty, Flaubert had originally planned to make him armless and legless rather than visionless; and he pointedly accentuated Emma's disillusion by the swish of the driver's whip that knocks the helpless beggar off the coach. This is coincident with the critical stroke that once laid Flaubert prostrate on a muddy Norman road. His blind man dogs his heroine's missteps to her very deathbed, with a terrible mimicry which is not unworthy of King Lear's fool; and there his unseasonable song, a lyric from Restif de la Bretonne about young girls' dreams of love, finds its long awaited echo of relevance. Emma's eyes open to a recognition scene "like a person waking from a dream," like Don Quixote when death restores his aberrant sense of reality.

The counterpoint set up in the cathedral attains its fullest resolution—far from the rented room at the Hôtel-de-Boulogne—in Emma's bedchamber. There priestly rites alleviate clinical symptoms; the unction allays the poison; and, taking formal leave of her five senses one by one, Flaubert breaks off his prolonged sequence of associations between sacred and profane love. In so far as orchestration is based on arrangement rather than statement, Flaubert's can best be appreciated by comparing this episode with a remotely analogous one from *The Old Curiosity Shop*, the famous sermon on the reiterated text: "Dear, gentle, patient, noble Nell was dead." Flaubert, who evokes what Dickens invokes and elaborates what the Englishman simplifies, dismisses his heroine more abruptly and absolutely: "She no longer existed." Thereafter Emma's death-watch unites "in the same human weakness" Father Bournisien, with his holy water, and M. Homais, with his bottle of chlorine. Since religion is served by the priest as inadequately as science is by the pharmacist, it is not surprising that neither force has operated benignly on Emma's existence, or that the antagonists—as Bournisien predicts—"may end by understanding one another." Homais, the eternal quacksalver, is a would-be writer as well as a pseudo-scientist, who practises the up-to-date art of journalism and is most adept at self-advertisement. Because his shop is the source of Emma's arsenic, he is an unconscious accomplice in her suicide; and he instigates the ill-advised surgery that poisons Hippolyte's leg and blackens Charles's reputation. When his own prescription, the antiphlogistic pomade, fails to cure the Blind Man's scrofula, it is typical of him to add insult to injury, persecuting his patient while continuing to pose as the benefactor of mankind. M. Homais is definitively shown up by the retarded arrival of Dr. Larivière, just as the introduction of Catherine Leroux is a standing rebuke to Emma's course of conduct. Hereupon, Flaubert, inspired by memories of his father, dedicates a strongly affirmative paragraph to the understanding physician, who pursues the compassionate calling of medicine as religiously as a medieval saint. But the doctor is no god-in-the-machine, and it is too late for an antidote. With a tear he discerns the prognosis at once and with a farewell pun he diagnoses the complaint of Homais. His difficulty is not *le sang* but *le sens*—neither anemia nor hypertension, nor indeed that lack of sense from which poor Emma suffered, but insensibility, the defect of her quality.

What is worse, the disease is contagious. With the rare exception of the stranger Larivière, and the dubious hope of agreement between the cleric and the anticlerical, nobody in Yonville seems to understand anybody else. And though collective misunderstanding is comic, failure to be understood is a personal tragedy. Though Emma, misunderstood by her husband and lovers and neighbors, misunderstands them and herself as well, at least she harbors a feeling of something missed; whereas the distinguishing mark of Homais is the bland assurance that he never misses anything. His Voltairean incantations, his hymns to progress, his faith in railroads and rubber, his fads and statistics, his optimism—a hundred years later—may seem as far-fetched as Emma's delusions of grandeur. His clichés, embedded like fossils in his newspaper articles, Flaubert was momentarily tempted to say, "would enable some future Cuvier of the moral sciences to reconstruct clearly all the ineptitude of the nineteenth-century middle class, if that race were not indestructible." Of that hardy breed M. Homais survives as our prime specimen. Neither a creation nor a discovery, he represents the fine flower of the species that pervaded the *Comédie humaine*, the ripe perfection of the philosophy whose accredited spokesman was M. Prudhomme. This was enthusiastically attested when Prudhomme's creator and actor, Henry Monnier, sought permission to dramatize and enact Homais. The latter is more successful in attaining their common ambition, the decoration of the Legion of Honor; while his predecessor, M. Prudhomme, must content himself, when the curtain falls, with "a decorated son-in-law." The curtain-line of their spiritual relative, that famous father-in-law, M. Poirier, is his resolve to be "peer of France in 'forty-eight," an aspiration which has meanwhile been thwarted by the revolution of that date. But the unabashed Homais goes from strength to strength; the Empire will shower its accolades upon him and his brethren; and the dazzling glimpse of him in his hydroelectric undervest is a virtual apotheosis.

When he equipped his personage with a motto, "Il faut marcher avec son siècle!," Flaubert may have remembered his newly decorated friend, Maxime Du Camp, whose *Chants modernes* were prefaced by a Whitmanesque declaration: "Tout marche, tout grandit, tout s'augmente autour de nous..." Those reverberations stridently blended with the journalistic watchword of Saint-Marc Girardin, "Il faut marcher, marcher toujours..." Any endeavor which aims to keep in step with one's century, as Flaubert realized better than most of his contemporaries, is bound to be outdistanced in the long run. He took the province for his ground because it was an available microcosm, because it exaggerated the ordinary, because its dearth of color sharpened its outlines; but he did not assume that provinciality was confined to the hinterland or, for that matter, to any territory. M. Homais is historically, rather than geographically, provincial. The habit of equating one's age with the apogee of civilization, one's town with the hub of the universe, one's horizons with the limits of human awareness, is paradoxically widespread: it is just what Russian novelists were attacking as *poshlost*, or self-satisfied mediocrity. It is what stands between Emma Bovary and the all-too-easily-satisfied citizens of Yonville. Her capacity for dissatisfaction, had she been a man and a genius, might have led to Rimbaldian adventures or Baudelairean visions: "Anywhere out of the world." As things stand, her retribution is a triumph for the community, a vindication of the bourgeoisie. Flaubert, who does not always conceal his tenderness toward those who suffer, not infrequently reveals his bitterness toward those whose kingdom is of this world. We cannot sympathize with the prosperous Homais as we could with Balzac's bankrupt César Birotteau; and, unlike his prototypes on the comic stage, Flaubert's druggist is not just a harmless busybody, a well-meaning figure of fun; he is the formidable embodiment of a deeply satirical perception which was adumbrated in Le Garçon and eventuates in *Bouvard et Pécuchet*. His Bovarism would be more illusive than Emma's, if the modern epoch did not conspire to support his bumptious ideology and to repay his flatteries with its honors. His *boutonnière*, like the one conferred on Tolstoy's Russian guardsman, symbolizes more than Napoleon intended—and less. For the symbol is an empty ornament, the badge of society's approval is meaningless, when it goes unsupported by reality.

What, then, is real? Not the mean guerdon awarded to Catherine Leroux, but the lifelong service that earned it so many times over. And what is realism? Not the pathology of Emma's case, but the diagnostic insight of Larivière. Charles Bovary, for all his shortcomings, remains the great doctor's disciple, and retains the peasant virtues of his own patients; he is led astray by other motives than his own, by sentimentalism through Emma and pretentiousness through Homais. As the thrice-injured party, conjugally betrayed, professionally humiliated, financially ruined, Dr. Bovary is the neglected protagonist. If Emma is a victim of the situation, he is her victim, and her revenge against the situation is to undermine his way of life. The depths of his ignominy can be gauged by the idealized achievements of Dr. Benassis in Balzac's *Médecin de campagne*. Flaubert's ideal, though it is more dishonored than observed, fortifies him against those negative values which triumph in his book, and rises to an unwonted pitch of affirmation with the character-sketch of Dr. Larivière: his disinterested skill, his paternal majesty, his kindness to the poor, his scorn for all decorations, his ability to see through falsehood. His most revealing epithet is *hospitalier*, since it connotes not only hospitality but Flaubert's birthplace, his father's hospital at Rouen, and also the stained-glass figure of Saint Julian the Hospitaller, whom the verger of the cathedral pointed out in an earlier draft, and who would later be Flaubert's knightly hero. The hospital and the cathedral: such, in retrospect, are the substance and the form of *Madame Bovary*. The attitude that embraces the distance between them, that comprehends both the painful actualities and the grandiose aspirations, and that can therefore make each paragraph comment dynamically upon itself, is Flaubertian irony. Irony dominates life, so Flaubert asserted by precept and example. So it does, particularly for those who are occupied with art as well as life, and unflinchingly face the problems of their interrelationship. Hence the irony of ironies: a novel which is at once cautionary and exemplary, a warning against other novels and a model for other novelists, the classic demonstration of what literature gives and what literature takes.

4. *The Dance of Kuchiouk Hanem*

The sun of romanticism had already started to set in 1843, with the failure of Hugo's trilogy, *Les Burgraves*. That was a pivotal year for the young Flaubert, culminating in the failure of his legal studies. "Merde pour le Droit!," he had cursed in a letter to Chevalier, and had gone on to describe the law as his *Delenda Carthago*. The echo from Cato's famous curse against Rome's greatest rival was to call forth an unpredictable reverberation from Flaubert as a writer. His first publication involved him in another brush with the law, from which he turned quite literally to Carthage. The acquittal of *Madame Bovary* was hailed as marking the triumph of realism; and, though he had no sympathy with the publicized movement, he found himself being hailed as one of its pontiffs. But his romantic strain had been no more than temporarily purged; soon he was yielding again to the *Tentation*. Then, having been somewhat intimidated by the clerical line of the government prosecution, he set aside his manuscript once more and searched for a pre-Christian subject. He still wished to locate his next work in the sultry climate of the Middle East. From first to last his Nordic imagination gravitated toward the Mediterranean, "that antique sea of which I have dreamed so much." An early trip to Corsica had opened up the prospect of escaping from home and ego: O, to be a renegado, a muleteer, a hermit! During most of the two-year interval between the first *Tentation* and *Madame Bovary*, he accompanied Du Camp on a journalistic and photographic tour of the Levant. Flaubert felt no emotion in Jerusalem—or rather, he felt "more hollow than an empty barrel." Ephesus, on the other hand, struck him as "orientally and classically splendid"—the order of the adverbs is revealing. It was on leaving Greece that he professed himself a bohemian—that is to say, a gypsy.

Temperamentally he was not cut out to become a poetic vagabond, an Arthur Rimbaud; indeed we could not imagine a Flaubert deracinated or exiled. His spiritual expatriation was all the more poignant because his material existence was so solidly rooted and so narrowly circumscribed. Like Heine's pine tree, he cherished his palmy dream. From Croisset, less than three months before his death, he wrote to his niece: "For two weeks I have been overcome with the desire to see a palm tree standing out against the blue sky, and to hear a stork tapping his beak at the top of a minaret..." Yet on the very first day of his journey down the Nile, the pyramids of Sakkara had somehow reminded him of his Norman farmhouse on the Seine: of fishing there in the moonlight, of strolling through the garden in his dressing-gown, of waiting for the buds of another spring. So Stendhal could dream about France in Italy, having dreamed about Italy in France. But the stay-at-home Flaubert had less and less occasion to be homesick; looking out through the northern mist, he could yearn more and more nostalgically for the desert sun. Bouilhet, who had vicariously shared his friends' Egyptian adventures while remaining at Rouen, could afford to have fewer illusions about them:

> Où fuir? où fuir? Par les routes humaines
> Le sable est dur et le soleil est lourd;
> Ma bouche ardente a tari les fontaines
> Et l'arbre est mort où j'ai cueilli l'amour.

Flaubert's exoticism was the old mirage of a great good place elsewhere. Like the destination of Baudelaire's poetic voyage, its esthetic principles were clearer than its concrete features; its order, beauty, luxury, calmness, and pleasure were happy antitheses of the confusion, ugliness, poverty, agitation, and discomfort that both Flaubert and Baudelaire discerned in their environing world. There was every literary reason, and notably Hugo's *Orientales*, why the quest for a visionary alternative should lead eastward as well as southward. Orientalism, whatever else it could mean, meant gorgeous color, in contrast to the greyish tonality of the French provincial landscape. It meant exciting spectacle instead of humdrum routine, the perennially mysterious in place of the all too familiar. Flaubert had tipped his hand in *Madame Bovary*, briefly departing from the orbit of Emma's awareness, when he envisaged the memory of Rodolphe entombed in her heart, "more solemn and still than the mummy of a king in a vault."

Here, as so often happens, the figure of speech was more congenial to Flaubert than the meretricious relationship on which it implies a comment. Willing as he was to accept the critical view that *Madame Bovary* might be the last bourgeois novel, for better or for worse, he was anxious to make a new departure from it. His self-conscious "need for metamorphoses," for exhausting subjects, experimenting with forms, and outdoing himself along with his predecessors, may well mark the effectual beginning of what we now call modernism in literature. Certainly he established a precedent for the self-changing styles and the self-succeeding periods of so many ingenious and restless artists in the twentieth century. What next? The question to be continually provoked by Apollinaire and Cocteau, by Joyce and Eliot, by Picasso and Stravinsky, acquired its pertinence when critics wondered what could be the sequel to *Madame Bovary.* It was a surprise to them, as well as a satisfaction to Flaubert, that it should be removed as far as possible in space and time from the local and the contemporary, that it should move all the way from the domestic to the exotic extreme. That remove, of course, brought it much closer to Flaubert's *beau idéal,* though he undertook it against the advice of Bouilhet and ended by disappointing the Goncourts. Victor Hugo was pleased, at all events, to recognize in it "the double sentiment of the real, which displays life, and the ideal, which reveals the soul." Whose soul? What soul? That question is too important to beg. Flaubert saw himself, in more technical terms, "applying to antiquity the methods of the modern novel." In the interests of first-hand observation, he revisited Tunisia and fixed the Carthaginian topography within his mind. He also set down a prayer, supplicating the "God of souls" to lend him strength and hope, to inspire him with "powers of plastic emotion," to crown his undertaking with "resurrection of the past."

Edmond de Goncourt would later eulogize Flaubert for having been a resurrectionist in the manner of Carlyle and Michelet, for having joined in the nineteenth century's effort to disinter ancient worlds and to breathe life into mummified kings. As for Taine, congratulating Flaubert on *Hérodias,* he would heartily agree with the problematic assumption that history and fiction were becoming indistinguishable. Among Flaubert's many unrealized conceptions were a novel about the Battle of Thermopylae and another based on his travels in Asia Minor. Yet for him, as for so many Frenchmen—for Napoleon and Tartarin, for Gide's *Immoraliste* and Camus' *Etranger*—North Africa cast an especially potent spell. In *Salammbô* he celebrated a scene not very far from that of *La Tentation de saint Antoine*, though separated from it chronologically by more than four hundred years, and culturally by the enormous gulf between the western tradition and the eastern rivals it left by the wayside. Originally, Flaubert had had some notion of composing an Oriental tale about a woman who wanted to be loved by a god, Anubis. That might have furnished Voltaire with substance enough for another two-dimensional satire, but it lacked the prerequisite solidity for the full Flaubertian treatment. His two African visits reinforced the idea of a novel about the struggle—"or rather, fusion" —of social forces: barbarism versus civilization, the Orient against the Occident. What better subject than the powerful Semitic city-state on the other side of the Mediterranean, outpost of Phoenician conquest and challenge to Roman supremacy, with its menacing panoply of armies and navies and merchant ships. It was a proud and garish and sinister theme. "Does not the name of Carthage fill us with horror and cynicism?" Flaubert had asked himself in a schoolboy essay on arts and commerce. Now he felt himself drawn back to it because, he explained to the Goncourts, "it is the most rotten place in civilization."

Madame Bovary presents "the wonderfully built-up catastrophe of a life," according to Hugo von Hofmannsthal; *Salammbô* presents "the wonderfully built-up catastrophe of a city." Paris must loom somewhere in the background for all French novelists, unless it occupies the foreground as centrally as it does for Balzac and Zola, and as it does for Flaubert in *L'Education sentimentale*. Its shadows have sometimes intermingled with those of fanciful capitals like Stendhal's Parma or penitential colonies like Proust's Sodom and Gomorrah. Dissatisfied by an early excursion to the Pyrenees, Flaubert had sweepingly longed for Babylon, Nineveh, Persepolis, Palmyra, and Alexandria: ruined cities were the inspiration for his lyrical dreams. "There," as on the acropolis of his Carthage, "one felt the succession of the ages and, as it were, the memories of forgotten fatherlands." Carthage, the heir of Tyre, beleaguered and foredoomed, was a Troy without an *Iliad*, and without the legend of a European posterity. It was brilliant and corrupt, as Byzantium would be; but where Byzantium stands for jewelled artifice, Carthage stood for sanguinary violence. "The great city, sleeping in the shadow beneath [its nocturnal visitors], frightened them with its clustering stairways, its tall black houses, and its vague gods, even more ferocious than its people." Geographically, if not historically, Carthage is not far from present-day Oran; and the plague Camus has chronicled is as grim as any state of siege; it is difficult to think of two French novels, however, which stand farther apart than *La Peste* and *Salammbô*. But, of all the cities inviting literary comparison, the eternal competitor is Rome. Rome's most formidable challenger, Hannibal, is still a child in the story; and it will be another century before Carthage is wholly destroyed; yet our retrospective knowledge lends an irony to the victories of the Carthaginians and a fatality to the predictions of Hamilcar Barca:

> You will lose your ships, your lands, your chariots, your hammocks, and your slaves who scrape your feet! The jackals will sleep in your palaces, the plowshare will level your tombs. There will be nothing left but the cry of eagles and the crumbling of ruins. Thou shalt fall, Carthage!

Destruction of so devastating a kind presupposes construction on a vast scale; and Flaubert spared no pains in building up and fitting out the citadels to be sacked, the palaces to be pillaged, and the temples to be profaned. His labors on *Salammbô* equalled the four-and-a-half-year period that he had spent on *Madame Bovary*, leading directly to publication in 1862. He enjoyed his daily stint much more than he had when writing the earlier book, and took special pleasure in his interlude of field-work at Carthage. Moreover, he could document his facts much more lavishly than when they had sprung from mere village gossip; at the same time, he could gratify his growing passion for the erudite and the encyclopedic. Théophile Gautier, in his *Roman de la momie*, had spun a popular romance of the Pharaohs and set it in an archaeological framework. Flaubert sought to make archaeology vivid, and fantasy solid, by fusing the two. He profited from the advice of the archaeologist, Ernest Feydeau, who had also made himself a *confrère* by bringing out a scandalous novel, *Fanny*. To his captious reviewers, Flaubert could reply by citing chapters and texts from ancient history. His heavy accumulation of notes and plans was grounded both on classical authorities and on the latest scholarship. For the outline of his plot he followed Polybius, the Greek historian who had sadly traced the spread of Roman domination. The latter part of Polybius' First Book deals with what, he tells us, is the cruellest and most inhumane of all the gory wars that he has ever written or heard about. Known as the Inexpiable War, it broke out in the middle of the third century B.C., during the lull between the First and Second Punic Wars. It was a revolt of mercenaries against the Carthaginian rulers under whom they had fought in the larger and, at the end, more catastrophic conflict.

No armchair strategist has ever taken his military responsibilities more seriously than the sedentary Flaubert, in plotting his tactics, deploying his troops, and specifying their archaic weapons. Their movement and counter-movement, out of the city and back again to besiege it, set an epic rhythm for the novel. As barbarians to the Carthaginians, these hordes could hardly have been more barbaric. Carthage itself is a hybridization of the primitive and the decadent, which should have satisfied Flaubert's appetite for contrasting extremes, a gaudy agglomeration of ritualized brutality and oppressive opulence. We are not allowed to forget that it was, after all, a mercantile oligarchy. Hamilcar, its leading magistrate, is torn between the greed of the elders, *les Riches,* and the need of the mercenaries, whose wages have been scanted. Carthage has reached the stage when it not only hires its heroes but pays them inadequately—a penultimate stage, by any reckoning. Their expulsion makes us feel the arrogance of the rich insiders, cushioned and fortified on their rocky heights and within their geometrical walls. The retreat of the muscular outsiders across the plain to the mountains reminds us that they live in a wider communion with nature, as opposed to the subterranean enclosures and labyrinthine passages inside. The aqueduct is the vital link between the two communities; and when it is cut off, their relation is reversed; the privileged precinct becomes a thirsting hell. The pattern of advance and withdrawal is timeless, and varies little from one declining cuture to another: from the Greco-Persian expedition of Xenophon's *Anabasis* to the anonymous hordes that swarm through St.-John Perse's *Anabase.*

Flaubert's concern for his hireling army is centered upon its far-flung intermixture of races. The misunderstanding that plunges them into battle can be traced to their confusion of tongues. And afterward, as they bury their respective dead, each ethnic group has its own nostalgia for its outlandish burial customs:

> The Greeks, with the points of their swords, dug graves. The Spartans, taking off their cloaks, wrapped the bodies in them; the Athenians turned the faces toward the rising sun; the Cantabrians immured them under a pile of pebbles; the Nasamonians doubled up and bound them with thongs of oxhide, and the Garamantes took them to be buried on the beach, so that they might be perpetually washed by the waves. The Latins were sorry they could not collect their ashes in urns; the Nomads missed the mummifying warmth of the sands, and the Celts three bare stones under a rainy sky, beyond a bay dotted with isles.

Flaubert has outdone himself in distancing this paragraph. Once we have recovered from its panoramic display of erudition—not unlike the systematic presentation of folklore in the painting of Brueghel—a less neutral reaction sets in. The generalization of death is particularized by the surviving warriors of different breeds, going through their tribal motions, or else unable to go through them, so far away from home. The pluralizing of repeated actions, a device we have noticed in *Madame Bovary*, finds more extensive scope among the cohorts and crowds of *Salammbô*. Individuals thread their way through the welter by means of the third-person singular pronoun, *il* or *elle*, heralded only when necessary by their proper names, yet detached from the impersonal narrator, who contents himself with external descriptions of their behavior. Emotion is so objectively depicted that, on occasion, eye-witnesses are brought in to support the narrator's testimony: "Hamilcar grew extraordinarily pale, and those who were leaning over the pit saw him put one hand against the wall to keep himself from falling." This is from a civic episode; an overt expression of feeling is more callously avoided when Hamilcar undergoes his personal ordeal, when he is called upon to sacrifice his own son. His stratagem for substituting the child of a slave is almost intercepted when the slave makes an agonized appeal; and here, as customarily with Flaubert, the underprivileged person is the emotional vehicle. Hamilcar, again the patrician general, can no longer see himself as a despairing father. "He had never thought, so immense was the abyss dividing the two, that there could be anything in common between them." When he does respond, it is with a sense of outrage and "a look colder and heavier than an executioner's axe." The metaphor brings us quickly back to the surface, to that realm of harsh and painful fact from which Flaubert has no intention of permitting us any sentimental escape.

He has deliberately chosen dramatis personae whose sentiments tend to be externalized into gestures, rites, or feats of prowess—Tyrian prototypes of Hemingway's extroverts. Such may be the "plastic emotion" he prayed for: the subordination of human feelings to the large pictorial composition. *Salammbô* makes its impact, and is remembered, as a striking series of visual impressions. As we might expect, it relies more implicitly upon the use of imagery than did *Madame Bovary*. The average count is about an image a page for Flaubert's contemporaneous novels; but it runs as high as seven images for every three pages of the more decorative *contes*. More important than the numerical difference is the functional distinction. The images of *Madame Bovary* are couched in a mood of ironic parallelism, juxtaposing glories of the past to the trivialities of the present, as in the poems of Jules Laforgue and T. S. Eliot. Since the vantage-point of *Salammbô* is objective rather than subjective, its predominant images are literal rather than metaphorical; they are objects, paraphernalia of the story, to be admired impassively for their own sake, as in the poetry of the Parnasse. Things-in-themselves are no less determinant than they are with Zola and the stricter naturalists; only these must be strange or beautiful objects—highly wrought ornaments, curious delicacies, rare perfumes—rather than crude or commonplace forms of unvarnished reality. Now, though a lapidary style is facilitated where the subject-matter consists of precious stones, not much room is then left for imaginative interplay. To live in a land where metaphors come true is to lack perspective for comparison. Furthermore, description can only be elaborated at the expense of narration: hence the diametrical opposition between the massiveness of Flaubert and the mobility of Stendhal. The site of Carthage offered Flaubert the maximum opportunity to develop a spatial dimension within his temporal medium.

He was criticized for becoming an antiquarian, a connoisseur, a collector of bric-a-brac. *Salammbô* can doubtless be classified within the genre of the "tapestry-novel," to cite Mann's term which *Death in Venice* formulates and which the *Joseph* cycle exemplifies. Mann too, in his Egyptian resurrection, has compounded learning and craftsmanship; and he has gone much farther than Flaubert in the effort to rationalize and psychologize a mythical *donnée*. Flaubert, though he gives his myth flesh and blood—both, perhaps, in inordinate quantities—seems reluctant to modernize it. He is concerned less with the individual consciousness than with the collective unconscious, the racial memory, the herd instinct. His motivating forces are mass movements, controlled and formalized from chapter to chapter by prayers and orations, songs and imprecations, parleys and processions. It is not surprising that the composer, Ernest Reyer, made an opera of *Salammbô*. Even in the book, the choruses tend to outnumber the arias. The solo parts are mainly accorded to leaders, mostly generals, official or outlaw, with a priest or two, and a heroine who might be regarded as a sort of high priestess. Though all of them enact their roles conscientiously, they leave us no further impression of personality. The gladiatorial hero, Mâtho, most readers feel, is as unshaped as any operatic tenor. As elected leader of the mercenaries, this guileless knight has a cunning squire: the Greek slave, Spendius, a characterization which hovers somewhere between *fallax servus* and *miles gloriosus*. In Salammbô herself, Sainte-Beuve, like other critics, saw an avatar of the Druid priestess Velléda, who loves the Christian soldier Eudore in Chateaubriand's *Martyrs*. Flaubert, in his generous rejoinder to Sainte-Beuve's condescending review, allowed that the pedestal might be too large for the statue. Yet the pedestal is a monument in its own right, and the statue seems—in a certain light —to be dancing.

To be sure, the statue is more or less fictitious, while the pedestal is firmly based upon history. Yet few historical novels—*pace* Taine—are pieced together indistinguishably. Polybius supplied the slightest of hints by mentioning the defection from the rebels of the Numidian chieftain, Narr' Havas, who is rewarded by being promised the hand of Hamilcar's daughter. We know nothing more about her; the documentation gives out at this tenuous point; and scholarly research, balked in retracing it, could conclude that Flaubert was at a loss without sources. Possibly; but the resourceful artist, by definition, is never without sources; and when these are not historic, they may better be legendary or iconographic. There were always Mohammed's houris and Delacroix's odalisques. There was Clésinger's sculpture, *La Femme au serpent*, whose interlacing sinuosity so fascinated Flaubert and his contemporaries. And, speaking of serpents, he would inevitably respond to the lure of that *femme fatale par excellence*, the unparalleled queen of tempt-resses, Cleopatra. Visiting the chateau of Chenonceaux, he had expressed a whim to sleep in the bed of the long-defunct beauty, Diane de Poitiers, and had exclaimed: "Oh! how gladly would I give all the women in the world to possess the mummy of Cleo-patra!" Fortunately, his choice was not confined to this dilemma between renunciation and necrophilia. Instead, as Theodor Reik has suggested, it wavered ambivalently between two typical her-oines, the mother and the prostitute. The maternal type has its idealized incarnation in Madame Arnoux. But the innocence of Frédéric's adolescence, with which Flaubert surrounds her, is jeop-ardized by the procuress, Zoraïde Turc—who, though she is hardly more than a glamorous name, wafts a musky aroma through the province of *L'Education sentimentale*. A more complete recoil, for the young hero of the semi-autobiographical *Novembre*, flings him into the arms of a world-weary harlot, whose favorite reading alter-nates between *Paul et Virginie* and *Les Crimes des reines*.

Flaubert's prototype for Eve was bound to be a Frenchwoman: the motherly, wifely, sisterly Elisa Schlésinger. His quest for an archetypal Lilith was likelier to be consummated in Africa, where the frustrated passion of a lifetime was slaked by a memorable night of fulfillment. At Esna, on the Nile, he was entertained by a dark-skinned dancing-girl from Damascus named Kuchiouk Hanem. So elusive a figure has she cut that her very name was misspelled with an R in the expurgated Conard edition of *Notes de voyage* —a consequence of Flaubert's elusive handwriting—and in the wist-ful poem that poor Bouilhet dedicated to his friend's carnal ad-venture. Yet it would be hard to recall any passage in Occidental literature which conveys more vividly the masculine cognizance of the feminine body in motion than the page or two in Flaubert's notebooks: "une petite fantasia." While she undulated and quivered and stripped in her dance of the bee, he thought of the corybants on Greek vases. Feeling her necklace between his teeth, in her bed, he "felt like a tiger." Lying awake while she slept, and snored, he "thought of Judith and Holofernes," remembering the exhibition paintings of Decamps and Vernet, and anticipating the episode where Salammbô, dagger in hand, visits Mâtho's tent. The heroine of the Apocrypha, who saved her city by seducing the enemy general, would eventually provide a distant source for the romantic underplot of *Salammbô*. At the moment Flaubert's immediate thoughts were of his sleeping companion as a potential assassin: "La Débauche et la Mort..." Some months afterward, on the way back from Thebes, he paid her a farewell call; but she had been unwell and he was disillusioned; being Flaubert, he relished the bitter taste in his mixed emotions. Writing to placate Louise Colet, he recollected that Kuchiouk Hanem had had vermin, and that their odor had mingled with her perfume. This for him had been the most exquisite touch of all, "the grand synthesis."

The physical aspect of the Egyptian courtesan, reincarnated in his portrayal of the Carthaginian princess, charges the atmosphere with its sensual fumes and swaying rhythms and tactile values. Salammbô's femininity is highlighted by the ambiance of brawling masculinity, from the opening crisis when the feast in her father's palace turns into an orgy and she emerges to dominate it with her ancestral rhapsodies. The mountains to which the soldiers are expelled, as if to emphasize the absence of women, are compared to succoring breasts. The temple of the goddess Tanit, which Mâtho and Spendius return in the dark to penetrate, is the very *sanctum sanctorum* of womanhood, the shrine of Astarte's mysteries which claim Salammbô as their hierophant. Yet, even under those erotic auspices, she is—she all but remains—a vestal virgin. The round of ceremonies and pageantries allows the lovers—or are they haters?— no more than two brief spells of privacy together. In her bedchamber she repulses him; in his tent she yields to him—or is it, rather, he who yields to her? For once the situation is presented subjectively and impressionistically, and the private climax is interrupted by a resumption of the public clamor. These tantalizing encounters are less voluptuous than the preparatory ritual dance, where the intimate partner of her writhings is the black python, her totemic snake, phallic symbol of much that goes unconsummated otherwise. With the apostasy of the eunuch Schahabarim, mentor of Salammbô and high priest of Tanit, the emphasis shifts from the female to the male principle, and to stranger gods than Baal himself. They are presumably propitiated by the terrible immolation of children that takes place in the temple of Moloch, piously abetted by the fanatical Carthaginian families. It is the cruel destructiveness of Moloch that prevails over sexual fertility; it is Mars over Venus, Thanatos over Eros, in the guise of crucifixion and cannibalism, lacerating tortures and consuming holocausts.

If Flaubert was haunted by the Marquis de Sade, as he told the Goncourts, here is where the ghost stalks most truculently. The sadism of *Salammbô* interacts with the masochism of *La Tentation de saint Antoine*. The *Tentation*, despite its negativism, culminates in a pantheistic affirmation. *Salammbô*, for all its heroics, subsides into nihilistic defeat. Though "the love of life" may be admirable, it is not enough to save animals at bay from the final carnage. The city-state revenges its famine upon its foes, through an unholy alliance between atrocity and perfidy. Mâtho, forced to run the gauntlet of every conceivable torture, has his heart cut out at Salammbô's feet. She, enthroned with Narr' Havas, succumbs to the shock, as the book concludes: "Thus died the daughter of Hamilcar for having touched the mantle of Tanit." The underlying motif of sacrilege, of desecrating the Holy of Holies, is present from the outset, when the revellers poison the sacred fish. The crucial profanation is the rape of the *zaïmph*, the goddess's veil stolen from her temple by Mâtho and recaptured by Salammbô from the mercenaries' camp. It is the loss and recovery of this palladium which determine the fate of the city, and speed the to-and-fro-conflicting marches of the campaigning battalions. Mâtho relinquishes it for Salammbô's love; for obtaining it, through her involvement with him, she sacrifices her life. What, then, is that fabric which human eyes are forbidden to look upon? "As bluish as night, as yellow as dawn, as crimson as sunlight, shadowy, diaphanous, glittering, flimsy"—it seems to represent the stuff of illusion. As a symbolic act, the tearing away of a veil betokens the defloration of sex. More simply, it is a disclosure of nakedness, which Flaubert equated with truthfulness and simplicity. His tendency to dwell on semi-nude dancers and half-naked athletes is an implicit reservation upon the overdressed stuffiness of his period.

In *Par les champs et par les grèves* he paused to protest against the fig-leaves of his century. In *Salammbô* he might be said to have symbolically removed them. If this be an iconoclastic gesture, his characters suffer for it, and it does not really point the way to any positivistic revelation of forbidden knowledge. Rather, it leaves us in a mood of calculated revulsion, more willing to detach ourselves completely than we would be from his nineteenth-century novels. Gautier called *Salammbô* an epic poem, and it earned his praise by its verbal artifice, as well as by a purview which is scaled to its stately parading of elephants back and forth. But we should be disappointed if we were led to expect hero-worship, idealization, or a past which is more benign or better ordered than our present. In the struggle—or fusion—between civilization and barbarism, Flaubert's sympathies are plainly with the barbarians. The mercenaries hold out with incredible bravery until they are betrayed by the bad faith of the Carthaginians. The civilization of Carthage is an institutionalized barbarism, all the more cruel and perverse because of its pretensions; and Flaubert's account of it, which seemed far-fetched or pedantic to some of his contemporaries, should seem less so to readers who have heard about gas chambers and atomic weapons. Typically ironic is the ending; Carthage is saved, but we know it is doomed in the long run; the advancing shadow of Roman conquest has already fallen upon it; and, as in Shakespeare's *Antony and Cleopatra*, the impending threat of a masculine and equestrian Rome rises over the prostrate specter of a feminine and serpentine Africa. To touch upon the imperial theme, if only at its *bas-empire* outposts, was a timely, if slightly hazardous, enterprise for a writer of the Second Empire. Flaubert made a more direct attack, fifteen years after *Salammbô*, in the concentrated form of *Hérodias*.

That tale, the last of his *Trois Contes*, was succinctly outlined in the gospels of Saint Matthew and Saint Mark. But Flaubert insisted that, as he understood it, the story had "no connection with religion." What had attracted him to it had been, first of all, "the official demeanor of Herod (who was a real prefect)"; then "the untamable visage of Herodias, a sort of Cleopatra and Maintenon";

and finally, predominating again, "the question of races." The citadel that hangs like a turreted crown above the Dead Sea, flaunting its eagles toward Galilee, stands at a fateful crossroad between east and west, paganism and Christianity, Judea and Rome. The admixture of nationalities is still more diverse than among the mercenaries of Carthage; the climactic banquet will be even more polyglot than theirs, and will offer a richer menu. Names of bizarre and luxurious dishes will season a theological disputation. When will he come, the Messiah, to liberate the Jews? Has he not arrived in the person of "a certain Jesus"? A mere illusionist—no, a performer of miracles! Presiding uneasily over this land of tensions and uncertainties is the Tetrarch Herod Antipas, son of the more celebrated Herod the Great, and Flaubert's portrait of the weak and harried provincial administrator. His recent and irregular marriage to his sister-in-law, Herodias, has been sharply questioned and denounced. Even now, as he gazes down from his terrace, he hears a sepulchral voice reechoing out of the vaults below. It is the imprisoned Joakanann, who, raging like a beast in his cage, continues to overwhelm the Tetrarch with accusations of incest and prophecies of biblical desolation. By an unpropitious coincidence, Herod must play the host to a state visit from his ambitious superior, the Roman governor, Vitellius. The air is thick with political rumors from the world's capital—who's in, who's out—a mundane parallel to the messianic speculations of the Pharisees and Sadducees.

Herod, the Romanized Jewish official, is caught between the proconsul and the prophet. It is his wife who pulls the strings, combining, as Flaubert had planned, the inscrutability of Cleopatra with the intrigue of Madame de Maintenon. Her daughter, Salome, is briefly glimpsed but not recognized in the first and second sections; in the third she makes a dramatic appearance at the height of Herod's birthday feast. "It was Herodias, as she had been in her youth. Then she began to dance." For the choreography of that libidinous dance, with its Nubian twists and twirls and jingling of jewelry, Flaubert again is indebted to Kuchiouk Hanem. Salome is past mistress of her art; yet, when the infatuated Tetrarch invites her to stipulate her grisly reward, she stammers and lisps her memorized speech like a child. Like Salammbô, she is too innocent for the vicious part in which circumstances have cast her, and Flaubert would have us savor the irony of it. So much for the heroine as prostitute; he seems to be more interested in her mother. Not so Mallarmé, whose fragmentary *Hérodiade* devotes itself to the daughter—granddaughter of Herod the Great—at a virginal and narcissistic phase of her ill-omened career. The focus seems to have shifted from Herodias to Salome with the vogue of Gustave Moreau's water-colors and oils, so extravagantly admired by the decadents, notably Huysmans. His eulogy in *A rebours*, endowing the dancer with all the vampire traits of the Trojan Helen or the convulsive depravities of the Babylonian Whore, alludes significantly to Salammbô. It remained for Oscar Wilde's Salome to be incited by necrophilic motives, in the *fin-de-siècle* drama so widely publicized by Beardsley's illustrations and Strauss's music. Given that trend of interpretation, which was doubtless encouraged by Flaubert's version, it is surprising that he should have been undistracted from his resolve to stress the bureaucratic maneuvering, the interracial unrest, and the matriarch's revenge.

What emerges from this seething cauldron is the single element that has been studiously underplayed, and indeed disclaimed by his statement that religion was not involved. In looking back at the early Christians, with his friend Renan, Flaubert's doctrinal skepticism was counterweighted by his historical sympathy. His facile imitator, Anatole France, would rework *Hérodias* in *Le Procurateur de Judée*; but he would merely be amused at obtuseness, where Flaubert was indignant over corruption. The devil's bargain, arranged by Herodias and enacted by Salome, has traded faith for debauchery; the voice that cried out in the wilderness is temporarily silenced; but, Joakanann will have the last word, canonized as Saint John the Baptist. His decapitation is the prologue to the crucifixion of Jesus, and Herod's levity is a rehearsal for a more solemn trial. The significance of that train of coming events is barely hinted in the restrained conclusion, where the three Essenes console themselves and depart, bearing the severed head toward Galilee. "As it was very heavy, they took turns in carrying it." Having been vocal when unseen in the pit, Joakanann when dead is visibly clamorous—"the lugubrious object, on the platter, amid the left-overs of the feast." When the accusing object is held up before the proconsul's son, Aulus Vitellius, the sleepy debauchee who is destined to be the calamitous emperor, their mute colloquy has prophetic undertones: "Through their parted lashes, the dead eyeballs and the dim eyeballs seemed to speak a word to each other." In the long run, the Galileans will conquer. Once they have ceased to be underdogs, once their adherents have scaled the heights of privilege, they will no longer have the ambivalent Flaubert on their side. So long as Salome is pitted against Saint John, or Salammbô against Saint Anthony, or Kuchiouk Hanem against Saint Polycarp, or the belly-dance of eroticism against the mental discipline of asceticism, he will be a votary of the saints.

5. Spleen and Ideal

Alternativement, the undulant adverb that dangles like a signature at the end of *Hérodias*, subsumes the creative rhythm of Flaubert's career. Alternately is the word; and the alternation starts from, and returns to, *La Tentation de saint Antoine*. On the rebound from his grandiose and abortive first attempt, he goaded himself into writing *Madame Bovary*. Then, recoiling by way of the second *Tentation*, he plunged into the voluptuous archaeology of *Salammbô*. After that, in the penultimate year of the Second Empire, came *L'Education sentimentale*: after the Inexpiable War of Carthage, the anticlimax of Paris in 'forty-eight. The realistic alternative was always for him *malgré lui*, and his kind of realism would be described by Sartre as "the condemnation of reality." On the other hand, at a time when Zola and the Goncourts were already raising the banners of naturalism, Flaubert fell back impenitently on the presumptions of an old-fashioned romanticism. To George Sand he subscribed himself "an old romantic," and to the Princess Mathilde he wrote: "For lack of the *real* one tries to console oneself through *fiction*." After the Revolution of 1870, his literary reaction was to publish the definitive version of the *Tentation*. Having thereby given his private solace of almost twenty-five years to a world which was far from eager to have it, he might well ask himself again what was now being asked of the century: what next? Was it not, on both personal and public grounds, a time for realism with a vengeance? He considered a culminating project based upon a contemporary theme, such as *Under Napoleon III* or *The Bourgeois in the Nineteenth Century*.

His ultimate commitment, *Bouvard et Pécuchet*, was the belated counterpart of *La Tentation de saint Antoine*, in that it became a vow and an onus, a wager with himself and a way of life. During his last decade, Flaubert lived it intensely, though distracted from it by ills and losses, and deviating from it toward more colorful and more tractable projects. The most successful of the deviations, indeed his one unqualified success with the immediate consensus of critics and readers, was the *Trois Contes*. Each of these miniatures, which took him no more months than the novels had taken him years to compose, was a pendant to one of the larger works. *Hérodias* was to *Salammbô* what *Un Coeur simple* was to *Madame Bovary*, as Jules Lemaître pointed out; it should be added that the same relationship holds good between *La Légende de saint Julien l'hospitalier* and *La Tentation de saint Antoine*. Yet nature makes no sudden jumps; Flaubert's alternations were not clean breaks from book to book, or from historical costume to *complet bourgeois*. It was the essence of his binocular vision to bring the past to bear on the present, and vice versa by turns, superinducing the contrasts implicit throughout his work, which become explicit among the *Trois Contes*. That double perspective, which sets him apart from his fellow prose writers, finds its unique affinity among the poets. It is much more than caprice that so often prompts us to cite Baudelaire when we discuss Flaubert. The novelist, in his quest for themes and values, alternates across a sliding scale which the poet, in the main section of his *Fleurs du mal*, has designated *Spleen et idéal*. Realistic spleen, romantic ideal.

Splenetic by disposition, Flaubert met with more and more to inflame his irritation. In his fifties, he retained no resemblance to the Viking Apollo of student days. Prematurely old and grossly paunched, red-faced and bald-headed, with heavy eyelids and drooping mustachios, he had only to look into a mirror to be reclaimed by the spirit of caricature. Among increasing bodily complaints, he suffered from shingles, more appropriately diagnosed in his case as Saint Anthony's fire. His old friends, wherever they were, seemed to be dropping off. He lost his cherished mother, who— despite his occasional protests against "le culte de la mère"—had centralized his bachelor's existence. His favorite niece, who had grown up under his tutelage, had married a man who proceeded to fail in business; willingly, and without much thanks, the uncle spent his available assets to help them. His income from his books was negligible: 500 francs for the first five years' sales of *Madame Bovary*. Some financial assistance was finally obtained for him, somewhat to his embarrassment, through a nominal post at the Mazarine Library. His half-hearted attempts in the theater merely confirmed his membership in the select group of *auteurs sifflés*, with Zola, Daudet, Goncourt, and Turgenev. But Flaubert was inured to artistic rebuffs, and stoical in facing domestic anxieties. What he blanched before, what he fulminated against, was the national calamity: the defeat of France by Germany, the ensuing fall of Louis Napoleon, and the scarifying interlude of the Commune. For a month and a half of the occupation, Prussian officers were billeted in the ivory tower at Croisset.

It was a crisis which offered the fullest scope to Flaubert's inherent pessimism. His esthetic credo had disavowed the claims of the fatherland upon the artist. Nationality would be regarded as an anachronism in the cosmopolitan future, he had written to Bouilhet from Athens twenty years before. But, with the Franco-Prussian War, he professed himself a French patriot. "Seriously, bestially, brutally," he wanted to fight; he drilled with the militia; he felt within him the warlike pulsation of that Indian blood which, he liked to boast, had been brought into the family by *voyageur* ancestors. As the wave of invasion subsided, and France once more was subdivided against itself, he lapsed into the old feeling of impotent anger. The revolutionary tradition had come full circle; the Commune would revert to the Middle Ages; "the International will triumph in the end, but not as it hopes or as one fears." Nor could he be cheered by the precarious birth of the Third Republic. Impartially, he called down plagues upon the contending parties of both the socialist left and the Catholic right. He made his principal play, *Le Candidat*, an acrid satire on universal suffrage, with its attendant graft and demagoguery. Small wonder that the playwright never achieved the popularity for which he made so inconsistent a bid. Hating all catchwords, he bridled at the prevailing one, democracy, because it exalted grace at the expense of justice, as he put it: social standards were debased by egalitarianism masquerading as Christian charity. "The whole dream of democracy," he argued with George Sand, "is to elevate the proletariat to the level of stupidity of the bourgeoisie."

That argument, for all its disparities, turned out to be his most fruitful meeting of minds. George Sand, surviving her own tempestuous generation, had ripened to a mellow humanity far surpassing her brittle heroines. No one in his succession of male confidants, with the probable exception of Turgenev, could have been rated as Flaubert's peer. None of her actual lovers seems to have touched such responsive chords of womanly insight. For his part, he derived more warmth from her than from any mistress. She was his senior by seventeen years, as Louise Colet had been by thirteen and Elisa Schlésinger by eleven. In the four years between his mother's death and George Sand's, her maternal intervention was the decisive influence upon him. It is she, among his various correspondents, whose letters have proved worthiest of being reprinted with his; and if the *Correspondance* constitutes a writers' bible, as André Gide has said, Flaubert's Old Testament severity has been alleviated by George Sand's evangelical sympathy. She is the *cher maître*, whom he respectfully addresses as *vous*; he is her *vieux troubadour*, with whom she uses the intimate *toi*. To her he confides his self-questionings, along with the terrible doubts that history has been casting up at their feet. How can we any longer believe in science, progress, civilization itself, after the devastating passage of these latterday Huns?

> Ready-made phrases are not lacking: France will rise again! We must not despair! It is a salutary punishment! We were really too immoral! Et cetera. Oh, eternal balderdash! No, there is no recovering from such a blow! I feel affected to the marrow!
>
> If I were twenty years younger, perhaps I would think otherwise, and if I were twenty years older I should be resigned . . . All the friends I had are dead or lost. I no longer have any center. Literature seems to me an empty and useless affair. Shall I ever be in a condition to take it up again?
>
> Oh, if I could only fly to a country where one would see no more uniforms, hear no drums and talk about no massacres, where one was not obliged to be a citizen! But the earth is no longer inhabitable for poor mandarins.

So runs his repeated plaint, which ranges from self-pity to a cynical contempt for the world. When she softens before the spectacle, he assumes a hard-boiled tone, and advises her to cultivate hatred. But the master, unwilling to write off a lifetime of humanitarian idealism as no more than a lost illusion, takes her mandarin disciple firmly to task through a printed *Réponse à un ami*. Why talk so much about classes? The people include you and me.

> No, no, one cannot isolate oneself, or break the ties of blood, or curse or scorn one's kind. Humanity is not an empty word. Our life is composed of love, and to give up loving is to give up living.

And so, betwixt misanthropy and philanthropy, the dialectic alternates. Pressing her charge of self-isolation, the philanthropist makes it a touchstone for their respective attitudes: his desolation as against her consolation. That is a distinction which the misanthrope will not accept. If his theories sound impersonal, if his characters look satirical, it is not because he lacks conviction. On the contrary, he has all too many ideals, and perhaps they are all too exacting. It may be a mere pedantic quip to sign a letter "Bourgeoisophobus," but it is a serious ethical proposition to maintain that "hatred of the bourgeoisie is the beginning of virtue." Such a conception of virtue may seem perverse, and must be difficult to put into practice, especially for one who has been born and bred a thoroughgoing bourgeois. Hence the conflict of the two Gustaves, and the preference of the inner idealist for past epochs and exotic climes. The history of the world, Flaubert had grown fond of saying, comprised three stages: "Paganisme, christianisme, muflisme." His terms for antiquity and for the Middle Ages are decently neutral. His term for modernity is scarcely translatable: *un mufle*, literally an animal's muzzle or snout, is slang for a boor. It is our decadent fate to live in the heyday of boorishness, an epoch which Flaubert elsewhere characterizes as "utilitarian, military, American, and Catholic as well." His pursuit of ideals had led him back to the pagan Salammbô and the Christian saint Antoine. In the same light, Emma Bovary and Frédéric Moreau must be looked upon as protagonists—or, since they are more acted upon than acting, as his agonists—for the age of *muflisme*.

To take up literature again in his final period, under conditions more bleakly antipathetic than ever, was to vent his spleen more fully, to concentrate more directly upon a pair of active *mufles*, to vomit on his contemporaries—in Flaubertian phrase—the disquietude that they inspired in him. "It is indignation alone that sustains me," he explained to George Sand's son, as well as to Edmond de Goncourt, who came closer to sharing his vein. But the indignation itself was hard to sustain indefinitely. In a gentler and more consolatory mood, he set aside *Bouvard et Pécuchet*, and turned out *Trois Contes* within an eighteen-month period between 1875 and 1877. All three of these tales are legends, or saints' lives, in one way or another. *La Légende de saint Julien l'hospitalier* is the earliest and most conventional. Not an expressionistic dialogue like the *Tentation*, it is a simple narrative whose concluding sentence brings the narrator close to home, with the acknowledgment that he has been animating a stained-glass window devoted to Saint Julian in the Rouen Cathedral. This is a reversal of the direction set by the trysting lovers when they flee from that brooding monument in *Madame Bovary*, evading a moral sanction which Julian seeks. *Hérodias* marks another return to the same ecclesiastical auspices, drawing its iconography from a sculptured tympanum of Salome and Saint John. Sinners and saints are played off against one another in the ancient tale; in the medieval legend, the sinner becomes a saint. Unlike the self-denying Anthony, Julian acts rashly and brutally. His redemption likewise has its artistic symbolism, if we recollect Flaubert's earlier remark about the current state of literature: "It would take Christs of art to cure that leper."

But the parable, responding to George Sand's benevolence, is primarily social rather than esthetic. At the other extreme from Anthony's withdrawal is Julian's "need to mingle with the existence of others." The surfaces of the story, naïve as a folk-tale, are richly decorated by its large and varied bestiary, like illuminations on vellum. The mute suffering of animals, which preoccupied Flaubert as much as Vigny, is caused by Julian's wanton cruelty. Through a dreamlike sequence of hunting scenes, pursuer and then pursued, he moves toward their fated revenge upon him. His sin is vastly bloodier than the Ancient Mariner's, and accordingly his expiation is more sacrificial. The primitive theme of unwitting parricide has continued to fascinate such moderns as Thomas Mann in *The Holy Sinner*, Albert Camus in *Le Malentendu*, and Robert Penn Warren in *The Ballad of Billie Potts*. For Flaubert it is something more than a ritual drama between generations; it foreshadows the guilty introspection of Proust on his mother's death. The purge of Julian's guilt, through the leper's embrace, is not without its Proustian undertones. In a broader sense, the moral is pointed by the fraternal gesture. Thus the life-denying tendencies are redeemed by the positive aspects of *La Légende de saint Julien*, just as they are upon the subtler plane of *Hérodias*. The remaining *conte*, which is substantial enough to qualify as a *nouvelle*, is *Un Coeur simple*. Written between *La Légende de saint Julien* and *Hérodias*, it ushers in the collective volume, which proceeds backward from the modern to the medieval and ancient. Yet *Un Coeur simple* is no less concerned with sainthood than the others. The most affirmative of Flaubert's writings, it is his counterstatement to *Madame Bovary*.

Its simple heart is the very antithesis of Emma's yearning confusion. The dignity of labor, the self-sacrifice, and the good will so fleetingly exemplified in the novel by the old peasant woman, Catherine Leroux, these are the qualities that make servitude a vocation for Madame Aubain's Félicité. Although the Goncourts had prided themselves upon portraying a servant, their Germinie Lacerteux was presented as a sordid sinner. Flaubert's exemplary figure has been remembered from his boyhood, and from the maid-of-all-work who held together his great-aunt's household at Pont-l'Eveque. There is such a person in many a well-established bourgeois ménage, upholding its traditions while it disintegrates. There is "nothing heroic" about Flaubert's portrait, not even the moment when the sometime farm-girl rescues her charges from an assaulting bull. Her sympathetic links with the animal kingdom are an intrinsic part of her religion: "she loved the lambs more tenderly through love of the Lamb, and the doves because of the Holy Ghost." Her capacity for love, personally frustrated, lavishes itself on her mistress's children—the boy is a disappointment, the girl dies young—and on a nephew who goes to sea and never comes back. Her sole comfort, as old age and loneliness and deafness close in around her, is the bright and noisy parrot, Loulou. Unwanted by a departing neighbor, the bird for her is "virtually a son, a lover." In its death, preserved by taxidermy, it becomes a fetish, and ultimately a pious offering on a festival altar. As she herself lies dying, it becomes the outlandish incarnation of Félicité's religious devotion; and the apotheosis of the parrot is her vision of the Paraclete.

When she insists on bearing her grotesque burden through the

winter night to Honfleur, and is laid prostrate on the Norman road
by a flick from a passing coachman's whip, we are reminded not
only of the Blind Man struck down behind Emma's coach, but of
the crucial seizure that took Flaubert under strikingly similar circumstances. That flash of secret identification may throw some
light on what Victor Hugo meant when he declared that Flaubert
reveals the soul by combining the ideal with the real. In these
succinct annals of forty-odd years, his realism functions at its least
eventful and its most meaningful levels. "Monotony of their existence—little facts," he has jotted among his notes. The selected
details, the faded souvenirs and damaged relics, are symbols of
spent emotion, treasures hoarded in Félicité's room and guarded
by her stuffed parrot. Each object, such as the little plush hat of
the dead daughter, has its moving association with the family. Dissociation, the disjunction of feelings and ideas, is Flaubert's cus-
tomary mode of treatment: compare Félicité's death-bed scene
with Emma's. For once he has allowed his pity to get the upper
hand over his irony; yet the genius of irony had its stroke of revenge; he had sought uniquely to please George Sand, who had
not survived to read the tale. *Un Coeur simple*, at all events, has
won the widest acceptance as a model of technique for shorter
fiction. Ezra Pound testified for his generation, when he averred
that it "contains all that anyone knows about writing." *Three
Lives*, the most convincing of Gertrude Stein's efforts to let the
inarticulate speak for itself, was roughly modelled on *Trois Contes*.

Release from his demons was temporary for Flaubert. With
the opuscula finished, published, and widely admired, he had
no excuse for not turning grimly back to the unfinishable opus
magnum, the child of spleen, *Bouvard et Pécuchet*. From the
contemporary nightmare he could see no means of prolonged
escape. When he collaborated on a musical fantasy, *Le Château
des coeurs*, it was set in the unmythical land of Pot-au-feu and
dominated by the savor of that homely stew, "emblem of material interests." He had announced to Turgenev, "1870 has
turned a good many people into fools or imbeciles or angry
men. I am in the latter category." As an *enragé*, he conceived
it his duty to put folly and imbecility in their place; but it was
a vicious circle; and he became all the more enraged while contemplating the targets of his rage. "The work that I am producing

could be subtitled *Encyclopedia of Human Stupidity*. I am over-whelmed by the undertaking and permeated by my subject," he told a neighbor. The parrot could somehow replace the dove, in the eyes of saintly simplicity; and yet, to keener observers, that displacement would carry with it a shocking implication, scarcely hinted at in *Un Coeur simple* but writ large in *Bouvard et Pécuchet*. Is the divine afflatus to be identified with the chattering squawk of repetitious mimicry? Has the Logos of civilization been addled by its own cult of Loulou: a mindless parroting of words, a meaningless re-echoing of sounds, a gigantic case of psittacism? No one can ever have labored more strenu-ously than Flaubert to validate the Word. His was a rear-guard action against the devaluation of language, the *mot juste* against the cliché. Parrots, like monkeys, engage in the crude imitation of human beings. Such antics have the additional consequence of reducing the realists to mimetic absurdity.

Ezra Pound recommended *Ulysses* to a French public by recalling *Bouvard et Pécuchet*. He seems to have had in mind the creation of a verbal medium out of subliterary materials. James Joyce has since put forward an even more challenging example of echolalia in *Finnegans Wake*. Flaubert also antici-pated Joyce in becoming, as Valéry impatiently remarked, "haunted by the demon of encyclopedic knowledge." Documentation in previous undertakings had been incidental and specific, filling in a historical background or lending concreteness to some technical matter. Research for *Bouvard et Pécuchet* was more systematic and comprehensive; everything in print was grist for the slow-grinding mill; and Flaubert counted some 1500 books which he would have read for no other reason. He was apparently garnering an album of citations, which might well have dis-couraged an up-to-date Faust from going on in the arts or sciences. Moreover, and we must not confuse the different sorts of documents, he had compiled a dictionary of accepted ideas, *idées reçues*, into which he would dip for turns of phrase we recognize in his fictional conversations. These banalities, in *Madame Bovary* and *L'Education sentimentale*, are highlighted by the sardonic narration; if *Le Candidat* seems painfully flat, it is because the dramatic form does not permit such relief. The *dictionnaire* is an alphabetical listing of clichés and howlers, prej-

udices and half-truths, hasty generalizations and popular fallacies
—a fairly heterogeneous body of statements and misstatements.
On the whole, its outlook is consistently philistine: literature is
defined as "occupation of the idle." Yet occasionally the encyclo-
pedist resumes his own caustic voice, defining optimist as "synonym
for imbecile."

It is hard to imagine any individual who would, seriously and
simultaneously, hold both of those contradictory opinions. It
would be the bourgeois who confounded art with idleness, and
consequently it would be Flaubert who was the implied pessimist.
The fact that certain notions are accepted does not make them
either false or true; it simply warrants their banality; and Flaubert
could still be enough of a romanticist to rank interesting falsehoods above banal truths. As an angry man, his problem was
to impersonate the mentality of the fools and imbeciles; and
since it was not easy to keep up a dead-pan impersonation,
now and then we seem to overhear the author's asides. In any
case, as his readers, we are expected to share his suspicion or
scorn of what he is exhibiting. This cajoles us into a superior
position, which can be a sequestered one. It is quite likely that
every country or era, however brilliant it may seem at a distance,
has its ideology of platitudes, which the satirist refuses to suffer
gladly. Swift's *Polite Conversation* comes to mind for Augustan
England, or Mencken and Nathan's *American Credo* for the
United States in the nineteen-twenties. These could take the
convenient and flexible shape of a manual or a corpus, whereas
Flaubert strove to build a work of fiction around his collection
of bromides. He may have followed the Balzacian example of
Le Cousin Pons, where the two old musicians wander into the
trammels of legalistic complication. More to his point would
have been Musset's *Lettres de Dupuis et Cotonet*, where the
partnership of stolid citizens sets up a romantic school of its
own, and proceeds to dabble through a sequence of fads and
follies. The immediate model seems to have been *Les Deux
Greffiers*, a humorous fiction about the bucolic retirement of two
clerks of court.

M. Homais would not soon be forgotten; yet, as the mouthpiece
of the bourgeoisie, he had played chorus rather than protagonist.
Le Garçon, the hypertrophied vulgarian, lingered on as a joke

from adolescence; his outrageous twentieth-century embodiment
would make a theatrical impact in Alfred Jarry's *Ubu roi*. But
Flaubert's heroes had shown, particularly in the two versions
of *L'Education sentimentale*, an innate disposition to hunt in
couples. The writer whose own personality was split between
deux bonshommes had a Noah-like addiction to pairs and braces.
He had first thought of his testamentary novel as *Les Deux
Cloportes*, the two woodlice. Then, needing a couple of appropriate surnames, he had gone through the usual onomastic search.
Bouvard was cognate with Bovary, and with the title of the
Count de Bouvigny in *Le Candidat*. What a shame that the
home-made cordial, "Bouvarine," which might have immortalized
François-Denys-Bartholomée Bouvard, was such an unmitigated
fiasco! As for Juste-Romain-Cyrille Pécuchet, he might have
traced his name to the Latin *pecus*, meaning herd of cattle,
and therefore harmonizing with *bos, bovis*, an ox. It was rather
embarrassing when an actual M. Pécuchet materialized in connection with Flaubert's depleted finances. But names have their
fates, as MM. Bouvard and Pécuchet realize, when they introduce
themselves to each other by deciphering their respective hatbands.
Characteristically, their initial action is to sit down on the
boulevard bench where they meet. There they discover that they
are colleagues, not to say predestined soul-mates. Happy coincidence! each is a copying-clerk, one of the white-collared legion
of petty employees, on whom the paper-work of business and
government depended in Flaubert's day.

Though they will engage in various feats and be discovered
in odd postures, they are by occupation as sedentary as heroes
could possibly be. The circumstance that henceforth pairs them
off, for the reasons that Bergson has analyzed, renders their
joint adventures automatically absurd. The threat of suicide, at
the nadir of their fortunes, becomes nugatory when both attempt
to hang themselves at once, and is capped by anticlimax when,
at the last minute, they decide that they must first draw up
their wills. If Flaubert could have finished *Bouvard et Pécuchet*,
sighed Hérédia, France would have had its *Don Quixote*. This
evocation, though it was inevitable, starts to waver just as soon
as we wonder which would be the knight and which the squire.
Pécuchet would appear to have the advantage, when he pops

out of their amateur museum with a pot on his head for a helmet; but it is Bouvard who commonly takes the initiative; and the two are differentiated with a nicety which assists their interplay as a comedy team. Bouvard is more typically bourgeois, corpulent and confident, more the man of the world and the man of property. Pécuchet is the highbrow, angular and diffident, high-strung, liberal, and—until an unfortunate episode—virgin. His intellectual aspirations predispose him to be a victim of physical discomfitures at the lowest comic level; when the right manure is not forthcoming from the local stables, he is not too proud to seek it out at its source upon the highroad. Whereas it is the irrepressible Bouvard who, blandly proposing to the shrewd widow, Madame Bordin, calls her attention to the convenience of having two sets of linen already marked with a B: "Let us unite our initials."

The clerks, released from copying by a windfall, undertake the townsman's classic relocation amid the countryside, and thereupon open up a maximum opportunity for the assorted humors of maladjustment. They pursue their dizzily parallel courses through a series of hobbies, which involve the major branches of practical and polite learning: agriculture, science, archaeology, belles lettres, politics, sex, metaphysics, religion, pedagogy. Bouvard and Pécuchet are autodidacts and self-helpers; all they know is what they have been reading; but they have been reading omnivorously; and they endeavor to carry out their homework methodically and quixotically. In each successive sphere the theories are spun, the experiments are set up, and the explosions logically follow. The experimentalists are slapstick-prone; they are gifted with the preposterous touch that turns gold to dross; things are foreordained to fall apart in their maladroit hands. Inanimate objects seem to display ingenuity, as well as malice, in avenging themselves upon such well-meaning and vulnerable creatures with such a flair for getting in everybody's way. When they fail to cure a hunchback by camphor, we are moved to recall Charles Bovary's failure with the club-footed Hippolyte. That was a specific disillusionment which, in *Madame Bovary*, was diffused into a general consciousness of ineffectuality. The generalization is completed, in *Bouvard et Pécuchet*, by taking a long view of many ridiculous instances. Flaubert ended by humorously accepting what was so bitter and depressing to the naturalists: the losing quarrel of men and women with things. In the early flush of their transplantation, the partners indulge in the national pastime of landscape gardening. Alas! the results are all too symptomatic of man's failures to improve on nature:

> In the twilight it was something frightful. The boulder occupied the lawn like a mountain, the tomb formed a cube in the midst of the spinach, the Venetian bridge a circumflex over the kidney-beans, and the cabin beyond a large black smudge—for they had set fire to its thatched roof so that it would look more poetic. The yews, in the shape of stags or armchairs, lined the way to the lightning-stricken tree, which extended crosswise from the hedge to the arbor, where tomatoes were hanging like stalactites. Here and there a sunflower displayed its yellow disk. The Chinese pagoda, painted red, seemed like a lighthouse on the mound. The peacocks' beaks, struck by the sun, reflected its beams; and behind the lattice, unframed by its slats, the flat fields bounded the horizon.

Naturally, this vista makes an unfavorable impression upon the Norman neighbors who, from chapter to chapter, forgather to pronounce the judgment of common sense. They are recognizable types with predictable responses: the mayor, the squire, the doctor, the priest, the widow—and, weaving in and out somewhat drunkenly, the workman Gorju, who is both a serviceable rogue and an emergent radical. The retired Parisians never manage to sink their roots in the village of Chavignolles. Like Emma at Yonville: "They were generally scorned." When they splash through their self-taught course in hydrotherapy, naked as savages, the villagers peek in and are scandalized. The latter, after all, are the choric spokesmen of public opinion, which Flaubert characterized in a letter to Turgenev as "the eternal and execrable *on.*" It is a function not unlike the role of the anonymous "they" in the limericks of Edward Lear, whose cue is to express loud disapproval of the leading character's eccentricities. Bouvard and Pécuchet seem to grow more earnest, as their enthusiasms and innovations persist, and Flaubert seems to grow more expressly critical of their provincial critics. When the Revolution of 1848 reaches Chavignolles, his *bonshommes* sympathize with it—and so, evidently, does he. He goes out of his way to include a mordant episode where the priest brings clerical pressure to bear on the freethinking schoolmaster. He is scathing in his depiction of the venal traffic in religiosity. His political conclusions are summed up symbolically when Bouvard and Pécuchet inspect the attic of the town hall, where plaster busts of Napoleon, Louis XVIII, Charles X, and Louis-Philippe lie discarded and dusty, behind some faded flags and a fire extinguisher.

Judged by the results of the culminating experiment, the book is an anti-educational novel, a *Bildungsroman* in reverse, wherein little is learned and nothing forgotten. In a burst of humanitarianism, Bouvard and Pécuchet adopt two children, and enter the arena of pedagogical controversy. Needless to say, Victor and Victorine prove to be precociously vicious brats, and the methods of their guardians are more inept and ineffectual than ever. Here Flaubert may have been ruefully glancing at his thankless relations with his niece and nephew-in-law. The intolerable situation further deteriorates into an adverse lawsuit, and then the text breaks off. From a detailed synopsis, we learn how Flaubert planned to round out the story. There would have been a scene— of the sort that Ibsen was even then dramatizing—in which the two reformers lectured their fellow citizens. Pécuchet would be pessimistic, Bouvard optimistic; the audience, convinced by neither, would be more hostile than ever; and the upshot would be scandal and stalemate. Yet, out of the depths of the ex-clerks' dejection, will come their simultaneous inspiration: "To copy, as in former days." The handy Gorju will make them a double desk; and, as the novel is scheduled to end, they are getting down to work: sitting down, of course, and resuming the contemplative posture, like two monks in a medieval scriptorium. What will they copy? It has been surmised that the *Dictionnaire des idées reçues* had been collected for that purpose, and was originally intended to appear as a second volume. It has also been conjectured that *Bouvard et Pécuchet* was itself envisaged as a prolegomenon to Flaubert's *sottisier*, the compilation of foolish extracts from famous writers.

But the anthology reads as if it were gathered for private amusement, while the dictionary has been drawn upon for commonplaces scattered through his other works. The ten extant chapters of *Bouvard et Pécuchet* make up a compact tome, which would be amply proportioned if the outline had been carried through. As the book stands, it has been thoroughly seasoned with fatuities quoted from both learned and vulgar sources. It seems possible that, if he had only been able to elaborate the sketchy final pages, Flaubert would have fulfilled his original design, *da capo al fine*. Speculation will never be conclusive; as it happened, the enterprise was literally interminable. When Turgenev and other friends advised him to cut it short, Flaubert replied with weary complaints about the trouble it gave him, yet insisted that it would be his terminal achievement. That it should terminate ambiguously seems altogether fitting. Insofar as it sends its protagonists back to work, to working without philosophizing, it re-enacts the ending of *Candide*, which Flaubert deemed "the greatest moral lesson that exists." Happily for the workers, this does not mean cultivating their garden; nor does it seem to mean a resumption of their former secretarial jobs. Presumably the copying will be done for copying's sake, at their parrot-like leisure, the imitation of imitation with no ulterior aim. Something like a circular movement is indicated, as it is on the last page of *Finnegans Wake*; and, just as Joyce parodies himself in Shem the Penman, so the mute farewell of Flaubert to literature is the scratching of his copyists' pens. His documentary labors had their reward in the historiographic guide of Langlois and Seignobos, where a footnote cites the unfinished monograph on the uninteresting Duke of Angoulême by Bouvard and Pécuchet.

Tiresome fellows! They bored their creator to death. Why then must we recapitulate their wasted motions, their magpie accumulations, their courses in self-improvement which left them worse off than before? Because we are their heirs, willy-nilly, because so much of our cultural heritage seems to have reached us via their copying-desk. It is not for nothing that our printers and publishers refer to manuscript as "copy." Nineteenth-century criticism, deeply immersed in the dense context of Bouvard and Pécuchet's dabblings, could afford to dismiss them as soulless clowns in cotton nightcaps. It is significant that twentieth-century reconsideration seems to be treating them more respectfully and sympathetically. Raymond Queneau has devoted three prefaces

to their defense and eulogy. René Dumesnil, the dean of Flau-
bertistes, would concede that "they have the souls of apostles,"
while so cogent an intellectual spokesman as Lionel Trilling would
enroll them in the company of Flaubert's saints. Without under-
cutting the hierarchy so freely, we may accept them as the ill-
starred champions of culture in its late and mechanized phase.
If they begin like Don Quixote, they conclude like Saint Anthony.
Slaves to words, they graduate to deeds, are repeatedly overthrown,
and return to their clerkly regimen. Yet, in the quixotic process,
they have educated themselves; they have been schooled in the
incompatibility between their ideal, which extends promiscuously
across the whole realm of belief, and the spleen of circumstances,
which is to be encountered in all things and in most men and
women. "Then"—and the realization significantly coincides with
the sight of a dead dog, which plunges them into their most
abysmal despair—"a pitiable faculty developed in their minds,
that of noticing stupidity and no longer tolerating it."

The Flaubert who wrote that sentence has clearly come out,
if but temporarily, on their side; and it is one of the great reversals,
like that of Swift, when he joins the horses against mankind.
As soon as the issue was formulated between the newcomers'
iconoclasm and the natives' routine, Flaubert's sympathies left
him no other choice. Bouvard and Pécuchet were as dear—and
as repugnant—to him, in their middle-aged foibles, as were
Frédéric Moreau and Deslauriers in their youthful illusions. The
parting recognition of L'Education sentimentale, "We were better
off then," might no less appropriately have brought his testament
to a close. In both cases, the situation is archetypal: a pair of
dilettantes surviving their own innocence and weathering the
undeceptions of the century. Such a duality seems to have been
ingrained within Flaubert's innermost sensibilities. Through his
celibate life ran a pattern of intimate friendships, from his
adolescent "fraternal love" for Ernest Chevalier to the mature and
mutual admiration between him and Turgenev—a pair of "moles
burrowing in the same direction." In the line of literary companions, the most devoted was Louis Bouilhet. A minor poet
and mediocre playwright, Bouilhet projected a poem on the
congenial theme of Le Boeuf and dedicated his Lucretian Fossiles
to Flaubert. They were exactly the same age, looked alike, and—

what was most important, given their isolation—Bouilhet visited Croisset every Sunday. The death of this trusted adviser in 1869 was a crushing loss to Flaubert. He reacted, in bourgeois fashion, by campaigning for a commemorative monument at Rouen. When the Municipal Council balked, he poured out the vials of his anti-bourgeois wrath, denouncing them—in a phrase he borrowed from Heine—as "conservatives who conserve nothing."

But the ideal is never far from the spleen. Turning away from bourgeoisophobe invective, Flaubert paid his personal tribute to Bouilhet in 1870 by prefacing his posthumous *Dernières Poèmes*. The preface says what it can to burnish the dim Parnassianism of the verse, and it puts some Flaubertian critical judgments into Bouilhet's mouth. Its peroration is pure self-revelation, addressing a poignant appeal to younger writers:

> Are there two young men anywhere who spend their Sundays reading the poets together, telling each other what they have been doing, plans for the works they would like to write, comparisons and phrases and words that have come to them—and who, though scornful of everything else, conceal this passion with a virginal shyness? Let me offer them a word of advice:
>
> Walk through the woods side by side, declaiming your verses, intermingling your souls with the moisture of trees and the timelessness of masterpieces; lose yourselves in the reveries of history, in the bewilderments of the sublime! Enjoy your youth in the arms of the Muse! Her love will console you for others, and replace them.
>
> Afterward, when you have felt the accidents of this world, if they seem transposed into illusions for you to describe, so that everything, including your existence, seems to have no other use, and you are resolute for all affronts, ready for all sacrifices, armed for all ordeals, then venture, publish!
>
> Then, whatever happens, you will view the miseries of your rivals without indignation and their glory without envy; for the less favored will console himself by the success of the more fortunate; he whose nerves are strong will sustain the companion who is discouraged; each will contribute his own accomplishments to the common store; and this mutual record will prevent vanity and put off decline.

Finally, when one of the two is dead—for life was too beautiful—let the other carefully preserve his memory in order to make it a bulwark against meanness, a refuge for weakness, or rather a private chapel where he will go to whisper his worries and relax his heart. How frequently at night, when staring into the darkness beyond that lamp which lit their two foreheads, he will vaguely seek a shade to ask him: "Is it right? What should I do? Tell me!" And if this memory is the eternal food of his despair, it will at least provide company for his solitude.

That lurking shade at the edge of the lamplight could not have been Bouilhet, though he must have played his loyal part in the composite remembrance. Rather, it was the alter ego within Flaubert, who had worn various external faces and had sometimes disappeared altogether. As between the *deux bonshommes,* it was the austere perfectionist, the self-created tutelary colleague, the idealization of the artist. By its very nature, it was a disembodied and depersonalized conception. "I believe that great art is scientific and impersonal," Flaubert disagreed with George Sand. "The first comer is more interesting than Gustave Flaubert," he flatly maintained, to this woman who was so much more interesting than her writings. "... The man is nothing. The work is everything." Yet the work was probably not quite so perfect as he desired it to be, and the man was a notable personality in spite of that constraining other self. His flat assertion that he had no biography is contradicted by all the contemporaneous witnesses. True, he seemed warm-hearted to the warmhearted Zola and calculating to the calculating Goncourts. But those reflexive testimonials, viewed across a temperament, show the interaction of a stronger temperament. Flaubert's all too human self, the pedestrian *bonhomme,* is his own best witness through the *Correspondance,* where—in contrast to the fastidious standards of taste that he propounds there—the tone is as torrential as Rabelais, and now and then as coarse. Writing *currente calamo,* without revision or reservation, he veers from the savagely indignant to the thumpingly enthusiastic. It is an unwonted pleasure to watch the erstwhile purist register conviction with so inexact and emphatic an adjective as "enormous," spelled *hénaurrrme!!!*

André Gide professed his willingness to trade Flaubert's novels for his letters. When the same revaluation is echoed in Proust's novel, it takes on the overtones of what a horrified Flaubert might have called an *opinion chic*. Paul Valéry restated it more concretely by declaring that he preferred Saint Flaubert to Saint-Antoine. However, a writer is never wholly separable from his writing, any more than he is wholly identifiable with it. Granted that there are degrees of proximity, Stendhal is at the opposite pole from Flaubert: a persona rather than an impersonal force, improvising rather than revising, gaining his effects through pace and spontaneity rather than deliberation and plasticity. The more deliberate procedure does not exclude the more casual impulses, as is evident from Flaubert's work-sheets. His style is the end-product of an arduous process of refinement, into which he has poured his sensibilities "drop by drop," in the metaphor of Remy de Gourmont, leaving nothing of himself but the lees. The inference is that the best of himself has been absorbed into the writing, which completes the life; the work perfects the man, even as *A la recherche du temps perdu* will resolve the imperfections of Marcel Proust. The resolution is less a depersonalization than, in Sartre's term, an objectivation. So Flaubert's realism obtains the effect of impersonality less by impassively watching than by aggressively resisting his environment. And the cost of such resistance comes high: an austere renunciation of selfhood and a tense estrangement from those assumptions and satisfactions which interlink the lives of most other men. Some of his more orthodox commentators have condemned this propensity as a form of suicide—a condemnation supported by literal rumors, among his fellow townsmen, as to the manner of his death.

But Flaubert, who died a thousand deaths with every book, also lived with each one a thousand lives. The pride that he took in his calling must be measured by its demands for sacrifice and discipline, as he rigorously augmented them. In a world where traditional values had been profaned, an epoch when so little was held sacred, what had survived uncorrupted from the past, if not art? What could durably be handed on to posterity, if not "sacrosanct literature"? This required the ministrations of a special priesthood, whose votaries had more often been the adherents of poetry than of prose. The originality of Flaubert's contribution was that it succeeded in consecrating that upstart genre which had heretofore been assigned to a modest, if popular, rank among the powers and dominions of literature. Others had done much, and others would do more, to broaden the sociological scope of the novel—Balzac, Zola—or to intensify its psychological penetration—Stendhal, Proust. With due regard for both and for other components, Flaubert brought them under the strict control of artistic technique. By establishing the norms that prose fiction could reckon by, insofar as it would be practised by artists, he established himself as "the novelist's novelist." That authoritative epithet was bestowed by Henry James, through whom the cycle revolved to Proust and Joyce, after whom the prospect is still unclear. It seems clear enough by now, however, that the mandarins have all passed. Probably we shall not look at first hand again upon the like of their incisive detachment, their elaborate cultivation, or their dedicated artistry. The retrospect has slightly dimmed already, so that it is becoming equally hard to understand why *Madame Bovary* was prosecuted and how it was ever produced. Some of our novelists, pursuing different aims and feeling pressures Flaubert never felt, wax impatient over his cult of stylistic perfection. He is by no means beyond their criticism. Yet to criticize him, as they should be aware, is to criticize nothing less than the novel itself.

VI

ZOLA

No subject whatever is impermeable to the formative energy of art. One of the greatest triumphs of art is to make us see commonplace things in their real shape and in their true light. Balzac plunged into the most trifling features of the "human comedy." Flaubert made profound analyses of the meanest characters. In some of Emile Zola's novels we discover minute descriptions of the structure of a locomotive, of a department store, or of a coal mine. No technical detail, however insignificant, was omitted from these accounts. Nevertheless, running through the works of all these realists great imaginative power is observable, which is by no means inferior to that of the romantic writers.

—ERNST CASSIRER

1. *Experience and Experiment*

THE DIFFERENCE between theory and practice is more evident, yet less deliberate, with Emile Zola than with other realists. This is because he theorized altogether too much. Flaubert, who hated being labelled a realist, once took him to task for his naturalistic manifestos. According to their witness, Edmond de Goncourt, Zola replied by pointing out that he had a living to earn, whereas Flaubert could afford to fight shy of critical labels. "Yes," agreed the younger novelist, who had already tried such alternatives as *actualisme.* "True enough, I really don't care any more than you do about the word 'naturalism.' However, I repeat it over and over because things need to be baptized, so that the public will regard them as new." He went on to subdivide his work into the books he wanted the world to judge and the incidental journalism that made propaganda for them. It should be added that, in the Goncourts' reported conversations, Zola takes on a tone of cynical frankness which seems more characteristic of his elder colleagues than of his more usual self. Elsewhere throughout their rueful *Journal* the brothers stake their claims as pioneers of the new movement, and deprecate Zola as a pushing young man who has been making his way by stealing their thunder—an "assimilator" and not an "innovator."

Now Zola possessed what they signally lacked: an understanding of literary dynamics, a posture not wearily defensive but strongly aggressive, a flair—reminiscent of Victor Hugo and Voltaire—for stirring up the interest of the public and gaining the adherence of disciples. One of his regular contributions to the liberal weekly *Le Voltaire* changed the life of an Anglo-Irish art-student, George Moore, and thereby passed a torch from France to Great Britain. The same inspiration would be relayed to America by Frank Norris, whose *McTeague* would aspire to do for San Francisco what Zola had done for Paris in *L'Assommoir*. If naturalism took the place of realism, even as realism had replaced romanticism over the course of two accelerating generations, Zola's sense of timing must have taught him that every slogan had its day, and prepared him for a later moment when his future editor and son-in-law proposed to substitute "naturism" for naturalism. His collected journalism now ranges through many volumes, devoting itself to many other causes than his own. The opportunism that sought the hazardous opportunity to vindicate Alfred Dreyfus clearly stems from a more complex motivation than the sheer will to arrive. Zola believed as sincerely in naturalism as in science and democracy; and those words, too, still held the untarnished promise of novelty during the opening years of the Third Republic.

Zola interconnected them somewhat naïvely, and took too hopeful a view of what they might bring; yet, unless we wholly repudiate them, we should appreciate his earnest effort to re-examine fiction against the changing conditions of knowledge and society, and thereby to reformulate the problem of literary expression for an increasingly scientific age. His criticism, which was calculated to pave the way for his novels, appears in retrospect to have done them much harm. Most of his followers, like Arno Holz in Germany, discounted his theories while emulating his practices. "Thank God he has not carried out in his novels the theories of his articles, which extol the infusion of positivism in art!" So his former follower, J. K. Huysmans, exclaims through the voice of a character in *Là-Bas*. Indeed it seems to have been his hostile critics who took his scientific pretensions most seriously, whereas his most appreciative contemporaries were symbolists or impressionists who evaluated him on their own terms. He had borrowed his revisionist term, with due acknowledgment, from Montaigne by way of Taine. *Naturalisme* has always belonged to the vocabulary of French philosophy, designating any system of thought which accounts for the human condition without recourse to the supernatural and with a consequent emphasis upon the material factors. Where *réalisme*, borrowed from the fine arts, need imply no more than detailed visualization, the philosophical catchword brings with it a further and more limiting implication: the conditioning effect of men's backgrounds upon their lives.

Sainte-Beuve, who professed himself "a naturalist of minds," had greeted the clinical spirit of Flaubert's generation. Balzac had proceeded through the species of humanity as if he were their natural historian. But it was not until 1859, with the argument over Darwin's *Origin of Species*, that it became conceivable to view man as wholly a product of natural history. Zola found his exemplar in the eminent physiologist Claude Bernard, and his text in Bernard's *Introduction à l'étude de la médecine expérimentale*, which appeared in 1865. He could not have found a more lucid handbook of the positivistic method that was currently revolutionizing the sciences. It is not for nothing that Dmitri Karamazov, when interrogated by medical experts, mutters "Bernard!" Zola, in his endeavor to redefine the novel as "a general inquiry into nature and man," unwisely invoked the support of this stimulating but none too relevant authority. Insofar as Balzac had introduced biological concepts in his foreword to the *Comédie humaine*, he had subordinated them to other considerations, sociological, psychological, ideological, and purely literary. Zola's manifesto, *Le Roman expérimental*, is substantially a paraphrase—one medical reader has termed it a parody—of Bernard's physiological treatise. In fact, it is largely composed of quotations wherein the word "doctor" has been blandly transposed to "novelist." Positivism has thus been converted to dogmatism.

The running parallel is justified, Zola argues, because "the same determinism should regulate paving-stones and human brains." Now Cabanis, the Ideologue, had linked psychology to physiology by asserting that the brain secretes thought as the liver secretes bile; but that was an organic linkage, contrasted with Zola's insensate juxtaposition. The laws that govern inorganic matter were applied to bodily organs in Bernard's discoveries; yet, between the internal secretions and the mental processes, there remained a gap which Zola could only bridge by confounding induction with deduction. He envisions Balzac as an experimentalist, subjecting his Baron Hulot in *La Cousine Bette* to "a series of tests." So far as this assertion is true, it must apply to others, even to the fanciful Hawthorne testing Arthur Dimmesdale; and Balzac's proof is no more empirical than Hawthorne's demonstration that the symptoms of adultery take the corporeal form of scarlet letters. Poets of old had cast horoscopes for their characters, and utilized the Ptolemaic universe as a backdrop. Zola simply adopted the assumptions of a more up-to-date science, which has badly dated since his day, and more especially the genetic studies of Dr. Prosper Lucas as expanded in his *Traité philosophique de l'hérédité naturelle*. Zola was not really experimenting; he was parroting Lucas' notions, when he showed hereditary weaknesses —such doubtful ones as criminality—being transmitted from parents to children. But it was a good excuse for creating an inordinately large cast of characters who turn out to be remarkably similar to one another.

Le Roman expérimental was actually a rationalization, formulated when *Les Rougon-Macquart* was already half completed. No one can have been taken in by its main thesis. Even his most loyal follower, Henry Céard, pointed out the fallacy in assuming that a writer can verify his own hypotheses, and helpfully suggested that readers might provide such verification. Such a hypothesis would be no more than a thesis, submitted to their responding experience. Zola's other commentators have sufficiently stressed the distinction between an author's head and a scientist's laboratory, the fact that nature herself must answer the questions raised by the experimentalist. What they have not allowed for

is that perhaps, through his literary experimentation, he earned
the right to mix his critical metaphors. Surely no comparable
man of letters, with the exception of Poe, had tried so hard to
grasp the scientific imagination. His contemporary, Jules Verne,
led the way for writers of science fiction to tinker with imaginary
gadgets. Science for them has been an Aladdin's lamp, a magical
fulfillment, an easy trick for outstripping the inventors. For Zola
it was much tougher than that; it was behavior under pressure;
and the literary experimenter was both the witness of the behavior
and the gauge of the pressure. "What is a good experiment then?"
the mathematician Henri Poincaré would later ask, and would
answer: "It is what lets us know more than an isolated fact; it
is what enables us to predict—in other words, to generalize." By
that broader definition, Zola's art may have something in common
with science after all.

"L'observation montre, l'expérience instruit." Here, as so often
when Zola uses Bernard's key-word, we are at a loss whether
to translate it by "experiment" or by "experience." This verbal
ambiguity is the basis of much confusion which might be appreciably lessened if we sometimes translated his notion as "the
experiential novel," thereby recognizing the large and free role
he assigned to the personality of the observer. "In arts and letters,"
be freely admitted, "personality dominates everything else." An
earlier formulation, which he liked to repeat, defines a work of
art as "an aspect of nature visualized through a temperament."
This gives the artist back almost everything that naturalistic rigor
would take away. Both components of that definition were amplified in a letter written at the very outset of his career, shortly
before his discovery of Claude Bernard: "I believe that in the
study of nature, *just as it is*, there is a great source of poetry; I
believe that a poet born with *a certain temperament* will in future
centuries be able to discover new effects by addressing himself
to exact investigations." Thus behind the experiment looms the
experience—or, at any rate, the observation. That, in Zola's case,
was less intensive or extensive than his printed avowals or his
publicized impact and image may have led us into believing.
The personal impression he made upon Henry James was that
of a man "fairly bristling with the betrayal that nothing whatever
had happened to him in life but to write *Les Rougon-Macquart*."

There were certainly more beasts in Zola's jungle than there would ever be in Lambert Strether's; yet the innocent-eyed American novelist could still discern another kind of innocence than his own; and *Les Rougon-Macquart* could become so widely discussed that a whole iconography would grow up around the studious exertions of its author. We actually know a good deal about Zola's temperament, as well as his physique, since in the interests of science he submitted to an exhaustive series of examinations, observing the Golden Rule like a good naturalist. The data, as obtained and published by Dr. Edouard Toulouse, reveal much inhibition and timidity, along with a persistent tendency to stay at home. His eyesight was both myopic and astigmatic, while his beribboned *pince-nez* proclaimed him to the skies as every inch an intellectual. The nose itself, that interrogative nose, with its capacity for smelling out issues like a hunting dog, is the theme of a remarkable sentence in the Goncourt journal. A medical dissertation has been devoted to the major part that odors admittedly played in his books. We scarcely need to recall the long purple passage on cheeses in *Le Ventre de Paris* or the asphyxiation by flowers in *La Faute de l'abbé Mouret* or, even more characteristically, the manure-sodden courtship in *La Terre*. When an expurgated translation of *L'Assommoir* first came out in the United States, one reviewer aptly remarked that it had been "deodorized."

Henri Massis, in his pioneering study of the documentation for that novel, concluded that Zola had observed little and invented much. To his interviewers he staunchly declared that he invented nothing; while *Le Roman expérimental* proposed to substitute novels of observation for novels of imagination. Concurrently, the younger Dumas was boasting: "Invention does not exist for us." Drama was becoming a slice of life, just as fiction was being a human document. The gathering of documents, however, can be a highly literary—not to say pedantic—mode of activity. Probably no ampler collection of novelists' notes and drafts and outlines was ever amassed than the eighty-eight volumes of Zola's manuscript in the Bibliothèque Nationale. A typical anecdote describes him preparing for *Nana*—since he was frankly a stranger to its world, the *demi-monde*—by taking an expensive prostitute out to dine and plying her, notebook in hand, with professional questions. His academic enemy, Ferdinand Brunetière, took pedantic pleasure in disclosing that the most outrageous scene in the book had a source in English literature. Such disclosures merely indicate that Zola was not the mechanical monster he set out to be in his obiter dicta. His procedures, though they may be extreme in some respects, should be judged by the same criteria we apply to other novelists.

Frequently, when observation flags and invention takes over, obsession tips its hand. Certain situations are so peculiar and so recurrent that we may accord to them a thematic significance. Then again Zola speaks explicitly through personages very close to himself such as Sandoz, the burgeoning writer in L'Oeuvre, or the eponymous hero of Le Docteur Pascal. He walks in and out as an incorruptible journalist through the corrupting sphere of L'Argent, or as a novelistic witness in Paris, "the man of crowds . . . alone in the midst of everybody." James was right to suspect that the principal happening in Zola's life—at least up to that stormy day in court, and that year of Dreyfusard exile in England—had been the twenty-four-year toil of putting together Les Rougon-Macquart. He never ceased to preach the gospel of labor; it was work, he affirmed, which gave life its meaning; and his standard message to his juniors could be summed up by the last words that Sandoz speaks in L'Oeuvre: "Allons, travaillez!" His powers of observation, imperfect though they may have been, were ambitious and resolute enough to have shown him the worlds he needed to see; and his early experience had taught him the fundamental and ineradicable lesson of poverty. The Goncourts would tax him with not having seen or suffered, but he had been there in the sense that they never were.

Flaubert, though his frame of mind was more worldly, disciplined himself by ascetic withdrawal, whereas Zola was moving toward his juridical confrontation. It might almost be suggested that, while Flaubert recoiled after the trial of Madame Bovary, Zola was gravitating toward the trial of J'accuse! Another suggestive contrast might be drawn between the sharp bleakness of Flaubert's Normandy and the lush warmth of Zola's Provence. But Zola was not—like their more outgoing colleague, Alphonse Daudet—a native Provençal; he was not even a French citizen, until naturalized on arriving at his majority. He was born at

Paris in 1840, the only child of an Italian engineer with some Balkan antecedents. The father had died in Emile's childhood, leaving a fragmented legend of large-scale projects, which cannot have been without influence over the son. The very surname is not without its symbolic overtones, for in Italian *zolla* means clod of earth. When Zola addressed the jury that was to condemn him, absolving himself from the anti-Dreyfusard charge of being a foreigner, he spoke of his mother and his grandparents from Beauce as "peasants of that vigorous soil"—the landscape he had depicted in *La Terre*.

Clearly he preferred the southern terrain of Aix-en-Provence, where he passed his adolescence. Here he contracted the most memorable friendship of his career, with Paul Cézanne, the son of the local banker, a friendship which was unhappily not to survive the publication of Zola's art-novel, *L'Oeuvre*. Meanwhile, during the period when Zola preceded Cézanne to Paris, their engaging correspondence prolonged the ties of their boyish readings, poetic efforts, and shared ambitions. But the Balzacian mood of youthful conquest and the fascination of the metropolis prompted an ambivalent response. Zola keeps nostalgically reverting from his cramped mansard to the open air; soon he will advise budding writers to deflect their gaze from the capital to the provinces; and even his most tainted heroines will recover a little of their virginity during holidays in the country. He failed his bachelor's examinations at Paris, as he had previously done at Aix, though he seems to have done a little better in science than in literature. Thrown out into the world, he worked at various menial employments, barely eking out a bohemian existence of a disappointingly unromantic kind. And then—a decisive step in his intellectual formation—he became clerk and subsequently chief of publicity for the well-known publishing firm of Hachette.

This means that he mastered the tricks of the trade at a time when the trade was becoming a big business, and that he was thoroughly versed in the techniques of bookselling before he wrote his own books. The welkin of the mid-century was then commencing to ring with the clamor of those whom he called "the lyric poets of advertisement." Their knack of making a noise in the market-place, of taking full advantage of *le tapage*, was one which he would go on to exercise in his own behalf. Small wonder that he became the first French writer whose publications sold by the hundreds of thousands. The literary stage was being set for productions of gas-lit melodrama. In outlining his grand design, he offered himself this shrewd counsel: "Don't forget that drama catches the public by the throat. They get angry, but they do not forget. Always give them, if not nightmares, at any rate excessive books which stick in their memory." The yellow backs of Charpentier's editions became a trademark for these excessive books, each of them designed to "make a killing," as he candidly put it to his publisher's wife, Madame Charpentier. Having served an apprenticeship in publisher's advertising, he moved on to journeywork as a journalistic free-lance. With the appearance of his first novel, *La Confession de Claude*, he and his employer agreed to a parting of the ways. M. Hachette is said to have told him off with the appraising epithet, "You are a rebel."

What would he be but a rebel, *un homme révolté*, in the restless line that Albert Camus would trace? And, what is more important, Zola would become one of those rebels whose rebellions were linked with successes. For rebellious success, *succès de scandale*, has been one of the mainsprings that animate modern French culture. Hugo and has romantic cronies had shocked the bourgeoisie; Flaubert had cursed them and turned his back; but Zola, through his newspaper work in the last years of the Empire and the first years of the Republic, joined in the effort of forming a liberal middle-class intelligentsia. The richest artistic experiments of those years were being carried on in the field of painting, among those painters whom the Emperor had grouped together by setting up the Salon des Refusés, after their canvases had been rejected by the official Salon. Zola would have liked to claim them as naturalists; and that claim had actually been asserted by the critic Castagnary in 1866; but the label that prevailed was Impressionist, after Monet's notorious eye-opener of 1874, *Impression: soleil levant*. Despite his myopia, Zola was fervent in defense of them and in attack on their enemies, the academic juries, with a particular regard for Manet, whom he may well have considered the most naturalistic representative of the school.

For his friend Cézanne, and for the increasing stylization of Cézanne's vision, he had less and less sympathy.

L'Oeuvre may be viewed as his modernized version of Balzac's Chef-d'oeuvre inconnu. Zola's truncated title focuses on the work or the idea of work, without denoting—as Balzac does—the idea of a masterwork which goes unheralded. Zola portrays his old friend as Claude Lantier, the monomaniac protagonist who comes to grief by setting his art against nature, and to whom the hard-working Sandoz—Zola's self-portrayal, with all of his "rage for production"—gives sound advice, which Cézanne must have found it hard to take. In the last analysis, it may have been nothing more than sheer biographical coincidence which led Zola to practise as an art-critic. His criticism in this field does not touch the high level sustained by a number of other French men of letters, from Diderot through Baudelaire to Malraux. Gradually he drew apart from the Impressionists; they had helped him to realize the value of sensation, in more ways than one; and his championship of their innovations proved to be good practice for his campaigning on behalf of naturalism. Always a new campaign! Two collections of articles bear the titles Une Campagne and Nouvelle Campagne. The battles and struggles of his career seem more palpable, less internal, than those of his forerunners. The targets are practical, and the aims professional, typically the fight for copyright through the Société des Gens de Lettres. Another collection is entitled Mes Haines; and it is prefaced by a hymn to salutary hatred; but its invectives are counterweighed by enthusiasms. Zola was a fighter but not a hater. Unlike Flaubert, he left hate to the other side, the bourgeoisie and its haine de la littérature.

His battle-ground, as Sandoz puts it, was the daily press. He was not a participant in the Franco-Prussian War, although he covered the government that emerged from it for a newspaper in the terrible year of the Commune. This double catastrophe, the central event of the epoch, furnished him with the major premise for his life-work, and shaped its underlying pattern through ways which we shall be considering in context. The twenty-volume cycle accumulated in almost yearly succession, interspersed with various by-products: stories, plays, and much discursive prose. If it was his aim to be chef d'école, he was able

to *faire école* with the School of Médan, the group of writers
named for the country house he had acquired and embellished
by means of his royalties. Thither he might have retired upon the
completion of the enormous undertaking he had set for himself.
Instead, he embarked upon an additional sequence of novels
rather more visionary in purport, and interrupted that task to
become the rallying figure in the polemical struggle at the end
of the century. His final turbulent decade was broken off by his
accidental death in 1902, asphyxiated by fumes from a stove in
his Paris apartment. Moralists were not lacking among the orthodox to invoke the judgment of providence; liberals merely suspected foul play; while fellow naturalists attributed this ironic
denouement to those gloomy forces which Zola had often assayed.

Hence he no more than crossed the threshold of the twentieth
century, which had seemed to him such a promised land, the
destination of his many crusades. The most famous of these was
launched by the open letter he addressed to the President of
France, which was headlined by the editor of *L'Aurore*, Georges
Clemenceau, with its more famous title, *J'accuse!* All of Zola's
excessive books could carry that title; they are all accusations
of one sort or another. It is seldom easy to distinguish the crusader
from the best-seller, but it was lucky for Dreyfus that Zola was
both altruistic and publicity-wise. He had learned how to profit
from the painful lesson that George Gissing stated in *The New
Grub Street:* "The simple, sober truth has no chance whatever
of being listened to, and it's only by volume of shouting that
the ear of the public is held." Into the pandemonium Zola
brought his temperamental equipment: his sense of smell, his
instinct for exposure, his reporter's professional curiosity, his
ability to create or convey sensation. He was not repelled by—
rather, he was attracted to—dirty linen; it is virtually the subject
of *L'Assommoir*; and the fight in the laundry, where Gervaise
Macquart quite literally exposes and spanks another washerwoman,
is symptomatic of his whole approach.

"Le naturalisme, c'est la nudité," he once explained. One of
his obsessions is female nudity—to be sure, no very abnormal
concern for a nineteenth-century Frenchman. It is ordained by
the situation at hand when Nana goes through her dazzling
strip-tease, or when Christine Hallegrain poses for Claude Lan-

tier's masterpiece, *Dans le plein air*, which seems to duplicate Manet's *Déjeuner sur l'herbe*. But mere sensuality is twisted into homicidal mania with Jacques Lantier in *La Bête humaine*, and into something like necrophilia with the Italian aristocrats of *Rome*; and it is reduced to gross absurdity on the bearskin rug of the parvenu Turkish bath in *La Curée*. There, at all events, Zola tells us what reaction he is trying to provoke; for he uses the expression "un frisson nouveau," which Hugo had coined to catch the shock-value of Baudelaire's poetry. Though *La Curée* is primarily concerned with real estate, and *La Bête humaine* with railroading, Zola was at pains to season such technical subject-matter with a hint of incest in one case and a crime of passion in the other. *La Curée* deliberately intermingled "the notes of wealth and the flesh." Sex is ordinarily the secondary motive, but it tends to dominate the main relationship. This tendency gave some color to Zola's scandalous reputation abroad, and to the reprehension of such a pure-minded Englishman as Algernon Charles Swinburne.

On the other hand, the French prosecutor investigating *La Confession de Claude* held that its disillusioned bohemianism offered a cautionary example to youth. *Pour une nuit d'amour* took its departure from a titillating escapade of Casanova's, but Zola stresses the price that is grimly paid for the night of love; the would-be lover, having earned his payment by disposing of two predecessors, is too fatigued to take advantage of it. Zola deals austerely with voluptuaries; his debauchees are prematurely enervated; his fallen women can never be rehabilitated; justly, an old Calvinistic servant pronounces the inexorable fate of the well-baptized Madeleine Férat. Here Zola is not following the puritan ethic so much as he is swallowing the pseudo-science of Michelet, who in *La Femme* had propounded the doctrine that a woman forever retains the psychic imprint of her first lover. The consequences of this aprioristic conception take the shape of a good many triangles, generally seen from a point of view sympathetic to that of the cuckold who is both anticipated and displaced—like Gervaise's husband Coupeau in *L'Assommoir*, preceded and succeeded by Lantier. The Enoch Arden theme of the long-lost husband's return to a wife who has given him up and remarried, similarly, is a haunting bugbear, most explicitly treated in the *nouvelle*, *Jacques Damour*. Here the sympathies, like Balzac's in *Le Colonel Chabert*, are with the returner.

This jealous suspicion becomes so obsessive that some of Zola's biographers have been ungallantly tempted to ascribe it to his own domestic plight. They would surmise that, if his preoccupation was not grounded on scientific experiment, it might have been based on intimate experience, mistaking a qualm of jealousy for a law of nature. But little is known of Madame Zola's prehistory, except that she had been her husband's mistress for a few years before she became his wife, and that—after the death of his dominating mother—she became the hostess of his circle. In the lascivious circle of the Goncourts, he was often rallied upon his relative chastity. His one dissatisfaction with his marriage, its childlessness, led him at the age of forty-eight into an affair with a girl of twenty. They were blessed with two children, adopted after his death by Madame Zola. That ultimate fulfillment is reflected in *Le Docteur Pascal*, the twentieth volume of *Les Rougon-Macquart*, which is partly a panoramic retrospect of what has happened to whom, but partly a celebration of the author's latterday romance. To his earlier frustration may be traced, in some measure, the numerous progeny of his problematic line of descent and their involvement with problems of heredity, procreation, and degeneration. In his master plan, after much calculating and schematizing, he had reminded himself: "Furthermore, put passion into it!" He cannot be said to have needed the reminder.

2. *The Poetry of Fact*

The most poignant letter from Zola in Paris to Cézanne at Aix describes a dream about a sublime book, written of course by the former and illustrated with sublime engravings by the latter, whereby their two names, embossed in gold upon the title-page, will inseparably go down to posterity. They have come down to us, but separately, so that we are almost surprised when biographers join them together. Yet some feeling for artistic experimentation may well have been transmitted to the novelist from the painter. Roger Fry has remarked: "If ever the art of Cézanne could be considered to have touched the art of his friend Zola, it is ... where an essentially romantic emotion is conveyed through a literal statement of commonplace matter of fact." In the correspondence, it is Cézanne who speaks of his researches; while their inseparable friend Baptistin Baille, who was destined to be an engineer, assumes a positivistic stance and accuses Zola of being a dreamer. Zola defends his escapist inclinations, motivated by homesickness for Provence and revulsion from Paris, by arguing that reality is all too sad. He is against realism; he is a romantic; he is a poet who has had the misfortune of being born into a prosaic century. This is pure Musset, whose bittersweet cadence echoes through juvenilia later to be published.

Meanwhile a periodical at Aix brought out Zola's first story, a fairy tale in prose which he described as "a long poetic dream." Together with similar reveries and sketches of southern inspiration and dream-like substance, it was gathered into his first book, *Contes à Ninon*, in 1864. The elusive Ninon, "daughter of a ray of light and a drop of dew," is to the narrator what the Muse had been to the Poet in Musset's *Nuits*. The following year—the year of the Goncourts' *Germinie Lacerteux*, which Zola saluted and would emulate—was also the year of his own *Confession de Claude*. Had he remained a dreamer, this would have been his *Scènes de la vie de Bohème*. But Claude finds, like Emile, that life in a garret is grim and hungry; the streets do not blossom with Mimis and Musettes; and his effort to redeem a prostitute—like Emile's, too, we gather—is bound to fail. "I am dream, and she is reality." So, in stating their relationship, he restates our classic opposition, and all the distance between Ninon and Nana. After the fashion of novelists, he could bestraddle both spheres and dramatize the conflict between them. He could see himself, clearly enough, in the role of Don Quixote. But, though he praised Gustave Doré's illustrations to Cervantes without reservation in 1863, in 1866 he criticized that same Don for "living wholly in the land of dreams" and "lacking a concern with reality." Quixotically, novels-within-novels will supply a means of seduction in *Pot-bouille* and a stratagem for murder in *La Bête humaine*.

The antithesis, *le rêve/la réalité*, runs through Zola's fiction from first to last. The formula, *réaliser son rêve*, sums up the attainment of desire for each of his protagonists, even though more often than not it is thwarted along the wayside, and though it varies from private ambitions in the earlier novels to collective ideals in the later ones. And yet, three-quarters of the way through the series, just after the devastating earthiness of *La Terre*, Zola could go to the other extreme in *Le Rêve*, a Cinderella story taking place against an ecclesiastical setting. His Cinderella dies at the end, it is true, but on the cathedral steps and not before her marriage to a Prince Charming, so that the happy ending is a kind of ascension. Desire is realized, with a Renanesque shrug: "All is but a dream." Zola's dreams do not have the texture of gossamer; but the pertinent consideration is that his fantasy never resigns before his facts; it comments and plays upon them; it amplifies them to the point of Hugolian elephantiasis. He remains a poet then, "contributing to creative literature as great works of fiction as have been written in the epic forms," according to William Dean Howells, "the Homer of the cesspool" according to the Duchesse de Guermantes. When Jean Cocteau, in recent homage, added "a neglected lyricist," he himself neglected to recall that Zola's lyricism had been hailed by innumerable critics in his day, who had refused to recognize his scientism. Though as Sandoz he had sought to extirpate "the romantic gangrene," he was down in their books as a romanticist.

He and they continually refer to his epic intentions. When he mapped out a new volume, he generally prefaced his specifications by announcing it to himself as *un poème*. Thus *La Bête humaine* would be the poem of a railway line; *Au Bonheur des Dames* would be the poem of a department store; and *Nana*, somewhat synecdochically, "le poème du cul." However that may be, we have the fastidious authority of Mallarmé for regarding the whole series as a "prodigious poem." For a middle term between such contradictory impulses, we might borrow a terse phrase from Dickens, "the poetry of fact." For Zola such a compounded outlook developed during the mid-'sixties, when he seems to have been moving from the gate of ivory toward the gate of horn. From the influence of Musset and Hugo, he moved into a passionate admiration for Balzac, about whom he wanted to write a study, "une sorte de roman réel." About George Sand he would soon be writing, "At this hour, in the struggle between truth and dream, the truth is winning." In his *Nouveaux Contes à Ninon* he confides that he has left the gallant paths of lovers, taken the highway, and been pushed into the gutter. To a younger poet remaining at Aix, in what Zola now viewed as an ivory tower, he explained his conversion to prose fiction and realism. He was aware that all modes of expression interpose a screen, as he now put it, between nature and the observing temperament; yet, as opposed to the classical and the romantic screens, the realistic had the virtue of transparency.

Still there would be distortions, and his corollary throws light on his future practice: "It is said that one either debases or idealizes a subject. In the long run it's the same thing." Giving a Flaubertian twist to a Horatian maxim, Zola had written to Cézanne that the artist is a composite of two men, the poet and the worker. "One is born a poet, one becomes a worker." He had become a worker under the hustling pressures of the Librairie Hachette; and, when he set out for himself, he confessed to one editor that he was seeking "the quickest notoriety." Such callow careerism, nevertheless, was disciplined by the newer literary models: the social consciousness of the Goncourts and the analytic criticism of Taine, along with the inimitable example of Flaubert and the inexhaustible lesson of Balzac. Zola's own thinking about his medium seems to have been crystallized by the invitation to read a paper before a scientific congress in 1866. He approached his topic, "Une Définition du roman," by contrasting Athens with Paris and the ancient epic with the *Comédie humaine*. Through an imaginary interview with Balzac, he defined the novelist as "a doctor of moral sciences" and the novel itself as "a treatise on moral anatomy, a compilation of human data, an experimental philosophy of the passions."

Attempting to work out this pattern, he framed his journeyman novels with certain philosophical presuppositions. He heralded *Thérèse Raquin* with an epigraph from Taine; while *Madeleine Férat*, rewritten from an unsuccessful play, was the doctrinal godchild of Michelet. Neither book was sufficiently excessive. Having in boyhood contemplated an epic poem on nothing less than Genesis, and growing up "after the confluence of Hugo and Balzac," he shared the opinion of his alter ego, Sandoz: "it was necessary to be encyclopedic in order to make books correspond to life." It was the heyday of what the Goncourts called "big machines," in the arts as in technology, and most spectacularly in Wagner's *Gesamtkunstwerk*. The brothers report Zola saying, with that calculation which he always seems to exhibit in their company: "After the infinitely fine analyses of sentiment as they have been accomplished by Flaubert in *Madame Bovary*, after the analysis of matters artistic, plastic, neurotic as you have done it, after those jewelled works, those chiselled volumes, there is no more room for the younger generation, no more to do in the way of constructing or creating a character. Only by the quantity of volumes, the power of creation, can we speak to the public." Flaubert would ironically assent when he came to deal with those exhaustive compilers of documents, Bouvard and Pécuchet.

What Zola failed to say, and what the Goncourts well understood, was that, in laying out a life-work in book-length installments, the free-lance bargained for steady employment at a rising income. He showed clear-eyed self-knowledge in understanding that his own talent was for excitement rather than detachment, not for penetration but for breadth, less for Balzac's *pourquoi* than for Bernard's *comment*. In that respect, he carried on the coarser strain so popularly exploited by Eugène Sue in those newspaper serials which the Goncourts despised. In his pot-boiling *Mystères de Marseilles*, Zola was not above an inept provincial imitation of Sue's *Mystères de Paris*. He went out of his way to repudiate the poetic master whose prose he sought to outrival, Victor Hugo. As Mallarmé perceived, it became the basis of Zola's achievement to establish a solid middle ground between the *oeuvre-bijou* and the *roman-feuilleton*—"between literature and something else, capable of satisfying the crowd and of continuing to astonish the men of letters." Zola thus succeeded in popularizing the insights of elders whom he insisted upon regarding as his fellow *naturalistes*. Balzac afforded the fullest precedent; he was the great precursor, as he had been for the *réalistes*; and Zola consciously designed *Les Rougon-Macquart* with an eye on *La Comédie humaine*.

Historically speaking, he wanted to do for the Second Empire what his predecessor had done for the July Monarchy. But his scientific canon would be stricter. "Balzac says that he wants to paint men, women, and things," Zola noted in setting down his plan. "I put men and women together, while allowing for the natural differences, and submit both men and women to things." The effect of this step is not merely to admit things to the cast, but to make them the leading characters in the drama, and to make men and women the victims of their surroundings. The paralyzed mother-in-law, in *Thérèse Raquin*, is not unique in becoming "like a thing." Here the contrast with Balzac is striking, if we oppose some of his defiant and self-reliant proponents of free will to some of the stunted growths and stultified minds whose sorry existence Zola has chronicled. But environment comes second to heredity in Zola's scheme for unifying his cycle, and therefore simplifying his characterization, whereas Balzac was free to set forth the varieties of man, without any special concern for the transmission of inherited traits. There are about 1200 characters in Zola's twenty tomes, somewhat more than half the population of Balzac's registry. Happily enough, a comparatively small number of them turn out to be either Rougons or Macquarts.

These are readily traceable by means of a genealogical tree, which Zola was to enlarge as he went along, from his original roster of twenty-six to a definitive thirty-six. There may be others, incidentally mentioned; but it is not really a very prolific family; and that is one of Zola's points, to be emphasized by Claude Lantier's grim portrait of his dead child, who is all but the last of his race. For hereditary madness and congenital alcoholism, dubious though they may be as medical concepts today, have affected and afflicted the genes of this line. Or rather, we should say, there are two diverging lines. Both can be traced across five generations to the cataleptic peasant woman, Adélaïde Foucque, known to her grandchildren as Tante Dide, "the mother of us all." The one derives from her brief marriage with the gardener Rougon; the other stems from her long-drawn-out liaison with the drunken smuggler Macquart. Stemming from the locale of Plassans—which is recognizable as Aix-en-Provence—and keeping pace with the rising and falling rhythms of the two imperial decades, they range across France toward Paris and into other provinces, where they consort with other families, such as the Maheux in the mines of *Germinal* or the Fouans on the farms of *La Terre*. Such dynastic continuities, extending far beyond the single existence, expanded the novel during the latter half of the nineteenth century, and paralleled the *Stammbaumsroman* of Zola with the ancestral surveys of Gustav Freytag.

That integrating device establishes a kind of cousinship among the successive volumes, which is varied by frequent changes of scene, though Paris is the inevitable cynosure. It is omnipresent, always there. "Toujours là!" We catch this breathless refrain after each section of *Une Page d'amour*, where the viewpoint is mainly confined to uncharacteristic drawing-rooms. Thence, from windows on the heights of Passy, we look down upon the sea of roofs at varying seasons and hours. Zola had to apologize for the anachronism of including a glimpse of the Trocadéro, which was being built and obstructing the panorama even as he wrote. "The transformation of Paris," into "the city of light" and "the capital of the world," through the demolition of its old buildings and the construction of its new boulevards, provides both theme and setting for *La Curée*. The master scene-designer is the Emperor's city-planner, Baron Haussmann himself; and the *curée*, the "spoils," are gained from the ensuing speculations, the lavish contracts and shady dealings in real estate. When the scene is not the city itself, it is likely to be a city in miniature, such as the central markets in *Le Ventre de Paris* or the department store in *Au Bonheur des Dames*. Either may be taken as a working model for Zola's developing series in all its planned miscellaneousness: the busy, noisy Halles Centrales, with their assortment of smells and savors, or the *grands magasins*, with their up-to-date merchandising schemes for driving the old-fashioned shopkeepers out of business. Like his brisk merchant, Octave Mouret, Zola kept installing new departments and bringing his inventories up to date.

He was the first to reconstruct on paper, with painful accuracy and completeness, the twin beehives of metropolitan co-existence: the squalid tenement of *L'Assommoir*, with its rickety stairs and dank cubicles, "a living organ at the very heart of a town," and the gimcrack apartment-house of *Pot-bouille*, with its modern improvements and middle-class pretensions, a buzzing hive of social climbing and marital misadventure. It was more to be expected that he should present, as others had already done though in his own dynamic manner, the political and financial organs of his society: the legislature in *Son Excellence Eugène Rougon* and the stock exchange in *L'Argent*. In short, he had that gift of institutional imagination which enabled Dickens to build his novels around such massive and pointed exaggerations as the Dust Heap and the Circumlocution Office. Zola greatly admired the vibrancy of Dickens' creations, albeit he was slightly put off by their evident lack of documentation. Zola's own sufficiency in that area has, in turn, been labored over more than sufficiently. From Paris he would go forth in quest of fact; in Médan he would write it up, with few erasures or corrections, at the steady rate of four pages every day. As a reporter, he was both enterprising and ubiquitous. For his railroad novel he rode both day and night behind an engine from Paris to LeHavre and back again, notebook in hand as usual. For his mining novel, he not only worked up technological information; he descended into the pits. And when he prepared for *Au Bonheur des Dames,* he went on tours of inspection and corresponded with the managers of the Bon Marché, the Samaritaine, and the Grands Magasins du Louvre.

He must have had the good reporter's faculty for impressing himself upon his interlocutors as a kindred spirit; it would not have been impossible to imagine him managing some rival enterprise. It must be confessed that he has something to answer for, insofar as he fostered the kind of pseudo-reportage so rife today, which is neither fact nor fiction but a contamination of both. His *Trois Villes* incline dangerously in that direction: *Lourdes* paves the way for Franz Werfel's plodding *Song of Bernadette.* Yet any comparison between his copious material and the use he finally made of it is bound to heighten our respect for his selectivity. Nor does he utilize factual digressions set apart from their fictional context, as novelists have so freely done from Scott to Dos Passos. Technical matters are apprehended directly, through the activities, sensations, and speeches of the characters. Occasionally Zola gets carried away, as by that savory episode in *Le Ventre de Paris* of which Barbey d'Aurevilly complained that it confounded the art of literature with the art of sausage-making. But, on such an occasion, it is not difficult for the impressionable—or simply the hungry—reader to be swept along in empathy. Again, when Zola depicts a white sale at the emporium, Au Bonheur des Dames, he rises to a pitch of lyricism which can only be compared with Melville's chapter on "The Whiteness of the Whale" in *Moby-Dick.*

Such a disproportion is explainable, when we remember that Zola started in advertising; but it does not justify itself by imparting any mysterious purity to the articles of linen on sale; they remain, in implication, blank. To that extent, however, they are exceptional; for most of the physical objects that Zola dwells on acquire some meaning above or beyond their immediate physical significance. Thus the poisonous exotic plant in the conservatory of *La Curée* makes an intermittent comment upon the strained relations of the household; while the title itself, repeated thematically, is a symbol, like a number of Zola's titles; if the booty is prey, the profiteering dealers are predatory animals, a pack of wolves. "It is around a symbol that a book is composed," André Gide has remarked, concluding that any well-composed work must therefore be symbolic, and that a work of art has to be the exaggeration of an idea. Gide's remark is borne out not only by Zola; it is corroborated by the very titles of lesser novels composed in his vein around American institutions—*The Octopus*, Frank Norris on the railroad; *The Jungle*, Upton Sinclair on the stockyards. As Anatole France discerned, concurring in a view which many critics surprised themselves by taking, the view of Zola as poet: "His grand and simple genius creates symbols, and brings to birth new myths."

That is the pith of the paradox: new myths. At a moment when fiction has been swinging away from naturalism, when the interplay of symbols is tending to obscure a primary sense of actuality, we scarcely need encouragement to look for archetypal recurrences amidst the accumulation of particular details. Flaubert struck a proper balance for Zola when he testified, "Nana turns into a myth without ceasing to be real." Rather more oracularly, the admirer of Kuchiouk Hanem added: "This creature is Babylonian. *Dixi*." Where the Flaubertian ironies play off the present against the past, Zola, by making every effort to be timely, somehow breaks through to the semblance of timelessness. Nana was completely designed to be a *demi-mondaine* of the Second Empire; she makes her appearance, singing atrociously, in a parody of an Offenbach burlesque; yet, under the aspect of the Blonde Venus, she is metamorphosed into a sempiternal goddess of love. Similarly in *La Curée*, where the love story is a modernized version of *Phèdre*, the analogy is pointed up when the aberrant wife and son attend Ristori's performance of Racine's tragedy. The mythical component is less explicit in *La Terre*; but there is a clear similarity between Père Fouan, who parcels out his land among three children, and the King Lear of Shakespeare—or of Turgenev.

The pious little embroideress in *Le Rêve*, who dreams particularly of the saints she has read about in *The Golden Legend*, achieves a kind of sainthood for herself. Legends of baser metal are current among the miners in *Germinal* to account for the sinister fumes that arise from the volcanic soil of the neighboring region; by naming that region Le Tartaret, Zola indicates Tartarus, the classical place of underground confinement. Conversely, in *La Faute de l'abbé Mouret*, the overgrown garden, where flora and fauna lushly surround the lovers with their sympathetic pullulation, is named Paradou; and the gloss is supplied in Zola's preliminary sketch: "Adam and Eve awakening at spring in the terrestrial paradise." Another biblical analogue is underlined several times in *Le Docteur Pascal*: the revival of love in the elderly King David, excited by the youthful beauty of Abishag the Shunammite. Dr. Pascal Rougon is the scientist of the family and—to his credit—its least typical member, a sport in the light of his own biological theories. Moreover, he is Zola's chief spokesman, the keeper of the records, the observant geneticist who sums it all up—and therefore, to a certain extent, an allegorical portrait of the artist. In his composite afterview, not inappropriately, poetry and science are blended together. "Ah!" he exclaims,

> these incipient sciences, these sciences where hypothesis stammers and imagination is still the mistress, they are the field of poets as well as scientists. The poets, pioneering in the advance guard, often discover virgin territories and point toward future solutions. Theirs is the margin between the established definitive truth and the unknown, from which the truth of tomorrow will be wrested . . . What an immense fresco to paint, what a colossal human comedy and what a tragedy to write, with heredity, which is the very Genesis of families, of societies, and of the world!

The exclamation, characteristically, looks backwards and forwards. "Every twenty years," the doctor elsewhere observes, "theories change." It happens that *Le Docteur Pascal* was written more than twenty years after it had been projected as the epilogue to *Les Rougon-Macquart*. Hence Dr. Pascal can paradoxically look backward when he speaks of genetics and forward when he speaks of Genesis. Significantly, he shifts from a scientific to a poetic terminology, and even more strikingly, to the vocabulary of art, with a word which Zola often employed in blocking out his books, and which may still retain some trace of his association with the Impressionists: *fresque*. Visiting and describing the Sistine Chapel would enlarge his conception of impressionism to include Michelangelo and the creation of his world. In answering a letter from Céard about *Germinal*, which raised the habitual question about his lyric exaggerations, Zola characterized that work as another vast fresco. Admitting to a "hypertrophy of detail," he confessed that he often leapt to the stars from the springboard of exact observation. "The truth ascends in winged flight to the symbol." Indeed the dark grotesquerie of his miners was precisely what Van Gogh had set out to paint, just a few years before in a neighboring province; while the two steam-wreathed terminals that bound the clangorous action of *La Bête humaine* are reminiscent of Monet's Gare Saint-Lazare.

It was entirely fitting that Courbet, the arch-realist among the painters, on reading *La Terre* should denominate Zola "the foremost painter of the epoch." On the other hand, his ventures into the theater discouraged him; he felt himself constrained by the Procrustean bed of the stage, and waged "war against conventions." None of his own eleven plays was successfully performed, though —with professional collaborators or adapters—he won a few lukewarm successes. As a dramatic critic, he concluded: "We are in the century of the novel." Yet the quality of his fiction is as highly theatrical as it is thoroughly pictorial. Actually, it is much easier to reconcile the contradictory epithets attached to his art, and to square its mechanical with its imaginative quality, if we view it as a forerunner of the cinema. Its cinematic potentialities have been effectively realized in a number of instances, notably in Jean Renoir's *Bête humaine*; and Alex Comfort has pointed out how admirably the gigantic scope, the oscillating movement, and the visual contrasts of *Germinal* would suit the screen. Such a film would have to represent the submission of men and women to things, the crushing of habits that reduced Etienne Lantier, like a true miner, "a little each day to the function of a machine." But it would also represent a sort of Bergsonian triumph of the organic over the mechanical, if it could somehow convey the epic throb that brings the mineshaft alive and turns its incessant pumping into the respiration of some crouching beast.

The situation is even more ominous in *La Bête humaine*, where human beings behave quite bestially, and the engine too is an animal—a mascot with a feminine name, La Lison. The heart of the engineer, Jacques Lantier, is nearly broken to see her lying wrecked and derailed in the snow. The climax, brought about by the cross-purposes of sex and machinery, is absurdly melodramatic: Jacques and his jealous fireman brutally wrestle, until they fall off the cab and are crushed to death under the wheels. But the berserk machine, the driverless train, speeds on blindly through the night, a historic allegory of things in the saddle. The cattle-cars are crammed with soldiers, "human cattle," youthful conscripts who have been drinking brandy, and have become vocal and happy. They do not know, as we do, that they are bound for the crushing defeat of the Franco-Prussian War. Zola's closing irony is heavy, and his bitterness waxes rhetorical. The creaking train, he has told us expressly himself, is "the image of France." But our attention should closely follow the verbal sequence from image to image, and come to rest on the last word, because it is the very last word of the book, and because it is the token of Zola's compassion:

> What mattered the victims crushed by the machine upon its way? Was it not going toward the future anyhow, care-less of the blood expended? Without a driver, surrounded by shadows, like a blind and deaf beast unleashed in the midst of death, it rolled along, rolled along, freighted with this cannon-fodder, with these soldiers already stupefied by fatigue, and drunk, and singing.

3. *The Human Beast*

The human condition, as classically stated by Pascal, is that of neither angel nor beast. Man, as incarnated in Tartuffe, was dem-onstrably no angel. To the horse-loving Gulliver, he was a yahoo. But it was for the generation of writers that followed Darwin to enroll themselves as naturalists and to keep the beast most rigor-ously in view. Balzac, committed to the religious dualism of spirit and matter, had contented himself with broad analogies between humanity and animality. Zola created "a pessimistic epic of human animality," said Jules Lemaître anent *Germinal*, and went on to say of *La Bête humaine* that the title would serve for the whole of Zola's work. In turning from the mine to the railroad, he was still concerned with the brutalizing effects of the machine on the lives of men and women. It was in part a fear of repeating himself that sidetracked the later novel to sexual crime and judicial investigation. It is the bad blood of the Macquarts pulsating in Jacques Lantier, "the beast howling in his depths," an atavistic reversion to the cave, that finally impels him to kill the woman he loves. "To possess and to kill meant the same thing within the dark bowels of the human beast." But the engine too was a beast, a mechanical beast, and so was the mineshaft. A special kind of animism operates to infuse life into machinery in *Les Rougon-Macquart*.

This neutralizes, to some degree, the kind of mechanism that imposes itself on human beings. The man who believed that the same laws determined brains and paving-stones elsewhere asserted his monistic belief that stones have souls. "Things speak to me," he might have claimed, with the heroine of *Le Rêve*. On the other hand, the intention of *La Joie de vivre* was "to study in a human being the disintegration that I have often studied in things." Thus he raised the inorganic to the organic level of existence, while levelling all the higher organisms—as in the double instance of the bestialized soldiers in the cattle-cars and the wounded engine in agony. Zola, who kept several cats and monkeys at Médan, happened to be especially fond of animals. It was an intrinsic part of his plan to assign them supporting roles in his novels, and they are documented in his *cahiers*. A number of these La Fontaine-like mascots, with justification, are listed in dictionaries of characters. The horse Zéphirin in *La Débâcle*, behaves heroically and compassionately; and the move from the battlefield to the concentration camp is protested by a heroic stampede of horses. The poor workhorses of *Germinal* are in no worse plight than the miners—to whose famine the pet rabbit, Pologne, is cruelly sacrificed.

It is not a long distance from *Le Roman expérimental* to *The Call of the Wild*. The lesson of mute suffering is underlined in Zola's bestiary, as it was in Flaubert's or Vigny's, but even more the stark ferocity that Balzac had discerned in Cooper's Indians. Those carpetbaggers of the Second Empire, the Rougons, are regularly compared to famished wolves. Prostitutes prowl the streets like "beasts in a cage." It may be significant that Zola's best play, *Les Héritiers Rabourdin*, was based upon *Volpone, or The Fox*;

and Zola admits that what he saw in Ben Jonson's satiric beast-fable was "the human beast unleashed with all its appetites." But where the English comic playwright was a traditionalist—like the author of the *Comédie humaine*—holding up beastly conduct to more humane standards, Zola bases his ethic upon the state of nature. "Ancient art deified Nature," he asserted in a sketch, *Aux champs*, "Modern art has humanized her." Where the ancients were pantheists, the moderns are Rousseauists, continuing to look toward the landscape for sympathy. "Nature," as Zola restates it in *Mes Haines*, "is associated with our griefs." He is careful not to commit a pathetic fallacy; nature may also be associated with our joys; but it is we who project the association. And, since we have relegated ourselves to the side of the apes, grief seems likely to prevail over joy.

The contrast between shadow and sunlight in *La Faute de l'abbé Mouret*, between the gloomy church and the teeming barnyard outside, reinforces that basic antithesis between religion and nature which Zola connected with "the eternal struggle of life against death." This conflict is pursued to the very ending, when the priest's imbecile sister, who "cares only for animals," interrupts a burial service to announce that her cow has just calved. Even more crudely, *La Terre* commences with the graphic description of a farm-girl, Françoise Mouche, stoutly assisting the local bull to mate with her cow. Later the accouchement of her sister, Lise, is closely paralleled by that of the cow. The latter's case has obstetrical complications, since one of the twin calves is born alive and one dead, and so the eternal struggle goes on. These touches, which many readers attributed to a congenital low-mindedness, are not bathetic nor even, for Zola, shocking. They are variations on his persistent theme, the cycle of fertility and sterility. When he depicted the initial onset of menstruation, in *La Joie de vivre* and again in *Germinal*, the Goncourts demurred because those misogynistic bachelors prided themselves on having been the first novelists to unveil, in *Chérie*, that intimate phase of feminine experience.

Clearly it signified more to Zola than it did to them, given his lifelong preoccupation with fecundity. It was the rite of passage to womanhood. The state of mind he bespeaks from the reader is that of Joyce's elemental heroine: "it didnt make me blush why should it either its only nature." However, the unblushing acceptance of sex is an attitude into which modern man has had to be reinitiated, as we have learned from the pedagogic instance of D. H. Lawrence. Zola's anticipation of *Lady Chatterley's Lover* is *La Faute de l'abbé Mouret*. Interestingly, the relationship of the lovers is there reversed; the hero, an ascetic young priest, succumbs to the innocent wildness of the dryad-like Albine, whom Zola characterizes in his notes as "la bête humaine amoureuse." The symbolic garden of Paradou frames their intercourse with pathetic fallacies, the tree of life presiding, the luxuriant foliage sympathizing, and the birds and butterflies providing voluptuous object-lessons. There is a large amount of botanizing in this overwritten book, but little psychologizing. With complete discontinuity, and no introspection at all, the Abbé becomes subject to physical impulse as soon as he fails to wear his *soutane*, and inhumanly virtuous again when he is refrocked. When Albine's uncle, the philosophical caretaker, hears of her flowery death, his emotions are those of La Mettrie's *homme machine:* "he had the rigid despair of an automaton whose mechanism was broken."

In contradistinction to creative forces, whether carnal or vegetative, the power of destruction works through mechanics, most expressly through the engines of war in *La Débâcle*. Under the surface of the earth, the mining operations of *Germinal* are ill-omened and suspect, enveloped in an almost primitive awe before the violation of nature's underground secrets, and grimly contrasted at the beginning and end with the sprouting beet-fields overhead. The title, signifying germination, was the name of the first month of spring in the revolutionary calendar; and its more orthodox counterpart, April, is noted for both cruelty and potentiality. The seasonal rhythm it sets is the prophecy of an ideological ripening for seeds and roots now crammed beneath the soil. The gesture of a countryman picking up a clod and hurling it at his wayward daughter, in *La Faute de l'abbé Mouret*, might well serve as a signature for the earthy Zola. *Fécondité* would stress the agricultural parallel between land-reclamation and repopulation. Yet Zola is at heart a city-dweller, especially when we compare him with so verdant a countryman as Jean Giono. The good earth, in spite of those fecundating virtues hymned by Zola-Sandoz, is not necessarily a healthy influence; it is whatever man makes of it. "Man makes the earth," runs a proverb from his ancestral Beauce, which Zola cites in *La Terre*. Robert Frost has given Americans a rough equivalent: "The land was ours before we were the land's."

It was *La Terre*, among all of Zola's novels, which met with the bitterest critical reception. Today it is regarded, by Angus Wilson, as the culmination of his genius. It is still the harshest and most uncompromising of all the agrarian novels for which it plowed the way, and it is truly an excessive book. Balzac's realism, in his late *Paysans*, had deflated the pastoral idealism of George Sand's *romans champêtres*; but the antagonism Balzac set forth was a class struggle between peasants and landlords, whereas the internecine struggles in *La Terre* are waged within the ranks of the peasantry, indeed within the bosom of one family. The countryside is by no means bereft of beauty, when viewed in its rhythmic progressions of sowing and reaping. When Jean Macquart first approaches the village, and when he finally leaves it, the sowers at some distance have the aspect of figures painted by the Barbizon School. But the sweat and blood and tears of the peasants' way of life, as he comes to know it, do not correspond with what he reads to his illiterate companions out of a well-meaning book about Jacques Bonhomme. The relations between these hard-working, land-grasping creatures are regulated less by *bonhomie* than by cupidity and low cunning; they are *bêtes humaines*. A rustic wedding lacks even the coarse jollity of the one that Flaubert presented in *Madame Bovary*; it merely offers a further occasion for the pinching and straining of family ties.

For Zola, the earth's productivity is impaired by the sense of property, the invidious distinction between *le tien* and *le mien*. Père Fouan's passion for land, "for as much land as possible," is like being in love with "a murderous woman for whom a man commits murder. Not wife nor children nor anybody—nothing human—but the land!" This single blinding trait, passed on to his children, sets brother against brother and sister against sister; and when he divests himself of the farm, they turn against him with a mounting violence which ends by out-Learing *King Lear*. The bourgeois tragedy of *Le Père Goriot* is decorous by comparison. The cow that miscarries, a donkey that gets drunk, a youth who cuts off his thumb to avoid the army—these are light touches, compared with the brutalities that enmesh the savage tribe of Fouan. The half-witted dwarfish cripple Hilarion revenges himself by rap-

ing his eighty-nine-year-old grandmother, the penny-pinching dowager La Grande. She has shut him out to live in squalor and incest
with his wan and emaciated sister Palmyre, who dies one day
among the gleaners in the screaming throes of a sudden fit. The
animal-like Mère Fouan is killed in the course of a family scuffle.
So is her niece, Françoise Mouche, but not before she has been
raped by her brother-in-law, with the complicity of her sister, his
wife.

As it happens, Père Fouan has been a witness to the rape; and
so the brutal couple must do away with him too, burning his body
in a final holocaust. Zola had not planned upon so sensational a
conclusion; he had planned to let the old man slip gradually into
the soil that he had so fanatically worshipped. It was a report in a
newspaper which had suggested that ultimate parricide. Thus he
could document his sensationalism with the sort of possible im-
probability that makes headlines precisely because it is lacking in
classical verisimilitude. The tragedy has comic relief, which proved
even more offensive to many sensibilities, in the person of the
shiftless son with "the face of a ravaged Christ, a drunken Christ,"
who is locally and blasphemously known as Jésu-Christ. He seems
to be somewhat more in the tradition of Panurge, since his single
definitive accomplishment is to make a fine art of flatulence. By
his Rabelaisian demonstrations, he flouts the tight-fisted values of
the community, thereby achieving some measure of independence
and even generosity of outlook. So much, as it were, for ownership! "Tout ça ne vaut pas un pet!" This drunkard, who is a cynical war veteran and a political freethinker, may be Zola's deeply
unsettling answer to the question writers often ask themselves:
"What would happen to Jesus Christ if he came back to earth
today?"

In any case, the notorious wind-breaking contest won by this
Jésu-Christ is the stuff of *fabliau* rather than parable. And Zola's
flair for the malodorous involves him in further scatology, such as
the dumping of a chamber-pot on the head of an invading bailiff,
or the distasteful method of fertilization used by a personage nicknamed Mère Caca. Yet even these feculent details may be linked
with an underlying cult of fertility. Jean Macquart, who has Zola's
own olfactory perceptions, loves the smell of manure because it is
"the very odor of the earth's coition." His troth with Françoise,

plighted amid those effluvia, reminds us of Hardy's *Jude*, meeting his "mere female animal" in a pigpen. Both of these situations are deliberate in their reduction to bestiality. But there is a tremor of moral revulsion in Hardy, where Zola remains unflinching and un-disgusted. The land itself remains his chosen heroine. Père Fouan's destiny has a certain amount of poetic justice in it, since "he had consumed his father in his time." Here Zola employs the verb-of-all-purpose, *manger*, which serves throughout his writing to reiter-ate this dog-eat-dog motivation. His imperial speculators are "ces mangeurs de curée." Men are devoured by Nana, workers by work-ers in *Germinal*, financiers by financiers in *L'Argent*, and small tradesmen by mercantile bigness in *Au Bonheur des Dames*. In *Rome* the Jesuits are the devourers—a reversal of Voltaire's canni-balistic rallying cry: "*Mangeons du jésuite!*"

In one of the *Contes à Ninon*, *Aventures du grand Sidoine et du petit Médéric*, the two adventurers find themselves in a strange country. "Here some eat and others do not eat," they are informed. "People belong to the one class or the other." So it is in France as Zola depicts it. *L'Assommoir* has more to do with drinking than with eating, and its heavy holiday meals merely serve to set off the gnawing hunger of the later chapters. "Hunger is the pivot," Zola noted in his manuscript. It is, without doubt, the most universal of drives, and no writer has brought it closer to home. He himself was more at home in the city than in the country; and *Le Ventre de Paris* is an earlier and more amenable work, dealing as it does with consumers instead of producers. Taking us to market in the cart of a suburban gardener, Zola spends his most wholesome and most appetizing pages on the smells and sights of the Nouvelles Halles Centrales. This gigantic clearing-house of foodstuffs is to Paris "a great central organ beating furiously, pouring the blood of life into all its veins." But all is not unmitigated good cheer; the metaphor of a heart is less appropriate than the image that lends the book its title and theme; and Zola comments upon it in much the same spirit as Shakespeare in his allegorical anecdote of the Belly and the Members.

The spokesman is the anti-romantic painter, Claude Lantier, at a younger and happier stage of his artistic career than the dena-tured perfectionism of *L'Oeuvre*. The heaps of provender that confront him upon all sides are still-lifes worthy of his naturalistic impressionism. From this strategic center, likewise, he watches what he describes—after a popular series of prints—as the battle between the Fat and the Thin:

> He cited certain episodes: the Fat, big enough to burst, preparing their banquets for the evening, while the Thin, wrinkled by fasting, look in from the street with the faces of envious sticks; and again, the Fat, with stuffed cheeks, chasing away from their table one of the Thin who had the audacity to make his humble entrance, and who resembles a ten-pin surrounded by people like bowls. He saw the entire human drama in it; he ended by classifying men into Fat and Thin, two hostile groups, one of which gobbles up the other, rounds out its belly, and relaxes.

The quarrel has been going on ever since the days when Cain was fat and Abel was thin; and though Sancho Panza was free to choose the Haves when his master sided with the Have-Nots, Claude and his friend Florent congenitally belong to the losing side of the lean and the hungry. Class antagonism is inherent in the naturalistic universe; Zola scaled it down to a drunken blood-feud between two fishermen's families in his humorous tale, La Fête à Coqueville; but it looms constantly larger in the relationships of his Rougons and his Macquarts. Florent, the political idealist of Le Ventre de Paris, has just returned from a prison colony in Cayenne. "J'ai faim" is his self-characterizing statement at the end of the introductory chapter. When his niece, the child of his prosperous butcher brother, asks for a fairy tale, he spins the autobiographical fantasy of "un monsieur qui a été mangé par les bêtes." Temporarily he finds employment as an inspector of sea-food, which entails a continual argument between his martyr-like austerity and the billingsgate of the buxom fishwives. He is spied upon, informed against, and sent back to his pre-Dreyfusard exile. The parable of exiled idealism and centralized authority reinforces the basic contrast between deprivation and abundance.

Zola subtitled Les Rougon-Macquart: l'histoire naturelle et sociale d'une famille sous le Second Empire. He prefaced his first volume with a promise to resolve "la double question des tempéraments et des milieux" by following the threads that connect man to man. But the parallel is not evenly sustained. In self-conscious differentiation from Balzac, he proposed to be primarily a natural historian and secondarily a social one, more directly concerned with genealogical than with regional lines of connection. But as the series developed, the emphasis shifted—we shall have fuller occasion to notice—from the temperamental to the environmental. *Thérèse Raquin*, his one substantial novel before *Les Rougon-Macquart*, had been attacked as a horrible example of "la littérature putride." Sainte-Beuve had lived long enough to read it, and to warn its author that his reliance on words like *brutal* could prove a boomerang. In his preface to the second edition, Zola defended the book on pseudo-scientific grounds, presenting it as a physiological case-history. "In a word, I had a single aim: given a potent man and an unsatisfied woman, to look for the beast in them, to see nothing but the beast, to hurl them into a violent drama and scrupulously note the sensations and actions of these creatures." Then, shifting his similitude from the clinical to the pathological, he adds: "I simply made, of two living bodies, the analytic study that surgeons make of corpses."

But is it a scalpel, the figurative instrument he had conceded to the Goncourts, or is it his usual sweeping brush that Zola wields in this shopkeeper's melodrama? Its morality would seem to be impeccable. The weight falls not so much upon the sexual triangle or the murder of the husband as upon the remorse of the guilty lovers in joyless union, haunted by the corpse of the man they have drowned. Well, murder will out; crime doesn't pay; and case histories may probe no more deeply than proverbs. When Ibsen abolished the supernatural from his theater, it came back in naturalistic dress; heredity is another name for Nemesis in *Ghosts*, as it is in *Les Rougon-Macquart*. In *Thérèse Raquin*, no less fatalistically, Zola was studying "temperaments, not characters," and presumably their chemical interaction. "A fatal force brings me back to your side," says Thérèse to her lover. The first edition had borne on its title-page a quotation removed at the instance of Sainte-Beuve, the famous assertion of Taine's determinism: "Vice and virtue are products like sugar and vitriol." The deletion was warranted, since the would-be industrial chemist had remained a moralist at heart; what he presented as end-products were really his starting-points; and the upshot of his research was to cast praise or blame on conditions and forces.

"My role," Zola explains in a letter to Gustave Geoffroy, "is to put man back into his place in the creation, like a product of the earth, still subject to all the influences of the environment; and with man himself, I have put the brain back in place among the organs; for I do not believe that thought is anything other than a function of matter." Conversely, differentiating his position from the criticism of Jules Lemaître, who considered Zola's characters mindless, he accused his critic of overemphasizing the brain at the expense of other organs, and of isolating man from nature, the earth from which he comes and to which he returns. To push materialism as far as this is virtually to profess a kind of pantheism. Art makes nature better by no mean, in Shakespearean terms, "But nature makes that mean." This broadened concept of nature comprehends environment as well as heredity. Accordingly, as Zola more solidly grounded his efforts, he became less interested in genetic traits and more interested in conditioning factors. There was less *histoire naturelle* and more *histoire sociale*. Thus it has been pointed out that the alcoholism is brought into *L'Assommoir* not through the degeneration of the Macquarts but by Gervaise's husband, no blood relation, the roofer Coupeau, who takes to drink after being crippled by a fall from a roof.

The spectacular later career of their daughter, in *Nana*, is fully explained by her juvenile delinquency in the earlier novel; and that, in turn, is a sociologically predictable response to the sordid circumstances of the *ménage à trois* within which she was brought up. Retrospectively, Zola called her a product, and wrote about her as he would write in *Travail* of the pathetic Josine, "Poor girl! she was a victim of her milieu." Yet he had not hesitated, even in dealing with Nana's childhood, to characterize her by the adjective "vicious"; when she becomes the most luridly glamorous of kept women, the Lesbian prostitute Satin is characterized as "her vice," and the chorus girls are personified "vices." Nor is it without significance that the lethal spirits brewed and consumed in *L'Assommoir* are known to the drinkers as "vitriol," for they are engaged in the distillation of vice. The chemistry may be vague, but the ethic is stern. Zola's portraiture seems strikingly harsh when it is compared with the virtuous courtesans of Victor Hugo or Dumas *fils*, or even with the corrupt enchantresses of Baudelaire and Flaubert. Evil is a growth, but not a flower, for Zola. Nature may be amoral, but society—as he observes it—is more productive of vice than of virtue, more addicted to vitriol than to sugar. Emile Verhaeren could note in his review of *L'Argent*: "Each volume affirms a vice." Again Zola had been preceded by Eugène Sue, with a sequence of seven respective novels on the Deadly Sins.

Life is not clean or neat. "La vie n'est pas propre," sighs Madame Hamelin, who somehow makes the best of the bad situations in *L'Argent*. But she also declares, "I want to go on living, to live forever." To accept the conditions of existence, on this basis, is to encounter what Victor Hugo, in one of the chapter-headings of *Les Misérables*, succinctly particularized as mire and yet soul: "La Boue, mais de l'âme." Zola's world is not devoid of goodness. He discerns a few lay saints amid the welter of human beasts—such as the heroine of his tale *La Soeur des pauvres*, or the legend-minded Angélique of *Le Rêve*. He was particularly attracted to feminine sainthood; in his youth he had wanted to write a poem about Joan of Arc, and in his last period he contemplated a biography of Bernadette of Lourdes. Perhaps the saintliest of his heroines is Pauline Quenu, "born for others," whose self-sacrifice keeps *La Joie de vivre* from becoming a chronicle of tragic desperation. It is not the joy of living but the fear of death that overshadows her cousin Lazare Chanteau, who composes a symphony on the theme of sorrow. A restless dabbler, he turns from music to chemistry; but all of his projects continue to go astray. As he walks along the Norman seashore, a latter-day Werther or René, his horizons are darkened by the pessimism of Schopenhauer and his current philosophy.

Was Zola himself a pessimist? Not surprisingly, he was so reputed. Though he sounds optimistic when he is writing as a journalistic propagandist, the note of sadness, more often than not, seems inherent in the universe of *Les Rougon-Macquart*. Yet Dr. Pascal's "terrible lesson in life," like the vision that comforts Saint-Antoine, stresses the value of any molecular place in the cosmic scheme. When Zola composed an opera libretto about the scriptural namesake of Lazare, it culminated with Lazarus deciding to return to the tomb. But Lazare Chanteau, despite his record of failures, is starting out again in America when we last hear about him through *Le Docteur Pascal*. The last words of *La Joie de vivre* are pronounced by his all but inanimate father, a basket case, rendered legless and armless by a wasting disease: "Faut-il être bête

pour se tuer." Suicide is stupid; and since the adjective *bête* is
homonymous with the noun, we are reminded that man, even
paraplegic man, maimed and helpless though he may be, can attempt to rise above the animal state. Zola had originally wanted
to call his book—more straightforwardly—*Le Mal de vivre*, or else
La Vallée des larmes, or even—after Lazare's symphony—*La Douleur*. There is massive irony behind his considered title, *La Joie de
vivre*. But there is also the positive affirmation, much like the resolution of the seasoned and battered Old Woman, dismissing suicide
in *Candide*, that life is worth living on any terms.

4. Faces in the Crowd

"Life is simpler," Zola had commented, on what he regarded
as the Machiavellian supersubtlety of Stendhal. His own practice,
as we have been finding, is not quite so oversimplified as his
theory. But life is seldom as simple as literature makes it. The
nature of things is bound to be subtler and more elusive than
any given rendering into language. It takes a Proust to begin to
express a genuine sense of that complexity and profundity.
Whereas the very compression of Zola's scheme, as he confessed,
made for "a constant simplification of the characters." His commitment to brute instincts and single-minded drives made him
a relatively primitive psychologist, ready to substitute tribal masks
for physiognomies. He was congratulated by Cesare Lombroso
for having adhered to the pseudo-scientific concept of the criminal
type. However, as Alfred de Vigny had foreseen, when justifying
the historical novel by way of his *Réflexions sur la vérité dans
l'art*, "in letters today a study of the general destiny of societies
is no less necessary than an analysis of the human heart." Ever
since Stendhal, the focus had been shifting from the psychological
to the sociological sphere. With Zola, the introspective tradition
is altogether abandoned, and the novelist becomes a behaviorist
who concentrates on material forces and conditioned reflexes.
Preoccupied less with his characters than with their characteristics,
he is finally interested less in temperament than in milieu.

Already, in his original working notes for *Les Rougon-Macquart*,
he had written: "The milieux, properly stated, milieux of place

and of society, determine the class of the personages (worker, artist, bourgeois—me and my uncles, Paul and his father)." The last was not a very cogent example of a functioning determinism, since it could only have been by recoil that Cézanne's paternity had determined his vocation. "Don't forget heredity," Zola had to remind himself in *La Curée*. As he worked his way through the series, he gave a larger and larger role to environment as a social determinant. His framework, the family tree of the Rougons and Macquarts, survived as a sort of literary parlor game, like that map of the Land of Tenderness devised as a guide to the once-famous romance of Mademoiselle de Scudéry. Interviewed by the press upon his visit to Lourdes, Zola affirmed that he was "irresistibly drawn toward the great collectivities." Since he conceived his subject collectively, encyclopedically, excessively, we can learn more about his method through cross-reference than through narrative recapitulation. We can learn something from such modest samples as *Comment on se marie* and *Comment on meurt*, a pair of sketches which scan the descending classes of society, illustrating their respective reactions to marriage and to death. Challenged by a questionnaire to name his favorite heroes in fiction, Zola replied: "Those who are not heroes."

One of his recurrent words, which reverberates with a peculiar self-expressiveness, is *pulluler*—to grow, to teem, to swarm. "To make his characters swarm and to make the central thing they swarm about as large as life"—Henry James might well have said "larger than life," but otherwise this appraisal seems just and apt. In magnifying his central objects to the point of gigantism, Zola necessarily dwarfed his characters. He visualized his institutions, like the Bourse, as anthills in revolution. Warfare, with its nameless battalions, is the greatest of collectivities. Paris at work is the most intriguing of spectacles. The little people of *L'Assommoir* are intimidated by the Louvre and dwarfed by the column of the Place Vendôme. "The era of crowds," with its concomitant symptoms of what might be a declining civilization, would soon be signalized by Gustave Le Bon in his influential if somewhat apocalyptic handbook *La Psychologie des foules*. The very plebiscite that established the Second Empire had been an alarming portent of what might be brought about in the future through new techniques of mass-manipulation; and, with the founding of the First International in 1864, the socialistic proponents of the masses had their re-echoing forum through Europe. "Zola was the prophet of a new age of mass-psychology, mass-analysis, and mass-entertainment, an age in which the part is never greater than the whole." So his recent English interpreter, F. W. J. Hemmings, summarizes his contribution, for better or for worse.

It was his intention, spelled out in *Le Roman expérimental*, to show the reciprocal interaction between society and the individual. His sense of collectivity, which at times brought him close to Walt Whitman, made him a harbinger for the twentieth-century exponents of *l'unanimisme*. Unlike his novelistic forerunners—even Balzac had individualized his humblest creatures—Zola never lost sight of "that anonymous personage, the crowd." To Paul Alexis he admitted, of *La Bête humaine*, that the story mattered little; the important matter was the railroad, and the network of swarming humanity caught up among the cogs of its machinery. The book is given its nervous rhythm of scheduled urgency by the goings and comings of the train. "Le train roulait, roulait toujours..." The white train in *Lourdes* keeps on rolling with the same phrase. A similar sense of movement—not wheels on rails, but the feet of armies marching to and from a battlefield —is conveyed in *La Débâcle* by a verbal refrain which echoes the Marseillaise: "Marchons, marchons..." The human race is envisioned as rolling stock, which transports everything else, in *Le Docteur Pascal*. The engineer of *La Bête humaine*, Jacques Lantier, is emotionally geared to the pulsations of his beloved engine. His watchword is "Rouler seul, rouler seul encore..." Most of Zola's protagonists, as distinguished from his faceless aggregation, turn out to be rolling stones.

Jacques, as it happens, was an afterthought in Zola's genealogy. In *L'Assommoir*, Gervaise Coupeau has two sons by Auguste Lantier. The elder, Claude, is the bohemian commentator of *Le Ventre de Paris* and the suicidal artist of *L'Oeuvre*. The younger, Etienne, is a rolling stone who casts his lot with the miners in *Germinal*. Zola had also planned to use Etienne in *La Bête humaine*, but thought better of it, and created the unforeseen middle brother to carry out a murderous impulse which Etienne had momentarily felt in *Germinal*. Mastering the residual cave-man within him, the latter survives to fight in the Commune, as we are told at the end of the cycle. Embodying the only thread of connection between *Germinal* and *Les Rougon-Macquart* at large, he is simply a young man of open-eyed good will, an observer who becomes a participant. To the extent that the novel has a center of consciousness, it is through his mind that its sense-impressions and processes are filtered. Commonly considered the most powerful of strike-novels, *Germinal* might also be viewed as a *Bildungsroman*, insofar as it presents the education of a worker. As usual, the men at work are enmeshed in the workings of mechanisms. Hence the practical details are not just sketched in the background; they implement the reciprocity between man and the machine.

In analogous fashion, the education of a farmer is presented in *La Terre*, as is that of a soldier in *La Débâcle*. In both cases, the migratory hero is Jean Macquart. So far as characterization goes, he might just as well be Etienne Lantier; and this resemblance is not quite satisfactorily explained by the fact that they are uncle and nephew. Each of them is transiently attached to the little community he serves, be it farm or mine, through a love affair fraught with pathos and jealousy. But, as a pupil in the school of experience, it is Jean who receives the hardest knocks; for he is both an outsider among the hostile peasantry and an infantryman in the ill-fated war. It is the vista that changes, not the visage. When Balzac employs the *retour des personnages*, his readers are fascinated by the alteration of familiar characters reappearing in different contexts. Character is functional in Zola; change is effected not by growth but by uprooting, by getting another job or moving on to another scene. Octave Mouret is the protagonist of two novels whose cast is more bourgeois, *Pot-bouille* and *Au Bonheur des Dames*. The one involves his sentimental education, the other his business success. The apartment house is the veritable protagonist of the one, the department store of the other. Octave grows, at least, in worldly wisdom; what he gains in the alcove, a knowledge of women, he exploits in the emporium.

As an uprooted provincial from the south, gaining a fortune at Paris, he follows in the footsteps of his uncle, Aristide Rougon,

who has changed his name to Saccard. Saccard's use of a pseudonym typifies the part he plays as a trimmer, who must trim his
sails to the winds of empire. Starting as a republican journalist
in *La Fortune des Rougon*, he betrays his principles in order to
profit from the new regime. In *La Curée*, he leads the wolf-pack
that thrives on the operations of replanning and rebuilding the
imperial metropolis. In *L'Argent*, having lost his previous fortune, he wins and loses another through speculation within its
central arena, the stock-exchange. And ironically, as we are informed by Dr. Pascal's postscript, he rises again to weather the
downfall of Louis Napoleon by returning to liberal journalism.
Throughout these vicissitudes, it is not Saccard but conditions
which are variable. He operates consistently, with a single-minded
venality, buying a wife and selling a son, "selling everybody who
fell into his hands." In his predictable conduct, he resembles
those theatrical types who reappear in one comedy after another,
like Molière's Sganarelle, who is now a shrewd peasant, again
a scheming bourgeois, still again a clever servant, and always a
sharper. Business is invariably business.

Balzac, since he puts more stress on the will, allows more scope
for villainy. The varieties of sharp practice—the buying and selling,
the getting and spending, the hoarding and lending—are more
evident in the *Comédie humaine*. Zola, who did not even maintain a bank account, did not have Balzac's consuming interest
in money as such, or his ambivalent feelings toward the plutocracy. Retail trade, as engaged in by Octave Mouret, is an
intensification of Darwin's struggle for life. Zola's theory of value,
like that of the Marxists, was based directly on labor. He managed
to work up the Bourse with such conscientiousness that *L'Argent*
has been cited as a document by such exacting economists as
Werner Sombart and Vilfredo Pareto; but even there he revealed a more personal predilection by dragging in the newspaper editor, Paul Jordan, who scorns money and later succeeds
as a reforming novelist. Zola himself, having been a parliamentary
reporter, was more at ease with politics than with finance. He
had deliberately chosen a family chronicle as the best means of
presenting a history of the Second Empire, so that the ascent
of the Rougons would run parallel to the ascendancy of the
imperial party. Every character represents a state of mind at

the time, he would remark to his English translator, Henry Vizetelly—a remark which admits that his creations are animated less by psychology than by ideology.

La Fortune des Rougon, the introductory volume, hailed in his own blurb as "une satire bourgeoise," registers the impact of the Bonapartist *coup d'état* at Plassans, together with the consolidation of a local dynasty. Pierre Rougon, the one legitimate son—and therefore heir—of the mad matriarch, Tante Dide, acquires the custody of his mother's property, settles into the bourgeoisie through marriage, and for his intriguing on behalf of Louis Bonaparte is rewarded with the lucrative post of tax-collector. The mother's incipient madness is confirmed when she witnesses the death of her favorite grandchild, Silvère Mouret, a youthful republican shot down by the police in the course of the uprising. The continuing intrigues of the town form the background of *La Conquête de Plassans*, while the foreground is the household of Pierre's weak-minded son-in-law, François Mouret, which gradually disintegrates and finally goes up in flames, consequent to the sinister visitation of a Tartuffe-like agent, the counter-intriguing Abbé Faujas. Such machinations need a Stendhalian finesse to make them convincing. Further novels shift the center of gravity to the capital and, with *Son Excellence Eugène Rougon*, to the legislature itself, the nerve center of political ambitions. Eugène, who is "the eagle of the family," who was once a provincial advocate, makes himself "one of the pillars of the Second Empire"—one of its tarnished pilasters, as it turns out.

"I made it," he boasts, "and it has made me." The qualities that make and unmake him stem from his native Provence: a facile eloquence, a warm gregariousness, and a coldly cynical view of human nature. A ruler should be known and judged by the men around him, Zola is arguing; and Eugène Rougon is his vulgarization of Napoleon III, in all the self-serving theatricality and all the regimented inefficiency of his flashy officialdom. To complete the parody, His Excellency is made and unmade by the men around him, the gang of henchmen and cronies who abet and profit from his power. "You have too many friends, M. Rougon," the Emperor tells him shortly before his dismissal as Prime Minister. The ups and downs of his public career set the pattern—self-advancement at the expense of principle—which is being privately pursued by his brother Saccard and by countless other fortune-hunters, the *hommes nouveaux* of the mid-century. To the extent that these energetic Rougons are self-made men, they would seem to transcend the pathological heritage with which Zola originally endowed them. Given his premises, we might expect them to show a worse record than the Jukeses. Perhaps a more appropriate comparison would be with Faulkner's memoirs of the Snopeses.

Though the breed as a whole is mean, self-seeking, and un-attractive, it has some exceptional offshoots who are wholly admirable. Witness the aptly named Angélique in *Le Rêve*, whose mother was the procuress Sidonie Rougon. Again, the lovely Clotilde, in *Le Docteur Pascal*, is the noble daughter of the ignoble Saccard—whose effete son Maxime fits in more readily with Zola's genetic presuppositions. Since each of those daughters has been brought up by decent foster-parents, we may observe some degree of concession to environmentalism. Zola is not reluctant to speak of innate, as opposed to inherited, character-istics. Dr. Pascal Rougon, the kindly and upright brother of Eugène and Aristide, spends his whole career at Plassans, where his own mother wonders from time to time, "Where did you come from?," and tells him, "You are not one of us." The clannish-ness personified by Félicité Rougon seems to be grounded more solidly on mutual self-interest than on instinctive physiological ties. In the perennial struggle of fat against thin, of rapacious greed against suffering fortitude, or of beasts of prey against beasts that are preyed upon, there could be no doubt as to which side the clan espoused. Nor should we need to remind ourselves that Zola, cheerfully incurring the charge of *"lèse-bourgeoisie,"* took the other side.

This ranges him with the bastard line, the Macquarts. There he finds his most characteristic material, and thither he conducts his readers' sympathies. He is less harsh with the emaciated slum-dwellers of *L'Assommoir* than with the obese tenants of *Pot-bouille*. Out of the twenty volumes, a critical consensus might select half a dozen titles for the first rank. *L'Assommoir* and *Nana*, *Germinal* and *La Bête humaine*, *La Terre* and *La Débâcle* —curiously enough, these six are interrelated by pairs. All of them conclusively belong to the simple annals of the Macquarts. Therein Zola was really breaking new ground, whereas his Rougons could have been predicted from Balzac and were being matched by Daudet and others. Charles Péguy observed that Zola's most widely read books included *Nana* and *La Débâcle*, whereas *La Fortune des Rougon* and *Son Excellence Eugène Rougon* were among those with the smallest circulation. Obviously, this preference had something to do with the sensational themes of the sought-after volumes; but some credit should be accorded to the author's gradual discovery of his vein and to his increasing mastery over his medium. That mastery, in turn, had the benefit of an increasing freedom from his scientific *mystique*. As he moved along, he was less and less bound to his biological dogmas; there are fewer digressions as to who begot whom; in following the misfortunes of those rolling stones, the Macquarts, he was freer to range farther afield.

Contrasted with the *Comédie humaine*, where the totality seems larger than the sum of its components, parts of *Les Rougon-Macquart* seem larger than the whole. When he depicted Plassans, he was adapting the Balzacian approach of *Scènes de la vie de province*; he could bring his predecessor up-to-date but hardly outdo him, when he depicted Parisian tradespeople. But there were gaps in Balzac's sociology, the most conspicuous of them almost large enough to discredit his pretensions as a sociologist— namely, the proletariat. The very word *prolétaire*, in its modern application, was not admitted into the *Dictionnaire de l'Académie* until 1862. When Balzac probed into the lower orders, his concern was crime, not poverty. Yet no writer, and much less one who has innovated so much, can be blamed for missing some innovation. Traditionally, after all, the novel has to do with the middle class. "What is a pauper?" inquired the rich man, Trimalchio, in one of the first experimental novels, the *Satyricon* of Petronius. Through the greater part of literature, the poor man, when he has not been ignored, has been shrugged off with a callous joke. When he lived in the country, of course, he could be sentimentalized for the envy of courtiers and burghers. Into that pastoral tradition George Sand infused radical sentiment, prefacing *La Mare au diable* by stating a classical predisposition for "ideal verity" rather than "positive reality." Her fellow socialist, Eugène Sue, adumbrated Zola more closely, through a string of historical novels tracing a long-suffering family of workers down the ages.

An age of expanding humanitarianism had found romantic means of expression for its philanthropy in the rhetoric of Michelet and the rhapsody of Hugo. But the *réalistes* of the 'fifties, Zola complained, were still too narrowly circumscribed by the bourgeoisie. In 1865 the brothers Goncourt utilized the preface of *Germinie Lacerteux* to set forth their naturalistic manifesto. At a moment when fiction was enlarging its purview and society was extending its suffrage, why, they wondered, should not the people have their "right to the novel"? *Germinie Lacerteux*, their answer to this question, was scarcely popular in any sense. It was not for the people; the preface berates the public. It was not by the people, but by a pair of mandarins writing *de haut en bas*. It was not of the people, since the heroine is a servant, who consequently plays a traditional part in introducing her betters to life backstairs. To be sure, the spotlight now centered upon her, bringing out many an uncouth detail. But the writers' point of view did not differ essentially from when it focussed on Japanese exoticism or eighteenth-century esthetics. Erich Auerbach, after keenly analyzing the detachment and self-consciousness of their prose, demonstrates Zola's originality by comparing their preface with two passages from *Germinal*. The confrontation is indeed a showdown, and the choice is well taken; for Zola intended *Germinal*, along with *L'Assommoir*, to portray the two faces of the working-man, mean and heroic.

From the very beginning, Zola had projected a novel dealing entirely with proletarians. *L'Assommoir* was published in 1877, eight years before *Germinal* and twelve years after *Germinie Lacerteux*. In his preface Zola flatly acknowledges no precedent: *L'Assommoir is* "the first novel about the people that does not lie, that has the smell of the people." Answering the remonstrances of its critics, he describes its plot as "morality in action." He wanted "to paint the fatal decline of a working-class family in the poisoned milieu of our slums." The upshot, he avers, is the most chaste of his books. It is true that the good-natured heroine pays and pays for her reunion with her premarital lover—

an old obsession with Zola, as we have seen, and one which she accepts as "a law of nature." The step-by-step account of her husband's deterioration into delirium tremens is narrated with the sententious fervor of a temperance tract. The most disturbing feature of L'Assommoir, Zola shrewdly suggested, was its form. "My crime is to have had the curiosity to collect and pour into an elaborated mould the language of the people." Here his professional ear made the écriture artiste of the Goncourts look amateurish. Not content with what he himself could pick up on the streets, he had listed the slang of métiers; he had pored over dictionaries of argot; and to a correspondent he acknowledged that the book had become, among other things, "a philological study."

The texture of Zola's writing was inherently coarse-grained; it suffered comparatively when it was printed along with nouvelles by more succinct and elegant disciples, notably Maupassant and Huysmans; but he had the perception to make good the virtue of its defect, its unliterary vigor. The gap between academic canons and the norms of la langue parlée has been wider in French than in many other languages, certainly much wider than in our own. Hence André Gide, though he rated Germinal among the ten best French novels, asserted with neo-classic asperity that it might just as well have been written in Volopük. More responsive, Mallarmé, in a letter to Zola on L'Assommoir, fully appreciated the novelty of the experiment. This was nothing less than to transpose a colloquial idiom into a literary style, a feat so much more easily accomplished by American writers from Mark Twain through Ernest Hemingway. The resulting narration does not assume any higher tone than the conversation, but mingles, by way of le style indirect libre, with the more relaxed syntax and the more pungent diction of vulgar speech. The innovation has subsequently developed into the stock-in-trade of such vernacularists as Charles-Louis Philippe, Louis-Ferdinand Céline, and Raymond Queneau. But it is still a salutary shock to open the book and listen at once to the vivid phraseology of the concierge's lodge and the neighborhood bistro.

Turgenev, when he arranged for a Russian translation, had to admit that unmentionable words were mentioned in L'Assommoir no less than 720 times. The translator's difficulties begin with the title: meaning literally a bludgeon and figuratively a drinking dive, where—figuratively and sometimes literally—the customers take a beating. Coupeau supplies a gloss with prophetic irony when, upon the occasion of his first drink with Gervaise, he expresses his lifelong desire to live in a decent quarter, because he believes that bad company is like "un coup de l'assommoir." The circumstance that his characters often stammer, that their speeches are repeatedly introduced by verbs like *balbutier* and *bégayer*, becomes peculiarly meaningful when we remember that Zola himself lisped slightly. Henri Barbusse, in fact, recollected that he spoke very much as they do. Through his habit of verbal immediacy he could identify himself with their outlook, even while, through his naturalistic perspective, he was tracing the pattern of their destinies. To cite one terse example: at the lowest point of Gervaise's degradation, wandering through the streets and nearly dying of cold, she sees a sign which promises a reward of fifty francs for returning a lost dog. The reaction occurs somewhere between her stream of consciousness and Zola's commentary: "Voilà une bête qui doit être aimé."

In a warm essay, *L'Amour des bêtes*, he had speculated: "Why does it give me a heartache to pass a stray dog on one of our noisy streets?" Here the bounty offered for the missing animal becomes an inverted measure of the sympathies withheld from the starving woman. Somebody must love that dog. Who loves that human beast, Gervaise Coupeau? She herself has been called upon, in the course of the novel, to exert an immense capacity for love. We have seen her as a mistress, freshly arriving at Paris with two infants, only to be deserted by her lover; as a wife, supporting her crippled husband by the laundry, until he drags her down toward his drunken level; and as a mother, falling through desperation into a dull promiscuity, which points the way toward the more glittering corruption of her daughter, Nana. Up to the chilling moment when her body is discovered under the tenement stairway, Gervaise is kept alive by a powerful and persistent female warmth, which makes her the most sympathetic and the most memorable of Zola's creations. He was consistent with his principle of subordinating person to thing, when he substituted *L'Assommoir* for his working title, *La Vie simple de Gervaise Macquart*. And yet she continues to loom above the squalor, like the maternal figure of Daumier's washwoman, climbing the weary steps up the bank of the misty Seine.

5. *Forward, Backward, Downward*

More perhaps than any other, Zola set the pace and delineated the sphere for the contemporary novelist, through his dynamic relationship to his age. George Moore, who admired him more as a personality than as an artist, testifies how much he impressed a younger generation with "the idea of a new art based on science." That problematic idea was primarily the index of Zola's determined contemporaneity, his willingness not merely to chronicle social and technological changes, but to face a public which was changing with them. If his excessive books were modernized myths, they were also fabulous feats of journalism. He not only dealt with news, he was able to make it. His documentation was the effort of a conscientious reporter, rather than an experimental scientist; and he had a reporter's nose for stenches in the nostrils of the community, which could be turned to journalistic account—for subjects which needed discussion, commanded attention, shocked, and sold. It is as a crusading journalist that his resemblance to Dickens comes out most clearly. A comparable gift for blending righteous indignation with a touch of *succès de scandale*—though, naturally, the scandal was milder in a country more easily scandalized—enabled Dickens to produce best-seller after best-seller, successively accusing the workhouse system, the Yorkshire schools, the law's delays, and many another institutional evil.

Most of Zola's French peers are conspicuous for their refusal to meet the common reader on his own ground. Stendhal addressed posterity, Flaubert damned the bourgeoisie, and Proust at times would be talking to himself. Balzac, to be certain, had Zola's motives, in writing for as much of a living as the traffic would bear; but Balzac's adherence to traditions kept him from plunging so whole-heartedly into the turbid movements of the time. In spite of Zola's vaunted genealogy, the sense of human connection is stronger from book to book in *La Comédie humaine* than in *Les Rougon-Macquart*. Zola is always restlessly moving on to some new thing or force or situation. *Les Rougon-Macquart* is more panoramic in its coverage of the Second Empire than *La Comédie humaine* in its treatment of the July Monarchy; but Zola wrote at a greater distance from the dating of his panorama. Balzac's vantage-point was a staunch commitment to the past, whereas Zola's was a rather more nebulous faith in the future. It is not altogether clear what he could have meant by his do-or-die slogan, "The Republic will be naturalistic, or it will not be." So many French republics have ceased to exist that the ultimatum has lost its force. Yet its overtones reverberate, beyond the vogue of his novels, to imply that a democratic society ought to be founded upon a positivistic philosophy.

Queen Victoria's poet laureate, who had once believed in the idea of progress, could look across the English Channel and shudder:

> Set the maiden fancies wallowing in the troughs of Zolaism,—
> Forward, forward, ay, and backward, downward too into the abysm!

Even in these pangs of revulsion, Tennyson reveals his sensitive ear; for *vautrer* is one of those earthbound expressions which stamp Zola's prose with his personal imprint, and therefore Tennyson's "wallowing" is the *mot juste*. Forward, forward and backward—this is the paradox of scientific advancement, in that it has tended to lessen humanistic stature. Man's increased understanding of nature has forced him to acknowledge his subordination to it, while the development of technology has mechanized not only ways of living but life itself. Hence the highly civilized researches of Claude Bernard could lend support to the atavism of *La Bête humaine*, and modern industry could produce the cave-men of *Germinal*. Downward, then, upward and downward —this is the timeless principle of tragedy, in that the highest aspirations seem to precede and invite the most cataclysmic downfalls. Zola was profoundly aware of that principle. Indeed his very point of departure became his most timely application of it. This is the inevitable collapse, the fall of the Emperor Napoleon III and the resultant *débâcle* of the Second Empire. It was the stroke of this "terrible and necessary denouement" which transformed the work into "the picture of a dead reign, a strange epoch of folly and shame."

Flaubert had dallied over a number of sketches for a novel to be entitled *Sous Napoléon III*. The War of 1870 was the nationalistic premise for those Alsatian collaborators who signed themselves Erckmann-Chatrian. Zola was planning *Les Rougon-Macquart*, and writing the first volume, while the Emperor was still on his shaky throne. But *La Fortune des Rougon* could not have been published until the opening year of the Third Republic; nor could many of the subsequent volumes have appeared under an authoritarian regime. Zola augmented his plan, as he fulfilled it, from eight or ten to twenty volumes; and the additions were less closely tied to the original nexus of social history. Since he had not expected Bonapartism to fall so soon, he was obliged to telescope some of his time-scheme, and thus to crowd the correlation between historic events and his characters' lives. When he started, he was dealing with more or less contemporaneous material. When he finished, his subject-matter was some twenty years behind him. The earlier novels, with their administrative intrigues and bureaucratic hierarchies, are more documentary in their approach and more directly satirical. The later ones, which range afield from the narrow road between Plassans and Paris, are less topical in their appeal and consequently more universal. By the time he arrived at his penultimate volume, *La Débâcle*, he was writing a historical novel. But the darkening cloud of national catastrophe hangs over *Les Rougon-Macquart* from first to last. Its collective theme is the fall of France.

Baudelaire and the poets, emulating Flaubert, alienated from society and cultivating art for its own sake, could celebrate a self-conscious decadence, "the phosphorescence of rottenness." Zola undertook the reformer's task of confronting and exposing corruption. Two of his most penetrating reviewers, Anatole France and Jules Lemaître, independently and in different contexts, characterized his work as "apocalyptic." The apocalypse toward which it tends is the defeat of the Franco-Prussian War and the vision of communist Paris in flames. All of his accusations and exposures point the way to that revelation. The Battle of Waterloo formed a grandiose overture to *La Chartreuse de Parme*; the Battle of Sédan forms a dissonant climax to *Les*

Rougon-Macquart. The aftermath of the first Napoleon had been anticlimactic for Stendhal. Zola could share that premise; and one of his stories, *Le Capitaine Burle*, portrays the degenerate son of a Napoleonic hero. But since the nostalgia of the magic name had been exploited to buttress the muddled dictatorship of Napoleon's nephew, Louis Bonaparte, Zola's tendency was to rush through those two decades toward deliverance with the special impetus of his driverless train and its carloads of drunken recruits. He looks back, as he writes, during the Third Republic; but his writing looks ahead to the disintegration of the Empire.

This double perspective frames his characters within an extra dimension of fatalistic irony. Their private calamities occur on the brink of the public disaster. Everyone is dancing on a volcano, everything is headed for the abyss. If *La Bête humaine* breaks off on a note of suspense, with the unguided wheels still racing down the tracks, the reader's mind can supply the fated crack-up. After we learn the destiny of anything, we can see it all as predestined; we become determinists after the fact; and our foreknowledge of what has been historically determined ends by reinforcing Zola's determinism. His subtitle dates his dramatis personae: *une famille sous le Second Empire.* The implied connection between family and state is less direct for the illegitimate branch; and the proletarian Macquarts, insulted and injured, remain the underdogs; yet, in being socially downtrodden, they are morally exculpated from the degradation of the epoch. It is the social-climbing Rougons who gain a stake in the country, through their Bonapartist plotting and counter-plotting, both locally and in the capital. The exiled Victor Hugo castigated France's erstwhile ruler as *Napoléon le Petit.* Eugène Rougon, appointed "vice-emperor" at the height of his power, is depicted mock-heroically as a little Napoleon the Little. He is the most reactionary among the politicians surrounding the Emperor; and Zola completes the sardonic portrait by making him a self-appointed censor of outspoken fiction.

Zola portrays Eugène's venal brother, Saccard, making and losing fortunes in stock and real estate, until he is driven into bankruptcy by a combination modelled on the house of Rothschild. This maneuver is a kind of revenge on Saccard's professed anti-Semitism. The financial crash, with its symbolic deflation of all over-inflated values, foreshadows the political doom. The careers of both brothers reach their apogee in "the great season of the Empire," when Napoleon III is potentially the "master of Europe" and Paris is becoming "the inn of the world"— years of commercial prosperity and military victory, self-crowned by the Great Exposition of 1859. Zola regarded the exhibitionistic style of the period, that garish classicism so reminiscent of Rome in Egypt, as "that opulent bastard of all styles." When he looked about and beheld Haussmann's reconstructed metropolis, he muttered allusions to Sodom, Babylon, Nineveh. "Now that we have the Empire, everything is moving, everything is for sale," mutters a thin malcontent in *Le Ventre de Paris*, and goes on to brand it "the reign of debauchery." Of this *demi-monde* the mock-empress is Nana Coupeau. Nana, in her bedazzling rise from *midinette* to *grande cocotte*, is no less distinctive a star of empire than her distant cousins, the financier and the statesman. She, too, enjoys her carnival apogee; when the horse that is named for her wins in the races at Longchamps, she is hailed as "queen of Paris."

Nana's success in her profession makes her at least a temporary exception to the rule that condemns the Macquarts to misfortune, and ranks them among the anonymous workers at the base of the pyramid. However, in all consistency, she has Bonapartist sympathies; she is shown drinking to the Emperor's health; and her apartment is located on the Boulevard Haussmann—a far cry from Gervaise's tenement, whence she first strayed to the streets in *L'Assommoir*. "Mamma was a laundress, papa got drunk, and he died of it," she shrugs. "Voilà!" Here as elsewhere, the diagnosis reverts from a biological to a sociological, and ultimately to a moral, plane. This reversion becomes explicit in Zola's asides: "With her, the rot that was allowed to ferment among the people welled up and corrupted the aristocracy." More generally, sexual habits observe class distinctions. *Pot-bouille* proceeds upon the assumption that adultery is to the middle class what prostitution is to the proletariat. Such is the pot-luck hinted at in the title. As for *Nana*, we could consider it a work of pornography, in the most literal meaning of the term, as writing about a prostitute; and that consideration would explain, at all events, why it outsold Zola's previous books.

But Nana is no ordinary street-walker; she is the most seductive of the show-girls ostentatiously kept by the Emperor's courtiers. Her impresario, frankly and cynically, refers to his theater as a brothel; but when the curtain goes up on its cardboard Olympus, and when its mimic Olympians are bedraggled with mud, and when we are taken into the atmosphere of makeshift and dishevelment and perspiration backstage, we realize that it also bodies forth the tawdry and tinselled spectacle of the Second Empire itself. That was truly Zola's house of ill fame. What he stresses is not the lubricity of Nana so much as her "rage for abasement." This comes to the surface most cruelly in the episode that so offended Brunetière, which—the conservative critic triumphantly claimed—had been plagiarized from a scene in Thomas Otway's *Venice Preserved*. Zola admitted that he had borrowed the business from an account of that Restoration tragedy in Taine's *Histoire de la littérature anglaise*. He could have found another account in Voltaire's *Lettres philosophiques*, and a pointed allusion to it in Balzac's *Melmoth réconcilié*. The lurid passage seems to have exercised a peculiar fascination over those French writers whose way it came. But Zola makes it his own, with certain adaptive touches which Brunetière was too obtuse to perceive.

The scene involves the caprice of a courtesan, who forces her elderly senatorial lover to crawl on all fours along the floor, and to bark like a dog while she goads him with a whip. There is something inherently Zolaesque in so naturalistic a reduction of human beings to bestiality; and Zola adds political significance by assigning the part of infatuated lover to the proud and austere Count Muffat de Beuville, who happens to be the Emperor's chamberlain. As he grovels and cringes, Nana fondly fancies that she is kicking the Tuileries, flagellating "the majesty of the imperial court." She takes a grim pleasure in walking over and spitting upon his court uniform, with its eagles and decorations. She is motivated less by perversion than by subversion, unconscious *lèse-majesté*. "It was her revenge, some recurring family rancor." Apart from this sadistic gesture, she is not cruel by nature; masochistically, and ironically, she allows herself to be brutally treated by Muffat's rival, her fellow actor, Fontan. Hardly a *femme fatale*, she has more in her of Moll Flanders than of Lilith or Astarte. Vulgar and stupid, she abases men because she is greedy, and her attraction for them is completely physical. She remains enough her mother's daughter to relapse on occasion into the *bonne fille*. But the parable is a study in corruption at every level, and it is her fate to be the corrupting agent.

In one of his botanical asides, Zola comments, "When tuberoses decompose, they have a human odor." The moralist joins the physiologist in pursuing Nana to an edifyingly horrible death. Wasted by the smallpox, her suppurating corpse lies in her deserted room on her voluptuous bed. After a harrowing clinical description, her "corrupted flesh" is pronounced to be that of "Venus in decomposition." The other harlots, recently so loud in their praise of the Emperor, have fled. Through the windows, from the boulevards, comes the clamor of crowds, gathering in enthusiastic response to announcements of war with Germany. Their shout comprises the last words of the book: "On to Berlin, to Berlin!" For this effective tag-line, with its ironic repercussions, Zola had a precedent in Augier's popular comedy, *Le Gendre de M. Poirier*. There the bourgeois hero ends by resolving to become a peer in 1848. Actually, the peerage was abolished in that year, as audiences well knew when the play was performed in the 'fifties, and M. Poirier's resolve was the emptiest of ambitions. Much louder and vastly more hollow, in view of what lies ahead for Paris, is the roar of the bellicose crowd at the close of *Nana*. Retrospective irony points the moral that goes unpronounced in *La Bête humaine*: the imperial adventure is as ill-starred as the dead adventuress.

Her recumbent body prefigures "France in the agonies of the Second Empire," Zola explicitly wrote to his Dutch translator, Van Santen Kolff, adding in qualification, "Perhaps this underlines the symbol a little too much. But, obviously, I should have wanted something comparable." Nana has contracted her fatal illness from her pathetic infant son, Louiset. It is part of Zola's pathological scheme that so many subfamilies should terminate in such sickly and moribund children. Hardy obtains a similar effect by means of a heavier symbolism, with the hapless little Father Time in *Jude the Obscure*. And the portrait of Claude Lantier's dead child has a precedent with Frédéric Moreau's in *L'Education sentimentale*. The last legitimate offspring of the Rougons, the feeble Charles, bleeds to death of a hemorrhage, in full view of his helpless and insane great-great-grandmother, herself "a living skeleton" in the asylum at Plassans. After her demise, a grand new mental hospital is erected by the dowager Félicité Rougon as a fitting memorial to the clan. Slightly at cross-purposes with himself, Zola had to compress the rise and fall of the Rougons within the lifetime of their centenarian ancestress, and particularly within her last twenty years. The young Thomas Mann, looking backward at the end of the nineteenth century, could concentrate on its elegiac aspect, and qualify his *Buddenbrooks* as the chronicle of a declining family, *Verfall einer Familie*.

The long-drawn-out processes of hereditary degeneration, Zola found, were much too slow to express the sudden decline in morale. He speeded them up in his valedictory volume, *Le Docteur Pascal*, when old Antoine Macquart, after a lifetime spent consuming alcohol, is himself consumed by spontaneous combustion —a casualty which recurs more often in symbolic fiction than in the annals of medicine. Dickens had used it in *Bleak House* to symbolize the danger of an explosion in Chancery—a precedent which Zola denied having known. The dynastic taint, in his foreground, is an omnipresent reminder of the Bonaparte dynasty, in the background, and its morally tainted government. Moreover, Napoleon III, "that equivocal dreamer," takes a personal hand in the proceedings here and there. The prince of opportunists, half adventurer, half reformer, he struts on and off the stage. We hear his high-pitched voice; we note his vaguely glazed eyes; and we watch the pallid light of his countenance, shining from behind his arrogant moustaches down upon the more favored characters. Uniformed amidst the panoply of the battlefield in *La Débâcle*, he cuts a thoroughly ignominious figure, which Zola accentuates by reporting the rumor that he berouged his cheeks to keep up the appearance of courage. Calculated echoes of his uncle's legend play up "the irony of the imperial household." When the French, capitulating to Bismarck, run a faded tablecloth up the flagpole on the citadel at Sédan, they complete the impression of mock-heroic bathos.

The Empire itself, "grown old … and rotten," is invariably displayed as a mock-empire. The shadow of Bismarck looms larger as that of Napoleon wavers. No rescuing god descends in a machine. Our final glimpse of the escaping Emperor takes place when he is hiding in a hotel-room, where the shabby walls mock France's plight with two pictures: Rouget de Lisle introducing the Marseillaise and the Last Judgment. But, if there is stern mockery in those symbols of France's demoralization, there is epic compassion in Zola's narrative of the routed army's retreat. Here he broke a path for the French novelists who would record their country's experience in the first World War, with the varying results that J. N. Cru has studied, in his comprehensive survey of war literature, *Témoins*. Zola was not writing from first-hand acquaintance with the actions he treated; but he took his habitual pains to gather the factual details with some exactitude; and hence he set a solid example for the writers of Henri Barbusse's generation. In another respect, M. Cru concludes, Zola's influence may have been less constructive. He listened to, and passed on, a number of exaggerated atrocity-stories, which could have no other consequence than to sharpen the animus on both sides in the next war. Yet there are humane touches, worthy of Tolstoy, such as the recognition at the ambulance station or the flight of swallows flushed out by a cannonade.

Zola's unheroic heroes are the hitherto unsung victims of what is becoming total war. They are the unknown soldiers, conscripted men in the ranks as distinguished from the vainglorious rigidity of their commanding officers, exhausted grandsons of the Revolution whose nobility is their patient willingness to trudge along in a losing cause. But Zola also compassionates the entrammeled civilians, the dwellers in the shelled towns and, above all, the farmers whose fertile fields are laid waste. He dramatizes the malign transition from plowshares to swords by enlisting Jean Macquart, who has worked among the peasantry in *La Terre*, as one of his two protagonists. The second is Jean's comrade-in-arms, Maurice Levasseur, and each in turn saves the other under fire. Surviving but separated politically afterward, they find themselves on opposite sides in the Commune; and "that mad dream," that civic nightmare, expires for them in the horror of fratricide. As an abysmal instance of men and women crushed by things, *La Débâcle* has an interesting pendant, *L'Attaque du moulin*, written at about the halfway point in the composition of *Les Rougon-Macquart* and standing somewhat aside from the main body of Zola's work, as a pure *nouvelle* rather than as a quasi-historical document. It is still a long way to Zola's mill in northerly Lorraine from Daudet's in peaceful and cheerful Provence; and documentary novels like *Le Nabab* are singularly devoid of the ideological shudder that marks their counterparts in *Les Rougon-Macquart*.

L'Attaque du moulin, treating another incident in the same war, presents the same conflicting values as *La Débâcle*—on the one hand, the productiveness of a village mill; on the other, the destructiveness of enemy troops. A wedding, scheduled against a bountiful setting, gives way to a siege where non-combatants are victimized. French reinforcements are expected to rescue them; but the bridegroom is shot, and the bride goes mad, and her father's mill is a smoking ruin, before they arrive. Their concluding shout of victory has the hollowness of Nana's cheering mob. The tale was published in *Les Soirées de Médan*, a collection which included tales by five younger writers who shared Zola's naturalistic program—and, more than that, his attitude toward the ironies of the Franco-Prussian War. The gem of the collection was Maupassant's masterpiece, with which he was making his literary début, *Boule de suif*. If Zola's *nouvelle* was surpassed by its pungent satire, it employed devices which Maupassant had acquired from the master of Médan. The stage-coach that breaks down, like the train in *La Bête humaine*, is an image of the Empire; the passenger who becomes an ethical touchstone for the others is a prostitute, like Nana. The collaborators had thought of calling their volume *L'Invasion comique*, because it grotesquely dwelt on the comic side of the German occupation. Yet the individual comedies were incidental to the collective tragedy, and the true matrix of naturalism was Zola's brooding apprehension of peripety.

6. Conscience and Consciousness

It was indeed the end of everything, an exacerbation of destiny, an accumulation of disasters greater than those which any nation has ever undergone—continual defeats, provinces lost, billions to pay, the most frightful of civil

wars drowned in blood, wreckage and corpses on all sides—
no more money, no more honor, a whole world to reconstruct!

Such is the meditation of Jean Macquart, as he walks away from
the smouldering ruins of devastated Paris at the end of *La Débâcle*.
He says farewell to Henriette Weiss, the woman he might have
married if he had not slain her brother, his best friend, through
a mishap of civil war. Now, as Jean looks up at the tranquil sky,
his mood changes, like the mood of Tolstoy's prostrate hero on
the battlefield of Austerlitz. There is an auroral gleam on the
horizon.

> . . . It was the sure rejuvenation of eternal nature, of eternal
> humanity, the renewal promised to those who hope and
> work, the tree that pushes out a vigorous new shoot when a
> rotten branch has been cut off, after the poisonous sap has
> yellowed its leaves.

And now that the regime has fallen at last, Zola's parting comment
is purged of irony:

> The ravaged field was fallow, the house was burned to the
> ground; and Jean, the humblest and the saddest of men,
> walked toward the future, toward the great and rough task
> of creating a whole new France.

It was in a more militant state of mind that Etienne Lantier
emerged from the underground caverns of *Germinal*. He conceived the budding crops as mythical dragons' teeth, which would
some day sprout to avenge the defeated miners. Much in Zola
is bitterly pessimistic; nature can be an insensate and unrelenting
foe; in the short story, *L'Inondation*, the happiness of a peasant
family is washed away overnight by the rising of the river Garonne.
Society, the family itself, can be a hotbed for the breeding of
enemies. Throughout *Les Rougon-Macquart*, as we have been
observing, Zola's catastrophic imagination tends to move in a
falling cadence. A fall is likewise the theme of *Finnegans Wake*,
where it heralds the theme of a rainbow, and thereby re-enacts
a cyclic pattern common to many myths of resurrection. *Felix
culpa!* the happiness of toil is the retribution in store for Adam

and Eve, as they take their solitary way eastward from Eden. *Allons, travaillez!*

So it is, in the long run, with the manic-depressive Zola. His pessimism is a trait acquired through confrontation with harsh realities, whereas his optimism seems innate. The Second Empire was over, after all; the problem was no longer survival but revival. Zola's epilogue—or perhaps we should call it his testament or his credo—carries us across the dividing line into the Third Republic, whence we look back upon the entire conspectus. Now, having been planned that way from the beginning, *Le Docteur Pascal* must pick up a good many of the genealogical threads, which have latterly been running slack. As he got farther away from his original theories, Zola got more interested in actual conditions. Now he must go back to his experimental framework; and, though it may have helped him to launch his ambitious program, at this mature stage it may be something of an encumbrance. Pascal Rougon, the elderly bachelor scientist, is the *raisonneur* of *Les Rougon-Macquart*. On his death, which he clinically observes as long as he remains conscious, a martyr to experimentalism, his scientific records are destroyed by his mother, Félicité, who is determined to shield the family honor. But it is his abiding "belief in life" which prevails, his love of life and hope for its final triumph, since his youthful niece and pupil Clotilde bears his posthumous and illegitimate child. The series concludes with the image of an infant at nurse, the hopeful pledge of the breed's continuation.

To be sure, the child is a product of incest, and a Rougon on both sides, with a father past sixty; but we need not stop to ask, since Zola does not, what might be the genetic consequences. Instead, we may well turn briefly from experiment to experience, and remind ourselves why a special fervor informs such passages. Why, again, would Zola declare of another madonna, in *Fécondité*, that "a mother nursing an infant" is the "highest expression of human beauty"? His belated satisfaction in becoming a father, albeit hugger-mugger, speaks out at such moments. Its symbol is the statue of Fecundity unveiled in *Paris*. But in this regard, it is significant that his numerous fictional infants are never very convincing. His *gamins* behave too much like adults. They are wizened waifs, like the little housekeeper Lalie, who meets a worse than Dickensian fate in *L'Assommoir,* or the crippled and twisted Jeanlin who turns into a killer in *Germinal,* or the spoiled and neurasthenic Jeanne who breaks up her mother's romance in that restrained and strained domestic drama, *Une Page d'amour.* Insofar as character equals relationship with Zola, women, on the whole, have more character than men, possibly because his situations demand so much in the way of adaptability. Wives and especially mothers, in accordance with well-observed facts of French sociology, hold families together; and here the author's point of view may be more filial than conjugal.

A salient instance is Gervaise Coupeau, and a flagrant exception is her daughter Nana. The most heroic figure in *La Débâcle* is Henriette Weiss, who crosses the battle lines in search of her husband, only to reach him facing a firing squad. Nor can we forget the long-suffering Maheude, that proletarian Niobe of *Germinal,* going to work in the mine at Montsou where she has lost her son and daughter, after her husband has been killed in the strike. In the tension of that male atmosphere, female qualities come out more strongly, as in her fragile daughter Catherine, who undergoes her crisis of adolescence, or in the easy-going Mouquette, ever "ready to submit to things and men." The battle of the sexes was never more brutal than when local womanhood revenges its indignities by mutilating the body of the philandering storekeeper. At the other extreme is the situation in *Au Bonheur des Dames,* where the grand bazaar of the title specializes in *articles de luxe* for Parisian ladies—or rather, it does not specialize, it adds one new department to another to form "a cathedral," the fane of "a new religion." The title, of course, is ironic; for, though the customers may be happy, the working and living conditions of the shop-girls are not. But commerce proves to be an effectual leveller. It humiliates a pretentious countess, who is caught red-handed in the act of shop-lifting. It elevates the modest Denise Baudu, who marries her employer—the ladies' man, Octave Mouret—after a Pamela-like resistance to his mercantile blandishments.

As the series progresses, it sallies forth from its middle-class ambiance and fraternizes with the working class. As its scope is broadened, its tone is transposed, from mild satire toward an epic note. Not that the proletariat is idealized. "Neither flatter the working-man nor slander him," Zola jotted in his sketches for *L'Assommoir.* He defended *Germinal* by arguing, "If the people are so

perfect, so divine, why try to improve their lot? No, they are degraded by ignorance, and hence we should labor to drag them out
of the mud." This metaphor is almost literally acted out in the
mire and fury of *Germinal*. The setting, so typically Zolaesque, is
a bemiring and engulfing milieu. The subject, so forthrightly stated
in Zola's notes, is nothing less than "the struggle between capital
and labor"—which, he announced, would be of paramount importance as the nineteenth century flowed into the twentieth.
Previously, he had aligned himself with the thin, in their univer-
salized conflict with the fat; but, given those simplistic labels, the
choice was easy, and not very much of a commitment. Claude
Lantier was an articulate bystander in *Le Ventre de Paris*. His
younger brother, Etienne, joins the miners after he has lost a previous job by hitting his employer. Zola himself seems to join the
hunger march in *Germinal*, and to strike a blow for organized labor,
in his contrasting picture of the manager's sumptuous luncheon.

In the 1880's, the world was shaken by a reverberating series of
strikes. Capitalism—capitalism unlimited—was still in the saddle,
yet not so firmly as before. Mechanization was more of a menace
than ever. Zola caught the new spirit, though he was actually tracing a chain of events which had occurred in the 'sixties. One of
his sources of strength is that, while he felt for the workers, he
was not without sympathy for the divided responsibilities and the
mounting insecurities of ownership and management. Hennebeau,
the general manager, is nearly paralyzed between the demands of
the miners and those of the stockholders; nor is he the master in
his own home; he wistfully envies the sexual opportunities of his
humblest employees. But the strikers are bound to be divided and
quelled. The failure of their cause is sealed by the counterblow
on their behalf, the explosion of dynamite, that sabotages the mine
and entraps the miners. The devil in the machine, who performs
this gesture of desperate violence, is the mysterious Russian an-
archist Souvarine. In disarming contrast with his "red vision of
revolution," we encounter in *L'Argent*—on the very premises of
his money-lending brother—the dreamy Sigismund Busch, who
not only reads *Das Kapital* but contributes to *Die Rheinische
Zeitung* and corresponds with its principal contributor, Karl Marx.

Never disdainful of watchwords, though never a party man, Zola
was increasingly willing to be regarded as a socialist. He would be

accepted as a fellow traveller by such leftist politicians as Jean
Jaurès and Léon Blum. Nor was *Germinal* his only "roman socialiste"; he informed a correspondent that *L'Argent*, which could
have been his most capitalistic enterprise, was "partly historical
and partly socialistic." He had come a long way from the position
of natural and social historian. In transferring his emphasis from
temperament to environment, he had moved from pseudo-scientific
determinism to humanitarian meliorism, and from the analytic
study of circumstances to the propagandistic control of them—in
two words, from sociology to socialism. He had gone far beyond
the intention set down in his working notes for *Les Rougon-Macquart*: "I simply observe, without sermonizing." Now it so happens
that a certain posture of detached observation figures as one of
Zola's fixed ideas from book to book. This is the situation where
an observer witnesses a crime or a disaster which he is either
powerless or unwilling to prevent, and which holds a serious consequence for him nevertheless. Some of the most clandestine deeds
he recounts, by this odd compulsion, have an unexpected beholder.
The entrapped witness, sharing some guilty secret, turns up again
and again under differing guises.

In *Thérèse Raquin* it is the mute old woman, whose son the
lovers have murdered, and who ends by staring them into a suicide
pact. In *La Terre* it is the enfeebled old man, who has to be put
out of the way because he has inadvertently witnessed the fatal
altercation. In *La Bête humaine* the train on which murder is committed flashes by while Jacques Lantier is watching, making him
an accomplice and ultimately a murderer himself. In *Le Docteur
Pascal*, Félicité Rougon looks on complacently without intervening, while her half-brother-in-law, Antoine Macquart, goes up in
flames. One might also notice that the senile Tante Dide is the
uncomprehending onlooker, while the sickly Charles bleeds to
death. In three of Zola's later novels, conformably, some individual
has foreknowledge of some dire event, but, for reasons of his own,
takes no step to hinder it: the poisoning in *Rome*, the dynamiting
in *Paris*, and the accident of the elevator shaft in *Fécondité*. Any
prolific novelist, exploring the patterns of human behavior, is likely
to repeat himself now and then; but when coincidence is strained
from the outset, and repetition makes it more emphatic, we are
entitled to draw thematic inferences. We need not suspect that

Zola harbored some personal burden of guilt, or that he was any more of a *voyeur* than any other curious-minded man. It was for Proust to play the supine eavesdropper.

For Zola, the very force of his moral revulsion from the imperial spectacle must have left him dissatisfied with his role as a mere spectator. We know that he had been exempted from the war as an only son, and that he had vainly sought a prefectship under the emergent republic afterward. He grew tired of watching, standing on the sidelines; clearly, he wanted to act. Insofar as he had been recording the passive submission to outrage, he recoiled from his self-imposed assignment. That recoil touched off an activism which was latent in *Les Rougon-Macquart* and which came to the surface in what he went on to write in the aftermath, as if the silent witness at last stepped forward and pointed his attestations with *J'accuse!* The full impact of his multiple undertaking had been assured with the publication of its seventh volume, *L'Assommoir*, in 1877. Ten years and eight volumes later, during the periodical publication of *La Terre*, the well-established Zola was attacked in an extremely hostile manifesto by five younger novelists. That attack seems to have been countenanced, if not inspired, by Edmond de Goncourt and Alphonse Daudet, who had come to suspect that Zola was exploiting the naturalistic movement for his own advantage. His project, at all events, had by then completed its fifteenth installment.

In 1891, when he was within two volumes of his goal, the journalist and critic, Jules Huret, circulated and publicized a set of questionnaires on the current trends in literature. One of his leading questions was whether naturalism was dead, and many of his respondents agreed that it was. Loyal to Zola, Paul Alexis disagreed, and foresaw the influence continuing well on into the twentieth century. Zola himself saw it taking another turn, which he labelled "a sort of classicism of naturalism." Jules Lemaître retorted that naturalism was Zola, and Zola alone; while Anatole France, in referring to the master as "less an exact realist than a perverted idealist," shrewdly hinted at what a naturalistic classicism might be. In reaction against his adolescent romanticism, Zola had taken issue with the idealistic esthetics of the socialist Proudhon, and had criticized the Parnassian school of poets for divorcing art from life. Yet, as a realist, he took fewer and fewer

pains to conceal his basic ideals. Flaubertian detachment was out
of date by the 1890's. Once again the influential men of letters
were ideologues, polemicists, or lay preachers, such as Nietzsche
and Ibsen, or the older Tolstoy and the younger Shaw. On completing *Les Rougon-Macquart,* Zola would probably have been glad
to put his doctrines of the experimental novel behind him; but
since he was inclined to be doctrinaire in any case, he was stimulated to go questing after other notions, more congenial to his bent
and the decade.

Hence the novelist becomes "an experimental moralist," in another sense from *Le Roman expérimental;* while, in still another
sense, he seems to be reverting to his early romantic idealism. He
toyed with the notion of turning historian; but his messianic passion, now released from historical controls, gained the upper
hand. "After forty years of analysis, have I not the right to finish
with a bit of synthesis?" In a letter raising this rhetorical question,
he answers it with a rhetorical flourish: "Hypothesis, Utopia, is
one of the rights of the poet." He had answered the critics of
L'Assommoir by insisting that one ought not to dream of Utopia
without having studied reality. The socialist of the trilogy, *Les Trois
Villes,* who was modelled upon his friend Jules Guesde, seeks to
"realize the dream of future society." These three successive volumes pursue the quest of their protagonist, the Abbé Froment, to
sound out the Christian virtues as they manifest themselves in the
modern world: faith in *Lourdes,* hope in *Rome,* and charity back
in *Paris.* Though Zola distrusted priests, he venerated saints, and
he had been particularly impressed by the legend of Bernadette.
But he was appalled by the "extraordinary perversion" that was
turning her Bethlehem into a modern counterpart of Sodom and
Gomorrah; and though he sympathized with the suffering pilgrims,
he impeached the sanctimonious sideshows that battened upon
their sufferings.

The absence of anticipated miracles is a test of faith for Alyosha
in *The Brothers Karamazov.* The Abbé Froment, returning from
Lourdes, remains more positivistic in his criteria. The next station
of his pilgrimage is Rome itself, where his hopes center upon the
renewed Catholicism of Pope Leo XIII. They are soon dashed by
the vista, spread before him, of dogmatic tradition and clerical
intrigue. Saint Peter's church seems to be not a rock but an opera

house. His hopeful tract, *La Nouvelle Rome*, has been put on the Index, and a papal audience does no more than reaffirm the condemnation. Here Zola, who was not received by the Pope on his tour of documentation, had to depend on hearsay for his depiction. After these two journalistic exposures of religious centers, he gravitated homeward toward the metropolis of the novel, where his ground was certain to be more secure. Lourdes had been "a glorification of the absurd." Rome had shown itself "incapable of renewal." Paris would reveal "a striking truth." He was not unaware —who could claim to know better?—that Paris had aspects of Sodom and Gomorrah. Abbé Froment is familiar with them from his endeavors on behalf of Catholic charities; amelioration has convinced him that what is needful should be justice rather than charity; and he cannot but flinch before that tasteless religiosity which is making the Sacré-Coeur its monument.

His search for a new religion leads him toward the religion of science, as expounded by one Bertheroy—a figure modelled on Marcelin Berthelot, the chemist and ideologue of the Third Republic, who was preaching a peaceful revolution through scientific evolution. Little by little the Abbé has become, what is quite untenable, an "unbelieving priest supervising the belief of others." Love, which was a lapse for the Abbé Mouret, becomes a second calling for the ex-Abbé Froment as a married layman. As we leave him, rededicating himself, the meaning of his name is emphasized, and with it the fruitfulness of his secular mission; for the city shines before him like a field of wheat, *froment*. "Paris was aflame, sown with light from the divine sun, gloriously stirring a future harvest of truth and justice." This prospect seems far brighter than that backward glance toward the Commune in *La Débâcle*, or that upward thrust through the soil in *Germinal*. But *Les Trois Villes* is a transitional effort, in its revaluation and rejection of the existing agencies of belief. There was nowhere else to look now, except ahead. Zola, who collected ecclesiastical objects, was never reluctant to assume the part of a lay apostle. Reversing the New Testament, he proceeded from the apocalypse to the gospels. Christening his projected tetralogy *Les Quatre Evangiles*, he baptized his four evangelist-heroes—scions of the unfrocked Abbé—Mathieu, Marc, Luc, and Jean.

The first of these secular scriptures is *Fécondité*, and here Zola's private cult of fertility combines with his public duty to admonish his fellow citizens on the hazards of the declining birth-rate. "He really did care more for the depopulation of France than for his novel," Frank Norris would protest. Characterization is therefore quantitative, according to the size of the character's family. Heroes are polyphiloprogenitive; villains make dastardly use of birth control; and pregnancy is the principal mode of suspense as, from chapter to chapter, new births are announced. The climax is the jubilee of Mathieu and his mate, under a familial oak tree, where —after forty years of child-bearing, child-rearing, and encouraging their children's children to reproduce themselves—they are surrounded with more than three hundred progeny. If *Fécondité* reads like *Les Rougon-Macquart* in reverse, *Travail*, the second gospel, rights the reverses that labor has suffered in *Germinal*. When certain familiar obstacles arise, they are easily overcome by a combination of Fourieristic socialism and Darwinian biology. The dying words of a dotard capitalist constitute a formula for conversion to the new system: "It must be returned . . ." Realizing his dream, Luc succeeds, not only in founding his "happy city of solidarity," but in using electricity to light its hygienic phalansteries.

Utopia, by definition, is nowhere; its figments are not expected to be flesh and blood; but flesh and blood were Zola's elements; and he is at his worst when he plays the reformer on paper, in the manner of Shaw. Happily, the reforming impulse behind his third gospel was real enough, since *Vérité* embodies Zola's response to the Dreyfus case. He himself plays Marc. "It is my triumph," he admitted. If it were not for the triumph, which was not yet complete when he wrote, this part would be similar to that of Dr. Stockmann, Ibsen's municipal iconoclast in *An Enemy of the People*. For Zola has scaled down to provincial dimensions, wisely enough, the affair that convulsed the whole country for twelve years and ended by supporting the authority of the political over the military, as well as by completing the separation of church from state. The issue, though proportionately reduced, is still a critical one. Zola has transferred it from the general staff of the army to the corps engaged in public instruction. Both the Jewish officer traduced and the defending crusader appear as country schoolmasters. The pedagogical matter is well suited to the unvarnished didacticism of Zola's later manner; and the final view of the old master, feted by the many generations of his pupils, seems to be a truer jubilee than the overteeming family group of *Fécondité*.

"Shut down the taverns, open up the schools." Those two brief injunctions, with which Zola pointed up the moral of *L'Assommoir*, sum up the transition from *Les Rougon-Macquart* to *Les Trois Villes* and *Les Quatre Evangiles*. It was fitting that his last novel, *Vérité*, should commemorate his greatest campaign and celebrate his alignment with "the France of Voltaire and Diderot, of the Revolution and the three Republics." Having set forth his views on the family in *Fécondité*, the city in *Travail*, and the nation in *Vérité*, what would there have been left for him to write about in the announced *Justice?* What could he have made, if he had lived, out of the unwritten fourth evangel of Jean Froment? *Vérité* had originally been Zola's running title for the four whole volumes, and he might just as well have named the Dreyfusard third volume *Justice*, although his gathering of journalistic contributions to the Affair is optimistically entitled *La Vérité en marche*. The categories are coupled off in the motto that runs through his later work, *La Vérité et la Justice*. The means of truth would forward the ends of justice in the Affaire Dreyfus; and the twin bywords are inscribed, with a warranted optimism, over the portals of the house that is given to the rehabilitated victim in *Vérité*. They had been the dying words of Bernadette and they were a kind of war-cry for Zola, who invoked them more than once in the courtroom as he had invoked them in the Salon. They ended by becoming interchangeable as well as inseparable. It may not be irrelevant that the old Russian language had but a single word for both truth and justice, *pravda*, even though we may not think of either in connection with the newspaper of that name.

Truth, as an end in itself, may be a broader abstraction than justice. It took Zola's peculiar force to render what Edwin Arlington Robinson has specified, in a sonnet addressed to him, as "the racked and shrieking hideousness of truth"—the kind that must be dragged resisting through the gates of horn. As an activist, in the pursuit of justice, Zola had to put letters behind him. He must have known that his perpetual candidacy for the French Academy would come to naught, when he espoused the cause of Captain Dreyfus. He lived through the pardon and amnesty, but missed—

by four years—the revision and vindication his efforts had insti-
gated. Anatole France, in his classic funeral oration, compared the
massive bulk of Zola's achievement with that of Tolstoy, and spoke
of both achievements as two cities reared by the lyre at the opposite extremes of European thought: on the western side the city
of labor, on the eastern side the city of resignation. Across that
distance, those two lyrists had closely followed one another's development, with mutual respect and dialectical reservations. For
Tolstoy, work was not enough; it had to be guided by faith. Such
guidance fostered a passiveness which Zola could never accept; he
had seen all too much at Lourdes of "the religion of human suffering"—and it is not without irony that he re-echoes this catch-
phrase introduced by the Goncourts, and popularized by the
Vicomte de Vogüé in his exploratory study of the Russian novel.

Yet, with due allowance for differences of temperament and
milieu, the two careers run curiously parallel. Both men, by their
middle years, had accomplished their monumental contributions
as novelists. Both became evangelists, as they proceeded toward
the intellectual and social problems of the twentieth century. The
Revolution of 1825 had been as strategic in Tolstoy's outlook as
the War of 1870 was in Zola's. The railroad, as a bearer of turbulence, made even more of an impression on Tolstoy than on
Zola. Both revered the soil, but the self-made Frenchman could
not idealize the folk as did the Russian nobleman. In *War and
Peace*, Count Pierre Bezuhov must leave his rifled mansion; in *La
Débâcle*, the accountant Weiss grabs a gun to protect his beleaguered home. And if the Rougons and Macquarts do not people
our minds as comfortably or as memorably as the Rostovs and
Bolkonskys, some of the many reasons might be reckoned by adopting the Tolstoyan distinction of Sir Isaiah Berlin: Zola was a hedge-
hog, purely and squarely, not a fox or a hybrid of the two. It is on
the extra-literary, the ideological side, we must admit, that Tolstoy
and Zola come closest to meeting. *What Is Art?* may be more cogent than *Le Roman expérimental* as an argument for *Les Rougon-
Macquart*. In the ninth chapter of Tolstoy's anti-esthetic treatise,
there is a remarkable sentence vindicating at length the dignity
and the variety of the laboring life. It is better justified by *Germinal* or *La Terre* than by that idyllic passage in *Anna Karenina*
where the landlord mingles with his reapers.

Anatole France completed his eulogy with an eloquent but slightly ambiguous statement: "Il fût un moment de la conscience humaine." The term *conscience*, like our preliminary *expérience*, has two interrelated meanings in French. Like our English "conscience," it can signify moral compunction: as, for example, when Gargantua warned Pantagruel that "science sans conscience" would ruin the soul. It can also be used, more neutrally and amorally, where we would use "consciousness"; and there is a sense in which Anatole France was comparing Zola's gesture to a momentary arrest in the temporal flow of historic awareness; but that conception brings us closer to Proust. Zola's final emphasis seems to be more ethical than psychological. His cycle of life and work had revolved from science to conscience, from natural to social history, and from sociological observation to socialistic action. Roger Martin du Gard continued in that direction when, speaking for the generation that grew up amidst the Dreyfus case, to his *Jean Barois* he prefixed an epigraph: "The sick conscience—there is the battle-ground." It was this Zolaesque quality of the French novel that the Swedish Academy recognized, with the award of the Nobel Prize to Albert Camus for "illuminating the problems of the human conscience in our time." It is the more philosophical meaning of *conscience*, together with the more personal phase of *expérience*, that André Malraux seems to have in mind, when he defines a man's task in *L'Espoir:* "To transform as large an experience as possible into consciousness . . ."

VII

PROUST

> Proust is perhaps the last great historian of the loves, the society, the
> intelligence, the diplomacy, the literature and the art of the Heartbreak
> House of capitalist culture; and the little man with the sad appealing
> voice, the metaphysician's mind, the Saracen's beak, the ill-fitting dress-
> shirt and the great eyes that seem to see all about him like the many-
> faceted eyes of a fly, dominates the scene and plays host in the mansion
> where he is not long to be master.
>
> —EDMUND WILSON

1. A Cork-Lined Room

IN TURNING from Zola to Proust, the contrast is obviously more
striking than the continuity. Side by side, they span the poles between which modern fiction seems to operate: on the one hand a
materialistic involvement, on the other an inward withdrawal.
Given two French novelists of successive generations, it would be
hard to discern less common ground between them, beyond the
arena of the Dreyfus case. It is true that Proust fetched his paternal ancestry from the same central region of France, La Beauce,
where the maternal forebears of Zola had dwelt. Yet it is impossible to believe that either of those fragrant paths immortalized
by Proust would take us from his father's village, Illiers, to the
thickly manured peasants' acres of *La Terre*. Both men, we might
desperately argue, were preoccupied with genealogy and with de-
generacy; but such a line of argument would bring out more crucial distinctions, polarities of inclusiveness and exclusiveness, of
extroversion and introspection, journalistic productivity as against
stylistic preciosity, a utopian prospect against a nostalgic retrospect. During the thirty-year span between them, while the French

novel was plodding somewhat wearily down its main road, it was being prodded in other directions by the vitalizing influence of the Russian novelists. After its conquests of the nineteenth century, its repeated assaults on objective reality, as Jacques Rivière pointed out in a prescient article, there was likely to be a strategic retreat, a season of questioning, a lapse into subjectivity.

During the first decade of Proust's literary career, when his tenuous published concerns were with estheticism and snobbery, Zola was portentously bringing forth his evangelical testaments. This chronological overlapping could scarcely have afforded a meeting of minds. Yet, when we view their respective work from a distance, following the continuous medium across the changing epoch, it all falls into a complementary relationship. Zola's dreams, whether realized or unrealized, did not come solely through the gates of horn, as we have seen; and we shall see that Proust, though his mood is often somnolent, though he was adept at interpreting fantasies, though he took steps to substantiate a myth of an ivory tower, never escaped by way of the ivory gate. Even the Duchesse de Guermantes, echoing Zola's more perceptive critics, could recognize the latent epic poet underneath the scientific pretensions. Whereas Proust was considered by Valery Larbaud to be the very incarnation of symbolism, further consideration will show that he retains—or rather, regains—a substantial element of naturalism. Indeed one of his earliest articles, *Contre l'obscurité*, which he would develop into a preface for a novel by Paul Morand, protested against the excesses of the *symbolistes*, and—what could not have then been foreseen—aligned Proust with that great tradition of French analysis which is finally independent of schools or periods. A year or two before his death, when his work was being hailed as a classic, he professed himself a classicist.

Questionless, since his twenties coincided with the 1890's, he came into his majority on a wave of reaction against the social novel. The minor poet he took as his mentor, whom he dubbed his "Professor of Beauty," Count Robert de Montesquiou-Fezensac, was one of the dandified lights of the *fin du siècle*. Now Huysmans, in his apostasy from the school of Médan, had made his most striking impact with *A rebours*—surely one of the curiosities of literature, whether we read it as a satire or as a fantasy. Its hero, Des Esseintes, with his flamboyant postures and far-fetched ges-

tures, resisting modernity in the name of decadence, is said to
have been modeled on Montesquiou. We can triangulate Proust's
development by bearing in mind that, a generation afterward,
Montesquiou served as a model for his pivotal character, the Baron
de Charlus. And we could connect Proust with the naturalistic
line—not through Zola, to be sure, but through those forerunners
whom Zola had eclipsed, the brothers Goncourt. Proust, as a fellow connoisseur, could share their meticulously esthetic approach;
and, as an exponent of the first person, he could profit from the
fact that their memoirs had proved to be more important than
their novels. One of the significant lessons learned in his novel
discloses itself through a passage imitated from the Goncourt
journal. It was altogether fitting that formal recognition should
belatedly come to him, in 1919, with the prize of the Goncourt
Academy.

"Memoirs are at best half sincere," wrote André Gide in the
margin of his memoirs, *Si le grain ne meurt*. "No matter how great
their concern for truth, everything is always more complex than
people say. Possibly one might even get nearer the truth in a novel."
If the truth is dialectical, then the novel permits its attainment
through dialogue, where memoirs would gloss it over into a monologue. Thus Gide, the apostle of sincerity, the witness who has left
us our twentieth-century counterpart of the Goncourts' record for
the nineteenth, the anecdotist who claimed the status of novel for
only one of his books, *Les Faux-monnayeurs*, seems to have been
pointing the way for Proust. With both, as with James Joyce and
other contemporaries, the novelist seems to be coalescing with the
autobiographer. Critical biographies are needful in order to gauge
the exact extent of this coalescence, as Richard Ellmann has so
delicately done for James Joyce. George D. Painter, who has been
facing a similar problem, has given us his solution to the first half
of it, in *Proust: The Early Years*. His premise is that *A la recherche du temps perdu* "occupies a place unique among great novels
in that it is not, properly speaking, a work of fiction, but a creative
autobiography."

Properly speaking, and bearing in mind the rather more literal
example of Joyce, one must qualify that large assertion. It is a
question of relative degree, and not of absolute uniqueness. Imaginative composition is much too variable and flexible to support

such distinctions of kind between one writer and all the rest. Proust, at first glance, might seem to invite Mr. Painter's endeavors; for, in his early manuscript novel, the introduction expresses his curiosity about a fictitious novelist—who, incidentally, has just died, and whose supposititious book, *Jean Santeuil*, contains all we ever learn about him. Therein Proust speculates that it might be worth while to spend a whole lifetime trying to find out "what are the secret links, the necessary metamorphoses existing between the life of a writer and his work, between reality and art." Yet, as he matured in his craft, he gave more weight to the complexity of the interrelationship and the importance of the finished product. It was not as a practising man of letters but as an accomplished work of art in himself that he praised Alphonse Daudet, though he knew the man well through close friendship with his sons. Proust resented the familiarity with which such a critic as Sainte-Beuve had treated such a contemporary as Balzac, on the grounds that the biographical method confused art with life. Such criticism, by invading privacies, downgraded literary works into human documents.

Proust seems to be speaking of himself, as well as of Balzac, when he comments: "A book is the product of another self than the one we display in our habits, in our social life, in our vices. If we would try to comprehend it, we can do so by seeking to re-create it within ourself at the very depth of our being." When he concludes that "art exactly recomposes life," the stress on exactitude is counterbalanced by the emphasis on re-composition. Zola's disclaimer of having invented anything is matched by Proust's claim of having invented everything. Declaring that there were no keys to his characters, Proust added that sometimes a single character had eight or ten keys—a seeming contradiction which brings him closer to the eclectic methods of other novelists, including Zola. Beginning with his own hints and admissions, and continuing through gossip and reminiscence, a welter of testimony has accumulated to identify his dramatis personae with living originals. No one, it is fair to say, would argue that A *la recherche du temps perdu* is a *roman à clef*, in the sense that it derives its significance from the events or persons to which it may allude. On the contrary, at the present stage of interpretation, actual lives seem to borrow vicarious glory from such identifications, however ambiguous. The names Proust dropped now glitter in a glamor reflected on them from his name and fame.

We should be grateful to Mr. Painter for having gathered and sifted the evidence so thoroughly, and for adding so much to it from his own researches. But we should still be wary of the circular reasoning that sometimes infers Proust's biography from his writing, and of the teleological assumption that approaches his friends in the light of presumptive models. When we have been told by our author that it was his habit to recombine many traits into one impression, then we must view his characters as composites, and the process of recombination as an act of creation. Nothing, of course, can be created *ex nihilo*; all human creations are bound to be re-creations. Proust merely carries this logic to its conclusion, through his special cultivation of remembrance. Memory has always been personified as the mother of the Muses. Her vast palace, as Saint Augustine envisioned it, housed innumerable images which had been accumulated by the diverse impressions of the senses. Imagination itself may be no more than what classical psychology, in Hobbes's phrase, called "decaying sense"; and even the romantic poets attempted no more than to distill their stored recollections. Since Proust himself was much concerned with discriminating the imaginary from the real, we may make—and must welcome—the effort to disengage his artistic achievements from their raw materials, always providing we do not forget that art to him became a higher reality, for which life itself was no more than a groping rehearsal.

Baudelaire had once written: "Life is a hospital, where every patient is possessed with a desire to change his bed. One of them might wish to suffer facing the stove; another might believe that he would convalesce near the window." The poet, for all his insight, could not have foreseen the coddled and talented valetudinarian who would want to lie near the stove and look out of the window simultaneously, and whose caprice would induce a luminous vision. But literature in France, which has so frequently felt the benefit of clinical analysis, was now beginning to reach its pathological phase. Decadentism, a touchstone for such post-romantics as Baudelaire and Gautier, became a self-conscious cult in the 1880's. It was one of the claims of the Goncourts that they had been the first to write about—or else to write with—their nerves, to be "écrivains des nerfs"; and after Jules de Goncourt's premature death, Edmond had told Flaubert, "We are all invalids." Others, more extroverted, saw themselves as doctors, ministering to the ills of the epoch. Balzac could set up as a practitioner of social medicine, and Zola could tear a page or two from Claude Bernard's *Médecine expérimentale*. Marcel Proust could not pretend to be anybody's doctor, perhaps because—like Flaubert—he was the son and brother of medical men, or because—like Flaubert again—he was all too literally a patient.

He was born into French history at its grimmest, in Paris—or rather, Auteuil, where his parents had taken refuge—during the terrible year of 1871, which saw the bloody parturition of the Third Republic in the ashes of the Second Empire and the wreckage of the Commune. His father, from a family of country shopkeepers, had risen to professional eminence as a specialist in public health, serving both the University and the government. His mother, whom he seems to have resembled more closely, and to whom he was bound by the strongest ties of mutual devotion, came from a Jewish family of culture and affluence. Hence his very origin presupposed *deux côtés*, and it has been pointed out that his intermixture of bloods was the same as Montaigne's. Certainly we can find affinities between the two in their introspective habits, their apt quotations, their fascinating digressions, their feeling for the diversity and the contrariety of human nature, above all their perpetual willingness to ask themselves what they really know: "Que sais-je?" But such a combination of qualities is far too rare to be accounted for on racial grounds. More to the immediate point, in shaping his temperament, was Proust's neurasthenia. When his sickly young protagonist meets the great writer whom he aspires to emulate, Bergotte tells Marcel that the pleasures of intellect should repay him for the constrictions of illness.

He was nine years old when his malady caught up with him, in the guise of an asthmatic attack. Naturally, consultants were not lacking to diagnose it, and some of them were not unaware of its psychosomatic implications. Like a familiar spirit, it came and went, moving in upon him at crises throughout his life. Life was beset with allergies on all sides, impeded by colds through the win-

ter and by fevers through the summer, and cadenced by suffoca-
tions and fumigations. If he loved the hawthorn hedges so fervidly,
it was because they endangered, as well as allured, his hyperesthetic
sensibilities. Since merely breathing the open air and freely roam-
ing the countryside were hazardous pursuits for him from boyhood,
a special poignance pervades his evocation of early memories recalling his father's Illiers—his Combray. Hay-fever paid for *le
parfum de Combray*. Not inconsistently, Albert Thibaudet once
described him as the most purely Parisian of novelists, and his
digression on street-cries goes far to substantiate that claim. From
his family apartment, seldom changed and never very far from the
grand boulevards, he would sally forth, when permitted, to seek
the artificial nature of the Champs Elysées or the Bois de Boulogne. When he went farther afield, on advice of physicians, it was
to a spa or the seaside—to a resort where existence was pampered
and passive, not unlike that of Thomas Mann's semi-recumbent
intellectual, watching the grace and vitality of a youthful band on
a beach.

Such vacations, *villégiatures*, sojourns in the country, would set
the rhythmic patterns of his novel, in accordance with the leisurely
seasonal practices of the old aristocracy, emulated more and more
by the upper bourgeoisie. The effect of that holiday rhythm, upon
impressionist painting, has been elucidated by Meyer Schapiro.
It presupposed the viewpoint of the cultivated *rentier*, indulging
his footloose sensibilities in picnics and promenades. A comparable
sort of impressionism was awakened within this indoor youth by
his occasional outings, an urban—not to say an urbane—rusticity.
We even find his Jean Santeuil flouting doctors' orders to cultivate
thunderstorms, because of their resemblance to Turner's seascapes,
with a spectatorial ardor which Proust himself had acquired from
Ruskin. One of his unpublished experiments is a dialogue entitled
Vacances, possibly after a story about children's holidays by the
exemplary Comtesse de Ségur. There his precocious hero and a
somewhat maturer heroine keep an assignation in the Bois which
will be repeatedly set and missed in his novel, wherein nonetheless
his girlish heroines will figure as the tutelary nymphs of parks and
beaches. The *vacances* of the dialogue seem to stand not so much
for interims of dalliance as for the empty spaces of the heart, a

disappointing vacancy left by one love to be not impossibly filled by another.

As a student at the Lycée Condorcet, his favorite subjects were history and natural history. For a while his favorite authors, accordingly, were Saint-Simon and Fabre, the duke who vivisected his fellow courtiers and the entomologist who treated insects so humanely. Both of these authorities are consulted throughout Proust's novel. He plays with the notion of becoming the Saint-Simon of his day, and reduces domestic situations to mock-heroic absurdity by invoking the precedent and protocol of Versailles in the *grand siècle*. Conversely, he offers entomological explanations for problems of human behavior: the cruelty of a cook to a kitchenmaid is like that of the hymenoptera to the spider. These habitual cross-references to science, with Proust as with Flaubert, put an ironic distance between the writer and his material; but the two planes are kept apart, where they are confounded by Zola. Although Proust had been destined by his father for academic training as a diplomat or an archivist, the son demurred, and was—as usual—indulged. In a letter to Dr. Proust, he asserted that anything other than literature or philosophy would for him be "du temps perdu." At the Sorbonne, he followed with especial interest the philosophical courses of his relative by marriage, Henri Bergson. Bergson's metaphysic of time and man's relation to it, "the cinematographic mechanism of thought" expounded in *Matière et mémoire*, seemed peculiarly apposite to the closing years of the century—or, in another way, to the opening years of the new one.

His newly graduated disciple was able, by Proust's own definition, to waste a good deal of time. Through school friendships and intellectual interests, he had begun to move in the charmed spiral of those salons which the French designate as the world, *le monde*. We make the same reduction when we spell society with a capital S. There his taste and intelligence were as much engaged as his wealth and charm in a reciprocal bedazzlement. He was soon cutting a figure at exhibitions and concerts. With other aspiring young writers he founded a little magazine, *Le Banquet*; he contributed elegant trifles to literary journals, notably the symbolistic organ, *La Revue blanche*; and he became a fashionable chronicler for the weekly *Figaro*. For several years, while hardly ever putting in an

appearance, he held the most nominal of unpaid sinecures at the
Mazarine Library, a fragile link with Flaubert. Whenever he could,
all too seldom and too briefly for his tastes, he travelled upon sentimental journeys to indulge his love of painting and architecture.
By the condescending Montesquiou, and by such professionals as
Maurice Barrès, he would always be patronized as "our young
man." André Gide would blandly turn down *Du côté de chez
Swann* without even reading it because its author seemed so pat-
ently a snob, a social climber, the merest amateur. And when it
came out under other auspices, *La Nouvelle Revue française* added
insult to injury with a review by Henri Ghéon beginning: "Voilà
une oeuvre de loisir . . ."

His earliest book, *Les Plaisirs et les jours,* had crystallized that
image. Rereading those fragile stories, impressionistic sketches, and
poems mainly in prose, we may well be fascinated by their tentative statement of many themes which he would fully orchestrate
in his maturity. But we can also understand how his original readers found him slight and precious, overpretentious and—in a *de
luxe* edition—overexpensive. Anatole France's preface added a few
master-touches to the self-portrait of a world-weary young man of
twenty-five, whose talent—France asserted, with an aptness which
might then have been mistaken for pedantry—somehow combined
the ingenuousness of a Bernardin de Saint-Pierre with the depravity
of a Petronius. Proust himself made a classical allusion through his
title, a dissonant echo of Hesiod's *Works and Days*, which not
only confirms the net impression of hedonism, epicureanism, and
dilettantism, but also announces a lifelong preoccupation with
time. Income and ill health guaranteed his leisure; and we now
know that, when he was not meeting his worldly engagements, he
was not necessarily being idle or frivolous. Secretly, he was engaged
in writing a novel of more than a thousand manuscript pages,
which has latterly been assembled and published—somewhat less
than definitively—as *Jean Santeuil*. Here again, the latter-day reader
can look for adumbrations of things to come, along with autobiographical glimpses and historical vignettes.

Here, as in the accomplished novel, everything begins with the
crisis of a child in bed, waiting for his mother's good-night kiss.
Much of the background is taken up by a first-hand account of
the Dreyfus affair, still at issue and engaging Proust's sympathies

as would no other public event: for, though his own position was not affected by the ensuing trend toward anti-Semitism, what was much worse, its aspersions could be cast upon the person nearest and dearest to him. *Jean Santeuil*, though it is episodically interesting, lacks the integrating quality that could make it uniquely Proustian. Still under thirty, he could not yet have attained the dimension of time or the perspective of memory. Since he abandoned the unpolished draft and reworked certain episodes in other contexts, his lifework still remains to be regarded as one ever-developing book, a *livre vécu* in the fullest sense of the term. We cannot imagine Proust finishing a novel and going on to write another. He would affirm, in *La Prisonnière*, that all great writers ended by composing single works. *A la recherche du temps perdu* would furnish a better warrant than *Jean Santeuil* for the prefatory remark: "This book has not been fabricated, it has been harvested." Apparently discouraged by this unripe effort, and increasingly bedridden by his malaise, he found solace and further inspiration in his reading. *Jean Santeuil* records, and later essays comment upon, his assimilation of the French masters, both in poetry and in fiction.

For fresh insights, he inclined responsively to Anglo-American literature: to Emerson and, more surprisingly, to Thoreau, both of whom must have helped him to sharpen the antithesis between society and solitude. From the line of English novelists, George Eliot and Thomas Hardy, in particular, fostered his appreciation for moral landscapes. But the master who commanded his utmost veneration, whose doctrine he embraced as an esthetic discipline, was John Ruskin. The churches and cathedrals that Proust visited and studied were monuments to this discipleship. Its milestones were his hard-won translations of *The Bible of Amiens* and *Sesame and Lilies*, a pair of spiritual exercises suggested and assisted by his mother, who knew English much better than he did. Proust approaching thirty-five—and what is mid-journey, for most, turned out to be two-thirds of the way for him—could scarcely have been looked upon as anything more than a clever esthete or an affable dilettante. That was the season of his catastrophe, the death of his mother in 1905. His father having died two years before, this spoiled child, so dependent on his parents, was left alone with his middle-aged remorse. Asked in a juvenile questionnaire his "idea of happiness," he had answered with naïve sophistication: "To live near those I love, with the charms of nature, a number of books and paintings, and the theater not too far away." Asked "your idea of misery," he had responded: "To be separated from Mamma."

His most intimate friend, the composer Reynaldo Hahn, cherished a poignant recollection of him, weeping and smiling beside his mother's deathbed. After a nervous prostration from which he recovered in a sanatorium, he returned to his Boulevard Haussmann apartment and settled down in austere reclusion to vindicate his survival, to become a writer in earnest, to make up for time lost. Significantly, he had envisaged his formal initiation into the profession of letters as one fine morning when his mother would unfold by his bedside a copy of *Le Figaro* containing his maiden article. He imagined himself outlining to her his plan for a sequel, which would be a critique of criticism, a counter-attack upon Sainte-Beuve for having failed to appreciate contemporaneous talents, especially Balzac's. When he went on to express his own appreciation of Balzac, through the voices of an aristocratic family named Guermantes, he had bridged the abyss between the critical and the creative, and was on the right road toward the object of his quest. With the sequence of papers most recently published, *Contre Sainte-Beuve*, the critic is proved to have been the real dilettante; and the man of the world, Sainte-Beuve, is left behind by the dedicated artist, Proust.

Dedication would not have been enough without technical mastery. A versatile and formidable mimic, starting out like many another novelist, he had mastered his medium through parody of his predecessors. The series reprinted in *Pastiches et mélanges* took off from an incident of the day which seems to have been truly Proustian in its purport, a scandal involving false diamonds. Proust, in recounting the hoax nine times, neatly hit off the styles of Balzac, Flaubert, the Goncourts, and other nineteenth-century men of letters. However, the climactic scene, a lavish reception dominated by Montesquiou, replete with genealogical parentheses and details of feminine attire, reflects the elaborate manner and the suspicious nature of Saint-Simon. At this point, Proust was ready to emerge with a style of his own—a style inheriting from symbolism, as Charles Bruneau has formulated it, "the search for novelty in substance and the concern for detail in form." In Proust's semi-isolation through some five years of writing, he managed to complete a projected trilogy. Since he encountered difficulties with publishers, the first volume, *Du côté de chez Swann*, was brought out at his own expense in 1913. During the first World War, which had intervened to delay further publication, he was constantly engaged in retouching, enlarging, and elaborating the unpublished residue. By 1922, when death overtook him still working at the novel, four component sub-novels had appeared. Three more, with a few gaps and rough edges, would round out the final version posthumously.

The cork-lined room in which he slept by day and worked abed at night, insulated from the noise of the boulevards and the pollen of the chestnut trees, has become a symbol of his regimen, both as a chronic invalid and as an artistic recluse. It becomes less arcane when we are reminded that Proust was adopting a mode of insulation already used by his lyrical friend, the Comtesse de Noailles, as well as by the boulevard playwright, Henry Bernstein. But it assumes deeper meaning when we recall the narrator tossing about on his pillow at Combray, and reviewing the long succession of bedrooms in which he has tried to sleep: country houses, city apartments, grand hotels, sanatoria, all of them prolongations of the womb. In the dedicatory epistle to *Les Plaisirs et les jours*, he compares his sick-chamber to Noah's ark, and his protective mother to the departing dove. "Then I understood that Noah could never see the world so well as from the ark, even though it was claustral and darkness covered the earth," Proust confessed, in a sentence which Gide would underline as prophetic. In *Jean Santeuil* there is a revealing episode where the protagonist quarrels with his parents over his choice of companions. Throwing a tantrum, he breaks their present to him, a piece of Venetian glass. Shamed before the servants, he hides in a wardrobe, whence he emerges contrite and ludicrous; for somehow an old cloak of his mother's has draped itself around him.

When he bespeaks her forgiveness, she replies: "This will be, as at the temple, the symbol of indestructible union." Though there has been no prior indication of Madame Santeuil's religion, she is evidently alluding here to the synagogue and to the rite that concludes the orthodox Jewish marriage ceremony, when the bridegroom seals the occasion by crunching glass underfoot, presumably to commemorate the destruction of the Temple. In other

words, she is affirming a psychic bond which is familial to the point
of becoming quasi-conjugal. What is even more revealing, both
this quarrel and this reconciliation really happened; and it was
Proust's mother who introduced the wedding allusion, in a letter
responding to her son's written apology. His impulsive response to
another's misfortune was even more expressive of the more than
filial emotion that charges *A la recherche du temps perdu*. One day
he picked up the *Figaro* and read that a casual acquaintance, with
whom he had lately exchanged paternal condolences, in a sudden
fit of madness, had murdered his mother. Through a bizarre coincidence, the case was being handled by a police investigator named
Proust. Marcel Proust was prompted to dash off a soul-searching
and self-accusing essay, which *Le Figaro* printed under the heading,
Sentiments filiaux d'un parricide. When he reprinted it in *Pastiches et mélanges*, for some reason he left out his namesake.

His theme might almost have been Oscar Wilde's: "Each man
kills the thing he loves." And Proust's variations on it give a serious inflection to Wilde's epigrammatic observation that women,
alas, become like their mothers, while men, alas, do not. The illustrations of filial sentiment are drawn from the very archetypes of
tragedy: the primordial instance of Oedipus, the conflict of parent
and offspring in *King Lear*, the patricide of *The Brothers Karamazov*, and the mute reproach of the little princess dying from child-
birth in *War and Peace*. Their common sorrow could be generalized further by comparing Tolstoy's heroine to the mistress
murdered by her lover, in Zola's *Bête humaine*, with *pourquoi* on
her lips. Why this suffering? Who is guilty? "What have you done
to me?" The question incites a questioning final paragraph, which
Proust appended shortly before the article went to press. One does
not need to be a murderer to accuse one's self of matricide. One
need only watch the daily attrition—and Proust is unsparingly detailed in his description—of those who love us and those to whom
we bring so little but anxiety. Not so eventful nor so melodramatic
as the classic catastrophes, but more universally tragic, is the grind-
ing business from day to day of aging, *vieillissement*, the tragedy
of time. We, who grow up while our parents grow old, share a
universal guilt. It is just as well that we cannot foresee the particular outcome; but even Don Quixote had his lucid intervals,
when the dream faded in the face of reality.

> With the majority of men so tragic a vision, assuming that
> they can rise to it, is very quickly effaced before the first
> rays of the joy of living. But what joy, what reason for liv-
> ing, what life can resist that vision? Between it and joy,

Proust ends by asking, and his answer is rhetorically implicit,

> which is true, which is the truth?

2. *The Telescope*

The strategic retreat that enabled Proust to accomplish his long-
deferred purpose was not so much a withdrawal from the world as
a sublimation of it within his work. His ark was grounded upon a
convenient beach, whither his close friends could bring an occasional olive branch in the guise of a recollected detail or a shared
anecdote, pertinent scraps of human documentation for the labor
at hand. In a letter to Hahn, he quoted the well-known but seldom
tested maxim of Pascal: "All men's ills result from their not being
able to shut themselves up in their chambers." Proust was unable
to shut out his illness; that was the price he had to pay for his
necessary seclusion; but he could well afford to circumscribe an existence which was materially cushioned as well as psychologically
insulated. No writer, including Proust himself, has ever been in
quite so recumbent a position as the persona through whom he
speaks in his novel. The latter is addressed as Marcel once or
twice by his heroine, and uses the *je* as intensively as any narrator
has ever done; and yet, as Proust in person elsewhere insists, this
alter ego is not always *moi* in the autobiographical sense. Since we
are permitted to take a familiar tone with fictional characters, let
us call him by his Christian name, reserving the surname for the
author as author.

Marcel, we should notice, is about a decade younger than Proust,
and a good deal lazier in postponing his literary efforts. He is much
too sickly to undertake his military service, whereas we know that
Proust volunteered and served cheerfully. We also know that
Proust once fought a duel, with the display of courage appropriate
to such occasions. It is hard to think of Marcel, in spite of his
vague allusions, cutting so active a dash. Baldassare Silvande, the

protagonist of the very first tale in *Les Plaisirs et les jours*, happened, by no accident, to be a young prince on his deathbed. Granted that in nineteenth-century fiction the heroes of each succeeding generation seem to behave more passively than those of the last, the hero of Proust—if he may still be so designated—lies supine. However, his unheroic function may be said to have radically altered; and his intellectual curiosity may compensate, in large measure, for his physical inactivity. Since writing is his major activity, he is primarily the writer as writer. Secondarily, immobilized further by the illness that Proust has passed on to Marcel, he is more of a sufferer than an actor. He has been deliberately cast in a spectatorial role, a role which is usually intermediate between the author and his character. Here it becomes a gigantic incubus, subsisting on both.

Thus the observed and the observer come together at the point of observation. A precedent which readily comes to mind is that of another claustrophile writer, Nathaniel Hawthorne, who immured himself in his study for twelve years and wore the mask of "a spiritualized Paul Pry." Proust's narration, like Hawthorne's, is dependent—to an unseemly degree—upon eavesdropping. That could be rationalized on technical grounds, inasmuch as the author is committed to the first person, and the narrator has no other way of finding out what the reader must learn. But the device is too deeply intrinsic, with Proust, to be mere convention. Rather, it is his technique for a shocking revelation, a frame for his vision of sexual abnormality. As such, it occurs at a central point of *A la recherche du temps perdu*, when the horrified Marcel—whose outlook remains intransigently heterosexual—peers from a hidden staircase into the courtyard of the Hotel de Guermantes. It is anticipated in the first volume, when he peeks through a window at Montjouvain; and it is recapitulated in the last, with the most abysmal of coincidences. Moreover, it has been strikingly foreshadowed in an early tale, *Confession d'une jeune fille*. But there it was the guilt-ridden narrator who is spied upon by her mother, who in turn is literally shocked to death at seeing her daughter in the embrace of a lover. In his subsequent revelations, Proust would change the sexes and shift the part of the spy.

We do not need to consult the abnormal psychologists, or to diagnose this obsession as scoptophilia; nor should we condemn it out of hand, in the New Testament phrase, as lust of the eye. If Proust was so intensely—even morbidly—ocular, such a point of view can be more easily shared by most of us than some of the keener olfactory perceptions of Zola. That cork-lined chamber, sealed off as it was from the street, had to be nonetheless a room with a view. Cyril Connolly would have said, with facetious aptness, "a womb with a view." Marcel is undeniably a *voyeur*, in the sense that he invariably looks out, looks down, looks into situations; in the sense, too, that he looks on while others act. Stylistic studies have shown that the verbal combination, A *voit* B *agir*, is peculiarly characteristic of Proust. Characteristically, someone *sees* somebody else *do* something. This, of course, is the usual stance of the critic; and it is closely related to those qualities which make Proust so discerning an interpreter of the plastic arts. Painting and music were harmonized with poetry, in accordance with the synesthetic ideal of the symbolists, by his slight and youthful sequence of lyrics, *Portraits de peintres et de musiciens*. In his prose he exercises his pictorial gifts, not only in the portrayal of his subjects, but in the imagery with which he surrounds them.

Yet the visual approach is no less germane to scientific investigation than it is to artistic depiction; and when he is metaphorically illustrating his intentions and attitudes, his images habitually take the form of optical instruments and devices—such as the kinetoscope, precursor of the cinema, through which his earliest evocations seem to appear. One of his favorite metaphors may well have been borrowed from Bergson, for whom it connotes self-knowledge. Proust turns it around, and points it directly at the Bergsonian subject and object, when he speaks of "a telescope levelled at time." For, he explains to a correspondent, "the telescope brings out stars which are invisible to the naked eye, and I have tried . . . to bring to consciousness those unconscious phenomena, wholly forgotten, which are sometimes located far back in the past." Literary imaginations, ever since the seventeenth century, have been exhilarated and exalted by such analogies. Stimulated by an astronomy which reckoned in light-years, Proust's innovation was to extend the telescopic conception from the spatial to the temporal sphere. In cultivating a parallelism with science, he was serious, consistent, and far more experimental than Zola had ever been, precisely because the experimentation took place within his medium, instead of being superimposed from outside. Critical analogies with Einstein's relativistic physics came afterward.

The phrasing of Proust's collective title announces that this will be a research as well as a quest. *A la recherche du temps perdu!* The overtones of *recherche* range widely enough to touch upon Balzac's search for the absolute, *La Recherche de l'absolu*, along with Stendhal's pursuit of happiness, *La Recherche pour le bonheur*. Given the unending difficulties of translation, Proust was fortunate in his fluent and sensitive British translator, C. K. Scott Moncrieff; but, faced with those inevitable and painful moments when translators must choose between beauty and fidelity, Scott Moncrieff invariably tended to make the esthete's—or the philanderer's—choice. He made an extremely misleading decision, which Proust lived long enough to agonize over, when he retitled the work with an inappropriate echo of Shakespearean lyricism, *Remembrance of Things Past*. Now "past"—the participle and the substantive agree both in French and in English—is unquestionably a key-word with Proust. He had thought of such titles as *Le Voyageur du passé*, *Les Stalactites du passé*, and *Le Passé prorogé*. Both "remembrance" and "things" are relevant concepts likewise. But *le temps*, with its ever-widening penumbra of vital meanings, should dominate; the word itself is sounded at the beginning and at the end; and *perdu* should complete the paradox of attempting to retrieve the irretrievable. Proust's first working-title was, purely and simply, *Le Temps perdu.*

His bewildered letter to Scott Moncrieff stresses the ambiguity of time wasted. *Making Up for Lost Time* would be a closer equivalent to his idea, and *An Experiment with Time* would not be so out of key as the prevailing makeshift. His original framework was chronological. He conceived his three projected parts as three successive ages: the Age of Names, the Age of Words, and the Age of Things. His personal development, from infancy to maturity, paralleled his novelistic progression: from the romantic suggestiveness of place-names and baronial nomenclature, by way of the power that comes with control of language, toward an apprehension of reality. His generation had been taught, by the geographer Elisée Reclus, that geography is history in space as history is geography in time. Proust's final arrangement, more concretely than this threefold time-scheme, presents itself in topographical terms.

On the one hand, there is Swann's way, the neighboring path by the river Vivonne toward Méséglise-la-Vineuse and the estate at Tansonville, along the hawthorn lane to the gate in the lilac hedge. On the other hand, in the opposite direction, there is the Guermantes' way, a world apart. Its remote chateau seems half obscured, half lit by a nimbus of magic-lantern slides and story-books. Its ducal inhabitants, glimpsed at church occasionally, seem to have just stepped down from the stained-glass windows or from the tapestries of their medieval ancestors.

Between those alternatives, walks to be taken on Sunday morning by the family after mass at Combray, two ways of life—the bourgeois and the aristocratic—are permanently engraved upon the infantile sensibility. Marcel will encounter the same dichotomy elsewhere, though much less clearly in Paris. There the crowded conditions—not to mention the long arm of coincidence—oblige his family to rent an apartment in the Hôtel de Guermantes, the private house of the Duke in the Faubourg Saint-Germain, where the absence of storied feudal landmarks might have brought despair to the soul of Henry James. That is the second stage, a quixotic disenchantment with castles which turn out to be inns, and it presages the third stage, a synthesis. But the identical social pattern persists, wherever the locale. When Marcel visits the seacoast at Balbec, he observes that Rivebelle and Marcouville-l'Orgueilleuse are situated at the opposite ends of the bay, and that neither can quite view the other through the mist. The situation is precisely what it has been, for him, with the disjunct and contiguous worlds of Guermantes and Méséglise. Nor has Proust been the only observer to have noted this law of peninsular opposites. F. Scott Fitzgerald, in *The Great Gatsby*, chronicled a similar disengagement on Long Island in the 1920's, between the suburbs of East Egg and West Egg.

"The true paradises," Proust would come to admit, "are the ones that we have lost." Genius itself had been defined by Baudelaire as "l'enfance retrouvée à volonté," childhood sought and found again—in other words, as a controlled projection of nostalgia. The first impressions that Proust relays to us are calculated to project a telescopic view, through the pathos of distance toward the dim enchantments of tender years, all very far away and long ago. When his first subnovel, *Du côté de chez Swann*, made its first appearance, readers may well have associated it with a current tendency for novelists to reminisce about youth. Alain-Fournier's memorable evocation of *le domaine perdu*, the private realm of adolescence in *Le Grand Meaulnes*, appeared in the very same year. But Proust had farther-reaching examples to heed: in one of his letters, attesting that English and American writers had exerted the most powerful influence over him, he especially singled out George Eliot, and confided that two pages of *The Mill on the Floss* could make him weep. One can imagine Proust's suscepti- bilities responding with particular warmth to that sentence of George Eliot's which sets forth the effect of earliest surroundings upon the juvenescent consciousness, and offers a botanical illus- tration:

> And there is no better reason for preferring this elderberry bush than that it stirs an early memory—that it is no nov- elty in my life, speaking to me merely through my present sensibilities to form and colour, but the long companion of my existence, that wove itself into my joys when joys were vivid.

Matter is thus interwoven with memory, and material objects endow our lives with their attributes of continuity. Marcel had al- ready found his talisman, or he could not have conjured up his past so vividly; but it remains a secret, barely hinted at the close of his drowsy and insomniac prelude. There, having somehow passed through the deep well, we are momentarily allowed to touch the tea-cup to our lips and taste the *madeleine*. Proust would not have us forget that the name and shape of that little tea-cake are trace- able to the shells that pilgrims wore on their hats as badges of their vocation. Let us make no mistake; we are at the commencement of a religious pilgrimage. The book is richly mined with anticipa- tions we miss, in reading it for the first time and in looking forward, not backward. The flowers that will expand, in the long afterview, are still no more than shrivelled bits of paper. Our attention focuses on the child, upon the Wordsworthian vista of lost innocence and upon the Freudian omen of lurking corruption. The critical inci- dent has already been rehearsed in the opening pages of *Jean San- teuil* and elsewhere—in the arresting story, *La Fin de la jalousie*, whose hero in boyhood could not go to sleep until his mother, dressed and perfumed for the evening, stopped at his bedside and gave him a good-night kiss.

The need for that kiss, which Marcel compares to the host at communion, is the starting point for A la recherche du temps perdu. Waiting in bed while his mother is delayed by unexpected company downstairs, the child agonizes to a neurotic crisis. Finally she climbs the stairs and calms him, by installing herself in his room for the night and reading him to sleep with an idyll of George Sand. The father, though in his nightshirt he looks like a painted Abraham, is somewhat less than stern with his whimpering Isaac; while the grandmother shakes her head, and voices the fear that her grandchild will be spoiled by overprotective indulgence. Her criterion is always "le naturel"; she is in favor of more fresh air from the outset; and she is to be the moral barometer. As Marcel will retrospectively recognize, he has just experienced "a puberty of grief," which will lead him to the traumatic consequence of "an abdication of the will." In the transposed Confession d'une jeune fille, the young girl very pertinently confesses, "What distressed my mother was my lack of will power." The irony of Marcel's situation, in retrospect, is that the visitor who caused the agonizing delay happens to be the one person who might have fully sympathized with the child's anxieties. This, then, constitutes our oblique introduction to Charles Swann, that introspective dandy, our hero's hero, the link between Proust's two worlds.

Hence Swann's preliminary impact is dazzlingly unclear; the sound of his name is "almost mythological." He seems to be an elegant and intelligent man-about-town, vaguely a stock-broker, specifically a clubman, a fastidious connoisseur of paintings and women, whose middle-class Jewish antecedents have not hindered his acceptance into the highest circles of society, but who is rumored to have compromised that position by marrying a beautiful woman of doubtful repute. In the latter part of the first book, when their respective families have returned to Paris, Swann's daughter Gilberte will become Marcel's favored companion in their children's games at the Champs Elysées. Meanwhile, the gap is bridged by the novelette, Un Amour de Swann. It is a flashback, which could stand by itself, in the delicately analytic genre of Adolphe or even La Princesse de Clèves. Contextually, Swann's relationship with Odette de Crécy functions as an unheeded object-lesson for

Marcel's prospective involvement with Albertine Simonet. There will be the same possessiveness on the part of the lover, and the same elusiveness on the part of the mistress, engendering the same enigmas of jealousy. *Un Amour de Swann* would seem to be the residual outcome of an earlier plan for a more conventional novel, now inserted like an old-fashioned cameo into a redesigned setting.

Out of gossip, hearsay, and the occasional confidences of his third-person protagonist, the first-person narrator, Marcel, is apparently piecing together an episode which happened before he was born; and since Swann himself, more often than not, is perplexed by Odette's behavior, we feel that she is at least three removes from us. Through Swann's eyes, we catch our first glance at those two Parisian spheres which Marcel will later frequent *in propria persona*. Again it is a question of *deux côtés:* Odette's friends among the upper bohemians, the "little clan" presided over by the shrill and high-handed lion-huntress, Madame Verdurin; and Swann's friends from the Faubourg Saint-Germain, the fashionable circle whose brightest luminary is the young Princesse des Laumes, later to be idolized as the Duchesse de Guermantes. Here we are but a decade removed from the Second Empire. When Odette eludes Swann and he seeks her on the boulevards at night, scanning the ghostly faces of the prostitutes in the shadows, he is likened to Orpheus seeking Euridyce in the underworld. Classical though the simile may sound, it is actually mock-heroic; seemingly archetypal, it has a topical resonance; for the version of the myth in the immediate background is Offenbach's operetta, *Orfée aux enfers,* and the scene vibrates to the discredited tinkling of the jaunty imperial cancan. Nana's apotheosis, from *cocotte* to goddess, is reversed with Odette.

The *nouvelle* breaks off with a shrug, as Swann realizes that he has wasted several years of his life, and his greatest love, upon an incompatible creature who has never quite suited—and never will suit—his taste. The reader is left to make the decisive connection, which links the novel at large with the interpolation, and provides a suitably ironic finale for Swann's romance. The glamorous Madame Swann, whom we have known mainly as Gilberte's mother, has become the very flower of the Parisian esthetic in the 1880's. Marcel is among those who eagerly stand and wait in the Bois de Boulogne for her carriage to pass by. One day he overhears from

other bystanders that, before her marriage, she was the notorious
Odette de Crécy. To learn that Swann has married Odette after
all is more of a shock of recognition for us than it is for Marcel,
since presumably he has not yet learned at that moment what we
already have from his foregoing narrative. *Du côté de chez Swann*
terminates with his efforts to recover an exquisite period-piece by
returning to his old station in the Avenue des Acacias and trying
to recollect his initial impression. But the place is different now
because the time is, if only because the carriages have been replaced
by automobiles. "The remembrance of a certain image is merely
the regret for a certain instant; and houses, roads, and avenues are
as fleeting, alas, as the years."

The effort at recapture has failed because it has been so deliberate. Marcel has not yet formulated the difference between voluntary and intuitive memory, though he has caught certain glimpses
of how a casual sensation can set off a whole train of associations,
and how forgotten gardens can unfold in a cup of tea, like Japanese paper flowers. The first subnovel ends, as it should, with an
anticlimax, which nevertheless prepares the ground for the ultimate goal. Proust had not planned to use this passage as a peroration, endlessly suggestive though it may be; as an afterthought, he
lifted it from a somewhat earlier context in his manuscript. The
whole of A *la recherche du temps perdu* constituted, in his mind,
one single, continuous novel, broken up into volumes by mere ex-
pediency, and sectioned off in lengthy, irregular chapters. In fact,
he liked to think of it as one single, continuous sentence—a thought
which throws some light upon its meandering style. Considering
that *Du côté de chez Swann* would not have any sequel in print
for six years, he was fortunate to conclude it on this note of eloquent questioning. Its publication was signalized by a newspaper
interview, in which he elucidated his undertaking with references
to Balzac and Bergson. In utilizing the novel as an instrument for
exploring the unconscious in depth, Proust explained with a geometrical metaphor, he was proceeding from a two-dimensional to a
three-dimensional psychology.

The simple-minded distinction between flat and round characters, promulgated by E. M. Forster among many others, and so
completely outmoded by the Proustian technique, makes this explanation a little too simple. It is amplified, in *La Fugitive*, by dif-

ferentiating between the spatial and the temporal, as between a plane and a solid psychology. But, obviously, Proust's psycho-geometry was non-Euclidean, if not Einsteinian. It should be considered four-dimensional, like the weathered church of Saint-Hilaire, since time is of the essence, and since the result is a relativity of outlook. Proust instanced, to his interviewer, a railway train from which, as it curved on its track, the same village would appear to be now on one side and again on the other. A more congenial instance in the novel is the ride that Marcel takes with the country doctor; as they follow the winding road, the two steeples of near-by Martinville, together with a third farther on at Vieuvicq, seem to be continually changing places; and Marcel is moved to sketch an essay about them. If the passing of time can thus be charted by our divagations through space, then we may infer from this working model that human beings reveal themselves by acting differently under differing circumstances. They behave with unvarying consistency only in caricature, or upon the comic stage, or in that society column—the *chronique* for *Le Figaro*—where Proust was fond of describing types by allusion to the masks of the *commedia dell'arte*.

Already, as a schoolboy of seventeen, he had announced to his schoolmate, Robert Dreyfus, "I don't believe that a type is a character." If it tends to become one, that is because our contacts with others are comparatively few and far between, and we fill in the interstices by association of ideas. Yet, confronted with any act, we cannot be sure of its motivation; and the adolescent Proust exemplifies by naming two actors whose interpretations of Molière's *Misanthrope* were diametrically opposed. The Proustian theory of characterization, like all important discoveries, was not without precedents. Aristotle had allowed for the workings of a consistent inconsistency. Montaigne had expatiated upon the inconstancy of our actions. Jules Michelet, correlating time with historiography, and recalling that Rembrandt had painted thirty varying portraits of one sitter, had exclaimed: "How many men in a man!" Similarly, contemplating an action, Proust would discern an unlimited number of motives; consequently, each of his leading sitters has a diversified gallery of portrayals. Character was monolithic, in early fiction, and motive was self-evident. The eighteenth century varied the formula by occasional concealment and surprise, when seemingly good characters turned out to be unexpectedly bad and *vice versa*. Jane Austen based her art on such misapprehensions, and *Pride and Prejudice* was written to show how misleading first impressions could be. The striking exception had been Diderot's *Neveu de Rameau*, whose inner contradictions dramatized the growth of psychic self-consciousness.

"If reason be judge," wrote Herman Melville in *The Confidence-Man*, "no writer has produced such inconsistent characters as nature herself has." But it was undoubtedly Henry James who made the closest anticipation to Proust. The two careers just overlapped enough for some degree of mutual awareness. Proust could admire *What Maisie Knew* for taking a little girl as its center of consciousness, while James—when Edith Wharton introduced him to *Du côté de chez Swann*—could glowingly respond to the French counterpart of his own stylistic endeavors. In the notes for his unfinished *Ivory Tower*, he seems indeed to be adumbrating Proust when he refers to "my law of successive Aspects." Proust himself acknowledged a standing debt to Balzac's *retour des personnages*: that trick of reintroduction, from book to book, of old characters in new lights, which bring out their ever-changing aspects. But Balzac, rather more the sociologist than the psychologist, remained the omniscient narrator. There are moments when Marcel sighs for the prerogatives he has relinquished, and wishes he could look into the heart of his heroine, like Stendhal's story-telling Canon of Padua, who penetrated to the innermost thoughts of the personages in *La Chartreuse de Parme*. Yet Albertine's emotions and habits mystify him, just as Odette's have mystified Swann. For that matter, Madame Swann beheld by Marcel has quite another aspect from Odette courted by Swann; and we must try to reconcile these contradictory figures with the dubious lady in pink, whom Marcel surprises with his gay bachelor uncle. Further incarnations will be reported by other witnesses, as we move from Proust's theory to his practice.

From Bergson, he had acquired a suspicion of the spatializing intellect, which distorts the instinctive flow of experience by turning fluid concreteness into static abstractions. Bergson's *Introduction à la métaphysique* had compared the metaphysician's viewpoint with that of the novelist. Any conception of character, viewed from outside, must be relative, no more than a fractional sum of the traits observed. Only by complete identification with the character can the narrator, or the philosopher, achieve the absolute. This illuminates the autobiographical compulsion, which not only throws Proust back upon himself absolutely, but is constantly sifting and qualifying his relativistic attitude toward others. All psychologizing in literature must be projected through the author's ego. He may subject it to discipline, with Pascal: "Le moi est haïssable." Or else he may seek estrangement, with Rimbaud: "Je est un autre." But he can never escape from the purview of self. Proust had the strength to accept and explore the conditions of this confinement. Hence he was able to make a searching inquiry out of what, to such gifted precursors as Chateaubriand, had been a passing insight: "The only heart one paints well is one's own, while attaching it to someone else, and indeed the greater part of genius is composed of memories." Truly, Virginia Woolf was warranted in declaring that human nature had changed around 1910. Not that it actually had, any more than sunsets had altered when Monet began to paint them. The change was Proust's perception of character.

3. The Microscope

The cherished sonata by Vinteuil, which furnishes a musical theme for the love of Swann and Odette, suggests a paradigm for the temporal structure of A la recherche du temps perdu. Proust was so little concerned with the articulation of his seven subnovels, which came out in two or three volumes apiece, that—for ulterior reasons —he printed the first part of Sodome et Gomorrhe with the last part of Le Côté des Guermantes. But he was deeply concerned with locales and seasons, and with the flow of associations that bound them together in the mind. His first and second subtitles seem to indicate two themes, which are being singly introduced, to be intermingled by further development. The second continues the first: Du côté de chez Swann moves from Combray to Paris, A l'ombre des jeunes filles en fleurs from Paris to Balbec. Emphasis falls on the countryside in the one, and upon the seaside in the other, as contrasted with the bustling and disillusioning city, which we mainly glimpse through parks and drawing-rooms or dining-rooms, where hints are dropped about the best shops for comestibles and luxury articles. Vacations seem to last indefinitely. Except for the servants, few of the characters ever seem to work. The basis of human relations, which is exchange with Balzac and production with Zola, is leisure with Proust.

Through the enamored eyes of Marcel, as infant and adolescent, we visualize the awakening idyll. Landscapes—those dreamy walks at Combray, the family, the figure of Swann, the romantic aura of Guermantes in the background. And seascapes—the Grand Hotel at Balbec, the grandmother, Albertine and those blooming girls on the beach, new acquaintances vaguely related to others that we have already met or shall soon be meeting. These first encounters, with their special enchantment and indelible imprint, are presented through a pair of subnovels, poetic in tone and philosophic in mood. A certain amount of Bergsonian exposition makes it explicit that this will be a novelistic experiment. There is more description than narration, and much less illustration than commentary. We seem to be confronting a sequence of essays and memoirs, rather than the usual sort of story. It is as if we were engaged in playing chess by mail, and going through correspondence after each move. Though Proust's ultimate concern is with recollection, here he is creating expectation, looking back at the budding consciousness that is looking forward; and, of course, the spells that are woven here will be exorcised by disenchantments. Later on, he would conceive his work as a conflation of *The Thousand and One Nights* and *The Memoirs of Saint-Simon*. To be growing up was to be moving from the arabesque of the former toward the acumen of the latter.

"Art," Proust wrote to the English friend whose pen-name was Stephen Hudson, "is a perpetual sacrifice of sentiment to truth." We are still in the sentimental stages. Boyish illusions, now under careful cultivation, will give way to grown-up disillusionment, as innocence yields to experience. Already this is beginning to happen, whenever some new aspect of character is disclosed and reality undercuts an ideal. Thus the gallant Marquis de Saint-Loup, who prefers brains to breeding, stands in danger of being blackballed from the Jockey Club because of his Dreyfusard romance with a capricious young Jewish actress of the *avant-garde*, Rachel. A diamond necklace seems to him scarcely worthy of her, though—when

Marcel is introduced to her—the narrator recognizes that he himself had once refused her favors at twenty francs in a house of prostitution. One man's passion is another's allergy. Ensnared like
Swann, or like Saint-Loup, Marcel will find that his friends have
no sympathy with his affections. Meanwhile, he can clear-sightedly
note that Saint-Loup's infatuation proceeds from "the golden gates
of the land of dreams." Proust does not quite invoke our classical
emblems; but he will concede that Marcel's enamorment with the
Guermantes has passed through "the golden gate of imagination,"
in contradistinction to those testing truths which must pass through
"the low and shameful gate of experience." The subjectivity of love
is summed up in the most succinct of the many maxims that crystallize his narrative: "Laissons les jolies femmes aux hommes sans
imagination." Imagination will supply its own attractions.

His schoolmates invented a verb, *proustifier*, to denote the florid
atmosphere of elaborate ceremony and exaggerated compliment
with which he managed to clothe the simplest transaction. There
are moments, long moments, particularly during the earlier volumes, when we may close the book and ask ourselves whether it is
not too Proustified—whether things are not all too overidealized,
too wonderful, too naïve. But, patience! The similarity with Henry
James or George Meredith is on the surface; it does not go very
deep because they glided over the depths that Proust would plumb;
there is more of a kinship with Jonathan Swift, who both magnified
and belittled mankind. Proust took such pains to build castles in
the sky, precisely, so that he could bring them down to earth and
demolish them. The metaphor of the telescope is appropriate for
the distant approach, the faraway view; it will not do for closer
observation, unless perchance we imagine him peering through the
wrong end. He went out of his way to affirm expressly that his
instrument was not a microscope. Yet he might well have claimed
the advantage that Hawthorne saw in works of medieval art: "They
combine the telescope and the microscope." The resourceful artist,
as Flaubert foresaw, would use each for its distinctive purpose:
"Everything depends on the word, the circumlocution, the lens one
uses—whether it be a telescope or a microscope."

As we advance through Proust's novel, the rarefied becomes
familiar and the remote comes under close scrutiny, under the kind
of analysis that can only be described as microscopic—and he does

not altogether avoid the comparison. The outlook shifts from the psychological to the sociological; the mode is not so lyrical or impressionistic as it is satirical and increasingly dramatic; the monologue branches out into dialogue. In contrast to Marcel's youthful reveries and reflections, we have an increasing number of conversations and drawing-room scenes designed to bring out personality. "The more we read of Proust," said Edith Wharton, "the more we see that his strength is the strength of tradition." He pokes fun at the self-appointed society novelist, who stands in the corner at a reception, squints through his monocle, and murmurs fiercely: "I am observing." So much for Paul Bourget! But what of Balzac? It was not for nothing that the *Comédie humaine* had formed the foundation of Jean Santeuil's avid reading, or the means by which Proust, in counter-attacking Sainte-Beuve, had found his way back from criticism to fiction. It is in *Contre Sainte-Beuve* that a Monsieur de Guermantes makes his first appearance, extolling Balzac; in *A la recherche du temps perdu* that enthusiasm is transferred to the Duke's brother, the Baron de Charlus; and when the Baron admires "such grand frescoes as the series of *Illusions perdues*" and *Splendeurs et misères des courtisanes*, his very words are the almost literal echoes of Proust's own in his correspondence.

When Marcel's importunate Jewish friend, Albert Bloch, asks him a financial question about his charming aristocratic friend, Robert de Saint-Loup, Bloch professes to be interested "from a Balzacian point of view." When Marcel asks Saint-Loup a similar question about his aunt, the Duchesse de Guermantes, Marcel characterizes his own point of view as Balzacian. The precedent is cited more and more, as Proust hits his narrative stride; he becomes less and less the amateur experimentalist and more and more the professional novelist in the grand manner, less the disciple of Bergson and more the heir of Balzac and the realists. This means that, temporarily, he abandons his quest for self-knowledge in favor of worldly wisdom and of that awareness of status which is known, to unsympathetic outsiders, as snobbery. The very word *snob*, with its intonation of looking down one's nose, happens to be an Anglicism in French; and thence it begins with certain snobbish overtones of Anglophilia; but if we push it back to its English origins, it designates the humble trade of a shoemaker's apprentice. The definition given in Johnson's dictionary, "one who meanly admires mean things," is almost synonymous with Flaubert's conception of the bourgeois, defined as "quiconque pense bassement."

As a pejorative epithet, the term had been used at Cambridge University to distinguish townsmen from gownsmen. It was the Cantabrigian alumnus, Thackeray, notably in A *Book of Snobs, by One of Themselves,* who adapted it to literary usage. Proust accords with the author of the *Newcomes* in assuming that snobs are would-be gentlemen, bourgeoisie who ape the nobility. But Thackeray's satire assumes that Judy O'Grady, whatever her pretensions and affectations, will never be as good as the Colonel's lady. Proust's implies not merely that they are sisters under the skin, but that the humbler may well be the morally superior. Hence one of his noblest characters, the trustworthy and omnicompetent servant, Françoise, significantly confuses *dame du monde* with *demi-mondaine.* It may be a further source of confusion that snob, as employed today, would seem to signify one who looks down at his alleged inferiors rather than up at his pretended betters. But this would merely demonstrate how securely the *arrivistes* of the nineteenth century have arrived in the twentieth. Furthermore, where everyone is climbing, there are bound to be setbacks and comedowns. The rise and fall of composers' reputations are reported by Proust like news from the stock-market. Conversely, if the arts are appraised by pecuniary standards, shares of stock are depicted esthetically; their engraving is comparable to the tracery of Gothic cathedrals; and Marcel's father is complimented upon the composition of his portfolio as if it were a collection of prints.

Proust invites the scientific observer—the botanist or entomologist or ichthyologist of souls—to study the patterns of habit and conformation and emulation among the strange breeds he has microscopically analyzed. Such a study was made by Thorstein Veblen, under the accelerated circumstances of American society; and there is much in his *Theory of the Leisure Class* which applies to the Proustian situation, with due allowance for the displacement of the decaying nobility by the newly rich. And yet, Proust argues with himself, if a sociologist could enter the mind of a snob, instead of viewing it from without, he would apprehend the blossoming of a whole social springtime. His image is suggestively redolent of fresh flowers and renewed juvenescence. That state of mind is what he liked to call "the poetry of snobbery," a poetry

dependent on the suggestiveness of names and especially their historic significance. Proust acknowledged this appeal in a journalistic
prose-poem dedicated "To a Snob," who might have been Montesquiou or himself. There he drew the picture of a soul embellished
with heraldic devices, a garden cultivated with genealogical trees.
To such a sensibility, a mere visiting-card could conjure up the
Crusades. The *Almanach de Gotha* was more than a European
social register; it was a glorious compendium of ancestral history.
"Your dream consolidates the present with the past," Proust tells
his snob. Thus it fits in with his enlarging purpose.

That prince of intellectual snobs, Paul Valéry, in a note of homage to Proust, refines his poetic conception of snobbishness into a
system of symbols. Society is seen as a concourse of abstractions
representing its values—money, beauty, politics, elegance, letters,
birth. Since its fallible representatives do not always live up to their
abstract roles, "this combination is marvellously propitious to the
designs of a subtle novelist." Friends were continually asking
Proust what Bloch asks Marcel in the subtle novel: "Tell me, are
you a snob?" The query reflects upon the questioner; for, according to one of Proust's observations, snobs are particularly sensitive
to the presence of snobs; most of us are extraordinarily quick to
perceive and condemn our own vices, when they are displayed by
others. Proust, to those who queried him on the subject, made
some tersely ambivalent disclaimers. He protested to Madame
Sert that some of his best friends were princes and dukes, while
others, perhaps more distinguished, included a valet and a chauffeur—rather an equivocal protestation, in the light of what we have
since been hearing about his intimate friendships. Yet he was able
to foresee unlikely combinations, even as he could resolve evident
contradictions; and in the affected minor poet, Legrandin, he presents a personage who is both a parlor socialist and a social climber.

Marcel's climb seems to be an easy one, not altogether accounted
for by what we are shown of his talent and charm; but that impression may be the result of another virtue, Proust's modesty. At
this stage of his initiation, Marcel confides quixotically, he knows
more of books than of men, more of literature than of the world.
Literature was his passport to society, wayward though his pursuit
of it may have been. Even in his *Figaro* articles, he could not
chronicle the salon of the Countess Potocka without mentioning

the rival assemblies of the Princesse de Cadignan in Balzac and the Duchesse de Sanseverina in Stendhal. His bookish preparation, blended with all the picturesque connotations of the Guermantes' way, had led him to approach the Faubourg Saint-Germain as if it were a spiritual state. The rarefaction of its titles and perquisites was sealed by the fact that they did not legally exist under the Republic. The charmed circles were further delimited by their allegiance to the legitimate dynasty of the Bourbon and the succeeding pretenders of Orléans. The Bonapartes had been the merest interlopers; Empire furniture was in bad taste; and history had consistently taken the wrong turn ever since the eighteenth century. At the gates of this legendary realm, calling the wrong turns, we encounter the Marquis de Norpois, Marcel's father's chief at the Ministry of Foreign Affairs. A traditionalist who has deigned to accept a government post, the past master of forms and protocols and clichés, he enunciates the formal criteria that will be called into question. If he is comparable to Count Mosca, as an insertion proposes, Stendhal's politician is admittedly "more intelligent, less pedantic."

The fabulous house of Guermantes makes itself manifest through the magic-lantern slides of its devotee, trailing clouds of romantic glory. Marcel fondly lingers over its pedigree and heraldry, its royal marriages and forfeited domains. The line embodies the oldest blood in France, and Proust took care to christen it after a long extinct duchy. The Duchess Oriane, eighteenth of her name, is its purest cynosure, since she is a Guermantes on both sides. Her impact on Marcel is a Stendhalian crystallization, a filial infatuation with an older woman, a Platonic devotion which he relays to the reader, compulsively sharing his own responses to her taste in dress, her style of wit, her air of perfect assurance on all occasions. Surely she resembles an epic goddess, condescending to interest herself in the lives of mortals, and exhibiting the birdlike beauty of an ornithomorphic deity. We first envision her formally, surrounded by her magnificent compeers, attending a benefit performance at the Opéra. The true operatic spectacle is not on the stage but in the boxes, a convocation of sea-gods and goddesses. The scene is the Opéra-Comique, in one of Proust's versions; and, as Marcel gets acquainted with the Guermantes, they will recall to him the Second Empire comic-opera manner of Meilhac and Halévy. The well-weathered moral, as Saint-Loup self-critically repeats it, is *sic transit gloria mundi*.

Marcel likes to think of his patricians as the sculptured apostles in the Sainte-Chapelle. Alas, they bear a closer resemblance to the dethroned kings in *Candide*. It is by design that they are given this brilliantly theatrical presentation. Finding such façades too beautiful to be real, we soon begin to suspect hypocrisies, mysteries unprobed, appearances precariously kept up. In a letter to Prince Antoine Bibesco, apologizing for the fashionable frivolity of his own existence in 1903, Proust inserted two Emersonian sentences in English: "This is the apparent life." "The real life is underneath all this." Taking up—and being taken up by—the apparent life, Marcel ascends the hierarchy of the salons. He is first received by an acquaintance of his grandmother's re-encountered at Balbec, a dowdy elderly bluestocking and a déclassé Guermantes, the Marquise de Villeparisis. Abetted by the coincidence that the Duc de Guermantes is now his family's Parisian landlord, he is soon being invited to their select parties, and even casually dropping in on them. On one such occasion, his fellow visitor is their close friend and his old idol, Charles Swann. Their host and hostess, it appears, are going out to dinner. Though the Duke is hungry and impatient to leave, he chats with them affably while he is waiting for the Duchess to complete her toilette. Finally, she makes her resplendent entrance, in a new red velvet evening gown.

Swann is not his urbane and sprightly self. He seems to be uncharacteristically haggard; the Dreyfus case is opening a rift between him and his royalist friends; and he is becoming more conscious of his own ancestry, an older and stranger lineage than the Guermantes. Rallied by Oriane about his plans for the following season, good manners desert him for the nonce, and he suddenly blurts out the verdict he has just received from his doctor. He cannot plan more diversions; he has less than a year to live. But the carriage is ready, and nothing in the fair-weather code of the Guermantes has taught them how to meet a heart-cry sympathetically. The best they can do is to overlook its burden of implication and hurry away, with a bland jest and a polite farewell. Raising her skirts to mount the carriage step, the Duchess reveals that she is wearing black slippers. That is the anticlimax, and it is countered immediately by the climax. The Duke finds time enough to send her back for slippers that will perfectly match her dress. The real life is underneath all that, underneath the apparent life; and Proust has laid it bare with this double stroke, the dying man's recognition of what he has lived for. Heretofore, the sphere of observation has been manners; hereafter it will be morals. Etiquette is discredited by ethics. What was so romantically built up by Proustification has been broken down by a process which a more realistic Proust termed "depoetization."

Marcel has traversed the distance from Swann's way to the Guermantes' way, in the path of his model whose world has just collapsed. *A la recherche du temps perdu* pivots around this crisis of snobbery, which terminates *Le Côté des Guermantes*. It does not terminate the gay round of pleasures for the Duke and the Duchess, which carry over into the subsequent volume. Their dinner-party precedes a grandiose reception, given by their cousins, the Prince and Princesse de Guermantes. Afterward, they are anticipating a masquerade. What could be more suitable for that ornamental couple? The Duke will impersonate Louis XI, and the Duchess will be Isabel of Bavaria. Arriving home to don their courtly finery, they are met with the news that a cousin has died, and their reaction again takes the form of moral deafness. Callously, they brush the announcement aside as an exaggeration. The obligations of mourning ought not to preclude their full enjoyment of a gala evening. However, Marcel by now has become disillusioned with other aspects of their personalities. They are accomplices in repartee, but not in love, he suspects. The Duchess, indeed, shows a certain complicity with the Duke's love affairs. Their childless marriage is botanically prefigured by the exotic and sterile plant in their courtyard window. Both are cavalierly inconsiderate with their domestics. The famous Guermantes wit is beginning to sound banal, and the Guermantes taste seems to have been copied from the moribund Swann.

With regard to the lack of consideration manifested in the treatment of Swann, there is a pertinent letter written by Proust in 1912 to a young man of eighteen, and recently printed—a reprimand quite as haughty and petulant as anything the Baron de Charlus would say to Marcel. Without attempting to read between the lines, we may notice that it makes a promise which seems to be fulfilled by the episode of *Les Souliers rouges de la Duchesse*.

"Some day I shall portray certain characters who will never know, even from a vulgar point of view, the true elegance of being dressed for a ball and renouncing it to keep a friend company." Proust could have found a literary source for such a situation near at hand in Balzac's *Père Goriot*, where, while the old man is dying, his daughters are dancing. But evidently the conjunction of circumstance touched some peculiarly resonant personal chord; for in his fledgling tale, *La Mort de Baldassare Silvande*, the heroine slips away from the hero's deathbed to take part in a ball. This must have mirrored a recurrent anxiety for Proust, when his illness shut him off from the world. Sheltered and indulged, he was haunted by the semi-invalid's worry that no one really appreciates his sufferings. They must all be off somewhere gayly waltzing. His special feeling for servants was grounded in his inordinate dependence upon them. He pays his debt of gratitude through the motherly Françoise, "standing in the little doorway to the corridor like the statue of a saint in its niche"—like Flaubert's long-suffering and saintly Félicité.

Proust knew himself well enough to observe that the sensibility of neurotics is a manifestation of egoism—often leading to the charge of insensitivity or indifference on the part of most others. There was no way out of that plight, except by transcending the ego, and extending those sympathies which the Guermantes had withheld from the ailing Swann. Their conduct, after all, had gracefully conformed to the mundane epigram of La Rochefoucauld on how bravely we bear the sufferings of our friends. Madame Verdurin, faithless to her faithful devotees, reaches heights of fortitude in disregarding their deaths. Swann's long-dead father has left a byword in Marcel's family, because he had mourned for his wife so cheerfully. He grieved for her often, he had attested, but only a little at a time. Marcel, who is not less morbidly sensitive, easily offended, or demanding in his friendships than Proust himself, feels bitterly insulted when he fancies that he has been ignored by Saint-Loup on horseback. A similar cut or slight is sulkily nursed by Jean Santeuil. For a snob, psychologically dependent on signs of recognition, a snub might be ironically just. Yet—more humanely speaking—to be excluded, when one has tried too hard to be included, marks a chilling failure of empathy. There is a critical digression in which Marcel, or Proust, discusses some of the dominant notes he discerns in particular novels, the figure in the carpet, the pattern that marks them distinctly as Hardy's or Tolstoy's or Dostoevsky's. With Stendhal, it is "a certain sentiment of altitude"; and with Proust, we might add, it is non-recognition. That is the "crisis of snobbery," the trial in which his worldlings are tested and are found wanting.

Le Côté des Guermantes is divided into two parts. In departure from the languorous rhythms of the preceding volumes, much of it takes place on two eventful days, culminating in a third which continues through the Guermantes' parties into *Sodome et Gomorrhe*. For Marcel it is a chronicle of theaters as well as salons, of a ripening friendship with Saint-Loup and an uneasy relationship with Charlus, and of various other attractions and distractions. What is most sincere and genuine, amid the pretence and hypocrisy, is attached to the portrayal of the grandmother. Both she and her daughter, Marcel's mother, were perspicuously inspired by Madame Proust. The grandmother closely resembles Proust's mother in old age, tragically but inevitably victimized by that universal *vieillissement* to which her son bore witness in *Sentiments filiaux d'un parricide*. To have watched his lifelong nurse becoming a fellow sufferer, in her turn, must have brought about some emotional transference within him. It must have been what finally gained him access to that negative capability, that sympathetic imagination, which enables great writers to place themselves in positions other than their own, to imagine exactly how someone else may feel. And only by such efforts have they succeeded in penetrating beyond the blank walls of callous indifference.

The grandmother has a flair like Madame Proust's, which comes out in her letters to her son, for marking all events with apt quotations from Madame de Sévigné—whose own finest letters, much as we may value them, were addressed to a notoriously ungrateful daughter. Marcel's mother inherits this flair, along with her mother's copy of Sévigné. The tragedy of the grandmother strikes in a vulgar setting and provokes a stoical agony. Walking along the Champs Elysées with her grandson, the old lady feels a stroke of heart disease coming on, and retires to a comfort station until it is over. Despite the levelling function of this convenience, its attendant is nicknamed "the Marquise" because she is so boastfully snobbish about the customers she condescends to admit. When

the stricken grandmother emerges, with a smile and a phrase from
Sévigné on her lips, she points out the telling analogy between
"the Marquise" and the Guermantes or the Verdurins. Her suffering, at the end of the first part, prepares the ground for Swann's
at the end of the second; and the obtuseness of the red-gowned
Duchess, along the Guermantes' way, is counterpoised by the insight of the dishevelled grandmother. Before she dies, the old
woman is subjected to a last Molièresque ordeal among the doctors.
One of them, an eminent specialist, scarcely has time for a consul-
tation because he is dining out; yet, like the Duchess going back
for her slippers, he does go back to his apartment in order to have
a decoration sewn on his new frock coat.

Amid the ensuing pages of gossip and scandal, the dead woman
drops out of sight and out of mind; but she re-arises, the ghost of
Marcel's inner life, to haunt the brief central passage of *Sodome et
Gomorrhe*, at the still midpoint of the whole novel, *Les Inter-
mittences du coeur*—"perhaps the greatest passage that Proust
ever wrote," in the opinion of Samuel Beckett. Voluntary memory
has hardly succeeded in keeping alive his sense of her. It is accidental association, via a return to the hotel room where he slept
when she was his companion at Balbec, which revives her presence.
She is no longer there to unbutton his shoes and kiss him good-
night, or in the next room to answer when he raps on the parti-
tion, but the delayed reaction is strong enough to restore his
feeling for continuity. The grandmother figures as the touchstone
of dignity and decency in *A la recherche du temps perdu*; and
when Marcel's maturing consciousness burgeons into a conscience,
it will be hers, "in whose heart I had always placed myself." In
the isolation and desolation of her immediate absence, he has
realized the import of the fatal diagnosis: "Each of us is truly
alone." What makes death so tragic is that perforce it must be a
solitary experience, almost as much so for the bereaved as for
the defunct. This is the realization of a truth which we spend
our lives evading, and which is brought home by the deaths of
those nearest to us, that deep truth which—as surviving parricides
—we attempt to efface by the shallower joys of living.

"That which you love always ends by deciding to leave you.
You are alone. You are always alone." So Léon-Paul Fargue, in echoing Proust's—or, at any rate, Marcel's—conclusion, reminds us of an

example we have still to ponder, the extreme example of Albertine. Thackeray had confirmed the bleak generalization, when the unhappy Beatrix cries out in *Henry Esmond*, "We are all alone, alone, alone!" Such loneliness is nothing less than the precondition of tragedy, as Shakespeare's Juliet comprehends when she takes the potion, soliloquizing: "My dismal scene I needs must act alone." The paradox, in Proust's case, was that an immersion in society could intensify that vision of solitude. Conversely, he would learn and teach that human relations could best be illuminated through introspection, through the exploration of the ego. The classic stratagem for setting one's world in perspective is to court it avidly and then to withdraw austerely. Did not Noah see everything more clairvoyantly from his ark? To have seen the best and retired, to have lived through the worst and survived, to be in the very midst of things yet out of them, to remain in touch while retaining one's reservations—what better role for the writer? When one correspondent hailed Proust as a social critic, he welcomed that designation as a title of honor. It may prove a more authentic title, in the long run, than many in the *Almanach de Gotha*.

4. *The Dostoevsky Side*

Afterthought is intrinsic to Proust's method, as well as to his theme. Working by slow accretion, revising and amplifying the later volumes while the earlier ones were being published, he did not live long enough to watch the impact of his darker second thoughts. His first two volumes, with their youthful reveries and idyllic enchantments, scarcely alerted the reader for a holocaust. The third, *Le Côté des Guermantes*, marked a maturation, shortened the distance between the two paths of childhood, and proved that Proust could use the naturalistic microscope as well as the symbolistic telescope. But it was not until the fourth, *Sodome et Gomorrhe*, which was published in the year of his death, that he opened up the lurid abysses over which his masqueraders were revelling. Consequently, his readers were likely to have been misled by their first impressions, precisely as Proust intended them to be, not to say bored by the naïve evocations of an adolescent romanticism. In a letter to the editor of *La Nouvelle Revue fran-çaise*, Jacques Rivière, we find him explaining that his thought would not be wholly unveiled until the end, which would reverse the tentative conclusion of *Du côté de chez Swann*. "That is just a stage, subjective and dilettantish in appearance, on the way to the most objective and affirmative of conclusions."

The glamor of names could be pedantically neutralized by his Curé, an amateur etymologist. Like his predecessors, but more self-consciously, Proust had created an illusion in order to destroy it; he had woven a veil of the apparent life in order to tear it away and reveal the real life underneath it. In order to show the passing of time, he needed time—which, of course, meant space, in terms of pages. He had to present familiar landmarks and recognizable visages before he could show how they had been changing through the years of development and decay. To demonstrate how misleading appearances could be, he had to bestrew the trail with false scents and misdirections, to lead his readers on with enticements and sidetrack them with surprises until they learned to expect the unexpected: by indirection to follow the "changement de direction dans les caractères." Once it was clear that certain values were false, it would be more urgent than ever to ascertain which values were true. "In the second half," Proust warned a friend, "my characters are the very opposite of what they were in the first half, and of what could be expected." Our initial glimpse of the Baron de Charlus could hardly have been more out of character, discolored as it was by a rumor from Combray, which was pleased to regard him as the lover of Madame Swann. As for the Duchess, Proust admitted in the candor of correspondence, that Marcel may have mistaken an old hen for a bird of paradise.

In a cryptic digression, amplifying—it would appear—the unprinted earlier version of *A l'ombre des jeunes filles en fleurs*, Proust comments on what he calls "the Dostoevsky side of the letters of Madame de Sévigné." It would seem that the French letter-writer depicted landscapes in much the same way as the Russian novelist portrayed characters. A later conversation between Marcel and Albertine more fully explains what that ill-assorted pair—the maternal Frenchwoman, the parricidal Russian—had in common. "Instead of presenting things in logical order—that is to say, be-

ginning from the cause—they show us first the effect, the illusion
that strikes us." But that is the side that strikes any passer-by, after
all. Dostoevsky penetrates more deeply, and differs from more conventional narrative, by registering further effects which lead more
directly to causes. Proust comes closer to the heart of the whole
quixotic process when he observes that novelists treat of war "in
reverse order, starting from beliefs and illusions, and correcting
them little by little, as Dostoevsky would tell the story of a life."
Thus Dostoevsky is given credit for that presentation of character,
in all its growth and change and fullness of potentialities and contradictions, which had been approximated only by certain highly
perceptive older writers, as in Henry James's law of aspects, and
which remained to be systematized by Proust.

The Proustian system affords a salient instance of what Mark
Schorer would term "technique as discovery." T. S. Eliot has
summed it up, for his own purposes, with his usual succinctness:

> What we know of other people
> Is only our memory of the moments
> During which we knew them. And they have changed since then.
> To pretend that they and we are the same
> Is a useful and convenient social convention
> Which must sometimes be broken. We must also remember
> That at every meeting, we are meeting a stranger.

Everyone else is a stranger to Marcel. Everything seems strange
except the memory of those moments. On the other hand, "Our
social personality is created by the thoughts of other people."
Obviously, the same people look different, when they are observed
from differing points of view. This is what makes Proust's psychology relativistic. Yet even when the observer continues to be
the same person, and assuming for the nonce that his own viewpoint does not change, he is confronted by conflicting evidence—
a discontinuous series of facts from which he must extrapolate a
personality. "Alas! Albertine was several persons." We are introduced to a character under one aspect; and then we discover another, quite unlike, and more often worse than better, since time
is so envious and calumniating, and since Marcel is growing up
and becoming more worldly and critical. Since these disillusioning
revelations frequently bring out some disparity between public

repute and private scandal, they account in some measure for the amount of effort Proust spends in overhearing and eavesdropping. Gossip plays a functional part in the drama. Marcel's epiphanies, those *moments privilègiés* of mystical insight, alternate with his *reconnaissances*, recognition-scenes where he puts two and two together and they add up to some irregular truth.

After the languid vacations and intermittent solitudes, three such recognitions came together in the course of a single crowded day, although the report on them spreads through two subnovels. That of the late afternoon, "The Red Slippers of the Duchess," is the culminating episode of *Le Côté des Guermantes*. That of the morning, the meeting between the Baron de Charlus and his homosexual accomplice, Jupien, is not recounted until the introductory chapter of *Sodome et Gomorrhe*. Proust did not actually delay this emergence of his "men-women"; for the introduction was published as *Sodome et Gomorrhe I* with the second volume of *Le Côté des Guermantes*, presumably to test the public's response to its problematic theme. The third *reconnaissance* occurs in the evening, between Swann and the Prince de Guermantes at the latter's reception; and the upshot, after so many undeceptions, is unexpectedly reassuring; but it continues the strain of *Le Côté des Guermantes* by completing Marcel's ascent to the innermost circles of the Faubourg Saint-Germain. The main direction of *Sodome et Gomorrhe*, as indicated by its sulphurous title, is more devious; it is a descent to the lowest circles of the underworld. After the two ways of the innocent countryside, braving the hazards that paralyzed Lot's wife, we turn our gaze to the cities of the plain.

The premonitory chapter builds up, through a welter of botanical and entomological illustrations, to a malediction in the manner of the Hebrew prophets, a cumulative sentence running over two pages, comprising a long review of the woes that have befallen the accursed breed of sodomites, with an anonymous but pointed allusion to the downfall of Oscar Wilde. It is clear, from an adumbration of this sentence in *Contre Sainte-Beuve*, that it was Proust's intention from the outset to open up discussion of a subject hitherto forbidden in modern literature of the West, except for prurient hints or sentimental euphemisms—plus the page or two in the all-inclusive *Comédie humaine* that made it M. de

Charlus' favorite reading. André Gide had fictionally broached a fuller discussion in *L'Immoraliste*, one of his early *récits*; he had privately and anonymously printed *Corydon*, where he offered an apologia; and he had frankly discussed his own experience in his autobiographical *Si le grain ne meurt*, which he confided to print —through a narrowly limited edition—two years before Proust made his contribution, and which became more generally available two years after *Sodome et Gomorrhe*. Having made his personal confession, which was surely an act of remarkable courage, Gide tended to think that Proust was somewhat evasive, in limiting himself to the third person and offering a purely fictional treatment. But Proust was writing fiction, not autobiography; and, unlike Gide, he was not an apologist for sexual inversion.

They could indeed have joined issue over Gide's war-cry, "Familles, je vous hais!" The biblical lamentations of *Sodome et Gomorrhe*, when we contrast them with the classical elegiacs of *Corydon*, are unrelentingly severe in their moral condemnation. Proust may well have been condemning himself, or else protesting too much, or taking what Rivière would describe as a kind of revenge. A recognition, according to Aristotle, is most effective when it coincides with a reversal. Both are involved in the attainder of homosexuality that sooner or later besmirches so many of Proust's dramatis personae. The searchlight of suspicion flashes through the darkness hither and yonder, bringing out unforeseen aspects of previously established acquaintances. Marcel's eyes, which may have been too naïvely shut, now open widely and suddenly. The principal object of this awakening also makes his impact visually. Together with Marcel, *le voyeur vu*, we feel the stare of the Baron de Charlus upon their first real encounter at Balbec. Charlus becomes the key figure in the drama because he aspires so high and sinks so low. He is both a celebrity and a celebrant, the dandy of dandies and the snob of snobs, arbiter of elegance and poet of society. His position, impeccable though it may be from a heraldic standpoint, is precarious because, to a more and more flagrant degree, he is the exponent, indeed the personification of the vice that Proust excoriates—and it is Proust who speaks of it, "for the convenience of language," as a vice.

All that has been upgraded by snobbery will be downgraded by pederasty. Seldom can such lofty pride have preceded so abysmal a fall. Again, there had been a precedent in Balzac: the degradation of the Baron Hulot in *La Cousine Bette*, straying from one heterosexual entanglement to another more sordid than the last, has been transposed by Proust to his minor key. No fuller portrait has ever been painted in literature of the homosexual temperament with its gifts and its weaknesses, its generous impulses and petty vanities, its unpredictable oscillations from the sensitive and affectionate to the histrionic and hysterical. Most paradoxical of all, as Proust examines it, is the cult of virility on the part of effeminacy; the tragedy of *vieillissement* is particularly poignant when an aging *tante* pursues an ephebic ideal; and perhaps the most tragic feature of the homosexual's destiny is that, to so many of his fellow men, he is predestined to seem slightly comic. The sorrows of M. de Charlus—his unlucky passion for the despicable violinist Morel, his crushing humiliation at the hands of the upstart Madame Verdurin, his vaunted duel which mockheroically fails to materialize—cannot but have a satirizing effect on all his poses and upon the pretensions he represents. Proust's attitude becomes overt in a gesture of ferocious comedy, which can be autobiographically traced to one of his own caprices, when the inarticulate Marcel replies to Charlus' toplofty reprimand by seizing and crushing and stamping upon his hat.

Sterility is a violation of nature because it impairs the family, which meant even more to Proust than it did to Zola. That bizarre plant which cannot be fertilized, because a rare insect cannot fly over the wall, bringing pollen from the tree in the courtyard, stands for the aristocratic degeneration of the whole tribe of Guermantes and particularly for the perversion of Charlus. Charlus is deemed perverse because the fulfillment of his impulse, whether it be natural or unnatural, is antisocial. It upsets so many norms, it demands so many conditions, that inherently it can never be satisfied. Can there be beauty in Sodom? So Dostoevsky averred in *The Brothers Karamazov*; but his vision of evil was not so specific. As for Gomorrah, following a hint from Alfred de Vigny, Proust equates it with Lesbos, and borrows his epigraph from the poem expressing Vigny's jealousy of a mistress whom he suspected of Sapphic deviations. Hence the two cities of the plain are specified by Proust as the respective capitals of male and female homosexuality. The apocalyptic horror of his concep-

tion is that the sexes, created to seek one another, should draw
apart, reversing the parable of Aristophanes in Plato's *Symposium*
and presaging the gradual extinction of the race. On the men in
Sodom and the women in Gomorrah, alike, the brimstone rains
down.

Now Proust confided to Gide that he too cherished some beautiful memories of youthful and graceful erotic relationships of this
kind, but that he had exhausted them in A *l'ombre des jeunes filles
en fleurs*. That would seem to imply a transposition, since the explicit
involvement there is Marcel's poetic infatuation with the band of
girls on the beach. Whenever he kisses Albertine's cheeks afterward, he embraces them all—or rather, he basks in a vicarious sunlight, imparting a highly sublimated emotion. This accords with
the oft-repeated suspicion that his heroine is a hero in travesty,
and with all the learned research and salacious conjecture attempting to show that Albertine was modelled on Proust's sometime
chauffeur and part-time secretary, Alfred Agostinelli. It is an interesting biographical question, the answer to which may throw
significant light on the success or failure of Proust's feminine
characterizations and on his somewhat negativistic treatment of
the love between man and woman. He is ready to admit that "the
invert imposes a masculine visage upon his heroines." But to argue
that we should read Albert, for Albertine, raises many more questions than it answers. It is tantamount to arguing that the most
indubitable female in the novel should nonetheless be denomi-
nated François. If we transpose the sex of Albertine, should we
not likewise assume that her most intimate friend, Andrée, was
similarly a masculine André?

That would reduce the dilemma to a sheer pederastic triangle
without the taint of Lesbian complications, and it would altogether eliminate the characteristically Proustian note of bisexual
rivalry. The jealousy of a heterosexual lover whose beloved had
mixed inclinations—that had been Swann's problem long before
it was Marcel's. Moreover, it had been the theme of Balzac's
story, later to be read by Swann's daughter, *La Fille aux yeux
d'or*. In his essay on Baudelaire, Proust underlines *Les Lesbiennes*
as the alternate title of *Les Fleurs du mal* and one of its major
themes. One of his own early sketches not reprinted, *Avant la
nuit*, is a dialogue about Lesbianism. Its representatives appear at

a much earlier stage than the pederasts, through the *reconnaissance* at Montjouvain and the notorious liaison between Mademoiselle Vinteuil and her vicious companion. Whether or not Albertine is inclined in that direction must, by the very nature of the inquiry, remain a moot point forever. But we must accept a character in a book as he or she is named and described and sexed by the author. There have been authors, like Pierre Loti, of whom it was rumored that their heroines were actually heroes in private life; but since the transformation was effected as a deliberate concession to the taste of most readers, what right have we to challenge it retroactively?

Proust normalized the emotions he was concerned with in order to bring out their universal implications. One of the most authoritative responses to Albertine is her acceptance by Pamela Hansford Johnson, who testifies that "she remains most beautifully a girl, in fact, a schoolgirl." If there had been no gossip, and if there were no Sainte-Beuve-like inquiries into Proust's life, there would be no issue as to her essential femininity. This does not exclude the inscrutable role that Proust's experience must have played in charging the portrayal with emotion, with "a tenderness at once filial and maternal." We are aware that Agostinelli, whom he confessed he loved best next to his mother, typed the manuscript of *Du côté de chez Swann*; that he had been Proust's driver on many an architectural tour; and that, having taken up aviation under the touching pseudonym of Marcel Swann, he was killed in a flying accident at the age of twenty-six. He is expressly memorialized in a footnote to one of his employer's Ruskinian articles. This may lend a note of special poignance to the interrelationship between Albertine and the chauffeur in the novel, an intimate of Morel who is eyed with disapproval by Marcel's mother, and to the imagery of flight by plane which more and more surrounds Albertine's relation with Marcel. Witness their drives to the airdrome together, their last visit to Versailles, and the symbol of the mythological aviator—is it Icarus?—who figures as "an image of liberty."

Those elusive images are played off against the more typical metaphor of a hermetically sealed compartment—as it were an ark, a vacuum jar, a cork-lined room—whose inmate is anxious both to shut out the world and to complain that he is shut off from it. Albertine's case affords not only a test for Proust's method of characterization but a demonstration of the precept, realized on the death of the grandmother, that each of us is truly alone. If the most intimate of human relations, the utmost possibility of mutual understanding, can be dissolved into a flux of fleeting sensations and contrasting impressions, can the self ever hope to know another? And, since the fragile ties of association and memory have their own ways of entangling and obscuring the data of consciousness, what indeed—we may echo Montaigne—can we know? Huysmans had complained that the so-called psychological novel rang the changes on one perennial query: will she or won't she? Proust would vary the tense of the formula: did she or didn't she? Antoine Bibesco once had a secret agreement with him to tell one another what others were saying about them behind their backs. Curious to hear about himself, Proust could not bear to repeat anything to Bibesco. Though the unilateral pact was a failure, it is not without relevance for the novel.

Proust turns the psychology of love into a sort of epistemological inquest, which he pushes to the point of solipsism. Who is real? What is truth? "C'est vrai?" becomes a query, not an assertion. Never was the rift wider between transparent selfhood and opaque otherness. "The sole reality" is "what one thinks." Marcel's preoccupation with Albertine, through the heavily augmented and posthumously published volumes of *La Prisonnière* and *La Fugitive*,—Proust had thought of them as *Sodome et Gomorrhe III*—constitutes a controlled experiment on her and on himself. The experimental conditions, under which he exercises his green-eyed despotism over his captive, are curiously arbitrary and have raised eyebrows in readers, pausing to wonder how such cohabitation could have been arranged with *une jeune fille bien élevée*. But the notion of *un jeune homme* would seem to fit even more awkwardly into the contextual circumstances. The many conflicting aspects of Albertine that manifest themselves may be roughly organized into two antithetical portraits, and may be judged by the principle that condemns Gomorrhe as contrasted with the girlish freshness of Balbec. The narrator, who is not above instancing Sherlock Holmes, all but compromises himself by the spying and prying and cross-examining that he employs to collect his evidence. Like Swann with Odette, Marcel takes the part of a collector, lodging his mistress in his father's tapestried chamber, showering her with the most extravagant presents, dressing her in Liberty and Fortuny silks, promising her a pianola, a yacht, a Rolls-Royce, even marriage.

His ardor, like his predecessor's, is a collector's zeal, a manifestation of the sense of property. No wonder he can only feel that he possesses his object when he watches her sleep, "la regarder dormir," when she is unconscious. One wonders whether, in spite of his lover's protestations, he ever really wanted to understand her own thoughts and feelings. "That the jealous will never understand," Dostoevsky had said. Whatever she says is scrutinized as an equivocation, while unquestioningly he entertains the worst reports about her. Every day his affection diminishes, bringing him much pain but little joy. Love, he concludes at one stage, is an expensive mechanical toy. Happiness is, in Leonardo's phrase, *una cosa mentale*, a state of mind which may not have much to do with rational reality. "About Albertine, I felt I would never find out anything, that I could never resolve the indiscriminate profusion of actual details and misleading facts, and that it would always be so to the very end, unless she were imprisoned—but prisoners escape." The opening of the window through which she escapes is as symbolic a liberation as the slamming of the door in Ibsen's *Doll's House*. It should let some fresh air into this atmosphere of asthmatic suffocation. However, we cannot escape with Albertine. We must stay within the solitary brain of the real prisoner, Marcel. Nothing can set him free from his predicament.

Even after he hears the news of her accidental death, he goes on tormenting himself about her, like Petrarch writing sonnets to a posthumous Laura. Albertine's existence is reduced so utterly to her imprint upon Marcel's mind that a mistaken signature on a telegram can, until it is corrected, momentarily revive her. She is a very Dulcinea in her evanescence and ambiguity. Lacking the faith of Dulcinea's champion, Marcel might be more relevantly compared to the Curious Impertinent of Cervantes, the husband whose consuming jealousy drove his faithful wife to infidelity. We might also recall the uncertain couple in Joyce's *nouvelle*, "The Dead," and their apprehension of those buried lives which the still living can never fathom. The completely subjective treatment of Albertine and the menace of Gomorrah, in all its tormented lyricism, are balanced by the satiric assault upon Sodom and the objectified depiction of the degraded Charlus, which has retrospectively tainted Marcel's picture of the Guermantes. From society as they represent it, he retreats to his metaphysical solitude, and A la recherche du temps perdu reaches its moral nadir with the passing of Albertine. Yet that negation, however inhumane, is not absolute; nothing is, with Proust. From his sound-proof cell, he makes occasional sorties into the arena of social criticism, with particular reference to the Dreyfus affair.

"And it came to pass," announces the book of Genesis, "when God destroyed the cities of the plain, that God remembered Abraham." The themes of homosexuality and anti-Semitism counterpoint one another in A la recherche du temps perdu. Inverts are constantly being compared with Jews as an unpopular minority, a lost tribe of Israel, "an Oriental colony." They offer parallel subjects for the psychological and the social pathologist respectively: on the one hand, an abnormal phase of love; on the other, an anomalous group among nations; in both cases, an international freemasonry which cuts across classes, recognizes members by oblique glances, and runs the continual risk of ostracism. Here, again, the approach is serio-comic. The hawk nose and curly beard of Bloch's uncle, M. Nissim Bernard, are regularly likened to the sculptured visage of some sculptured Assyrian monarch, while apt allusions to Racine's Esther and Athalie invest Proust's Israelites with semi-tragic dignity. The ghetto, in its exclusion, is Proust's parody on the exclusiveness of the Faubourg Saint-Germain. The pushing Bloch, who makes the ascent from the one coterie to the other, plays the zany to Marcel throughout. Bloch lives in a world of à peu près, approximations to what might be considered the real thing by persons whose aspirations are more securely supported. He seems to embody the Jewish element in Proust's personality, and to function as a scapegoat for such embarrassments as that may have occasioned him.

Proust had little reason to think of himself as a Jew, given his paternity and cognomen. If his exposure to Catholicism had been perfunctory, he was passionate in his esthetic devotion to churches. Yet, given the conjunction of entering the haut monde at the moment when its traditional alliance between clerical and militaristic forces made for an indiscriminate hostility to anyone associated with Dreyfus by race or conviction, Proust was surprised by an uncalculated and incalculable set of vicissitudes. As he put it, invoking an optical device which was more of a toy than an instrument, the social kaleidoscope had been brusquely shaken, interposing recombinations and novel patterns. Most of these were quite predictable; it could be foreseen that M. de Norpois would equivocate, or that most of the servants would react at least as seignorially as their masters. The anti-Dreyfusism of the Duke and the Duchess completes the disillusionment of Marcel and widens their rift with Swann. Swann's way and the Guermantes' way once more seem far apart, the former still infused with the old familial values, the latter gradually undermined by homosexual suspicions, and now—to sharpen the alignment— the Jews and the Gentiles taking opposite sides. The technique of reversal is carefully utilized in shifting from the anti-Dreyfusard atmosphere of *Le Côté des Guermantes* to the pro-Dreyfus tone of *Sodome et Gomorrhe*.

The unpredictable climax is Swann's confrontation with the Prince de Guermantes, as retold by Swann—his final appearance in the novel and the Prince's first. Step by step, we have been prepared for the awesome pinnacle of the hierarchy, the most exclusive house in the Faubourg. The Prince Gilbert is reputed to be the stuffiest and most hieratic of the Guermantes, and consequently expected to be the most feudal in his opinions. When Swann appears, no longer a dandy of the Jockey Club but suddenly a patriarch of the Old Testament, the other guests expect their host to show him the door. Their interview, in contrast with the slight to Swann administered an hour or two before by the Prince's easier-going cousins, the Duke and the Duchess, turns out to be a delicate and sympathetic meeting of two sensitive minds, temporarily estranged by external contingencies. The Prince, whose active conscience has privately led him to the conviction that Dreyfus is innocent, apologizes to Swann because his deepest commitments—the church and the army—scarcely allow him to join the public cause. Instead—and the paradox, superficially so absurd, becomes profoundly moving—he and the Princess are having masses said for Dreyfus' intention. Here, then, is a character whom we meet in a mood of undeception with all he embodies; and here is an utterly unforeseeable aspect, which brightens instead of blackening.

Proust's successive denigrations fall within the sophisticated French tradition, in that they see through pretenses and expose motives. But they extend beyond that to the Russian, the Dostoevsky side, through recognitions which bring out an extra dimension, not merely self-interest and perversity but hidden merits and unlooked-for beauties. Such is Marcel's realization that the dowdy old Marquise de Villeparisis has been the most dazzling heartbreaker of her day, and is still dragging out a lifelong romance with the stilted old Marquis de Norpois. Even more surprising, because M. Verdurin has so cruelly made M. Saniette the feeble butt of his dinner-table jokes, is the anonymous benevolence that takes the place of malice when need arises. The decency was always there, Marcel surmises, just as America or the North Pole had been before they were discovered by Columbus or Peary. The discovery, in this instance, is confirmed by further reversals: the testimony of the brothers Goncourt that that professional host, who seemed to Swann a philistine interloper amid the fine arts, was in fact a discriminating patron, and that his aggressive wife was in no mere ironic sense, *La Patronne*. Where there is degradation there may be rehabilitation, especially when life goes badly and art offers compensations. Charles Morel, the vile catamite, is a highly gifted violinist. Mademoiselle Vinteuil and her infamous companion, though they have desecrated the composer's memory, bring him new fame by transcribing the score of his greatest work, the posthumous septet.

When Captain Dreyfus was finally rehabilitated, Proust exchanged letters of congratulation with the woman he most admired after his mother, Madame Emile Strauss. His comment was based on the observation that life was behaving like a novel for once. For the past decade, he and she and nearly everyone else had undergone torments and disappointments. For the next, they could be sure of further ills and losses. But, for Dreyfus, life had been providential "in the manner of fairy tales and serial romances." The difference was that their unhappiness was grounded on physiological and emotional truths, whereas his troubles were due to legal fictions. "Happy those who are the victims of errors,

judicial or otherwise! They are the only human beings for whom
there are revenges and reparations!" For the rest, a happy ending
would be fictitious. This may be taken as Proust's considered answer to the questions posed at the end of *Sentiments filiaux d'un
parricide*. The true conclusion is sorrow, more frequently than
joy. When a wedding announcement arrives which surprisingly—
shockingly, to those who can read between the lines—unites the
two ways in an aristocratic marriage, Marcel and his mother
respond to it differently. "It is the recompense of virtue," says
the mother, harking back to that epiphany of his childhood, when
she lulled him to sleep by reading an idyllic romance of George
Sand. But her son has now grown up, and sadly knows better,
and so he thinks to himself without replying: "It is the reward
of vice; it is a marriage at the end of a novel by Balzac." In a
letter to George Sand, as we may well recall, Balzac had written:
"You look for man as he ought to be; I take him as he is."

5. A Metamorphosis of Things

> At first sight experience seems to bury us under a flood of
> external objects, pressing upon us with a sharp and im-
> portunate reality, calling us out of ourselves in a thousand
> forms of action. But when reflexion begins to act upon
> those objects, they are dissipated under its influence; the
> cohesive force seems suspended like a trick of magic; each
> object is loosed into a group of impressions—colour, odour,
> texture—in the mind of the observer . . . Every one of those
> impressions is the impression of the individual in his isola-
> tion, each mind keeping as a solitary prisoner its own
> dream of a world.

The speaker here is neither Marcel nor Proust. It is Walter Pater,
enunciating his esthetic credo in the postscript to *The Renaissance*.
The flux of existence, the "perpetual weaving and unweaving of
ourselves," is the premise for his cult of experience, his hedonistic
exhortation to burn with a gemlike flame. Up to a point, and that
is the point where Marcel detaches himself from Swann, Proust
may be said to have followed Pater's exhortation. No one, indeed,
has gone farther, in magnifying connoisseurship into a world-

view, in visualizing one's self as heir of all the ages, as the soul
adventuring among masterpieces. But Proust, the pupil of Bergson,
was more deeply preoccupied with another premise, on which
Pater touches but lightly: the dissipation of objects under analysis,
the perpetual flow that carries all things away. Mobility was
counterbalanced by stability in the nineteenth century, which
consequently offered the freest scope for the development of individuality. As a surviving child of that century, Proust is our witness
to the disintegration of personality during the subsequent period.
It is more than coincidental that the three climactic revelations
of A *la recherche du temps perdu* occur through a day and a night
of the year 1900.

Realities seem rather less tangible in the twentieth century,
even as personalities seem less knowable, and Marcel withdraws
more and more into the prison of self. This withdrawal accords
with the tendency toward the psychological novel as Freud has
conceived it. From the psychoanalytic standpoint, the author tends
to identify himself with a single character whom he depicts from
within, while depicting all other characters from the outside. "The
psychological novel in general probably owes its peculiarities to
the tendency of modern writers to split up their ego by self-
observation into many component egos, and in that way to personify the conflicting trends in their own mental life in many
heroes." This process is by no means peculiar to the psychological
novel: something like it is at work in all the broader forms of
fiction. It is bound to affect the efforts of any given human being
to imagine other existences than his own. Shakespeare himself
could not escape from it, although his imaginative sympathy multiplied it to the *n*th degree through the diversity of his dramatis
personae. Stendhal, at least, was prolific in the ingenuity with
which he disguised his returning alter ego in masks and pseudonyms. Proust made a virtue of the increased limitations that turned
the writer back upon himself, through his very approach to the
problems of characterization, via a single "continuous character"
groping for others amid the discontinuities. That left him, in
Bergsonian terms, with one absolute personage, Marcel, and some
two hundred others in the relative.

These are related to their creator in varying degrees of closeness.
Proust the man becomes Proust the author, who projects himself

into Marcel the narrator, who is singularly bewildered by the elusiveness of Albertine in particular, but of nearly everyone else to some extent. Yet, in the manner of his nineteenth-century forerunners —Stendhal as Count Mosca, Balzac as Daniel d'Arthez, Flaubert as Saint-Antoine, Zola as Doctor Pascal—Proust may be seen to double in certain roles which are near his heart or, at any rate, on his conscience. Thus the initial relation between Marcel and Swann comes close to a conventional novelist's idealization of himself as hero, while the exponents of the various arts—especially the writer, Bergotte—come to figure as the proponents of Proust's artistic ideals. At the other extreme, when he immolates the Baron de Charlus on the altar of snobbery and homosexuality, clearly Proust is excoriating those qualities in himself. "Qui aime bien châtie bien" is one of the Baron's maxims. It is also evident that Bloch plays the whipping-boy for whatever Proust may have disliked about his Jewish connection. Bloch's mundane course runs parallel to Marcel's. Slightly older and very knowing, Bloch takes the lead at the earlier stages; later, as a rising playwright, he seems to be dogging Marcel's steps in every salon. Their affinity is reluctantly conceded, in an instant of non-recognition, when Bloch is mistaken for Marcel.

The bond between the two is forged by the kind of Semitic anti-Semitism that had prompted Heinrich Heine to caricature himself under the jeering name of Hirsch-Hyacinthe. But Proust has a way of imposing his conflicts and compulsions on any person who comes within his ken, however slight or conventionalized. Consider, for a moment, this anecdote, which somehow gets into A la recherche du temps perdu, not in its context there, but as it has so often been repeated in American smoking-rooms. Its simplest outline involves a dark-haired woman whose bastard child is red-headed. When she is asked an obvious question, whether the child does not take after its father, she replies that she does not know, that she had never seen him with his hat off. The point here, as in a good many crude jokes, is simply the offhand brusquerie with which the act of procreation is taken, regardless of whatever its personal consequences may be. Now it so happens that this tale is retold on a page of A l'ombre des jeunes filles en fleurs, and it is revealing to watch for the Proustification. Proust's explicit point, reflecting back on the early Albertine, is that in

love so much can be made of so little. The implicit moral, heralding the late Albertine, is that we scarcely know anything about
those with whom we may have been most intimate.

In the retelling, the sexes have been transposed. The parent
who cannot reply is an old man, unlikely as it may seem, under
the circumstances, that he never saw the color of the mother's
hair. At all events, the woman has long been dead; it is he who
has brought up the child; and his parental devotion has been
aided, most characteristically, by financial support from Marcel's
grandmother. She feels this obligation to him, moreover, because
he had once been her drawing-master, and is therefore an artist
after his humble fashion. If Proust could work this transfiguration
upon so casual and trivial a bit of material, what could he not do
with themes of his own predilection? The theme of art, which
gradually gains momentum in A la recherche du temps perdu, is
tentatively sounded from the outset. Its representative in Combray
—a spiritual cousin of the grandmother's drawing-master—is Vinteuil, the silly old music-master, whose image is so scandalously
degraded by his daughter and her Lesbian friend. In the Parisian
flashback, he is mentioned as an all but anonymous composer,
whose haunting phrase, remembered by Swann and Odette, becomes the national anthem of their love. In much the same way,
the cattleya orchid given by Swann to Odette becomes the symbol
of their love-making. Esthete that he is, he must endow every
action with a corresponding association.

Odette's attraction for Swann is enhanced through his fancy
that she resembles a figure from a painting by Botticelli. His connoisseur's eye finds pictorial prototypes to transfigure everyone he
encounters. When he ascends the grand staircase to a musicale at
the Marquise de Sainte-Euverte's, where again we hear the Vinteuil
sonata, the liveried footmen remind him successively of works by
Mantegna, Dürer, Goya, and Cellini. The youthful Marcel has
yet to achieve that cultivation of taste which will end by making
his world a kind of museum; but his grandmother has already
begun it by surrounding him with pictures of churches and other
landmarks; and these are engravings, not photographs, thereby
involving another mode of artistry as a framing perspective. Ecclesiastical architecture, along with the sculpture that embellishes
it, will constitute his illustrated Bible—and, even more personally,

his Noah's Ark. Bloch will look less bumptious when envisaged as an Oriental potentate by Bellini, and a pregnant kitchenmaid will be beatified with an epithet comparing her to Giotto's allegorical representation of Charity. That allusion, according to Proust's unrealized final plan, was to be extended into a section entitled "The Virtues and Vices of Padua and Combray," where presumably the frescoes of the Arena Chapel would provide a symbolic transition from esthetics to ethics.

Marcel's boyish interests, ever since that night when his mother read aloud to him from George Sand, were bound to be chiefly literary. When he grew interested in the writing of contemporaries, his favorite was the urbane and erudite Bergotte. The old-fashioned M. de Norpois, borrowing an expression from Anatole France, dismisses Bergotte as "a flute-player." When Marcel is suddenly introduced to his idol at a luncheon of Madame Swann's, he is taken by surprise but we are not; for previously the name of *Phèdre* on a boulevard poster has seemed like a hostess announcing a fellow guest as "M. Anatole France." By putting words of sympathy and encouragement into Bergotte's mouth, Proust acknowledged France's sponsorship of his first book. But Marcel is somewhat disappointed by the rather coarse features and undistinguished manners of this exquisite stylist, and somewhat shocked, on coming to know him better, by his malicious tongue. A comparable disappointment awaits him in a neighboring sphere; and both spheres are interconnected by a rare pamphlet on Racine, the gift of Gilberte, which celebrates the genius of that great actress, Berma, in the role of Phèdre. Marcel's expectations are aroused to a pitch of esthetic enthusiasm which cannot be sustained by the long-awaited performance. He will have to see it again, and brood upon it afterward, before he can rejoin the ranks of Berma's ardent admirers. Second impressions teach him a lesson by reinforcing novelty with familiarity, and by calling memory to the aid of discovery.

Insofar as La Berma—like Bergotte, she shares the better part of a syllable with Bergson—may have a model, it could only be the incomparable Sarah Bernhardt. Our curiosity with regard to keys could be more legitimately focussed on Proust's artists than on his other personages, since with them he is not merely characterizing; he is criticizing, and, by means of concretely fictitious examples, formulating his general views on the arts. Yet, with the important exception of Berma, whose demeanor on the stage was Sarah Bernhardt's in *Phèdre*, and whose private life in the novel is wholly Proustian, the other artistic performances are composites. Inscribing a copy of *Du côté de chez Swann* to Jacques de Lacretelle, Proust recalled, at length and in detail, the melodic phrases that echoed through his mind's ear when he was describing Vinteuil's sonata—phrases from Saint-Saëns, Fauré, Franck, Schubert, and two from Wagner. If Proust was able to harmonize those components, he might well claim to *égaler la musique*, if not to compose his own music, as Ernst Robert Curtius has suggested. Music was primary in the *Art poétique* of the Symbolists, as expounded by Verlaine, though their ultimate aim was a simultaneous appeal to all the senses through a deliberate intermixture of genres. By achieving that state of synesthesia, they hoped to converge upon their exemplar, Wagner, who was not less their arch-musician because he was likewise a man of letters.

Proust makes consciously musical use of *leitmotiv* when the violin sounds the theme of Swann's love, or of Marcel's in the resurrected Vinteuil septet. More literary and parodistic is the association whereby Marcel salutes each entrance of Saint-Loup's Rachel with the opening line of an aria from *La Juive*. But Proust was well aware of the difference between a phrase composed of notes and a phrase compounded in words. His preoccupation with time and memory had taught him that the temporal structure of the novel has its own modes of duration and recurrence, and he had set other perceptions in movement by speaking of other senses than that of sound: the smell of hawthorn, the taste of linden tea, the sight of Venice, the touch of a paving-stone. Like Thomas Mann, he is more effective when he handles words and associations thematically than when he attempts to equal music by writing program notes to imaginary compositions. When Proust turned to painting, he could speak with more authority through the person of Elstir, in whom he painted a verbal portrait of the generic impressionist. Though the foreign-sounding and slightly anagrammatic name is suggestive of Whistler, the description of his paintings is not, in spite of the butterfly signature. Proust is much more successful than Zola in evoking Cézanne at L'Estaque, when Marcel evokes the recessive vistas of seaside and hillside at Carquethuit; and when he conjures up the water-lilies in the Vivonne, he rivals Monet in another medium.

Elstir, the man, could not have gained his mastery without having served a rigorous apprenticeship to life, as well as to art. Readers of Henry James may well be reminded of the expatriate sculptor Gloriani, who is presented under such contrasting aspects in *Rodrick Hudson* and in *The Ambassadors*. We are permitted a premature glimpse of Elstir, as the raffish bohemian, M. Biche, in one of the flashbacks to the Verdurin circle; while, under the title of Miss Sacripant, 1871, we are allowed to peek at a Nana-like aspect of the as yet unmarried Odette. More fortunate than Swann because he is more creative, the painter could take advantage of his illusions by portraying not his mistress but his love. Elstir is the principal esthetician in *A la recherche du temps perdu*. His conversations, together with Marcel's reactions to his canvases, highly elaborated by Proust in rewriting, form a running commentary on the Ruskinian dialectic between art and life. Elstir's studio, chaotic though it might seem, impresses Marcel as a laboratory for the new creation of a world. There is godlike aspiration here, though not the demiurgic conception of Flaubert or Joyce, wherein the artist must create an individual cosmos; for Elstir, the creation pre-exists in nature, and must be re-created through the artist's personal view of it. Mallarmé's objective was "to paint not the thing, but the effect it produces." Looking at some of Elstir's seascapes of Balbec, Marcel observes:

> I could notice that the charm of each consisted in a sort of metamorphosis of the things represented in it, analogous to that which is known as metaphor in poetry; and that, if God the Father had created things by naming them, Elstir recreated them by taking away their names or by giving them another.

Moving from the age of names toward the age of things, and from the garden of innocence toward the holocaust of experience, Marcel is learning how artists revive our awareness, which is constantly being dulled by the force of habit. He is reaching the intermediate stage, the age of words, which are to be the source of his craft; and Proust's formulation seems to echo an essay of Emerson's, which speaks of the poet as accomplishing "a metamorphosis of things." In his own essay, A propos du style de Flaubert, Proust amplifies this transition from the visual arts to literature. Arguing that Flaubert's modulation of tenses has done as much as Kant's categories to renew our "vision des choses," he goes on to affirm that it is metaphor which confers the touch of immortality upon style. In short, he reaffirms the Aristotelian principle that metaphor is the poet's chief criterion. Surely, it is the imaginative gift that Proust has in common with Homer, Dante, and Shakespeare, far-fetched though the comparison might seem from any other point of view. Strictly speaking, Proust—in his formal way —employs similes more frequently than metaphors. Counts of his images vary with the computer; but all the samplings seem to indicate an average incidence of at least one to a page; and they are significantly lower in the third-person Amour de Swann than in the first-person narrative elsewhere. What is most Proustian is the elaboration, which prolongs a detailed analogy and finds so many unexpected points of resemblance that the figure might almost be classified, in rhetorical terms, as an allegory.

Unclassical mixtures are frequent. Sensation is made more vivid by synesthetic transpositions, where metaphors are deliberately mixed. The transcendental and the actual are brought very close together, either by ennobling the commonplace or by adding a common touch to the esoteric. An altarpiece may be the counterpart of a kitchen utensil. On the other hand, Françoise's kitchen is regulated by as nice a dietary code as was laid down in the Old Testament. In other respects, Françoise is like the chorus of a Greek tragedy; and when she goes to market to purchase meat for her boeuf à la mode, she is likened to Michelangelo, visiting Carrara to quarry marble for his latest sculptural masterpiece. Cookery, along with gowns and gardens, thus holds its traditionally French place among the fine arts, and Françoise holds her own with Berma and Bergotte, Vinteuil and Elstir. Just as Marcel associates Bergotte with Gilberte, so he associates Elstir with Albertine, and A l'ombre des jeunes filles en fleurs is particularly rich in metaphorical transformations. Proust transforms an elevator ride into an esthetic adventure, with elaborate virtuosity, by regarding the operator as an organist who is pulling out the stops. The airplane, the automobile, the telephone, the electric light, and other such mechanical inventions have become the merest routine of our daily lives; but they were the astonishing innovations of Proust's day; and his sense of wonder has estranged them anew and quickened them into tutelary divinities.

The "lift," quite apart from its magic or its convenience, serves an ulterior purpose which is characteristic; it tests the motives of both Saint-Loup and Bloch, as well as Marcel's ability to interpret them. Does Saint-Loup blush because Bloch has pretentiously mispronounced the Anglicism, *lift*, or because—as we are later led to suspect—he himself has an illicit relationship with the *liftier*? In any case, the focal simile is one which may have been added in proof to the passage describing the pampered and indolent guests at the Grand Hotel of Balbec: how they occasionally look up from their afternoon game of cards toward the sea, which appears to them through a window like a pleasant canvas hung on the wall of a luxurious bachelor apartment, all flatness, artifice, unreality. Then at night, the simile continues, oscillating from art to natural history, the hotel's wide-windowed dining room becomes a vast illuminated aquarium, exhibiting strange species of fish and molluscs to the fishermen and the townspeople without, who are pressing their noses against the glass. Among the latter— Proust puts himself in the corner of the picture—perhaps there may be some curious writer, some specialist in human ichthyology, eager to study and record the habits of these rare specimens. And, as he stands in the outer darkness among the working-class population of Balbec, Proust raises one of his parenthetical questions:

(A great social question is to know whether the glass wall will always protect the banqueting of those marvellous creatures, or whether the obscure people watching so hungrily in the darkness will not come to snatch them from the aquarium and devour them.)

The sciences, almost as much as the arts, have been encyclopedically ransacked for imagery. Plants are compared to people, people to plants. Medicine furnishes its expected quota, both from the doctor's and from the patient's side. The influence of asthma on the rhythms of Proust's prose, with its respiratory prolongations, has become a topic for monographic research. His syntactic devices are not less distinctive than his figures of speech. What rhetoricians would term enumeration, a series of parallels in apposition, branching out to explore divergent areas and yet converging upon a single many-sided idea, this is what extends the length of his sentences, while qualifying and reinforcing his predicates. If they must be construed like a sentence in Greek or Latin, Leo Spitzer has remarked, it is because the complexity of Proust's world can only be reflected through such construction. He himself bears out that remark in a comment: "For style, with a writer as with a painter, is a question not of technique but of vision." The technique, complex as it may seem, is no more than the means of projection. The content determines the form, and that is why—to paraphrase Buffon again—style becomes an emanation of personality. The special character of Proust's vision is metamorphic; not without warrant, he himself adduces Ovid's *Metamorphoses*; and though he does not specifically mention Picasso, he cannot see an object or situation without envisioning a Cubist sequence of past and future states, of growth and wane, renewal and decomposition.

One of Odette's Anglicisms, which Proust too uses, and for which he has been criticized by such purists as Gide, is the key-word *réaliser*. French usage here is objective and external; the word means to materialize, to bring something about. In English, and sometimes in Proust, the meaning is more subjective and psychological: to become aware, to have something brought home to one. It spells the difference between the attainment of a surface reality and the apprehension of an internal reality. A similar distinction is blurred in Proust's translation of Ruskin's *Bible of Amiens*, where "actually"—in reality—gets rendered by the more ephemeral *actuellement*—at the moment. The problem, in two words, is to metamorphose *actualités* into actualities, to absorb events into consciousness. "Car on ne se réalise que successivement." The reader can only realize what the writer presents through, let us say, the successive aspects of Albertine; and his realization, as Georges Poulet reminds us, is bound to be a *re-cognition*. Knowledge is most securely based on previous acquaintance. This explains the importance of memory; one must look back and sum up, in order to understand fully. The creations of artistry are most meaningful when they touch emotions we have experienced. Proust could recapture many a lost sigh from the facile and faded poetry of Alfred de Musset, because he had been so fond of it in his youth. He could not have forgotten the counsel offered by the Muse to the poet in *La Nuit d'octobre*, since that dialogue—though scorned by Bloch in *Du côté de chez Swann*—is recited by Rachel in *Le Temps retrouvé*:

> Aimerais-tu les fleurs, les prés et la verdure,
> Les sonnets de Pétrarque et le chant des oiseaux,
> Michelange et les arts, Shakespeare et la nature,
> Si tu n'y retrouvais quelques anciens sanglots?

Thus the greatest artists are perpetually engaged in sending us back to ourselves for corroboration. Reciprocally, their light re-kindles an interior warmth. Its insights are intermissions of the heart, such as the impact of the grandmother's death or of Marcel's delayed reaction to Berma; hence they cannot be arbitrarily willed. They flash upon the inward eye, in spontaneous recollection, even as they must have done for Wordsworth. Proust prefers a more technological metaphor: the mind has become a dark room, wherein the continuous film of its impressions and sensations is being developed over and over again. Along with photographic reproductions of works of art, we know that he enjoyed collecting snapshots of his friends. We treasure the albums now available, which show him in a variety of poses, half-reclining à la Récamier, or as a child with his mother and brother, or as a traveller with his father in Venice, or ill at ease in his military uniform, or wearing a Charlie Chaplin derby on a balcony, or sitting for the slick portrait by Jacques-Emile Blanche, or on his deathbed with a prophet's beard. Through all these metamorphoses of self, we discern the same penetrating and penetrable eyes. But the shots remain unique precisely because they are segments of a continuum, stills displayed outside the theater to advertise the cinema of an existence.

6. The Undiscovered Country

A la recherche du temps perdu is a work which changed with its ever-changing subject, grew with the growing awareness and skill of its author, and expanded like those metaphorical Japanese pellets which open up into flowers. Proust's undulating conception of human nature, which inspired him to present his characters under such diverse aspects, was mirrored in the growth and development through which he composed his novel. His original plan envisaged a trilogy, to have been subtitled *Du côté de chez Swann, Le Côté des Guermantes,* and *Le Temps retrouvé;* and he seems to have actually completed a novel which followed that clear-cut outline. The first subnovel had been published, and the second was in the hands of the printer, when the first World War broke out. The extended delay caused Proust to revise and rework the material that he had planned for a single intermediate installment, and to amplify it ultimately to the extent of five successive subnovels. The fifth of these, the sixth of the total seven, *La Fugitive*—originally published as *Albertine disparue,* and ineptly presented in English under a title from Walter de la Mare, *The Sweet Cheat Gone*—remains fragmentary, since Proust was at work upon it when he died. Hence the seventh and last subnovel, *Le Temps retrouvé,* was never fully revised, and reverts to the earlier stratum of *Du côté de chez Swann,* where it was to have been the third subnovel. Apparently, the final chapter of the latter book was written directly after the opening chapter of the former, in order to frame the whole within Proust's unfolding time-scheme.

Except for Walt Whitman and his *Leaves of Grass,* it would be hard to think of another writer living from day to day and year to year in such an organic relation to his writing; even Goethe had many other concerns than *Faust;* and it would be even harder to think of Proust completing *A la recherche du temps perdu* and going on to write something else. "Who touches this, touches a man." Whoever writes such a book must be, by his own definition, *homo unius libri.* Partly upon the basis of galley proofs from the unpublished recension of *Le Côté des Guermantes,* and partly upon the basis of conjectures which may well be modified by the continuing study of Proust's manuscripts, Albert Feuillerat has analyzed the process of composition, applying to Proust a method not unlike that which Proust applied to his characters. The additions were not necessarily digressions, though they were often essayistic in manner. Enrichment seems to have brought with it a good deal of calculated depreciation. Consistently, in the characterization, the *retouches* brought out darker traits, especially in Charlus and Albertine, while enlarging the presentation of Sodom and Gomorrah. This increasingly critical tone corresponds with Proust's increasing tendency toward social criticism in the Balzacian vein. Symptomatically, one of his many verbal revisions substitutes *intelligence* for *mémoire,* as if to indicate that the maturer Proust depended less on Bergsonian intuition and more on conscious control.

The narrative seems to cover some thirty years in its total span, though not consecutively. It moves back and forth, retrospectively augmented by the preparatory episode of Swann in love, and heavily syncopated as it nears its unrevised conclusion. Since the continuity is internal, and since the narrator's mind is continually moving from one epoch to another, the chronology is perforce rather vague. There are times when Marcel seems to divide his interest between playing marbles with Gilberte on the Champs Elysées and reading Bergotte about Berma in Racine, to enjoy the company of a nursemaid in the daytime and a prostitute at night. As Ernst Robert Curtius has discerned, Proust reckons time by seasons of the soul. Yet time must be concretely related to the times. On occasion the book can wax knowingly topical, as when the *rentier* author speaks of the rise and fall of Royal Dutch, De Beers, and his other stocks, or when the dilettante narrator feels the impact of the Russian Revolution through the vogue of the *Ballets Russes* and the emigrating grand duchesses. The chronicle itself is linked by two decisive external events, the long-drawn-out Dreyfus case, which after so much conflict ended happily, and the first World War, with its cataclysmic twist of the social kaleidoscope.

The overcrowded pages of *Le Temps retrouvé* constitute a seismographic register of those ultimate changes. Combray itself is occupied by the Germans; and, since their look-out is the tower of its storied church, Saint-Hilaire, it is shelled by the allies and its stained glass is shattered. The hawthorn lane, so redolent of youthful associations, is now relabelled Incline 307 on the military charts. We have indeed traversed the time-span from names to things. In Paris, a soldier on furlough from the trenches, wistfully stopping to gaze at the restaurants, where the order of the day is to feed civilians as usual, reminds Marcel—with a pang—of the fishermen at Balbec, pressing their noses against the panes of the dining-room aquarium. By way of contrast we glance at Madame Verdurin, thriving upon the latest misinformation, and breakfasting upon a scarce *croissant* which consoles her for the news in the morning papers, the sinking of the *Lusitania.* The German air-raids are envisioned as rides of the Valkyries, the zeppelins heralding a Wagnerian *Götterdämmerung*. Bombing also suggests the rain of ashes at Pompeii and Herculaneum, where in their day—as Charlus reminds Marcel—the names Sodoma, Gomorra had been scrawled on the ruins. The hecatomb of civilization itself, with concomitant lighting and sound effects, forms the backdrop for a last homosexual revelation.

Marcel again plays the coincidental eavesdropper and keeps one more vigil in Sodom; for, during a sudden blackout, he has taken refuge at an establishment which the infamous Jupien conducts for those who share his patron's sentiments. Proust's point, however, is that such sentiments can never be really shared; the Baron de Charlus' masochistic perversion cannot find an answering sadism. The partners Jupien finds for him are vulgar rather than vicious, callow young men out to pick up a dishonest franc or two, but by no means wicked enough for his tastes, as Charlus complains; and with his self-torturing plaint, we reach the lowest and most vicious circle in the Dantesque abasement of all that Proust himself has been castigating. We see the Baron just once more, utterly aged and nearly paralyzed, attended by Jupien as if by a governess; yet, even in the recesses of second childhood, Charlus is still attempting to debauch other children. "Nothing," Marcel seems justified in concluding, "is more limited than pleasure and vice." The second coincidence, which has also taken place during the air-raids, is even more devastating for Marcel, since it corroborates his suspicions of his best friend, Robert de Saint-Loup. Likewise a visitor to the sodomite brothel, Saint-Loup betrays himself by dropping his Croix de Guerre. That equivocal emblem presages another aspect—the Dostoevsky side of his character—and his heroic ending shortly afterward, killed at the front with a song of Schumann on his lips. As irony or emulation will have it, when the hero of Thomas Mann's *Magic Mountain* is lost in battle on the other side, he too is singing a *lied* by the same composer.

Marcel, the perennial spectator, who lay so prostrate in a hotel room at Doncières while Robert was undergoing his military service, breaks down altogether and languishes through the war years in a sanatorium. For a while thereafter, he stays at Tansonville, formerly the estate of the long-dead Swann. The *châtelaine* is now Marcel's old playmate, Gilberte, who has meanwhile become the wife and then the widow of Robert de Saint-Loup. Consequently, the two ways—worlds apart, when viewed through the wide eyes of childhood—are reunited in the person of their daughter, Mademoiselle de Saint-Loup. Marcel even discovers that it is possible to include both *le côté de Méséglise* and *le côté des Guermantes* in the same walk along the Vivonne. In the diminishing universe of adulthood, *le monde* has become absurdly small; and Marcel's postwar return to the salons, his farewell appearance upon that darkening stage, is a scene of kaleidoscopic reorientation. His last hostess turns out to be our old friend, Madame Verdurin, who, by the ironic interplay of death, remarriage, and ultra-snobbery, has pushed her pertinacious way to the apogee of the Faubourg Saint-Germain. It is she, for whatever there still may be in a name, who is now the Princesse de Guermantes. This is more of a surprise for us than it can have been for Marcel, like the transfiguration of Odette into Madame Swann. The reception of the parvenu princess, as Marcel beholds it, is therefore neither a recognition nor a reversal; rather, it surprisingly becomes an estrangement and an impulsion.

Not that the Guermantes and their friends—and Marcel is now surprised to be greeted as one of the oldest—have appreciably altered their habits. In a corner, the octogenarian Duke is carrying on a senile flirtation with the dowager Odette. As for the Duchess, she can no longer recall what slippers she wore with her red velvet gown, on that evening when Swann and Marcel saw her off to that no longer famous dinner party some twenty years before. So far as she can recollect, they were golden. All who have survived, true to their idle and frivolous natures, are still going through their characteristic motions. Bloch is welcomed, as he might not have been twenty years before; and what does it matter? He is twenty years nearer his death. But the *coup de théâtre*, the dramatic effect that strikes us along with Marcel, is the sense of taking part in a masquerade. All these familiar figures with powdered hair, their arteries visibly hardened, seem to turn into statues before our eyes, in a final metamorphosis, a kind of collective *vieillissement*. With the *tableau vivant* comes the realization that aging is not, as youth may naïvely assume, a gradual experience. As Goethe's friend, Rahel, pointed out, one grows old suddenly. This truth, which one learns by living through it, Proust gathered through intuition, since he himself was not destined to experience old age. From the long-

sought-after spectacle we back away, with something of the revulsion that Swift embodied when he conceived those monstrosities
of old age, the Struldbrugs.

If that revulsion seems a lame and impotent conclusion, a de-
pressingly negative consummation of Marcel's persistent quest for
glamor, it is accompanied by a climactic affirmation, a conclusive
moment of self-discovery. This is effected, not by coincidences,
which always seem for Proust to wear an air of fatality, but by the
most casual of chances—a chain of circumstances, as he would say,
so trivial that they would probably be meaningless to anyone other
than Marcel. A stone in the courtyard feels underfoot like the hallowed pavement of Venice. The tinkle of a spoon against a plate
sounds like the bell that rang downstairs at Combray, when Swann
paid his evening visit so long ago. A book, picked up by chance in
an anteroom, happens to be *François le champi*, that innocent tale
which will forever be linked with Marcel's mother, reading at his
bedside. And finally—an eternity in a teacup—the *madeleine* renews the all but forgotten taste of Aunt Léonie's linden tea. This
conjunction, the fortuitous linkage of those sensations and memories which surround and possess us simultaneously, it is this then
which is truly real, much more real than the ensuing vista, from
which Marcel will soon be turning away; for in one dazzling insight
he has chanced upon that "Open, Sesame" which can help him to
regain lost time and recover the past.

There will be one more party; but it will receive very little attention; we shall only learn about it indirectly. It is a funereal affair,
given by La Berma in honor of her most ungrateful daughter together with her uncongenial son-in-law. The aging actress, we are
now made aware, is no longer the undisputed tragedy queen.
Among the knowledgeable and fashionable she has been superseded
by a new star, under whose lacquered aspect we may recognize the
feline Jewess, Rachel, who had once been so demanding a mistress
to Saint-Loup, and had still earlier been a call-girl rejected by
Marcel. Her career in the theater, it appears, has paralleled his
climb through the Faubourg. She is now at the height of fashion,
and her recitation is scheduled to be the *pièce de résistance* at the
Guermantes reception. Since Berma's tea has been scheduled for
the same hour, it is sparsely attended. All the invited guests are
dancing attendance upon her triumphant rival. When even the two

guests of honor leave the old woman to swallow the insult alone, departing to beg invitations from the insolent Rachel, Berma's humiliation is as complete as Vinteuil's had been so long ago. In her most tragical role—"par son enfant Madone transpercée"—she joins a chorus whose muffled ululation has been intermittently voiced throughout *A la recherche du temps perdu*, and which has been mentioned in a mysterious allusion to "les mères profanées."

These profaned mothers might have been the subject of an unwritten chapter, hinted at parenthetically in *Sodome et Gomorrhe*. There, in discussing the symptoms of the homosexual neurosis, Marcel alludes to those sons whose faces, instead of resembling their father, turn out instead to be the profanation of their mother. Now Proust had been a mother's boy in every conceivable sense: in his physical resemblance to Madame Proust, in the tenderness with which she had coddled his invalidism, and in the complex of feminine attitudes and responses which had resulted. At this point, we may pertinently recall that, when Jean Santeuil quarrels with his parents and apologizes, Madame Santeuil forgives her son by comparing their relationship to a Jewish marriage. The comparison, in all actuality, had been made by Madame Proust; and it is all the more pertinent because there is no other indication that the mother of the novel is Jewish. That self-revealing chapter of *Jean Santeuil* terminates with a footnote in which Jean starts to add a codicil to his will. If his parents survive him, he would like them to preserve the furniture of his room, as well as his mother's old cloak, which has so symbolically draped itself around him during his hysterical scene with them. If they predecease him, he wants to bequeath this intimate legacy to his best friend, Henri de Réveillon—"the furniture, yes, but not the little cloak, for that would seem to be worse than a profanation."

Here he seems to hesitate, and the episode breaks off, but the reason for the hesitation is discernible. It had been the parents' suspicion of Henri, and of his seductive influence over Jean, which had brought about the preceding quarrel. Although the symbolic cloak has disappeared from *A la recherche du temps perdu*, along with the rest of the incident, the definitive work contains some curious allusions to a set of furniture which Marcel has inherited from his Aunt Léonie, memorabilia of Combray and its innocent affections. Some of these pieces, he confides rather casually, he gave away to the brothel he first patronized, where their presence brought home to him a contrast between profane and sacred love. Revolted, he eschewed the call house; he would "rather have violated a dead woman." To turn back again from fiction to confession, and to grant some degree of credit to the scabrous recollections of Maurice Sachs in *Le Sabbat*, we hear that Proust was a patron of an actual establishment similar to the one kept by Jupien for Charlus, and presided over by a certain Albert, where the waiting room was furnished with a sofa and other items formerly in the possession of Proust's family. In that peculiar manner, so deviously and yet so precisely, so near at hand and yet so far away, he seems to have stigmatized his own inversion as a perversion, an express violation of the family's sanctity.

His guilty fear of having profaned, having outraged, nay, having assassinated his mother had come out during his lifetime in the *Confession d'une jeune fille* and shortly after her death in the *Sentiments filiaux d'un parricide*. In the curse of *Sodome et Gommorhe*, inverts are condemned as "motherless sons." One of the violent fantasies of Charlus, who has shockingly insinuated that Marcel did not care for "his old grandmother," takes the form of suggesting that Bloch should beat his "bitch of a mother." That transposition is striking because it makes the maternal image, cruelly victimized by unfilial conduct, a Jewess. Once again the anti-Semitism complements the homosexuality. Yet mere self-accusation is not enough; there must be some decisive act of restitution. Mademoiselle Vinteuil, having shamed the image of her father with "ritual profanations," has expiated her sin by restoring his masterpiece. Marcel has no gift to match the little phrase of Vinteuil, or the brush-stroke of Elstir, or even—so he humbly believes—the flute-playing of Bergotte. Yet those artistic milestones along Swann's way and the Guermantes' way are both to be transcended by a third way, *le côté de Martinville*. Swann himself, preceding Marcel along the two ways, had sensed it through his connoisseurship of art; but he had been a sterile dilettante, a collector rather than a creator, "un célibataire des arts"; while Charlus was an even more striking instance of the artist *manqué*. The antithesis between sterility and fertility, here as elsewhere, reinforces the parallel between creative and familial values.

"To create is to live twice," Camus would observe. Though

Marcel aspires to be a writer, he has heretofore been uncertain of his talent. One day, inspired by the changing roadside view of the Martinville steeples, he has endeavored to set down his verbal impressions in such a manner as to indicate the passage of time. He has sent the resulting article to *Le Figaro*, in spite of M. de Norpois' disapproval, and he learns that it has been accepted several volumes later. Proust's mother has been associated with this acceptance—since she brings the paper to her son's bedside in *Contre Sainte-Beuve*—and hence with his emergence as a full-fledged author. But she was no longer at his side in this ark; it was as if the dove had flown away; and that is the precondition of Noah's insight. Belatedly, laboriously, precariously, Proust had to set up his own intercourse with the world. Could he overcome his innate narcissism, which she had done so much to foster? Just possibly, but only by following her example of self-sacrifice, and thereby doing penance for the suffering that he had inflicted upon her. The years of desecration had to be atoned for by a long and testing consecration. Marcel's mother has felt that her son's worst vice was the lack of will-power. Could this spoiled child, this spendthrift of time, ever really make up for what he had so cavalierly wasted? Could he redeem himself? Was it not already too late for such a calling?

After his retirement from society, many legends grew up around Proust's monumental endeavors. Montesquiou, uneasily, spitefully, hopefully, sneered that they were sure to come to naught. Proust joked nervously about the character of Mr. Casaubon in *Middlemarch*, whose research was unending and unproductive. In an essay on Ruskin, he paused to worry about the brilliant procrastinations of Coleridge. Having diagnosed his own case as a paralytic syndrome, "a sort of moral ataxy," Proust had prescribed for himself a cure which he knew would kill. It was to put his life into a book, and to make that book a way of life. Echoing a scriptural trope which has provided a text for so many percipient modern writers, and which Gide would invoke as a title for his confessions, *Si le grain ne meurt,* Proust likened himself to a seed which must be buried so that the plant may ripen in the fullness of time. His discovery—that art could be the master of time, "que l'oeuvre d'art était le seul moyen de retrouver le Temps perdu"—brought with it his vocation. Nothing was lost, after all. The indolence and the

frivolity were the very conditions of the experiment. The outcome
would be everything that had gone into it, an *apologia pro vita sua*.
It has been said that all of Kafka's work constitutes an epistle to
his father. So we might say, of Proust's novel, that it may be read
as a letter to his mother.

Since he could not believe—though after her death he tried—
in a personal immortality, and since he knew he would never live
to see full publication, he was addressing himself, as Stendhal had
more expressly done, to an anonymous posterity, a "happy few."
In order to accomplish this self-appointed labor, his passive sick-
room had to be vitalized into an active work-room. Marcel contemplates the task before him in one of Proust's enumerative sentences, which branches out synesthetically into the many spheres
of his artistic curiosity, promising "to bear it like a fatigue, accept
it like a rule, construct it like a church, follow it like a regimen,
overcome it like an obstacle, win it like a friendship, feed it like
a child, create it like a world." Nor, among these burgeoning analogues, wherein the infant becomes a master architect and the
pampered invalid a demiurge, does he exclude the object-lesson of
Françoise's cookery. When, scarcely seeing an end in sight, he
exclaims, "How many great cathedrals remain unfinished!," his
ecclesiastical metaphor expresses the religious ardor of his own
dedication—as did the *madeleine*, the churches at Martinville, or,
for that matter, his intellectual apprenticeship to Ruskin. For the
latter, Proust had written, "that beauty to which he found himself
consecrating his life was not conceived as an object of enjoyment
fashioned to charm him, but as a reality infinitely more important
than life, for which he would have given his own life."

It is worth remembering that the point of departure, as it were
the precondition, for *Jean Santeuil* had been a writer's death. That
implicit notion of an esthetic martyrdom is fully dramatized by the
magistral set-piece of *La Prisonnière* depicting the death of Bergotte. As it happened, Anatole France could not have served as a
model for this phase of the portrait of a great writer, since he survived Proust's death by a year or two. Moreover, there has been a
persisting report that Proust was engaged in retouching this very
passage upon his own deathbed. The malady from which Bergotte
suffers, however, is that which afflicts Marcel's grandmother in
the novel, and which in fact afflicted Proust's mother, uremia.
Proust himself, like Bergotte, had made very nearly his last sortie

from his chamber to visit an exhibition of Dutch paintings, featuring the celebrated *View of Delft* by Vermeer. With the ripening of the novel, it came to reflect a gradual disillusionment over the narrator's early idol. Marcel tells us that latterly he has come to prefer a newer and more original novelist, who happens to look like Bloch, and whose style—as Proust describes its complexities—happens to sound like Proust's. Marcel learns the bad news about Bergotte from the papers, which report it next day with typical inaccuracy. Self-revealingly, in detailing the symptoms, the dreams, and the expiring thoughts of Bergotte, Proust for once escapes from the prison of Marcel's ego and completely identifies himself with the sensibilities of the dying writer.

In short, the final key to Bergotte is Proust, Proust as his philosophy has taught him how to die, Proust enunciating his ethical credo. "He was dead," announces Proust-Marcel, and counters the announcement with an inquiry: "Mort à jamais?" Dead forever? Question counters question: "Qui peut le dire?" The speculation harks back to the opening section and the initial doubt: whether the adolescent view of Combray can ever be resurrected. "Mort à jamais? C'est possible." There Marcel consoled himself with animistic fancies, based on the Celtic belief that the souls of the dead are confined in stones or trees or animals, whence our passing touch may release them accidentally.

> So it is with our own past. In vain we try to conjure it up; all our intellectual efforts are futile. It lies hidden beyond the realm and reach of the intellect in some unsuspected material object, in the sensation which that object will convey to us. As for the object, it depends upon chance whether or not we encounter it before dying.

Among the models cited for Bergotte, along with France and Bergson and Ruskin, was Ernest Renan, who had raised the same inquiry in an eloquent paragraph upon the beliefs of the ancient Hebrews—a paragraph which Proust seems to have echoed from Renan's *Avenir de la science*. Had they lived in vain, asked the biblical critic, all those unremembered generations whose experience has preceded ours? "Mortes, mortes à jamais?" And Renan had answered himself, "No, they live in humanity; they have served to build that great Babel which mounts toward the sky, wherein every layer is a race." In Proust's considered reply to the reiterated query, he combines the Kantian precept of esthetic disinterestedness with the Platonic myth of an unknown land and the Talmudic doctrine of pre-natal wisdom. Why should Vermeer, whoever he may have been, why should that artist of genius expend his allotment of days on endeavors predestined by the nature of things to survive him? Why should anyone feel any obligation to do good or be polite? Because, though temporarily reborn into this life, such a person belongs to a different world and somehow retains his allegiance to its sanctions—kindness, scrupulousness, and sacrifice—

> those laws which are brought nearer to us by every profound work of intellect, and which are imperceptible only —and always—to fools. So that the idea that Bergotte was not dead forever is not without probability.

Swann had perceptively realized, when he first heard the *motifs* of Vinteuil's music, that they were "the veritable ideas of another world." Marcel, when he listens to the last opus of Vinteuil, perceives that the musician has been returning to a lost fatherland, "une patrie perdue." Through his parable of that undiscovered country, Proust interlinks the recognitions of art with those of ethics, the disinterested imperatives of Vinteuil and Bergotte with the unselfish motives of Marcel's mother and grandmother. Moralistic critics, like Jacques Maritain, have taken Proust to task for lacking standards of value. They have confused the decadence that he chronicles with his damnation of it; and, what is worse, they have overlooked his sympathetic reaffirmation of the parental virtues. The pilgrimage has unexpectedly led from the *Almanach de Gotha* to the Old Testament. Thus, despite the subjective and dilettantish beginning, the ending—as Proust had predicted—is affirmative and objective. Dead forever? Possibly. Who can say? The books of Bergotte, with candles burning between them across the windows, are angels which foreshadow a resurrection. Poets have sighed for snows of yesteryear and counselled readers to gather ephemeral rosebuds, have beseeched the fair moment to tarry a while and repeatedly called upon time to suspend its flight. Proust's emphasis on changing fashions, superficially viewed, may well seem to make him the very laureate of mutability.

He did indeed preoccupy himself, not less elegiacally than Henry

James in *The Spoils of Poynton*, with "the poetry . . . of something sensibly gone." Indeed we seem to glimpse, with the disposal of Marcel's furniture, a disintegrating sense of property in its last corrupted stages. Yet things, the cherished things, the real things in their evanescence, dissolve into ideas. Bergson, himself the apostle of flux, understood exactly what was happening; for, in his review of Proust's interpretation of Ruskin, the French metaphysician had written of the English esthetician, "He is then an idealist to the highest degree, but he is also a realist, because for him matter is but the expression of the spirit." Proust had stated the proposition in theological terms, with a quasi-mystical reference to communion, when he wrote to Hahn, "You should know then that, in the Catholic liturgy, real presence actually means ideal presence." *Présence réelle* is the heading of one of his *Regrets et rêveries* in *Les Plaisirs et les jours*, and *l'adoration perpétuelle* was his phrase for a culminating section which never seems to have been committed to paper. He touches upon the subject more philosophically when he speaks of apprehending essences, moments common to both past and present, and therefore more essential than both. "We could not have asked," George Santayana has commented, "for a more competent or a more unexpected witness to the fact that life as it flows is so much time wasted, and that nothing can ever be recovered or truly possessed save under the form of eternity which is also, as he tells us, the form of art."

Art, Proust tells us, again religiously, is the true Last Judgment. It is our one chance for a conquest over time, as André Malraux would more belligerently put it, the single triumph of man, the time-binding animal, over circumstances highly unfavorable to the survival of anything. Survival does not promise immortality for books, any more than for authors, Proust concedes in one of his last marginalia. Yet art is a path for man's escape from history, the fulfillment of his yearning for timelessness, or eternal return, which Mircea Eliade has shown to be at the base of so many fundamental mythologies. In the endless issue between the schools of Heraclitus and Parmenides, exponents of the Many and of the One, which has been joined by innumerable moderns, poetized by Valéry in *Le Cimetière marin* and by T. S. Eliot in *Burnt Norton*, Proust seems to gravitate from the pole of change toward that of permanence. Joyce, in one of his notebooks under the heading of

"Proust," jotted down the formulation "analytic still life." It was the tribute of stasis to kinesis; for *Ulysses* is ultimately spatial, even as *A la recherche du temps perdu* is temporal in its element. But the adjectival focus is thoroughly warranted because, as Joseph Conrad noted, Proust had pushed analysis to the point where it became creative. He could only have reached that point through self-analysis, which he termed *auto-contemplation*, and through the most intimate sort of transference to those other selves, his readers.

In his youthful manifesto, *Contre l'obscurité*, he had praised the characters of *War and Peace* and *The Mill on the Floss* for achieving universality by way of individuality. *A la recherche du temps perdu*, as an achievement of that kind, is even more surprising, because its premises are so idiosyncratic, so far-fetched and special. Yet it bridges, as every great novel must do in its own way, the vast distance between the *moi* and the *nous*. Marcel retells his dreams and fantasies, but he remains essentially an insomniac, who stays wide awake while others sleep. Among the various optical instruments with which he metaphorically supplements the naked eye, he suggests that his book could be used as a sort of magnifying glass for studying ourselves—scanning the fine print, no doubt, and reading between the lines. Elsewhere, apropos of *Sesame and Lilies*, he remarks of books in general what seems to be particularly true of *A la recherche du temps perdu*: "reading is our guide whose magic keys open the door of dwellings we could not have entered within the depths of ourselves." Not so much for the modelling of his characters as for the training of our perceptions, for our enhanced awareness of the way things happen to happen, of how human beings respond or do not respond to one another, we may talk of keys in connection with Proust. That is why the serious reader, completing the final page of the many-volumed novel, is not the same person who opened the first volume some time ago.

VII

REALISM AND REALITY

2.063   The total reality is the world.

2.1   We make to ourselves pictures of facts.

2.12   The picture is a model of reality.

2.161   In the picture and the pictured there must be something identical in order that the one can be a picture of the other at all.

2.17   What the picture must have in common with reality in order to be able to represent it after its manner—rightly or falsely—is its form of representation.

2.21   The picture agrees with reality or not; it is right or wrong, true or false.

2.22   The picture represents what it represents, independently of its truth or falsehood, through the form of representation.

2.221 What the picture represents is its sense.

2.222 In the agreement or disagreement of its sense with reality, its truth or falsity consists.

2.223 In order to discover whether the picture is true or false we must compare it with reality.

—LUDWIG WITTGENSTEIN

1. From Essence to Existence

THE MOST EFFECTIVE of those whom, in retrospect, we have agreed to call realists, like Proust, have had little use for the term. His particular kind of realization, the rediscovery of self through the modalities of art, had little in common with simplifications preached on behalf of literary populism, denunciations launched against a besieged ivory tower, or the other rallying-cries that sounded while he was trying to complete his book. There is a sense in which reality was more elusive for him than it had been for his predecessors, to whose grasp it offered a harder core. For the epicurean Stendhal

it seemed to lay just around the corner, even though that corner
had been turned by moving on from the eighteenth into the nineteenth century. To have lived under the *ancien régime*, its survivors
were fond of repeating, was indeed to have known *la douceur de
vivre*. That nostalgic sweetness seems to have suffered a gradual
dilution of flavor, so that our elders now tell us what we have
missed by not living in the nineteenth century; and the adolescence
of the twentieth, the epoch of Proust's maturation, is reminiscently
sighed over as *la belle époque*. But the taste of life, to the author
of *Sentiments filiaux d'un parricide*, was more often bitter than
sweet; and A *la recherche du temps perdu* completes the tendency
of the novel to become a tragic medium. We may well agree with
Edmond Jaloux that Proust was "a man of the nineteenth century," the age that is both presumed and subsumed by his work.
Whether we should also regard the latter as the last of all novels,
with Ortega y Gasset, is one of the largest questions it leaves us
to face.

The novel, by historical definition, tends to pursue the real—an
unending quest, since the object changes its appearance in differing contexts and to different observers. "Every epoch has its own
realism, invented more or less in relation to the preceding epochs,"
remarked the late semi-abstractionist Fernand Léger. "Sometimes
it reacts against them—often it continues in the same line." The
line that we have been tracing may seem overdrawn, insofar as it
links together five unique personalities. Yet they unite in their
cumulative response to a continuous train of historic circumstance;
they occupy intercommunicating worlds. Each, in his turn and
after his fashion, strikes through the masks of received opinion and
flattering illusion, penetrates to still another facet of changing actuality, and complements and corroborates the others' testimony.
Thus Zola and Proust, from temperamental extremes, converge at
a moment of difficult truth, the vindication of Dreyfus. The radical
Stendhal and the orthodox Balzac are mutually consistent in their
diverse accounts of the Napoleonic aftermath. Flaubert, disagreeing so mordantly with the cultural establishment of his day, finds
substantial agreement with Baudelaire and other artists who will
have their day in culture. In political terms, our novelists are oppo-
sitionists, as in scientific terms they are experimentalists, and artistically they compose an advance guard. We have noted how closely

some of their efforts correlate with parallel undertakings in politics, the sciences, and the fine arts. But the sphere from which they learn most, to which they contribute most, is their own. Hence their names are decisive points of reference, not only for one another, but for all subsequent practitioners of novelistic technique.

It is through such concrete links that these masters constitute a tradition, untraditional though any one of them may be in his approach to a given situation. Jean Cocteau has resolved the paradox by maintaining that "the great French tradition is a tradition of anarchy." From the sidelines, through our witnesses, we have watched the anarchic forces at work in the continual movement and countermovement of revolution and reaction, throwing the relations between individuals and the social order—or social disorder—into peculiarly high relief. No nation in the modern world has been caught more strategically between the glories and the griefs of military conquest. Among the countries washed by the tidal waves of romantic sensibility, France, with its bulwarks of self-conscious rationality, was in the strongest position to react. The dialectical interplay goes on at the very level of education, where the cult of logic may be contrasted with the habit of rhetoric. Auspices have combined, then, to school the French in the realistic outlook, whereas it has been deprecated and qualified by the English. Sentiments, ideologies, and conventions variously presented themselves to our writers; but the generic pattern of deflation, reexamination, and readjustment has been constant. Each of them, in his own way, was at odds with vested authority; each found himself through personal crises and renunciations of conventional success. Three of them died at fifty-nine, two at fifty-one; their average creative span is between twenty-five and thirty years. Though none of them survived into old age, all left heavy backlogs of youthful apprentice-work. None had families, except for Zola, who had two ménages and two illegitimate children. Balzac is no exception to the rule of bachelorhood, since he did not marry until the end of his effectual career.

Vital statistics, in all their austerity, bring out the *disponibilité* of the five, the freedom of their uncommitted talents to meet the disposition of circumstances. One of them was disinherited; another failed in business; two were publicly tried, one exculpated, one pardoned. Flaubert and Proust were semi-invalids, living on private means; Stendhal subsisted as a minor bureaucrat, while his books went unsold; Balzac and Zola were hardy professionals, setting the pace for fiction among the best-sellers. None of them, of course, became an Academician; all of them engaged in occasional journalism, save Flaubert. It was the central figure of Saint Flaubert who incarnated and handed on the legend of the artist, who brought the discipline of poetry to the composition of prose, whose religion of style canonized a pedestrian genre into work of high art. For the next two generations of writers, French and Anglo-American, *fin-de-siècle* and *entre-deux-guerres*, he was the patron and intercessor. Serious writing underwent an alchemical process which Roland Barthes has named *Flaubertisation*. Ernest Hemingway genuflected before Flaubert's bust in the Luxembourg Gardens, "heavy now in stone as an idol should be." This tribute included a hint of the disaffection that would emerge in the second World War, the "petrifying fountain" of which Jean Prévost would complain in his diagnostic symposium, *Problèmes du roman*. The cultivation of the Flaubertian virtues, marmoreal and plastic, monumental and statuesque, presupposes both unlimited leisure and assured income. Consequently the long-neglected and casual Stendhal, the veteran improvisator responding to pressures by dashing off masterworks, has become "the anti-Flaubert," who supersedes the master of Croisset as a model for the present generation.

Proust's culminating place has had less occasion to change; but, since today's novelists grew up in his shadow, like Marcel growing up in Bergotte's, their attitude is bound to be charged with ambivalence. His example has confirmed the metaphysical bent of the French novel, its use as a mode of investigation in depth, an abstraction of philosophical essence from psychological experience. Vulgarly he has been identified with the more orchidaceous aspects of his subject-matter, been denounced for the moral decadence that he so sternly renounced, and been volubly blamed for the fall of France in 1940. Jean-Paul Sartre has even paused to sneer at his sexual mores, before going on to venerate his amoral saint, Jean Genet. The time that Proust evokes so elegiacally, it is all too clear, will never again be recaptured. The writer no longer is likely to appear as a dandy or a *rentier*, a spoiled child or a pampered neurasthenic. In recoil from such passivity, which has its epitaph in the posthumous volumes of *A la recherche du temps perdu*, he makes his reappearance among the activists of the 1930's, a Saint-Exupéry or a Malraux. Instead of Flaubertian detachment from fatherland and all else, or Proustian attachment to the esthetic and ethical values of a lost fatherland, he professes and practises commitment. Commitment to what? The question is by no means an idle one, as we try to follow André Malraux from cause to cause or from land to land. Just as revolution transcends the individual's fate, so action for its own sake seems to justify his fluctuating allegiances. It seems equally significant that he has long since given up novel-writing, and that—in spite of, or perhaps because of, his political activism—he looks for final principles within the sphere of art.

Faced with the instability and discontinuity of the government, French literature has carried more than its share of institutional responsibilities. Whenever the occasion has arisen, a remarkably articulate group of intellectuals, whether *clercs* or *philosophes*, has felt called upon to act as spokesmen for public issues. The realists, as polemical free-lances, belong with this group; as self-dedicated artists, they stand somewhat aloof. When Flaubert referred to himself and a few of his friends as mandarins, he implied that they formed a literate elite in an illiterate society. The contemporary writers depicted by Simone de Beauvoir in her mid-century novel, *Les Mandarins*, seem too harassed by controversies and crises of the moment to produce anything other than pamphleteering. "You are writing an essay, good enough," says one of them, "but to write a novel just now, you must admit, would be discouraging." Not surprisingly, *Les Mandarins* is a rather journalistic production. Madame de Beauvoir expresses a general viewpoint which gained respect in the lacerating years of German Occupation and French Resistance, when the enemy was no mere personification of ennui, and when the struggle was for existence itself. The resistants were fortified by their philosophy of survival, Existentialism, and by their deployment of propaganda, *la littérature engagée*. Some of them, beset by further urgencies, continue to feel that it is much too late for the leisurely practice of belles lettres or the painstaking concentration on masterpieces. The title of Jean-Paul Sartre's monthly review, *Les Temps modernes*, resolutely proclaims its disengagement from the past and from posterity. Its table of contents is notably stronger in human documentation than in imaginative fiction.

Here we have left the studio of the artist for the platform of the publicist. We do not seem to be very far removed from the humanitarian naturalism of the later Zola. But from that old mandarin, Flaubert, no effort has been spared to widen the distance. M. Sartre is even more contumelious with him than with Proust, and for the crowning reason that Flaubert is too bourgeois. It is true that Flaubert's hatred of the bourgeoisie seems retrospectively milder when we compare it with Sartre's, which has been exacerbated by infusions of Marxism. For the writer's engagement, his best exemplar is a Negro, the late Richard Wright, whom conditions forced so unequivocally to take a militant stance. Sartre's own novels might be briefly instanced, by way of comment on his commentary. The first and most successful, *La Nausée*, is classic, almost Cervantesque, in ironically juxtaposing the colorful past, as seen through the protagonist's bookish researches, with the sordid present that surrounds him at Bouville—and what a Flaubertian address! Where the two periods are integrated by Proust, who harmonizes names with things, for Sartre: "Things become detached from their names." From the resulting nausea, he has presumably sought a liberation in the tetralogy, *Les Chemins de la liberté*. But the three published volumes show the consequences of his disregard for artistry. A fairly numerous cast is handled by devices of montage borrowed from John Dos Passos, who has borrowed them from James Joyce, whom Sartre hardly seems to know at first-hand. His technical weakness as a narrator is his facile dependence on conversation to make up for the defects of characterization. His abilities are primarily those of the accomplished *causeur*, the café interlocutor and *lycée* dialectician.

Les Chemins de la liberté is so entirely preoccupied with the topical events of its period, so *engagé* by slogans and party-lines, that it seems to be already outdated, with less chance every year of solving its dilemmas by an unlikely fourth volume. It is truly discouraging to couple this breakdown of an ambitious project with Malraux's abdication from the field after the elegiac first volume of *La Lutte avec l'ange*, especially when we must register the immeasurable loss of Albert Camus in mid-career. Partly because of his North African background, partly because of his expressed affinities with Dostoevsky, Kafka, and Faulkner, Camus seems to have gazed into deeper abysses than most of his compatriots. The feeling of nostalgia is provincial; the mood of alienation is universal. Every man who looks before and after can see himself as a wanderer between worlds, but that transitional anguish is more acute when he feels uncertain of both his starting-point and his destination. Such is Camus' account of man's condition in *Le Mythe de Sisyphe:*

> ... in a universe suddenly deprived of illusions and illuminations, man feels himself a stranger. From this exile he has no resort, since he is deprived of both the memories of a lost fatherland and the hope of a promised land. This divorce between man and his life, between the actor and his setting, is precisely the sentiment of absurdity.

This passage not only heralds the disorientation of *L'Etranger;* quite as expressly, but vainly, it yearns for the Proustian region, *une patrie perdue;* nor does it encourage utopian aspirations toward *une terre promise.* The lunar landscape to which it abandons us, with its chilling silences and its unmeaningful disproportions, may be a far cry from Flaubert's Normandy; yet we should not forget the pioneering experimentation of *Bouvard et Pécuchet,* which demonstrated likewise the divorce between names and things, and which challenged the whole framework of paraphernalia that clutter up human endeavors. In that direction lies nihilism, the celebration of nothingness that posits the rejection of everything, ultimately arriving at the deranged underworlds and nightmarish perspectives of Céline and, latterly, Samuel Beckett. To exist, on the other hand, is not so much to indulge in Cartesian introspection as it is to plod through a Sisyphian predicament. Sartre poses the absolute alternative, and formulates his reasons for existing, in his ontological treatise, *L'Etre ou le néant.* Camus, less of a philosopher, more of a novelist, and just as much of an existentialist, pursues a roughly similar course from the nausea and negation of *L'Etranger* through the liberation and affirmation of *La Peste.* There, in therapeutic allegory, the individualistic doctor-hero proves his humanity by his devoted acceptance of a collective destiny.

Solutions are more provisory than problems, however. The end-

less task of Sisyphus, pushing his rock up the hill from which it is
fated to roll down ad infinitum, might well serve as an archetype
for the ups and downs of the novel from generation to generation.
The rock itself might be taken to prefigure the increasingly heavy
burden of materiality, under which each successive novelist is expected to struggle upwards. Things, etymologically and otherwise,
have been the determining factor in realism from its beginnings;
and its history has been, to a grimly sobering degree, a record of
losing battles fought against them by men and women. That conflict has its basis in man's own physical composition and in his
relationships with outer nature. Its happy episodes have been his
triumphs over his fleshly frailties or over the obduracy of his environment. Yet his control is limited, and is endangered by the
machinery he has devised to enforce it. The hazard may be succinctly illustrated from one of Nathalie Sarraute's delicate *Tropismes*: "Things. Objects. Ringing doorbells. Things that must not
be neglected." It is a commonplace of observation, which the realists have amply documented, that the development of technology
has tended to mechanize human beings. Understandably, American fiction has reflected this trend in a certain behaviorism, producing such creatures of sensation and reflex as Ernest Hemingway's
characters. France, despite its well-attested intellectuality, has its
exceptional counterpart in the insensate behavior of Camus' stranger, Meursault. But while such persons have been reified into virtual automata, scientists have been teaching machines to perform
many functions of humans, and it is even conceivable—for a poet
like Francis Ponge—to humanize things: *Le Parti pris des choses*.

Balzac may be said to have been the precursor of *chosisme*, as he
was of so many other possibilities which his more single-minded
successors have developed. Zola assigned a more causative function
to Balzac's catalogued profusion of *les choses*; Flaubert and Proust
selected them with rigorous care and endowed them with symbolic
purport. Generally speaking, the inclination of post-Balzacian novelists has been toward what Willa Cather called, in a suggestive
essay, "The Novel *Démeublé*": the streamlining of old-fashioned
techniques has entailed the stripping-down of overfurnished descriptions. Yet *les meubles* play the leading part in Madame Sarraute's novel, *Le Planétarium*, much as they did in James's *Spoils
of Poynton*. Character and plot, as structural elements, currently

yield ground to furnishings and surroundings. Objects are neither associations nor symbols but things-in-themselves, virtually fetishes. The impress of the centipede on the wall, in Alain Robbe-Grillet's *Jalousie*, is more concrete in its presence than any person. It is objective because it is irreducible, whereas the psychologizing of previous novelists—of Proust, above all—has reduced personalities to a state of subjectivity. The current aim is a total—albeit limited —objectivity, not unlike that *Neue Sachlichkeit* envisaged by German writers some decades ago, an impersonality so self-denying that Flaubert may seem sentimental by comparison. Michel Butor sketches a conception of *Le Roman comme recherche*, which owes a good deal to Proust and to some of the Anglo-American experimentalists. But his analysis is applied to the novel, rather than exercised within it; whereas his own experiments, sticking fairly close to the surfaces, are existential in their immediacy and phenomenological in their emphasis on "the appearance of reality."

By reacting against its predecessors, the younger contemporary generation does no differently than they have done in their time; by waving the banner of *alittérature*, it fully complies with the realistic convention of repudiating literariness. But it also seems to repudiate humanness, straining toward the technician's dream of incorporeal form: *le roman pur, le roman blanc*. While appropriate labels are being proposed, critics might consider *le roman-gageure*, which at any rate suggests the venturesome ingenuity of these novelists, in imposing handicaps on themselves and playing games with their readers. It is decidedly not an accident that *le nouveau roman*, by whatever name we invoke it, coincides with the sequence of films, at once inventive and enigmatic, known as *la nouvelle vague*. The influences of the American novel upon the French, as Claude-Edmonde Magny discerned, began with the impact of the film. It has seemed a logical step for M. Robbe-Grillet to transpose his energies from prose fiction to cinema and *le ciné-roman*. *Le Voyeur*, his characteristic book, moves from the angle of vision through a protagonist's mind to *choses vues*; but words and deeds have surrendered to images; as John Weightman points out, "interior monologue is replaced by interior film." The result is pure exteriority, which may well be what was intended, and which brings home the effect of dehumanization. It is as if the long-dreaded bombs were dropping on cities at last, leaving intact the buildings and all their equipment, and simply vaporizing the people. In a civilization where matter itself has proved to be so destructible, where non-existence can be such an imminent reality, fiction can be no more inhuman than truth. One of Carlo Levi's spokesmen raises, with harrowing literalness, the question of an ultimate reification:

> What kind of novels do you expect after Auschwitz and Buchenwald? Have you seen the photographs of women weeping as they buried pieces of soap made from the bodies of their husbands and their sons? That's the way the confusion came to an end: the individual exchanged for the whole. . . . There it is, your *tranche de vie*—a piece of soap.

2. *The Banal Canvas*

With a shudder of momentary relief, we turn back to the nineteenth century once more. By retroactive contrast with the disasters that mankind has subsequently faced or still faces, it looms behind us as a citadel of comfort and stability, harboring the accumulations of culture and fostering the self-expressions of individualism. If the defects of its safety were dullness and smugness, if its official tone often took on a philistine edge, then its sensitive minds could freely and brilliantly object. Sin and guilt were perennial for Baudelaire, and crimes of violence were all the more monstrous when they were inhibited by the time-spirit of Ennui.

> Si le viol, le poison, le poignard, l'incendie
> N'ont pas encor brodé de leurs plaisants dessins
> Le canevas banal de nos piteux destins,
> C'est que notre âme, hélas! n'est pas assez hardie.

Such is the poet's warning to his other self, the hypocritical reader, which prefaces *Les Fleurs du mal,* and which was first published in the *Revue des deux mondes* during 1855. Two years later Flaubert gave him occasion to recall his artistic term, and to transpose the image from tapestry to painting. In his penetrating review of *Madame Bovary,* Baudelaire speaks of the wager that the novelist has made with himself, as it were: the primary condition is to pick "un canevas banal" and to lay on "un style nerveux, pittoresque, subtile, exact." Life is the easel for the banal canvas of our pitiful destinies; art is what it should be, the brush and the palette; and the reviewer elaborates the paradox, which no one could have appreciated better than he, of vulgar subject-matter treated with stylistic elegance. This was a traditional premise for the mock-epic, with its implicit ironies. But the realistic method held further consequences which, as Ernst Cassirer perceived, "were able to overcome the conventional dualism between the poetic and the prosaic spheres." The classicists and the romanticists were alike in their esthetic assumption that subjects had to be beautiful or wonderful in order to be worthy of serious treatment. On the contrary, the realists believed that in the arts, as in the sciences, everything ought to be studied that elicited human interest. Critical theories, by adhering to the old concept of imitation, were sidetracked into controversies over the value of what was being imitated. Cassirer's interpretation of symbolism, presupposing the wholeness of experience, authorizes the artist to impose his forms on any aspect of it.

When Balzac's artist, Théodore de Sommervieux, paints his picture of the drapery shop in *La Maison du Chat-qui-pelote*, the shopkeeper is not amused. "Is it so very amusing to see a painting of what you meet with every day in our street?" asks M. Guillaume. His naïve reaction is typically bourgeois, and Balzac himself does not altogether deserve it. Like his painter, he was concerned with what happens in our street, and to some extent with what happens every day. To a greater extent, he was concerned with the exceptional happening. To make the ordinary interesting, he made it extraordinary; he embellished his metropolis by exaggerating its crimes and romances; in this respect, they do not greatly diverge from the *faits divers* of sensational journalism; but in context we may classify him, with Dickens and Gogol, as a romantic realist. Theirs was a normal stage of transition between romanticism, with its sense of fantasy, and what might strictly be called quotidian realism, with its notation of the commonplace. Behind the romantics lay revolution and empire, and—along with their tarnished watchwords—a more eventful notion of reality, whose dying horn was unforgettably sounded by Stendhal. The canvas of current events seemed banal by the mid-century, perhaps more banal than the actual situation warranted; for, though the Revolution of 1848 erupted through the streets of Flaubert's Paris, it is deliberately evaded by Frédéric Moreau. Here and now is everyday occurrence; then and there—in Carthage? Alexandria?—was grandiose adventure. Through the course of a single book, *Ulysses*, in parallel lines which never meet, Joyce would poise the grandeur of the past against the triviality of the present. Like his master, Flaubert, he would construct a monument to banality by utilizing the utmost resources of artistry.

Flaubert professed a scorn of literary platforms; Zola used them adroitly to display his own works; both of them, in their different ways, transcend their doctrinal associations. The names that are ineluctably associated with the name of Naturalism are those of Edmond and Jules de Goncourt. Though their claims to the doctrine have priority over Zola's, they followed the example of Flaubert. Indeed they sought to outdistance their exemplar by moving in two directions simultaneously: on the one hand, by choosing sordid themes and, on the other, by cultivating a precious style. They too had their temporal and geographical respite, from the daily ugliness they forced themselves to transcribe, in their hobbies of eighteenth-century antiquarianism and Japanese exoticism. They heightened the drabness of their fictional canvases by laying on the local colors of vice and pathology. Above all, in that resounding preface to the anticlimactic *Germinie Lacerteux*, they laid down a principle of progression for future novelists, novel-readers, and even novel-characters: *le droit au roman*. Accordingly, as fiction has developed, it has widened its purview, until it has become the most capacious of genres; and newer aspects of experience, whenever they have been recognized as such, gradually yet continually, have been encompassed by the expanding medium. To a large degree, this has been a matter of social representation, and decisively so when the emphasis shifted from the aristocracy to the bourgeoisie. In their manifesto, the Goncourts demanded that the common people be accorded their right to the novel: that is to say, their recognition within the novel—we need not assume that they would care to read such novels, any more than that *Uncle Tom's Cabin* was addressed to a Negro audience.

Zola, if not the Goncourts, met that demand during the course of his comprehensive undertaking. The following generation, the first to be heard in the twentieth century, looking toward a full spread of the democratic franchise, brought forth such wholly proletarian novelists as Maxim Gorky and Martin Andersen Nexø. Though it might now be taken for granted that every class had a voice, there were other elements of society which struggled toward expression: minorities heretofore unrepresented in literature, races on the point of becoming vocal, regions newly opened to psychophysical exploration, taboos being lifted by changes in custom or taste. Extending its conquests over a wider and wider domain, fiction keeps on looking for worlds to conquer. Sooner or later it hopes to get everything down on paper and into print, to approximate a one-to-one correspondence between language and actuality: *pouvoir tout dire,* in the bold phrase of Paul Eluard. Each emergent writer stakes out and exploits his own terrain in the area of the unwritten. The objective of Henry Miller, "the recording of all that which is omitted in books," does not differ in kind from the formula of Cervantes. But since so many books have accumulated meanwhile, later additions to the record have become increasingly specialized. Since the theme of sex has been hedged about by convention or censorship until quite recently, it has remained—so Norman Mailer states in an interview—"perhaps the last frontier of the novel which has not been exhausted by nineteenth and twentieth-century novelists." In England, where realism and its congeners were distrusted as importations from France, a native school was known to mid-Victorians as the Sensation Novelists. Whether the sensation is willfully sought or was inadvertently created, the epithet seems more widely appropriate.

When an admirer of Mr. Miller declares that he "has given us the last *frisson,*" the reassuring implication is that we have lived through all the shocks and surprises likely to come our way. No frontiers are left, everything has been recorded, and there is really nothing more to say. We have indeed been reaching limits, limits of expression if not of experience; for times continue to change, and neo-realists do their pedestrian duty in keeping up with them. The well-meaning epigones of naturalism—Romain Rolland, Roger Martin du Gard, Georges Duhamel, Jules Romains—have at least preserved the intimate annals of the Third Republic through their meandering *romans-fleuve.* Professional novelists will always be stirred, as Zola was, by the challenge of providing an up-to-date *Comédie humaine.* Balzac has been the inevitable patron of the imposing fictional synthesis, from the *Episodios nacionales* of Pérez

Galdós to the Mississippi legend of William Faulkner. Naturalism
still claims an annual godchild when the Prix Goncourt is awarded,
and our popular novels have standardized those techniques which
the realists fought for and suffered over. When stories in *The New
Yorker* invite our concern for the most trivial details in the least
significant lives, when J. D. Salinger accompanies his characters
into the bathroom and pauses there to itemize the contents of the
family medicine-chest, we may not have experienced the last shudder, but we have attained a definitive yawn. We need not sigh for
new privacies to invade. We have come a long way, for better or
for worse, since Diderot praised Richardson for the rendition of
"toute la réalité possible." Not that the whole of reality is, by
nature, exhaustible; but the quantitative approach to it is, by definition, limited. Hence we seem to have run through that cycle of
possibilities, and to be due for some sort of qualitative change.

In 1891 Zola's disciple, Paul Alexis, responding to a much discussed questionnaire on literary trends, sent a telegram reading:
"Naturalism not dead. Letter follows." The oracle proved to be
more or less correct; making up in inertia for what it lost in momentum, the naturalistic movement has survived as a quasi-official
tradition. That this involves a reversal of its historic role even its
pious historian, Charles Beuchat, vaguely admits; for, having
gained its characteristic impetus by reacting against the established
schools, *le naturalisme* became reactionary in the more orthodox
sense, serving its turn as a target for forthcoming -isms. Among
these latter, the most pyrotechnical manifestation was that of
surréalisme. Whether we accept it at face value as super-realism or
share the doubts that would construe it as sub-realism, it was un-
ambiguous in its anti-realism. Although their pyrotechnics produced less light than heat and less heat than noise, the Surrealists
were serious in their efforts to revive and exalt the latent imaginative strain: the visionary, the oneiric, the phantasmagorical currents
that ran underground through the nineteenth century seeking escape from its external realities. André Breton, in his manifesto of
1924, called for an "absolute nonconformism." That would not
merely have been an impractical gesture; it was an unrealizable
contradiction. Absolute conformity may be conceivable, however
regrettable; nonconformity could hardly be other than relative,
since—like liberty, or realism itself—it can only flout certain sanc-

tions by observing others. *Surréalisme* was most meaningful in its refusal to conform with *le réalisme*. In that revolt it was joined by pseudo-movements, which produced little else except manifestos: the mindless Dadaists and the futureless Futurists.

But the cyclic pattern, whereby the *avant-garde* captured the establishment over previous generations, can no longer be said to prevail. Instead, the neo-naturalists sustain a rear-guard action, reinforced by defectors from the insurgent coteries of the 1920's. The situation has been stabilized by the supply and demand of the literary market. "*Don Quixote, Manon Lescaut, La Cousine Bette,* and all the masterpieces of fiction have not had the success of *Uncle Tom,*" lamented Flaubert, all the more uncomfortable because his outstanding success, *Madame Bovary,* had also attracted its public on problematic grounds. Standard products of later novelists, applying smoothly conventional techniques to mildly novel subjects, regularly head our best-seller lists. In pursuit of their Balzacian aim—"to compete with the civil registry"—they have populated sphere after sphere. With Zolaesque enterprise they have covered territory, exposed problems, and worked up the tricks of the various trades. They go on contributing, not to the novelistic craft, but to the common stock of *petits faits vrais* and *documents humains.* "The American desire for the real has created a journalistic sort of novel which has a *thing* excitement, a glamor of *process*: it specializes in information," writes Saul Bellow. "...It merely satisfies the reader's demand for knowledge." Precisely; and though that satisfaction is by no means unworthy, it can be better served by more literal sources of information. Fiction is bound to lose out in its competition with fact. The merest newspaper holds the advantage of authority over the novel of reportage, which combines watered-down fact with water-logged fiction. A first-hand reminiscence of concentration camps, such as David Rousset's, is bound to be far more impressive than any fictitious approximation.

These considerations may throw some light on the predominance of observation over imagination in, among so many others today, Jean-Paul Sartre and his followers. Our concern for a matter-of-fact authenticity, which turns the more outgoing novelists into reporters, confirms the more introspective in their natural bent, and drives them back upon the facts of their respective autobiographies. "All serious work in fiction is autobiographical," according to Thomas Wolfe, whose word may be a weathervane if not a touchstone. William Butler Yeats filled in the generalization with his wry remark "that in every novel that has created an intellectual fashion from Huysmans' *La Cathédrale* to Ernest Hemingway's *Farewell to Arms*, the chief character is a mirror." Hemingway's mirror has at least been portable, like Stendhal's; and yet, unquestionably, there has been a mounting trend toward self-scrutiny; the author has come out of his Flaubertian hiding-place and offered himself as his own fullest case history. Hence Gide gave us many *récits*, though only one *roman*, and Proust's one finished novel turned out to be the most intensive of all exercises in the first person singular. Only by focussing upon himself could the novelist look beneath the habitual surfaces of realism—and Proust, rejecting that label, would probably have welcomed the metaphorical overtones of Ortega's prefix, "infra-realism." The Proustian analysis, as Ramon Fernandez was quick to observe, shifted the center of gravity from the characters in a novel to the mind of the novelist. He could be accused of developing his ego at the expense of his dramatis personae. Speaking for the new school, Nathalie Sarraute argues shrewdly that this has been a temporary displacement which would scarcely do for other novelists than Proust, and that even the characters he has taken apart are mentally reassembled into classical types by the reader.

Madame Sarraute's collection of essays bears the warning title, *L'Ere du soupçon*. For her the relation between writer and reader seems marked by suspicion, rather than by that willing suspension of disbelief which once united them in mutual trust, and in a triadic identification with the leading character. Subjectivism could not profitably be carried beyond the involvements of the Proustian *moi*. After a generation of commitments to disappointing causes, once again—as with the apolitical generation of Flaubert—the striving is for detachment. Technically, it goes beyond all the precedents for dissolving characterization into sequences of discrete impressions. Though Edouard Dujardin is credited with the invention of internal monologue, French writers have not developed it so fully as Joyce or Faulkner, while Sartre has contended plausibly that its rendering of the so-called stream-of-consciousness is more of a rhetorical convention than a psychological reality. Properly speaking, it is with point of view rather than with center

of consciousness that our contemporary objectivists have been experimenting, since their mode of presentation is visual rather than
cognitive, and their focus is transposed as sharply and suddenly as
if the organ of apprehension were literally the lens of a camera. At
a distance the narrative technique becomes a prosopopoeia, a
speaking thing. This may well complete the tendency of the novelist to disappear behind his creation. Even Flaubert had gone no
farther than to hide behind his protagonist, not always invisibly.
Stendhal had been himself-as-raconteur, and Balzac the secretary
of society. Moving toward the opposite extreme of depersonalization and impersonation, Zola was the scientific temperament, while
Proust was whom but Marcel? "The demise of the narrator is the
death of the novel," Wolfgang Kayser has predicted.

Other critics, more interested in morale than in form, have
been struck less by the withdrawal of the narrator than by the
eclipse of the hero. Insofar as heroism meant warlike prowess, this
decline may be an index of ideological progress, which was already
observable in the transit from Corneille to Racine. Not that the
wars are all over, unhappily. During the intervals between them,
our writers have been searching for moral equivalents: Malraux
in all manner of revolutions, Hemingway in bull-fights, prize-
fights, fights with other writers. But the military image has been
shrinking, ever since Fabrice del Dongo's misadventures at the
turning-point of Waterloo, which left potential heroes unemployed and ready to compromise in their civilian careers, like
Eugène de Rastignac. If the ruling personage was the bourgeois
rampant, he was incarnate in such anti-heroes as Birotteau or
Homais. The tired young man of the mid-century, a Frédéric
Moreau, or the stylish dilettante of the *fin du siècle*, a Charles
Swann, was reduced to an ineffectual onlooker. Meanwhile the
proletarian underdog was acquiring dignity, if not stature, partici-
pating with Etienne Lantier or Jean Macquart in the large collectivities of mine or farm—or the army, for it seemed to some that
heroic values might be recaptured on an anonymous scale. This
has offered one answer to the restlessly reiterated anxiety of Malraux: "It is difficult to be a man." Such difficulties constitute the
stuff of tragedy, especially when they are overcome or heroically
resisted, as they so notably were in *La Condition humaine*. But all
too frequently twentieth-century literature has had to record a

total surrender to them, a relinquishment of the humane to the inhuman or of the virile to the perverse. Thus Jean Genet's *Notre Dame des fleurs* reads curiously like a homosexual burlesque of *Le Rouge et le noir*.

Franz Kafka was fascinated by an account of Balzac's famous walking-stick, which was reported to have borne the motto: "I break every obstacle." For himself the relationship with things was reversed, he ruefully commented: every obstacle broke him. He could not have more succinctly exemplified the difference between his heroes and Balzac's, or between the paralytic rhythm of Proust and Joyce and many of their contemporaries and the dynamic tempo of their nineteenth-century forerunners. This deceleration was by no means a deterioration, since it provided compensating opportunities for reflection, inwardness, and depth. Moreover, it combined with formal developments to promote an esthetic ideal, and to secure the standing of the novel as a fine art. In the case of Proust, the novelist coalesces with the protagonist, who ends by rising from his supine position in order to personify the artist. His self-portraiture is not only spiritual autobiography but, like Courbet's painting of his studio, realistic allegory. Baudelaire, who figured in that picture, maintained in an essay that modern life was not without its heroics, however disguised. Its raw material might be a banal canvas, such as both he and Flaubert had chosen to work with. But if it was shapeless and colorless, crude and vague, it could be wholly transfigured by a style like Flaubert's, as Baudelaire described it: sinewy, picturesque, subtle, exact. Zola, in describing what he regarded as Flaubert's naturalism, conceded a crucial point about his own: "Inevitably, the novelist kills the heroes off, if he recognizes only the ordinary course of common existence." But if he is acute enough to grasp the meaning of this homely substance, and enough of an artist to preserve and convey it, then he may be a hero for the nonce in his own right.

3. *Toward Mythology*

"All possible fields for the novel have been so often cropped, as the farmers say, that nobody will be able to get much from any of them unless he is a cultivator of very rare ability." This bit of rustic wisdom is culled from an editorial on "The Decline of the Novel," which appeared in *The Nation* (New York) during 1868, arguing—somewhat *pro domo*—that an increasing sociological emphasis would end by turning the functions of the novel over to the daily and weekly press. The prophecy could not have been worse timed. Henry James was just beginning his career; Tolstoy was completing *War and Peace*; indeed, it would be hard to think of a date when more of the world's great novelists were active. When we think of all that has happened to fiction since, and of the similar prophecies that are circulating today, perhaps we should feel encouraged to disregard them. Even Zola in 1872, rereading Balzac between his own early bouts with *Les Rougon-Macquart*, could lament that the novel was undergoing its death-throes. The *Nation* article failed to foresee that the very cropping of obvious fields might provide a special incentive for cultivators of rare ability. Yet it did point out an inherent weakness of that incipient naturalism which, now after nearly a hundred years, has revealed many signs of attenuation and possible exhaustion. So clairvoyant an observer as Ortega y Gasset noted the possibility when he first read Proust, and his *Notes on the Novel* are significantly coupled with his essay on *The Dehumanization of Art*. The diagnosis has been widely and loudly echoed in recent years, most impressively by novelists themselves. Thus Alberto Moravia, in an interview, frankly declares that Proust and Joyce have killed off the novel "as we knew it in the nineteenth century."

The saving clause almost restores the situation that has been abandoned, inasmuch as it is in the nature of the novel to out-distance its antecedents. The virtuosity of the 1920's seems to have carried this impetus to its *ne plus ultra*—or, at least, its point of diminishing returns. Up to that point, the recognizable mode was naturalism, which has been the last prolongation of realism. Be-yond that point, the quality of the attempt may be sufficiently different to require—what Diderot bespoke for Richardson—a new category. Those *nouveaux romans*, which go by so many other names, might be said to wear the look of post-novels. Paul Valéry considered the art of novel-writing to be "all but inconceivable." He did conceive, as an instance of its futility, one hypothetical sentence: "The Marquise went out at five o'clock." And Claude Mauriac has lately accepted the wager by publishing a novel entitled *La Marquise sortit à cinq heures*, thereby proving that Valéry exaggerated, and that obituaries are premature. Well, we have reached the stage where ingenuity is being strained to prove that the old game can still be played. The old themes can be varied indefinitely; and those who perform the variations deserve our thanks for keeping the spirit of craftsmanship alive; yet all the cinematographic contrivance of *La Jalousie* leaves us farther away from a human relationship than the baffled jealousy of Marcel over Albertine. There is a kind of *pointillisme* in the technique of M. Robbe-Grillet and his colleagues which may remind us of the later, the more mathematical Impressionists. Seurat and Signac are both clever and charming; but they seem elusive and manneristic after Cézanne and Renoir. The *roman-gageure* is a symptom of, and not a solution to, the present crisis of the novel.

Now the decline, or even the demise, of any particular genre need not in itself be a cause for alarm, though the underlying circumstances may claim our serious concern. Fabulation, "la fonction fabulatrice," which Bergson located at the midpoint between the communications of intellect and the expressions of instinct, is an integral part of man's psychic endowment. Storytelling has always been, and will probably go on being, one of the main continuities of culture; by that token it has been, and should continue to be, especially protean in its successive adaptations to cultural change. Certain genres seem to enjoy their heyday under certain historical conditions; the epochs of the drama have presupposed, in every case, a favoring social equilibrium; and we have seen something of those institutional factors which have helped the novel to become what Georg Lukács has repeatedly characterized as "the peculiar genre of bourgeois society." We also see the primacy of the form being currently undermined, not merely by specific changes in literary taste but by a general regression from literature itself. It is not only that fiction cannot keep pace with journalism, but that the verbal medium cannot vie with the audiovisual, in supplying tangible satisfaction for factual curiosities. Mechanical and electronic reproduction has not yet made literature a thing of the past, as was predicted a generation ago by the populist writer, Henri Poulaille; but there can be little doubt that books occupy a far less central place in the lives of average readers than in the days when George Sand was a household word. A contemporary

Emma Bovary would indulge her fantasies through films and be a reader of movie-magazines. The cinema has taken the place of the library as an agency of sentimental education. The novelist's silent collaborator, the reading public, has altered more than he, to his perplexity.

It is the photograph, according to André Malraux, which has most effectually competed with the civil registry. The novelist, in spite of Balzac's intention, might prefer to emulate the impressionistic painter, whom the invention of photography had released from the demand for literal representation—not to say photographic realism. The novel, we say, has consistently moved in a realistic direction: in other words, closer and closer to reality, as continually reinterpreted with reference to a changing style of life and view of the world. This progression seems to be normally irreversible; it is a species of tropism, animated by its own freedom of movement; it cannot move backwards, unless its forward path is blocked or counterpressures are brought into play. The novel was set in motion by breaking loose from the romance, which had been dominated by conventions. In hierarchical cultures, where status is frozen and values are fixed, the arts tend to be strictly conventionalized, as they were through the longstanding dynasties of Egypt or China and, to a lessening degree, in Byzantium or the medieval West. Realism, which is perennially at odds with convention yet cannot altogether dispense with it, cannot thrive except among the mobile institutions of an open society. "The novel was born with modern capitalism; it is saturated with individualism and liberal culture; it is characteristically middle-class," writes V. S. Pritchett, and then asks: "Is the novel tied to the fate of capitalism and the liberal view of life?" Not knowing the fate of capitalism, we should be begging the question if we tried to divine it from the state of the novel. But we would have the glimmering of an answer, if we could inquire how the novel has fared in one of its great fatherlands, which repudiates capitalism and looks askance at the liberal view of life.

Without presuming to press such an inquiry, which would be a most exacting and illuminating study for those who were competent and free to pursue it, we may relevantly ask what realism can mean in Soviet Russia. We know that Stendhal, Balzac, Zola, and other French realists are as highly esteemed there as foreign writers can be. Maxim Gorky, acknowledging their part in his own intellectual formation, gave eloquent expression to that esteem. Accepting the fact of their middle-class origin, along with the Marxian principle of the class struggle, he hailed them as "apostates of their class," who, by resisting its ideology, had been enabled to "elucidate its life, traditions, and deeds in a critical light." In this respect, they are not unlike the Russian realists of the nineteenth century, whose insight was so deeply rooted in their resistance to the Tsarist autocracy, and whose long exiled heir was Gorky himself. After the Revolution, he became the pivotal figure in an official effort to connect the realistic tradition with the Communist ideology. The two positions are not incompatible, insofar as both uphold the *droit au roman,* in criticizing the bourgeoisie and sympathizing with the proletariat. But, where such a position took independence under a bourgeois regime, it takes no more than conformity under a proletarian dictatorship. The realists have been nothing if not individualists; if they have shown any single trait in common, it has been the habit of viewing things—to echo Gorky's phrase—in a critical light. Consequently, it would be pleonastic for us to speak of critical realism; yet it denotes a necessary distinction, whenever the Marxists invoke their conventional slogan of socialist realism—sometimes condensed to "socrealism," which seems quite appropriate, since it sounds like an *ersatz* product.

It would be just as logical to speak of capitalist realism, Abram Tertz has suggested, or of Christian or Mohammedan realism, as if it were a doctrine rather than a method. Tertz is the pseudonym of a Soviet writer who has managed to publish outside Russia, and who has divulged how Russian writing must conform to the directives of the Communist Party line: "Socialist realism starts from an ideal image to which it adapts the living reality." So did Don Quixote, and that is why Cervantes started the novel off on its realistic course. Could any viewpoint be more remote from the untrammeled observation of Tolstoy? Among the many questions raised by Boris Pasternak through *Doctor Zhivago,* perhaps the most searching was: ". . . where is reality in Russia today?" Literature has been lagging behind it, Georg Lukács testifies ambiguously, and the ambiguity seems to hinge on whether reality is given a public or private definition. Fiction is richly detailed in its

poster-like presentation of wartime experiences, industrial processes, or colorful regions of the Soviet Union. Such incidental
naturalism is used to fill in plots and to fill out characters which,
more often than not, are blueprints and stereotypes controlled by
ideological preconceptions. While Western critics deplore the
dearth of heroes, Russians call upon their novelists for a positive
hero—and, so long as the living reality can be adapted to the ideal
image, they are likely to get him. In short, their socialist realism is,
more precisely, an uncritical idealism—or, as they would put it in
candid moments, a revolutionary romanticism. The books it fosters,
projecting the ideals of their closed society, may in themselves be
either good or bad; but they will be closer to epic legends than
novels, as we have known them in the self-critical West.

The epic strain, to be sure, had never been quite defunct. Both
Tolstoy and Melville touched it, as Zola did momentarily, conferring moral stature on simple men by bringing them out into the
open air and away from cities, the depreciating zones of realism.
Joyce's paradox was his conflation of modern urbanism with his
anti-hero's re-enactment of classical epos. In the 1920's, Louis
Aragon joined in the counterattacks of the Surrealists, wrote his
Paysan de Paris to renew "the sentiment of quotidian wonder,"
and scornfully declared that the word *réalité* was worth no more
than the musicality of its component syllables: *"La ré la ré la
réalité."* In the 1930's, having brought his anti-realism into the
Marxist camp, Aragon was campaigning *Pour un réalisme socialiste*, and equating reality with the rise of the working class. The
heresiarch of the Russian Revolution, Leon Trotsky, recognized
that realism was never an unmixed element, and that symbolism
constituted an important part of the intermixture. In an essay
on the Symbolist poets, he allowed: "Artistic creation, no matter
how realistic, has always been and remains symbolist." Art does not
blindly copy life; it singles out what is typical; and Trotsky instances the enduring significance of such types as Mephisto, Faust,
Hamlet, and Othello. Few, if any, of these would qualify as positive heroes; they are all much too individualistic to typify those
attributes which excite hero-worship and which might egg the
worshippers on to heroics of their own. On the other hand, when
Wagner presented his musical-dramatic tetralogy of the *Ring*, its
enlightened audiences must have felt immeasurably far removed

from the barbaric primitivism of his Volsungs and Valkyries. "People who go to Bayreuth," exclaimed Georges Sorel, "never dream of becoming Germanic heroes!"

The large irony that has overtaken the small irony here need hardly be underscored. It is additionally ironic that Sorel, of all political theorists, who pointed out the guise that Marxism would take as a twentieth-century mythology, overlooked the ominous potentialities of the Teutonic revival. Yet he went farther than other minds that were framed by the prosaic and well-ordered perspectives of the nineteenth century, and whose consequent view of life was the banal canvas of quotidian realism, by heralding a reality which has been eventful to the point of becoming millennial, where truth has been stranger than fiction and fiction more dangerous than ever because no clear-cut line has divided it from the truth. To be able to tell the true from the false, the real from the fictive, with any sense of certainty, presupposes a reasonably solid world-view. Art can be viewed and judged as imitation only when men are in confident touch with the realities that have been imitated. Otherwise there can be no critical act of comparison, no empirical test for delusive appearances. Appearance itself has been the criterion in most artistic traditions, with what may be behind it either left in a mystical limbo or consigned to a transcendent other world. Esthetically, the crucial relation has therefore been what Erich Auerbach called figural, the correspondence between one symbol and another, rather than the literal relation of image to object. Historically, as in other ways, the realistic approach has been exceptional; and there have been hints at many levels suggesting that its epoch, which began with the humanism of the Renaissance, will soon have receded into the past. In order "to exalt the present and the real," as Walt Whitman did so loudly and firmly, man must feel more thoroughly at home in his world and in his time.

Instead, he faces that feeling of alienation which Camus has so poignantly attested. Instead of living for the immediacy of the moment or living with the concreteness of the real thing, he looks for comfort in ultimates and abstractions. From the self-conscious attitude of modernity, of nowness, newness, novelty, he reverts to timeless patterns and traditional sanctions. "From the bourgeois and individual to the mythical and typical"—so Thomas

Mann, in recapitulating his own development, traced the trajectory of the novel during the past generation. That it might, in its most interesting manifestations, be no longer a novel, that the superimposition of myth was creating a new or transitional form—such was the programmatic argument of T. S. Eliot when he reviewed *Ulysses*. No fiction, of course, has ever existed without some sort of mythical substratum. Picasso could envisage *Les Demoiselles d'Avignon* as African primitives. "Literature is a decomposed and rationalized mythology," to the psychologist, Théodule Ribot. "... The myth approximates the ordinary conditions of human life until it becomes a romantic, and finally a realistic, novel." From the vantage-point of comparative religion, Mircea Eliade has lately added the remarkably stimulating suggestion that the novels of the nineteenth century be reconsidered as a corpus of myths. This would entail a whole series of thematic studies, some of which—I would venture to hope—have been adumbrated through the foregoing chapters: for example, the Napoleonides, the impact of a heroic image upon declining generations of progeny; the *femme incomprise*, her quest for feminine roles beyond the merely sexual or familial; the underworld, with the criminal as lapsed hero flinging his protest in the teeth of society; the machine, its metamorphoses of things and the adjustments or maladjustments of lives; and art, the esthetic consciousness of the artist as a point of departure and return.

Such is the folklore of civilization: neither the biography of writers nor the pseudo-biography of their characters, but the stuff of collective experience as it has been sensitively registered and compactly preserved. Though history supplies it with dates and names and settings and appropriate changes of costume, its themes can be reduced to self-repeating archetypes. The passage of time seems temporarily arrested by our very awareness of time. Proust, its registrar, found a touchstone for timelessness in the architecture of medieval churches; and, in one of his essays about them, he stressed the effectiveness of the liturgical background in the death-scene of Emma Bovary. If he himself was close to the *Symbolistes*, Flaubert was a penitent romanticist constantly backsliding, and both were only less interested in the fabulous than they were in the true. Zola, for all his scientific pretensions and journalistic exertions, gained more effect through his symbolic conceptions and epic sweep. As for Balzac, his many claims included the visionary, and of *La Peau de chagrin* he boasted: "Everything in it is myth and figure." Of our five authors, Stendhal remains the most intransigent in his worldly rationalism, possibly for chronological reasons, allowing little to distract his attention from the immediate and the actual. Yet the current trend toward mythography is so impelling that, along with Albert Béguin's well-grounded *Balzac visionnaire*, we now have Gilbert Durand's over-argued *Décor mythique de la Chartreuse de Parme*. We have seen that the realists make their use of romantic conventions, and we may grant that a recessive element of symbolism is powerful in their work. But if the myth has been the source of modern fiction, it has come down to earth; its collapse, as Ortega taught us, was the basic occasion for the novel, the anti-mythical novel of Cervantes.

With all due reverence for origins, we ought not to forget how far we have travelled from them, or how strenuously the realists have labored to counteract the influences of simple-minded credulity. Happily, we can take fantasy for granted; it springs eternal in human situations; civilized cultures may well distinguish themselves from primitive tribes by their habit of bringing reason to bear on imagination. Mythology has generously endowed us with our parable, in the ancient allegory of the twin gates. The ivory gate has always been the one surrounded by welcoming crowds, since its apparitions are so attractive and easy. To stand at the hornèd gate is an anxious and difficult vigil, since it is conceived as our only means of access to the portents of reality. Realism, we may by now be willing to admit, is a rigorous discipline. Image-breaking, for man, is harder than image-making. All the other forms of fiction may delude and delight. The novel, though born among them, must turn against them. Ungrateful task! Yet it is by becoming iconoclastic, mythoclastic, rationalistic, analytic, self-critical, that it has sublimated a casual pastime into a mode of knowledge. Literature, of every kind and in every age, belongs to life and reveals it somehow or other, sometimes obliquely or incidentally. The direct and deliberate revelation, the confrontation of life by literature, is uniquely characteristic of the modern outlook as Matthew Arnold has defined it, with its challenge to life and its criticism of life. André Malraux has broadened that panorama, broad as it is, with his dictum: "Our art . . . is becoming an interrogation of the world." To strike the interrogative note is to realize anew how the pace has been set by experimental science and—here M. Malraux would enlarge his question-mark—by liberal democracy. Better a question-mark than a period, where there is so much at stake.

At all events, there can be no doubt about the cohabitation, tense as it must have been throughout, between the realistic movement and the bourgeois life-style. So far as life had been banalized —to adopt M. Durand's word—by the middle class, it could be redeemed by the cult of art; and the Flaubertian concept of the artist's vocation, as Thomas Mann has reconsidered it, was itself a perquisite of the high bourgeoisie which twentieth-century writers can ill afford. With this personal dedication to goals set beyond the values of a materialistic environment went an inborn propensity to protest against that environment, which André Gide has both exemplified and formulated. In a digression inspired by Wagnerian music-drama, Proust is moved to reconsider the *Comédie humaine* and some of the other large-scale works of its century as examples of what he terms *auto-contemplation*. The term is not elegant, though it suits the circumstances better than *autocritique*—which has come to mean the very opposite, the renunciation of independence by Soviet artists. Whereas the critics of middle-class society, free in their semi-detachment to attack its wrongs and expose its defects, crowned it with the redeeming virtues of self-contemplation, self-awareness, self-knowledge. Those works of theirs became, in the fullness of irony, its monumental glories. Proust spoke of them as frescoes, in his praise of Balzac, and Zola applied the same artistic metaphor to his own project. From this distance they seem more like windows, opening through the opaque walls of time past, to disclose varieties of existence which we could never have known in other ways. There are many windows in the house of fiction, as we should always be glad to hear James remind us; but few of them are wider or clearer than these, and none has let in more light on the darker places of time and fate and human will.

Chronology

1783   Henri Beyle born at Grenoble, January 23.

1789   Fall of the Bastille, July 14. Revolution begins.

1790   Death of Stendhal's mother.

1792   FIRST REPUBLIC proclaimed by National Convention. *La Tyrannie Raillane.*

1795   DIRECTORY.

1795–99   Beyle attends Ecole Centrale at Grenoble.

1796   Bonald, *Théorie du pouvoir.* Maistre, *Considérations sur la France.*

1799   CONSULATE. Honoré Balzac born at Tours, May 20. 18 Brumaire (November 9). Beyle comes to Paris.

1800   Madame de Staël, *De la littérature considérée dans ses rapports avec les institutions sociales.*

1800–02   Beyle with Sixth Dragoons in Italy.

1801   Chateaubriand, *Atala.*

1802   Bonaparte named First Consul for life. Chateaubriand, *René; Le Génie du christianisme.*

1804   EMPIRE. *Code Napoléon.* Sénancour, *Obermann.* Destutt de Tracy, *Eléments d'idéologie.*

1805   Beyle follows Mélanie Guilbert to Marseilles, and works in a wholesale grocery establishment.

1806–09   Beyle attached to French military commissariat in Germany and Austria.

1807–13   Balzac in Oratorian College at Vendôme.

1807   Madame de Staël, *Corinne.*

1810   Beyle auditor for the Council of State, Inspector-General of Crown Chattels. Madame de Staël, *De l'Allemagne.*

1812   Beyle in Moscow with the Grand Army.

1813   Beyle Intendant of Sagan in Silesia.

1814 RESTORATION of the house of Bourbon. Beyle has published his first book, Vies de Haydn, Mozart et Métastase under a pseudonym. Leaves for Italy. Balzac family moves to Paris.

1814–21 Beyle in Milan.

1815 Napoleon returns for a hundred days, and is finally exiled after Waterloo. Louis XVIII reascends the throne.

1816 Balzac studies law. Constant, Adolphe.

1817 Beyle publishes Histoire de la peinture en Italie under his initials, Rome, Naples et Florence under the pseudonym of Stendhal.

1819 Death of Beyle's father.

1821 Exiled from Milan, Beyle returns to Paris, travels to England. Flaubert born at Rouen, December 12.

1821–25 Balzac turns out pot-boiling novels under various pseudonyms.

1822 Stendhal, De l'amour.

1823–25 Stendhal, Racine et Shakespeare.

1824 Charles X ascends throne. Saint-Simon, Catéchisme des industriels.

1826 Vigny, Cinq-mars.

1827 Stendhal, Armance. Hugo, Préface de Cromwell.

1828 Liquidation of Balzac's printing enterprises.

1829 Stendhal, Promenades dans Rome. Balzac, Le Dernier Chouan; Physiologie du mariage. Mérimée, Chronique du règne de Charles IX.

1830 JULY MONARCHY. Duke of Orleans crowned as Louis-Philippe. Beyle appointed consul to Trieste, rejected by Austrian government. Balzac publishes La Maison du Chat-qui-pelote, Gobseck, and other stories which will find their place in La Comédie humaine. Hugo, Hernani.

1830–42 Comte, Cours de la philosophie positive.

1831 Stendhal, Le Rouge et le noir. Balzac, La Peau de chagrin. Hugo, Notre-Dame de Paris. Balzac assumes the prefix de.

1831–41 Beyle French consul at Civitavecchia.

1832 Balzac, Le Colonel Chabert; Le Curé de Tours; Louis Lambert. Sand, Indiana.

1832–37 Balzac, Contes drolatiques.

1832–40 Flaubert attends lycée at Rouen.

1833 Sand, Lélia. Balzac, Le Médecin de campagne. Balzac meets his Polish correspondent, Countess Hanska, at Neuchâtel. Beyle accompanies George Sand and Alfred de Musset from Lyon to Marseilles.

1834   Balzac, *Eugénie Grandet; La Fille aux yeux d'or; La Recherche de l'absolu.* Lamennais, *Paroles d'un croyant.*

1834–35   Beyle writing *Lucien Leuwen,* to be published posthumously.

1835   Beyle writes his autobiographical fragment, *La Vie de Henry Brulard.* Balzac, *Le Père Goriot; Séraphita.* Tocqueville, *De la démocratie en Amérique.*

1835–36   Gautier, *Mademoiselle de Maupin.*

1836   Flaubert meets Elisa Schlésinger. Balzac, *Le Lys dans la vallée; La Vieille Fille.* Musset, *Confession d'un enfant du siècle.*

1836–39   Beyle, on leave of absence, travels with Mérimée, writes memoirs of Napoleon.

1837   Balzac, *César Birotteau; Les Employés.*

1837–43   Balzac, *Les Illusions perdues.*

1838   Balzac travels to Sardinia. Flaubert attempts to write a novel, *Mémoires d'un fou.* Stendhal, *Mémoires d'un touriste.* Balzac, *La Maison Nucingen.*

1839   Stendhal, *La Chartreuse de Parme; L'Abbesse de Castro.* Balzac, *Une Fille d'Eve; Le Curé de village.* Daguerre's photographic process acquired by the state and divulged to the public.

1839–40   Beyle writing his uncompleted novel, *Lamiel.*

1840   Balzac edits *La Revue parisienne,* and reviews *La Chartreuse de Parme.* His play, *Vautrin,* forbidden. Flaubert, having taken the baccalaureate, travels in Corsica and the Pyrenees. Proudhon, *Qu'est-ce que la propriété?* Sainte-Beuve, *Port-Royal.* Zola born at Paris, April 2.

1841   Balzac, *La Rabouilleuse; Ursule Mirouët; Une Ténébreuse Affaire.*

1842   Stendhal dies at Paris, March 22. Balzac, *Avant-propos de la Comédie humaine.* Balzac in St. Petersburg with Countess Hanska. Flaubert completes another youthful novel, *Novembre.*

1843   Flaubert fails his law examinations, has a nervous breakdown, begins his first *Education sentimentale.* Sue, *Les Mystères de Paris.*

1844   Dumas, *Les Trois Mousquetaires.* Balzac, *Modeste Mignon; Les Paysans* (completed by Charles Rabou). Flaubert at Croisset.

1844–45   Dumas, *Le Comte de Monte-Cristo.* Sue, *Le Juif errant.*

1845   Flaubert, in Genoa, sees Brueghel's painting of the temptation of Saint Anthony.

1846   Balzac, *La Cousine Bette.* Sand, *La Mare au diable.* Arsène Houssaye, *Histoire de la peinture flamande et hollandaise.*

1846–55   Flaubert's affair with Louise Colet.

1847   Balzac, *Le Cousin Pons*. Visits Countess Hanska's estate in the
          Ukraine. Flaubert's travels in Brittany with Du Camp. Michelet,
          Lamartine, and Louis Blanc publish histories of the Revolution.
          Death of Zola's father.

1848   SECOND REPUBLIC. February revolution. Marx and Engels,
          Communist Manifesto. Attempts to organize labor end in massacres
          of the "June days."

1849–51   Flaubert abandons first version of *La Tentation de saint Antoine*,
          travels with Du Camp in the Near East.

1849–69   Sainte-Beuve, *Causeries du lundi; Nouveaux lundis*.

1850   Balzac marries Countess Hanska in Russia, March 14; dies at Paris,
          August 18. Sand, *François le champi*.

1851   Murger, *Scènes de la vie de Bohème*. *Coup d'état* of Louis Napoléon.

1852   SECOND EMPIRE.

1855   Courbet, rejected from the Exposition, sets up his Pavillon du
          Réalisme. Gérard de Nerval, *Aurélia*.

1856   A periodical, *Réalisme*, edited by Duranty, runs for several months.
          Madame Bovary appearing in *L'Artiste*.

1857   Flaubert and his publishers tried and acquitted for alleged immoral-
          ity of *Madame Bovary*, which appears in book form. Baudelaire,
          Les Fleurs du mal. Champfleury, *Le Réalisme*. Second *Tentation de
          saint Antoine*.

1858   Flaubert in Tunisia. Zola and his mother move to Paris. Taine's first
          Essais de critique et d'histoire.

1859   Zola fails bachelor's examinations, at Paris and Marseilles. Darwin,
          Origin of Species.

1862   Flaubert, *Salammbô*. Hugo, *Les Misérables*. Zola naturalized.

1862–65   Zola employed by house of Hachette.

1862–69   Literary dinners at Magny restaurant.

1863   *Salon des refusés*. Renan, *Vie de Jésus*. Taine, *Histoire de la littéra-
          ture anglaise*.

1864   First International organized at London. Zola, *Contes à Ninon*.

1865   Zola, *La Confession de Claude*. Goncourt, *Germinie Lacerteux*.
          Bernard, *Introduction à l'étude de la médecine expérimentale*.

1866   Zola writes literary and artistic criticism for *L'Evénement*. Zola, *Mes Haines; Mon Salon. Le Parnasse contemporain*.

1867   Paris Exposition with exhibits by Courbet and Manet. Zola, *Thérèse Raquin*.

1868   Baudelaire, *Petits Poèmes en prose*.

1869   Flaubert, *L'Education sentimentale*.

1870   THIRD REPUBLIC proclaimed, after defeat of Napoleon III in Franco-Prussian War. Flaubert a lieutenant in National Guard at Rouen. Zola marries Alexandrine Mesley, goes south to engage in republican politics.

1871   PARIS COMMUNE from March 18 to May 23. Proust born in Auteuil, July 10. Zola, *La Fortune des Rougon; La Curée*.

1872   Bouilhet, *Dernières Chansons*, with preface by Flaubert.

1873   Zola, *Le Ventre de Paris*. Rimbaud, *Une Saison en enfer*. Flaubert begins *Bouvard et Pécuchet*.

1874   Flaubert, *La Tentation de saint Antoine*. His play, *Le Candidat*, performed unsuccessfully. Zola, *La Conquête de Plassans*. Zola becomes French correspondent of Russian *Messenger of Europe*. First Impressionist exhibition.

1875   Zola, *La Faute de l'abbé Mouret*. Taine begins to publish *Les Origines de la France contemporaine*.

1876   Mallarmé, *L'Apres-midi d'un faune*.

1877   Flaubert, *Trois Contes*. Zola, *L'Assommoir*. Daudet, *Le Nabab*.

1878   Zola settles at Médan.

1880   Flaubert dies at Croisset, May 8. Zola, *Nana; Le Roman expérimental. Les Soirées de Médan*. Proust experiences his first asthmatic attack.

1881   Zola, *Le Naturalisme au théâtre; Les Romanciers naturalistes*. Flaubert, *Bouvard et Pécuchet*. France, *Le Crime de Sylvestre Bonnard*.

1882   Zola, *Pot-bouille*.

1882–89 Proust at Lycée Condorcet.

1883   Zola, *Au Bonheur des Dames*. Brunetière, *Le Roman naturaliste*.

1884   Strikes break out in northern France and Belgium. Huysmans, *A rebours*.

1884–92 Publication of Flaubert's *Correspondance*.

1885   Zola, *Germinal*. Maupassant, *Bel-Ami*.

1886   Zola, *L'Oeuvre*. Melchior de Vogüé, *Le Roman russe*. Symbolist
        Manifesto.

1887   Antoine founds the Théâtre Libre. Zola attacked in *Le Figaro* by
        five younger novelists. Zola, *La Terre*. First publication from *Le
        Journal des Goncourt*.

1888   Maupassant, *Pierre et Jean*. Dujardin, *Les Lauriers sont coupés*.

1889   Boulanger crisis. Zola has a daughter by Jeanne Rozerot. Proust
        performs his military service. Bourget, *Le Disciple*. Bergson, *Les
        Données immédiates de la conscience*.

1890   Zola, *La Bête humaine*. Villiers de l'Isle Adam, *Axël*.

1891   Zola, *L'Argent*. Jeanne Rozerot bears Zola a son. Huret, *Enquête sur
        l'évolution littéraire*.

1892   Zola, *La Débâcle*.

1893   Zola, *Le Docteur Pascal*.

1894   Zola in Rome. Court-martial of Alfred Dreyfus.

1894-98 Zola, *Les Trois Villes*.

1895   Dreyfus degraded and sent to Devil's Island.

1896   Proust, *Les Plaisirs et les jours*. Valéry, *La Soirée avec M. Teste*.

1896-99 Proust writes *Jean Santeuil*.

1897   Zola, *Lettre à la jeunesse*. Barrès, *Les Déracinés*. Gide, *Les Nourri-
        tures terrestres*. Proust's duel with Jean Lorrain.

1898   Colonel Esterhazy acquitted in Dreyfus case. Zola's letter to the
        President, *J'accuse*, published in *L'Aurore*. Tried and condemned,
        he escapes to England. Proust, encouraged by Anatole France, cir-
        culates a petition on Zola's behalf.

1899   Reopening of Dreyfus case after suicide of Colonel Henry. Zola re-
        turns to France. Zola, *Fécondité*.

1900   General amnesty to those involved in the Dreyfus affair. Proust in
        Venice.

1901   Zola, *Travail*.

1902   Zola asphyxiated at Paris, September 29. Gide, *L'Immoraliste*.

1903   Zola, *Vérité*. Death of Proust's father.

1904   Proust translates Ruskin's *Bible of Amiens*. Dreyfus appeal allowed.

1904-12 Rolland, *Jean Christophe*.

1905	Proust retires after the death of his mother.
1906	Ruskin's *Sesame and Lilies* translated by Proust. Rehabilitation of Dreyfus.
1908	Zola's remains transferred to the Pantheon. Sorel, *Réflexions sur la violence*.
1909	Founding of *La Nouvelle Revue française*.
1913	Proust, *Du côté de chez Swann*. Alain-Fournier, *Le Grand Meaulnes*. Apollinaire, *Alcools*.
1914	Gide, *Les Caves du Vatican*. Death of Alfred Agostinelli.
1914–18	First World War.
1916	Barbusse, *Le Feu*.
1919	Proust receives the Goncourt Prize for *A l'ombre des jeunes filles en fleurs*. Valéry, *La Crise de l'esprit*. Proust, *Pastiches et mélanges*.
1920	Proust, *Le Côté des Guermantes*. Three volumes of poems by Valéry.
1922	Proust, *Sodome et Gomorrhe*. Proust dies at Paris, November 18.
1923	Proust, *La Prisonnière*.
1924	First Surrealist Manifesto.
1925	Proust, *Albertine disparue* (*La Fugitive*). Gide, *Les Faux-monnayeurs*.
1927	Proust, *Le Temps retrouvé; Chroniques*. Gide, *Voyage au Congo*.
1932	Céline, *Voyage au bout de la nuit*.
1933	Malraux, *La Condition humaine*.
1938	Sartre, *La Nausée*.
1939–45	Second World War.
1941–44	VICHY REGIME.
1943	Prévost (ed.), *Problèmes du roman*.
1946	FOURTH REPUBLIC.
1947	Camus, *La Peste*.
1952	Proust, *Jean Santeuil*.
1954	Proust, *Contre Sainte-Beuve*.
1958	FIFTH REPUBLIC.

Acknowledgments

THE MOST GRATIFYING PART of the present volume, for the author, is the opportunity to render thanks for aid and comfort received along the way. The backlog of reading that I have drawn upon was started during the second term of a Junior Fellowship in the Society of Fellows at Harvard University from 1937 to 1939. The stimulus to round out these researches came through an invitation to discuss Zola and Proust with the Christian Gauss Seminars in Literary Criticism at Princeton University in the spring of 1961. Though I was granted a Guggenheim Fellowship for another project in 1943–44, the Foundation showed its characteristic magnanimity in allowing me further time for this one. The mechanical problems of preparation have been facilitated by a grant from the Joseph H. Clark Bequest to Harvard University. No words can express the debt that I have accumulated over the years to the Widener and the Houghton collections of the Harvard College Library. I am also grateful for courtesies extended by the Bibliothèque Nationale (Paris), the Boston Public Library, the Boston Athenaeum, and the libraries of Columbia and Princeton Universities.

Since portions of this book have been appearing in various other forms, it would seem appropriate here to indicate those appearances, with due thanks to the publications involved. Under the title, "Literature as an Institution," most of the second and third sections of Chapter I were first printed in *Accent*, V, 3 (Spring, 1946), and have been reprinted and translated on several other occasions. The opening section of Chapter II has been published in Portuguese translation by *Pensamento da America*, III, 7 (July 4, 1944); while the fifth section was published in *Yale French Studies*, 6 (Autumn, 1950). Earlier versions of Chapters III and IV, under the respective titles of *Toward Stendhal* (1945) and *Toward Balzac* (1947), came out as separate brochures under the imprint of New Directions. The first section of Chapter V appeared in *The Yale Review*, XXXVIII, 1 (Autumn, 1948), entitled "Flaubert and the Spirit of '48," the second in *The Kenyon Review*, X, 1 (Winter, 1948) as "Flaubert: Portrait of the Artist as a Saint," and the third in *Essays in Criticism*, II, 1 (January, 1952) as "*Madame Bovary:* The Cathedral and the Hospital"—all of them abridged, and subsequently revised. An abridgment of the last two sections of the final chapter, under the title "Apogee and Aftermath of the Novel," is appearing in *Daedalus* concurrently with the publication of the present volume.

Perhaps I should also mention certain correlative articles, since I have plagiarized from myself here and there. These would include my introductions to English translations of Flaubert's *Three Tales* by Arthur McDowall (Norfolk: New Directions, 1944), *Letters of Marcel Proust* by Mina Curtiss (New York: Random House, 1949), and Stendhal's *Charterhouse of Parma* by Lowell Bair (New York: Bantam Books, 1960). The semantic discussion of Chapter II is epitomized in "What Is Realism?," which served originally as the introduction to a symposium on that subject in *Comparative Literature*, III, 3 (Summer, 1951). This article reappears in my *Contexts of Criticism* (Cambridge: Harvard University Press, 1957), which also contains a lecture based on my preliminary sketch of the nineteenth-century background, "Society as Its Own Historian." Two other closely related essays are gathered in that collection, "The Example of Cervantes" and "Balzac and Proust"—the latter having previously been part of a French tribute, under the auspices of UNESCO, to the Balzac centennial in 1950. My use of certain concepts is amplified by "Notes on Convention" in *Perspectives of Criticism* (Cambridge: Harvard University Press, 1950) and "The Ivory Gate," *Yale French Studies*, 13 (Spring, 1954).

I am happy to thank the following authors and publishers for permission to quote at some length from copyright material: Miss Marianne Moore and Messrs. The Macmillan Company (New York) and Faber and Faber, Ltd. (London) for the quotation from "Light Is Speech" in *Collected Poems* (1951); Mr. T. S. Eliot and Messrs. Harcourt, Brace & World, Inc. (New York) and Faber and Faber, Ltd. (London) for the quotations from "John Ford" (*Selected Essays*, 1932), "Burnt Norton" (*Four Quartets*, 1943), and *The Cocktail Party* (1950); and Mr. Robert Fitzgerald and Messrs.

Doubleday and Company, Inc. (New York) and William Heinemann, Ltd. (London) for the quotation from the Fitzgerald translation of Homer's *Odyssey* (1961). I only wish it were possible to be equally specific in acknowledging general obligations of a more personal kind, particularly the influence of teachers and the incitement of students. The number of those who have helpfully advised and encouraged me, I feel uncomfortably certain, extends far beyond any list of names which I could set down here.

There is a special sadness in recalling those who have not lived to judge how I have profited from their kind advice: Fernand Baldensperger, Albert Léon Guérard, F. O. Matthiessen, André Morize, and Theodore Spencer. It is an unmitigated pleasure, however, to record the generous interest of old and continuing friends and colleagues: R. P. Blackmur, Mina Curtiss, Herbert Dieckmann, André du Bouchet, F. B. Deknatel, Leon Edel, W. M. Frohock, Henry Hatfield, Howard E. Hugo, Walter J. Kaiser, Philip Kolb, James Laughlin IV, Vladimir Nabokov, Henri Peyre, Renato Poggioli, Jean Seznec, Maurice Z. Shroder, John L. Sweeney, Wiktor Weintraub, and Edmund Wilson. My gratitude goes out to John Brett-Smith and Sheldon Meyer for an exercise of patience which has gone far beyond the duty of publisher or editor. Four student assistants from Radcliffe and Harvard—Elisabeth Commager Ainger, Marina Levin, Susan Scarff, and Peter Ott—have greatly lightened the labor of checking references, while the typing of the manuscript has been in the very competent hands of Elizabeth Ann Farmer. I cannot thank my wife for all her diverse contributions; yet I must note that she has not merely lived with this book; she has, at times, kept it alive.

H. L.

Notes

The notes that follow, which are linked to the text through page numbers and key-phrases or names, simply indicate the bibliographical references in their most compact form. It will be seen that most of the quotations or citations have been directly translated or paraphrased from the original French. The place of publication for books, unless it is stated otherwise, is Paris. The publishers of the editions chiefly used are Le Divan for Stendhal, Conard for Balzac and Flaubert, Fasquelle (Bernouard) for Zola, and Gallimard (Pléiade) for Proust. It has seemed more convenient to cite chapters or section headings rather than pages, in referring to certain standard works which have been frequently and variously reprinted.

I PREMISES

3 T. S. Eliot/"John Ford," *Selected Essays* (New York, 1932), p. 178.

1. Toward a Critical Method

3 Henry James/*The Ambassadors*, preface.
4 Goethe/J. P. Eckermann, *Gespräche mit Goethe*, June 11, 1825.
5 "separable content."/R. P. Blackmur, *The Double Agent* (New York, 1935), p. 285.
   "belletristic philandering."/V. L. Parrington (ed.), *The Connecticut Wits* (New York, 1926), p. xxiv.
   content and form are not detachable/See A. C. Bradley, *Oxford Lectures on Poetry* (London, 1911), pp. 17ff.; Mark Schorer, "Technique as Discovery," *Forms of Modern Fiction*, ed. W. V. O'Connor (Minneapolis, 1948), pp. 9ff.
   James/"The Art of Fiction," *Partial Portraits* (New York, 1888), p. 400.
   Buffon/*Discours sur le style*.
6 Aristotle/*Poetics*, iv, 6.
   Otto Rank/*Art and Artist* (New York, 1932), p. 11.
   Francis Bacon/*The Advancement of Learning*, bk. ii.
   Ernest Renan/*L'Avenir de la science* (1890), p. 201.
7 disciple of Bacon/C. A. Sainte-Beuve, *Nouveaux Lundis* (1870), III, 24.
   botanizing/Sainte-Beuve, *Portraits littéraires* (1878), III, 546.
   "a kind of botany,"/H. A. Taine, *Philosophie de l'art* (1893), I, 13.
   H. F. Amiel/*Fragments d'un journal intime* (1931), II, 17.

7 "From the novel to criticism . . ."/Taine, *Essais de critique et d'histoire* (1866), p. 108.

8 Zola/*Le Roman expérimental*, ed. Maurice Le Blond (1928), p. 181.

2. TAINE AND HIS INFLUENCE

8 Vicomte de Bonald/*Législation primitive* (1817), II, 228.

moment/See W. H. Ree, "The Meaning of Taine's Moment," *Romanic Review* (1939), XXX, 273ff.

Milieu/See Leo Spitzer, "Milieu and Ambiance," *Essays in Historical Semantics* (New York, 1948), pp. 179ff.

Flaubert/*Correspondance* (1929), V, 160.

9 George Plekhanov/*Essays in the History of Materialism* (London, 1934), p. 235.

Jean-Paul Sartre/*L'Imagination* (1936), p. 27.

"Vice and virtue are products . . ."/Taine, *Histoire de la littérature anglaise* (1866), I, xv.

"History, Its Present and Future."/S. J. Kahn, *Science and Aesthetic Judgment: A Study in Taine's Critical Method* (London, 1953), p. 64.

10 With Shakespeare/*Littérature anglaise*, II, 164.

". . . psychological mechanics."/*Ibid.*, I, xxxii.

"master faculty"/See Irving Babbitt, *The Masters of Modern French Criticism* (Boston, 1912), p. 181.

Dostoevsky/*The Brothers Karamazov*, tr. Constance Garnett (New York, 1916), p. 785.

11 "Not in Greece . . ."/*Littérature anglaise*, II, 52.

"the exact imprint of the century . . ."/*Ibid.*, II, 3.

12 "the very age and body of the time . . ."/*Hamlet*, III, ii, 27.

quantities of charters/*Littérature anglaise*, I, xlvi.

Ferdinand Brunetière/*L'Evolution des genres dans l'histoire de la littérature* (1892), p. xii.

Flaubert's gloomy prediction/Louis Bouilhet, *Dernières Chansons* (1872), p. 4.

"What shocks me . . ."/*Lettres inédites à Tourgueneff*, ed. Emile Gérard-Gailly (Monaco, 1946), p. 15.

13 "the social destination of art."/P. J. Proudhon, *Du principe de l'art et de sa destination sociale* (1865).

14 Granville Hicks/*The Great Tradition* (New York, 1933); cf. *Harper's*, CXCII, 1153 (June, 1946), unnumbered last pages.

Karl Marx/and Friedrich Engels, *Sur la littérature et l'art*, ed. and tr. Jean Fréville (1936), p. 59.

15 Johnson/*Preface to Shakespeare*.

"neither to pardon . . ."/Taine, *Philosophie de l'art*, I, 12.

3. LITERATURE AS AN INSTITUTION

16 that organic principle/See F. O. Matthiessen, *American Renaissance* (New York, 1941), p. 133.

German estheticians and cultural historians/See Karl Viëtor, "Deutsche Literaturgeschichte als Geistesgeschichte," *Publications of the Modern Language Association of America* (1945), LX, 899.

17 Bernard De Voto/*The Literary Fallacy* (Boston, 1944), p. 43.

An enterprising sociologist/P. A. Sorokin, *Social and Cultural Dynamics* (New York, 1937), I, 423.

17   Those volumes testify/Cf. Roger Caillois, *Sociologia de la novela* (Buenos Aires, 1942), p. 64; Régis Messac, *Le "Detective Novel" et l'influence de la pensée scientifique* (1929).

18   Goethe/"Natur und Kunst."
     Schiller/*Die Braut von Messina*, "Über den Gebrauch des Chors in der Tragödie."
     masculine straightforwardness/Taine, *Littérature anglaise*, pp. 496ff.
     Francisque Sarcey/"Essai d'une esthétique de théâtre," *Quarante ans du théâtre* (1900), I, 132.
     Guy de Maupassant/*Pierre et Jean* (1892), pp. xviif.
     José Ortega y Gasset/*Meditaciones del Quijote* (Madrid, 1914), p. 105.

19   Stendhal/*Le Rouge et le noir*, ed. Henri Martineau (1927), I, 132.
     Taine/*Les Origines de la France contemporaine: l'Ancien Régime* (1909), I, 312.
     Plato/See Richard McKeon, "Literary Criticism and the Concept of Imitation in Antiquity," *Modern Philology* (1936), XXXIV, 12.
     Cicero/Aelius Donatus, *Excerpta de comoedia.*

20   "abstract and brief chronicles . . ."/*Hamlet*, II, ii, 547f.
     ". . . so abominably."/*Ibid.*, III, ii, 39f.
     Oscar Wilde/*The Picture of Dorian Gray*, preface.
     James Joyce/*Ulysses* (New York, 1934), p. 8.
     E. E. Stoll/*From Shakespeare to Joyce* (New York, 1949), p. 28.
     This formula/Gustave Lanson, "L'Histoire littéraire et la sociologie," *Revue de métaphysique et de morale* (1904), XII, 635.

21   Leslie Stephen's phrase/*English Literature and Society in the Eighteenth Century* (London, 1907), p. 13.
     Prosper de Barante/*De la littérature française pendant le dix-huitième siècle* (1824), p. 5; cf. Max Lerner and Edwin Mims, Jr., "Literature," *Encyclopedia of the Social Sciences* (New York, 1933), IX, 523.

22   "natural history of minds,"/Sainte-Beuve, *Portraits littéraires*, III, 546.
     Sartre/*Critique de la raison dialectique* (1960), I, 45ff.
     Walter Bagehot/*Physics and Politics* (New York, 1901), p. 32.

23   Edgar Quinet/C. L. Chassin, *Edgar Quinet: sa vie et son oeuvre* (1859), pp. 57ff.

II ROMANCE AND REALISM

24   D. H. Lawrence/*Studies in Classic American Literature* (New York, 1930), p. 3.

1. TRUTH AND FICTION

24   Alfonso Reyes/*El Deslinde: prolegómenos a la teoría literaria* (Mexico, 1944), p. 71.
     André Gide/*Les Faux-monnayeurs* (1925), p. 236.

25   James/*Portrait of a Lady*, preface.
     Kipling/"In the Neolithic Age."
     D. H. Lawrence/*Letters*, ed. Aldous Huxley (New York, 1932), p. 299.
     "feigned history,"/Francis Bacon, *The Advancement of Learning*, bk. ii.
     ". . . ficta quam facta."/See Bernard Weinberg, *A History of Literary Criticism in the Italian Renaissance* (Chicago, 1961), I, 164.
     Johnson/*The Rambler*, xcvi.
     The dangerous prevalence of imagination/*Rasselas*, ch. xliv.

26   Pablo Picasso/In *Picasso: Forty Years of His Art*, ed. A. H. Barr (New York, 1939), p. 11.
     Alfred de Vigny/*Cinq-mars*, ed. Fernand Baldensperger (1914), p. vii.
     Emile Hennequin/*La Critique scientifique* (1888), p. 135.
     The novelist is a witness/Lady Murasaki, *The Tale of Genji*, tr. Arthur Waley (New York, 1935), p. 501.
     "intended to give artistic verisimilitude . . ."/W. S. Gilbert, *The Mikado*, act ii.
27   Two French writers/M. A. Leblond, *La Société française sous la Troisième République, d'après les romanciers contemporains* (1905), p. 176.
     Maxime Du Camp/*Souvenirs littéraires* (1883), II, 417.
28   Bernardin de Saint-Pierre/*La Vie et les ouvrages de Jean-Jacques Rousseau* (1907), p. 45.
     Schiller/*Über naive und sentimentalische Dichtung*.
     Aristotle/*Poetics*, xxv, 17.
     Nature, as an esthetic norm/A. O. Lovejoy, *Essays in the History of Ideas* (Baltimore, 1948), pp. 68ff.
29   Jean Hytier/*Les Romans de l'individu* (1928), p. 3.
     Boileau/*L'Art poétique*, iii, 118.
     Roger Fry/*Vision and Design* (London, 1937), p. 16.
     "the literary rules."/Alfred de Vigny, *Journal d'un poète*, ed. Fernand Baldensperger (1928), p. 45.
30   Arnold Hauser/*The Social History of Art* (London, 1951), II, 715.
     Zola/*Roman expérimental*, p. 60.
     the turbulence of the Revolution/See Pierre Hamp, "La littérature, image de la société," *Encyclopédie française* (1935), XVI, 64-2.
     Some have maintained/Brander Matthews, *The Historical Novel and Other Essays* (New York, 1901), p. 105; Bliss Perry, A *Study of Prose Fiction* (Boston, 1903), p. 187; cf. Roger Picard, *Le Romantisme social* (New York, 1944), pp. 59ff., 422ff.
31   Johnson/*Preface to Shakespeare*.
     Boileau/*Epîtres*, ix, 43ff.

2. THE THIRD ESTATE

32   "the modern burgher epic"/G. W. F. Hegel, *Aesthetik* (Berlin, 1955), p. 983.
     Zola/*Roman expérimental*, p. 118.
     Hesiod's Muses/*Theogony*, 27f.
     W. P. Ker/*Epic and Romance* (London, 1922).
     a seventeenth-century essay/P. D. Huet, *De l'origine des romans*, in *Ana, ou collection de bons mots* (Amsterdam, 1796), VIII, 350; cf. M. L. Wolff, *Geschichte der Romantheorie* (Nuremberg, 1915), pp. 47ff.
33   Ariosto/*Orlando Furioso*, I, 1.
     John Lyly/*Euphues and His England*, dedication.
     Madame de Staël/"Essai sur les fictions," *Oeuvres* (Brussels, 1830), II, 147.
     E. M. Forster's words/*Howard's End* (New York, 1921), p. 171.
     John Galsworthy/*The Forsyte Saga*, preface.
     Balzac/*Scènes de la vie privée*, ed. Marcel Bouteron and Henri Longnon (1912), I, xxvii.
     Sterne/*Tristram Shandy*, IV, xxxii.
34   "things having more of a role . . ."/Edmond and Jules de Goncourt, *Journal*, ed. Robert Ricatte (1956), I, 257.

34   Sister Carrie would be stared at/Theodore Dreiser, *Sister Carrie*, ch. iii.
     "The Man That Was A Thing."/H. B. Stowe, *Uncle Tom's Cabin*,
     ed. K. S. Lynn (Cambridge, Mass., 1962), p. xxv.
     Emile Durkheim/See H. S. Hughes, *Consciousness and Society* (New
     York, 1958), p. 283.
     Locke/*An Essay concerning Human Understanding*, III, x.
     spread of literacy/See Ian Watt, *The Rise of the Novel* (Berkeley,
     1957), pp. 47ff.
     Sainte-Beuve/"De la littérature industrielle," *Portraits contemporains*
     (1870), II, 444ff.
     Joseph Bédier/*Les Fabliaux* (1925), p. 371.
     The Council of Nicea/See A. David-Sauvageot, *Le Réalisme et le natu-
     ralisme dans la littérature et dans l'art* (1889), p. 48.
35   John Dunlop/*The History of Fiction* (London, 1845), p. 187.
     seventeenth-century Japan/See Howard Hibbett, *The Floating World in
     Japanese Fiction* (New York, 1959).
     Thomas Mann/"Lübeck als geistige Lebensform," *Gesammelte Werke*
     (Oldenburg, 1960), XI, 398.
     Bourgeois/See Raymond Giraud, *The Unheroic Hero in the Novels of
     Stendhal, Balzac and Flaubert* (New Brunswick, N. J., 1957), pp. 13ff.
     individual enterprise/See Pierre Laserre, *Le Romantisme français* (1928),
     p. 340.
     liberty . . . property/See Charles Morazé, *La France bourgeoise* (1946),
     pp. 71f.
36   . . . above all, mobile/See Fernand Baldensperger, *Le Mouvement des
     idées dans l'émigration française* (1924), I, 230.
37   "I won't sit in the kitchen . . ."/W. M. Thackeray, *The Newcomes*, I, iv.
     the landed and the moneyed interests/Joseph Addison, *The Spectator*,
     cxxvi.
38   "Land of Tenderness."/Mlle. de Scudéry, *Clélie: histoire romancée*
     (1656), I, i, 398.
     Bernardin de Saint-Pierre/*Paul et Virginie*, ed. Maurice Souriau (1930),
     p. 97.
     Marquis de Sade/*Idée sur les romans*, ed. Octave Uzanne (1878), p. 36.
39   "between the idyll and the carnival."/Francesco de Sanctis, *History of
     Italian Literature*, tr. Joan Redfern (New York, 1931), I, 440.

3. ANTI-ROMANCE

39   a new kind of anecdotal narrative/See Karl Vossler, *Die Dichtungsfor-
     men der Romanen* (Stuttgart, 1951), p. 300.
     Goethe/Eckermann, *Gespräche mit Goethe*, January 25, 1827.
40   "marvellous and uncommon incidents,"/Walter Scott, *Essays on Chiv-
     alry, Romance, and the Drama* (London, 1887), p. 65.
     Clara Reeve/*The Progress of Romance* (Colchester, 1785), I, 14, 111.
     a transitional form/See Robert Petsch, *Wesen und Formen der Erzähl-
     kunst* (Halle, 1934), p. 280.
     Boileau/*Les Héros de roman*, ed. T. F. Crane (Boston, 1902), p. 175.
41   the last citadel of feudalism/See F. W. Chandler, *Romances of Roguery*
     (New York, 1899), I, 20.
42   Stendhal/*De l'amour*, ed. Henri Martineau (1927), II, 179.
     "The fictitious . . ."/Miguel de Cervantes Saavedra, *Don Quijote de la
     Mancha*, I, xlvii.

42   "Better versed in misfortunes . . ."/*Ibid.*, I, vi.
      Miguel de Unamuno/*Vida de Don Quijote y Sancho* (Madrid, 1928),
      p. 33.

43   José Ortega y Gasset/*Meditaciones del Quijote*, p. 35.
      Américo Castro/*El Pensamiento de Cervantes* (Madrid, 1925), pp. 88ff.

44   Byron/*Don Juan*, XIII, xi, 81.
      "the Quixotism of R. Crusoe."/Daniel Defoe, *Serious Reflections during
      the Life and Surprising Adventures of Robinson Crusoe*, preface.

45   Marivaux/*La Vie de Marianne*, II, avertissement.
      histoire/See Frédéric Deloffre, "Le Problème d'illusion romanesque et le
      renouvellement des techniques narratives entre 1700 et 1715," *La Littéra-
      ture narrative d'imagination* (Strasburg, 1961), p. 115.
      romanesque/See L. P. Smith, *Words and Idioms* (Boston, 1925), pp.
      66ff.
      Friedrich Schlegel/"Brief über den Roman," *Gespräche über die Poesie*.
      Heinrich Heine/*Reisebilder*, "Die Stadt Lucca," xvii.

46   Hegel and Schopenhauer/See J. J. A. Bertrand, *Cervantes et le roman-
      tisme allemand* (1914), pp. 459f.
      Oswald Spengler/*The Decline of the West*, tr. C. F. Atkinson (New
      York, 1937), I, 31.
      Franz Kafka/"Die Wahrheit über Sancho Panza," *Parabeln* (Berlin,
      1935).
      Dostoevsky/*The Diary of a Writer*, tr. Boris Brasol (New York, 1949),
      p. 260; cf. E. J. Simmons, *Dostoevsky: The Making of a Novelist* (New
      York, 1940), p. 211.
      Mark Twain/See O. H. Moore, "Mark Twain and *Don Quixote*," *PMLA*
      (1922), XXXVII, 324.
      Melville/See Harry Levin, "*Don Quixote* and *Moby Dick*," *Cervantes
      across the Centuries*, ed. Angel Flores and M. J. Benardete (New York,
      1947), pp. 217ff.
      William Dean Howells/*My Literary Passions* (New York, 1895), p. 26.
      William Faulkner/*Writers at Work*, ed. Malcolm Cowley (New York,
      1958), p. 136.
      nineteenth-century France/See Maurice Bardon, "*Don Quichotte* et le
      roman réaliste français: Stendhal, Balzac, Flaubert," *Revue de la littéra-
      ture comparée* (1936), XVI, 63.

47   Alphonse Daudet/*Tartarin de Tarascon* (1890), p. 35.
      "The conscience of mankind . . ."/Flaubert, *Correspondance* (1927),
      III, 281.
      "comic epic poem in prose"/Henry Fielding, *The Adventures of Joseph
      Andrews*, preface; cf. *Don Quijote*, I, xlvii.
      Thomas Mann/*Doktor Faustus* (Stockholm, 1947), p. 454.
      Henry Miller/*Tropic of Cancer* (New York, 1961), p. 2.
      "parody-novel,"/Viktor Shklovsky, *O teorii prozy* (Moscow, 1925), p.
      139; cf. Aurélien Digeon, *Les Romans de Fielding* (1923), p. 127.
      André Malraux/*Les Voix du silence* (1951), p. 310.
      Bernard Shaw/*John Bull's Other Island and Major Barbara* (London,
      1924), p. 148.

4. The Gates of Ivory

48   Irving Babbitt/*Spanish Character and Other Essays* (Boston, 1940), p. 4.
      Georg Lukács/*Die Theorie des Romans* (Berlin, 1920); "Es geht um
      den Realismus," *Das Wort* (1938), III, 112.

48 Christopher Caudwell/*Illusion and Reality: A Study of the Sources of Poetry* (London, 1937).

Pierre Abraham/*Proust: recherches sur la création intellectuelle* (1930); *Créatures chez Balzac* (1931).

Students of the French novel/Gustav Jakob, *L'Illusion et désillusion dans le roman réaliste français: 1851 à 1890* (1911), p. 16; René Girard, *Mensonge romantique et vérité romanesque* (1961), p. 120.

a recent study of the German novel/Robert Brinkmann, *Wirklichkeit und Illusion* (Tübingen, 1957), pp. 78ff.

49 Homer/*Odyssey*, XIX, 562ff.

Archaeologists/See E. L. Highbarger, *The Gates of Dreams* (Baltimore, 1940).

Vergil/*Aeneid*, VI, 894ff.

François Rabelais/*Tiers Livre*, ch. xiii.

"two ivory gates…"/C. A. Sainte-Beuve, *Portraits contemporains*, II, 177.

epistle to Villemain/Sainte-Beuve, *Poésies complètes* (1910), p. 378.

Johnson/James Boswell, *The Life of Samuel Johnson*, ed. G. B. Hill (Oxford, 1887), I, 49.

50 Jules Vallès/*Les Réfractaires* (1935), pp. 159ff.

Renan/*Feuilles détachées* (1892), p. 232.

Wallace Stevens's phrase/*Notes toward a Supreme Fiction* (Cummington, 1942), p. 29.

Dickens/*Bleak House*, preface.

Baudelaire's portrait of Tasso/*Oeuvres*, ed. Y. G. Le Dantec (1935), I, 175.

Joubert's maxims/Joseph Joubert, *Pensées* (1883), II, 144.

Carlyle/"Biography," *Critical and Miscellaneous Essays*.

Thomas Kyd's *Spanish Tragedy*/*Works*, ed. F. S. Boas (Oxford, 1901), p. 68.

51 expressing the inexpressible/Walt Whitman, *Leaves of Grass* (1855), preface.

"True eloquence…"/Blaise Pascal, *Pensées*, préface générale, 24.

"beauty and the beast."/Victor Hugo, *Cromwell*, préface.

"mire, and yet soul."/Hugo, *Les Misérables*, "Jean Valjean," ch. iii.

"a new shudder,"/Hugo, *Correspondance* (1898), II, 11.

Byron's proverbial line/*Don Juan*, XIV, ci, 801ff.

52 Gérard de Nerval/*La Bohême galante*, ed. Jules Marsan (1926), p. 124.

Paul Valéry/*Variété* (1930), II, 113.

Taine's own theory/*De l'intelligence* (1878), II, 6.

inner conflicts/See S. O. Lesser, *Fiction and the Unconscious* (Boston, 1957), p. 150.

Courbet's definition/See Malraux, *Les Voix du silence*, p. 299.

53 Jane Austen/*Emma*, ch. xxxiii.

T. S. Eliot/*Four Quartets* (New York, 1943), p. 14.

"Abstract words…"/Ernest Hemingway, *A Farewell to Arms* (New York, 1932), p. 196.

André Gide/*Les Faux-monnayeurs* (1925), p. 261.

54 E. H. Gombrich/*Art and Illusion: A Study in the Psychology of Pictorial Representation* (New York, 1956), pp. 87, 291.

Malraux/*Les Voix du silence*, pp. 647, 299.

55 Baudelaire/*Oeuvres*, II, 220.

55   "By what art . . ."/Henry James, *The American*, preface.
     Virginia Woolf/*A Room of One's Own* (New York, 1929), p. 124.
     Karl Mannheim/*Ideology and Utopia* (London, 1936).
56   Disraeli's dictum/*Lothair* (London, 1904), I, 169.

                    5. FROM PRIAM TO BIROTTEAU
56   William Dean Howells/*Criticism and Fiction* (New York, 1892), p. 13.
57   Stendhal/*Racine et Shakespeare*, ed. Henri Martineau (1928), p. 106.
     Hawthorne/*The Scarlet Letter*, ch. i.
     le genre dramatique sérieux/P. A. Caron de Beaumarchais, *Théâtre com-
     plet*, ed. G. d'Heylie and F. Marescot (1869), II, 15.
     Goncourt/*Journal*, I, 522.
58   Taine/*Philosophie de l'art*, I, 102.
     Thomas Mann/"Goethe als Repräsentant des bürgerlichen Zeitalters,"
     Gesammelte Werke, IX, 297.
59   Napoleon Bonaparte/See Georg Brandes, *Main Currents in European
     Literature* (London, 1906), I, 23.
     Corneille/Comte Emmanuel de Las Cases, *Mémorial de Saint-Hélène*
     (1935), I, 385.
     "I need solitude . . ."/J. H. Rose, *The Life of Napoleon* (New York,
     1924), I, 181.
60   John Livingston Lowes/*The Road to Xanadu* (Boston, 1927), p. 243.
     Marquis de Sade/See André Breton, "Limits not Frontiers of Surreal-
     ism," *Surrealism*, ed. Herbert Read (London, 1936), p. 107.
     "Set man apart . . ."/Aristide Marie, *Henry Monnier, 1799-1877* (1931),
     p. 65.
     Coelina/Henry Monnier, *Scènes populaires* (1836), p. 18.
61   Edmond Estève/*Byron et le romantisme français* (1907), p. 4.
62   "Whoever thinks basely"/Flaubert, *Correspondance*, V, 550.
     Marquise de Lambert/See Sainte-Beuve, *Causeries du lundi* (1881), IV,
     230.
     Thomas Mann/"Tonio Kröger," *Gesammelte Werke*, VIII, 337.
     Hugo's equivocation/*Océan* (1942), p. 267.
63   *Méphis, ou le prolétaire*/See J. L. Puech, *La Vie et l'oeuvre de Flora
     Tristan* (1925), p. 402.
     Dostoevsky/See Avrahm Yarmolinsky, *Dostoevsky: A Life* (New York,
     1924), p. 156.

                    6. THE CONTEXT OF REALISM
64   a general tendency/See Jean Hankiss, *La Littérature et la vie* (Sao Paolo,
     1951), p. 122.
     Karl Mannheim/*Ideology and Utopia*, p. 228.
     Benedetto Croce/*Aesthetics*, tr. Douglas Ainslie (London, 1912), p. 70.
65   Howells/*Criticism and Fiction*, p. 104.
     Charlotte Brontë/*The Brontës: Their Lives, Friendships, and Corre-
     spondence*, ed. Thomas J. Wise (Oxford, 1932), p. 181.
     Diderot/*Eloge de Richardson*.
66   Eugene Zamyatin/"On Literature, Revolution and Entropy," *Partisan
     Review* (1961), XXVIII, 378.
     Rabelais/See Johan Huizinga, "Renaissance und Realismus," *Wege der
     Kulturgeschichte* (Munich, 1930), pp. 159ff.
     Schiller/*Über naive und sentimentalische Dichtung*.

66   Léon-Paul Fargue/*Sous la lampe* (1929), p. 15.
      George Moore/*Confessions of a Young Man* (London, 1933), p. 148.
67   Baudelaire/*Oeuvres*, II, 66.
      Dostoevsky/See Renato Poggioli, "Realism in Russia," *Comparative Literature* (1951), III, 263.
      George Pellissier/*Le Réalisme du romantisme* (1912).
      Emile Faguet/"Le Réalisme des romantiques," *Revue des deux mondes* (1912), sixth series, VIII, 694.
      Mario Praz/*The Hero in Eclipse in Victorian Fiction* (London, 1956).
      Westminster Review/See R. G. Davis, "The Sense of the Real in English Fiction," *Comparative Literature* (1951), III, 214.
68   as early as 1826/See E. B. O. Borgerhoff, "*Réalisme* and Kindred Words: Their Use in Terms of Criticism in the First Half of the Nineteenth Century," *PMLA* (1938), LIII, 837.
      the same things that romanticism stood for/See Bernard Weinberg, *French Realism: The Critical Reaction, 1830-1870* (New York, 1937), pp. 98, 137.
      conservative periodicals/T. E. Du Val, Jr., *The Subject of Realism in the Revue des deux mondes, 1831-1865* (Philadelphia, 1936), p. 37.
      "the landscape-painter of humanity,"/Camille Lemonnier, *G. Courbet et son oeuvre* (1868), p. 38.
      "Les bourgeois sont ainsi!"/See Emile Bouvier, *La Bataille réaliste, 1844-1857* (1913), p. 238.
      The technique of photography/See Gisèle Freund, *La Photographie en France au dix-neuvième siècle* (1936), p. 37.
69   the diorama/Balzac, *Scènes de la vie privée* (1912), VI, 272.
      "That terrible word 'realism' . . ."/Edmond Duranty, *La Cause du Beau Guillaume* (1920), II, 8.
      "a transitional term . . ."/Champfleury, *Le Réalisme* (1857), pp. 5, 3, 10, 4, 2.
70   parallel columns/Champfleury, *Chien-Caillou* (1860), p. 8.
      a republican paper/*Le Salut Public*, ed. Ferdinand Vandérem (1925).
      "a latent and unconscious aspiration . . ."/See Pierre Martino, *Le Roman réaliste sous le second empire* (1930), p. 85.
      L'Atelier du peintre/See Meyer Schapiro, "Courbet and Popular Imagery," *Journal of the Warburg and Cortauld Institutes* (1941), IV, 182.
71   Louis Peisse/Weinberg, *French Realism*, p. 112.
      M. Prudhomme/Monnier, *Mémoires de M. Joseph Prudhomme* (1857), II, 215.
      the Goncourts/*Germinie Lacerteux* (1865), v, vi, vii.
      synonymous with impressionism/See John Rewald, *The History of Impressionism* (New York, 1946), p. 126.
72   "human documents."/Edmond de Goncourt, *La Faustin* (1882), p. ii.
      Zola/*Roman expérimental*, p. 250.
73   Brunetière/*Le Roman naturaliste* (1883), p. 11.
      Jules Janin's horrendous parody/*L'Ane mort* (1860), pp. 80, 82.
      Georg Lukács/*Essays über Realismus* (Berlin, 1948), p. 128.
      Proust/*A la recherche du temps perdu* (1954), III, 726.
      Erich Auerbach/*Mímesis: Dargestellte Wirklichkeit in der abendländischen Litteratur* (Bern, 1946), pp. 405ff.

7. THE DYNASTY OF REALISM

74 a remark of André Gide's/*Interviews imaginaires* (New York, 1943), p. 105.

a sociological study/Ernst Kohn-Bramstedt, *Aristocracy and the Middle Classes: Social Types in German Literature, 1830-1900* (London, 1937), p. 332.

Tolstoy advised Maxim Gorky/Maxim Gorky, *Reminiscences*, tr. S. S. Koteliansky (New York, 1948), p. 53.

Henry James wrote Howells/*The Letters of Henry James*, ed. Percy Lubbock (New York, 1920), I, 104.

". . . more life for my money."/Henry James, "The Story in It."

moeurs/Cf. Henri Peyre, *The Contemporary French Novel* (New York, 1955), p. 22.

75 Mrs. Grundy/See J. G. Patterson, *A Zola Dictionary* (London, 1912), p. xix.

Guizot/Charles Dickens (ed.), *Household Words: A Weekly Journal* (December 18, 1858), XIX, 50.

Stephen Spender/*European Witness* (London, 1946), p. 115.

76 "the great French tradition . . ."/H. J. Laski, *Authority in the Modern State* (New Haven, 1919), p. 169.

Renan/*Discours et conférences* (1887), p. 9.

77 Matthew Arnold/*Literature and Dogma* (London, 1892), p. 322.

Bonald/*La Pensée chrétienne: textes et études*, ed. Paul Bourget and Michel Salomon (1904), p. 315.

Michelet/*Introduction à l'histoire universelle* (1834), pp. 104, 106, vi.

78 Taine/*Le Régime moderne* (1904), II, 197.

Marianne Moore/*Collected Poems* (New York, 1951), p. 102.

Kléber Haedens/*Paradoxe sur le roman* (Marseille, 1941), p. 7.

Fanny Burney/*The Wanderer, or Female Difficulties* (London, 1814), I, xiii.

79 Friedrich Lange/*The History of Materialism*, tr. E. C. Thomas (London, 1925), II, 245, 257.

Alfred de Musset/*La Confession d'un enfant du siècle*, ed. Robert Doré (1937), p. 24.

80 M. Prudhomme/Henry Monnier, *Mémoires de M. Joseph Prudhomme* (1857), I, 2.

the Goncourts/*Charles Demailly* (1888), p. 98.

Bernhard Groethuysen/*Die Entstehung der bürgerlichen Welt- und Lebensanschauung in Frankreich* (Halle, 1927), p. xvi.

Werner Sombart/*Der Bourgeois* (Munich, 1920), p. 461.

83 No lack of conviction/Flaubert, *Correspondance* (1930), VII, 280.

III STENDHAL

84 Maxim Gorky/"Les Ecrivains et l'histoire, ou Stendhal examiné à la lumière du Marxisme," *Le Mois* (February, 1932), II, 153.

1. THE PURSUIT OF HAPPINESS

84 *Vies de Haydn, de Mozart et de Métastase*/Ed. Henri Martineau (1928), p. 407.

tickets for a posthumous lottery/*Vie de Henry Brulard*, ed. Martineau (1927), II, 8.

85 around 1880/*Correspondance*, ed. Martineau (1933-34), X, 267.

85   until 1900/*Souvenirs d'égotisme*, ed. Martineau (1951), p. 69.

86   "he was our sole religion."/*Mémoires sur Napoléon*, ed. Martineau (1930), p. 31.

   Homer or Tasso/*Lucien Leuwen*, ed. Martineau (1929), I, 114.

   the bourgeoisie/See A. L. Guérard, *Reflections on the Napoleonic Legend* (New York, 1924), p. 204.

   "The merest lad . . ."/*Vie de Napoléon*, ed. Martineau (1930), p. 186.

87   ". . . to pass the time."/*Racine et Shakespeare*, ed. Martineau (1928), p. 87.

   "always about frivolous subjects."/*Vie de Rossini*, ed. Martineau (1929), I, 1.

   Napoleon's *Code civil*/Paul Arbelet, "La Véritable Lettre de Stendhal à Balzac," *Revue d'histoire littéraire de la France* (1917), XXIV, 552.

   "He respected a single man . . ."/*Vie de Henry Brulard*, ed. Henry Debraye (1913), II, 329.

   the jaunty figure/See Alain, *Stendhal* (1935); Henry Debraye, *Stendhal: documents iconographiques* (Geneva, 1950).

   "the unsuccessful lover . . ."/*Vie de Henry Brulard*, ed. Martineau, I, 25.

88   Childhood, Ambition, and Dilettantism/Casimir Stryienski (ed.), *Comment a vécu Stendhal* (1900), pp. 7, 22.

   la voie oblique/See Victor Brombert, *Stendhal et la voie oblique* (1954).

   T. S. Eliot/*The Use of Poetry and the Use of Criticism* (Cambridge, Mass., 1933), p. 60.

89   "That curious epicurean . . ."/Friedrich Nietzsche, *Jenseits von Gut und Böse*, ed. Alfred Baümler (Stuttgart, 1959), pp. 190f.

   Léon Blum/*Stendhal et le Beylisme* (1914), p. 88.

   diagram of a crossroad/*Vie de Henry Brulard*, II, 104.

   The calendar of his life/Henri Martineau, *Le Calendrier de Stendhal* (1950); cf. *L'Itinéraire de Stendhal* (1912).

90   What Greece had been for Byron/*Correspondance*, V, 9.

   "his dream in Italian costume."/Benedetto Croce, *Poesia e non poesia* (Bari, 1923), p. 92; cf. L. F. Benedetto, *Arrigo Beyle, Milanese* (Florence, 1942).

   an English sea-captain/*Rome, Naples et Florence*, ed. Daniel Muller (1919), I, 96.

   The word *touriste*/*Mémoires d'un touriste*, ed. Louis Royer (1932), I, lix.

91   *Promenades dans Rome*/Ed. Martineau (1931), I, 284.

   It was in France/See Pierre Martino, *Stendhal* (1934), p. 231.

   Albert Thibaudet/*Stendhal* (1931), p. 83.

92   characterized by his acquaintances/Pierre Jourda (ed.), *Stendhal raconté par ceux qui l'ont vu* (1931), pp. 43, 107.

   over two hundred different pseudonyms/Henri Martineau, *Le Coeur de Stendhal* (1953), II, 217.

   Winckelmann's Prussian birthplace/*Stendhal: collection des plus belles pages*, ed. Paul Léautaud (1908), p. 511.

   thirty-two wills/*Mélanges intimes*, ed. Martineau (1936), I, 7ff.

93   *vie romancée*/Paul Hazard, *La Vie de Stendhal* (1907).

   Rousseau's *Confessions*/*Correspondance*, ed. Adolphe Paupe and P. A. Chéramy (1908), III, 95.

   Georges Blin/*Stendhal et les problèmes de la personnalité* (1958), I, 41ff; *Stendhal et les problèmes du roman* (1954), pp. 108ff.

93   Giuseppe di Lampedusa/"Notes sur Stendhal," *Stendhal Club* (1960), II, 157.
     Jean Prévost/*La Création chez Stendhal* (1951), pp. 23, 129, 210, 350.
94   Jean Starobinski/*L'Oeil vivant* (1961), p. 196ff.
     a wishing-ring/'*Les privilèges du 10 avril 1840*,' *Mélanges intimes*, I, 197ff.
     "the reality of experience"/James Joyce, *Portrait of the Artist as a Young Man* (London, 1924), p. 288.
95   one biographer/Arthur Chuquet, *Stendhal-Beyle* (1912), p. 5.
     "The magnificent memories of Italy . . ."/*Vie de Henry Brulard*, I, 134.
     he confessed his blunder/*Ibid.*, II, 242.
     the same blunder/*Le Rouge et le noir*, ed. Martineau (1927), II, 32.
     psychoanalysts/Edmund Bergler, *Talleyrand-Napoleon-Stendhal-Grabbes: Psychoanalytisch-biographische Essays* (Vienna, 1935), p. 117.
96   "La chasse du bonheur"/*Vie de Henry Brulard*, I, 41.
     "la promesse du bonheur."/*De l'amour*, I, 80.
     he had abandoned his mistresses/*Vie de Henry Brulard*, I, 41.
97   Walter Pater/*The Renaissance*, conclusion.
     l'esprit de l'escalier/Laurent Dugas, *Les Grands Timides* (1922), p. 17.
98   "Paris . . . n'est-ce que ça?"/*Vie de Henry Brulard*, II, 224.
     "Le Saint Bernard . . ."/*Ibid.*, II, 298.
     ". . . I believe it comes from imagination."/*Ibid.*, II, 304.
     "Comment, ce fameux amour . . ."/*Lamiel*, ed. Martineau (1948), p. 171.

2. The Comedy of the Nineteenth Century

98   Balzac/*Oeuvres diverses*, ed. Marcel Bouteron and Henri Longnon (1940), III, 382, 374, 377.
99   he looked upon Metternich/*Correspondance*, X, 273, 286.
     "the most knavish of kings,"/*Vie de Henry Brulard*, I, 11.
100 "set the murderous Machiavel to school."/*3 Henry VI*, III, ii, 193.
     "those gusts of sensibility,"/*Mémoires sur Napoléon*, p. 47.
     Pascal/*Pensées*, iv, 277.
     "The discovery of this book . . ."/*Vie de Henry Brulard*, I, 123.
     "abominable illusions"/*Ibid.*, I, 89.
     espagnolisme/*Ibid.*, I, 270.
     "All my life . . ."/*Ibid.*, II, 283.
     "Ariosto shaped my character."/*Ibid.*, I, 125.
     La Nouvelle Héloise/*Ibid.*, I, 251.
101 "I, who regarded myself . . ."/*Ibid.*, II, 217.
     rereading the thirty volumes/*Journal*, ed. Martineau (1937), II, 217.
     the Chevalier des Grieux/*Ibid.*, II, 221.
     Werther and Don Juan/*De l'amour*, II, 152.
     "The trouble . . ."/*Journal*, II, 146.
     "de-Rousseauize"/*Ibid.*, I, 131n.
     "To know men thoroughly . . ."/*Ibid.*, I, 52.
     his *philosophe* grandfather/*Vie de Henry Brulard*, II, 32.
     "The imagination . . ."/*Mélanges intimes*, I, 246.
     his Anglicized intention/See Victor del Litto, *En marge des manuscrits de Stendhal* (1955), p. 106.
102 ". . . hypocrisy and vagueness."/*Vie de Henry Brulard*, I, 152.
     "True or false . . ."/*Ibid.*, II, 165.

102 The Central Schools/See François Picavet, *Les Idéologues* (1891), pp. 489, 584ff.
Jefferson's opinion/Gilbert Chinard, *Jefferson et les idéologues* (Baltimore, 1925), pp. 241, 203.
"Your Ideologues destroy every illusion..."/J. H. Rose, *The Life of Napoleon I* (New York, 1902), II, 169.
its own adherents/See Emile Cailliet, *La Tradition littéraire des Idéologues* (Philadelphia, 1943), p. 131.
Stendhal told his sister/*Correspondance*, I, 303f.

103 Sterne... had parodied Locke/See Kenneth MacLean, *John Locke and the English Literature of the Eighteenth Century* (New Haven, 1936), p. 84.
Scott/*Waverley*, general preface.
dissuade him from writing novels/*Souvenirs d'égotisme*, p. 44.
"A human being..."/*Correspondance*, ed. Paupe and Chéramy, II, 201.
Taine/*Littérature anglaise*, I, xlv.

104 Amiel/*Journal intime*, II, 287.
"M. de Tracy..."/*Le Rouge et le noir*, ed. Jules Marsan (1923), I, 389.

105 The passions/*Mélanges d'art*, ed. Martineau (1932), p. 43.
"a book of ideology."/*De l'amour*, I, 40.
"I am constantly afraid..."/*Ibid.*, I, 57.
"the accumulation of charming illusions."/*Ibid.*, I, 214.

106 "to write comedies, like Molière..."/*Vie de Henry Brulard*, I, 13.
employed as a clerk/See Paul Arbelet, *Stendhal épicier* (1926), pp. 2, 16.
Du rire/See Henry Debraye, "En feuilletant les manuscrits de Grenoble," *La Revue Critique* (1913), XX, 652; cf. *Molière, Shakespeare, la comédie et le rire*, ed. Martineau (1930).
always playing the comedian/*Comment a vécu Stendhal*, p. 134.
study the classical repertory/See Paul Arbelet, *Stendhal au pays des comédiens* (Grenoble, 1934), p. 99.
Horace Walpole's epigram/*Letters*, ed. Peter Cunningham (London, 1857), VI, 366.
scorn is not incompatible with gaiety/*Molière, Shakespeare*, p. 326.
"the habit of viewing society..."/*Journal*, I, 252.
a Machiavelli/Henri Cordier, *Molière jugé par Stendhal* (1898), p. viii.

107 "...intellectual pleasure."/*Mélanges de littérature*, ed. Martineau (1933), III, 397.
un sourire/See J. P. Richard, *Littérature et sensation* (1954), p. 39.
La Comédie est impossible en 1836/*Mélanges de littérature*, III, 421ff; *Ibid.*, II, 227.
capitalism unworthy/See del Litto, *En marge des manuscrits*, pp. 160ff.

108 "...the century of ridicule is past."/*Correspondance*, ed. Martineau, X, 21.
"...the comedy of the nineteenth century."/Paul Arbelet, "Stendhal relu par Stendhal," *Revue de Paris* (November 15, 1917), XXIV, 412.
"Transform your comedies into novels..."/*Racine et Shakespeare*, p. 133.
"From that moment..."/*Le Rouge et le noir*, ed. Martineau, II, 36.
"Here is a scene of comedy."/*Le Rouge et le noir*, ed. Marsan, I, 418.

109 Zola/*Les Romanciers naturalistes* (1925), p. 104.

109   Albert Sorel/*Lectures historiques* (1894), p. 166.
      Henri Sée/"Stendhal et la vie économique et sociale de son temps,"
      Mercure de France (July 1, 1929), CCXIII, 104.
      the Civil Code/Adolphe Paupe, *La Vie littéraire de Stendhal*, pp. 51f.
      "More details . . ."/*Lucien Leuwen*, IV, 209.
      It is estimated/*Vie de Napoléon*, ed. Louis Royer (1929), p. xii.
      a sadder and wiser postscript/*Mélanges intimes*, I, 83.
110   Balzac/*Oeuvres diverses*, III, 277.
      Sainte-Beuve/*Premiers Lundis* (1874), I, 165.
      Johnson/*Racine et Shakespeare*, ed. Pierre Martino (1925), II, 14ff.
      novel has eclipsed all the other genres/*Racine et Shakespeare*, ed. Mar-
      tineau, p. 133.
      Béranger/*Le Rouge et le noir*, ed. Martineau, II, 62; cf. ed. Marsan, II,
      561.
111   the liberal Italian vein/See Victor del Litto, *La Vie intellectuelle de
      Stendhal, 1801-1821* (1959), p. 684.
      "Dandyism appears . . ."/Charles Baudelaire, *Oeuvres*, II, 350f; cf. Mar-
      garet Gilman, "Baudelaire and Stendhal," *PMLA* (1939), LIV, 684ff.
      Goethe/J. P. Eckermann, *Gespräche mit Goethe*, July 5, 1827.
      "comic bard"/*Journal*, III, 286; cf. Harry Levin, "A Letter in English by
      Stendhal," *Harvard Library Bulletin* (1948), II, 123ff.
112   "le romanesque des idées"/*Vie de Henry Brulard*, I, 134, 224.
      Mérimée/*Portraits historiques et littéraires*, ed. Pierre Jourda (1925), p.
      155.
      "less exact than prose,"/*Correspondance*, X, 269.
      Chateaubriand/*Ibid.*, V, 364.
      Apropos of Mme. de Staël/del Litto, *En marge des manuscrits*, p. 306.
      affreux/See Antoine Albalat, *Le Travail du style* (1903), p. 267.
      Prévost/Cf. Paul Hazard, "Sur une édition principe de *La Chartreuse
      de Parme*," *Formes et couleurs* (1943), V, 4.
      "My talent . . ."/*Lamiel*, ed. Casimir Stryienski (1889), p. xii.
      "Characters depicted by poets . . ."/See Jules Alciatore, "Stendhal et
      Lancelin," *Modern Philology* (1942), XL, 85.

3. THE HAPPY FEW

113   "It is hard to escape . . ."/*Armance*, ed. Martineau (1927), p. 109.
      "The least energetic . . ."/*Ibid.*, p. 146.
114   "Ah how I'd like to operate a cannon . . ."/*Ibid.*, 149.
115   "the devil's daughter"/*Lamiel*, p. 39.
      "the professor of energy,"/Maurice Barrès, *Les Déracinés* (1922), I, 248.
      the Horatian lesson/*Le Rouge et le noir*, ed. Martineau, II, 26.
      Like Lucien Leuwen/*Lucien Leuwen*, ed. Martineau (1929), I, 109.
      Michelangelo/*Histoire de la peinture en Italie*, ed. Martineau (1929), II,
      414.
      "In France . . ."/*Rome, Naples et Florence*, I, 161.
      In Italy/*Chroniques italiennes* (1855), p. 7.
116   Charles Nodier/*Romans* (1862), p. 164.
      Nietzsche/*Götzendämmerung*, ed. Alfred Baümler (Stuttgart, 1954), p.
      167.
      "Probably all great men . . ."/*Promenades dans Rome*, ed. Martineau
      (1931), III, 201.
      Oscar Wilde/*The Picture of Dorian Gray*, ch. xviii.

116 Lacenaire/See Jean Prévost, *Essai sur les sources de Lamiel* (Lyon, 1942), pp. 31ff.
Dostoevsky/*Crime and Punishment,* tr. Constance Garnett (New York, 1914), p. 239.

117 "too ardent a soul..."/*Romans et nouvelles,* ed. Martineau (1928), I, 209.
Romain Rolland/*Vies de Haydn, de Mozart et de Métastase,* ed. Daniel Muller (1914), p. xviii.
"noble and tender souls"/*Promenades dans Rome,* II, 190.
"à la Don Quichotte"/*Lucien Leuwen,* ed. Henry Debraye (1926), IV, 442.
le naturel/See Francine Marrill-Albérès, *Le Naturel chez Stendhal* (1956), pp. 271ff.

118 "Such is the danger..."/*Lucien Leuwen,* ed. Martineau, II, 38.
"Vous avez une belle âme,"/*Chartreuse de Parme,* ed. Martineau (1927), II, 59.
"Naturalness or lack of hypocrisy"/*Vie de Henry Brulard,* II, 90.
Auguste Bussière/Jean Mélia (ed.), *Stendhal et ses commentateurs* (1911), p. 221.
like Fielding/*Mélanges intimes,* II, 230; cf. Blin, *Stendhal et les problèmes du roman,* p. 48.
Egotisme/See André Monglond, *Le Préromantisme français* (Grenoble, 1930), II, 346.

119 "Il a de l'imprévu."/See Martin Turnell, *The Novel in France* (New York, 1958), p. 154.
Somerset Maugham/*The Summing Up* (New York, 1940), p. 69.
Ovid/*Metamorphoses,* vii, 20.
Aristotle/*Nichomachean Ethics,* vii, 2.
Rousseau/*Profession de foi du Vicaire Savoyard,* ed. P. M. Masson (1914), p. 167.
Diderot/*Le Neveu de Rameau,* ed. Herbert Dieckmann (1957), p. 104.
Abbé Prévost/*Oeuvres choisies* (1810), III, 242.
"...egoism and sensibility."/Benjamin Constant, *Adolphe,* ed. J. H. Bornèque (1955), p. 148.

120 Mortonval's *Tartuffe moderne*/*Courrier Anglais,* ed. Martineau (1935), I, 184.
Lemontey's *Famille de Jura*/*The New Monthly Magazine,* XIX (1827), original papers, I, 200; III, 302; cf. Doris Gunnell, *op. cit.,* pp. 163, 276ff.
particularly fond of memoirs/*Vie de Henry Brulard,* I, 12.
André Gide/*Les Faux-monnayeurs,* p. 147.
"odious truths"/*Cent Soixante-quatorze Lettres à Stendhal,* ed. Martineau (1947), I, 221.
"The French nation..."/See Louis Maigron, *Le Roman historique* (1912), p. 59.

121 "to recount an adventure..."/*Mélanges de littérature,* III, 217.
essay on Scott/*Ibid.,* III, 308.
a recent Italian critic/Mario Bonfantini, *Stendhal e il realismo* (Milan, 1958), p. 50.

123 "Whatever happens..."/*Le Rouge et le noir,* I, 163f.
Armance/p. 3.
In those days/*Le Rouge et le noir,* II, 174.

123 Musset/*La Confession d'un enfant du siècle*, p. 9.
"... the uniform of my century."/*Le Rouge et le noir*, II, 171.
"Under Napoleon ..."/*Ibid.*, I, 313.

125 "N'est-ce que ça?"/*Ibid.*, I, 153; II, 81.
Les Deux Hommes/*Pensées*, p. 73.
"Madame de Rênal ..."/*Le Rouge et le noir*, II, 448.
"... sentiments of the liveliest hatred."/*Ibid.*, II, 212.

126 "Beware of that young man ..."/*Ibid.*, II, 154.
"the unhappy man ..."/*Ibid.*, II, 176.
Goethe/Eckermann, *Gespräche mit Goethe*, January 17, 1831.
Emile Faguet/*Politiques et moralistes du dix-neuvième siècle* (1900),
III, 54.

127 "Gentlemen ..."/*Le Rouge et le noir*, II, 448.
Prince Korasoff's advice/*Ibid.*, II, 93.
"No, man cannot put his trust ..."/*Ibid.*, II, 479.
"The powerful idea of duty ..."/*Ibid.*, II, 481.
a tiger/*Ibid.*, II, 355.

128 "What the pride of the rich calls society ..."/*Ibid.*, II, 448.
"Tender and honest ..."/Casimir Stryienski, *Soirées du Stendhal Club*
(1905), p. 96.

129 "O nineteenth century!"/*Le Rouge et le noir*, II, 481.
"new energy"/Jean Lucas-Dubreton, *La Restauration et la Monarchie de
Juillet* (1926), p. 86.
C'est à vous .../Molière, *Le Tartuffe*, IV, vii.

4. A Pistol-Shot at a Concert

129 "A novel is a mirror ..."/*Le Rouge et le noir*, I, 133; II, 232.
130 No one would guess/*Correspondance*, VI, 153.
"Politics in a work of literature ..."/*Chartreuse de Parme*, II, 306; Armance, p. 151; *Le Rouge et le noir*, II, 266f.

131 the suicide of Chatterton/*Mélanges intimes*, II, 256.
"He would rather pay court ..."/*Lucien Leuwen*, I, 3.
"perfect model."/*Correspondance*, V, 83.
"They are just ..."/*De l'amour*, II, 67.
"Washington ..."/*Lucien Leuwen*, I, p. 114.

132 *D'un nouveau complot contre les industriels*/*Mélanges de littérature*, II,
232.
"between raving legitimists ..."/*Lucien Leuwen*, I, 231.
"crowned price-list,"/*Ibid.*, III, 269, 266.
"with no other sentiment ..."/*Ibid.*, III, 366.
"combine the profits ..."/*Lucien Leuwen*, ed. Debraye (1926), IV, 370.

133 "the Talleyrand of the Bourse,"/*Lucien Leuwen*, ed. Martineau, III, 314.
"Think it over ..."/*Ibid.*, II, 240f.
on the Balzacian terrain/See Maurice Bardèche, *Stendhal romancier*
(1947), p. 246.
"the French under King Philippe"/*Lamiel*, ed. Martineau, p. 302.

134 "I make war on society ..."/*Ibid.*, p. 261.
"the rule of the ivy,"/*Ibid.*, p. 95.
"The world ..."/*Ibid.*, p. 127.
Charles Maurras/See Adolphe Paupe, *Histoire des oeuvres de Stendhal*
(1903), p. 207.

135 Henry James/"Henry Beyle," *The Nation* (September 17, 1874), XIX, 188.
136 the cancelled dedication/*Histoire de la peinture en Italie*, p. 4.
      "Was that battle Waterloo?"/*Chartreuse de Parme*, I, 133.
      "The amount of blood . . ."/*Ibid.*, I, 126.
137 of Byron's Don Juan/Gunnell, *op. cit.*, p. 152.
      "that is to say, nothing."/Chuquet, *op. cit.*, p. 415.
      paradox of the unheroic soldier/J. N. Cru, *Témoins* (1929), p. 15.
      Tolstoy/Aylmer Maude, *Life of Tolstoy* (Oxford, 1929), I, 103.
      T. S. Eliot/"A Cooking Egg," *Collected Poems* (New York, 1936), p. 53.
138 "the validity of the Word"/Archibald MacLeish, "Post-War Writers and Pre-War Readers," *The New Republic* (June 10, 1940), CII, 790.
      "The vile Sancho Panzas . . ."/*Chartreuse de Parme*, I, 310.
      Manzoni/*Del romanzo storico*.
      In a Neapolitan manuscript/See Pierre Martino, *Stendhal*, pp. 232ff.
139 Benvenuto Cellini/See Harry Levin, "La Citadelle de Parme: Stendhal et Benvenuto Cellini," *Revue de littérature comparée* (1938), XVIII, 346ff.
      André Malraux/"The Cultural Heritage," *The New Republic* (October 21, 1936), LXXXVIII, 315.
140 "la meilleure des républiques."/See Charles Rozan, *Petites ignorances historiques et littéraires* (1888), p. 510.
      "With that word republic . . ."/*Chartreuse de Parme*, II, 320.
      a discreet hiatus/*Rome, Naples et Florence*, I, p. 141.
      Lionel Trilling/*E. M. Forster* (Norfolk, Conn., 1943), pp. 13ff.
141 Souvenir of Rossini/*Journal*, V, p. 58; Farges, *Stendhal diplomate* (1892), p. 67.
      "No more immoral . . ."/*Chartreuse de Parme*, I, 188.
      the Americans have no opera/*Ibid.*, II, 355.
142 ". . . the game of whist . . ."/*Ibid.*, I, 215f.
      "the confessor and the mistress."/*Ibid.*, II, 318.
      Mandeville's couplet/Bernard Mandeville, *The Fable of the Bees*, ed. F. B. Kaye (Oxford, 1924), I, 24.
143 Rebecca-Rowena problem/Harry Levin, *The Power of Blackness* (New York, 1958), pp. 23, 176.
      "like a son."/*Chartreuse de Parme*, I, 248.
      the stuff of folklore/See Stith Thompson, *Motif Index of Folk-Literature* (Bloomington, Indiana, 1934), IV, 414; cf. John Webster, *The Duchess of Malfi*, IV, i.
      Henri III et sa cour/See *The New Monthly Magazine*, XXV (1829), original papers, I, 495.
144 "aerial solitude,"/*Chartreuse de Parme*, II, 131.
      The fall from horseback/See Gilbert Durand, "Lucien Leuwen, ou l'héroisme à l'envers," *Stendhal Club* (1959), I, 209.
145 "to fulfill his duties as a citizen."/*Chartreuse de Parme*, II, 227.
      "tribune of the people,"/*Ibid.*, II, 229.
      Balzac/*Oeuvres diverses*, III, 393.
146 Princess des Ursins/See *The New Monthly Magazine*, XVI (1826), original papers, I, 217.
      "Without me . . ."/*Chartreuse de Parme*, II, 317.
      "to make a republic . . ."/*Ibid.*, II, 333.

147   "the perfume of profound melancholy,"/*Ibid.*, II, 433.
      "It is better to kill the devil . . ."/*Ibid.*, I, 305.
148   John Adams/See Chinard, *op. cit.*, p. 261.
      like Wordsworth's/*The Prelude*, xi, 108ff.
149   ". . . the agile air of youth"/*Histoire de la peinture en Italie*, II, 156.
      Jean Dutourd/*L'Ame sensible* (1959), p. 31.

IV BALZAC

150   Hugo von Hofmannsthal/"Honoré de Balzac," tr. Kenneth Burke, *The Dial* (May, 1925), LXXVIII, 364.

1. THE LAW OF DISORGANIZATION

151   *Exegi monumentum* . . ./*Etudes philosophiques*, ed. Marcel Bouteron and Henri Longnon (1925-27), I, 199.
152   invented the nineteenth century/Oscar Wilde, *Intentions*, "The Decay of Lying."
      De la littérature industrielle/Sainte-Beuve, *Portraits contemporains*, II, 446.
      "It is a mistake . . ."/*Scènes de la vie parisienne*, ed. Bouteron and Longnon (1913-14), V, 342.
153   Société des Gens de Lettres/See Louis de Royaumant, *Balzac et la Société des Gens de Lettres* (1913).
      Béatrix/*Scènes de la vie privée*, ed. Bouteron and Longnon (1912-13), V, 4.
      Georg Lukács/*K istorii realisma* (Moscow, 1939), p. 204.
154   "ce trouveur (trouvère) moderne."/*Vie privée*, I, xxviii.
      Mercadet/*Théâtre*, ed. Bouteron and Longnon (1929), II, 188.
      Mercadet/*Nineteenth Century French Plays*, ed. J. L. Borgerhoff (New York, 1931), p. 373.
155   the miser Grandet/*Scènes de la vie de province*, ed. Bouteron and Longnon (1913), I, 358.
      Grandeur et décadence de César Birotteau/*Vie parisienne*, II, 57.
      "a martyr of commercial probity,"/*Ibid.*, II, 340.
      his historic original/Georges Lenôtre, *Paris révolutionnaire* (1921), II, 183.
      César's accounts/René Bouvier, *Balzac homme d'affaires* (1930), p. 62.
156   Louis Lambert/*Etudes philosophiques*, V, 120.
      Count de Saint-Simon/Georges Weill, *Saint-Simon et son oeuvre* (1894), p. 55.
      Renan/*L'Avenir de la science*, p. 37.
      Autre Etude d'une femme/*Vie privée*, VII, 385.
      Anton Bettelheim/*Balzac* (Munich, 1926), p. 22.
157   "the gospel in action."/*Correspondance* (1876), I, 249.
      he advertised the products/Henri Clouzot and R. H. Valensi, *Le Paris de la Comédie humaine* (1926), p. 47.
      he speculated on tickets/Léon Gozlan, *Balzac chez lui* (1862), p. 129.
      a sort of lottery/Emmanuel Failletaz, *Balzac et le monde des affaires* (Lausanne, 1932), p. 134.
158   Taine/*Nouveaux Essais de critique et d'histoire* (1866), p. 63.
      Souverain/*Lettres à l'Etrangère* (1906), II, 52.
      one of his previous publishers/Edmond Werdet, *Portrait intime de Balzac* (1859), p. 199.

158 Alexandre de Berny/Albert Arrault, *Madame de Berny, éducatrice de Balzac* (Tours, 1945), p. 250; see also Gabriel Hanotaux and Georges Vicaire, *La Jeunesse de Balzac* (1921), p. 114.
"His first operations . . ."/Balzac, *Oeuvres* (Brussels, 1837), IV, 206.
the occasional note of parody/See Maurice Bardèche, *Balzac* (1943), pp. 56, 100.
"the life of a Mohican."/*Correspondance* (1876), I, 100.
". . . fighting like Mohicans."/*Scènes de la vie militaire,* ed. Bouteron and Longnon (1914), p. 21.

159 a later appreciation/*Oeuvres diverses,* ed. Bouteron and Longnon (1940), III, 285.
"a passion and spirit . . ."/*L'Etrangère,* II, 246.
neckties/*Oeuvres diverses* (1938), II, 47.
To advise other men/*Etudes analytiques,* ed. Bouteron and Longnon (1927), I, 71.
Lytton Strachey/*Landmarks in French Literature* (New York, 1912), p. 227.

160 ". . . a phenomenon of moral paternity."/*Vie parisienne,* IV, 146.
flesh-and-blood immortality/André Billy, *Vie de Balzac* (1944), II, 214; cf. Charles Léger (ed.), *Balzac mis à nu et les dessous de la société romantique* (1928), p. xxxviii.
Histoire des Treize/*Vie parisienne,* I, 4.

161 ". . . he traverses the centuries without dying."/*Le Centenaire* (1837), p. 146.
". . . two francs a page."/*Letters to His Family,* ed. W. S. Hastings (Princeton, 1934), p. 50.
"As for me . . ."/*L'Etrangère,* II, 302.
Paul Bourget/Anatole Cerfberr and Jules Christophe, *Répertoire de la Comédie humaine* (1887), p. xiii.
Pedro Salinas/*La Responsabilidad del escritor* (Barcelona, 1961), p. 241.
". . . with the sword."/Gozlan, *Balzac chez lui,* p. 36.
project for presenting a battle/See Bernard Guyon, *La Création littéraire chez Balzac; la genèse du Médecin de campagne* (1951), p. 37.
"No more eagles."/*Scènes de la vie de campagne,* ed. Bouteron and Longnon (1922-23), II, 188.

162 Nucingen and Keller/*Vie parisienne,* II, 406.
". . . somewhat degenerate,"/*L'Etrangère,* I, 158.
more than one chair/*Ibid.,* I, 89.
Writing day and night/*Correspondance* (1876), I, pp. 245, 322; *L'Etrangère,* I, pp. 283, 273.

163 ". . . always creating!"/*Ibid.,* p. 37.
La Cousine Bette/*Vie parisienne,* V, 244.
"Work!"/*Correspondance,* II, 113, 160.
Théophile Gautier/*Honoré de Balzac* (1859), p. 57.
"to be celebrated and to be loved,"/*Correspondance,* I, 48.
"Mais il paraît . . ."/*L'Etrangère,* I, 537.

164 "Fuge, late, tace . . ."/*Vie de campagne,* II, 234.
"the perpetual creation . . ."/*Ibid.,* II, 249.
the voluptuous setting/Gautier, *Balzac,* p. 85.
"I have written my desires . . ."/*L'Etrangère,* I, p. 16.

165 Les Ressources de Quinola/*Théâtre,* I, 314.
Cézanne/Emile Bernard, *Souvenirs sur Paul Cézanne* (1926), p. 35.

166 "the first and foremost . . ."/Henry James, *Notes on Novelists* (New York, 1914), p. 109.
The Wild Ass's Skin/F. O. Matthiessen, *Theodore Dreiser* (New York, 1951), pp. 38f.
Mercadet/*Théâtre*, II, 305.

2. DOCTOR OF SOCIAL MEDICINE

167 *Le Colonel Chabert*/*Vie privée*, VII, 79.
". . . conscience, property, health."/*Vie de campagne*, II, 60.
Sainte-Beuve/*Portraits contemporains*, I, 328.

168 George Sand/*Histoire de ma vie* (1854), IV, 136.
Madame Firmiani/*Vie privée*, III, 356.
"a doctor of social medicine"/*Vie parisienne*, V, i.
Doctor Horace Bianchon/Cerfberr and Christophe, *Répertoire*, p. 34; see also Docteur Cabanès, *Balzac ignoré*, 1902, pp. 257ff; Fernand Lotte, "Le Retour des personnages dans la *Comédie humaine*," *L'Année Balzacienne* (1961), p. 234.
"Pathology of Social Life,"/Charles Spoelberch de Lovenjoul, *Un Roman d'amour* (1896), p. 146.
nosography/See Moïse Le Yaouanc, *Nosographie de l'humanité balzacienne* (1959).
"those two eagles of thought,"/*Vie de province*, IV, 216.
this axiom/*Oeuvres diverses*, I, 205.

169 *La Muse du département*/*Vie de province*, III, 107.
". . . religion and monarchy."/*Vie privée*, I, xxx, xxi.
"The family is society."/*Vie de province*, I, 144; *Vie privée*, I, 204; *ibid.*, II, 81.

170 an example not to follow./*Vie privée*, V, 310.
to modernize the *Imitatio Christi*/*Correspondance*, I, 237.
". . . universal social communion"/*Vie de campagne*, II, 151.
Bernard Guyon/*La Pensée politique et sociale de Balzac* (1947), p. 108.

171 his conservative principles/Billy, *Vie de Balzac*, I, 140; see A. Prioult, *Balzac avant la Comédie Humaine* (1936), p. 258; L. J. Arrigon, *Les Années romantiques de Balzac* (1927), p. 123.
L'Eglise/Ed. Jean Pommier (1947), pp. 8, 19, 33.

172 "Believing is living . . ."/*Etudes philosophiques*, I, 314.
. . . spokesman for social Catholicism/See Charles Brun, *Le Roman social en France au XIXe siècle* (1910), pp. 215ff.
"The religion of Balzac . . ."/Philippe Bertault, *Balzac et la religion* (1942), p. 495.
"politically."/*L'Etrangère*, II, 48.
His Catholicism/*Ibid.*, II, 417.
"wholly terrestrial."/*Ibid.*, II, 422.
". . . the best people."/*Vie parisienne*, I, 235.

173 similarity to Ferrante Palla/*Oeuvres diverses*, III, 392.
"mediocracy."/*Les Paysans* (1923), p. 163.
Fourier's socialism/See H. J. Hunt, *Le Socialisme et le romantisme en France* (Oxford, 1936), p. 212.
Hugo and Zola and Friedrich Engels/Victor Hugo, *Actes et paroles* (1937), I, 296; Zola, *Les Romanciers naturalistes*, p. 47; F. Schiller, "Marx and Engels on Balzac," *International Literature* (1933), III, 113.
a pernicious influence/Paul Thureau-Dangin, *Histoire de la Monarchie de juillet* (1888), I, 360.

173 *Index Librorum Prohibitorum*/See Louis Bethléem, *Romans à lire et romans à proscrire* (1932), p. 28.
Les Comédiens sans le savoir/*Vie parisienne*, VII, 344.

174 Félix Davin/Charles Spoelberch de Lovenjoul, *Histoire des oeuvres de Honoré de Balzac* (1886), p. 201.
Béatrix/*Vie privée*, V, 22.
Marquis Damaso Pareto/*Vie privée*, IV, 203.
"magnificent combinations,"/*Vie parisienne*, II, 256.
"I am by no means orthodox . . ."/*L'Etrangère*, I, 403.
Louis Lambert/*Etudes philosophiques*, V, 128.
Balzac's will to believe/See Geoffroy Atkinson, *Les Idées de Balzac* (1949), II, pp. 86ff.
the theosophy of Swedenborg/See Pauline Bernheim, *Balzac und Swedenborg* (Berlin, 1914), p. 49.
Henry Miller/*The Wisdom of the Heart* (Norfolk, Conn., 1941), p. 198.

175 Aldous Huxley/*Music at Night* (New York, 1931), p. 288.
Goethe/Eckermann, *Gespräche mit Goethe*, August 2, 1830.
"the greatest poet of our century,"/*Etudes philosophiques*, I, 25.

176 Jean Cassou/*Quarante-huit* (1939), p. 116.
Monsieur Grandet/*Vie de province*, I, 283.
La Vieille Fille/*Vie de province*, III, 265.
César Birotteau/*Vie parisienne*, II, 87.
different animals/E. P. Dargan (ed.), *Studies in Balzac's Realism* (Chicago, 1932), p. 60.
"the chemistry of the will"/*Etudes philosophiques*, II, 188.
Académie des Sciences/D. L. King, *L'Influence des sciences physiologiques sur la littérature française* (1929), p. 114.

177 Vesuvius as its inkwell/Heinrich Heine, *Die Nordsee*; *Scènes de la vie politique* (1914), p. 406.
Walter Scott/*Vie privée*, I, xxviii.
"the social movement"/*Oeuvres diverses*, I, 391.
men, women, and things/*Vie privée*, I, xxix.

178 "French society . . ."/*Ibid.*, xxix.
". . . on human nature"/Taine, *Nouveaux Essais*, p. 170.
". . . scenes of bourgeois life."/*Etudes philosophiques*, III, 256.

179 Ferragus/*Vie parisienne*, I, 15.
"The Thousand and One Nights . . ."/*L'Etrangère*, I, 206.
Apartments were beginning/See Georges d'Avenel, *Le Mécanisme de la vie moderne* (1900), III, 9.
"the province jealous of Paris . . ."/*Vie de province*, III, 81.
"social antithesis,"/*Vie privée*, I, xxxvi.
"a branch office . . ."/*Etudes philosophiques*, I, 320.
Leslie Stephen/See Irving Babbitt, *Rousseau and Romanticism* (Boston, 1919), p. 107.
"admirable scenes . . ."/*Vie parisienne*, IV, 373.
"divine comedy of marriage."/*Etudes analytiques*, I, 332.
La Fille aux yeux d'or/*Vie parisienne*, I, 330.

180 "stupid"/*L'Etrangère*, I, 503.
Le Père Goriot/*Vie privée*, VI, 222.

181 "a written comedy?"/*Etudes philosophiques*, V, 19.

181   Cervantes and Sterne/*L'Etrangère*, I, 471.
      Richardson's accomplishment/*Vie privée*, I, xxxv.
      The Undivine Comedy/See Marcel Françon, "The Title of the *Comédie humaine*," *Slavonic Review* (1943), XXI, 56ff.
      Maison du berger/Alfred de Vigny, *Poèmes*, ed. Fernand Baldensperger (1948), p. 180.
      The Prince/*L'Etrangère*, II, 397.
      Don Quixote/Ibid., II, 330.
      comedy of the nineteenth century/See Marie-Jeanne Durry, "Apropos de la *Comédie humaine*," *Revue d'histoire littéraire de la France* (January, 1936), XLIII, 96ff.
      A combien l'amour revient aux vieillards/*Vie parisienne*, III, 207.
182   Daguerre's invention/*L'Etrangère*, II, 38.
      pictorial supplement/*Baudelaire*, II, 328.
      Bixiou/See Edith Melcher, *The Life and Times of Henry Monnier* (Cambridge, Mass., 1950), pp. 169ff.
      Grandeur et décadance de Joseph Prudhomme/See D. Z. Milatchich, *Le Théâtre de Honoré de Balzac* (1930), p. 233.
183   rogues and fools/*Vie privée*, VI, 303.
      Molière is mentioned/Geneviève Delattre, *Les Opinions littéraires de Balzac* (1961), p. 77.
      Baudelaire/"Le Voyage," *Oeuvres*, I, 144.

              3. SUBTRACTING THE DISCOUNT
184   another Molière/Alphonse de Lamartine, *Cours familier de la littérature* (1856), II, 298.
      banality or hyperbole/Gilbert Mayer, *La Qualification affective dans les romans d'Honoré de Balzac* (1940), pp. 389f.
      "a garment"/*L'Etrangère*, II, 49.
      "like a gentleman."/W. M. Thackeray, *Paris Sketch Book* (London, 1869), p. 96.
      a novel a month/*Correspondance*, I, 44.
      twenty days/Champfleury, *Balzac: sa méthode de travail* (1879), p. 12.
      Le Secret des Ruggieri/W. L. Crain, "An Introduction to *Le Secret des Ruggieri*," in *The Evolution of Balzac's Comédie Humaine*, ed. E. P. Dargan and Bernard Weinberg (Chicago, 1942), p. 298.
      Illusions perdues/*Le Manuscrit de la collection Spoelberch de Lovenjoul*, ed. S. J. Bérard (1959), pp. 261ff.
185   Taine/*Nouveaux Essais*, pp. 11f.
      Le Cousin Pons/*Vie parisienne*, VI, 23.
      Le Lys dans la vallée/J. M. Burton, *Honoré de Balzac and His Figures of Speech* (Princeton, 1921), p. 38.
      Barbey d'Aurevilly/Edouard Maynial (ed.), *L'Epoque réaliste* (1931), p. 118.
186   foreshortened narration/Henry James, *The Question of Our Speech* (Boston, 1905), p. 109.
      the *roman noir*/A. M. Killen, *Le Roman terrifiant et son influence sur la littérature française* (1924), p. 178.
      Histoire des Treize/*Vie parisienne*, I, 4.
      Chance/*Vie privée*, I, xxix.
      "the ape of Walter Scott,"/*Vie de province*, V, 72.
187   Cooper's hold/See T. R. Palfrey, "Cooper and Balzac," *Modern Philology* (February, 1932), XXIX, 335ff.

187 *Quentin Durward*/Laure Surville, *Balzac: sa vie et ses oeuvres d'après sa correspondance* (1858), p. 104.
     Melmoth réconcilié/*Etudes philosophiques*, I, 322.

188 Chasles/Abraham Levin, *The Legacy of Philarète Chasles* (Chapel Hill, N. C., 1957), I, 145.
     Sainte-Beuve/*Causeries du lundi*, II, 450.
     his visionary side/Gautier, *Balzac*, p. 38; Baudelaire, *Oeuvres*, II, 473; cf. Albert Béguin, *Balzac visionnaire* (Geneva, 1946).
     a somnambulist/Goncourt, *Journal*, I, 167.
     La Peau de chagrin/*Etudes philosophiques*, I, 38.
     scores of anecdotes/André Le Breton, *Balzac: l'homme et l'oeuvre* (1905), p. 31.
     "Consult Doctor Bianchon."/André Billy, *Vie de Balzac*, II, 310.
     competing with the civil registry/*Vie privée*, I, xxviii.
     "demographic authenticity,"/Louis Chevalier, *Classes labourieuses et classes dangereuses à Paris pendant la première moitié de la XIXe siècle* (1958), p. 17.
     Pierre Abraham/*Créatures chez Balzac*, p. 189.

189 "une pathologie romancée."/Docteur F. Bonnet-Roy, *Balzac: les médecins, la médecine et la science* (1944), p. 74.
     "juriste romantique."/See Adrien Peytel, *Balzac: juriste romantique* (1950).
     Howells/*Criticism and Fiction*, p. 17.
     Benedetto Croce/*Poesia e non poesia*, p. 246.
     "le romanesque réel . . ."/*Correspondance*, I, 344.
     "those elements of the epic . . ."/*Vie privée*, I, xxviii.
     Chimeras were changing/*Ibid.*, xxv.

190 Baudelaire/*Oeuvres*, II, 147.
     George Sand/*Autour de ma table* (1853), p. 210.

191 James/*French Poets and Novelists* (London, 1878), p. 91.
     gobe-sec/Félicien Marceau, *Balzac et son monde* (1955), p. 330.
     "aggrandized by the play of social interests,"/*Vie privée*, V, 390.
     "the penetration of all the springs . . ."/*Ibid.*, V, 390.
     Marlowe's Barabas/*The Jew of Malta*, I, i, 72.
     ". . . subtract the discount . . ."/*Ibid.*, V, 389.
     "Power and pleasure . . ."/*Ibid.*, V, 398.
     "Gold contains everything in essence . . ."/*Ibid.*, V, 390.

192 Balzac's notes/Jacques Crépet (ed.), *Pensées, sujets, fragments* (1910), p. 114.
     a series of transactions/See George Downing, "A Famous Boarding House," in Dargan, *Studies in Balzac's Realism*, pp. 149ff.
     "money is life"/*Père Goriot*, p. 457.
     "life is a business."/*Vie de province*, I, 454.
     "Poor young man,"/*Ibid.*, I, 345.
     Flaubert/*Correspondance*, IV, 65.
     ". . . to buy and sell men."/*Vie de province*, I, 464.
     "a miser cannot sing . . ."/John Ruskin, *Works*, ed. E. T. Cook and Alexander Wedderburn (London, 1905), XX, 74.

193 "I have covered this canvas . . ."/*Etudes philosophiques*, I, 32.
     "Gradually the ideas of exchange . . ."/Gide, *Les Faux-monnayeurs*, p. 244.

193 "the most vividly materialized of human ideas,"/*Etudes philosophiques*, III, 269.

George Moore/*Avowals* (London, 1933), p. 126.

The Goncourts/*Journal*, I, 970.

La Fille aux yeux d'or/See Georges Hirschfeld, *Balzac und Delacroix* (Basel, 1946), p. 131; Béguin, *op. cit.*, p. 109.

194 like crows around a corpse/*Vie parisienne*, VI, 252.

Flaubert/*Bouvard et Pécuchet* (1923), p. 169.

his fashionable *milieux*/J. L. Dangelzer, *La Description de milieu dans le roman français de Balzac à Zola* (1938), pp. 48ff.

195 "social man,"/*Une Fille d'Eve*, préface de la première édition, in *Oeuvres complètes* (1879), XII, 522.

the lower class/See Chevalier, *Classes laborieuses*, p. 58; Georges Pradalier, *Balzac historien* (1955), p. 79.

"the poetry of evil."/*Vie parisienne*, IV, 118.

François Mauriac/Preface to Claude Mauriac, *Aimer Balzac* (1945), p. 22.

a poet who acts out his poems/*Vie privée*, VI, 334.

an artist in crime/*Vie parisienne*, IV, 448.

a disciple of Rousseau/*Vie privée*, VI, 430.

Vidocq/See Gozlan, *Balzac chez lui*, p. 214.

196 Affaire Peytel/Fernand Roux, *Balzac jurisconsulte et criminaliste* (1906), p. 354.

197 "Prostitution and theft . . ."/*Vie parisienne*, IV, 167.

a provincial comedian/*Ibid.*, V, 10.

"Madame Marneffe left Crevel . . ."/*Ibid.*, V, 353.

4. THE THIRTY-THIRD MANDARIN

199 "the great social force . . ."/*Vie parisienne*, VI, 352.

"Tell me what you have . . ."/*Vie de campagne*, I, 127.

". . . M. Marneffe."/*Vie parisienne*, V, 305, 310.

200 Maurice Bardèche/*Op. cit.*, p. 468.

Baudelaire/*Oeuvres*, II, 473.

"individualizing the type . . ."/*L'Etrangère*, I, 205.

"secret saturnalia . . ."/*Vie privée*, IV, 123.

"the Milo of Crotona . . ."/*Vie de campagne*, I, 291.

"the Cromwell of the prison,"/*Vie parisienne*, IV, 136.

"the Christ of paternity,"/*Vie privée*, VI, 442.

Arnold Bennett/*Journal*, 1924-28 (New York, 1933), p. 65.

Ernst Robert Curtius/*Balzac* (Bern, 1951), pp. 346ff.

Jules Vallès/*Les Réfractaires*, p. 182.

201 Michel Butor/*Répertoire* (1960), p. 83.

reappearing characters/Ethel Preston, *Recherches sur la technique de Balzac: le retour systématique des personnages dans la Comédie humaine* (1926), p. 279.

202 the Baron de Nucingen/Fernand Lotte, *Dictionnaire biographique de la Comédie humaine* (1952), p. 345; "Le Retour des personnages," p. 234.

his sister/Laure Surville, *op. cit.*, p. 97.

203 Taine's metaphor/*Nouveaux Essais*, p. 147.

"passion is all humanity."/*Vie privée*, p. xxxiv.

"other people's money."/Alexandre Dumas *fils*, *Théâtre complet* (1909), II, 294.

204   Taine/*Littérature anglaise* (1869), V, 122.
      "Hatred and Vengeance"/*Vie parisienne*, V, 128.
      "get around God."/*Op. cit.*, V, 475.
205   "Everything collapses . . ."/*Vie privée*, VI, 497.
      "There is no such thing as absolute virtue . . ."/*Vie parisienne*, II, 354.
      an image of evil/*Etudes philosophiques*, IV, 384.
206   "*C'est enfin le bourgeois moderne*,"/*Vie privée*, II, 488.
      "Pent-up youth . . ."/*Vie politique*, ed. Bouteron and Longnon (1914),
      p. 425.
      "Intelligence is the lever . . ."/*Vie de province*, VII, 21.
      "lupanar of thought,"/*Ibid.*, VIII, 91.
      candidate for posthumous honors,/*Vie parisienne*, IV, 317.
207   "*A nous deux maintenant.*"/*Vie privée*, VI, 516.
      the first American translator/See Benjamin Griffith, *Balzac aux Etats-
      Unis* (1931), p. 11.
      Balzac's favorite walks/*Correspondance*, I, 24.
      Le Vicaire des Ardennes/*Oeuvres* (Brussels), IV, 104.
      ". . . thirty-third mandarin."/*Vie privée*, VI, 361.
208   Dostoevsky/See J. W. Bienstock, "Dostoevski et Balzac," *Mercure de
      France*, CLXXVI (December 1, 1924), p. 425.
      "Fortune is virtue."/*Vie privée*, VI, 304.
      Ben Jonson/*Sejanus*, III, iii.
      a sacred book/W. B. Yeats, *Essays and Introductions* (London, 1961),
      p. 438.
      "Here the point of departure . . ."/*Etudes philosophiques*, V, 116.
209   Goethe/See Georg Brandes, *Main Currents in Nineteenth Century Lit-
      erature*, V, 173.
      "Vouloir et Pouvoir . . ."/*Etudes philosophiques*, I, 38.
      Napoleon/*Vie privée*, VII, 395.
      "the morality of the comedy . . ."/*Etudes philosophiques*, I, 111.
      resistance and movement./*Ibid.*, I, 202, 489.
      Nietzsche/See Curtius, *Balzac*, p. 138.
210   Anatole France/See Marc Blanchard (ed.), *Témoignages et jugements
      sur Balzac* (1931), p. 187.
      Antonio Labriola/*Essays on the Materialistic Conception of History*
      (Chicago, 1908), p. 218.
      Edmond and Jules de Goncourt/*Journal*, I, 398.
      "that terrible social question . . ."/*Vie de campagne*, I, 123.
      "We have written poetry about criminals . . ."/*Ibid.*, I, 1.
      ". . . logic of Democracy."/*Ibid.*, I, 119.
211   V. Grib/*Balzac*, tr. S. G. Bloomfield (New York, 1937), p. 34.
      Cooper's redskins/*Vie de campagne*, I, 30.
      Vautrin/*Théâtre*, I, 11.
      Le Père Goriot/*Vie privée*, VI, 335.
      André Le Breton/*Balzac*, p. 83.
212   Marche-à-Terre/See G. C. Bosset, *Fenimore Cooper et le roman d'aven-
      ture en France* (1927), p. 55.
      ". . . beneath dirty shirts."/*Vie de campagne*, III, 214.
      "Obedience, Struggle, and Revolt . . ."/*Vie privée*, VI, 480.
      catchwords of his correspondence/*Correspondance*, I, 281, 374.
      "combat for money . . ."/*L'Etrangère*, I, 66.
      Victor Hugo/*Actes et paroles*, p. 297.

212 "...a continual struggle between teachers and pupils."/*Etudes philoso-phiques*, V, 73.
Le Curé de Tours/*Vie de province*, II, 247.
"I must struggle,"/*Ibid.*, V, 113.

213 "a perpetual combat between the rich and the poor."/*Oeuvres diverses*, I, 65.
Karl Marx/*Das Kapital* (Berlin, 1928), I, 524; cf. III, 14.
Engels/See F. Schiller, "Marx and Engels on Balzac," p. 114.
Dostoevsky/J. W. Bienstock, *op. cit.*, p. 418.
Brunetière/*Les Epoques du théâtre français* (1892), p. 65.

V FLAUBERT

214 Irving Babbitt/*Rousseau and Romanticism* (Boston, 1919), p. 107.

1. A SENTIMENTAL EDUCATION
214 "France is bored ..."/See Louis Barthou, *Lamartine orateur* (1916), p. 89.
"the coffin of a dead illusion."/Théophile Gautier, "La Comédie de la mort," *Poésies complètes*, ed. René Jasinski (1934), II, 6.
moralists/Ernest Seillière, *Le Romantisme des réalistes* (1914), p. 3.
sociologists/Cesare Lombroso, *L'Uomo di genio* (Turin, 1894), p. 61.
psychologists/Emile Tardieu, *L'Ennui: étude psychologique* (1903), pp. 56, 217.

215 the onset of boredom/*Racine et Shakespeare* (1925), II, 182.
"permanent lassitude"/*Notes de voyages* (1910), I, 202.
"...a thinking phantom."/*Correspondance* (1926-33), I, 151.
"absence of all illusion ..."/See Jean Cassou, *Quarante-huit*, p. 237.
Louis Reybaud/*Jérôme Paturot à la recherche de la meilleure des répu-bliques* (1849), p. 565.

216 "unemployed public thought ..."/Goncourt, *Charles Demailly*, p. 23.
unflattering comparisons/See J. R. Bloch, "Le XIXme siècle," *Encyclo-pédie française*, XVI, 12-11.
'fifty-one the people/*Correspondance*, III, 349.
"a triple thinker,"/*Ibid.*, III, 183.
"...literature is the only confession."/Goncourt, *Journal* (1888), II, 84; cf. *Journal* (1956), I, 1224.
the four purest men of letters in France/*Ibid.*, I, 852.

217 Edmond About/See René Descharmes and René Dumesnil, *Autour de Flaubert* (1912), I, 34.
"the long lie we have lived."/*Correspondance*, VI, 161.
Its socialism/*Lettres inédites de Gustave Flaubert*, ed. Auriant (1948), p. 65.
"The reaction of 'forty-eight ..."/*Correspondance*, V, 258.

218 "Blasé at eighteen!"/*Ibid.*, I, 47.
"...peoples, crowns and kings ..."/*Ibid.*, I, 22.
"In literary terms ..."/*Ibid.*, II, 343.
"a poet cold-blooded enough to be clear-sighted."/Zola, *Romanciers na-turalistes*, p. 116.

219 Latin and Nordic blood/See Gustave Lanson (ed.), *Pages choisies de Gustave Flaubert* (1904), p. xi.

219   such racial connoisseurs as Gobineau/See E. E. Freiemuth von Helms, *German Criticism of Gustave Flaubert* (New York, 1939), p. 52.
"radically cured of the malady of René,"/Sainte-Beuve, *Causeries du lundi*, VI (1853), 229.
as if it were a scalpel/*Ibid.*, XIII (1858), 297.
novel as "anatomy"/*Correspondance*, IV, 3.
"cigar lying on her foot."/*Ibid.*, I, 27.
220   "a child of literature."/*Ibid.*, I, 14.
Lara/*Théâtre* (1927), p. 92.
an academic re-examination/Louis Maigron, *Le Romantisme et moeurs* (1910), pp. 30, 94.
Baudelaire/"A Sainte-Beuve," *Oeuvres*, I, 226.
"an unhealthy tale . . ."/*Oeuvres de jeunesse inédites* (1910), I, 148; cf. 406, 527; II, 182.
a king and an ape/M. J. Durry, *Flaubert et ses projets inédits* (1952), p. 62.
"I never know . . ."/*Notes de voyages*, I, 15.
221   Le Garçon/Goncourt, *Journal*, I, 729.
Dostoevsky/*Stavrogin's Confession*, tr. Virginia Woolf and S. S. Kotelian-sky, with a psychoanalytic study of the author by Sigmund Freud (1947), p. 91.
René Dumesnil/*Gustave Flaubert: son hérédité, son milieu, sa méthode* (1905), p. 101; cf. G. M. Gould, "A Biographic Clinic on Flaubert," *Medical Record* (April 14, 1906), p. 39; Hélène Frejlich, *Flaubert d'après sa correspondance* (1933), pp. 52ff.
222   "neurosis,"/*Correspondance*, VII, 236f; cf. I, 229; IV, 169.
Maxime Du Camp/*Souvenirs littéraires* (1883), I, 245ff.
the contemplative life/*Correspondance*, I, 277.
she aspired to play opposite Flaubert/See J. F. Jackson, *Louise Colet et ses amis littéraires* (New Haven, 1937), p. 224.
"monstrous personality"/Louise Colet, *Lui* (1860), pp. 334, 337.
223   he had no biography/*Correspondance*, IV, 326.
Hugo's stoical recommendation/*Ibid.*, VI, 442; VIII, 196, 263; cf. Hugo, "A un poète."
"Tout m'a manqué . . ."/*Oeuvres de jeunesse*, III, 120.
224   grand Platonic passion/See Emile Gérard-Gailly, *L'Unique Passion de Flaubert* (1932).
"looked like the women in romantic books,"/*L'Education sentimentale* (1923), p. 12.
"like the dread of incest."/*Education*, pp. 605f.
a last farewell/*Correspondance*, IV, 128.
the Paris insurrection/See Alexis François, "Gustave Flaubert, Maxime Du Camp, et la révolution de 1848," *Revue d'histoire littéraire de France* (January-March, 1953), LIII, 44ff.
footsteps of Maxime Du Camp/Maurice Parturier, "Autour de Méri-mée," *Bulletin du Bibliophile* (December, 1931), p. 487.
"I want to write a moral history . . ."/*Correspondance*, V, 158.
225   Proust/*Contre Sainte-Beuve* (1954), p. 423.
"Some see black . . ."/*Education*, p. 67.
an illusion-ridden age/Georg Brandes, *Moderne Geister* (Frankfurt, 1882), p. 295.
"that man with every weakness,"/*Education*, p. 429.

225   Henry James's description/*Notes on Novelists*, p. 82.
      Edmund Wilson/*The Triple Thinkers* (New York, 1948), p. 101.
      "the Walter Scott of France,"/*Education*, p. 19.
      the heroes of the *Comédie humaine*,/*Ibid.*, p. 24.
226   "The gas-lamps gleamed . . ."/*Ibid.*, p. 71.
227   ". . . a considerable number of Orleanists."/*Ibid.*, p. 421.
      "The majority of the men . . ."/*Ibid.*, p. 342.
      "heroes smell bad."/*Ibid.*, p. 415.
      "Oh, these revolutions!"/*Ibid.*, p. 486.
      ". . . the faith of an inquisitor."/*Ibid.*, p. 195.
      "Vive la République!"/*Ibid.*, p. 599.
228   "secret of success in life"/Walter Pater, *The Renaissance*, conclusion.
      Wilhelm Meister/See Léon Dégoumois, *Flaubert à l'école de Goethe*
      (Geneva, 1934), p. 45.
      history-lessons/Du Camp, *op. cit.*, II, 474.
      Georges Sorel/See René Dumesnil, *En marge de Flaubert* (1928), p. 23.
      "those who have . . ."/*Education*, p. 255.
      "I have been present . . ."/*Correspondance*, IV, 171.
229   He wrote to Du Camp/*Lettres inédites*, ed. Auriant, p. 49.
      "We were better off then!"/*Education*, p. 612.
      "a mother in mourning . . ."/*Ibid.*, p. 551.
      "a veritable *nature morte*,"/*Ibid.*, p. 576.
230   ". . . this scene of poignant cruelty . . ."/See René Dumesnil, *Gustave
      Flaubert, l'homme et l'oeuvre* (1932), p. 381.
      "our *Odyssey* . . ."/See René Dumesnil, *L'Education sentimentale de
      Gustave Flaubert* (1936), p. 201.
      "a nostalgia for the boulevards."/*Education*, p. 363.
      "the great city with all its noises,"/*Ibid.*, p. 97.
      "impressionism"/See Walter Melang, *Flaubert als Begründer des litera-
      rischen "Impressionismus" in Frankreich* (Münster, 1933).

            2. THE MARTYRDOM OF ST. POLYCARP
231   "I have always put myself in what I have written . . ."/*Correspondance*,
      II, 461.
      "born lyrical"/*Ibid.*, III, 375.
      "the book of my whole lifetime."/*La Tentation de saint Antoine* (1924),
      p. 666.
232   "Enthusiasm for works of art . . ."/Jean Seznec, *Les Sources de l'épisode
      des dieux dans La Tentation de saint Antoine* (1940), p. 160.
      La Spirale/See E. W. Fischer, *Etudes sur Flaubert inédit* (Leipzig,
      1908), p. 119.
      Freud/See Ernest Jones, *The Life and Work of Sigmund Freud* (New
      York, 1953), I, 174f.
      voluntary hallucination/Taine, *De l'intelligence*, I, 90.
      Arthur Rimbaud/*Une Saison en enfer*.
      Albert Thibaudet/*Gustave Flaubert* (1935), p. 119.
      a predisposition for contrasts/see Frédéric Paulhan, *Les Caractères*
      (1902), p. 236.
      use of verbal antithesis/See Rudolf Lehman, *Die Formelemente des Stils
      von Flaubert* (Marburg, 1911), p. 78.
      exhibit of silverware/*Education*, p. 225.
      "Ah, some day . . ."/*Correspondance*, I, 206.

233 "... the bitterness of interrupted sympathies."/*Education*, p. 600.
Tertullian/*Tentation*, p. 661.
"My God, my God ..."/*Correspondance*, III, 312; IV, 32.
That prince of decadents/J. K. Huysmans, *A rebours* (1955), p. 223.
Le Poittevin/René Descharmes, *Gustave Flaubert: sa vie, son caractère et ses idées avant 1857* (1909), p. 49.

234 Renan/*Souvenirs d'enfance et de jeunesse* (1926), p. 62.
"some ceremony of a remote religion ..."/*Correspondance*, I, 203.
"I am mystical at heart ..."/*Ibid.*, II, 412.
Spinoza/*Ibid.*, VII, 327.
Voltaire/*Ibid.*, IV, 363.
Live like a monk/*Ibid.*, IV, 247; II, 253; VIII, 100.
Antoine Arbalat/*Le Travail du style* (1921), p. 65.
François Mauriac/See Henri Guillemin, *Flaubert devant la vie et devant Dieu* (1939), p. v.
Spinoza's deity/Marianne Bonwit, *Gustave Flaubert et la principe de l'impassibilité* (Berkeley, 1950), pp. 277f.
Hugo/*Cromwell*, préface.
"everywhere present and nowhere visible,"/*Correspondance*, III, 61; IV, 164.

235 "... paring his fingernails."/James Joyce, *Portrait of the Artist as a Young Man*, p. 243.
Theodor Reik's monograph/*Flaubert und seine Versuchung des heiligen Antonius* (Minden-Westfalen, 1912).
Barbey d'Aurevilly/*Le Roman contemporain* (1902), p. 107.
the qualifications for living/*Correspondance*, VI, 2.
mere hypochondria/Goncourt, *Journal*, II, 902.
the very notion of literary property/Louis Bertrand, *Gustave Flaubert, avec des fragments inédits* (n. d.), p. 253.

236 "the last of the Fathers of the Church."/Caroline Commanville, *Souvenirs de Gustave Flaubert* (1895), pp. 28, 49.
"the fatherland of my breed,"/*Notes de voyages*, II, 171.
"he practised all the bourgeois virtues;"/Goncourt, *Journal*, III, 1266.
painting and writing/See Bouvier, *La Bataille réaliste*, 45ff; cf. L. L. Schucking, *The Sociology of Literary Taste* (New York, 1944), p. 29; also Maurice Sponck, *Les Artistes littéraires* (1889), p. 20.
Fromentin/Quoted by Antoine Albalat, *Gustave Flaubert et ses amis* (1927), p. 144.
the abyss that the Goncourts noted/*Journal*, I, 603.
"ivory tower"/*Correspondance*, III, 54; see also Harry Levin, "The Ivory Gate," *Yale French Studies* (Spring, 1954), XIII, 17.

237 *auteurs sifflés*/Zola, *Romanciers naturalistes*, p. 151.
an authentic Raphael/Gautier, *Mademoiselle de Maupin* (1899), p. 22.
"my master,"/*Correspondance*, V, 85.
Arsène Houssaye/*Confessions* (1891), VI, 95.
"art for art's sake"/See G. V. Plekhanov, *Art and Society*, ed. Granville Hicks (New York, 1936), p. 48; Albert Cassagne, *La Théorie de l'art pour l'art en France* (1906), pp. 86, 157; R. F. Egan, *The Genesis of the Theory of Art for Art's Sake in Germany and in England* (Northampton, 1921), pp. 33, 39.
Victor Cousin/*Cours de philosophie sur le vrai, le beau, et le bien* (1836), pp. 224, 201.

238   "truth by means of beauty."/*Correspondance*, IV, 182.
His scientific inclinations/See Lucien Lévy-Bruhl, "Flaubert philosophe," *Revue de Paris* (February 15, 1900), IV, 842.
the form came before the idea/Goncourt, *Journal*, I, 308, 1031; cf. *Correspondance*, II, 143, 416, 448, 469.
Guy de Maupassant/*Pierre et Jean* (1893), p. xxxiii.

239   "our vision of things,"/Proust, *Chroniques* (1927), pp. 193, 205.
the verb-of-all-work, *faire*/Albalat, *Le Travail du style*, p. 93.
Pater/*Appreciations*, "Style."
Anthony Trollope/*An Autobiography* (Oxford, 1923), p. 24.
the squeaks of the puppet-saint/Dumesnil, *Gustave Flaubert*, p. 82.
". . . it makes me dream endlessly."/*Tentation*, p. 667.

240   *Le Stylite*/Alfred Le Poittevin, *Une Promenade de Bélial*, ed. René Descharmes (1924), p. 114.
four days of reading/Du Camp, *op. cit.*, I, 427.
"le dégoût d'être homme . . ."/Louis Bouilhet, *Oeuvres* (1891), p. 97.

241   A more immediate model/See Fernand Baldensperger, *Goethe en France* (1904), p. 144.
"pour me désennuyer."/Edgar Quinet, *Ahasvérus* (1881), p. 286.
Smarh/See Algernon Coleman, "Some Sources of Flaubert's *Smarh*," *Modern Language Notes* (April, 1925), XL, 205.
"a shroud stained with wine,"/*Oeuvres de jeunesse*, II, 56.
The impulse to revive the epic/See H. J. Hunt, *The Epic in Nineteenth-Century France* (Oxford, 1941).
George Saintsbury/"Gustave Flaubert," *Fortnightly Review* (April, 1878), CLXXIII, 575.
Renan/*Feuilles détachées* (1892), p. 349.

242   "Quelle solitude!"/*Tentation*, p. 7.
"the folly of crowds . . ."/*Ibid.*, p. 150.
"all action is degrading."/*Ibid.*, p. 42.
". . . a refined gluttony?"/*Par les champs et par les grèves* (1927), p. 197.
Baudelaire/"Les Deux Bonnes Soeurs," *Oeuvres*, I, 129.

243   "the Holy of Holies . . ."/*Tentation*, p. 165.
"not a woman but a world."/*Ibid.*, p. 36.
Ennoïa/*Ibid.*, p. 266.
the Mona Lisa/See Mario Praz, *La Carne, la morte, e il diavolo nella letteratura romantica* (Milan, 1930), p. 242.
". . . the reality of things."/*Tentation*, p. 115.
"the world of Ideas . . ."/*Ibid.*, p. 116.

244   Antoine calls him the Devil/*Ibid.*, p. 166.
"The continuity of life . . ."/*Ibid.*, p. 187.
"Where is the line . . ."/*Ibid.*, p. 393.
"How can I tell . . ."/*Ibid.*, p. 589.
a materialistic synthesis/See Jean Seznec, "Saint-Antoine et les monstres," *PMLA* (March, 1943), I, 195.
Taine himself was overwhelmed/*Tentation*, p. 683.

245   Victor Hugo/"Suite."
"fled from all contact,"/*Tentation*, p. 86.

3. THE FEMALE QUIXOTE

246   Anatole France/*La Vie littéraire* (1895), III, 303.
some flamboyant cathedral/*Correspondance*, III, 130.

246   more poetic than illusion/*Ibid.*, I, 163.
      his artistic origins/*Ibid.*, II, 442.
      "perpetual fusion of illusion and reality."/*Ibid.*, III, 53.
      Alphonse Daudet/*Oeuvres complètes* (1930), XII, p. 79.
      Emile Montégut/*Dramaturges et romanciers* (1890), p. 262; cf. *Correspondance*, VII, 369.
      Søren Kierkegaard/*Either/Or*, tr. D. F. and L. M. Swenson (Princeton, 1944), I, 210; cf. Maurice Bardon, "*Don Quixote* et le roman réaliste français," *Revue de littérature comparée* (January, 1936), XVI, 78.

247   Alfred Nettement/*Etudes critiques sur le feuilleton-roman* (1845), I, 355.
      A prize-winning discourse/Charles Menche de Loisne, *L'Influence de la littérature française de 1830 à 1850 sur l'esprit et les moeurs* (1852), p. 318.
      "a scene from *Les Mystères de Paris*."/L. W. Wylie, *Saint-Marc Girardin, Bourgeois* (Syracuse, 1947), p. 100.
      influence of the *roman-feuilleton*/Martino, *Le Roman réaliste*, p. 97.
      the suicide rate/Louis Proal, *Le Crime et le suicide passionels* (1900), p. 309.
      Paul Bourget/*Essais de psychologie contemporaine* (1893), I, 148f.

248   denouncing the librarian/*Madame Bovary* (1921), p. 175.
      original manuscript/*Madame Bovary: nouvelle version*, ed. Jean Pommier and Gabrielle Leleu (1949), pp. 211, 327.
      Maxime Du Camp and Louis Bouilhet/Du Camp, *op. cit.*, I, 437.
      critical midwifery/*Correspondance*, VI, p. 102.

249   "... I cried out in pain."/*Madame Bovary*, p. 483.
      M. Bouvaret/*Voyages*, ed. René Dumesnil (1948), pp. 44, 591; *Correspondance*, VI, p. 107; cf. A. M. Gossez, "Homais et Bovary, hommes politiques," *Mercure de France* (July 16, 1911), XCII, 282.
      "in the midst of fatality"/*Notes de voyages* (1910), I, 60.
      Henry James/*French Poets and Novelists*, p. 258.
      contradistinction to Don Quixote/See Helmut Hatzfeld, "*Don Quijote* und *Madame Bovary*," *Idealistische Philologie* (April, 1927), III, 55ff.

250   Jules de Gaultier/*Le Bovarysme* (1902), p. 13; cf. Dr. Genil Perrin and Madeleine Lebreuil, "Don Quichotte paranoïaque et le bovarysme de don Quichotte," *Mercure de France* (September 15, 1935), CCLXII, 45ff.
      Denis de Rougemont/*L'Amour et l'occident* (1939).
      "He reread René ..."/*Oeuvres de jeunesse*, III, 143.

251   *Madame Bovary c'est moi*/René Dumesnil, *La Vocation de Flaubert* (1961), pp. 222ff.
      Amor nel cor/*Madame Bovary*, p. 264.
      suppression of his own personality/*Correspondance*, IV, 164; II, 361.
      the bourgeois vulgarity of his material/*Ibid.*, III, 276, 339.
      will some day wither away/*Ibid.*, II, 345.
      Baudelaire/*Oeuvres*, II, 444.

252   Matthew Arnold/*Essays in Criticism* (London, 1896), II, 276.
      Brunetière/*Le Roman naturaliste*, p. 156.
      her range of perception/See B. F. Bart, "Aesthetic Distance in *Madame Bovary*," *PMLA* (December, 1954), LXIX, 1112ff.

253   things are attributes/See H. A. Stein, *Die Gegenstandswelt im Werke Flauberts* (Blescherode-am-Harz, 1938), pp. 68, 32.

253 the soil no richness/*Madame Bovary*, p. 96.
"as flat as a sidewalk."/*Ibid.*, p. 57.
"a small, ignoble Venice."/*Ibid.*, p. 11.
"budded like a springtime."/*Ibid.*, p. 13.
254 the Sandwich Islands/*Ibid.*, p. 98.
the butt of Malmsey/*Ibid.*, p. 266.
le style indirect libre/See Marguérite Lips, *Le Style indirect libre* (Geneva, 1926), p. 186.
"She gave up music . . ."/*Madame Bovary*, p. 88.
"What sunny days they had had!"/*Ibid.*, p. 172.
"Never before . . ."/*Ibid.*, p. 367.
255 Elizabeth Bowen/*Collected Impressions* (London, 1950), p. 25.
technique of characterization/*H. A. Taine: sa vie et sa correspondance* (1904), II, 232.
twenty French villages/*Correspondance*, III, 291.
Madame Delamare/See René Herval, *Les Véritables Origines de "Madame Bovary"* (1957); René Vérard, *Epilogue de "L'Affaire Bovary": La Victoire de Ry* (Rouen, 1959).
Zola/*Romanciers naturalistes*, p. 119.
Louise Pradier's confidences/See Gabrielle Leleu and Jean Pommier, "Du nouveau sur *Madame Bovary*," *Revue d'histoire littéraire de la France* (July-September, 1947), XLVII, 216ff; cf. René Dumesnil, "La véritable Madame Bovary," *Mercure de France* (November 1, 1948), CCCIV, 431ff.
an exact science/*Ibid.*, III, 285.
Réalisme/Martino, *Le Roman réaliste*, p. 93.
256 "He ate omelets . . ."/*Madame Bovary*, p. 84.
"This must be made very clear."/*Nouvelle version*, p. 84.
257 "fatality."/*Madame Bovary*, p. 480.
farewell letter to Emma/*Ibid.*, p. 281.
"Charles conjugal night . . ."/*Nouvelle version*, p. 94.
"a drop of wine . . ."/*Ibid.*, p. 224.
"a continual traffic . . ."/*Madame Bovary*, p. 137.
258 "I have a lover!"/*Ibid.*, p. 225.
"the platitudes of marriage"/*Ibid.*, p. 401.
"the words that looked so fine . . ."/*Ibid.*, p. 47.
"Balzac chateaubrianisé."/*Correspondance*, II, 316.
"the complexion of wealth . . ."/*Madame Bovary*, p. 71.
"Edgar Lagardy,"/See Léon Bopp, *Commentaire sur Madame Bovary* (Neuchâtel, 1951), p. 348.
259 . . . both sets of characters/*Madame Bovary: ébauches et fragments inédits*, ed. Gabrielle Leleu (1936), I, 562ff.
biographical rather than dramatic/*Correspondance*, III, 247.
"dialogue should be written . . ."/*Ibid.*, III, 359.
"She had loved him after all."/*Madame Bovary*, p. 26.
260 "She wanted simultaneously . . ."/*Ibid.*, p. 84.
Keepsakes/*Nouvelle version*, p. 43.
"Agony precise medical details . . ."/*Ibid.*, p. 32.
261 a map of Yonville/See Ernest Bovet, "Le Réalisme de Flaubert," *Revue d'histoire littéraire de la France* (January-March, 1911), XVIII, 14.
some 3600 pages of manuscript/*Nouvelle version*, p. v.

261 worse than pornography/*Madame Bovary*, p. 562; cf. Alexander Zévaès, *Les Procès littéraires au dix-neuvième siècle* (1924), pp. 71ff.
Bishop Dupanloup/Goncourt, *Journal*, II, 1089.
Joyce/*Finnegans Wake* (New York, 1939), p. 349.

262 "a realism which would be the negation . . ."/*Madame Bovary*, p. 629.
Taine/*Vie et opinions de M. Fréderic-Thomas Graindorge* (1870), p. 185.
Lamartine/*Madame Bovary*, p. 587.
Albert Thibaudet/*Gustave Flaubert*, p. 96.

263 "as sad as an unfurnished house."/*Madame Bovary*, p. 42.
"Every notary . . ."/*Ibid.*, p. 401.

264 "Leave by the north portico . . ."/*Ibid.*, p. 336.
"impassive,"/*Ibid.*, p. 542.
"A request for money . . ."/*Ibid.*, p. 429.
"corruption"/*Ibid.*, p. 384.
"prostitution."/*Ibid.*, p. 425.
"poor devil,"/*Ibid.*, p. 250, 369.
"poor boy,"/*Ibid.*, p. 291.
"her poor hands."/*Ibid.*, p. 446.
"poor garments"/*Ibid.*, pp. 208ff.

265 stealing the twenty-five francs/*Nouvelle version*, p. 367.
the broken window-panes of the chateau/*Madame Bovary*, p. 72.
Courbet/See Louis Hourticq, *La Vie des images* (1927), p. 211; H. A. Hatzfeld, *Literature through Art* (New York, 1952), pp. 167ff.
the goat Djala/See L. P. Shanks, *Flaubert's Youth* (Baltimore, 1927), p. 43.
Conjugal Love/*Madame Bovary*, p. 344.
"monster,"/*Nouvelle version*, p. xxx.
Restif de la Bretonne/*Ibid.*, p. 124.

266 "like a person waking from a dream,"/*Madame Bovary*, p. 447.
"She no longer existed."/*Ibid.*, p. 449.
"in the same human weakness"/*Ibid.*, pp. 458, 460.

267 not *le sang* but *le sens*/*Ibid.*, p. 445.
some future Cuvier/*Ebauches et fragments inédits*, II, 576.
Henry Monnier/Dumesnil, *Gustave Flaubert*, p. 233.
"a decorated son-in-law."/*Nouvelle version*, p. 111n.
M. Poirier/Emile Augier et Jules Sandeau, *Le Gendre de Monsieur Poirier*, IV, iv.

268 "Il faut marcher avec son siècle!"/*Madame Bovary*, p. 102.
Maxime Du Camp/See E. M. Grant, *French Poetry and Modern Industry* (Cambridge, Mass., 1927), p. 86.
journalistic watchword/Wylie, *Saint-Marc Girardin*, p. 154.

269 *hospitalier*/*Madame Bovary*, p. 441.
an earlier draft/*Nouvelle version*, p. 497.
Irony dominates life/*Correspondance*, II, 407.

4. THE DANCE OF KUCHIOUK HANEM

270 "Merde pour le Droit!"/*Correspondance*, I, 108.
one of its pontiffs/*Ibid.*, VII, 285.
From first to last/See Bertrand, *Gustave Flaubert*, p. 52.
"that antique sea . . ."/*Notes de voyages*, I, 84.
O, to be a renegado/*Ibid.*, I, 72.

270   "more hollow than an empty barrel."/*Ibid.*, I, 291.
        "orientally and classically . . ."/*Ibid.*, II, 17.
        a bohemian/*Ibid.*, II, 171.
        Heine's pine tree/"Ein Fichtenbaum steht einsam."
271   "For two weeks . . ."/*Correspondance*, VIII, 391.
        his Norman farmhouse/*Notes de voyages*, I, 74; cf. Francis Steegmuller,
        Flaubert and Madame Bovary (New York, 1939), pp. 202f.
        Bouilhet/*Oeuvres*, p. 43.
        the French provincial landscape/See B. F. Bart, *Flaubert's Landscape
        Description* (Ann Arbor, 1956).
        "more solemn and still . . ."/*Madame Bovary*, p. 297.
272   the last bourgeois novel/Champfleury, *Souvenirs et portraits de jeunesse*
        (1872), p. 246; cf. Albalat, *Gustave Flaubert et ses amis*, p. 68.
        "need for metamorphoses,"/*Correspondance*, III, 320; cf. J. P. Richard,
        Littérature et sensation, p. 147.
        the advice of Bouilhet/L. Letellier, *Louis Bouilhet: sa vie et ses oeuvres*
        (Rouen, 1919), p. 232.
        Flaubert's *beau idéal*/See E. L. Ferrère, *L'Esthétique de Gustave Flau-
        bert* (1913), p. 231.
        disappointing the Goncourts/*Journal*, I, 912.
        Victor Hugo/Flaubert, *Salammbô* (1921), p. 501.
        "applying to antiquity . . ."/*Ibid.*, p. 415.
        "the God of souls."/*Voyages*, ed. Dumesnil, II, p. 585.
        Edmond de Goncourt/*Journal*, III, 1265.
        Taine/Flaubert, *Trois Contes* (1921), p. 227.
        unrealized conceptions/Durry, *op. cit.*, 11ff.
273   Anubis/L. F. Benedetto, *Le Origini di Salammbô* (Florence, 1920), p.
        36.
        "or rather, fusion"/*Notes de voyages*, II, 359.
        "Does not the name . . ."/*Oeuvres de jeunesse*, II, 4.
        explained to the Goncourts/*Journal*, I, 554.
        Hugo von Hofmannsthal/*Die Berührung der Sphären* (Berlin, 1931),
        p. 141.
        excursion to the Pyrenees/*Par les champs et par les grèves*, p. 478.
        ". . . forgotten fatherlands."/*Salammbô*, p. 68.
274   "The great city . . ."/*Ibid.*, p. 10.
        "You will lose . . ."/*Ibid.*, p. 155.
        his captious reviewers/*Correspondance*, V, 75.
275   Polybius/*Histories*, I, lxxxviii.
276   "The Greeks . . ."/*Salammbô*, p. 280.
        "Hamilcar grew extraordinarily pale . . ."/*Ibid.*, p. 287.
277   "He had never thought . . ."/*Ibid.*, p. 337.
        "a colder and heavier look . . ."/*Ibid.*, p. 338.
        the average count/D. L. Demorest, *L'Expression figurée et symbolique
        dans l'oeuvre de Flaubert* (1931), p. 652.
278   a spatial dimension/See Joseph Frank, "Spatial Form in Modern Litera-
        ture," *Sewanee Review* (April, 1945), LIII, 221ff.
        collector of bric-a-brac/Barbey d'Aurevilly, *Le Roman contemporain*, p.
        100.
        an operatic tenor/See Goncourt, *Journal*, I, 912.
        Sainte-Beuve/*Nouveaux Lundis*, IV, 50, 437, 446; *Correspondance*, V,
        57, 69.

279 scholarly research/Arthur Hamilton, *Sources of the Religious Element in Flaubert's Salammbô* (Baltimore, 1917), p. 98.
"Oh! how gladly . . ."/*Par les champs et par les grèves*, p. 35.
Theodor Reik/*Op. cit.*, pp. 39n, 93ff.
Zoraïde Turc/Auriant, *Koutchouk-Hanem, l'almée de Flaubert* (1942), p. 38.

280 "une petite fantasia."/*Voyages*, ed. Dumesnil, II, 87.
"like a tiger."/*Ibid.*, II, 595.
". . . Judith and Holofernes."/*Ibid.*, II, p. 90; cf. Steegmuller, *Flaubert and Madame Bovary*, p. 210.
the exhibition paintings/See Hourticq, *La Vie des images*, p. 205.
Some months afterward/*Notes de voyages*, I, 212.
"the grand synthesis."/*Correspondance*, III, 137.
succoring breasts/*Salammbô*, p. 37.

281 the Marquis de Sade/Goncourt, *Journal*, I, 553; cf. 730, 900.
"the love of life"/*Salammbô*, p. 366.
"As bluish as night . . ."/*Ibid.*, p. 99.

282 he paused to protest/*Par les champs et par les grèves*, p. 299.
Gautier/*Salammbô*, ed. René Dumesnil (1944), I, cxii.
the Gospels/Saint Matthew, xiv, 1ff; Saint Mark, vi, 17ff.
"no connection with religion."/*Correspondance*, VII, 309.

283 "a certain Jesus?"/*Trois Contes*, p. 176.
"It was Herodias . . ."/*Ibid.*, p. 184.

284 Huysmans/*A rebours*, p. 87; cf. Praz, *La Carne, la morte e il diavolo*, pp. 289ff.
"As it was very heavy . . ."/*Trois Contes*, p. 190.
"Through their parted lashes . . ."/*Ibid.*, p. 189.

5. Spleen and Ideal

285 Sartre/*Critique de la raison dialectique* (1960), I, 49.
"an old romantic,"/*Correspondance*, V, 242; cf. VI, 47.
"For lack of the *real* . . ."/*Ibid.*, V, 378.
a culminating project/Durry, *op. cit.*, pp. 255, 325.

286 Jules Lemaître/*Les Contemporains* (1918), VIII, 112.
Saint Anthony's fire/*Correspondance*, VII, 296.
"le culte de la mère"/*Correspondance*, IV, 304.

287 500 francs/René Dumesnil, *La Publication de Madame Bovary* (1927), p. 94; cf. *Correspondance*, I, xxxvi.
auteurs sifflés/Zola, *Romanciers naturalistes*, p. 151.
Nationality/*Correspondance*, II, 279.
a French patriot/*Lettres à Tourgueneff*, p. 45.
"Seriously, bestially . . ."/*Correspondance*, VI, 151.
"the International . . ."/*Ibid.*, VI, 276.
the socialist left/See Eugen Haas, *Flaubert und die Politik* (Berlin, 1933), p. 28.
grace at the expense of justice/*Correspondance*, VI, 227.
"The whole dream of democracy . . ."/*Ibid.*, VI, 287.

288 "Ready-made phrases . . ."/*Ibid.*, VI, 184f.

289 "No, no . . ."/*Correspondance entre George Sand et Gustave Flaubert* (n. d.), p. 268.
he lacks conviction/*Correspondance*, VII, 280.
"*Bourgeoisophobus*,"/*Ibid.*, III, 75.

289   "hatred of the bourgeoisie . . ."/*Ibid.*, V, 300.
       "Paganisme . . ."/*Ibid.*, VI, 201.
       "utilitarian . . ."/*Ibid.*, VI, 184.
       "It is indignation . . ."/*Ibid.*, VIII, 64; cf. Goncourt, *Journal*, II, 927.

290   Iconography/Hourticq, *La Vie des images*, p. 218.
       ". . . to cure that leper."/*Correspondance*, II, 254.
       "the need to mingle . . ."/*Trois Contes*, p. 116.

291   his great-aunt's household/See Emile Gérard-Gailly, *Flaubert et les fan-
       tômes de Trouville* (1930), pp. 101ff.
       "nothing heroic"/*Trois Contes*, p. 15.
       "she loved the lambs . . ."/*Ibid.*, p. 24.
       "virtually a son . . ."/*Ibid.*, p. 49.

292   "Monotony of their existence . . ."/*Ibid.*, p. 68.
       over his irony/*Correspondance*, VII, 307.
       to please George Sand/*Ibid.*, VIII, 65.
       Ezra Pound/*The Letters of Ezra Pound*, ed. D. O. Paige (New York,
       1950), p. 89.
       Gertrude Stein/*The Autobiography of Alice B. Toklas* (New York,
       1933), p. 41.
       "emblem of material interests."/*Théâtre*, p. 263.
       "1870 has turned . . ."/*Lettres à Tourgueneff*, p. 47.
       "The work that I am producing . . ."/*Lettres inédites à Raoul-Duval*, ed.
       Georges Normandy (1950), p. 211.

293   Ezra Pound/"James Joyce et Pécuchet," *Polite Essays* (Norfolk, Conn.,
       n. d.), p. 403.
       Valéry/"La Tentation de (Saint) Flaubert," *Variété* (1945), V, 204.
       some 1500 books/*Correspondance*, VIII, 356.
       turns of phrase/See René Descharmes, *Autour de Bouvard et Pécuchet*
       (1921), pp. 240ff.

294   "occupation of the idle."/*Bouvard et Pécuchet* (1923), p. 436.
       "synonym for imbecile."/*Ibid.*, p. 439.
       Les Deux Greffiers/Descharmes and Dumesnil, *Autour de Flaubert*, II,
       7ff.
       Le Garçon/See René Dumesnil, *La Vocation de Flaubert* (1961), p. 49.

295   *Les Deux Cloportes*/Durry, *op. cit.*, pp. 210, 111.
       appropriate surnames/See Shanks, *Flaubert's Youth*, p. 39; D. L. Demo-
       rest, *À travers des plans, manuscrits et dossiers de Bouvard et Pécuchet*
       (1931), pp. 20f.
       "Bouvarine,"/*Bouvard et Pécuchet*, p. 68.
       Hérédia/Quoted by Albalat, *Flaubert et ses amis*, p. 83.

296   "Let us unite our initials."/*Bouvard et Pécuchet*, p. 236.
       Inanimate objects/See Claudia Neuenschwander-Naef, *Vorstellungswelt
       und Realität in Flauberts Bouvard et Pécuchet* (Winterthur, 1959), pp.
       36ff.

297   "In the twilight . . ."/*Bouvard et Pécuchet*, p. 61.
       "They were generally scorned."/*Ibid.*, p. 177.
       "the eternal and execrable on."/*Lettres à Tourgueneff*, p. 105.

298   "To copy . . ."/*Bouvard et Pécuchet*, p. 395.
       Dictionnaires des idées reçues/ed. E. L. Ferrère (1913).
       Flaubert's *sottisier*/See Dumesnil, *En marge de Flaubert*, pp. 35ff.

299   Turgenev and other friends/See *Lettres à Tourgueneff*, p. 81; Claude
       Digeon, *Le Dernier Visage de Flaubert* (1946), p. 66.

299 "the greatest moral lesson . . ."/*Correspondance*, VII, 203.
historiographic guide/C. V. Langlois and Charles Seignobos, *Introduction aux études historiques* (1897), pp. 16n., 263n.
Raymond Queneau/*Bâtons, chiffres et lettres* (1950), pp. 53ff.

300 ". . . the souls of apostles."/Dumesnil, *En marge de Flaubert*, p. 43.
Lionel Trilling/*The Opposing Self* (1955), p. 205.
"a pitiable faculty . . ."/*Bouvard et Pécuchet*, p. 292.
"fraternal love"/*Correspondance*, I, 6; cf. M. Z. Schroder, *Icarus: The Image of the Artist in French Romanticism* (Cambridge, Mass., 1961), p. 156.
"moles burrowing in the same direction."/*Ivan Tourgueneff d'après sa correspondance*, ed. E. Halpérine-Kaminsky (1901), p. 48.

301 "Conservatives who conserve nothing."/*Correspondance*, VI, 471; Heinrich Heine, *Lutetia* (December 11, 1841).
"Are there two young men . . ."/*Correspondance*, VI, 487.

302 "I believe that great art . . ."/*Ibid.*, V, 257.
"The first comer . . ."/*Ibid.*, V, 253.
no biography/*Ibid.*, IV, 326.
Zola/Gabriel Revillard, "L'Amitié d'Emile Zola pour Gustave Flaubert," *Les Amis de Flaubert* (1953), IV, 12.
Goncourts/*Journal*, I, 1079.

303 André Gide/*Interviews imaginaires*, p. 96.
Proust's novel/*A la recherche du temps perdu*, II, 490.
Paul Valéry/*Variété* (1945), V, 207.
Stendhal is at the opposite pole/See Paul Hazard, "Sur une édition principe de la *Chartreuse de Parme*," *Formes et couleurs* (1943), V, 4.
Remy de Gourmont/*Le Problème du style* (1888), p. 107.
Sartre's term/Sartre, *Critique de la raison dialectique*, p. 90.
the effect of impersonality/See René Canat, *Une Forme du mal du siècle: du sentiment de la solitude morale chez les romantiques et les parnassiens* (1904), p. 186; also Lucien Laumet, *La Sensibilité de Flaubert* (1951).
a form of suicide/Albert Béguin, *Balzac visionnaire*, p. 21; cf. Dmitri Merezhkovsky, *The Life-Work of Flaubert*, tr. G. A. Mounsey (London, n. d.), p. 11.
literal rumors/*Lettres à Raoul-Duval*, pp. 266ff.
"sacrosanct literature?"/*Correspondance*, VIII, 235.
a special priesthood/*Ibid.*, V, 253.

304 Henry James/*Notes on Novelists*, p. 108.

VI ZOLA

305 Ernst Cassirer/*An Essay on Man* (New Haven, 1944), p. 157.

1. EXPERIENCE AND EXPERIMENT

305 Flaubert/Goncourt, *Journal*, II, 1172.
actualisme/F. W. J. Hemmings, *Emile Zola* (Oxford, 1953), p. 117.

306 "assimilator"/Goncourt, *Journal*, III, 64.
George Moore/*Confessions of a Young Man*, p. 80.
McTeague/See Lars Aahnebrink, *The Influence of Emile Zola on Frank Norris* (Upsala, 1947), pp. 25ff.
his future editor/See Marcel Batilliat, *Emile Zola* (1931), pp. 68f.

306   Arno Holz/See W. H. Root, *German Criticism of Zola, 1875-1893* (New York, 1931), pp. 88f.
307   J. K. Huysmans/*Là-Bas* (1908), p. 4.
      due acknowledgment/*Une Campagne*, ed. Maurice Le Blond (1928), p. 105.
      Sainte-Beuve/*Portraits littéraires*, III, 546.
      "Bernards!"/*Dostoevsky, Brothers Karamazov*, p. 781.
      "a general inquiry . . ."/*Roman expérimental*, ed. Maurice Le Blond (1928), p. 38.
      one medical reader/Henri Martineau, *Le Roman scientifique d'Emile Zola: la médecine et Les Rougon-Macquart* (1907), p. 34.
308   "the same determinism . . ."/*Roman expérimental*, p. 22.
      Cabanis/Picavet, *Les Idéologues*, p. 234.
      "a series of tests."/*Roman expérimental*, p. 16.
      Henry Céard/*Lettres inédites à Emile Zola*, ed. C. A. Burns (1958), pp. 107f.
      Zola's other commentators/J. M. Guyau, *L'Art au point de vue sociologique* (1923), p. 147; Max Nordau, *Degeneration* (New York, 1905), pp. 488ff.
309   Henri Poincaré/*Science et hypothèse* (1903), p. 169.
      "L'observation montre . . ."/*Roman expérimental*, p. 18.
      "In arts and letters . . ."/*Ibid.*, p. 35.
      "an aspect of nature . . ."/*Ibid.*, p. 92; *Mes Haines*, ed. Maurice Le Blond (1928), p. 24. Cf. *Salons*, ed. F. W. J. Hemmings and R. J. Niess (Geneva, 1959), pp. 25, 75. See also J. M. Matthews, *Les Deux Zola: science et personnalité dans l'expression* (Geneva, 1957), p. 19.
      "I believe that in the study of nature . . ."/*Correspondance, 1858-1871*, ed. Maurice Le Blond (1928), p. 244.
      Henry James/*Notes on Novelists*, p. 31.
310   a whole iconography/See John Grand-Carteret, *Zola en images* (n. d.).
      Dr. Edouard Toulouse/*Enquête médico-psychologique sur les rapports de la superiorité intellectuelle avec la névropathie*: I, *Emile Zola* (1896), pp. 163, 184, 261.
      the Goncourt journal/III, 248.
      A medical dissertation/Léopold Bernard, *Les Odeurs dans l'oeuvre d'Emile Zola* (Montpellier, 1889).
      "deodorized."/Quoted by A. J. Salvan, *Zola aux Etats-Unis* (Providence, 1943), p. 34.
      Henri Massis/*Comment Emile Zola composait ses romans* (1906), p. 329.
      To his interviewers/Edmondo de Amicis, *Ricordi di Parigi* (Milan, 1882), p. 253.
      novels of observation/*Roman expérimental*, p. 23.
      Alexandre Dumas *fils*/*Théâtre complet*, III, 211.
      Bibliothèque Nationale/See *Emile Zola: exposition organisée pour la cinquantaine anniversaire de sa mort* (1952).
311   Ferdinand Brunetière/*Le Roman naturaliste*, p. 127.
      "the man of crowds . . ."/*Paris*, ed. Maurice Le Blond (1929), p. 567.
      it was work/*Mélanges, préfaces et discours*, ed. Maurice Le Blond (1929), p. 291.
      "Allons, travaillez!"/*L'Oeuvre*, ed. Maurice Le Blond (1928), p. 397.
      The Goncourts/*Journal*, II, 66, 1048.

312 "peasants of that vigorous soil"/*Le Procès Zola devant la Cour d'assizes de la Seine et la Cour de cassation* (1899), II, 222.
     "the lyric poets of advertisement"/"Une Victime de la réclame," *Contes et Nouvelles*, ed. Maurice Le Blond (1928), II, 514.
313 *le tapage*/*Correspondance, 1858-1871*, p. 303.
     "Don't forget that drama . . ."/*La Fortune des Rougon*, ed. Maurice Le Blond (1928), p. 356.
     "make a killing,"/*Correspondance, 1872-1902*, ed. Maurice Le Blond, p. 488.
     "You are a rebel."/Paul Alexis, *Emile Zola: notes d'un ami* (1882), p. 61.
     Castagnary/See John Rewald, *The History of Impressionism* (New York, 1946), p. 126.
314 "rage for production"/*L'Oeuvre*, p. 411.
     His battle-ground/*Ibid.*, p. 175.
315 headlined by the editor/See Marc Bernard, *Zola par lui-même* (1957), p. 141.
     George Gissing/*The New Grub Street* (New York, 1926), p. 488.
316 "un frisson nouveau,"/*La Curée*, ed. Maurice Le Blond (1925), p. 187; cf. *Documents littéraires*, ed. Maurice Le Blond (1928), p. 136.
     "the notes of wealth and the flesh."/*Curée*, p. 313.
     Algernon Charles Swinburne/See C. R. Decker, "Zola's Literary Reputation in England," *PMLA* (December, 1934), XLIX, 1141.
     La Confession de Claude/Ed. Maurice Le Blond (1928), pp. 66, 145.
     the pseudo-science of Michelet/Marcel Cressot, "Zola et Michelet: essai sur la genèse de deux romans de jeunesse," *Revue d'histoire littéraire de la France* (July-September, 1928), XXXV, 387f.
317 some of Zola's biographers/Matthew Josephson, *Zola and His Time* (New York, 1928), pp. 88ff; Armand Lanoux, *Bonjour, Monsieur Zola* (1954), pp. 67f, 106ff.
     "put passion into it!"/*Fortune des Rougon*, p. 355.

2. THE POETRY OF FACT

317 letter from Zola in Paris/*Correspondance, 1858-1871*, p. 53.
     Roger Fry/*Cézanne* (London, 1927), p. 23.
318 Cézanne who speaks of his researches/See John Rewald, *Cézanne et Zola* (1936), pp. 124f.
     Baptistin Baille/*Correspondance, 1858-1871*, p. 101.
     reality is all too sad/*Ibid.*, p. 141.
     against realism/*Ibid.*, p. 59.
     he is a romantic/*Ibid.*, p. 129.
     "a long poetic dream"/*Ibid.*, p. 22.
     ". . . a drop of dew,"/*Contes à Ninon* (1864), p. 22.
     Zola saluted/*Correspondance, 1858-1871*, pp. 264f.
     Like Emile's too/See Henri Guillemin, *Zola: légende et vérité* (1960), pp. 15ff.
     Mimis and Musettes/*Confession de Claude*, p. 90.
     "I am dream . . ."/*Ibid.*, p. 38.
     the role of Don Quixote/*Correspondance, 1872-1902*, p. 580; cf. *Les Mystères de Marseilles*, ed. Maurice Le Blond (1928), p. 112.
     Gustave Doré's illustrations/*Salons*, pp. 13f.
319 "All is but a dream."/*Le Rêve*, ed. Maurice Le Blond (1928), p. 208.

319 William Dean Howells/"Emile Zola," *North American Review* (November, 1902), LXXV, 595.

Duchesse de Guermantes/Marcel Proust, *A la recherche du temps perdu*, II, 499.

Jean Cocteau/In *Présence de Zola*, ed. Marc Bernard (1953), p. 241.

"the romantic gangrene,"/*L'Oeuvre*, p. 66.

La Bête humaine/Ed. Maurice Le Blond (1928), p. 385.

Au Bonheur des Dames/Ed. Maurice Le Blond (1928), p. 459.

Nana/Auriant, *La Véritable Histoire de Nana* (1942), p. 58.

"prodigious poem."/*Dix-neuf lettres de Stephane Mallarmé à Emile Zola*, ed. Léon Deffoux and Jean Royère (1929), p. 58.

"The poetry of fact"/*All the Year Round*, 438 (September 14, 1867), p. 277.

the influence of Musset and Hugo/See Carl Francke, *Emile Zola als romantischer Dichter* (Marburg, 1914).

"une sorte de roman réel."/*Correspondance, 1858-1871*, p. 307.

About George Sand/*Documents littéraires*, p. 185.

Nouveaux Contes à Ninon/(1889), p. 8.

320 "It is said . . ."/*Correspondance, 1858-1871*, p. 250.

"One is born a poet . . ."/*Ibid.*, p. 59.

"the quickest notoriety."/*Ibid.*, p. 276.

"Une Définition du roman,"/"Trois Textes inédits de Zola," ed. Guy Robert, *Revue des sciences humaines*, 51-2 (July-December, 1948), p. 205.

"after the confluence of Hugo and Balzac,"/*L'Oeuvre*, p. 47.

Goncourts/*Journal*, II, 586.

321 "between literature and something else . . ."/*Lettres de Mallarmé à Zola*, p. 55.

"Balzac says . . ."/*Fortune des Rougon*, p. 357.

322 "like a thing."/*Thérèse Raquin*, ed. Maurice Le Blond (1928), pp. 174, 150.

about 1200 characters/See F. C. Ramond, *Les Personnages des Rougon-Macquart* (1901).

a genealogical tree/*Fortune des Rougon*, p. 8.

"the mother of us all."/*Le Docteur Pascal*, ed. Maurice Le Blond (1928), p. 67.

323 *Une Page d'amour*/ed. Maurice Le Blond (1928), p. 355.

"The transformation of Paris,"/*Curée*, p. 32.

"the capital of the world,"/*Ibid.*, p. 31.

"a living organ . . ."/*L'Assommoir*, ed. Maurice Le Blond (1928), p. 45.

the vibrancy of Dickens' creations/*Le Naturalisme au théâtre*, ed. Maurice Le Blond (1928), p. 64.

324 Barbey d'Aurevilly/*Le Roman contemporain* (1902), p. 209.

325 André Gide/*Journal, 1889-1939* (1948), p. 94.

Anatole France/See *Bête humaine*, p. 394.

Flaubert/*Correspondance*, VIII, 388.

326 "Adam and Eve awakening . . ."/*La Faute de l'abbé Mouret*, ed. Maurice Le Blond (1927), p. 418.

"these incipient sciences . . ."/*Docteur Pascal*, p. 107.

"Every twenty years . . ."/*Ibid.*, p. 296.

327 *fresque*/E. g., *Bête humaine*, p. 377.

327 describing the Sistine Chapel/*Rome*, ed. Maurice Le Blond (1928), I, 208.

"hypertrophy of detail,"/*Correspondance*, 1872-1902, p. 637.

Courbet/See Guy Robert, *La Terre d'Emile Zola: étude historique et critique* (1952), p. 104.

"war against conventions."/*Naturalisme au théâtre*, p. 100.

"We are in the century . . ."/*Nos Auteurs dramatiques*, ed. Maurice Le Blond (1928), p. 170.

Alex Comfort/*The Novel in Our Time* (London, 1948), pp. 38ff.

". . . the function of a machine."/*Germinal*, ed. Maurice Le Blond (1928), p. 147.

328 "human cattle,"/*Bête humaine*, p. 368.

"the image of France."/*Ibid.*, p. 389.

3. THE HUMAN BEAST

328 Jules Lemaître/*Contemporains* (1884), I, 284; *Bête humaine*, p. 395.

329 "the beast howling . . ."/*Ibid.*, p. 29.

"To possess and to kill . . ."/*Ibid.*, p. 179.

stones have souls/Jacques Kayser, "Emile Zola, journaliste d'actualité," *Cahiers laïques*, 51 (May-June, 1959), p. 193.

"Things speak to me,"/*Rêve*, p. 179.

La Joie de vivre/Ed. Maurice Le Blond (1928), p. 367.

"beasts in a cage."/*L'Assommoir*, p. 430.

330 "the human beast unleashed . . ."/*Théâtre*, ed. Maurice Le Blond (1927), II, vii.

"Ancient art . . ."/*Contes et nouvelles*, I, 59ff.

"associated with our griefs."/*Mes Haines*, p. 66.

"the eternal struggle . . ."/*Faute de l'abbé Mouret*, p. 432.

"cares only for animals,"/*Ibid.*, p. 74.

the Goncourts/*Journal*, III, 282f.

Joyce's elemental heroine/*Ulysses* (New York, 1934), p. 762.

331 "la bête humaine amoureuse."/*Faute de l'abbé Mouret*, p. 419.

"he had the rigid despair . . ."/*Ibid.*, p. 396.

a city-dweller/See Robert, *La Terre d'Emile Zola*, pp. 92ff.

"Man makes the earth,"/*La Terre*, ed. Maurice Le Blond (1929), p. 40.

332 Robert Frost/"The Gift Outright."

Angus Wilson/*The Earth*, tr. Ann Lindsay (London, 1959), p. 5.

an excessive book/Cf. Jared Wenger, "The Art of Flashlight: Violent Technique in *Les Rougon-Macquart*," PMLA (December, 1942), LVII, 1137ff.

le tien and *le mien*/*Terre*, p. 130.

"for as much land as possible,"/*Ibid.*, p. 83.

"a murderous woman . . ."/*Ibid.*, p. 26.

333 a report in a newspaper/Maurice Le Blond, *La Publication de La Terre* (1937), pp. 56ff.

"the face of a ravaged Christ . . ."/*Terre*, p. 23.

"Tout ça ne vaut pas . . ."/*Ibid.*, p. 338.

"the very odor . . ."/*Ibid.*, p. 405.

334 the land itself/Robert, *La Terre d'Emile Zola*, p. 168.

"he had consumed his father . . ."/*Terre*, p. 33.

"ces mangeurs . . ."/*Curée*, p. 304.

devoured by Nana/*Nana*, ed. Maurice Le Blond (1928), p. 195.

334 workers/*Germinal*, p. 156.
financiers/*L'Argent*, ed. Maurice Le Blond (1928), p. 101.
small tradesmen/*Au Bonheur des Dames*, p. 27.
the Jesuits/*Rome*, p. 414.
"Mangeons du jésuite!"/*Candide*, xvi.
Contes à Ninon/P. 283.
"Hunger is the pivot,"/See Massis, *op. cit.*, p. 299.
"a great central organ . . ."/*Le Ventre de Paris*, ed. Maurice Le Blond (1927), p. 36.
335 the battle between the Fat and the Thin/*Ibid.*, p. 221.
"un monsieur qui a été mangé . . ."/*Ibid.*, p. 99.
"la double question . . ."/*Fortune des Rougon*, p. 7.
336 "la littérature putride,"/See *Thérèse Raquin*, p. 240.
Sainte-Beuve/*Correspondance* (1878), II, 315.
"In a word . . ."/*Thérèse Raquin*, p. ix.
conceded to the Goncourts/*Mes Haines*, p. 55.
"temperaments, not characters,"/*Thérèse Raquin*, p. viii.
"A fatal force . . ."/*Ibid.*, p. 40.
337 "My role . . ."/*Correspondance*, 1872-1902, p. 641.
differentiating his position/*Ibid.*, p. 634.
in Shakespearean terms/*The Winter's Tale*, IV, iv, 89.
it has been pointed out/Gustave Lanson, *Histoire de la littérature française* (1912), p. 1079.
Zola called her a product/*Correspondance*, 1872-1902, p. 469.
Travail/Ed. Maurice Le Blond (1928), I, 78.
"vicious"/*L'Assommoir*, p. 334.
"her vice,"/*Nana*, pp. 299, 153.
338 "Each volume affirms . . ."/*L'Argent*, p. 456.
"La vie n'est pas propre,"/*Ibid.*, p. 143.
"I want to go on living . . ."/*Ibid.*, p. 75.
"born for others,"/*Joie de vivre*, p. 40.
"terrible lesson in life,"/*Docteur Pascal*, p. 333.
"Faut-il être bête . . ."/*Joie de vivre*, p. 358.
339 *La Douleur*/See N. O. Franzen, *Zola et la Joie de vivre* (Stockholm, 1958), p. 72f.

4. FACES IN THE CROWD

339 "a constant simplification . . ."/*Correspondance*, 1872-1902, p. 636.
Alfred de Vigny/*Cinq-mars*, p. v.
Cesare Lombroso/"Illustrative Studies in Criminal Anthropology," *The Monist* (January, 1891), I, 2.
"The milieux . . ."/*Fortune des Rougon*, p. 353.
340 "Don't forget heredity,"/Quoted by F. Doucet, *L'Esthetique d'Emile Zola et ses applications critiques* (The Hague, 1923), p. 145.
"irresistibly attracted . . ."/*Mes Voyages: Lourdes, Rome*, ed. René Ternois (1958), p. 13.
a questionnaire/Reprinted in the *Bulletin de la Société des amis d'Emile Zola*, 4 (1924), p. 18.
Henry James/*Notes on Novelists*, p. 43.
anthills in revolution/*L'Argent*, p. 41.
Paris at work/*L'Oeuvre*, p. 236.
341 F. W. J. Hemmings/*Op. cit.*, p. 291.

341 *Le Roman expérimental*/P. 24.
"that anonymous personage . . ."/*Bête humaine*, p. 388.
Paul Alexis/*Op. cit.*, p. 124f.
". . . roulait, roulait toujours . . ."/*Bête humaine*, p. 369.
"white train"/*Lourdes*, ed. Maurice Le Blond (1929), p. 534.
"Marchons, marchons . . ."/*La Débâcle*, ed. Maurice Le Blond (1927), I, 121.
as rolling stock/*Docteur Pascal*, p. 119.
"Rouler seul . . ."/*Bête humaine*, p. 58.
Jacques, as it happens/*Emile Zola's Letters to J. Van Santen Kolff*, ed. R. J. Niess, Washington University Studies, New Series: Language and Literature, 10 (May, 1940), pp. 6, 29.

343 "selling everybody . . ."/*L'Argent*, p. 236.
struggle for life/*Au Bonheur des Dames*, p. 459.
Werner Sombart/*Der Bourgeois*, pp. 122, 403, 484.
Vilfredo Pareto/*The Mind and Society* (New York, 1935), I, 329.

344 Henry Vizetelly/*La Débâcle* (New York, 1925), p. xi.
"une satire bourgeoise,"/*Fortune des Rougon*, p. 378.
"the eagle of the family"/*Docteur Pascal*, p. 109.
"one of the pillars . . ."/*Curée*, p. 13.
"I made it . . ."/*Son Excellence Eugène Rougon*, ed. Maurice Le Blond (1927), p. 79.
"You have too many friends . . ."/*Ibid.*, p. 315.

345 "Where did you come from?"/*Docteur Pascal*, p. 18.
"lèse-bourgeoisie,"/*Pot-bouille*, ed. Maurice Le Blond (1928), p. 450.

346 Charles Péguy/"Les Récentes Oeuvres de Zola," *Cahiers de la Quinzaine*, IV, 5 (Paris, 1902), p. 57.
gaps in Balzac's sociology/Charles Brun, *Le Roman social en France au dix-neuvième siècle* (1910), p. 130.

347 the *réalistes* of the fifties/*Roman expérimental*, p. 250.
the two faces of the working-man/*Zola's Letters to Kolff*, p. 33.
dealing entirely with proletarians/*L'Assommoir*, p. 461.
"the first novel about the people . . ."/*Ibid.*, p. vi.

348 "a law of nature."/*Ibid.*, p. 285.
slang of *métiers*/See Massis, *op. cit.*, pp. 171ff.
dictionaries of *argot*/See Léon Deffoux, *La Publication de L'Assommoir* (1931), pp. 8off.
"a philological study."/*Correspondance, 1872-1902*, p. 453.
André Gide/*Incidences* (1924), p. 155.
Mallarmé/*Lettres à Zola*, p. 38.
Turgenev/*M. M. Stasulevich i ego sovremenniki v ikh perepiske*, ed. M. K. Lemke (Saint Petersburg, 1902), III, 113.

349 "un coup de l'assommoir."/*L'Assommoir*, p. 47.
Henri Barbusse/*Emile Zola* (1932), p. 110.
"Voilà une bête . . ."/*L'Assommoir*, p. 428.
L'Amour des bêtes/*Nouvelle Campagne*, ed. Maurice Le Blond (1928), p. 45.

350 *La Vie simple de Gervaise Macquart*/Massis, *op. cit.*, p. 107.

5. FOREWARD, BACKWARD, DOWNWARD

350 George Moore/*Confessions of a Young Man*, p. 82.
resemblance to Dickens/Cf. Angus Wilson, *Zola* (New York, 1952), p. 130.

351   "The Republic will be naturalistic . . ."/*Roman expérimental*, p. 301.
      Tennyson/"Locksley Hall, Sixty Years After."
      the timeless principle of tragedy/See Gerhard Walter, *Emile Zola, Der
      Denker des Fin de Siècle* (Munich, 1959), pp. 233ff.
      "terrible and necessary denouement"/*Fortune des Rougon*, p. 9.

352   Baudelaire and the poets/Edgar Allan Poe, *Oeuvres en prose*, tr. Charles
      Baudelaire (1951), p. 1058.
      Anatole France/See *L'Argent*, p. 454.
      Jules Lemaître/*Les Contemporains* (1889), IV, 278.

353   "vice-emperor"/*Docteur Pascal*, p. 339.
      the politicians surrounding the Emperor/See R. B. Grant, *Zola's Son
      Excellence Eugène Rougon* (Durham, North Carolina, 1960).

354   "the great season of the Empire,"/*L'Argent*, p. 245.
      "the master of Europe"/*Ibid.*, p. 212.
      "the inn of the world"/*Ibid.*, p. 245.
      "that opulent bastard of all styles."/*Curée*, p. 21.
      Sodom, Babylon, Nineveh/*L'Argent*, p. 272.
      ". . . everything is for sale,"/*Ventre de Paris*, pp. 170ff.
      "queen of Paris."/*Nana*, p. 348.
      "Mamma was a laundress . . ."/*Ibid.*, p. 306.
      "With her, the rot . . ."/*Ibid.*, p. 200.
      adultery is to the middle class/*Pot-bouille*, p. 429; cf. *Une Campagne*,
      p. 140.

355   "rage for abasement."/*Nana*, p. 408.
      Brunetière/*Le Roman naturaliste*, p. 127. See also Auriant, *op. cit.*, pp.
      125ff.
      Voltaire/*Lettres philosophiques*, xviii.
      Balzac/*Etudes philosophiques*, I, 331; cf. 70.
      "the majesty of the Imperial court."/*Nana*, p. 409.

356   "When tuberoses decompose . . ."/*Ibid.*, p. 132.
      "corrupted flesh"/*Ibid.*, p. 436.
      "Venus in decomposition."/*Ibid.*, p. 436.
      "France in the agonies . . ."/*Zola's Letters to Kolff*, p. 22.

357   "a living skeleton"/*Docteur Pascal*, p. 69.
      a precedent which Zola denied/*Zola's Letters to Kolff*, p. 52.
      "that equivocal dreamer,"/*Curée*, p. 137.
      reporting the rumor/H. L. Rufener, *Biography of a War Novel: Zola's
      La Débâcle* (New York, 1946), pp. 83ff.
      "the irony of the imperial household."/*Débâcle*, I, 144; cf. I, 72.
      "grown old . . ."/*Ibid.*, p. 16.

358   J. N. Cru/*Témoins*, pp. 49, 74.
      "that mad dream,"/*Débâcle*, II, 547.

359   a pure *nouvelle*/*Zola's Letters to Kolff*, p. 43.
      L'Invasion comique/See Léon Deffoux and Emile Zavie, *Le Groupe de
      Médan* (1920), p. 11.

6. CONSCIENCE AND CONSCIOUSNESS

361   "belief in life"/*Docteur Pascal*, pp. 40, 46.
      "a mother nursing an infant"/*Fécondité*, ed. Maurice Le Blond (1928),
      I, 253.

362   "ready to submit . . ."/*Germinal*, p. 54.
      "a cathedral,"/*Au Bonheur des Dames*, p. 80.
      "a new religion."/*Ibid.*, p. 449.

362 "Neither flatter the working-man . . ."/See Massis, *op. cit.*, p. 101.
"If the people are so perfect . . ."/*Correspondance*, 1872-1902, p. 633.
363 "the struggle between capital and labor"/*Germinal*, p. 557.
"red vision of revolution,"/*Germinal*, p. 470.
as a socialist/See J. M. Gros, *Le Mouvement littéraire socialiste depuis 1880* (1904), p. 251.
364 Jean Jaurès/See *Travail*, p. 615.
Léon Blum/"Les Livres," *La Revue blanche* (January-April, 1898), XV, 554.
"roman socialiste"/*Correspondance*, 1872-1902, p. 611.
"partly historical . . ."/*Zola's Letters to Kolff*, p. 36.
"I simply observe . . ."/*Fortune des Rougon*, p. 354.
365 Paul Alexis/Jules Huret (ed.), *Enquête sur l'évolution littéraire* (1891), p. 189.
Zola himself/*Ibid.*, p. 11.
Anatole France/*Ibid.*, p. 2.
Proudhon/*Mes Haines*, pp. 21ff.
the Parnassian school/*Documents littéraires*, p. 139.
366 "an experimental moralist,"/*Roman expérimental*, p. 29.
turning historian/*Présence de Zola*, p. 149.
"After forty years . . ."/*Correspondance*, 1872-1902, p. 853.
He had answered the critics . . ./*Ibid.*, p. 465.
"realize the dream of future society."/*Paris*, p. 56.
"extraordinary perversion"/*Lourdes*, p. 315.
an opera house/*Rome*, I, 188.
367 "a glorification of the absurd."/*Paris*, p. 537.
Sodom and Gomorrah/*Ibid.*, p. 110.
"an unbelieving priest . . ."/*Ibid.*, p. 14.
"Paris was aflame . . ."/*Ibid.*, p. 553.
368 Frank Norris/*The Responsibilities of the Novelist* (New York, 1903), p. 30.
"It must be returned . . ."/*Travail*, p. 419.
"happy city of solidarity,"/*Ibid.*, p. 155.
"It is my triumph,"/*Vérité*, ed. Maurice Le Blond (1928), II, p. 673.
369 "Shut up the taverns . . ."/*Correspondance*, 1872-1902, p. 467.
"the France of Voltaire and Diderot . . ./*Vérité*, I, 169.
Having set forth his views/*Ibid.*, II, 668.
La Vérité et la justice./*Ibid.*, II, 601, I, 193; cf. *Germinal*, p. 544; see also C. S. Brown, *Repetition in Zola's Novels* (Athens, Georgia, 1952), p. 67.
the dying words of Bernadette/*Rome*, II, 658.
in the courtroom/*Le Procès Zola*, II, 224f.
in the Salon/*Salons*, p. 52.
Edwin Arlington Robinson/"Zola."
370 For Tolstoy, work was not enough/L. N. Tolstoy, *Zola, Dumas, Guy de Maupassant*, tr. E. Halpérine-Kaminsky (n. d.), p. 61.
"the religion of human suffering"/*Lourdes*, p. 537; cf. Melchior de Vogüé, *Le Roman russe* (1886), p. 203; Goncourt, *Journal*, III, 536.
371 Anatole France/*Funerailles d'Emile Zola* (1902), p. 16.
Albert Camus/*Speech of Acceptance upon the Award of the Nobel Prize for Literature* (New York, 1958), p. v.
André Malraux/*L'Espoir* (1937), p. 284.

VII MARCEL PROUST

372   Edmund Wilson/*Axel's Castle: A Study in the Imaginative Literature of 1870-1930* (New York, 1931), p. 190.

1. A CORK-LINED ROOM

373   Jacques Rivière/"Reconnaissance à Dada," *Nouvelle Revue française* (August 1, 1920), XV, 225.
      the Duchesse de Guermantes/*A la recherche du temps perdu*, ed. Pierre Clarac and André Ferré (1954), II, 199
      Valery Larbaud/Quoted by Eméric Fiser in *La Théorie du symbole littéraire chez Marcel Proust* (1941), p. 9.
      he professed himself a classicist/See Walter A. Strauss, *Proust and Literature: The Novelist as Critic* (Cambridge, Mass., 1957), pp. 217f.
      "Professor of Beauty,"/*Contre Sainte-Beuve, suivi de Nouveaux mélanges* (1954), p. 430n.

374   André Gide/*Si le grain ne meurt* (1928), p. 282.
      George D. Painter/*Proust: The Early Years* (Boston, 1959), p. xiii.

375   "what are the secret links . . ."/*Jean Santeuil* (1952), I, 54.
      Alphonse Daudet/*Contre Sainte-Beuve*, p. 339.
      "A book is the product . . ."/*Ibid.*, p. 137.
      "art exactly recomposes life,"/*A la recherche*, III, 898.
      having invented everything/*A la recherche*, III, 846.
      no keys to his characters/Jacques de Lacretelle, "Les Clefs de l'oeuvre de Proust," *Hommage à Marcel Proust* (1927), p. 190; see also Antoine Adam, "Le Roman de Proust et le problème des clefs," *Revue des sciences humaines*, N. S. 65 (January-March, 1952), pp. 49ff.

376   Saint Augustine/*Confessions*, X, 8.
      Hobbes/*Leviathan*, bk. i, ch. ii.
      Baudelaire/"Le Spleen de Paris," *Oeuvres*, I, 487.
      the 1880's/See A. E. Carter, *The Idea of Decadence in French Literature* (Toronto, 1958), pp. 21ff.

377   "écrivains des nerfs"/Goncourt, *Journal*, II, 476.
      "We are all invalids."/*Ibid.*, II, 903.
      Bergotte/*A la recherche*, I, 569.

378   Illiers/See P. L. Larcher, *Le Parfum de Combray* (1945).
      Albert Thibaudet/*Histoire de la littérature française* (1936), p. 536.
      Meyer Schapiro/"Nature of Abstract Art," *Marxist Quarterly* (January-March, 1937), I, 83.
      Vacances/Harry Levin (ed.), "An Unpublished Dialogue by Marcel Proust," *Harvard Library Bulletin* (Spring, 1949), III, 257ff.

379   his favorite subjects/Léon Pierre-Quint, *Marcel Proust: sa vie, son oeuvre* (1935), p. 27.
      the hymenoptera/*A la recherche*, I, 123.
      "du temps perdu."/*Correspondance avec sa mère*, ed. Philip Kolb (1953), p. 53.
      "the cinematographic mechanism of thought"/Henri Bergson, *L'Evolution créatrice* (1908), p. 295.

380   "our young man."/Robert de Montesquiou, *Les Pas effacés* (1923), II, 284.
      the merest amateur/*Lettres à André Gide* (Neuchâtel, 1949), p. 10.

380   Henri Ghéon/"Notes," *La Nouvelle Revue française* (January 1, 1914), VI, 139.

a Bernardin de Saint-Pierre/*Les Plaisirs et les jours* (1924), p. 9.

381   composing single works/*A la recherche*, III, 375.

"This book has not been fabricated . . ."/*Jean Santeuil*, p. 31.

"idea of happiness,"/See *Proust: documents iconographiques*, ed. Georges Cattaui (Geneva, 1956), p. 20.

382   Reynaldo Hahn/*Notes: journal d'un musicien* (1933), p. 99.

383   "Then I understood . . ."/*Les Plaisirs et les jours*, p. 13; *Lettres à André Gide*, p. 120.

". . . the symbol of indestructible union."/*Jean Santeuil*, I, 315; *Correspondance avec sa mère*, p. 103.

384   a police investigator named Proust/*Pastiches et mélanges* (1919), p. 221; cf. *Le Figaro*, LIII, iii, 32 (February 1, 1907), p. 1.

Sentiments filiaux d'un parricide/*Pastiches et mélanges*, p. 224.

Oscar Wilde's/"The Ballad of Reading Gaol."

2. THE TELESCOPE

385   maxim of Pascal/*Lettres à Reynaldo Hahn*, ed. Philip Kolb (1956), p. 97.

addressed as Marcel/*A la recherche*, III, 75, 157.

younger than Proust/See Willy Hachez, "Chronologie et l'age des personnages de *A la recherche du temps perdu*," *Bulletin de la Société des amis de Marcel Proust*, 6 (1956), pp. 205ff; see also "Retouches à une chronologie," *Ibid.*, 11 (1961), pp. 392ff.

386   Nathaniel Hawthorne/"Sights from a Steeple."

387   Cyril Connolly/*The Unquiet Grave* (New York, 1945), p. 122.

Stylistic studies/A. G. Hatcher, "*Voir* as a Modern Novelistic Device," *Philological Quarterly* (October, 1944), XXIII, 363ff.

the kinetoscope/*A la recherche*, I, 7.

Bergson/*Matière et mémoire* (1911), p. 181; cf. Kurt Jaeckel, *Bergson und Proust* (Breslau, 1934), p. 104; Floris Delattre, "Bergson et Proust," *Les Etudes Bergsoniennes*, I (1948), p. 63.

"a telescope levelled at time."/*Correspondance générale* (1932), III, 194f.

388   such titles as . . ./*Lettres à Reynaldo Hahn*, p. 224.

Le Temps perdu/*Marcel Proust et Jacques Rivière: Correspondance*, ed. Philip Kolb (1955), p. 122.

letter to Scott Moncrieff/Miron Grindea (ed.), "In Search of Our Proust," *Adam: International Review* (1957), XXV, 48.

Elisée Reclus/See André Ferré, *Géographie de Marcel Proust* (1939), pp. 12f.

389   Marcouville-l'Orgueilleuse/*A la recherche*, I, 704.

"The true paradises . . ."/*Ibid.*, III, 870.

Baudelaire/*Oeuvres*, II, 331.

390   a current tendency/See Justin O'Brien, *The Novel of Adolescence in France* (New York, 1937), p. 208.

one of his letters/Robert de Billy, *Marcel Proust: lettres et conversations* (1930), p. 181.

George Eliot/*The Mill on the Floss*, II, i; see also L. A. Bisson, "Proust, Bergson, and George Eliot," *Modern Language Review* (April, 1945), XL, 104.

391   "le naturel"/*A la recherche*, I, 734.
      "a puberty of grief,"/*Ibid.*, I, 38.
      "an abdication of the will."/*Ibid.*, III, 343.
      Confession d'une jeune fille/*Les Plaisirs et les jours*, p. 148.
      "almost mythological."/*A la recherche*, I, 144.

392   a more conventional novel/See André Maurois, *A la recherche de Marcel
      Proust* (1949), pp. 152ff.
      Orpheus seeking Eurydice/*A la recherche*, I, 230.

393   "the remembrance of a certain image . . ."/*Ibid.*, I, 427.
      as an afterthought/Anthony Pugh, "A Note on the Text of Swann,"
      Adam (1957), XXV, 260.
      a newspaper interview/Reprinted by Marie Scheikévitch, *Souvenirs d'un
      temps disparu* (1935), p. 171.

394   the spatial and the temporal/*A la recherche*, III, 557; cf. *Ibid.*, p. 1031.
      "I don't believe . . ."/*Correspondance générale* (1933), IV, 175.
      Jules Michelet/*Histoire de la Révolution française* (1869), II, 420.

395   Herman Melville/*The Confidence-Man* (London, 1923), p. 90.
      What Maisie Knew/See Walter Berry, "Du coté de Guermantes," *Hom-
      mage à Marcel Proust*, p. 73.
      Edith Wharton/*A Backward Glance* (New York, 1934), pp. 322ff.
      "my law of successive Aspects."/F. O. Matthiessen (ed.), *The American
      Novels and Stories of Henry James* (New York, 1947), p. 996.
      Balzac's *retour des personnages*/See Harry Levin, "Balzac et Proust," in
      Hommage à Balzac (1950), pp. 281ff.
      Stendhal's story-telling Canon of Padua/*A la recherche*, III, 551.
      Bergson's *Introduction à la métaphysique*/*Revue de métaphysique et de
      morale* (January, 1903), XI, 2.

396   Pascal/*Pensées*, 136.
      Rimbaud/*Oeuvres complètes* (1954), p. 270.
      Chateaubriand/*Le Génie du christianisme*, II, i, 3.
      Virginia Woolf/*Mr. Bennett and Mrs. Brown* (London, 1924), p. 4.

3. THE MICROSCOPE

397   *The Thousand and One Nights*/*A la recherche*, III, 1043f.
      "Art . . . is a perpetual sacrifice . . ."/*Correspondance générale*, III, 10.

398   "the golden gates of the land of dreams."/*A la recherche*, II, 175.
      "the golden gate of imagination,"/*Ibid.*, I, 698.
      "Laissons les jolies femmes . . ."/*Ibid.*, III, 440.
      proustifier/Fernand Gregh, "Promenade," *Hommage à Marcel Proust*,
      p. 36.
      his instrument was not a microscope/*A la recherche*, III, 1041; cf. *Cor-
      respondance générale*, III, p. 297.
      Hawthorne/*Passages from the French and Italian Note-Books* (Boston,
      1883), p. 282.
      Flaubert/*Oeuvres de jeunesse*, III, 194.

399   Edith Wharton/"The Writing of Fiction," *Marcel Proust: Reviews and
      Estimates in English*, ed. G. D. Lindner (Stanford, 1942), p. 75.
      "I am observing."/*A la recherche*, I, 327.
      "such grand frescoes . . ."/*Ibid.*, II, 1050; cf. René Boylesve, *Marcel
      Proust: quelques échanges et témoignages* (1931), p. 32; *Correspondance
      générale*, IV, 152.
      "from a Balzacian point of view."/*A la recherche*, II, 219, 100.

400   Françoise/*Ibid.*, I, 485.
      the composition of his portfolio/*Ibid.*, I, 454.
      a whole social springtime/*Ibid.*, II, 750.
      "the poetry of snobbery,"/Lucien Daudet, *Autour de soixante lettres de
      Marcel Proust* (1929), p. 157.
401   "To a Snob,"/*Les Plaisirs et les jours*, p. 78.
      Paul Valéry/*Hommage à Marcel Proust*, p. 109.
      ". . . are you a snob?"/*A la recherche*, I, 740.
      Madame Sert/See Princess Bibesco, *Au bal avec Marcel Proust* (1928),
      p. 181.
      more of books than of men/*A la recherche*, II, 470.
      the Countess Potocka/*Chroniques*, p. 55.
402   "more intelligent . . ."/*A la recherche*, II, 106.
403   *sic transit . . ./Ibid.*, II, 509.
      the Sainte-Chapelle/*Ibid.*, II, 301.
      "This is the apparent life . . ."/*Lettres de Marcel Proust à Antoine Bi-
      besco* (Lausanne, 1949), p. 90.
404   "depoetization."/See Claude Vallée, *La Féerie de Marcel Proust* (1958),
      p. 260.
405   "Some day I shall portray . . ."/"Hommage à Marcel Proust," *Le Disque
      vert* (Brussels, 1952), p. 19.
      "standing in the little doorway . . ."/*A la recherche*, I, 53.
      "the sensibility of neurotics . . ."/*Ibid.*, II, 10.
      but only a little at a time/*Ibid.*, I, 15.
      a critical digression/*Ibid.*, III, 376ff.
406   "crisis of snobbery,"/*Ibid.*, I, 744.
407   Samuel Beckett/*Proust* (New York, 1931), p. 25.
      "in whose heart . . ."/*A la recherche*, II, 313.
      "Each of us is truly alone."/*Ibid.*, II, 318.
      Léon-Paul Fargue/*Poèmes* (1944), p. 92.
408   Thackeray/*Henry Esmond* (London, 1869), p. 345.
      a title of honor/*Correspondance générale*, III, 168.

                    4. THE DOSTOEVSKY SIDE
409   "That is just a stage . . ."/*Marcel Proust et Jacques Rivière*, p. 2.
      "changement de direction . . ."/*A la recherche*, I, 431.
      "In the second half . . ."/Léon Pierre-Quint, *Marcel Proust*, p. 157.
      an old hen/See André Maurois, *Le Monde de Marcel Proust* (1960), p.
      71.
      a cryptic digression/See Albert Feuillerat, *Comment Marcel Proust a
      composé son roman* (New Haven, 1934), p. 44.
      "the Dostoevsky side . . ."/*A la recherche*, I, 654.
      "Instead of presenting things . . ."/*Ibid.*, III, 378.
410   "in reverse order . . ."/*Ibid.*, III, 983.
      T. S. Eliot/*The Cocktail Party* (New York, 1950), pp. 71f.
      "Our social personality . . ."/*A la recherche*, I, 19.
      "Alas! Albertine . . ."/*Ibid.*, III, 337.
411   a malediction/*Ibid.*, II, 615f.
      an adumbration/*Contre Sainte-Beuve*, pp. 255ff.
412   Gide's war-cry/*Les Nourritures terrestres* (1947), p. 74.
      a kind of revenge/*Marcel Proust et Jacques Rivière*, p. 193.
      "for the convenience of language,"/*A la recherche*, II, 613.

413   Dostoevsky/*The Brothers Karamazov*, p. 111.
       Alfred de Vigny/*A la recherche*, II, 601.
414   confided to Gide/*Journal*, p. 694.
       Alfred Agostinelli/See Robert Vigneron, "Genèse de *Swann*," *Revue
       d'histoire de la philosophie et d'histoire générale de la civilisation*, N. S.,
       17 (January 15, 1937), pp. 67ff; see also Justin O'Brien, "Albertine the
       Ambiguous," *PMLA* (December, 1949), LXIV, 933ff; and Harry Levin,
       "Proust, Gide, and the Sexes," *Ibid.* (June, 1950), 648ff.
       "the invert imposes . . ."/*A la recherche*, III, 910.
       essay on Baudelaire/*Chroniques*, p. 228.
       Avant la nuit/La Revue blanche (July-October, 1893), IV, 381f.
415   Pamela Hansford Johnson/*Proust Recaptured* (Chicago, 1958), p. 133.
       "a tenderness . . ."/*A la recherche*, III, 79.
       best next to his mother/*Correspondance générale* (1935), V, 92.
       memorialized in a footnote/*Pastiches et mélanges*, p. 95.
       "an image of liberty."/*A la recherche*, III, 105.
416   Huysmans/*A rebours*, p. iv.
       a secret agreement/*Lettres à Antoine Bibesco*, p. 120.
       "C'est vrai?"/*A la recherche*, III, 21.
       "the sole reality,"/*Ibid.*, II, 518.
       Sherlock Holmes/*Ibid.*, III, 456.
417   "la regarder dormir,"/*Nouvelle Revue française* (November 1, 1922), X,
       514ff.
       Dostoevsky/*The Brothers Karamazov*, p. 407.
       a mechanical toy/*A la recherche*, II, 158.
       una cosa mentale/Ibid., I, 500.
       "About Albertine . . ."/*Ibid.*, II, 734.
418   Genesis/XIX, 29.
       "an Oriental colony."/*A la recherche*, II, 632.
       à peu près/Ibid., I, 770.
419   the anti-Dreyfusard atmosphere/*Correspondance générale*, II, 19.
420   America or the North Pole/*A la recherche*, III, 327.
       "in the manner of fairy tales . . ."/*Correspondance générale* (1936), VI,
       48.
421   "It is the recompense of virtue."/*A la recherche*, III, 658.

                       5. A METAMORPHOSIS OF THINGS

422   Freud/"The Relation of the Poet to Day-dreaming," *Collected Papers*
       (London, 1949), IV, 180.
       "continuous character"/*Lettres à Antoine Bibesco*, p. 175.
       related to their creator/Louis Martin-Chauffier, "Proust et le double *je*
       de quatre personnes," Jean Prévost (ed.), *Problèmes du roman* (Algiers,
       1946), p. 55.
423   "Qui aime bien chatie bien"/*A la recherche*, II, 559.
       Bloch plays the whipping-boy/Cf. Maurois, *A la recherche de Marcel
       Proust*, p. 30.
       Bloch is mistaken for Marcel/*Ibid.*, III, 974.
       this tale is retold/*A la recherche*, I, 859.
424   the liveried footmen/*Ibid.*, I, 323ff.
       his illustrated Bible/*Ibid.*, I, 840.
425   "The Virtues and Vices of Padua and Combray,"/Feuillerat, *op. cit.*,
       pp. 218ff.

425 "a flute-player."/*Ibid.*, I, 473; cf. Anatole France, *La Vie littéraire* (1898), IV, x.
"M. Anatole France."/*A la recherche*, I, 442, 547.
426 Jacques de Lacretelle/"Les Clefs de l'oeuvre de Proust," *Hommage à Marcel Proust*, pp. 190ff.
égaler la musique/See Georges Piroué, *Proust et la musique du devenir* (1960), p. 272.
Ernst Robert Curtius/*Französischer Geist im Zwansigsten Jahrhundert* (Bern, 1952), p. 283.
427 not his mistress but his love/*A la recherche*, III, 440.
elaborated by Proust in rewriting/Feuillerat, *op. cit.*, p. 59.
a laboratory/*A la recherche*, I, 834.
Mallarmé/*Propos sur la poésie*, ed. Henri Mondor (1945), p. 43.
"I could notice . . ."/*A la recherche*, I, 835.
"a metamorphosis of things."/R. W. Emerson, *Essays: Second Series* (Boston, 1890), p. 25.
428 *A propos du style de Flaubert*/*Chroniques*, p. 193.
similes more frequently than metaphors/See Charles Bruneau, *La Prose littéraire de Proust à Camus* (Oxford, 1953).
Counts of his images/V. E. Graham, *The Imagery of Proust* (Summary, *Dissertation Abstracts*, XIV, 1409); see Stephen Ullmann, *The Image in the Modern French Novel* (Cambridge, 1960), p. 129.
synesthetic transpositions/See Stephen Ullmann, *Style in the French Novel* (Cambridge, 1957), pp. 189ff.
Michelangelo/*A la recherche*, I, 445.
an elevator ride/*Ibid.*, I, 665.
429 added in proof/See Feuillerat, *op. cit.*, p. 46.
"(A great social question . . ."/*A la recherche*, I, 681.
monographic research/Georges Rivane, *Influence de l'asthme sur l'oeuvre de Marcel Proust* (1945).
rhetoricians would term enumeration/Jean Mouton, *Le Style de Marcel Proust* (1948), p. 166; cf. Yvette Louria, *La Convergence stylistique chez Proust* (Geneva, 1957).
430 Leo Spitzer/"Zum Stil Marcel Prousts," *Stilstudien* (Munich, 1928), II, 367.
"For style, with a writer . . ."/*A la recherche*, III, 895.
Ovid's *Metamorphoses*/*Ibid.*, I, 754, 976.
réaliser/*Ibid.*, II, 273; cf. Spitzer, *op. cit.*, p. 403; Gide, *Journal*, p. 844.
Ruskin's *Bible of Amiens*/Emile Audra, "Ruskin et la France," *Revue des cours et des conférences* (January 15, 1926), XXVII, 283.
"Car on ne se réalise . . ."/*A la recherche*, III, 379.
Georges Poulet/*Etudes sur le temps humain* (Edinburgh, 1949), p. 386.
Alfred de Musset/See Jean Pommier, "Musset et Proust," *Bulletin de la Société des amis de Marcel Proust*, 2 (1951-52), pp. 59ff.
431 a dark room/*A la recherche*, III, 895.
albums/Cattaui, *op. cit.*; André Maurois, *Le Monde de Marcel Proust*.

6. THE UNDISCOVERED COUNTRY

432 Walter de la Mare/"The Ghost," *Collected Poems* (New York, 1920), p. 182.
the final chapter of the latter book/*Correspondance générale*, III, 72.
Walt Whitman/"So Long!"

433   intelligence . . . mémoire/Feuillerat, op. cit., p. 128.
       Ernst Robert Curtius/Französischer Geist, p. 291.
       a soldier on furlough/A la recherche, III, 735.
       Madame Verdurin/Ibid., III, 772.
434   Sodoma, Gomora/Ibid., III, 807.
       ". . . more limited than pleasure or vice."/Ibid., III, 827.
435   Bloch is welcomed/Ibid., III, 995.
       Goethe's friend, Rahel/See Karl Vietor, Goethe the Poet (Cambridge,
       Mass., 1949), p. 177.
436   "Open, Sesame"/A la recherche, III, 538.
437   "les mères profanées."/Ibid., II, 908. Cf. Jean Frétet, L'Aliénation poé-
       tique: Mallarmé, Rimbaud, Proust (1946), pp. 239ff; also Georges
       Bataille, "Marcel Proust et les mères profanées," Critique (December,
       1946), I, 608ff.
       "the furniture, yes . . ."/Jean Santeuil, I, 315.
       a set of furniture/A la recherche, I, 578.
438   Maurice Sachs/Le Sabbat (1946), p. 283.
       "motherless sons."/A la recherche, II, 615.
       "his old grandmother"/Ibid., I, 767.
       "bitch of a mother."/Ibid., II, 288.
       "ritual profanations,"/Ibid., I, 162.
       "un célibataire des arts"/Ibid., III, 892.
       Camus/Le Mythe de Sisyphe (1942), p. 130.
439   Montesquiou/Les Pas effacés, II, 286.
       Mr. Casaubon/Marie Nordlinger (ed.), Lettres à une amie (Manchester,
       1942), p. 5.
       an essay on Ruskin/Pastiches et mélanges, pp. 251f.
       "a sort of moral ataxy,"/A la recherche, I, 815.
       "que l'oeuvre d'art . . ."/Ibid., III, 899.
440   a personal immortality/Ibid., III, 1043.
       "to bear it like a fatigue . . ."/Ibid., III, 1032.
       Ruskin/La Bible d'Amiens (1926), p. 55; Pastiches et mélanges, p. 155.
       a persisting report/See André Maurois, A la recherche de Marcel Proust,
       p. 327.
441   an exhibition of Dutch paintings/See Maurice E. Chernowitz, Proust
       and Painting (New York, 1945), p. 74.
       "Mortes, mortes à jamais?"/Ernest Renan, L'Avenir de la science, pp.
       219ff.
       "He was dead."/A la recherche, III, 187.
       "So it is with our own past."/A la recherche, I, 44.
442   "those laws . . ."/Ibid., III, 188.
       "the veritable ideas of another world."/Ibid., I, 349.
       "une patrie perdue."/Ibid., III, 257.
       Jacques Maritain/L'Art et scolastique (1935), p. 298.
443   Henry James/The Spoils of Poynton, ch. xxi.
       Bergson/Séances et travaux de l'Académie des sciences morales et poli-
       tiques (July 1, 1904), CLXII, 491f.
       "You should know . . ."/Lettres à Reynado Hahn, p. 34.
       l'adoration perpétuelle/Feuillerat, op. cit., p. 231.
       more essential than both/A la recherche, III, 872.
       George Santayana/"Proust on Essences," Obiter Scripta (New York,
       1936), p. 277.

443 the true Last Judgment/*A la recherche*, III, 880.
André Malraux/*Les Voix du silence*, p. 639.
one of his last marginalia/*A la recherche*, III, 1043.
Mircea Eliade/*Le Mythe de l'éternel retour* (1943).
James Joyce/*Scribbledehobble*, ed. T. E. Connolly (Evanston, 1961),
p. 104.

444 Joseph Conrad/In *Marcel Proust: An English Tribute* (London, 1923),
p. 126.
auto-contemplation/*A la recherche*, III, 160.
Contre l'obscurité/*Chroniques*, p. 143.
a sort of magnifying glass/*A la recherche*, III, 911.
apropos of *Sesame and Lilies*/*Sésame et les lys* (1896), p. 38.

VIII   REALISM AND REALITY

445 Ludwig Wittgenstein/*Tractatus Logico-Philosophicus*, tr. C. K. Ogden
(New York, 1933), pp. 39ff.

1. FROM ESSENCE TO EXISTENCE

445 little use for the term/*A la recherche*, III, 881.
446 Edmond Jaloux/*Avec Marcel Proust* (1953), p. 29.
Ortega y Gasset/*Obras completas* (Madrid, 1947), III, 403.
historical definition/See René Tavernier, "Les Problèmes du roman," in
Problèmes du roman, ed. Jean Prévost (Algiers, 1943), p. 14.
Fernand Léger/"The Visual Arts Today," *Daedalus*, special issue (Winter, 1960), p. 87.
447 Jean Cocteau/*Lettres aux américains* (1949), p. 70.
448 Roland Barthes/*La Dégré zéro de l'écriture* (1953), p. 94.
Ernest Hemingway/*Green Hills of Africa* (New York, 1935), p. 71.
Jean Prévost/*Problèmes du roman*, p. 22.
"anti-Flaubert,"/Jean Dutourd, *L'Ame sensible*, p. 54.
449 the writer's engagement/Jean-Paul Sartre, *Situations* (1948), II, 21.
group of intellectuals/See Victor Brombert, *The Intellectual Hero* (New
York, 1961).
Simone de Beauvoir/*Les Mandarins* (1954), p. 225.
450 Flaubert is too bourgeois/J. P. Sartre, "The Case for Responsible Literature," *Horizon* (May, 1945), XI, 307.
"Things become detached . . ."/J. P. Sartre, *La Nausée* (1938), p. 160.
451 man's condition/Albert Camus, *Le Mythe de Sisyphe* (1942), p. 18.
452 succinctly illustrated/Nathalie Sarraute, *Tropismes* (1957), p. 41.
Francis Ponge/*Le Parti pris des choses* (1942).
"The Novel *Démeublé*."/Willa Cather, *Literary Encounters* (Boston,
1938), p. 235.
453 *Le Roman comme recherche*/Michel Butor, *Répertoire* (1960), p. 8.
Claude-Edmonde Magny/*L'Age du roman américain* (1948).
John Weightman/"Alain Robbe-Grillet," in *The Novelist as Philosopher*,
ed. John Cruickshank (London, 1962), p. 248.
454 an ultimate reification/Carlo Levi, *L'Orologio* (Milan, 1950), p. 70.

2. THE BANAL CANVAS

454 Charles Baudelaire/"Au lecteur," *Oeuvres*, I, 18.
"un canevas banal"/Baudelaire, *Oeuvres*, II, 444.

455   Ernst Cassirer/*An Essay on Man*, p. 157.
      La Maison du Chat-qui-pelote/Balzac, *Vie privée*, I, 25.
457   Paul Eluard/*Choix de poèmes* (1951), p. 411.
      Henry Miller/*Tropic of Cancer* (New York, 1961), p. 11.
      Norman Mailer/*Advertisements for Myself* (New York, 1959), p. 270.
      an admirer of Mr. Miller/Anaïs Nin, preface to Henry Miller, *op. cit.*,
      p. xxxi.
458   Paul Alexis/Huret, *Enquête sur l'evolution littéraire*, p. 188.
      Charles Beuchat/*Histoire du naturalisme français* (1949), II, 12.
      sub-realism/P. E. More in *Humanism and America*, ed. Norman Foerster
      (New York, 1930), p. 63.
      André Breton/*Les Manifestes du surréalisme* (1946), p. 75.
459   "*Don Quixote . . .*"/Flaubert, *Correspondance*, VI, 480f.
      Saul Bellow/"Facts that Put Fancy to Flight," *New York Times Book
      Review* (February 11, 1962), p. 28.
460   Thomas Wolfe/*Look Homeward, Angel* (New York, 1929), preface.
      William Butler Yeats/Ed., *The Oxford Book of Modern Verse* (New
      York, 1936), pp. xxviif.
      Ortega/*Obras completas*, III, 373.
      Ramon Fernandez/"La Vie sociale dans l'oeuvre de Marcel Proust,"
      Répertoire des personnages de "A la recherche du temps perdu," ed.
      Charles Daudet (1927), p. viii.
      Nathalie Sarraute/*L'Ere du soupçon* (1956), pp. 39, 83f.
      a rhetorical convention/Sartre, *Situations II*, p. 200.
461   Wolfgang Kayser/*Enstehung und Krise des modernen Romans* (Stutt-
      gart, 1954), p. 34.
      from Corneille to Racine/See Paul Bénichou, *Morales du grand siècle*
      (1948), pp. 97ff.
      reiterated anxiety of Malraux/See W. M. Frohock, *André Malraux and
      the Tragic Imagination* (Palo Alto, 1952), p. 116.
462   Franz Kafka/Max Brod, *Franz Kafka: eine Biographie* (Berlin, 1954),
      p. 68.
      ". . . course of common existence."/Zola, *Romanciers naturalistes*, p.
      109.

            3. TOWARD MYTHOLOGY
463   "The Decline of the Novel,"/*The Nation*, VI, 150 (May 14, 1868), p.
      390.
      rereading Balzac/Zola, *Mélanges*, p. 100.
      Ortega/*Obras completas*, III, 403.
      Alberto Moravia/*Writers at Work*, ed. Malcolm Cowley, p. 228; cf.
      Cyril Connolly, *The Unquiet Grave*, p. 22.
      Paul Valéry/*Hommage à Marcel Proust*, p. 105; cf. Breton, *Manifestes*,
      p. 18.
464   "la fonction fabulatrice,"/Bergson, *Les Deux Sources de la morale et de
      la religion* (1933), p. 112.
      Georg Lukács/"Essay on the Novel," *International Literature*, 5 (May,
      1936), p. 58.
      Henri Poulaille/*Le Nouvel Age littéraire* (1930), p. 433.
465   André Malraux/*Les Voix du silence*, p. 120.
      V. S. Pritchett/"The Future of Fiction," *New Writing and Daylight*,
      ed. John Lehmann (1946), VII, 77.

466   Maxim Gorky/*Problems of Soviet Literature: Reports and Speeches at the First Soviet Writers' Congress* (New York, 1935), p. 41.
Abram Tertz/*On Socialist Realism* (New York, 1951), pp. 23, 76.
Boris Pasternak/*Doctor Zhivago*, tr. Max Hayward and Manya Harari (New York, 1958), p. 224.
Georg Lukács/*Essays über Realismus*, p. 71.

467   Louis Aragon/*Le Paysan de Paris* (1926), pp. 14, 69.
Leon Trotsky/See Isaac Deutscher, *The Prophet Armed* (New York, 1954), p. 51.

468   Georges Sorel/*Les Illusions du progrès* (1911), p. 320.
Walt Whitman/"Song of the Exposition."

469   Thomas Mann/"Freud und die Zukunft," *Gesammelte Werke*, IX, 493.
T. S. Eliot/"Ulysses, Order, and Myth," *The Dial* (November, 1923), LXXV, 483.
Théodule Ribot/*Essai sur l'imagination créatrice* (1922), p. 114.
Mircea Eliade/*Images et symboles* (1952), p. 12; cf. Roland Barthes, *Mythologies* (1957), p. 245.
liturgical background/Proust, *Pastiches et mélanges*, p. 207.

470   the visionary/Balzac, *Correspondance*, I, 567.
toward mythography/Gilbert Durand, *Le Décor mythique de la Chartreuse de Parme* (1961), p. 127.
Ortega y Gasset/*Meditaciones del Quijote*, pp. 16off.
Matthew Arnold/"On the Modern Element in Literature," *Essays* (1914), p. 454.
André Malraux/*Les Voix du silence*, p. 601.

471   Thomas Mann/*Pariser Rechenschaft* (Berlin, 1926), p. 98.
André Gide/"Discours prononcé au congrès international des écrivains," *Littérature engagée* (1950), p. 93.
autocontemplation/Proust, *A la recherche*, III, 160.
self-knowledge/See Karl Vossler, *Frankreichs Kultur im Spiegel seiner Sprachentwicklunng* (Heidelberg, 1921), p. 366.

Index